THE PHONOLOGY OF THE WORl

Series Editor: Jacques Durand, Université de

The Phonology of German

THE PHONOLOGY OF THE WORLD'S LANGUAGES

The phonology of most languages was once and to a large extent still is available only in a fragmented way, through unpublished theses, or articles scattered in more or less accessible journals. Each volume in this series offers an extensive treatment of the phonology of one language within a modern theoretical perspective, and provides comprehensive references to recent and more classical studies of the language. The following are normally included: an introduction situating the language geographically and typologically, an overview of the theoretical assumptions made by the author, a description of the segmental system and of the rules or constraints characterizing the language, an outline of syllable structure and domains above the syllable, a discussion of lexical and postlexical phonology, an account of stress and prominence, and, if space allows, some overview of the intonational structure of the language.

Each volume is cast in a modern theoretical framework, but there has been and will always be scope for a diversity of approach which reflects variations between languages and in the methodologies and theoretical preoccupations of the authors.

Published in the series:

The Phonology of Norwegian
Gjert Kristoffersen

The Phonology of Hungarian
Péter Siptár and Miklós Törkenczy

The Phonology of Portuguese
Maria Helena Mateus and Ernesto d'Andrade

The Phonology of English
Michael Hammond

The Phonology of Dutch
Geert Booij

The Phonology of Armenian
Bert Vaux

The Phonology of German
Richard Wiese

The Phonology and Morphology of Kimatuumbi
David Odden

The Lexical Phonology of Slovak
Jerzy Rubach

THE
PHONOLOGY
OF
GERMAN

—

Richard Wiese

OXFORD
UNIVERSITY PRESS

OXFORD
UNIVERSITY PRESS

Great Clarendon Street, Oxford OX2 6DP

Oxford University Press is a department of the University of Oxford.
It furthers the University's objective of excellence in research, scholarship,
and education by publishing worldwide in

Oxford New York

Athens Auckland Bangkok Bogotá Buenos Aires Calcutta
Cape Town Chennai Dar es Salaam Delhi Florence Hong Kong Istanbul
Karachi Kuala Lumpur Madrid Melbourne Mexico City Mumbai
Nairobi Paris São Paulo Shanghai Singapore Taipei Tokyo Toronto Warsaw
with associated companies in Berlin Ibadan

Published in the United States
by Oxford University Press Inc., New York

Published new as paperback 2000

British Library Cataloguing in Publication Data
Data available

Library of Congress Cataloging in Publication Data
The phonology of German / Richard Wiese.
(The phonology of the world's languages)
Includes bibliographical references.
1. German language—Phonology. I. Title. II. Series.
PF3131.W54 1996   431'.5—dc20   95–22081
ISBN 0–19–824040–6 (hbk.)
ISBN 0–19–829950–8 (pbk.)

1 3 5 7 9 10 8 6 4 2

Typeset by Graphicraft Typesetters Ltd., Hong Kong
Printed in Great Britain on acid-free paper by
Biddles Ltd., Guildford and King's Lynn

PREFACE

As a student of linguistics, I experienced phonology as the least interesting of the core areas of linguistics. It seemed obvious that classical phonology involved a few mechanical procedures, leading to the (never quite satisfactory) discovery of phonemes and allophones, while generative phonology (if presented at all) seemed to suffer from excessive abstractness and other problems. The general picture presented was that the important questions of linguistics were asked (if not answered) in other domains, such as in syntax, semantics, and pragmatics. This experience (doubtlessly shared by many contemporary students) led me to pursue other interests for a long period.

But eventually it turned out that phonology was not just a stock of uninteresting pieces of dead knowledge. Rather, in phonology, general questions on the nature of human language and its principles can be studied, which are of the same kind as questions and problems in other domains of grammatical theory. Following this discovery, I started to think about the phonological structure of my own language a number of years ago. The present book is the result and summary of these considerations.

Many colleagues have helped and supported this project in various ways during the past years. Jacques Durand has been the instigator of the study by kindly suggesting that I write it for this series and by helping me along all the way. I have been very fortunate and privileged in that a number of colleagues in various places, particularly along the lower Rhine in Düsseldorf and Cologne, have provided numerous occasions for discussion and have read large parts of the manuscript. Heinz Giegerich and Tracy Hall have been particularly constructive and critical with their many insights and suggestions. It is quite likely that I should have taken better notice of their advice. Geert Booij, Ray Fabri, Michael Jessen, Renate Raffelsiefen, Karl Heinz Ramers, Monika Rothweiler, Heinz Vater, Dieter Wunderlich, and Si-Taek Yu have also been very helpful by reading various parts of the manuscript and pointing out problems and weaknesses. Hans-Willi Cuypers and Tim Skellett have been very careful in helping me with proofreading, and with work on the references and indexes.

For this paperback edition, some obvious errors have been corrected, while the main text and the analyses proposed there have not been changed. I thank the following colleagues for helping me in spotting the mistakes: Wilbur A. Benware, Tracy Alan Hall, Bettina Isensee, Martin Neef, and Joseph C. Salmons. The discussion on phonological topics in general and on the phonology of German has continued and, arguably, increased since the present book was written. The book therefore now contains a postscript in which I briefly introduce those studies within the relatively new framework of Optimality Theory that have focused on German.

In addition, the reformed spelling for German words has been adopted for the paperback edition and the word index has been expanded to include page references. I thank Barbara Pfisterer and Dorothea Stresing for their invaluable help in these tasks.

CONTENTS

Abbreviations and Symbols   x

1. INTRODUCTION   1

1.1. Major Aims and Principles   1
1.2. A Brief Survey of the Content   5
1.3. Notational and Other Technical Matters   7
1.4. Phonetic Symbols   8

2. THE PHONEME SYSTEM OF GERMAN   9

2.1. The Phonemic Contrasts   10
2.2. Problems of Phonemization   11
   2.2.1. The system boundary problem   11
   2.2.2. The problem of complex segments: Affricates and diphthongs   13
   2.2.3. The problem of phonetic similarity   15
   2.2.4. The problem of phonemic choice   16
   2.2.5. The central vowel: schwa   16
2.3. The Contrastive Features   19
   2.3.1. Vowels   19
   2.3.2. Consonants   22

3. THE PROSODIC STRUCTURE OF GERMAN   27

3.1. Segmental Architecture   27
3.2. Syllables   33
   3.2.1. The skeleton   37
   3.2.2. More on subsyllabic structure   43
   3.2.3. Extrasyllabicity   47
   3.2.4. Syllabification   49
3.3. The Foot   56
   3.3.1. Glottal stop and the foot   58
   3.3.2. Plural formation and the foot   61
   3.3.3. Hypocoristics or clippings   62
3.4. The Phonological Word   65
3.5. The Phonological Phrase   74
3.6. The Intonational Phrase   77
3.7. Concluding Remarks   82

4. PROSODIC MORPHOLOGY   85

4.1. Phonology-dependent Affixations   85
   4.1.1. +*ei*   85
   4.1.2. Unstressed prefixes *be*+ and *ge*+   89

4.1.3. Allomorphy of +*heit* and +*keit* 98
4.1.4. On some supposed allomorphies 100
4.2. A Prosodic Constraint on Compounds 103
4.3. Inflection, Schwa, and Prosodic Structure 105
4.3.1. Schwa in nouns 106
4.3.2. Adjectives 109
4.3.3. Verbs 110
4.3.4. On various approaches to inflectional schwa in German 113

5. ASPECTS OF LEXICAL PHONOLOGY AND MORPHOLOGY 115

5.1. Lexical Phonology and Morphology 116
5.2. More on Morphology and the Lexicon of German 119
5.2.1. Two classes of morphology 119
5.2.2. Level ordering in the German lexicon 127
5.2.3. Lexical levels or lexical categories? 129
5.3 Lexical Principles and the System of Nominal Inflection 132
5.3.1. Principles in Lexical Phonology 132
5.3.2. Plural formation 136
5.3.3. On the status of the *Fugenmorpheme* 143
5.4. On Some Open Problems 147

6. UNDERSPECIFICATION: AN ANALYSIS OF MARKEDNESS AND DEFAULTS 150

6.1. The Vowel System Underspecified 151
6.1.1. The diphthongs 159
6.1.2. On Contrastive Underspecification 162
6.2. The Consonant System Underspecified 163
6.2.1. On coronals 165
6.2.2. Other place features 167
6.3. The Major Classes and their Features 168
6.3.1. The feature phonology of /ʀ/ 170
6.3.2. Markedness rules and defaults 172
6.3.3. Laryngeals 173
6.4. Some Open Questions 175

7. PHONOLOGICAL RULES AND ALTERNATIONS 178

7.1. Rule Formalism 179
7.2. Rules of Vowel Alternation 181
7.2.1. Umlaut 181
7.2.2. Vowel shortening 194
7.2.3. Alternations with schwa 198
7.3. Rules in the Consonant System 199
7.3.1. Final Devoicing 200
7.3.2. g-Spirantization 206

7.3.3. Dorsal Fricative Assimilation   209
7.3.4. Nasal Assimilation   218
7.3.5. g-Deletion   224
7.3.6. Degemination   229
7.3.7. Consonant epenthesis   232
7.4. Syllables and Related Matters   234
7.4.1. Consonant–vowel transitions   235
7.4.2. The distribution of schwa   242
7.4.3. Some clitic forms   248
7.4.4. r-Vocalization   252
7.5. Phonotactic Constraints and Principles   258
7.5.1. The sonority hierarchy   258
7.5.2. Consonant clusters and complex segments   261
7.6. Phonology or Phonetics?   269

8. WORD STRESS, COMPOUND STRESS, PHRASE
   STRESS   272

8.1. Representations for Stress   272
8.2. Simplex Words   276
8.2.1. Vowel length and stress   277
8.2.2. Marked and unmarked stress patterns   280
8.2.3. Stress rules   282
8.3. Complex Words   287
8.3.1. Stress in suffixed words   287
8.3.2. Stress in prefixed words   293
8.4. Compounds   296
8.5. Phrasal Stress and Stress Shifts   302
8.5.1. Rules of phrasal stress   302
8.5.2. Stress shifts   306
8.6 Concluding Remarks   311

9. CONCLUDING REMARKS   312

Postscript 2000   314

Appendix: Word Index   319

References   342

Subject Index   356

ABBREVIATIONS AND SYMBOLS

A	adjective	nom.	nominative
abb.	abbreviation	NP	noun phrase
acc.	accusative	O	onset
adj.	adjective	P	preposition
ATR	advanced tongue root	part.	participle
Aux	auxiliary	pl.	plural
C	coda, consonant	PP	prepositional phrase
cond.	conditional	pres.	present
dat.	dative	R	root node of segment
dim.	diminutive	s	strong
F	foot	sg.	singular
f.	feminine	*SPE*	*The Sound Pattern of English*
fem.	feminine (feature)	subj.	subjunctive
gen.	genitive	V	verb, vowel
imp.	imperative	VP	verb phrase
infl.	inflection	w	weak
IP	intonational phrase		
iter.	iterative	α	variable ranging over + and −
m.	masculine	φ	phonological phrase
MHG	Middle High German	σ	syllable
N	noun, nucleus, underspecified nasal	ω	phonological word
n.	neuter		

1

INTRODUCTION

1.1. MAJOR AIMS AND PRINCIPLES

This volume is intended primarily as a thorough and in-depth survey of the phonological system of present-day German. Secondarily, it is intended as an application of recent theories and models as developed in phonology to the German language, and as a guide to and critical discussion of the standard literature relevant to the topics and problems under discussion. My empirical analyses reflect many hypotheses and theoretical constructs from recent works. In other words, emphasis is put both on empirical coverage and on theoretical argumentation and analysis.

There is ample room for discussion here; as Vennemann (1992: 399) has recently pointed out, 'Modern Standard German [. . .] is one of the best-studied languages in the world, yet its phonological system is only poorly understood. Just about any aspect of it is a matter of debate.' This book is intended as a contribution to the debate, which has in recent years increased considerably in quantity and, hopefully, in quality. I also hope to summarize much of this recent literature.

The language studied here is German, as it is spoken at the present time, and in the German-speaking countries (Germany, Austria, parts of Switzerland, and minorities elsewhere), but perhaps most frequently and directly in the northern parts of (former East and West) Germany.

Furthermore, the standardized form of present-day German, termed *Modern Standard German*, is chosen as the major object of the present study. As with other languages, it is by no means trivial to determine what the standard language, the norm, is. As far as the phonology is concerned, the main media concerned with establishing a standard are pronouncing dictionaries of German. Pronouncing dictionaries in Germany have a relatively short history compared to those of the other larger national languages of Europe. This is due to the rather late unification of the German-speaking *Fürstentümer* in the second half of the nineteenth century with the election of the Prussian king as the German *Kaiser* in 1871 as the most prominent event. It was only at the close of the nineteenth century that Theodor Siebs first published his *Deutsche Bühnenaussprache* (Siebs 1898). This was intended primarily as instruction on how to articulate on the stage, but subsequently it was also regarded as a definition of what was received German pronunciation in general. The Prussian dominance in nineteenth-century Germany was also responsible for the fact that Northern German pronunciation was chosen and elevated to the status of the *Hochsprache*.

At present, there are, besides the *Siebs* (1969, latest edition), two main pronouncing dictionaries that can be taken as defining the standard pronunciation: The *Duden-Aussprachewörterbuch* (Duden 1990, latest edition) published in West Germany, and the *Großes Wörterbuch der deutschen Aussprache* (Krech et al. 1982, latest edition) published in Leipzig, East Germany. Both works (besides the *Siebs*) are referred to occasionally in the present study. In some instances, however, deviations in transcription and judgement from both of these dictionaries are made. If such a case occurs, it is noted and reasons for it are discussed.

All of the pronouncing dictionaries have opted for a *gemäßigte Hochlautung* ('modified received pronunciation') as the basis of standardization. The main aim is to promote a pronunciation of German which is free of dialectal and other variation.[1] Basically, the pronouncing dictionaries claim both to be based on observation of actual speech and to be prescriptive for some forms of (public) communication. The level of speaking described in the dictionaries is set apart on the one hand from the articulation on the stage (the variant described in older editions of the *Siebs*) and on the other hand from the *Umgangslautung* ('colloquial pronunciation'), although some features of the latter register are sometimes described (e.g. Duden 1990: 55–9). Features of colloquial pronunciation will be discussed in the present work at a number of places.

It is certainly debatable whether there is an actual pronunciation which is totally purified of all regional connotations. This question is contained in a large body of literature on questions of defining and differentiating between the standard language, the colloquial language(s), and regional or social dialects. I will try to note whenever I discuss data which belong not to the codified standard but somewhere else. Often, these latter forms are part of *casual* (but not *fast*) speech in the sense of Kaisse (1985), with the additional qualification that such casual speech is usually under the influence of a major regional dialect. Modern Standard German proper, on the other hand, is relatively *formal* speech.

Although the focus of the present book is on present-day standard German, both on the standardized and the colloquial variants, important diverging features of closely related major dialects (such as Northern vernacular, Bavarian, Viennese German) will be referred to on appropriate occasions. There is no space, however, for thorough discussion of the large number of German dialects. For a recent survey of these see Russ (1990).

The book is meant to serve various types of readers. For the linguist, especially the phonologist, it may be used as an overview and a manual of the phonology of German. If successful, the book hopefully can be used as a ref-

---

[1] One may well ask whether there is not a contradiction in creating 'a dialect-free form of pronunciation [. . .] which does not create social distance' (Krech et al., 1982: 12, my translation).

erence work for many further studies in the field. At the same time, it argues for specific theoretical notions, but I shall make an effort to consider also facts which are not easily amenable to the particular model I have in mind. For teachers and students of German, especially at college and university level, the present book will provide wider and deeper information on the phonology of this language than any other book available up to now. In this respect, I hope to provide a fresh case for the inclusion of phonology into the teaching of German. Some areas covered here are treated very superficially or not at all in studies to date.

The one major area of the phonological system of German which I will not cover in the present work is that of intonation. While there is some discussion of the intonational phrase in Chapter 3, the general questions of the descriptions of intonational contours in German are not treated. Intonation studies are another large field of study for German as for other languages, and the concepts and methods used here are somewhat different from that of other domains of phonology. The reader is referred to works such as Fox (1984), Wunderlich (1988), Uhmann (1991), and Féry (1993) for coverage of intonation from different approaches and points of view.

The work starts from the assumptions that there is a considerable need for a handbook and an overview of this kind, and that there is, up to the present, no monograph available that can possibly serve the functions sketched above. On the whole, I can only hope to strike the right balance between the motivation of theoretical concepts and the presentation of empirical results. The book starts from a very elementary description presupposing no specific phonological knowledge. On the other hand, limitations of space have prevented me from discussing at length the more basic phonetic and phonological concepts used in the course of the book. Prior acquaintance with one of the recent textbooks on phonology might therefore be helpful to some readers.[2] Nevertheless, I attempt to explain all theoretical notions used at the time when they are needed.

The theoretical framework in which the description and analysis is couched can be called 'generative phonology' in three different senses. First, it is assumed here that representations (phonological representations, in this case) are not merely a matter of arbitrary conventions or notations, but an integral part of the theory and description. As in probably all models of generative phonology, a difference in representation implies a difference in the theory or in the description. For example, matters of markedness and simplicity are reflected directly in representational complexity. It is also assumed that the notion of *derivation* plays some role in characterizing the phonological component, although it is

---

[2] Fortunately, there is a good number of recent textbooks in phonology. I should name the volumes by Durand (1990), Goldsmith (1990), Kenstowicz (1994), and Roca (1994) as very useful and thorough introductions to many of the issues of current phonological theory. None of these books is based on a consideration of a specific language. These books are recommended for those interested in more general issues in phonological theory, such as non-linear models and Lexical Phonology.

currently an open question how much derivation (specified changes to a form set up as the underlying one) has to be assumed.

In a second sense, one fundamental assumption of generative phonology is that linguistic description in fact characterizes a small, but real and significant, part of human mental function. The domain of phonology is not of a physical or physiological nature, but psychological or mental. One methodological consequence of this view is that language users' judgements about aspects of a sound system constitute valid data for the phonologist.[3]

Thirdly, in accordance with the tradition of generative phonology since its beginnings, I will treat many of the so-called 'morphophonemic alternations' as an integral part of the phonological system. In consequence, without denying their special properties, I reject any view which holds that morphophonology and phonology proper are independent areas of grammar. Thus, the understanding of 'phonology' in this book is rather broad, compared to other works. Consequently, the empirical domain to be covered is wider as well, reaching to a considerable extent into aspects of morphology or word formation.

Many other aspects of what is often connected with generative phonology are of lesser importance, a matter of debate and discussion, or simply not held to be true. Thus, the degree of abstractness allowed will be much smaller in this study than it was assumed in Chomsky and Halle (1968; abbreviated as *SPE*) and work on German based on this theory (most notably Wurzel 1970; Kloeke 1982). Similarly, the idea of what a rule is and what it can do, is quite distinct here from the conception in earlier generative phonology. For the specialist we might add that the theoretical framework of this study is a combination of Lexical Phonology, non-linear phonology, and underspecification theory. The discussion of prosodic structure and its role is considerably enlarged as compared to older treatments.

In due course, I will have to justify these fundamental choices within the realm of theoretical options.

Another cautionary remark may be appropriate. Since the main aim of this book is to provide an analysis of the sound system of German, very little attention is paid to other languages. Thus, it may sometimes appear to the reader that particular phenomena or rules and representations set up to deal with these phenomena are rather unique and exotic. In many cases, quite the opposite is true. It is my belief that the phonological system of German contains only a small, although significant, part which must be seen as being language particular. For the larger part, the properties of this system are universal and shared by all or at least many other languages. But reasons of space allow neither for the discussion of related phenomena in other languages nor for reference to relevant theoretical proposals which are very similar to the ones made here for German.

---

[3] This is not to mean that judgements on matters of linguistic form are automatically *phonological* judgements.

1.2. A BRIEF SURVEY OF THE CONTENT

Given that this book attempts to explore all phenomena of German that can reasonably be covered by the term 'phonology', it may be useful to give a brief overview of what can be expected in the following chapters. (The uninitiated reader may want to skip this section, since it mentions concepts explained only in later chapters.) As pointed out above, morphophonological phenomena are not excluded from consideration. As shown in §§ 7.3.4 (Nasal Assimilation) and 7.3.6 (Degemination), the exclusion would in fact be unfortunate, since a number of processes seem to be such that they apply both in interaction with the morphology and as 'proper' phonological processes. Secondly, questions of suprasegmental or prosodic phonology loom rather large in the present study. This is partly due to the recent upsurge in theoretical work on suprasegmental properties. Non-linear models of various kinds seem to provide a better basis for the study of entities such as the syllable and other prosodic categories, stress, and intonation, which are usually treated rather cursorily or not at all in preceding surveys.

As an introduction (after the usual preliminaries), a first survey of the domain of study is given in the form of a *phoneme analysis* of the language. This serves the useful purpose of providing the minimal introduction possible to the phonological system of German; at the same time, it provides a good point of departure to justify further inquiries into the phonology of this language. Paradoxes of phonemization, questions of phoneme classes, and prosodic issues all justify the introduction of more elaborate phonological models.

In the second half of Chapter 2, a featural analysis of the phonemes (or rather, of all segments that play a role in the phonology of German) is presented. Features are, in this study just as in phonology in general, justified by the role they play in rules and combinatorial restrictions. Thus, it will be necessary here to just refer to regularities that are treated systematically later on.

While this is one necessary foundation for any subsequent analysis, the higher-level prosodic structure and the overall geometry of the feature representations provides another such groundwork. An *overview over prosodic structure*, conceptualized in the broad sense of including all kinds of sub- and suprasegmental phonological structure, is therefore presented in Chapter 3. Categories such as the syllable, its internal structure, the foot, the phonological word and phrase, and the intonational phrase are introduced and briefly motivated here. All of these elements will be seen to function in the description of some phonological regularities. This chapter introduces notions of non-linear representation, designed to express the non-segmental properties of the categories in question.

The discussion of prosodic structure is continued in Chapter 4 on the role of prosodic categories and constraints in morphology. Under the heading *Prosodic Morphology* I argue that diverse morphological formations in German must obey specific prosodic constraints which have not received much attention so

far. Here and in the following chapter, I also introduce and discuss a considerable amount of the morphology of German, including inflection, derivation, and
compounding.

The study also introduces the framework of *Lexical Phonology*. Lexical phonology assumes that one ingredient of the lexicon are the morphological rules
which, working in tandem with the phonological rules and principles, give words
their formal structure and their phonological shape. Chapter 5 motivates such an
approach and the principles formulated in this theory from some regularities of
German, in particular from noun inflection. In this chapter, I also outline a model
of level ordering for German, and raise some critical questions on problems in
this area.

The question of full versus non-redundant representation of segments is treated
in Chapter 6. Important theoretical notions introduced here are those of
underspecification and of default rules. A rather radical underspecification analysis
is presented for all segmental features, including those of the major classes.
Various rules are proposed to fill in the redundant values.

In accordance with the general spirit of current phonological theory, the *rules*
for alternations and processes should more or less follow, if the representations
chosen are the correct ones. Most of the rules that can be identified within the
phonology of German are discussed in Chapter 7. Rules relevant for the description of vowels (Umlaut, Schwa Distribution, and Vowel Shortening) are covered
as well as the larger number of rules pertaining to the consonantal segments,
such as Final Devoicing, Dorsal Fricative Assimilation, Nasal Assimilation, *g*-
Deletion, and Degemination, to name only a few of the better known. Special
attention is also paid to a number of syllable-related processes of consonantization
and vocalization and to phonotactic constraints at the syllable level.

From the list of rules mentioned above, it may seem that the approach is
highly (or excessively) rule-based. That impression might be corrected by emphasizing that the rules are usually blank-filling. Thus, they do not change one
structure into another, but simply fill in redundant information. In a way, the
rules are conceptualized as a consequence of the basic feature structure of the
German language.

The morphological information is also needed in the discussion of *word stress*.
After introducing (some version of) metrical representation, this system is applied
in Chapter 8 to stress in monomorphemic and complex words, and then to phrases,
in which stress shifts can also be observed.

While in this volume an attempt is made to cover all relevant areas and parts
of the phonology of Modern Standard German, it is natural that some domains
receive more attention than others. My proposals on segmental feature structure and the material on higher prosodic categories presented in Chapter 3,
the discussion of prosodic morphology in Chapter 4, the particular version of
underspecification I develop in Chapter 6, and the analysis of word stress in
Chapter 8—these parts present relatively new and unique results of phonological research.

1.3. NOTATIONAL AND OTHER TECHNICAL MATTERS

Phonology is one of the sciences of the form of language. Therefore, some amount of notation to refer to the entities we are dealing with, and some formal apparatus to state clearly and precisely the regularities we want to capture, cannot be avoided. For the former purpose—reference to phonological entities— the most important tool is the notation for segments developed by the *International Phonetic Association* (IPA). All transcriptions of sounds in this book follow the conventions of the IPA, in the latest version as it is described by the International Phonetic Association (1989). Tables (1), (2), and (3) in § 1.4 below represent a subset of the relevant IPA conventions and give a survey and a preliminary phonetic description of all the sound symbols used in discussions in this book. While the preliminary classification of the consonants in (1) is unproblematic, the classification of vowels in (2) will be defended in later chapters. For reasons explained in § 2.2.1, I regard the two *a*-sounds of German as being distinct only in length, but not in quality. Another deviation from the IPA format is the use of the tense–lax distinction for vowels. In the vowel quadrangle of the IPA, this distinction (as in [i] vs. [ɪ]) is expressed by a difference in vowel height and degree of centralization.

Following customary conventions, I will signify purely phonetic forms by enclosing the transcriptions in square brackets ('[ ]'), while phonological representations are denoted by slashes ('/ /'). When the assignment to underlying, intermediate or surface-phonetic levels is irrelevant or unclear, slashes (or just normal orthography) are used, with a minimum commitment as to the level addressed. For the benefit of brevity and readability, examples are sometimes referred to in their orthographic form. In such a case, italic characters are used if an example occurs in running text. The reader should also note that mixed notations, with phonetic symbols included in orthographic forms, occur as well: (*Lie*[b]*e* vs. *lie*[p]*lich*). As the two preceding words are the first two pieces of German data I present, I should also mention that all German words used in this book are given a gloss in the Appendix, while all longer phrases are given an English translation where they appear.

Apart from symbols for segments, it is necessary to be able to refer to various types of boundaries. In accordance with one well-known convention, I will denote morpheme boundaries by '+' and syllable boundaries by a dot '.' (see (3) below). In a way, the blank can also be seen as a symbol for a word boundary. A word such as *silbisch* can thus be transcribed as [zɪl.b+ɪʃ] or *sil-b+isch* in the orthography; the more complex word *Nationalität* as [naˈ.ts+ i̯o.n+a.l+i.tɛːt] (with length, including half-length, according to the judgement of Krech et al. (1982)).

It may be important to stress that the use of boundary symbols carries no commitment to a boundary approach in phonology or morphology. As the following chapters will show, just the contrary holds. Symbols such as '+' and '.' are merely convenient forms of notation. The same is true for the stress markers introduced in (3) below.

1.4. PHONETIC SYMBOLS

(1)

	Bilabial	Labio-dental	Alveolar	Palato-alveolar	Palatal	Velar	Uvular	Glottal
Plosive	p b		t d			k g		ʔ
Fricative		f v	s z	ʃ ʒ	ç ʝ	x ɣ	χ ʁ	h
Nasal	m	ɱ	n		ɲ	ŋ		
Approximant		ʋ	l, r		j		ʀ	

a. Transcription of consonants (IPA conventions following the revisions up to 1989)[4]

b. Diacritics

   voicelessness: ̥ (C̥)   syllabic: ̩ (C̩)
   aspiration: ʰ (Cʰ)

(2)

	Front				Central	Back	
	Tense		Lax		Lax	Lax	Tense
High	i	y	ɪ	ʏ		ʊ	u
Mid	e	ø	ɛ	œ	ə	ɔ	o
					ɐ		
Low					a	ɑ	

a. Classification and transcription of vowels (IPA-conventions) In each pair of vowels, the round vowel is given to the right of the corresponding non-round vowel.

b. Diacritics

   non-syllabic: ̯ (V̯)
   nasalized: ˜ (ṽ)

(3) Diacritics for suprasegmental aspects

   half-long: ˑ (Vˑ)   long: ː (Vː)
   primary stress: ' ('CV.CV)   secondary stress: ˌ (ˌCV.'CV)
   extra-heavy stress: " ("CV.'CV)
   syllable break: . (CV.CV)

---

[4] The recent IPA chart (International Phonetic Association 1989) does not provide room for an *approximant* uvular r-sound (except by means of a diacritic). Consequently, there is no symbol for an r-sound which is neither fricative, nor trilled, nor tapped. Since there seems to be a good case for such an approximant in German, I use the symbol [ʀ] for this sound segment. [ʀ] in the IPA chart stands for a *trilled* uvular r-sound. Ladefoged (1982: 154 *et passim*) recognizes an approximant uvular r-sound, but transcribes it as [ʁ], identical to the corresponding fricative.

THE PHONEME SYSTEM OF GERMAN

One of the cornerstones of phonological thought, and, in fact, the leading idea in early phonological theory, is the insight that behind the almost unlimited variability in the realization of sounds there is a rather small set of contrastive segments, the phonemes. Each language is characterized by a set of such phonemes, which are defined largely by the contrastive function they carry with respect to each other within a particular language system. The literature on phonemes, their possible definitions and their function, is vast; see Fischer-Jørgensen (1975) and Anderson (1985) for overview and discussion of various approaches and further references. Discussion of phonemes of German is also widespread; Trubetzkoy (1939), Moulton (1962), Ungeheuer (1969), and Philipp (1974) are some important authors; much of the literature is summarized by Werner (1972), Meinhold and Stock (1980), Benware (1986), and Ramers and Vater (1991).

The aim of this chapter is not so much to present a phonemic analysis of German, as to show that it is necessary to go beyond such an analysis. In later chapters, it will become even clearer that attempting to find a definition of 'phoneme' is perhaps more of a dead end than was believed for a long period. Nevertheless, it is useful for a number of reasons to put forward an inventory of phonemes for German. The idea that a phonological system is in one respect a system of units which are in distinctive contrast to each other has remained constant over the development of phonological theory and description. In the second part of this chapter, the phonemes will also be characterized in terms of phonological features.

The standard method for finding the set of phonemes for a language is to construct *minimal pairs*; that is, pairs of semantically distinct words that differ only in one segment at a particular place. Exchanging a minimal element in a word, to see whether this leads to an acceptable form with a different meaning, is known as the *commutation test*. Below, a set of minimal pairs is given for each phoneme of German; first for consonants in (1), and then for vowels in (2). Notice that phonemes are justified here by their ability to express lexical contrasts; something is a phoneme only if it helps to distinguish at least one morpheme from other morphemes. For the sake of completeness it should be mentioned here that word stress can also carry lexical contrasts, as in *'Tenor* 'tenor, substance' vs. *Te'nor* 'tenor singer'. We could therefore speak, within a strictly phonemic framework, of a stress phoneme in German. However, stress only functions marginally in the expression of lexical contrasts. Chapter 8 treats stress more comprehensively.

2.1. THE PHONEMIC CONTRASTS

A very general assumption about the phonemic system of German (as perhaps of all other languages) is that there are two basic subsystems, that of vowel phonemes and that of consonant phonemes. Accordingly, these two parts of the inventory will be presented here as distinct systems, but we will note from the start that there are consonant–vowel transitions that seem to be ruled out under such a perspective. In later sections, it will be seen that [j] and [ʊ] can be allophones of /ɪ/ and /ʊ/, respectively, and that the consonant /r/ can be vocalized. The consonant–vowel distinction is, thus, not as sharp as the usual treatment implies.

As far as possible, minimal pairs are displayed in (1) for three different positions in the word: word-initially, word-medially between vowels, and word-finally.[1] Although a pair of sounds reveals a phonemic contrast if there are minimal pairs in one of these positions only, it will be shown later on that the three positions differ systematically in their potential for displaying a phonemic contrast. In (1) and (2), sounds whose status as phonemes is actually debated in the pertinent literature, are bracketed. A dash appears in those positions where some phoneme is absent for systematic reasons, which will be explained below.

(1) Consonant phonemes and corresponding minimal pairs

Unit	Initial	Medial	Final
/p/	Pein ~ Bein	Mappe ~ Matte	Lob ~ Lot
/b/	Bus ~ Kuss	lieben ~ liefen	——
/t/	tot ~ rot	leiten ~ leiden	Tat ~ Tal
/d/	drei ~ frei	Leder ~ Leber	——
/k/	Kind ~ Rind	recken ~ retten	Kalk ~ Kalb
/g/	geben ~ leben	Bogen ~ Boden	——
(/pf/)	Pfau ~ Tau	schlupfen ~ schlucken	Kopf ~ Koch
(/ts/)	zahm ~ lahm	reizen ~ reißen	Sitz ~ Sinn
(/tʃ/)	Tscheche ~ Bäche	latschen ~ lahmen	Rutsch ~ Ruck
(/dʒ/)	Job ~ Mob	Loggia ~ Lotta	——
/f/	Fisch ~ Tisch	Affe ~ Asche	Graf ~ Gras
/v/	Wahl ~ Saal	Oval ~ Opal	——
/s/	Stil ~ Stiel	Masse ~ Masche	das ~ dann
/z/	Saal ~ Tal	reisen ~ reißen	——
/ʃ/	Schal ~ Saal	Esche ~ Ecke	harsch ~ hart
(/ʒ/)	Genie ~ Genius	Rage ~ Rabe	——
(/ç/)	China ~ Tina	reichen ~ reißen	Elch ~ Elf
(/x/)	——	rauchen ~ rauschen	Bach ~ Ball
(/j/)	Jugend ~ Tugend	Bojen ~ Boden	——
/m/	Mund ~ Schund	kämmen ~ kennen	Alm ~ Alp
/n/	Note ~ Schote	Kenner ~ Keller	Lohn ~ Los
(/ŋ/)	——	ringen ~ rinnen	Ding ~ Dill
/l/	Laub ~ Raub	fallen ~ fangen	viel ~ vier
/r/	Riss ~ Biss	waren ~ waten	dürr ~ dünn
(/h/)	Haus ~ Maus	Bernhard ~ Bernward	——
(/ʔ/)	aus ~ Haus	Pol?let ~ Prolet	——

[1] The contrast provided for the three positions is not the same; in agreement with general practice, the word class within a minimal pair is kept constant. In some cases, the words include more than

In the following list of vowel phonemes, minimal pairs are offered for contrasts in vowel quality alone, and also, keeping the quality constant as much as this is possible for each case, for contrasts in vowel quantity (length). Thus, in *lieben* vs. *leben*, both vowels are long, while in *bieten* vs. *bitten*, a vowel which is very similar in quality appears both long (*bieten*) and short (*bitten*).

(2) Vowels and corresponding minimal pairs

/iː/	lieben ~ leben, bieten ~ bitten	[iː] ~ [eː], [iː] ~ [ɪ]
/ɪ/	Wille ~ Welle, binnen ~ Bienen	[ɪ] ~ [ɛ], [ɪ] ~ [iː]
/yː/	Tür ~ Tier, Hüte ~ Hütte	[yː] ~ [iː], [yː] ~ [ʏ]
/ʏ/	Müll ~ Mull, füllen ~ fühlen	[ʏ] ~ [ʊ], [ʏ] ~ [yː]
/eː/	legen ~ lügen, Beet ~ Bett	[eː] ~ [yː], [eː] ~ [ɛ]
/ɛ/	Geld ~ Gold, schellen ~ schälen	[ɛ] ~ [ɔ], [ɛ] ~ [ɛː]
(/ɛː/)	säen ~ sehen, äße ~ esse	[ɛː] ~ [eː], [ɛː] ~ [ɛ]
/øː/	schön ~ schon, Höhle ~ Hölle	[øː] ~ [oː], [øː] ~ [œ]
/œ/	Hölle ~ Halle, Rösslein ~ Röslein	[œ] ~ [a], [œ] ~ [øː]
/aː/	Tat ~ Tod, Schal ~ Schall	[aː] ~ [oː], [aː] ~ [a]
/a/	Bass ~ Biss, Stall ~ Stahl	[a] ~ [ɪ], [a] ~ [aː]
/oː/	loben ~ leben, Ofen ~ offen	[oː] ~ [eː], [oː] ~ [ɔ]
/ɔ/	locken ~ lecken, schoss ~ Schoß	[ɔ] ~ [ɛ], [ɔ] ~ [oː]
/uː/	Huhn ~ Hahn, spuken ~ spucken	[uː] ~ [aː], [uː] ~ [ʊ]
/ʊ/	Lust ~ List, muss ~ Mus	[ʊ] ~ [ɪ], [ʊ] ~ [uː]
(/ə/)	fehlend ~ elend, Gebein ~ geben	[ə] ~ [ɛ], [ə] ~ [eː]
(/ɐ/)	Lehrer ~ Lehre, Vater ~ Vati	[ɐ] ~ [ə], [ɐ] ~ [i]
(/aɪ/)	Teil ~ Tal, Leib ~ Laub	[aɪ] ~ [aː], [aɪ] ~ [aʊ]
(/aʊ/)	Raum ~ Rahm, Laute ~ Leute	[aʊ] ~ [aː], [aʊ] ~ [ɔʏ]
(/ɔʏ/)	läuten ~ löten, neun ~ nein	[ɔʏ] ~ [øː], [ɔʏ] ~ [aɪ]

The two lists of phonemes presented in (1) and (2) are maximal in the sense that every segment ever considered as a serious candidate for phonemic status has been included.[2] Most authors dealing with this problem have proposed more or less divergent lists. In other words, not all decisions made in the lists above are self-evident. There are, on the contrary, quite a few problematic cases to which I will now turn. The discussion of these problems in the phonemization of German will provide the grounds for a different treatment and perspective on the phonological system in general. That is, only by going beyond the phonemic analysis given above, and by studying concepts such as phonological features, syllable structure, and phonological alternations, can one (hope to) eventually solve the puzzles and paradoxes that are apparent in the phoneme system as such and that loom large in the classical treatises on these topics.

2.2. PROBLEMS OF PHONEMIZATION

2.2.1. The system boundary problem

A first difficulty in setting up the phoneme system for probably any language is the unclear status of some sounds occurring in a subset of the vocabulary that

---

one morpheme. Philipp (1974), Meinhold and Stock (1980), and in particular Ortmann (1983) provide extensive lists of various other minimal pairs.

[2] I must admit that the *zero phoneme* has not been included in the lists.

is known to have entered the language in question by borrowing from foreign languages. In other words, some boundary has to be drawn between words that are regarded as belonging to the language, and others that are not members of this language. The latter are, in other words, unassimilated loanwords. For example, neither [ɔʊ] nor [ɛɪ] have been included among the diphthongs in (2), although many speakers of German will use the expression *ok* with [ɔʊkɛɪ] as a possible pronunciation quite frequently.[3]

Other relevant examples are the nasalized vowels in the French words such as *Balkon* [balkõ], *Restaurant* [ʀɛstoːʀã], *Parfum* [paʀfœ̃], or *Teint* [tɛ̃], or the phonemes /ʒ/ and /dʒ/ which occur in a relatively small class of borrowed words. Given that some speakers will use nasalized vowels and that the pronouncing dictionaries allow these forms, do we have to say that the vowel system of German includes such nasal vowels? Most accounts would answer negatively, but others (such as Duden 1990: 30) list nasalized vowel phonemes. Such problems are found not only in establishing the phoneme inventory, but also in other domains of phonology. For example, the possibility of having consonant clusters such as /sf/ and /sm/ as in *Sphäre* and *Smaragd* is generally felt to be restricted to non-native words. In a similar vein, the distribution of voiceless /s/ is restricted in that it occurs word-initially before vowels only in unassimilated loan words; see the analysis in § 6.4. The voiceless initial in *Sex*, for example, is often changed to the voiced counterpart /z/ (though not in those southern varieties which do not have voiced /z/).

Obviously, the problem of determining the system boundaries goes beyond the decision of what is a phoneme of German and what is not. It has to be faced in any phonological description. There are several possible strategies and methods to determine the set of properties that falls within the domain of the respective language. Frequency of occurrence (measured in word types or in word tokens?) is perhaps the first candidate that comes to mind, but is certainly not very convincing in itself. A much better criterion, which will be adopted in this study, is the following: if the speakers of a language accept particular sounds or sound clusters in borrowed words without any noticeable tendency to change the sound or cluster in some way, it may be concluded that this item (even if it did not occur in the language so far) is an acceptable element of the phonological system under consideration.

Voiced /ʒ/ provides exactly such a case. Speakers of German readily accept this fricative, for example, in *Genie*, *Garage*, *Orange*. There seems to be no tendency to assimilate /ʒ/ to the system of more native sounds. On the other hand, the nasalized vowels, which are also borrowed from French, and probably in a larger number of words than /ʒ/, rarely occur in normal speech. These words are readily assimilated, usually in such a way that the non-nasalized vowel plus the velar nasal [ŋ] is used instead of the nasalized vowel.[4] I discuss

---

[3] Alternatively, [ɔʊ] and [ɛɪ] can be monophthongized: [okeː].

[4] The pronouncing dictionaries generally allow for both pronunciations in those words with a nasalized vowel that are borrowed from French.

an explanation for this particular pronunciation of the assimilated nasalized vowels in § 3.1.

A distinction related to the one just discussed is that between *central* and *peripheral* properties of a sound system. Some authors assume that a phonological description may concentrate (first) on those characteristics which are regarded as central, while other properties are relegated to a peripheral domain. Regularities postulated for the central or core area may be violated in the periphery of the system. Thus, /ʒ/ can be labelled as being a phoneme of the periphery, but not the core. Similarly, certain combinatorial patterns, such as the combination /sk/, may be excluded from the central domain; but see § 7.5.1.

In the present work, I will not allow for phonological regularities to be restricted to the periphery. First, arguments for such a distinction are often based on nothing but the observation that a specific regularity is violated in a number of examples. Claiming peripherality as being responsible is of course only an escape strategy as long as no independent evidence is offered for the assignment to core or fringe. Second, the relationship between properties of core and fringe remains unclear. It must be possible to specify in which way peripheral phenomena are allowed to deviate from central properties. As far as I can see, such a theory is lacking. Any arbitrary property can be assigned to core or fringe.

Instead of the division into central vs. peripheral, I will regard a certain property or structure as *marked* with respect to its *unmarked* counterpart within *one* system. Markedness is used here in the sense of a relative naturalness within a given phonological system, namely, Modern Standard German. Furthermore, the relative markedness difference must be expressed in the richness of the representation. In Chapter 6 and elsewhere, we will have ample occasion to observe differences in markedness and discuss the possibilities and problems of this approach.

2.2.2. The problem of complex segments: Affricates and diphthongs

Notice first that some phonemes are included in (1) and (2) that are superficially different from the other segments even in transcription: /pf/, /ts/, /tʃ/ and /dʒ/ consist of two sounds each, while all other phonemes show a certain unity which is reflected by using only one symbol of transcription. The problem is not resolved, but only indicated, by transcribing /pf/ and /ts/ as /pᶠ/ and /tˢ/, respectively.

As stop-fricative sequences, at least /pf/ and /ts/ are examples of affricates. The adequate analysis of affricates is one of the classical problems of phonological theory. Trubetzkoy (1939) set up a series of criteria for the adequate phonemic treatment of sound sequences and concluded that German /pf/ and /ts/ must be monophonemic.

In the subsequent literature, there is a strong disagreement on the phonemization of the affricates. Moulton (1962), for example, does not include /pf/, /ts/, /tʃ/ in his list of phonemes, while other authors accept at least /pf/ and /ts/. (Diphthongs, however, are treated as monophonemic by Moulton 1962: § 7.6.)

One reason given by Moulton for not treating affricates as phonemes is the following: a morpheme boundary in *Rat+s* would cut right through the phoneme /ts/. Heike (1972: 44) argues for a biphonemic analysis of the affricates on the basis of the commutation between /ts/ and /st/; cf. *Latz* [lats] to *Last* [last]. Ramers and Vater (1991: 85–91) survey the argumentation on mono- vs. biphonemic treatment of various affricates.

To conclude this discussion, we should also note that there are other sound sequences with a similar structure in German, namely (at least) /ps/ and /ks/. Although rarer, these special clusters do occur and must be dealt with (see § 7.5.2, where I argue that they are affricates as well). They are often excluded from the set of affricates since they are not formed homorganically, that is, at an identical place of articulation for the stop and the fricative part. But to include this requirement in the definition of affricates is questionable since then only /pf/ and /ts/ could be called affricates. /tʃ/ and /dʒ/ are not homorganic at the underlying level, since /t/ and /d/ are alveolar sounds, while the fricatives /ʃ/ and /ʒ/ are palato-alveolar. Whatever the precise status of this distinction is, it must be phonemic, since /s/ contrasts with /ʃ/ in German. (Phonetically, [pf] is not homorganic either, since [p] is bilabial and [f] is labiodental. In other words, it seems as if homorganicity in the case of affricates is not necessarily required either on the phonological or on the phonetic level. The homorganicity of [tʃ] on the phonetic level is unclear; see Wängler (1974: 164–5) who states that [ts] and [tʃ] are often but not always homorganic.) It has generally been assumed[5] that only /pf/ and /ts/ are phonological affricates of German in the sense that they are monophonemic. In § 7.5.2, this assumption will be questioned.

Among the vowels, there is also a set of elements whose members behave like monophonemic units in some ways, although they are bisegmental. Thus, there exists a situation that seems somewhat parallel to the description of affricates above. German has (at least) the following three diphthongs: [aʊ], [aɪ], and [ɔʏ]. Here we are only concerned with the phonemic status of these entities, not with their phonetic characterization, on which I will briefly comment in § 6.1.1. All other logically possible diphthongs (at least if they are falling diphthongs: a glide or non-syllabic vowel following a full vowel) are excluded. This fact, together with the observation that the diphthongs have, by and large, the same distribution as the long vowels, might lead to the conclusion that the three diphthongs mentioned (as a small subset of all possible vowel combinations) are phonemes to be added to the list of the other vowel phonemes.

Unfortunately there are counter-arguments here that seem equally valid: notice first that the diphthongs consist of sounds that occur independently as phonemes of German, namely /a/, /ʊ/, /ɪ/, /ɔ/, and /ʏ/. Again, we indeed find disagreement whether these sequences of vowels are mono- or biphonemic units. The argument that the diphthongs have to be seen as biphonemic units was

[5] Since Trubetzkoy (1939: 51), who in his 'rule II' for monophonemic status made homorganicity an a priori condition.

mainly advanced by Moulton (1956), who showed that diphthongs are phono-tactically equivalent to the sequence of a short vowel plus a consonant. This equivalence to a sequence which is clearly biphonemic constitutes a second argument for the biphonemic treatment of diphthongs. In spite of this rather clear-cut distributional argument, it has generally been felt that the diphthongs should be included in the inventory of vowel phonemes. Consequently, most authors treat diphthongs as monophonemic units (e.g. Trubetzkoy 1939: 51; Philipp 1974: ch. 1; Werner 1972: 34; Benware 1986: 47–9).

The proposal that the diphthongs are combinations of phonemes might even be (and has been) extended to the long vowels: the distribution of long vowels is almost identical to that of a short vowel plus a following consonant.[6] The phonemic analysis of the vowels in German, we may conclude, is remarkably inconclusive: only for the short vowels (and here again, certainly not for schwa) is it uncontroversial how many vowel phonemes there are in the German language.

2.2.3. The problem of phonetic similarity

Example (1) includes two potential phonemes, /h/ and /ŋ/, that turn out to stand in a rather special relationship. On closer examination, /h/ and /ŋ/ can be analysed as being in complementary distribution with each other. While the occurrence of /h/ is restricted to initial position and (with a few exceptions as in *Bernhard*) to a position after a long vowel, /ŋ/ cannot occur in precisely these contexts. It occurs only after short vowels. Another way of stating this particular distribution would be to say that [h] occurs only at the beginning of a syllable (foot-initial syllable, to be precise, see § 3.3.1), while [ŋ] is restricted to a syllable-final position.

But saying that [h] and [ŋ] are allophones of a single phoneme seems some-what counter-intuitive. If we want to reject an analysis which postulates two allophones [h] and [ŋ] of one phoneme, it is necessary to introduce a further criterion, that of phonetic similarity. Presumably, [h] and [ŋ] are not phonetically similar enough in order to qualify as members of one phoneme. The criterion seems like a plausible one, although it is not at all clear where to draw the boundary between similar and dissimilar sounds. Minimally, it would be reasonable to require that some measure of 'similarity', for example in terms of segmental features, can be offered. In addition, the decision which of the two sounds, [h] or [ŋ], should be taken as the phoneme would be very difficult to make. Under a Trubetzkoyan phonemic theory, it would actually be impossible to decide, since [h] and [ŋ] have no common phonological content, that is, they share no features. This is the problem of adequate phonemization to which we will now turn.

---

[6] This series of equivalences (diphthongs—long vowels—short vowels plus consonant) will be taken up again in § 3.2. The phonotactic constraints which lead to the exclusion of all other vowel combinations as falling diphthongs will be presented in § 6.1.1.

2.2.4. **The problem of phonemic choice**

In this chapter, it has been assumed without comment that phonemes are concrete entities, that is, for any phoneme it is possible to name one particular phonetic sound as the representative of the phoneme. Only under these circumstances is it possible to speak of the phoneme /p/ (with [p] as a typical allophone). However, the 'representative allophone' is not always easily established. In German, the two fricatives [ç] and [x], the classical (though much-debated) example for an allophonic relationship, provide an example.[7] It is not clear at all whether the phoneme in question should be seen as /ç/ or as /x/. In § 7.3.3, it will be shown that the assumptions of underspecification force a different answer to this question.

Problems of phonemization also arise with a sound such as the glottal stop, [ʔ]. While there is agreement that this sound should not be treated as a phoneme, it is obvious that a phonological description of German should be able to say something about its distribution, that is, the conditions under which it can or must occur (see § 3.3.1 for an analysis). In a phonemic analysis, distributional statements can be made either about phonemes or about allophones. Thus, the question is which phoneme the glottal stop belongs to as an allophone. There is no sensible answer to this question, unless one proposes that there is a phoneme 'zero', with [ʔ] and Ø as allophones. To avoid the problem, [ʔ] is sometimes treated as a *boundary signal*, following the assumption that boundary signals may exist alongside the phonemes and allophones. But in words such as *The[ʔ]later*, the glottal stop signals no boundary.

2.2.5. **The central vowel: schwa**

Turning to the vowel system again, there is one vowel in (2), namely [ə], usually called by its Hebrew name *schwa*, which seems in many ways like a sound with a predictable distribution. (§ 7.3.2 is devoted to a further analysis of this vowel; § 4.3 to a first discussion of its distribution.) It occurs, for example, only in unstressed syllables. It also has other particular distributional properties, such as its non-occurrence in word-initial position or its exclusion as the only vowel of a word. For all of these reasons, it seems desirable not to view schwa as a phoneme in German. But on the other hand, (near-)minimal pairs can be found. Second, if schwa is not a phoneme, in phonemic theory it must be an allophone of some other phoneme, and again it is not obvious what this phoneme should be (/eː/ and /ɛ/ suggest themselves, see Moulton 1947 and Wurzel 1981 for such proposals).

The curious properties of schwa are most certainly not captured in either type of solution. Whether schwa is taken to be a phoneme or is considered an allophone, additional statements must be made about its restricted occurrence and its

---

[7] Kohler (1977, 1990*b*) convincingly argues for three allophones of the dorsal fricative: [ç], [x], and uvular [χ]. For more discussion see § 7.2.3.

properties. Most phonemic treatises leave the question open, and often treat schwa as a phoneme in a separate subsystem, namely in unstressed syllables (e.g. Moulton 1956, 1962; Ungeheuer 1969; Kufner 1971). These analyses are often made with some uneasiness, since they go against the intuition which sets schwa apart from all other vowels.[8]

The vowel [ɐ], also mentioned as a possible vowel phoneme in (2), is akin to schwa in that it is also restricted to unstressed syllables. Its nature is discussed in § 7.4.4, where I will treat this vowel as a vocalized /r/. However, in a strictly phonemic framework, we must note the surface contrasts such as those given in (2), and regard /ɐ/ as being phonemic. Some authors, such as Moulton (1962: § 7.9) use a phonemic sequence /ər/ instead and admit [ɐ] ([ʌ] in Moulton's transcription) as one of its allophones.

To conclude the discussion of vowel phonemes, I should add that there is one example of an argument against a phoneme of Modern Standard German which I regard as ill-founded, however. Scholars of Modern Standard German phonology such as Moulton (1962), Sanders (1972), and Reis (1974) have argued that the threefold contrast between /eː/ vs. /ɛː/ vs. /ɛ/ does not really exist. Many (most, all?) dialects are claimed not to make a distinction between [ɛː] and [eː]. The vowel [ɛː] is considered a *ghost phoneme*, a spelling pronunciation at best. But to make this point, examples such as those in (3) are relied on. Note that the vowel in question is always followed by /r/ here.

(3) [ɛː]   [ɛ]
    Speeren ~ sperren
    nähren   ~ Närrin
    hehren   ~ Herren
    zähren   ~ zerren

The relevance of the examples in (3) to the phonemic status (or indeed, any status at all) of [ɛː] is that the sequence of [e(ː)] followed by [r] does not exist. In other words, the contrast between /eː/ and /ɛː/ is neutralized in this position. That is, while in many varieties of German the distinction between [eː] in *sehen* and [ɛː] in *säen* is quite stable, no such distinction is possible (unless in hypercorrect pronunciation) between *Beeren* and *Bären*. This type of neutralization of phonemic contrast does not extend to high vowels. In (4), examples are given to demonstrate the contrast between /iː/ and /ɪ/ in pre-/r/ position.

(4) [iː]   [ɪ]
    wir   ~ wirr
    ihren ~ irren
    Bier ~ Birne

The overall conclusion to be drawn from these considerations is that there is a large number of indeterminacies and potentially contradictory statements in

---

[8] Moulton (1956: 380) feels that treating schwa as a phoneme is necessary but against 'good taste'.

any presentation of the phoneme system of German, even before allophonic and other alternations are considered in more detail. It is for this reason that we must look beyond the list of phonemes. Perhaps the whole notion of the phoneme and phonemic contrast is not as clear-cut and fundamental as it seemed (and seems) to many students of phonological structure. (For the general point, see also Kaye 1989.)

Another conclusion might be that a phonological system is not a closed one. On the one hand, foreign loan words are assimilated and made to conform to this system. The processes taking place in this assimilation can actually provide considerable evidence concerning the regularities of a phonological system. On the other hand, foreign words may carry properties into a language which, perhaps by historical accident, are lacking in that language. The language may, in such a case, change and accommodate the feature or unit in question. The phoneme /ʒ/ seems to be a good example for such a change in the case of Modern Standard German. In the light of these considerations, restricting the phonological study to a (rather arbitrarily delimited) set of native words seems inappropriate.

The discussion above was limited to the system of phonemes as individual items; it should be added that classical phonemics regarded a phonemic description as complete only if two other aspects were treated: first, the combinatorial possibilities for the phonemes, that is, the *phonotactics*; and, second, the relationship between phonemes and their realizations in terms of allophones. The phonotactic regularities are treated in § 7.4, but without the presupposition that these regularities must be described on the phonemic level.

Phonemic theory regards phonemes as abstract entities which are systematically related to their *phones*, the sound entities in actual speech. If there are alternative ways of realizing a phoneme, the respective phones are called *allophones*. The allophonic realizations of phonemes will be seen in this study as part of the larger issue of how underlying structures are converted by rules into their surface forms, a major issue of this whole study, especially of Chapters 6 and 7. At this point, I should mention some of the major allophonic relationships as they have been treated in the literature, with no commitment to the completeness or adequacy of these claims. In (5), some phonemes (or phoneme classes!) and their corresponding allophones are listed.[9]

(5) *Phonemes*   *Allophones*
    long (tense) vowels   long/short vowels
    voiceless plosives   aspirated/non-aspirated plosives
    /i/   [i], [ɪ], [j], [j̊]
    /x/   [x], [ç], [χ]
    /ʀ/   [ʀ], [ʁ], [ɐ]
    /ə/   [ə], syllabicity of following consonant
    /ɛ/   [ɛ], [ə]

---

[9] One may note again the inconsistent treatment of schwa. In Ch. 7, all of the allophonic alternations illustrated here are covered by phonological rules.

2.3. THE CONTRASTIVE FEATURES

Setting up a mere list of phonemes is insufficient as an adequate account of the phonological regularities in yet another sense: there are a number of regularities in the sound system of German (as most likely in any other language) that can be described adequately only by referring to *classes* of segments where, furthermore, all members of the class have some identifiable property in common. Even the superficial statements on allophonic relations in (5) above reveal this point. To isolate the 'natural classes' which show up here and, at the same time, to describe them in terms that are in principle interpretable phonetically, phonological theory has given the notion of the phonetic/phonological feature a rather prominent place since the pioneering work of Trubetzkoy (1939: ch. 4) and Jakobson (1939).

While a definitive set of features has still not been established, more knowledge of necessary and/or useful phonological features has been accumulated, especially through the strong hypotheses proposed in *SPE* and subsequent work. With respect to German, see in particular Wurzel (1970; 1981) and Kloeke (1982).

The features used below for the characterization of the segments of German are those that have been found to be required in the present overall description of the system. They can therefore be justified by reference to their usefulness in descriptions of various regularities which are given in later chapters. It is also an important part of following considerations in § 3.1 to consider other ways of representing the relationships of the features to each other. Below, I present the features separately for vowels and for consonants. However, another premise of the present feature model is that the features for vowels and consonants are largely identical (as assumed by Clements 1989). From the descriptions below, it might seem as if I am only proposing the use of binary features, while many present-day phonologists would use unary (monovalent) features instead. However, it will become evident in § 3.1 that I am in fact advocating a mixture of binary and unary features.

2.3.1. Vowels

Example (6) attempts a description of all the vowels mentioned so far, using a fairly uncontroversial set of features. Nevertheless, many other options in the choice of particular features could have been taken. Even the values of particular features are not always self-evident, let alone under the issue of (non-)binarity. While [consonantal] is included here, because [− consonantal] defines the class of vowels, all other features mentioned are those which potentially could be distinctive for the vowels. Of course, all vowels are additionally classified as [+ voice], [+ continuant], and [− obstruent]. On these features see § 2.3.2.[10]

---

[10] Example (6) does not include the short tense vowels ([i] etc.) and the vocalized variant of /ʀ/ ([ɐ]), both mentioned as allophones in (3). On the first, see the discussion in § 8.2.1; on the treatment of the /r/-related vowel see § 7.4.4.

(6) Features of the vowel system

	iː	ɪ	eː	ɛː	ɛ	aː	a	oː	ɔ	uː	ʊ	yː	ʏ	øː	œ	ə
consonantal	−	−	−	−	−	−	−	−	−	−	−	−	−	−	−	−
high	+	+	−	−	−	−	−	−	−	+	+	+	+	−	−	−
low	−	−	−	−	−	+	+	−	−	−	−	−	−	−	−	−
front	+	+	+	+	+	−	−	−	−	−	−	+	+	+	+	−
back	−	−	−	−	−	−	−	+	+	+	+	−	−	−	−	−
round	−	−	−	−	−	−	−	+	+	+	+	+	+	+	+	−
ATR	+	−	+	−	−	−	−	+	−	+	−	+	−	+	−	−
long	+	−	+	+	−	+	−	+	−	+	−	+	−	+	−	−

The feature matrix in (6) is based on the phonetic judgements expressed in the vowel chart (2) in the final part of Chapter 1. It expresses the distinctions of that chart by means of binary features. The features used here are generally those of *SPE*, with the deviations explained below. The feature [front] is less commonly used than [back], but will be argued to play an important role in the system, both for the contrasts and for the alternations. Furthermore, given that the three-way frontness distinction of the vowel chart in § 1.4 is correct, a second feature for the dimension of front–back is necessary in any case. Analogous to [back], [front] denotes a fronting movement of the tongue body.

The feature abbreviated as [ATR] (short for 'advanced tongue root') is similar to a property more commonly known by the name of [tense]. According to a theory first advanced by Halle and Stevens (1969), the peculiar distinction of vowel quality denoted by this feature is produced in such a way that tense vowels require a forward movement of the root of the tongue which is not present for the so-called lax vowels. Since this is a way of expressing the contrast by a specific articulatory gesture (just as the other features), and since the feature fits well into the description of the vowel system developed later, the feature [ATR] is used here.[11] It is also assumed that the /a/-sounds are both [− ATR].

A solution more along the lines of the IPA representation for vowels would be to rely on vowel *height* in distinguishing /i/ from /ɪ/, and /e/ from /ɛ/, and analogously for the back vowels. Using the features [high] and [mid], which allow for a fourfold distinction of vowel height, Lass (1984: 94) actually applies this idea to the German vowel system. Such a proposal cannot, however, express the fact that the [− ATR] vowels behave as a natural class, for example with respect to syllabification. In Lass's proposal, the vowels /i, y, e, ø, o, u/, that is, the tense vowels, do not appear as a natural class opposed to the lax vowels of /ɪ, ʏ, ɛ, œ, a, ɔ, ʊ, ə/.

Finally, it is important to stress that the feature [long] will shortly be reanalysed

---

[11] There is an extended debate about this feature or, rather, the property which has to be captured here. Halle (1977) rejects the proposal by Halle and Stevens (1969) and reintroduces [tense]. Ladefoged and Maddieson (1990) argue that [ATR] as used for some African languages is not identical to the contrast found in German vowels such as [i] vs. [ɪ]. For some discussion, see also Durand (1990: 45–8).

as a feature of a different kind. It appears here as a shorthand notation for a prosodic feature treated in § 3.2.1.1. Occasional claims that a three-way length contrast exists in German ([i], [iː], [iːː]) are totally unjustified; see Kohler (1977: § 4.10.4).

The vowel system of Modern Standard German as presented in (6) includes all features that can possibly be regarded as distinctive in this language. Notice that both tenseness and length are required, tenseness for the contrast between /eː/ and /ɛː/, which are [+ ATR] and [− ATR], respectively, and length as the only contrastive feature for /eː/ vs. between /ɛː/, and for /aː/ vs. /a/. Notice that the latter two sounds are, as argued below, identical in quality. Long /ɛː/ is sometimes (Wurzel 1981; Vennemann 1991b) classified as being [+ front, + low] for reasons of symmetry in the vowel system. Since [ɛː] simply is distinct from [æː] as it occurs in other languages and displays no qualitative difference to [ɛ], I reject this proposal. I return to the relationship between length and [ATR] in §§ 6.1 and 7.2.2.

The use of the feature [front] in addition to the more commonly used feature [back][12] requires some comment. [front] is chosen first because it enables us to contrast [ɛ] ([+ front]) with [ə] ([− front], but not [+ back]). Admitting, in the tradition of *SPE*, the feature [back] only, it is impossible to treat the central vowel schwa as distinct from [ɛ]. Secondly, without articulatory motivation, the two /a/-sounds can be classified only arbitrarily as being [+ back]. Therefore, the classification, although the predominant treatment, should be given up. If the two /a/-sounds are non-back sounds, it appears difficult at first sight to explain why they take part in the umlauting process, which generally is the fronting of a non-front (or back) segment (see § 7.2.1). But treating /a/ and /aː/ as [− front] and interpreting Umlaut as an assignment of [+ front] makes it possible to subsume /a/ under the Umlaut rule without saying that the /a/-sounds are articulated with the posterior part of the tongue.[13]

As (6) shows, the use of [front] has no other negative consequences. The additional, though not contrastive, use of the feature [back], on the other hand, allows us to distinguish three degrees of backness, the front vowels [+ front, − back], the central vowels [− front, − back], and the truly back vowels [− front, + back]. This feature system is not only faithful to the phonetic facts, it also, perhaps more importantly, brings out exactly the natural classes that seem to play a role in the sound pattern of German.

Some authors have followed Moulton (1962) in assuming that short [a] is 'higher and more central' (p. 61) than long [aː]. Others (Wängler 1974; Krech et al. 1982; Basbøll and Wagner 1985) have assumed that [a] is front, while [aː] is back, that is, should be transcribed as [ɑː].[14] A third group, finally, describes

---

[12] This is true both for general phonological works (see *SPE*; Halle and Clements 1983) and for studies of German (cf. Wurzel 1970; Kloeke 1982). Wurzel (1981: § 7.3) proposes an analysis of the German vowels which also relies on the feature [front]; there are differences, however, in the treatment of [ɛː] and in his use of the feature [centralized] instead of my [ATR].

[13] This argument derives from Wurzel (1981: 906).

[14] Basbøll and Wagner first judge [a] to be fronted with respect to [ɑː] (1985: 40); subsequently they claim the distinction to be 'negligible' and 'uncertain' (1985: 52).

[aː] as tense and [a] as lax, while Wängler (1974: 105), supported by Wurzel (1981: § 7.3.2.1), makes the claim that the opposite is true. To the extent that these descriptions are not plainly contradictory, they may be true to some extent (and for some speakers) on a phonetic level. However, the differences between the two /a/-sounds are not very clear and reliable, as witnessed by the disagreements among authorities.

The confusion is increased by the description in the IPA *Principles* (1949: 25), where long [aː] is described as 'rather front', while short [a] is supposed to be 'less front (= ɑ+)' (i.e. a short, advanced back vowel). All this gives rise to the suspicion that there is no systematic fronting difference between the two sounds. The most recent IPA chart has no symbol for a low, central vowel. Nevertheless, Kohler (1990a: 49) also uses [a, aː] to illustrate German vowels within the IPA system of conventions.

In a sizeable body of descriptions, the two /a/-sounds are assumed to be identical in quality; see, for example, Duden (1990), Siebs (1969), Ungeheuer (1969), Kohler (1990a), and Martens and Martens (1961). Furthermore, none of the putative distinctions assumed seems to play a role in phonological regularities. For example, any putative qualitative differences are certainly neutralized in the umlauting of /a/ and /aː/, which are [ɛ] and [ɛː], respectively. Since in the umlauting of all other vowels properties of length and tenseness ([ATR]) remain the same, this provides an argument from the phonological patterning for treating the two /a/-sounds as [− ATR].

For a final argument to the effect that the two /a/-sounds in Modern Standard German should not be distinguished as front vs. back vowels, consider the difference from the vowel system of American English: here there is a clear case of a low front vowel ([æ] or [a]) as in *mat* and a low back vowel ([ɑ]) as in *pot*. The two German vowels in question are not identical to either of these. Furthermore, they are not as distinct from each other as the two American English vowels are. Thus, current featural descriptions hardly have the means available to express the putative distinction.

Besides length and/or tenseness/ATR, a prosodic feature of 'contact type' (*Anschlußart*) is sometimes used to distinguish the two classes of vowels in German. Originally proposed by Sievers (1901) as the feature of *syllable cut*, discussed by Trubetzkoy (1939), and recently used by Vennemann (1991a, b; 1992), this position holds that the 'short, lax' vowels display abrupt syllable cut, while the 'long' vowels display smooth syllable cut. This latter group of vowels is long only if stressed. Ramers (1988: § 2.3) provides a review of the controversies in the literature. Note that I in fact treat length as a prosodic feature in § 3.1.

2.3.2. Consonants

In the featural analysis of the German consonant system (7), all segments which play any role at all in the language are broken down into their constituent features. In other words, not only phonemes or underlying segments are treated here, but all surface segments, except perhaps for some which arise through low-level phonetic assimilations. I follow the principle that a feature specification has to be given for any segment that is phonologically relevant, that is, that plays a role in some phonological regularity. In later chapters, more will have to be said about segments such as [ɣ] (the voiced counterpart of [x]), uvular [χ], [ɟ], which may also be the approximant [j], or glottal stop [ʔ].

(7) Features of the consonant system

voice −	p	t	k	f	s	ʃ	ç	x	χ						h	?
+	b	d	g	v	z	ʒ	j	ɣ	ʁ	m	n	ŋ	l	ʀ		
consonantal	+	+	+	+	+	+	+	+	+	+	+	+	+	+	+	+
obstruent	+	+	+	+	+	+	+	+	+	−	−	−	−	−	+	+
continuant	−	−	−	+	+	+	+	+	+	−	−	−	−	+	+	−
nasal	−	−	−	−	−	−	−	−	−	+	+	+	−	−	−	−
spread glottis	−	−	−	−	−	−	−	−	−	−	−	−	−	−	+	−
constr. glottis	−	−	−	−	−	−	−	−	−	−	−	−	−	−	−	+
Labial	+			+						+						
Dental				+												
Coronal		+			+	+					+		+			
Dorsal			+				+	+	+			+		+		
front			−				+	−	−			−		−		
Tongue position	+	+	+	+	+	+	+	+	+	+	+	+	+	+		
high	−	−	+	−	−	+	+	+	−	−	−	+	−	−		
low	−	−	−	−	−	−	−	−	+	−	−	−	−	+		

In this case, the set of features used departs in several ways from those used in *SPE* or the standard literature on German phonology. For [obstruent], most authors have used the complementary term [sonorant] (but see already Wurzel 1970: 195). One reason for choosing the former term is that the criticism of the definition of [sonorant] in terms of spontaneous voicing levied by Ladefoged (1971: 109) and others does not hold for [obstruent]. This latter feature is defined as a massive obstruction in the vocal tract, a configuration which prevents spontaneous voicing to take place. In accordance with this definition, obstruents are voiceless in the unmarked case, while sonorants are usually voiced. Note that consequently /h/ should be classified among the obstruents, and /ʀ/ among the sonorants, in contrast to other existing proposals. Another reason for preferring [obstruent] over [sonorant] will emerge in the discussion of underspecification in § 6.4.

The 'glottal' sounds /h/ and /ʔ/ are sometimes classified as belonging to the [− consonantal] set, on the grounds that the narrowing of the vocal tract characteristic for consonants is not present in these sounds and that the articulatory organs are usually in the position necessary for the following vowel. With respect to German, both Wurzel (1970; 1981: § 7.4.2.2) and Kloeke (1982) follow this proposal. Here I follow another line of reasoning (Lass 1976; Durand

1990), according to which these segments are consonants. But no particular oral-articulatory gesture is defined for these sounds. This theory can explain both the indeterminacy in many feature values for /h/ and /ʔ/, and the very particular phonotactic behaviour of these two sounds.

The feature [continuant] is defined here in such a way that only a complete blockage of the airstream in the mid-sagittal region of the oral tract counts as [− continuant].[15] This allows us to distinguish /r/ and /l/ with this feature, given that in the production of /l/ there is a mid-sagittal complete closure but a lateral release of air. The feature [lateral], suspicious for its positive value for /l/ alone, will then be a completely redundant feature to be introduced in § 6.2.2. The supposed non-continuancy of /l/ will shown to be correct in § 7.3.7.

The 'densest' set of segments is the set of fricatives [f], [s], [ʃ], [ç], [x], and [χ], to which [h] may be added, if one follows the assumptions made in (7) on the feature markings of [h]. None of these fricatives is easily distinguished in a way that captures all natural classes and necessary distinctions at the same time. In the feature model proposed here, [Labial], [Coronal], and [Dorsal] are terms denoting the major articulators (the lips, the tongue-tip (corona), and the tongue-body (dorsum)) that provide the basic distinctions of place of articulation (see § 3.1 for further explanation and discussion). The place features [high], [front], and [low] are minor features dependent on articulator features, the particular dependence indicated by the indentation in (7). On the special status of [high] and [low], see below and also § 3.1. To distinguish bilabial from labiodental articulation, I tentatively propose to use the articulator [Dental], the area behind the upper front teeth.[16]

The *SPE*-feature [anterior], useful to contrast /s/ and /ʃ/, is rejected here because of its arbitrary relationship to articulatory gestures. As some authors have rightly noted, it divides the scale of places of articulation with no relationship to major articulators and to any natural class. Instead, the feature [high] can serve the function of expressing the necessary distinction of /s/ and /ʃ/. Generally, there seems to be good reason to use [high] in this function, and not to rely on *SPE* features such as [anterior] or [distributed].[17] The distinction between /s/ and /ʃ/ versus /ç/ is captured by the articulators [Coronal] vs. [Dorsal]. I also reject [strident] and [distributed] on the grounds that they do not specify articulatory gestures. For discussion of problems related to the latter features see Keating (1988).

Three features in (7), namely [voice], [spread glottis], and [constricted

---

[15] See Chomsky and Halle (1968: 318) for discussion and Halle and Clements (1983: 7) for the same proposal.

[16] An alternative would be to use [front] as a minor feature under [Labial] for the characterization of [p] vs. [f], i.e. for distinguishing the bilabial from the labiodental place of articulation. But another reasonable use for [Dental] is in the specification of (English) [θ, ð]. As Theo Vennemann has kindly pointed out to me, sound change from /f/ to /θ/ can occur, a process which becomes more natural if the two segments share the feature [Dental], but switch from [Labial] to [Coronal].

[17] Palatalization in English e.g. is the transfer of [+ high] from a high vowel to the preceding consonant as in *tense* vs. *tension*, see, e.g. Rubach (1984).

glottis], relate to states of the vocal folds in the glottis. As argued by Halle and Stevens (1969), properties traditionally identified as voicing and aspiration should be broken down into features describing states of the vocal folds ([± stiff vocal cords], [± lax vocal cords]) and degrees of opening of the glottis ([± spread glottis], [± constricted glottis]). The glottal stop is the only segment (in German!) characterized by a constricted glottis; both [h] and aspirated stops bear a marking [+ spread glottis]. As shown in (7), all other sounds have negative values for both of these features.

This proposal has raised some criticism especially with respect to the vocal-cord features. Thus, in accordance with the features proposed in Halle and Clements (1983), I continue to use [voice] instead of the vocal-cord features proposed by Halle and Stevens. But the two features describing states of the glottis seem less controversial and are in fact quite appropriate for the regularities surrounding [h], [ʔ], and aspiration; see §§ 3.3.1 and 6.3.1 for further discussion.

Example (7) contains a number of gaps in the cells of the matrix, which are studied further in Chapter 6. The major articulators are supposed to be active (+) or not. There is thus no possible way of using negative specifications such as [− Labial], since the articulator features are not binary-valued, in contrast to other features.

Notice further that [high] is used in (7) for all segments except for the laryngeals. It is interpreted as a raising (or non-raising) of the tongue as a whole. Only a raising of this articulator above the neutral rest position counts as [+ high]. The other minor feature, [front], is used in German as a feature for the dorsal articulator only. Here, the fronting movement of the body of the tongue counts as [+ front]. In other words, these two features are assumed to be binary-valued, but they are dependent on the presence of their articulators. Otherwise, no value can appear in the table. The use of the features [high], [front] as secondary features also helps to avoid the recruitment of those additional features which are usually seen as problematic, such as [strident] and [anterior].

Finally, we note that two particular allophones of /ʀ/ are described here, namely the uvular approximant [ʀ] and the uvular fricative [ʁ]. These are the principal consonantal allophones of the /r/-sound, with the uvular place of articulation having the widest distribution in the standard language and in many dialects. Others of the many variants are described in §§ 6.3.1 and 7.4.4. There the particular choice of features for /ʀ/ is also justified, but one can note at this point that the place features chosen for /ʀ/ are very similar to those for /a/. In other words, uvular articulation (for [ʁ], [ʀ], and [χ]) is defined basically as a lowering of the tongue body. /ʀ/ is sometimes classified not as an approximant (i.e. [− obstruent]) but as a fricative (most recently by Kohler 1990a). Even if [ʀ] can be produced with the turbulent airstream characteristic for fricatives, the phonological regularities strongly argue in favour of its classification as an approximant; see the non-application of Final Devoicing to /ʀ/ (§ 7.3.1), the /r/-vocalization (§ 7.4.4), and its phonotactic distribution.

The features introduced here have to serve a double function: the classes of segments that behave in a parallel way in some regularity must be expressible as simple sets of (one or more) features. These are the *natural classes* of phonological theory. Secondly, the features are meant to describe the segments of Modern Standard German (whether in contrast to other segments or not) in at least an abstract way. Consequently, if a segment's featural description obviously contradicts the phonetic observations on this segment, something must be wrong with either the choice of the feature system or the particular values chosen for the segment. This two-fold function of the feature system is one reason why up to now no agreement has been reached on the adequate set of features which can serve both for the description of an individual language such as German and as a universally valid and sufficient tool for all languages.

3

THE PROSODIC STRUCTURE OF GERMAN

The preceding sections have provided a first look into subsegmental units of phonology, the segmental features. This chapter will first consider the relationship between these features in a hierarchical structure and then turn towards units larger than the segments and hierarchically above them. Here we are on not so well-studied ground; accordingly the results will be more tentative. Although classical phonology was primarily concerned with the segment and its internal structure, this does not mean that higher-level units, the so-called prosodic units, are negligible. One of the aims of later chapters is to show that many regularities within the phonology of Modern Standard German can only be captured if some notion of a fairly rich prosodic structure is taken into account. Therefore the present chapter deals, in turn, with the syllable, the foot, the phonological word, the phonological phrase, and the intonational phrase as the prosodic units which are probably the most relevant ones. Preliminary evidence is given for the role of these entities, and some description of their internal structure is developed. It may, at first blush, seem somewhat contradictory that the segment, the category that was traditionally set apart from the suprasegmental or prosodic aspects of phonological structure, is also treated here, but the rich structure associated with the segment in the following section makes the distinction between the segmental and the suprasegmental aspects almost disappear. This claim is made more concrete in the discussion of phonological rules which make features 'belong' to more than one segment.

In the present state of phonology, much more is known about the units of the 'lower' levels, such as the segments, their parts, and the syllables. Consequently, the discussion of these units is more extended in this chapter. Higher levels such as the phonological and intonational phrases are treated as well, but less can be said on their precise nature and on how they are derived systematically.

3.1. SEGMENTAL ARCHITECTURE

In the past, most phonological theories and descriptions have assumed that the unordered set of feature specifications is sufficient to characterize the segments of a language.[1] Each segment was analysed as a feature bundle, that is, as the assignment of exactly one value to each feature, with no structure imposed upon

---

[1] Goldsmith (1990), who provides one of the useful introductions of the aspects of phonology treated in this chapter, shows that not all phonological theories in the past have relied on unilinear feature representations. The two most influential phonological frameworks, American structuralism and *SPE*-type generative phonology, have used simple feature matrices of the kind introduced in Chapter 2.

the set of features and with no overlap between adjacent segments; however, this model, also used in § 2.3, is too simple and prevents the phonologist from accounting in an elegant and more adequate way for many observable regularities. There are basically two senses in which the segmental approach to feature representation must be modified: first, it is necessary to allow for feature specifications with domains larger than a single segment. Second, some of the features internal to a segment tend to behave in a parallel way; that is, it is possible to identify sub-bundles of features which are sensitive to particular phonological environments. This recurrent clustering of features should be expressed in the representation for segments.

If a feature value can hold for a domain larger than a single segment, then this state of affairs should not be represented by just writing sequences such as [+ back] [+ back]. As was shown in initial work leading to current models of non-linear phonology (see especially Goldsmith (1976) on tonal features), some explanatory mechanism is required which will express directly the particular one-to-many relationship between a feature specification and its points of realization. This mechanism is the (multiple) *association* of features (and categories in general) with other suitable categories. Thus, if the value for [back] is identical for two adjacent segments, an adequate representation should represent directly that the domain of this feature is greater than one single segment. The representation may take the form of (1), with 'S' representing the category of a segment for present purposes. Here, [+ back] is associated to two segment nodes. There is thus no one-to-one relationship between segments and feature values. This is the first way in which the representation of features in the present study and in most current theories of phonology, differs from that of *SPE*-type theories. The simple illustration in (1) indicates how a typical segmental feature can become part of a suprasegmental (prosodic) structure, if the simple, fundamental assumption of a one-to-one relationship between features and segments is abandoned. By dropping the assumption of a one-to-one relationship, we have moved into the field of non-linear phonology. In some sense, the two segments associated to a single—[back]—constitute one (suprasegmental) domain.

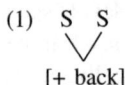

(1)   S   S
         \ /
       [+ back]

Turning to the second point, the clustering of segment-internal features, the introduction of a *subsegmental* hierarchy of features is achieved by introducing organizing nodes which group some of the features by reference to the notion of an articulator. Phonetically, there are a few major active articulators whose gestures specify the different places of articulation for vowels and consonants in Modern Standard German: the lips, the tongue-blade (corona), and the tongue-body (dorsum).[2] While these three articulators (labelled Labial, Coronal, and

---

[2] For other languages, additional articulators for consonants might enter the picture, such as the tongue-root (or the pharynx) for some Arabic languages. Such an articulator will also be used for the vowel representation later in this section. Note that non-terminal nodes are capitalized, while terminal features are not and are placed in brackets.

Dorsal) provide the basic distinctions (e.g. for /p/, /t/, /k/), other more detailed places of articulation arise through modifying specifications for each of the articulators; see (3) below. Furthermore, Tongue Position is used as an additional independent articulatory gesture.

Finally, it turns out that all the features which determine the place of articulation behave independently of other features, in particular those of the so-called major-class features and of the larynx, where properties of voicing, aspiration, and, perhaps, tensing are determined. Furthermore, a number of features are not defined for the laryngeal segments [h, ʔ]. Initially, this consideration may give plausibility to the introduction of the Supralaryngeal node and the Laryngeal node as organizing nodes in the hierarchy. In (2), all these features are represented in a hierarchical structure which has the root node (R) as its anchoring point. R is the symbol for the unit which, in this framework, encodes the notion of the phonetic segment. The possibilities illustrated in (2) are those for the consonants of Modern Standard German and have to be slightly enlarged in order to account for the vowel articulations (see (4)).

(2)

$$
\begin{array}{c}
\text{R: } \begin{bmatrix} \text{consonantal} \\ \text{obstruent} \end{bmatrix}
\end{array}
$$

Laryngeal   Supralaryngeal   [continuant]   [nasal]

$$\begin{bmatrix} \text{spread} \\ \text{glottis} \end{bmatrix} \quad \text{[voice]} \quad \begin{bmatrix} \text{constricted} \\ \text{glottis} \end{bmatrix}$$

Place   Tongue position

Labial Dental Coronal Dorsal   [high] [low]

[front]

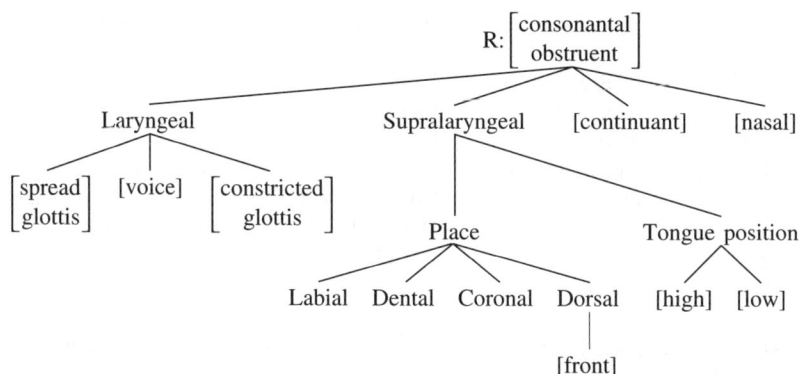

Ultimately, the proper shape of such a feature tree and the nodes used in it must be motivated through its use in the description of phonological regularities. From the numerous alternatives, I have chosen the one which seemed necessary or most useful in the characterization of phonological rules. The proposal introduced here is similar in most of the non-terminal parts to that of McCarthy (1988: 105), while the terminal elements used are different; for a related system also see Halle (1992). (All terminal elements needed later for consonants are introduced in (2) at the appropriate places.)

The need for, and the value of, the articulator nodes was first stressed by Halle (1983); also see Ladefoged and Halle (1988: 580) and others. The particular distribution of [consonantal] and [obstruent] as parts of the root node R and of [continuant] and [nasal], which are dependents of this node, is also borrowed from McCarthy's model. The latter features are allowed to be multiply associated, in the sense of (1), to more than one segment, while [consonantal] and [obstruent] are analysed as making up the content of the individual segment. The Laryngeal node contains all those features which have their articulatory basis in the state of the larynx, that is, in particular the voice feature (or features), and features forming the basis for [h] and [ʔ], as described in § 2.3.2. Possibly, the feature [voice] has to be replaced by the more specific laryngeal features describing elementary states of the glottis.

The maximal number of different places of articulation needed for Modern Standard German is illustrated (with an example each) in (3), where the necessary distinctions are translated in the categories introduced here. Notice that the special status of /h/, which was mentioned in § 2.3.2, is partially accounted for by not specifying any major articulator for this segment. This means that there is simply no Place node for this segment (as well as for [ʔ]). As proposed in § 2.3.2, I also add a new articulator, [Dental], to the existing list of such articulators, in order to differentiate labial [p] and [b] from labiodental [f], in which the labial articulator (the lower lip) is advanced towards the area of the upper front teeth. It must be admitted that [Dental] as an articulator is somewhat atypical, in that it is clearly not an active, movable organ which can perform an articulatory gesture of its own.

(3) Example	Traditional term	Articulators	Modification
p, m	bilabial	Labial	
f	labiodental	Labial, Dental	
s, t, n	alveolar	Coronal	
ʃ	palato-alveolar	Coronal, Tongue Position	+ high
ç	palatal	Dorsal, Tongue Position	+ front, + high
x, k	velar	Dorsal, Tongue Position	+ high
χ, ʀ	uvular	Dorsal, Tongue Position	+ low
h, ʔ	glottal	——	

The features [high], [front], and [low] are used here only as dependent, secondary features of the articulator nodes. In contrast to earlier proposals, Lahiri and Evers (1991) have argued that the upward or downward movement of the tongue should be regarded as an independent articulator, [Tongue Position]. I follow this proposal since it will turn out to be necessary for an optimal account of the phonotactics of some consonant clusters as described in § 7.5. In other words, some of the articulators related to the tongue can be modified by a fronting, raising, or lowering movement. These are the particular articulatory gestures necessary for the production of German consonants.

The features here are given with an eye towards the elimination of redundancy. [Tongue Position], for example, is present in more than just those places in (3) in which it is specified. But for other places of articulation, it is never distinctive. Notice also that according to the hypothesis proposed here there are secondary features allowing for binary values (in (3) only '+', with '−' taken to be the redundant value), while the articulator nodes and the higher class nodes present in (2) are simply present or absent. Only the positive specifications for the binary features are admitted as representing particular articulatory gestures. The gaps in the final column of (3) will eventually be filled by negative specifications; see Chapter 6 for detailed discussion.

It is relatively easy to argue for the correctness of the grouping which is induced by the articulators of [Labial], [Coronal], and [Dorsal]. Labial, coronal, and dorsal consonants can be shown to behave as groups or natural classes. See, for example, the special role of coronal obstruents as syllable 'appendices' (§ 3.2.3). The choice of the particular secondary features in (3) is less obvious. But there are two arguments for the solution adopted here: first, the segments marked by secondary features are the ones which appear to be 'marked' in the phonological sense, that is, they have a specific distribution or other properties which make them appear to be special with respect to their unmarked counterpart.

Second, features grouped together by a common articulator often belong together with respect to some regularity of the phonological system. Thus, /ʃ/ clearly patterns with /s/ and not with /ç/, although in terms of a simple model of articulatory places it is equally a neighbour to either of these sounds (see the second column of (3)). But /ʃ/ and /s/ share the articulator node of [Coronal], while /ç/ belongs to [Dorsal]. Several examples of this grouping will occur later in various analyses. In § 7.5.2, coronal [s] and [ʃ] will be shown to interact, while the dorsal fricatives [ç], [x], and [χ] are the well-known allophones involved in the rule treated in § 7.3.3. Note that [ʃ] patterns with the palatal and velar segments in sharing the [+ high] specification with these.

The exact status of the dependent features is not as clear. For example, it is questionable whether bilabial [p] and labiodental [f] should be distinguished by means of [front]. I propose that all articulator-dependent features should be interpretable as articulatory gestures of the respective articulator. Instead of [front], the feature [back] as another dependent of the Dorsal node could also be used. As will be argued in § 7.3.3 in connection with the alternation of the dorsal fricatives, there seems to be evidence that the proposal in (3) is correct for Modern Standard German. The dorsal feature [back] will be used, but only as a redundant feature, both for vowels and consonants. My use of the specification [+ low] for uvular consonants is also different from that of *SPE* or Halle and Clements (1983), who take uvular sounds to be [− low]. The justification for the present proposal comes from the close similarity between [R] and [a] in Modern Standard German, as discussed in § 7.4.4.

Finally, it must be added that the *vowel* features, introduced in § 2.3.1, are also dependent features of the articulators [Dorsal], [Labial], and [Tongue Position]. The vowel features [high], [front], [back], and [low] are clearly specifications of gestures executed by the body of the tongue, while [round] is a particular gesture of the lips. A phonological argument for the involvement of [Dorsal] is given on pages 32–3. A round vowel such as /y/ is more explicitly represented in the structure given in (4). The terminal values are those of (6) in § 2.3.1.

(4) /y/

$$
R \begin{bmatrix} - \text{consonantal} \\ - \text{obstruent} \end{bmatrix}
$$

Laryngeal   Supralaryngeal   [+ continuant]   [− nasal]

$\begin{bmatrix} - \text{spread} \\ \text{glottis} \end{bmatrix}$ [+ voice] $\begin{bmatrix} - \text{constricted} \\ \text{glottis} \end{bmatrix}$ Place   Tongue Position

[+ high]

Labial   Dorsal   Radical

[+ round]   [+ front]   [+ ATR]

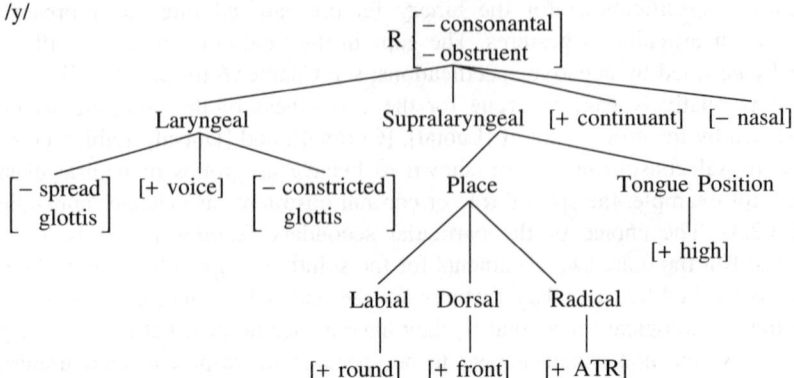

The reader may note that an additional articulator node is introduced here, the Radical node to which the feature [ATR] is attached. This proposal (from Clements 1989) seems correct, in so far as the feature ATR is supposed to be a gesture of the tongue-root (rather than the pharynx, the wall of the throat opposite the tongue-root as in other models), but there seems to be no other positive evidence for this proposal. Of course, the proposal also hinges on the correctness of the assumption that it is indeed the ATR feature which expresses the contrast between the tense and the lax vowels in German.

The representation of /y/ in (4) also illustrates that the Labial articulator may bear a secondary feature [round] in the case of vowels. In general, much of the evidence for this representation for vowels depends on the consonant–vowel interactions. It can be shown for German as well as for other languages that such interactions (assimilations, phonotactic constraints) usually involve elements specified for the same articulator. Thus, dorsal consonants may be influenced by the vowels, which always involve the Dorsal articulator, and only labial consonants may interact with round, that is, labial, vowels. The claim follows that coronal consonants should be independent of vowels.

An argument for the analysis of the velar/uvular articulation of consonants and of the articulation of vowels as instances of [Dorsal] can be provided from the way nasal vowels are treated in Modern Standard German. In § 2.2.1 it was observed that words with nasalized vowels, usually borrowed from French, are not normally pronounced with such vowels. Instead, we find pronunciations in which the vowels are followed by a nasal consonant. But this nasal consonant is, unexpectedly, the velar nasal [ŋ], as in [balkɔŋ] or [ʀɛstoʀaŋ]. On the basis of markedness alone, one would expect the unmarked [n] here. But if vowel articulation is seen as dorsal, then the adjustment consisting in assigning the feature [+ nasal] to a following position in the string naturally is completed by also taking over the dorsal articulation from the vowel position. That is, converting a nasalized vowel such as [ɔ̃] into [ɔŋ] simply consists in spreading the features of the first unit on to a second, new segment. Such an explanation for the velar nasal presupposes that the place of articulation features do not change if we move from vowels to consonants. Note that [Tongue Position] is also shared by consonants and vowels. But, as it is not part of the Place node, any features of [Tongue Position] will not be spread together with the feature [Dorsal]. This is a correct prediction, since [ɔ] and [ŋ] are both [Dorsal], but they differ in [high], as inspection of (6) and (7) in Chapter 2 will show.

The crucial difference between the treatment of segmental features as an unordered and unstructured set and their treatment as forming a hierarchical structure in which each node and each elementary feature occupies its own tier is that under the latter view each simple or complex unit in the structure can behave autonomously. It may, for example, be deleted or may spread to neighbouring segmental units. I disregard the question of how far the spreading of features extends: if in *kalt* [kalt] the final two consonants differ in their values for [obstruent] and [voice] only, do they share all other features in the way depicted in (1)? Questions of featural representations of segments are taken up again in Chapter 6 with respect to redundant vs. predictive specification of values, and in Chapter 7 with respect to phonological rules. We now turn to other, larger units in phonological structure. This discussion should also make it very clear that the segment as just treated is taken in this work as only one of many units.

3.2. SYLLABLES

Syllables are the most obvious and salient prosodic units of German as in many other languages. Speakers of German can (usually) agree on the number of syllables of a word. Nevertheless, it is possible that they are not relevant to a systematic phonological description. Before turning to the concept of the syllable itself, we will therefore provide evidence for the very clear and important role of this concept.

Syllables are quite obviously units in linguistic behaviour. In many types of linguistic performance, syllables play a prominent role. For example, children (and non-literate adults) find the dissection of speech into syllables easy and natural, but any other dissection (such as into segments or morphemes) much more difficult. Syllables are also often used as rhythmic units, such as in singing, chanting, or poetry. This is certainly true for German.

While this type of evidence for the syllable sounds quite convincing to some people, others wish to see evidence from structural linguistic patterns. After all, the syllable could be a unit of linguistic behaviour, but not directly involved in statements of phonological regularities, a position which was adopted in *SPE* and in analyses following this theory. It is quite easy to show that this move prevents the expression of a number of generalizations.

Here is one such argument for the role of the syllable in the phonology of German: Moulton (1962: 65) notes that the non-syllabic vowel [i̯] and the voiced fricative [j] are in complementary distribution, that is, are allophones of one single phoneme.[3] He presents near-minimal pairs such as the ones in (5) and concludes: '[ɹ̩] occurs after long syllables (long vowel + consonant, as in ['aːzɹ̩ən], or short vowel + two consonants, as in ['ɪndɹ̩ən]), whereas [j] occurs after short syllables (short vowel + one consonant)'.

(5) [daːlɹ̩ə] Dahlie ~ [taljə] Taille
    [ʃpaːnɹ̩əʀ] Spanier ~ [ʃampanjəʀ] Champagner
    [liːlɹ̩ə] Lilie ~ [vaːnɪljə] Vanille

Relying more directly on the concept of the syllable, the list of conditions in the description just cited is unnecessary. It appears that [j] occurs only in the initial position of the syllable, as in [tal.jə], and that [ɹ̩] cannot be found syllable-initially (cf. [daː.lɹ̩ə]). We will return to this complementary distribution in § 7.4.1.1, where it is described in detail.[4] Here it provides a first argument for the view that phonological regularities rely to a large extent on the syllable. Chapter 7 presents a number of rules which, similar to the one introduced here, rely on the syllable edge as a crucial part of the regularity.

It will also be argued that the syllable provides the major domain for statements about phonotactics, that is, the sequencing constraints for segments. If we want to describe the possibilities for combining consonants into clusters (as in § 7.4.1), the constraints must be stated as holding within some domain. Across word boundaries, for example, any two sounds can be combined. But also within words, combinations which are usually seen as impossible can occur. Thus, the sequence /tm/ is not taken to be a possible consonant cluster of German, mainly because no word starts or ends in this way. But such a sequence does in fact occur, as in *atmen* or *widmen*. The phonotactic statement ruling out this sequence might nevertheless be correct, since there is a syllable break between the two consonants, so that /t/ belongs to the first and /m/ to the second syllable. If the syllable is the relevant domain for this sort of regularity, the words cited above do not count as counterevidence. The morpheme is the other major domain for phonotactic restrictions; morpheme structure constraints seem to exist independently of syllable structure constraints, although the separation of these two levels is not always self-evident.

What is a syllable? We will eschew all attempts at a phonetic definition (see von Essen (1951) and Ladefoged and Maddieson (1990: 93f–4), who claim that this might indeed be impossible) and simply assume that it is a phonological unit organized around a syllabic peak (typically consisting of a vowel) of which speakers have a relatively high awareness. Speakers of German readily agree that *Phonologie* consists of four syllables, while *deutsch* has only one. This is

---

[3] The transcription is slightly adapted to the one used here. Moulton quotes the Siebs dictionary as also claiming a contrast between [ɹ̩] and [j] in pairs such as *Bill[ɹ̩]on* vs. *Bill[j]et* or *Mill[ɹ̩]arde* vs. *Brill[j]ant*. These distinctions are also made in Krech et al. (1982). Both I and a number of informants I consulted feel unable to confirm this contrast in a systematic way. In accordance with Moulton's classification, I transcribe the 'voiced fricative' as [j] and the other segment as a non-syllabic [ɹ̩]; in § 7.4.1. I argue, however, that the latter sound should be interpreted as the voiced approximant [j].   [4] For an extended discussion see also Hall (1992b: ch. 3).

not to say that there are no doubtful cases. First, it is not the case that every syllable in German has to contain a vowel: for words such as *Segel*, *Betten*, and *rotem*, there is a pronunciation in which the second syllable does not contain a vowel. Instead, the final consonant in each of these words can appear as the head of the syllable: [zeːgl̩], [bɛtn̩], [ʀoːtm̩].

Second and more important, while the number of syllables is usually obvious (though see remarks on deletion in § 7.6), the precise position of the syllable break is much harder to determine. Although syllable structure is predictable on the basis of the segmental information, there are some cases with a certain degree of ambiguity. Intervocalic consonants are not always unambiguously syllabified. Vennemann (1982: 262) gives the judgements for the syllabification of *erstens* listed in (6), a constellation for which (7) gives some more examples, which perhaps allow similar multiple assignments of intervocalic consonants to syllables (for more examples, see Vennemann 1988: 60). I will return shortly to those cases where a consonant is judged to belong to two syllables, that is, as ambisyllabic.[5] (One conclusion from the existence of several well-formed syllabifications for one string of segments that ought to be drawn is that there is a certain amount of optionality in the application of phonological rules which assign prosodic structure.)

(6) *a.* [ɛːʀ.stn̩s]   *b.* [ɛːʀs.tn̩s]   *c.* [ɛːʀ̇stn̩s]   *d.* [ɛːʀsɪ̇n̩s]

(7) Fenster   [nst]
    Elster   [lst]
    Ängste   [ŋst]
    edles   [dl]/[tl]
    regnen   [gn]/[kn]/[çn]
    extra   [kstr]

The model of the syllable in the present framework has to answer several questions. First, it must enumerate the possible syllables in Modern Standard German. This will be done here by specifying the structure of a well-formed syllable in German, using various hierarchically arranged categories. Second, the theory must fit the syllable into the overall phonological representation, that is, relate it to other parts of the phonological structure. Finally, the derivational status of the syllable must be clarified. If, as assumed here, the syllables are not given in underlying representations, some account of their generation must be given.

The first step in a model of the syllable might be to assume that syllable boundaries are interspersed with segments. Thus, we might transcribe *Phonologie* as [fo.no.lo.giː]. But the observation made above that consonants can be ambisyllabic casts doubt on the appropriateness of this model. It seems that for the pronunciation of *fallen*, neither (8*a*) nor (8*b*) is a correct transcription. (It is

---

[5] The dot is the IPA symbol for syllable boundaries as introduced in § 1.4; other conventions include the dash (–) or the dollar-sign ($), which are perhaps less easily overlooked. A dot above a consonant marks this consonant as ambisyllabic.

true, however, that speakers of German, if forced to separate such words into syllables, prefer (8*b*).)

(8) *a.* *fal.ən   *b.* ?fa.lən   *c.* falᵊn

That intervocalic consonants can be ambisyllabic in Modern Standard German is not universally assumed, but is held by Vennemann (1972; 1982) and Benware (1986: § 7.2.3); see also Ramers (1992) for a survey of the discussion. All consonants of German except for /h/ and /ʔ/ can be ambisyllabic, but ambisyllabic voiced fricatives are rare to non-existent. It is not clear if there is a systematic reason for this gap, since a few forms such as the name *Struwwelpeter* occur. Ambisyllabicity might then be captured by a notation such as in (8*c*), where the symbol for the syllable boundary is meant to co-occur with some phonetic segment.

But in this move, the assumption that syllable boundaries occur between segments has silently been abandoned. In fact, the whole notion of the syllable as something to be represented exclusively by *boundaries* between segments is called into question. Thus, we might preferably express the syllable as a superordinate structural unit in its own right. In the minimal way, this is done in (9), where the syllable (σ) occurs as a category dominating the segments belonging to it. An ambisyllabic consonant, under this view, is a segment dominated by two syllable nodes.

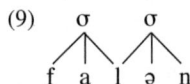

(9)   σ   σ

      ⟋⟋⟋ ⟋⟋⟋
     f a l ə n

The lines between the segments and the syllable nodes are again the association lines introduced in § 3.1 for intrasegmental relations. The syllable model illustrated in (9) is surely the simplest non-linear model possible. It is perhaps worth stressing, however, that each of the phonetic symbols occurring as a terminal symbol in this structure abbreviates a complex feature structure of the kind introduced in the preceding section. We have therefore to a considerable extent moved away from the unilinear view on phonological representations.

The intervocalic consonant in (9) represents the clearest case of an ambisyllabic consonant. There is some uncertainty how far the concept of ambisyllabicity can and should be extended. As shown in (6), one view has it that there are many other possible situations in which consonants can be ambisyllabic. In the following, I assume that only *single* intervocalic consonants can be ambisyllabic. Furthermore, they must follow a short lax vowel. This is the context where they are required by the phonotactic constraint disallowing a syllable to end in a short lax vowel. But in contrast to other authors (e.g. Ramers 1992), I would like to claim that not only stressed vowels can be followed by an ambisyllabic consonant. In the name *Matthias* as well as in *Matte*, in *Frikassee* as well as in *Kasse* /t/ and /s/, respectively, are ambisyllabic.[6] Unfortunately, there is little clear-cut

---

[6] One may note the geminate spelling in all of these cases. For more examples, see (28) below.

evidence for the ambisyllabic status of consonants (but see the non-application of Final Devoicing to ambisyllabic consonants illustrated in § 7.3.1). As for intervocalic consonant clusters, as in (6) and (7), it will be assumed that a restricted amount of optionality exists in assigning these consonants to syllables. Thus, both (6a) and (6b) will be seen as well-formed syllabifications of the word in question.

3.2.1. The skeleton

Concentrating on words of one syllable, it turns out that one of the fundamental phonotactic regularities of Modern Standard German is the following: after a long vowel, a certain number of consonants can occur. The same number of consonants is possible after a diphthong. But after a short vowel, one more consonant is possible in the same monosyllabic words. Thus, a long vowel is equivalent to a diphthong, while it looks as if a short vowel leaves room for an additional consonant in the same syllable. This regularity is illustrated in (10). The words given here have a maximal number of final consonants, leaving out some well-defined additional final consonants, namely /t/, /s/, and /st/. But, as shown in (11), the picture does not change if these additional consonants, such as /st/ maximally, are added.[7] There is always room for one additional consonant if the vowel in the word is a short one.

(10) *a.* viel   *b.* feil   *c.* Film
        doof   drauf   Dorf
        schön   neun   gern
        Stab   Raub   halb
        Bahn   Bein   Bank

(11) *a.* Dienst   *b.* raubst   *c.* Herbst
        Obst   läufst   wirfst
        lobst   streichst   denkst

Again abstracting away from some systematic exceptions which will be treated in the discussion of *extrasyllabicity* in § 3.2.3, it is apparent, on the basis of (10), that a syllable in German does not allow for the strings of segments given in (12). Here, v and k are simply variables standing for vocalic and consonantal segments, respectively. If the subscripts i, j have the same value, the sequence $v_i v_j$ is a long vowel; for $i \neq j$, the sequence symbolizes a diphthong. (Of course, such strings can be found in words containing more than one syllable, but this is only evidence that the syllable is the crucial unit for this fundamental phonotactic constraint.)

(12) $*v_i v_j k k$ $*v k k k$

---

[7] Some of the words in (11) are morphologically complex, since there are too few monomorphemic words of this type. It is a fact, however, that complex words in Modern Standard German have the same phonotactic possibilities and constraints as monomorphemic words.

The regularity discussed here was first described by Moulton (1956), who, on the basis of this evidence, suggested that long vowels should be analysed as geminates such as /aa/. The equivalence of long vowels, diphthongs, and a short vowel plus one consonant is then expressed directly.

Here a different approach will be followed, which takes seriously the notion that a syllable contains a certain, variable number of 'places' or 'positions' which can be filled by segments. (The gemination approach in the spirit of Moulton's analysis will be discussed briefly in § 7.2.1.) Suppose that one of these positions is singled out as the one with which vowels are associated. It will be denoted by 'V'. The phonotactic constraints given above can then be captured neatly by postulating that there are two more positions following the V, positions which we will denote by 'C'. Combining this claim with the proposition that there are also two such C-positions to the left of V in each syllable (for which evidence will be given in § 3.2.3), we can express all these statements in a structure such as (13), where the syllable node now dominates five such C- and V-positions in a particular order.

(13)   σ

        C   C   V   C   C

(13) is a template for maximal syllables in MSG which introduces a further structural layer for phonological representations, the so-called *CV-tier* or, because of its central place in phonological structure, *skeletal tier*. It derives from work by McCarthy (1981) on the analysis of Arabic and, more directly, by Clements and Keyser (1983) who argue that the syllable node and the CV-tier are the two representational ingredients for an adequate treatment of syllable-related regularities.[8] The exact nature of the skeletal tier is the subject of some debate (see also below), while its general importance seems well-established.

To return to the issue of ambisyllabicity, which was used at the beginning of this section to motivate the syllable as a non-segmental unit, we may now use the assignment of segments to skeletal positions to represent ambisyllabic consonants. An ambisyllabic consonant is a configuration in which a single segment is linked to two skeletal positions, which in turn belong to different syllables.

3.2.1.1. *Vowel length*

The CV-tier serves the very useful purpose of representing the length (or quantity) of vowels. Taking (for the present) (13) as the syllable template of German and associating a long vowel with two positions in the skeletons, the phonotactic constraint observed above is immediately accounted for, since the template has only a limited number of positions which can be filled. In (14), some more words illustrating various smaller or larger combinations of vowels and

---

[8] Wiese (1988a: pt. I) is largely an application of these concepts to German (and Chinese), pursuing Clements and Keyser's hypothesis that except for the CV-skeleton no additional structural elements are needed in the description of the syllable.

consonants are given. The phonetic symbols here and in the following of course represent segments in the sense of § 3.1. That is, the categories directly associated with the skeletal positions are the root nodes (R).

(14) *a. in*   *b. aus*   *c. mit*   *d. durch*

e. Knie   *f. Graf*   *g. klein*

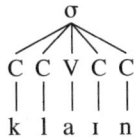

Long vowels are plainly single segmental feature structures, but those which are associated with two prosodic positions. In connection with syllable schema (13), nothing more needs to be said to account for the structural constraint outlined above. This, then, is the prosodic reinterpretation of the feature [long] mentioned in § 2.3.1.

One of the points to be noted in (14g) is the representation of *diphthongs*. The second segment of the diphthong is represented as a vowel segment of the 'normal' kind, but one which is associated not to a V-position, but to a C. This is a proposal for the representation of glides or semi-vowels, according to which the structural position of a vowel in a syllable is the factor responsible for its status as a full (syllabic) vowel or as a glide. No matter how we transcribe a glide (for the high, front, unrounded one, the transcription might be [ɪ], [y], or [j]), structurally it is now interpreted as a segment identical to the vowel [ɪ], but associated to a position of a different type, namely C.

At this point, it might be asked what the difference between C and V is beyond a difference simply in naming. One possibility is to assume that the feature [syllabic] provides the crucial distinction. The two units in question can then be defined in featural terms as in (15), assuming that a feature [segmental] defines the content of the CV-tier in general. It is also possible to define a generalized version of C and V by only specifying this latter feature: see X as defined in (15c). The unit defined in this way is also used in some models of the syllable, but since the C–V distinction is useful for the representation of glides, I will assume the existence of [syllabic] as part of the prosodic skeleton (following Clements and Keyser 1983, and Clements 1990). Most arguments against its use refer to this feature as part of the segmental matrix. Note that X (used as a simpler alternative to C and V by some authors) is not distinct from C and V, but a generalization over these two entities.

(15) *a.* C: $\begin{bmatrix} + \text{segmental} \\ - \text{syllabic} \end{bmatrix}$ *b.* V: $\begin{bmatrix} + \text{segmental} \\ + \text{syllabic} \end{bmatrix}$ *c.* X: [+ segmental]

3.2.1.2. *Affricates and other complex segments*

So far, the discussion of the CV-skeleton has revealed two relevant points in its favour: the skeleton allows for a representation of (vowel) length that fits well with phonotactic patterns in Modern Standard German; and it allows for a natural way of distinguishing between full vowels and glides. An additional line of reasoning derives from the nature of affricates. As observed in the introduction to the phonemic system, the status of affricates has been an area of debate, since affricates seem to display properties which make them look like single units. On the other hand, equally compelling arguments lead to a biphonemic treatment.

Consider, for example, the pattern in (16*a*). The data shows that, in the word-initial postion before /l/, exactly one consonant can appear. But, as shown in (16*b*), the labial affricate /pf/ is also possible in this context. Instead of simply noting the exceptional nature of this combination, a better solution would be to assume that this affricate is a unit equivalent to a single consonant—a single phoneme, in a phonemic analysis, or a single segmental unit in a feature-based generative phonology.

(16) *a.* $_w[\_\_\_]...$ *b.*

blau	Pflaume
Flanke	Pflanze
Glück	pflücken
klirren	Pflicht

This particular argument is valid only for /pf/ in Modern Standard German, but similar arguments can be put forward at least for /ts/.[9] The overall result is that at least these particular stop-fricative combinations behave as if they were units equivalent to single segments. To capture this, a feature such as [delayed release] was used in *SPE*, while Ladefoged (1971) and Wurzel (1970) utilized [fricative] for the same purpose. By postulating that stops and affricates are both [− continuant], and fricatives are [+ continuant], all three relevant classes can be kept apart by distinguishing stops from affricates with the help of [+ delayed release] defining the affricates. (The feature [fricative] groups the sounds in such a way that stops are [− continuant] and [− fricative], affricates are [− continuant] and [+ fricative], while fricatives are [+ continuant] and [+ fricative].)

But as it turns out, this monosegmental treatment of the affricates runs into problems, and for this reason the monophonemic analysis was never totally accepted. One argument for the bisegmental nature of affricates comes from their behaviour with respect to degemination. As shown in § 7.3.6 and further analysed there, whenever two identical consonants occur adjacent to each other in a word, the second of the two is deleted. This occurs mainly when the inflectional verbal suffixes /t/ (3 sg. pres.) and /st/ (2 sg. pres.) are attached to

---

[9] In Prinz and Wiese (1991) it is argued that *all* stop-fricative combinations in German should be analysed as potential phonological affricates. The following additional cases occur: /tʃ/: *deutsch*; /ps/: *Psychologie*; /pʃ/: *Pschorr*; /dʒ/: *Dschungel*; /ks/: *Xaver*. If this hypothesis is true, no monosegmental description can work, since these combinations are made of sounds with different places of articulation. This problem will be taken up again in § 7.5.2.

stems from the class of strong verbs that end in /t/ or /s/, respectively. In (17) and (18), some examples for each case are given.

(17) *a.* /raːt/ + /t/   *rat* + 3 sg. pres.   underlying form
     [rɛːt] *rät*   Degemination (plus Umlaut)
    b. /treːt/ + /t/   *tret* + 3 sg. pres.   underlying form
     [trɪt] *tritt*   Degemination (plus Ablaut)

(18) *a.* /raɪs/ + /st/   *reiß* + 2 sg. pres.   underlying form
     [raɪst] *reißt*   Degemination
    b. /leːz/ + /st/   *les* + 2 sg. pres.   underlying form
     [liːst] *liest*   Degemination (plus Ablaut)
    c. /haɪs/ + /st/   *heiß* + 2 sg. pres.   underlying form
     [haɪst] *heißt*   Degemination

It turns out that verbs ending in the affricate /ts/ behave exactly like those ending in /s/ or /z/, but not like those ending in /t/. In other words, degemination applies to words such as *sitz* /zɪts/ (see (19)) just as it does to words such as those in (18). If the stem-final segment in, for example, *tanz*, was not /s/ but some affricate distinct from both /t/ and /s/, we would either have to assume a special clause in the rule of Degemination, which says that the affricate /ts/ as well as /s/ causes the deletion if /s/ is affixed. Alternatively, we could say that the feature [delayed release] somehow does not 'count' for Degemination. In fact, § 7.2.6 confirms that identity with respect to [voice] is not required for this rule. But notice that degemination does not occur when /t/ and /s/ become adjacent (in either order) through inflection, as in *rät* + *st* or *lies* + *t*. That is, the feature [continuant] matters in degemination. Arguably, in determining identity of segments, Degemination considers all features except for those under the Laryngeal node.

(19) *a.* /zɪts/ + /st/   *sitz* + 2 sg. pres.   underlying form
     [zɪtst] *sitzt*   Degemination
    b. /tants/ + /st/   *tanz* + 2 sg. pres.   underlying form
     [tantst] *tanzt*   Degemination

Of course, assuming that the affricate /ts/ consists of precisely the two segments mentioned in the transcription will be enough to cause the Degemination rule to apply in (19). The rule only requires the presence of two (nearly) identical bundles of segmental features, and this condition is fulfilled in /zɪts+st/ just as it is in /haɪs+st/. Making the rule more complicated by treating the affricate as a separate type of segment is unfortunate, since it robs the Degemination rule of its primary motivation, namely the constraint that disallows two identical adjacent segments.

Not surprisingly perhaps, the differentiation between segmental structure and skeletal positions provides the means for treating the affricates as units on the one hand and as bisegmental strings on the other hand. If affricates are represented as in (20), both types of argument can be properly taken care of. The phonotactic unity of affricates is only natural, since phonotactic well-formedness is computed largely on the level of the skeleton. Segmentally, however, an affricate is simply the concatenation of the stop and the plosive. It is for this reason that affricates were not included in the table of segments (17) in § 2.3.2.

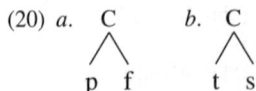

(20) *a.*   C   *b.*   C

        p   f   t   s

We are now able to state the syllabic representation of other types of words. As (21*a*) shows, the relationship between segments and skeletal positions can be many-to-one in both directions.

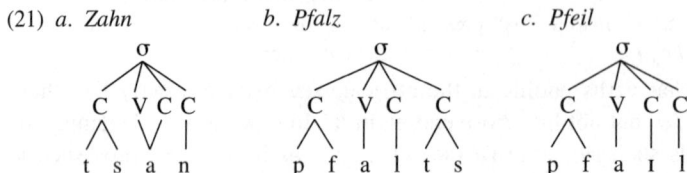

(21) *a. Zahn*   *b. Pfalz*   *c. Pfeil*

          σ   σ   σ

     C   V C C   C   V C   C   C   V C C

     t   s   a   n   p   f   a   l   t   s   p   f   a   ɪ   l

Affricates are well known as (at least potentially) complex segments. The next class of segments to be analysed here has not been studied to such an extent. Modern Standard German allows, besides the plosive-fricative combinations, that is, affricates, the mirror-image sequence of segments. In words such as *Spaß*, *Stein*, *Skat*, a word-initial fricative is followed by a plosive. The three combinations which occur with high frequency are /ʃp/, /ʃt/, and /sk/. As the data in (22*b*) shows, the plosives can also be combined with /s/, where (22*a*) has /ʃ/, and vice versa. These are definitely the more marked options. But the pronouncing dictionaries require the use of these initial fricatives in a large number of forms.

(22) *a.* /ʃp/   Spiel, Sprache, Splitter
       /ʃt/   Stuhl, Streit
       /sk/   Skelett, Sklave, Skrupel
   b. /sp/   Spezies, Spirans
       /st/   Stil, Stoiker
       /ʃk/   Schkeuditz, Schkopau

As the words in (22) show, there seems to be a further problem here for the assumption made earlier that syllables in German allow for only two prevocalic consonantal positions. There are numerous words with clusters such as /ʃpr/ or /skr/, even if one decides, as most authors do, not to include in the analysis the more marked options of (22*b*).[10] A straightforward solution to this problem consists in the proposal that the fricative-plosive sequences are totally analogous in structure to the affricates. That is, they are complex segments in the sense defined above, where two sets of featural information are associated to a single skeletal position, as illustrated in (23).

---

[10] The reason they are considered here is that there is only a partial tendency for assimilating these words to the unmarked pattern of (22*a*). There is some variation in the pronunciation of the [st] vs. [ʃt] and [sp] vs. [ʃp] clusters, also witnessed by the options offered in the pronouncing dictionaries. But the (few) words with initial [ʃk] are stable. Furthermore, North German dialects like that of Hamburg have [st] and [sp] as the unmarked or only form.

(23) *Spruch*

σ

C   C   V   C

ʃ   p   ʀ   ʊ   χ

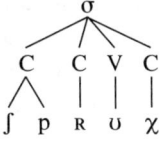

There are several arguments in favour of this analysis. First, the distributional possibilities for affricates and the complex segments covered here are to a large extent the same. Notice, for example, that /sk/ also fits the distributional context given in (16) for single units including the affricate /pf/, as in *Sklave, Sklerose*. Thus, if the classical arguments for the unity of affricates are valid, they are equally valid for /ʃp/ and the like. Incidentally, no term analogous to *affricate* exists for these structures. One could coin the term *suffricate*, by analogy with *affix* and *suffix*.

Second, it would complicate the phonological description of German to allow for the association of a plosive and a fricative segment *in this order* to a single prosodic position, but to disallow a complex structure where the two segments are in the opposite order. In other words, the existence of affricates leads one to expect the fricative-plosive combinations, the suffricates, if nothing else is being said.

Finally, in historic precursors of German, the clusters in question behave quite clearly as single units. For example, in Gothic a type of reduplication exists where the first consonant is reduplicated, for example, the preterite form *fáifráis* from *fráisan* 'try'. But if the word begins with the consonant cluster /sp/ or /sk/, as in *skáiskáid* from *skáidan* 'separate', these consonants both appear in the reduplicative prefix. If one takes the prosodic position as the relevant unit for reduplication, and if the clusters in question are indeed single units at this level, everything else follows. The same observation can be made with respect to Germanic alliteration (*Stabreim*), where /sp/ and /sk/ behave as single units, while 'regular' clusters such as /pr/ do not.[11] The analysis of fricative-stop clusters as suffricates will again be applied, with some success, to the consonant clusters in § 7.5.2.

3.2.2. More on subsyllabic structure

One of the open questions in syllabic phonology is how much more structure in addition to a CV- or X-tier the syllable needs to have. While the 'pure' CV-approach to syllable structure attempts to limit syllable structure to the categories illustrated in the syllable template (13), other models have argued for a further set of subsyllabic constituents. Clear evidence for one or the other solution is not always easy to come by, but there seems to be accumulating evidence for a fairly rich syllabic model. Candidates for such categories will therefore be introduced at this point.

---

[11] For this argument, see also Durand (1990: 217). For the data on Gothic, see Kienle (1969).

This is also the point at which we move from the non-linear phonological structure in which one-to-many and many-to-one associations between elements may occur, to the more constrained area of the prosodic hierarchy, which is tree-like. That is, all the units treated from here on belong to exactly one higher category (except for the top category, the 'root' in the graph-theoretic sense).

The particular model of the syllable discussed here will be the one in (24), where the onset, the rhyme, the nucleus, and the coda mediate between the CV-tier and the σ-node. Instead of C and V, elements on the skeletal tier could then also be undifferentiated Xs, as indicated in § 3.2.1.1. The head or syllabic core of the syllable could be defined as the first (sometimes the only) X dominated by the nucleus.[12]

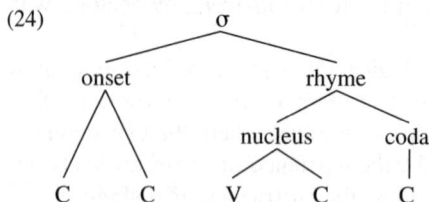

(24)

```
                    σ
         _____
        onset              rhyme
        / \               /\
       /   \          nucleus   coda
      /     \          /\        |
     C     C     V    C         C
```

To take up each of these categories in turn, the onset is clearly the category to which all prevocalic consonants belong. All phonotactic constraints governing the different combinatorial combinations in this area (see § 7.4) thus seem to refer to the onset as the relevant domain. This observation provides the basic justification for this category.

The rhyme, on the other hand, is less obviously involved in phonotactic regularities. Also, the division of labour between the rhyme and the two subordinated categories is unclear. I will simply leave this question open for further inquiry. For purely formal reasons, there should be a rhyme if there is an onset, unless one postulates a tripartite structure of onset-nucleus-coda, as Noske (1993) and Hall (1992b) do for German, and as I do in § 3.2.4 below. One argument in favour of a rhyme category seems to be the distribution of different variants of /ʀ/. As discussed further in § 7.4.4, /ʀ/ in Modern Standard German is usually vocalized in the rhyme, but not elsewhere. On a purely formal side, the rhyme category allows for a binary structuring of the syllable, under the assumption that there is an onset. But it is of course an open question in itself whether prosodic structure is binary or not.

It may also be worthwhile to remark on the relationship between the phonological category of rhyme and the 'rhyme' as it is commonly used in poetic work and analysis, since the relation exists but is not straightforward. If, in a poetic line, the final word ends in a stressed syllable, the string of segments considered to rhyme with some other poetic line is indeed identical to the rhyme as it is

---

[12] This latter option is found, e.g. in Sagey's model (Sagey 1986). There are syllable models based on other categories, such as the mora-based model and the metrical (strong-weak) model. For applications of the latter model to German, see Giegerich (1985; 1992b).

used here. Thus, in the beginning lines of the poem in (25), where 'rhymes' appear in bold, the first rhyming element consists of /ɪnən/. This is not a constituent in anybody's theory of the syllable, since it consists of a part of the prefinal syllable and of the final syllable. The second 'rhyme' /ɪn/ concludes lines 3 and 6 and it does correspond to a phonological rhyme. The third of the 'rhymes' contains two vowels again and is not a phonological rhyme. Note also that here we have two different vowels (/ɛ/ and /œ/ in lines 4 and 5, respectively), so that this counts as an impure poetic rhyme (though perhaps not for Friedrich Schiller with his Swabian dialectal background, in which front and round /ø/ as a distinctive unit did (and does) not exist).

(25)   Er stand auf seines Daches **Zinnen**,
                       Er schaute mit vergnügten **Sinnen**
                       Auf das beherrschte Samos h**in**.
                       Dies alles ist mir untert**änig**,
                       Begann er zu Ägyptens K**önig**,
                       Gestehe, daß ich glücklich b**in**.
            (Friedrich Schiller, *Der Ring des Polykrates*)

Poetic rhymes in German may also span more than two syllables, as in the trisyllabic *heitere* rhyming with *weitere*. Looking ahead somewhat, we may say that a poetic rhyme consists of all the material in a line-final foot except for the segments in the foot-initial onset. The onset consonants in rhyming pairs have to be *distinct*, in whatever way; *Herz* does not rhyme with *Herz*, but it does rhyme with *Schmerz, Erz, Scherz, März*, which also rhyme with each other. Somewhat surprisingly, the poetic rhyme provides rather clear evidence for the onset and for the foot, but not really for the phonological rhyme.

One of the often-noted facts about syllables in German is that word-final syllables cannot end in a short vowel (except for schwa). Thus, words ending in any of short /ɪ, ɛ, a, ɔ, ʊ, œ, ʏ/ do not occur. Turning towards word-internal syllables containing one of these vowels, one notes that consonants are ambisyllabic in the sense defined above precisely under the condition that otherwise the syllable would end in such a short vowel. Ambisyllabic consonants arguably do not occur with preceding long vowels. This leads to the conclusion that no syllable in German can end in a short vowel. Unfortunately, the situation is much less clear if the vowel in question is tense. These cases will be discussed below in § 8.2.1 in connection with questions of stress. Focusing on the clear cases, one way of accounting for the facts would be to postulate that the nucleus in a syllable must always branch in German, that is, have the shape given in (26). If this structure is seen as a well-formedness condition on German syllables, it will not allow for a syllable such as that displayed in (27).

(26)   nucleus

         V   C

(27)   *σ

```
      onset    rhyme
        |       /\
        |   nucleus  coda
        |      |
        C      V
```

In (28), further evidence is presented that a nucleus condition such as that in (26) is indeed active in German. A rule shortening (and consequently, laxing) long vowels can apply optionally particularly, but not exclusively, to those vowels which do not bear the primary stress in the word (more on this rule in § 7.2.2).[13] As the transcriptions indicate, if there is only one consonant following the short-ened vowel this consonant is ambisyllabic. The syllabification is always such that there is a consonant closing the syllable with a short vowel. In other words, the nucleus condition (26) is fulfilled.

(28) Afrika   [aː.fʀiː.kaː] ~ [af.ʀɪkaː]
     Metall   [meː.tall] ~ [mɛtall]
     zumal   [tsuː.maːl] ~ [tsʊmaːl]
     Philosophie [fiː.lo.zoː.fiː] ~ [fɪlɔzɔfiː]
     Kalender   [kaː.lɛn.dɐ] ~ [kalɛn.dɐ]
     Kuli   [kuː.liː] ~ [kʊliː]

There are certainly other ways of expressing the phonotactic condition dis-allowing syllable-final short, lax vowels than through the condition (26). (One alternative would be to use a structure such as (27) as a filter, disallowing short syllable-final vowels.) But if condition (26) provides the correct description, it provides the evidence for the category of nucleus which is the focus of this discussion. Later, especially in Chapter 8 on word stress, I tie the presence or absence of stress to the presence or absence of a nucleus; see also § 4.3.

The coda could, parallel to the onset, be seen as the node for final consonants in the syllable. But now a problem becomes apparent. In (24), the nucleus was analysed as a branching node, that is, one that contains two skeletal positions. This seems to be the right move, given that long vowels and diphthongs should be preferably in one single syllabic constituent, and that the nucleus was just analysed as a branching node for all syllables in German. In this case, however, the first postvocalic consonant should also become a part of the nucleus and not of the coda. Only a second consonant, if present, is dominated by the coda. An alternative would be to place all sonorants (vowels or sonorant consonants) under the nucleus. Evidence found by Treiman (1983) from word games and by Stemberger (1983) from speech errors confirms this view, at least for /r/ and /l/ which seem to form a unit with the preceding vowel. The most restrictive position on the content of the nucleus is held by Goldsmith (1990: 109) who identifies it with the V-slot, which can contain only a single short vowel.

[13] The shortening illustrated in (28) is only one of several such cases, as I demonstrate in § 7.2.2.

Unfortunately, there are arguments for even further ways of assigning consonants to subsyllabic structure. For example, the nucleus is taken as the domain for all vowels (syllabic or not), while all consonants are assigned to the coda.[14] But in this formulation, there is a strange interaction between the nucleus and the coda: if the nucleus is branching (containing a long vowel or a diphthong), the coda cannot be branching; and vice versa. It is hard to see why this should be the case, or even how to formalize the constraint. One of the reasons for the simple syllable schema in (13) was precisely the avoidance of such awkward statements. By simply saying that the syllable contains a certain number of skeletal positions, of which the third from the end is the V-position, all of these problems are avoided. Alternatively, it is possible to argue that the length restriction constitutes evidence for the rhyme to the exclusion of nucleus and coda, since the maximality is a property of the positions from the syllabic vowel position to the end of the syllable.

I therefore conclude this section on the structure of the syllable in German in a somewhat tentative way. There is at present no one single and convincing solution to the descriptive and theoretical issues. Hopefully, as in general work on the structure of the syllable, competition between various syllable models and their proponents will lead to the separation of necessary and unnecessary categories in a theory of the syllable. Later, in § 3.2.4, I will assume that the onset, the nucleus, and the coda are necessary elements of a syllable, besides the CV-positions.[15]

3.2.3. Extrasyllabicity

The syllable was presented here as an organizing category for the segments in a particular domain, perhaps the word. One of the natural assumptions here might be that *all* segments have to belong to a particular syllable. But as we have already seen that a segment might belong to more than one syllable (that is, be ambisyllabic), it might also be possible that a particular segment is not assigned to any syllable. Such a segment will be called *extrasyllabic*, and I argue that the concept of extrasyllabicity is useful or even necessary in the analysis of some segments which have been neglected in the discussion so far.

The class of cases that have not been covered at all in the discussion of syllables of Modern Standard German so far is illustrated in (29) and (30); here we see that a sequence of segments which is covered by a syllable which is maximally filled according to the schemata in (13) or (24) can be followed by either /t/, /s/, /d/, or /st/. The resulting words may be monomorphemic (29) or morphologically complex (30).

---

[14] This proposal is actually followed below. More discussion on what can fill the nucleus can be found in § 7.4.2.

[15] Another influential model of syllable structure is that of Hayes (1989) which claims that the major syllabic constituent is the *mora*. For a critical discussion see Noske (1992; 1993).

(29) *a.* Werft   *b.* Mumps   *c.* Herbst   *d.* Mond
     Haupt   Krebs   Obst   Freund
     Markt   Murks   Arzt   Feind

(30) *a.* lehn+t   *b.* Schal+s   *c.* lehn+st   *d.* lächel+nd
     glaub+t   Laub+s   glaub+st   ruder+nd

These words show that the coronal obstruents can be attached to any syllable which is well formed according to the criteria set up so far (except for the disallowed identical final consonants introduced in (17) to (19)). These final obstruents are not subject to any of the phonotactic restrictions that usually hold for German. It is even possible to form sequences consisting of two stops, such as /pt/ or /kt/. This partial independence of the final obstruents of the preceding structure leads to the hypothesis that these segments are perhaps not part of the syllable, but are *extrasyllabic* instead. In *Mond* and *Herbst*, /d/ and /st/ (respectively) are structurally outside of the syllable. Since it seems to be true that such an additional coronal obstruent appears only at the end of the word and not inside the word, the correct description should say that German allows an extrasyllabic coronal obstruent word-finally. (It will be shown later, in § 7.5.2, that /st/ constitutes a single unit here, and that it is not an accident that the obstruent must be coronal.) A preliminary representation of *Mond* and *Herbst* will then be as in (31). These structures are probably converted in a later syllabification into ones where the final consonants lose their extrasyllabic status, see (41).

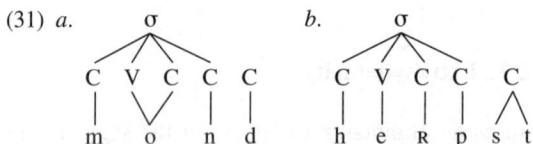

(31) *a.*   σ   *b.*   σ

More arguments for this type of extrasyllabicity will be given in the sections on phonotactics (§ 7.4); the eventual fate of extrasyllabic segments will be considered at the end of § 3.2.4.

It remains an open question whether more than one additional coronal obstruent can appear in the word-final position. While words such as, for example, **Herbsts*, **Obsts* are probably not well formed and are clearly avoided (see Wiese 1988: 101), there are words with an additional /s/ as in *Monds*, *Markts* (although even here, *Mondes* and *Marktes*, with the vowel schwa breaking up the cluster, clearly are the preferred options). For *Monds* and similar words, the extrasyllabic item consists, on the surface, of [ts], that is, the coronal affricate. It is therefore not necessary to admit more than one extrasyllabic position, but sufficient to admit the coronal affricate to occur as a marked option in this position. In addition, there is a very limited number of words for which one would have to assume two extrasyllabic consonants even if /st/ and /ts/ count as one complex segment: (*du*) *feil[σsch+st*, (*er/sie/es*) *lech[σz+t*, *schluch[σz+t*. I should point out, however, the following facts: this list is practically complete; no

monomorphemic words of this type exist; the last two words are onomato-
poeic; and the first example is not at all easy to pronounce for speakers of
German. For these reasons, these cases do not provide very forceful evidence
against the claim that only one (complex) segment may be extrasyllabic.

In the literature on extrasyllabicity in German, some other versions for final
extrasyllabicity have been considered. Giegerich (1985; 1989), Hall (1992*a*, *b*),
and Yu (1992*a*, *b*) have all proposed an even more restricted syllabification,
where only the sequence V C would be syllabified, at least in some early cycles
of syllabification, under the assumption that syllabification occurs repeatedly
during the derivation of words. Thus, in the examples in (31), an additional
consonant (/n/ and /p/, respectively) would be regarded as extrasyllabic.

Finally, a counterpart to final extrasyllabicity might also exist in the initial
position of words. While I proposed in § 3.2.1.2 that clusters such as /ʃpʀ/ and
/skl/ contain a complex initial segment (see (23)), an alternative analysis would
see the initial fricative /ʃ/ or /s/ as extrasyllabic (see Halle and Vergnaud 1980;
Wiese 1988*a*: § 3.8.1 for German). However, there is an important difference
between the initial and the final clusters, in that the shape of the initial fricatives
([s] vs. [ʃ]) depends directly on the following stops to the point of being predictable from these stops, while the final obstruents are almost independent of
the preceding material, as shown in (29) and (30). This asymmetry in the closeness between the segments in question is well represented by postulating a slot
for final, but not for initial, extrasyllabicity.[16]

3.2.4. Syllabification

The final task in this discussion of syllable structure of MSG is to determine
how words receive their syllabic structure. It should by now be obvious that the
syllable structure is indeed predictable. The cases cited by Vennemann (1982:
264 ff.) for non-predictable syllabification which are presented here in (32) are
less than convincing. In (32*a*), the position of the syllable boundary is not
predictable from the segment sequence (long or short vowel followed by /kl/)
alone, but it becomes predictable if the morphological boundary is taken into
account as well.[17] It is a fact about German that syllabification cannot 'cross'
over the boundaries before affixes such as +*lich* (more on this in § 3.4 where
I will argue that +*lich*, but not +*ig*, is a phonological word). These differences
in the syllabification always correlate with a difference in the morphological
structure.

A similar observation can be made for the cases in (32*b*), for which a pronunciation exists where only the position of the syllabic segment varies. The

---

[16] These questions are discussed more thoroughly in Wiese (1991).

[17] Vennemann's theory of *word phonology* explicitly disallows reference to morphological information in phonological descriptions.

(32) *a.* täglich ~ eklig   (/taːg/ + /lɪç/ ~ /eːkl/ + /ig/)
    [k.l̩]   [.kl̩]
    schicklich ~ pricklig   (/ʃɪk/ + /lɪç/ ~ /prɪkl/ + /ig/)
    [k.l̩]   [kl̩]

  b. eklen ~ ekeln   (/eːkl/ + /n/_A ~ /eːkl/ + /n/_V)
    [kl̩n̩] [kl̩n]
    lockren ~ lockern   (/lɔkʀ/ + /n/_A ~ /lɔkʀ/ + /n/_V)
    [kʀn̩]   [kʀ̩n]

  c. Knäuel ~ Geheul   Pollen ~ Köln
    [ɔYl̩]   [ɔYl]   [ɔl̩n]   [œln]
    Barren ~ Farn   Barrel ~ Kerl
    [aʀn̩] [aʀn]   [ɛʀl̩]   [ɛʀl]
    wieher(n) ~ wir   Herren ~ Herrn
    [iːʀ̩]   [iːʀ]   [ɛʀn̩] [ɛʀn]

left-hand examples are always inflected adjectives, the right-hand examples are verb forms. Again, under the assumption that syllabification can be sensitive to morphological categories such as word classes, the syllabification is predictable. It is also worth noting here that all of these examples involve an unstressed *schwa syllable*, that is, one containing either schwa or a sonorant consonant as the syllabic nucleus. These alternations are the subject of §§ 4.3 and 7.4.2. Schwa syllables in the sense just defined will play an important role in some of the later discussions.

The words in (32*c*) are not quite homogeneous and are slightly less straight-forward. Vennemann argues that here an identical segmental sequence is alternatively syllabified in the form of one or of two syllables. Notice first that the second syllable is always a schwa syllable in the sense defined above. (Instead of the syllabic consonant, there can be a sequence of schwa plus the consonant in the left-hand examples of (32*c*).) Some of these words are arguably or certainly morphologically complex, in particular *Knäu+el*, *Poll+en*, *Barr+en*, *Herr+en*, *Herr+n*.[18] The last two examples show a subtle contrast between the plural form of *Herr*, which is bisyllabic in the standard pronunciation, and the dative singular form, which can be (though it does not have to be) pronounced monosyllabically. I argue in the next section and in § 4.3.1 that plural nouns always end in an unstressed syllable. Thus, the morphology enforces a particular phonological shape for some words. The remaining two words in (32*c*), *Barrel* and *wieher(n)*, are indeed somewhat exceptional. *Barrel* is a recent loan word from English. The pronouncing dictionaries require a schwa vowel (and not a syllabic consonant) in the second syllable. This is one of the cases where schwa (or rather, as I will argue in § 7.4.2, an empty prosodic position)

---

[18] There is a stem-forming suffix *+en*, which is clearly present in words such as *Garten* (cf. *Gärtchen*) and *Balken* (cf. *Bälkchen*). Its presence in *Pollen* and *Barren* is less obvious, since alternative morphological forms not including *-en* are not easy to find. (There is a verb *barren*, however.) There is also an admittedly non-productive suffix *+el* (Fleischer 1982: §§ 2.2.4, 2.2.32), with *Knäuel* as an isolated formation from a Middle High German base *kluiwe* 'ball'.

is distinctive and part of the underlying representation. The verb *wiehern* may be either analysed in an analogous way or treated on the basis of the generalization that (nearly) all verbs are bisyllabic in most forms (more details on this in § 4.3.3). The overall conclusion is that very few clear cases for non-predictable syllabification are available. Note also that all of these cases involve a non-alternating schwa in one form in contrast to its absence in another form.

In the following, I give a sketch of syllabification, of a rule-governed assignment of syllable structure to a string of segments in a word of Modern Standard German. The set of rules is not explicit enough to constitute an algorithm, but it connects the segmental information to the elements of syllabic structure as it has been presented in this chapter. As subsyllabic structure, I assume the onset-nucleus-coda sequence in addition to and dominating the CV-tier.[19] It is presupposed here that the domain in which syllabification takes place is the *phonological word*. This concept will be made more precise in § 3.4 below.

Furthermore, I assume the existence of a set of phonotactic wellformedness constraints, determining which segment sequences are phonologically well formed. These, such as the sonority sequencing constraint, are discussed in detail in § 7.5.2. For the purposes of syllabification, it can simply be assumed that such conditions exist.

Where does syllabification start from? The reader should recall that a CV-approach to the syllable is argued above to be at least a necessary ingredient of a syllable model, and that underlying entries contain only unpredictable information. Given that segments (root nodes and their dependents) are generally in a one-to-one relationship to elements of the skeleton, with deviations from this only in special cases such as length (two positions—one segment) and complex segments (two segments—one position), skeletal positions need not be part of the underlying entries, except in the case of long vowels. Since length is, as argued in Chapter 2, a distinctive feature for vowels of Modern Standard German, and since length is a prosodic feature, this aspect of prosody is to be included in underlying entries. On the other hand, the structure of complex segments, the affricates and suffricates of § 3.2.1.2, is predictable. Discussion of such structures is resumed in § 7.5.1.

Skeletal positions are assigned by the very simple rule given in (33). The rule associates an X to every root node that is not associated with X already. Long vowels and perhaps other exceptional structures such as affricates are not affected by the rule. (33) is the first of a number of *default rules* I will present in due course.

(33) Skeletal structure
    Assign X to all root nodes.

---

[19] Within a psycholinguistic model of language production, Levelt (1989: ch. 9) also assigns a special status to the onset-nucleus-coda sequence: it acts as the frame for the final stage in the generation of the *phonetic plan*, the set of instructions to the articulatory component.

We are now in a position to indicate how syllable structure might be erected over a string of such Xs. In the following, I present what might be seen as the sketch of an algorithm, under the influence of similar proposals by Hall (1992*a*) and Giegerich (1992*b*). The hardest problem to solve is the correct derivation of prevocalic and postvocalic glides. Given that diphthongs are underlyingly just two adjacent vowel segments, the procedure has to pick only one of them (and the right one) as the syllabic head of a syllable and predict which of two vowels surfaces as the glide. In other words, diphthongs are completely subsumed under the nucleus node. As mentioned in § 3.2.2, this is only one of several existent and reasonable analyses. Alternatively, the nucleus dominates the sequence V-C independently of the segments associated with it. Finally, Hall (1992*a*) subsumes all syllabic vowels (long or short) under the nucleus, while consonants and diphthongal glides are in the coda.

Given that V-positions are X-positions enriched by the feature specification [+ syllabic] (see (15) above), a rule such as (34*a*) will turn some X-positions into V-positions. Obviously, diphthongs of the type /aʊ/ will be treated correctly in that only the first of the vowel segments will be dominated by V. Even in the exceptional diphthongs /ʊɪ/ to be found in the interjections *hui*, *pfui*, it is the left-most vowel which is syllabic: [ʊɪ̯]. As shown in (40) below, long vowels are also treated adequately. In (34*b*), I assume that a nucleus node N dominates all and only the vowels. This view of the nucleus is different from the one proposed in (26), but identical with the proposal of Vater (1992: § 3.2.2).

(34) Syllable head assignment[20]
    a. Assign [+ syllabic] to an X, unless another X immediately precedes.

              | |

          [− consonantal]   [− consonantal]
    b. Join all X dominating [− consonantal] into a nucleus N.

The major remaining task is to assign intervocalic consonants to the syllables in such a way that onsets are maximized. The principle of *onset maximization*, observed in numerous studies of syllabic phonology, also holds for German. The /t/ in *Fil.trat* is part of the second syllable, not the first, although /lt/ is a perfectly well-formed syllable ending. Basically, there seem be two ways to instantiate onset maximization in the syllabification procedure. First, it is possible to syllabify a string directionally, that is, from 'right to left' or vice versa. If syllables were erected over a string while proceeding *from the right edge to the left*,

---

[20] The *unless*-clause in (34*a*) is not valid if the vowel preceding the vowel to be syllabified is a long vowel, because sequences of syllabic vowels clearly exist in German, as in *Ruine* or *Theo* (see (40)). In theoretical phonology, an exhaustiveness condition (Hayes 1986) has been proposed which ensures the correct application of the condition: a long vowel is one associated to *two* skeletal positions, while the *unless*-clause explicitly asks for a vowel associated to only *one* position. Exhaustive application of the rule to the vowel is thus not ensured and prevents the rule's application. See § 7.3.1 for another application of this condition.

onsets would automatically be onset-maximal, given that syllables are always built up to their maximal size.[21]

The alternative way of ensuring onset maximization is simply to build onsets first, and codas later. Again assuming a maximality principle, onsets will contain all the possible consonants, and codas the remaining material. Arbitrarily following this second way, the following two rules can be proposed. In both of them, I assume that the constraints on possible well-formed onsets and codas are independently given.

(35) Syllable onsets
   a. Create an onset O to the left of each N.
   b. Join all Xs to the left of a V to the onset, obeying wellformedness constraints for syllabic structure.

(36) Syllables codas
   Join all Xs to the right of a V into a coda, obeying wellformedness constraints for syllabic structure.

Rules (35) and (36) assume the existence of an asymmetry between onsets and codas: note that (35*a*) makes onsets obligatory constituents, even if there is no material to fill them (see (40) for an example). This move is motivated by the facts of Glottal Stop Insertion to be discussed in §§ 3.3.1 and 6.3.3. I am not aware of similar arguments for the obligatoriness of the coda.

If onsets, nuclei, and codas are generated, syllable nodes (and perhaps also rhymes) are automatically given. To say that a syllable is a projection of every V-node or every nucleus might be sufficient. In the light of the discussion of schwa syllables and their role in prosodic morphology (§ 4.3), it would however be required to say that syllables without a nucleus are also admitted. On this conception it would be possible to say that any subsyllabic constituent (onset, nucleus, or coda) will establish a syllable node. Finally, every X not assigned the value [+ syllabic] by (34*a*) will be a C, that is, [– syllabic]. This is achieved by another default rule, stated in (37).

(37) Default for skeletal positions
   Assign [– syllabic] to every X.

It remains to illustrate the approach chosen with some representative examples.[22] In (38), the treatment of consonant clusters is of special importance, while (39) and (40) show how various vowel sequences are syllabified. In these examples, phonemic transcription symbols stand for more complex feature structures dominated by a root node. Note that 'C' on the skeletal tier stands for the coda, quite a different category from 'C' on the syllable-structure tier. *Filtr+at* is an affixed word, while the following examples are monomorphemic. This

---

[21] Talking about 'right' and 'left' really is of course just a spatial metaphor for the temporal order of phonological units. Maximality of syllable structure is sometimes regarded as a possible parameter in which languages may vary, see Itô (1989).

[22] I assume syllabification of so-called non-native words not to be substantially different from syllabification of other words. Only a few interjections such as *pfft* or *sst* are outside of the regularities of syllable structure and syllabification in Modern Standard German.

distinction is irrelevant for present purposes. In § 3.4, the indirect relevance of morphological structure for syllabification is discussed.

(38) Syllabification of *Filtrat*

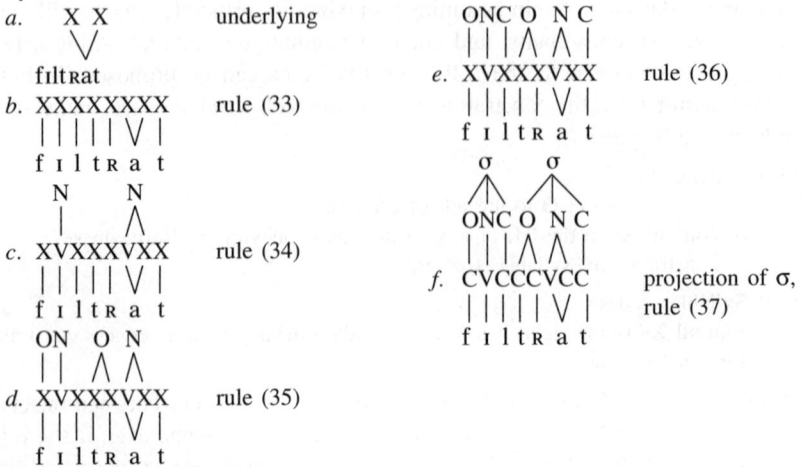

a.　　X X　　　　　underlying
　　　　 V
　　　 fıltʀat

b. XXXXXXXX　　rule (33)
　 | | | | | V |
　 f ı l tʀ a t
　　 N　　 N
　　 |　　 ∧
c. XVXXXVXX　　rule (34)
　 | | | | | V |
　 f ı l tʀ a t
　 ON　 O　 N
　 | |　 ∧ ∧
d. XVXXXVXX　　rule (35)
　 | | | | | V |
　 f ı l tʀ a t

　　ONC O　N C
　　| | | ∧ ∧ |
e. XVXXXVXX　　rule (36)
　 | | | | | V |
　 f ı l tʀ a t
　 σ　　 σ
　 ∧　　 ∧
　ONC O　N C
　| | | ∧ ∧ |
f. CVCCCVCC　　projection of σ,
　 | | | | | V |　rule (37)
　 f ı l tʀ a t

(39) Syllabification of *Taifun*

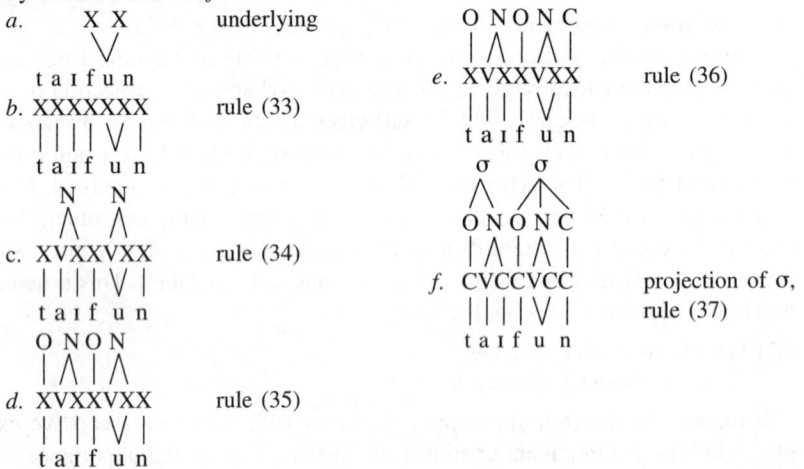

a.　　X X　　　　　underlying
　　　　 V
　　　 t a ı f u n

b. XXXXXXX　　rule (33)
　 | | | | V |
　 t a ı f u n
　　 N　 N
　　 ∧　 ∧
c. XVXXVXX　　rule (34)
　 | | | V |
　 t a ı f u n
　 O NO N
　 | ∧ | ∧
d. XVXXVXX　　rule (35)
　 | | | V |
　 t a ı f u n

　 O NO N C
　 | ∧ | ∧ |
e. XVXXVXX　　rule (36)
　 | | | V |
　 t a ı f u n
　 σ　　 σ
　 ∧　　 ∧
　 O NO N C
　 | ∧ | ∧ |
f. CVCCVCC　　projection of σ,
　 | | | V |　rule (37)
　 t a ı f u n

In the first syllable of *Taifun* as well as in both syllables of *Theo* below, I assume that no coda is generated. On the other hand, the second syllable of this latter word receives an empty onset by means of (35a). There is actually an alternative pronunciation of these bisyllabic sequences in which a glide is inserted in the position of the onset: [teː.jo], although this is more common if the first vowel is high, as in *Trio* [tʀiː.jo].

The outline of a scheme for syllabification given above has relied on a constituent model of the syllable, although not in the version used in other recent proposals, in which the full constituent structure (i.e. O-N-C) is always assigned to the segmental string (see e.g. Noske 1992). Such a constituent model can perhaps express the length constraint presented above for

German (see § 3.2.1) in the following way: assume that universally every constituent can be maximally binary branching. This would give six (instead of the required five) positions in the syllable. German might therefore exhibit an additional constraint stating that only one of the two constituents N or C may branch. These two principles together would yield the adequate length conditions.

(40) Syllabification of *Theo*

a. XXXX   underlying
   V V
   t e o

b. XXXXX   rule (33)
   | V V
   t e o
   N N
   Λ Λ

c. XVXVX   rule (34)
   | V V
   t e o
   O N O N
   | Λ Λ

d. XVX VX   rule (35)
   | V V
   t e o

e. ——   rule (36), not applicable
   σ   σ
   Λ   Λ
   O N O N
   | Λ Λ

f. CVC VC   projection of σ, rule (37)
   | V V
   t e o

Later discussions in Chapters 4 and 5 demonstrate that syllabification must be assumed to operate *cyclically*. That is, every addition of a morpheme leads to a new application of the rules of syllabification, as long as the domain for syllabification remains the same. That is, in [[[[*Kräft*]ig]ung]en] syllabification will take place four times, leading to [kʀɛf.ti.gʊŋən]. I leave the question open how the intervocalic consonants are resyllabified from coda to onset at each new cycle; see Giegerich (1992*b*), Hall (1992*b*), and Yu (1992*a*) for different approaches to this problem. A possible general approach is that of Rubach and Booij (1990) who propose to erase a coda at the beginning of each new cycle of syllabification. All other syllable structure is preserved once constructed, only coda consonants can possibly change their affiliation.

The extrasyllabic consonant postulated above, that is, the position outside the syllable, still needs discussion. While it seems to make sense to assume that coronal obstruents are extrasyllabic at some point, there are also arguments to the effect that these extrasyllabic consonants are integrated into the syllable at some point. As indicated in (41), some adjunction rule connects the extrasyllabic consonant to the syllable. Hall (1992*a*) and Giegerich (1992*b*) present arguments for such a rule which in fact applies late in the derivation, because there are other rules which have to apply before this rule.

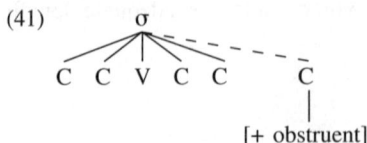

(41)

C C V C C   C
                   |
              [+ obstruent]

If this rule were to apply early in the derivation, its application would create violations of syllabic wellformedness conditions such as the sonority hierarchy (§ 7.5.1). Therefore, the lateness of this rule probably follows from the fact that it is only allowed to apply at a point at which these structural conditions are not valid any more. In § 7.5, I argue that the relevant conditions are indeed defined on relatively abstract levels of representation.

An alternative to rule (41) would be to postulate that extrasyllabic consonants are those which are directly associated, not to the syllable, but to the word-node (in final position). There would then be no need for an adjunction rule such as (41). This move has the advantage of accounting for the fact that there is no evidence that extrasyllabic consonants can ever appear word-internally. A word-internal coda (two consonants) plus an extrasyllabic consonant plus a following coda (two consonants) would yield a maximum of five word-internal consonants. This maximum is never met within words.

3.3. THE FOOT

There has been great debate about the phonology of the syllable, of which I attempt to cover major aspects in the preceding section. Much less is known or suspected about the other prosodic categories to which I now turn. According to most models of prosodic structure, the unit immediately above the syllable is the *foot*. It has not received as much attention as other concepts of phonological representation have. In studies of German, the foot has hardly been used systematically. Nevertheless, the foot seems to play a very clear role in the prosodic structure of German, as the following three arguments demonstrate. In particular, besides being involved in purely phonological regularities, the category of the foot seems to constrain some types of word formation in a way that is hard to describe straightforwardly without reference to the foot; see Chapter 4 on these cases. The category of the foot will also figure prominently in the discussion of stress regularities in Chapter 8.

For the following discussion, it is assumed (following the standard definition) that a foot is a sequence of one or more syllables. In the latter case, the first syllable must carry stronger stress than the subsequent syllables in that foot. That is, the foot consists of the string of syllables starting from one stressed syllable up to (but not including) the next one. Note that a sequence of two syllables may, depending on circumstances to be discussed later, consist of either one foot or two feet. The syllables in the weak position in a foot may be schwa syllables or not. Schwa syllables are unable to be in the strong position in a foot, all other types of syllables in German head a foot. This also means that 'normal' syllables can be in a strong or weak position without any change. Since this point is of some importance in later discussions, I will clarify it with some contrastive examples.

In (42a), the syllable erected over the adjectival suffix +*isch* has weaker stress than the preceding syllable and consequently is in the weak position of a bisyllabic foot. The same is true for the similar suffixes +*lich* and +*ung* in (42b, c). But what about the corresponding examples in (43)? Are the syllables similar or identical to those in (42) in a strong or a weak position in a foot? The answer depends on a judgement of stress difference or identity between the final three syllables in *malerische*, *widerliche*, and *Steigerungen*. In this respect, intuitions are not clear-cut, but an argument for the correctness of the structures proposed in (43) will be given immediately. F denotes the foot category. Intrasyllabic structure is disregarded here since it is not in the focus of discussion.[23]

(42) *a.* närr+isch   *b.* hand+lich   *c.* Acht+ung

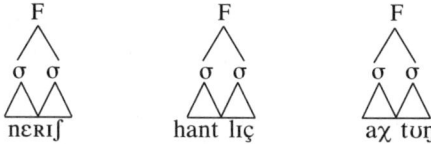

(43) *a.* mal+er+isch+e   *b.* wider+lich+e

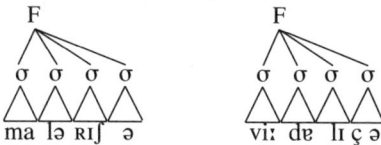

     c. Steig+er+ung+en

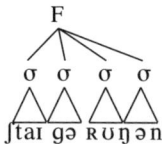

The foot as it is used here is quite compatible with the metrical foot as used in studies of poetic metre. In fact, as argued in § 3.2.2, the foot seems to be a crucial ingredient in determining the regularities of rhyming in poetry. On the basis of this assumption, we can find an argument for the foot structures in (43). A word rhyming with *widerliche* as in (43b) would be *liederliche*, but not any word ending in just -*iche*. That is, at least for the purposes of poetic rhyming, the words in (43) count as one single foot, but not as two. The uncertainty found

---

[23] Ambisyllabic consonants are also indicated. The segmental details and the level of abstractness or concreteness are however not relevant for the present purposes.

here is related to the unclarity in the perception of the stress patterns: is it indeed the case that there is a secondary stress in '*male,rische* and '*wider,liche*, or are the final three syllables unstressed to an equal degree? I leave this contrast unresolved; while it is possible that the foot in rhyming is not identical to that in phonological representation, it seems preferable to assume that the assumed stress difference is one of segmental structure (full vowels vs. schwa) alone. Words in (43) will then consist of one single foot. This is the solution I will actually make use of in § 3.4 and in Chapter 8, when discussing stress. A further question ignored here, but discussed in § 8.1, is the internal structure of feet containing more than two syllables.

3.3.1. Glottal stop and the foot

A first line of argumentation for the category of foot relies on the distribution of the glottal stop ([ʔ]) in German.[24] The occurrence of this sound in Modern Standard German is generally seen as a characteristic trait of the language (as opposed to, say, English). But phonemically, the distribution of glottal stop is predictable. It can occur only at the beginning of syllables that would begin with a vowel if the glottal stop were not present. Furthermore, the presence of glottal stop is optional. In no context does the non-occurrence of glottal stop lead to an ill-formed result, although different frequencies can be observed for different contexts. These two observations are of course the reasons why [ʔ] should not be analysed as a phoneme of Modern Standard German, as I indicated in (1) of § 2.1.

It is the pattern behind the variability that is in the focus of the discussion here. We first observe that a glottal stop can occur (and often does, in fact) word-initially, as illustrated in (44). This in itself is not very revealing, since at this point a number of units, morphological as well as phonological, begin simultaneously. The examples are also intended to show that the occurrence of [ʔ] is also not constrained by the following vowel or by morphological factors. (In the following, the glottal stop symbols are inserted into orthographic representations. They are always interpreted as *potential* glottal stops.)

(44) [ʔ]Atem
    [ʔ]Opa
    [ʔ]offen
    [ʔ]Igel
    [ʔ]Übung
    [ʔ]edel
    [ʔ]eine

The next set of examples in (45) is concerned with word-internal glottal stop.[25] The generalization is that a word-internal syllable beginning (on the level

---

[24] Yu (1992*b*: § 2.8.1) and Hall (1992*b*: § 2.4.4) make essentially the same point. For phonetic observations on [ʔ], see Krech (1968) and Stock (1971). If the first vowel in the sequence is a high vowel, a corresponding glide may occur instead of [ʔ] as the onset: for *Diode*, [dijoːdə] seems to stand in free variation to [diʔoːdə]; and, similarly, *Luise* allows for [luviːzə] and [luʔiːzə].

[25] Some examples are taken from Kloeke (1982: 46).

of the distinctive segments) with a vowel can only contain a glottal stop if it receives stronger stress than the preceding syllable—that is, foot-initially.

(45) Theodor ~ The[ʔ]oderich
     Thea ~ The[ʔ]ater
     Poesie ~ Po[ʔ]et
     ruinös ~ Ru[ʔ]ine
     Trio ~ Di[ʔ]ode
     Chaos ~ cha[ʔ]otisch
     Georg ~ Ge[ʔ]orgien

In these examples, there is no morphological boundary between the two vowels separated by glottal stop, although morpheme-initial glottal stop occurs as well, see *ver*+[ʔ]*eisen* or *ein*+[ʔ]*atmen*. Finally, it can be shown that the amount of stress in itself is not the crucial condition. As the pairs in (46) show, a relatively unstressed syllable (i.e. with secondary stress in the word domain) can start with a glottal stop. But in these cases, there is no preceding syllable with greater stress. The syllable beginning with a glottal stop clearly is not necessarily the one under primary word stress or in word-initial position; the glottal stop is also possible (though it occurs less often according to Kohler (1977: 173)) word-internally in '*Micha*ₗ[ʔ]*el* and not only in ₗ*Micha*'[ʔ]*ela* with the reverse stress pattern.

(46) [ʔ'lAnton ~ [ʔₗ]An'tenne
     [ʔ'lEkel ~ [ʔₗ]le'gal
     [ʔ'lAtem ~ [ʔₗ]A'tom
     [ʔ'lIden ~ [ʔₗ]lI'dee ~ [ʔₗ]lIde[ʔ'lal

Many descriptions of glottal stop distribution in Modern Standard German refer to the disjunction of contexts 'word-initially or in syllables with primary stress'. But the foot provides us with the means of handling the context for glottal stop in a unitary way. As this category was defined above, all glottal stops in the preceding examples occur exactly in foot-initial position and nowhere else; presupposing, however, that initial syllables with non-primary stress are dominated by their own foot, as in ₍Fll₎F[dee]. The foot, therefore, makes it possible to state a rule such as (47) which seems to allow for the most direct characterization of glottal stop. Whatever the merits of this rule (see § 6.3.3 for a reformulation in featural terms), the crucial point here is the usefulness of the foot as providing the context for the insertion.

(47) ʔ-insertion
     Insert [ʔ] in: ₍F[_____ [– consonantal]

A more precise characterization of ʔ-insertion would have to reflect on the features of the glottal stop and on the role of the prosodic skeleton or the onset in this process. Conceivably, [ʔ] fills an empty onset node as introduced in § 3.2.4. That is, ʔ-insertion is a means to avoid an empty onset. Also, it is necessary to account for the fact that across word boundaries [ʔ] cannot occur if word-final consonants are resyllabified to become an onset consonant of the following word. *Bin ich* 'am I' may be realized as [bɪn.ʔɪç] or [bɪɲɪç], the latter in a relatively casual style of speech. Of course, in the latter version, glottal stop is impossible. These examples suggest again that ?-insertion depends on the syllabification and the construction of prosodic structure in general. If syllabification crosses a word boundary (as it may in fast speech), creation of a consonantal onset bleeds ?-insertion.

The foot-initial distribution of non-phonemic [?] may also be related, although tentatively, to the distribution of the phoneme /h/. The occurrence of /h/ in *Uhu, Ahorn, Mahagoni, Alkohol,* and a few similar words, gives no clue to a particular restriction on the distribution of /h/ (except that it occurs only syllable-initially), since the /h/-initial syllable carries weaker stress than the preceding syllable, but there is no clear way of deciding whether a foot starts with the onset of the /h/-initial syllable. The set of alternations in (48) is more revealing.

(48) Bahnhof ~ Bahnhof   Wilhelm ~ Wilhelm (Willem)
     [baːn.hoːf] [baː.nof]   [vɪl.hɛlm] [vɪˈi̯əm]
     Bernhard ~ Bernhard   Leonhard ~ Leonhard
     [bɛʀn.haʀt] [bɛʀ.naʀt]   [leːɔn.hart] [leːɔn̯art]

It turns out that a syllable beginning in /h/ can undergo reduction. If reduction takes place, /h/ cannot appear. This dovetails with another fact about /h/: schwa syllables can begin with any consonantal phoneme except for /h/. Pronunciations such as [geːhən] for *gehen* are hypercorrect or spelling pronunciations. Since schwa syllables are the only syllables which cannot be strong in German, the lack of schwa syllables beginning in /h/ is immediately accounted for if /h/ is restricted to foot-initial position. Thus, the foot is also relevant in the description of the defective distribution of /h/. But this analysis is only possible if *Uhu* and similar words are seen as consisting of two feet, while other bisyllabic words such as *Duo* are dominated by a single foot. Interestingly, both Duden (1990) and Krech et al. (1982) transcribe *Alkohol* as [ˈalkohoːl], that is with a long final vowel, although in similar words with a non-stressed vowel this vowel is not marked as being long. We may interpret this transcription as an indication that there are indeed two feet here. Otherwise, no /h/ would be possible. (The clearest counterexample to the hypothesis that /h/ is always foot-initial is the (almost unique) word [ˌmahaˈgoːni] *Mahagoni,* where /h/ is clearly in the weak syllable of a foot.)

It must be stressed that in spite of the handful of lexical counterexamples to the proposed distributional constraint for /h/, there are still various broad generalizations which hold for both [h] and [?]: they form the class of laryngeal segments (see § 6.3.3); they never cluster with any other consonant; they can only appear syllable-initially; and they are alone in not beginning a schwa syllable (*[?ə . . .], *[hə . . .]). It is this remarkably parallel behaviour which gives rise to the proposition that these segments are both restricted to the foot-initial onset.

Taking all of these facts and analyses together, another conclusion becomes evident. In words such as *Antenne* or *Idee* (see (46)), the initial syllable also constitutes a foot, although this syllable does not carry word stress. (Such a foot is often called *pre-tonic*; see § 8.3.1 for more examples.) Our analysis of the glottal stop leads to this conclusion; but fortunately it makes a revision of the definition of the foot unnecessary. According to the definition, the foot cannot start with a syllable weaker than its right neighbour. An analysis of *Idee* using only a single foot would contradict this definition.[26]

I illustrate the notion of foot defended here in (49) by giving the prosodic structure for the word *Bibliothekar*, which has two secondary stresses before the final main stress, and therefore two pretonic feet in addition to the tonic foot. The word node combining the three feet will be the topic of § 3.4.

(49)

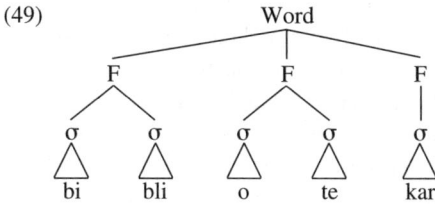

3.3.2. **Plural formation and the foot**

Glottal stop insertion provides a purely phonological argument for the category of the foot. (Possibly, as argued by Yu (1992*b*: § 2.8.2) and Hall (1992*b*), the distribution of aspirated vs. non-aspirated plosives provides a similar argument, though see the remarks on aspiration in § 7.6.) In contrast, the following two arguments depend on the interaction of morphology and phonology, which is the main topic of the two following chapters.

There are a number of (partly unpredictable) ways to form the plural of nouns in German which will be studied further, in its relation to the appearance of schwa, in § 4.3.1. For now it will just be noted that, with the exception of nouns taking +*s* as the plural marker, nouns in the plural are such that the last syllable must be a schwa syllable, while the preceding syllable is stressed. (50) and (51) give examples from the relevant noun classes. The plurals are always (at least) bisyllabic in such a way that the last syllable contains schwa or a syllabic consonant. These are the syllables earlier called *schwa syllables*. But the mono-syllabic stems in (50) receive suffixes which, together with schwa, create the bisyllabic structure. In contrast, the bisyllabic stems in (51) receive either no suffix or a purely consonantal one.

(50) *a.* Frau ~ Frau+en
    b. Kind ~ Kind+er
    c. Baum ~ Bäum+e

---

[26] In an alternative use of the foot (implicit in Giegerich's analysis (1985: 35–6, 270)), words with an initial weakly stressed syllable (for example *Dekan, Salat, Harmonika*) would contain only one foot. There is an interesting class of remaining cases, namely with schwa syllables in initial position as in *genau, ge+fallen*, or *be+fehlen*. On these examples see § 4.1.2, where the left-strong type of foot proposed here will also prove itself to be crucial in the analysis of *ge-* and *be-*prefixation.

(51) *a.* Vater ~ Väter
     b. Lehr+er ~ Lehr+er
     c. Schwester ~ Schwester+n

The noticeable fact about all noun plurals in (50) and (51) is that the suffixes and schwa occur in such a way that the constraint ('a final sequence consisting of a stressed syllable plus a schwa syllable') is obeyed, in nouns from these classes, without exception. If the noun in the singular form ends in a stressed syllable, either schwa or schwa plus a consonant is suffixed (50*a–c*) for the plural forms. Only if the noun already contains a final schwa syllable (either in the stem or in a derivational suffix as in *Lehrer*) can plural nouns without suffixes appear. The plural suffix -*n*, which is the unmarked suffix for feminine nouns, confirms this view, since it appears as [ən] if the constraint is not yet met, and as [n] if there already is a schwa syllable, see (51*c*) and many other feminine nouns such as *Steuer+n*, *Mauer+n*, and *Nummer+n*, see also (35) in § 4.3.1.

The overall result of these constraints on plural formation is that every plural noun (with the systematic exception of the *s*-plural nouns) ends in a stressed syllable followed by exactly one schwa syllable. This is the minimum structure for plural nouns, and several rules seem to conspire to create such a structure. Here we are not concerned with these rules (however, see §§ 4.3.1 and 7.4.2), but with the characterization of the structure itself. The question is how to describe the type of pattern in a non-arbitrary way. If we simply say that the sequence of a stressed syllable plus an unstressed syllable constitutes a *bisyllabic foot* of the kind amply illustrated above in (42), (43), and (49), then the observed constraint on plural nouns is sufficiently described by requiring these words to end in such a bisyllabic foot. Again, the foot provides the unit for a unitary characterization of the constraint which is obviously prosodic in nature. This discussion is continued in Chapter 4, where I present other evidence that the foot is a rather ubiquitous unit in the morphology of Modern Standard German.

3.3.3. Hypocoristics or clippings

As a second example for a foot-based word formation I will introduce a type of noun coinage that is not easily accounted for in standard theories of word syntax (for German see Toman 1983; or Olsen 1986). The reason is that in these words, nouns are derived from other nouns by a process of clipping or shortening and not by the concatenation of morphemes or words. In (52), I present a list of nouns formed by reducing a noun with an arbitrary number of syllables to two syllables. The first syllable in the short form is stressed, the final syllable invariably ends in /i/. It is important to stress that this is a highly productive way of deriving nouns.[27] One aspect not treated here is that the segmental material in

---

[27] If phonologists in Germany were finally to achieve the fame they undoubtedly deserve, they could easily (and affectionately!) be dubbed *Phoni+s*. Students of linguistics (*Sprachwissenschaft*) are actually being called *Sprawi+s*. This part of Ch. 3 was written during 1989 to 1990 before and during the unification of former East and West Germany, when some of the terms in (52) still had a referential meaning.

these hypocoristics ('terms of endearment') is partially reduced, perhaps to a minimum. The open question is whether there is a systematic reason for the fact that we find *Wessi* and not **Westi*, but *Fundi* instead of **Funni*.

(52) Profi   Professioneller
     Bundi   Bundesdeutscher
     Zoni   Zonenbewohner
     Wessi   Westdeutscher
     Fundi   Fundamentaler
     Zivi   Zivildienstleistender
     Nazi   Nationalsozialist
     Studi   Student

For the sake of completeness, I add examples from another group of words showing similar properties. The words in (53*a*) are slightly less systematic than the ones in the preceding list, but follow a similar pattern. They consist of, or end in, a bisyllabic sequence with the stress pattern 'strong before weak'. The segmental material is sometimes derived by taking the consonantal onset plus the vowel from two or more syllables of the input word. Usually the segments chosen in this clipping process are the first ones from the morphological constituents of the complex word. There is not necessarily, then, a fixed vowel at the end of these words, similar to the *−i* in (52).[28] Final *−o* occurs either in the origin forms, perhaps even as a phonological condition on these word formations, or as a pre-specified vowel, as in examples of (52). The forms in (53*b*) are generally known examples of the hypocoristic word formation illustrated above. They probably provide the bases on which the more recent forms in (52) are modelled.

(53) *a.* Juso   Jungsozialist
         Kripo   Kriminalpolizei
         Realo   Realpolitiker
         Gestapo   Geheime Staatspolizei
         Prolo   Proletarier
     b. Mutti   Mutter
         Vati   Vater
         Bubi   Bube

For the words in (52) and (53*b*), the result of this particular way of coining words is such that a sequence of two (minimal) syllables with the stress pattern strong-weak is derived. Furthermore, the word always ends in /i/. Thus, the word seems to conform with a structure which can only be described in phonological terms. Its suprasegmental aspects can be directly expressed by reference to the bisyllabic foot of the kind already encountered in plural formation. Since feet (at least in German) seem to prefer to have this particular shape, most aspects of the hypocoristics in (52) are adequately expressed by simply saying:

---

[28] These words are different from those in which the first one or two syllables from a longer word are taken to derive a so-called *Kurzwort*: *Auto*(*mobil*), *Krimi*(*nalroman*), *Lok*(*omotive*). See Fleischer (1982: 230) for some discussion.

'Build a prototypical foot ending in /i/ from a noun.' The complications in (53a) derive mainly from the fact that the word can be longer than one single foot (*Realo*, *Gestapo*). Just as with the plural nouns, the relevant foot is found here in the final position of the words; main stress is on the penultimate syllable.

As soon as one begins looking for cases of this sort, other examples with similar properties come to mind. In the domain of personal names, there are short forms of names (pet names, terms of endearment) which pattern in the same way. This is particularly striking with a name such as *Elisabeth*, which is four syllables long. It happens that (in different dialects of German) almost all possible combinations (with preservation of linear order) of syllables taken from the original name are used as short forms for this name, as (54a) shows. In (54b), I list other bisyllabic names coined from the same base. All these forms and many other pet names conform to the pattern by now very familiar as the bisyllabic foot.[29] The stress pattern of the original form ([ɛ.ˈliː.za.bɛt]) plays no role in determining the stress pattern of the foot-based short forms. Overall, the recurrence of this foot structure in different types of word formation could hardly be a coincidence.

(54) Elisabeth: *a.* Eli, Lisa, Sabeth
               b. Else/a, Liese, Libeth, Elsbeth, Liesbeth

It is also not coincidental that some of the expressions mentioned, those in (53b) and (54), are strongly connected to the language of children. There is ample evidence that the prosodic pattern displayed here is the preferred one in early language acquisition. The bisyllabic foot seems to be a structure to which children assimilate many words which are more complex in the language of adults.

The preceding discussion has shown that the foot plays an important role in the interaction of phonology with morphology. Another case for this role of the foot is provided by the often overlooked reduplicative constructions in German. As I argue in Wiese (1990b), reduplications such as *Tingeltangel* or *Hokuspokus* are best seen as prefixations of a foot category, to which all or most of the material of the base is copied. As shown by the rather numerous reduplicative words such as *Larifari* or *Schickimicki*, the type of foot ending in /i/ as identified in the discussion above also plays a role in reduplications.

It is equally clear, however, that the foot can serve as a domain for the application of phonological rules. In § 3.3.1, I argued that the occurrence of the glottal stop must be described with reference to the foot. These two types of regularities are certainly sufficient to give the foot a place among the phonological categories. As will be shown in §§ 8.1 and 8.2, the foot is also, not unexpectedly, a crucial unit in the description of stress regularities. Since the assignment of feet to strings of syllables also depends on stress regularities, this topic will also be treated there.

---

[29] Trisyllabic *Elisa/e* has this foot in final position, while *Lisabeth* does not. In this latter name, the first syllable of the base form, which also constitutes a foot, is deleted.

Finally, it should be mentioned that the phenomenon of *isochrony* also relates to the foot. It has often been observed that certain chunks of speech are judged to occupy equal amounts of time.[30] At least for languages such as German (or English), it is the stretch of speech covered by the foot which constitutes the elementary unit involved. As this perception of equidistant speech events, of rhythm, can best be described by reference to the foot, we have here another argument for the foot category.

3.4. THE PHONOLOGICAL WORD

The category of the *word* is both central and very elusive in linguistic theory and description. Without discussing the problems around the word in detail (see di Sciullo and Williams (1987) for one approach), I simply present some evidence from German that the category of *phonological word* is needed alongside that of *morphological word*. The phonological word will be taken as a node in the prosodic hierarchy superordinated to the foot.[31] In diagrams of prosodic trees, the phonological word will be denoted by Greek ω.

The thrust of the argument for the phonological word is that several regularities crucially involve the same type of unit, which should therefore be available for all of these processes. Furthermore, the phonological word can be derived from the morphological structure.

The first type of evidence derives from syllabification. In the discussion of syllabification in § 3.2.4, it was left open how the domain of the rules of syllabification should be defined. But it is clear that it is rarely the whole utterance which is covered by syllabification. Consider now the various morphologically complex words given in (55), where syllable and morphological breaks are indicated.

(55) *a.* Tier.+art, Tief.+ebene, Stand.+uhr
    b. täg.+lich, schad.+haft, farb.+los
    c. Ur.+oma, Ver.+antwortung, Un.+art
    d. kin.d+isch, far.b+ig, Ach.t+ung
    e. Leh.r+er, le.b+en, Män.n+er+n

In compounds, the internal word boundary coincides with a break for syllabification. The words in (55*a*) are chosen such that the right-hand member always begins in a vowel. But in spite of the fact that onset-less syllables are generally avoided, there is no syllabification across the internal word boundary.[32] The

---

[30] The precise status of the isochrony hypothesis is quite controversial; see Auer and Uhmann (1988) for one review.

[31] The phonological word is also discussed with respect to various aspects of the phonology of German in Giegerich (1985), Booij (1985), and Yu (1992*b*), although none of these authors proposes a notion identical to the one adopted here.

[32] Syllabification across the boundary certainly does occur in casual, reasonably fast speech, but it is not accepted as being well-formed. The so-called semi-suffixes (*Halbsuffixe* or *Suffixoide*) such as + *artig* do not allow resyllabification across the preceding boundary, even if vowel-initial: *gut.+artig*. This simply means that they are not suffixes but words. That this is true is shown on purely morphological grounds by Olsen (1988).

words in (55*b*) are suffixed by derivational suffixes. Again, the morphological boundary coincides with the syllable boundary in Modern Standard German, although the consonant cluster, in cases such as /bl/ in *farb.+los*, would allow for a different syllabification.

In (55*c*), the same observation is made for various types of prefixes. Prefixes in general constitute their own, separate domain of syllabification. There are two well-defined sets of exceptions. The prefixes *her+*, *hin+*, and *vor+* in combination with prepositions (*her+an*, *hin+aus*, *vor+an*) are syllabified so that their final consonant is onset to the second syllable: [hɛʁan], [hɪnaʊs], [fɔʁan]. To deal with these exceptions, one might propose that the phonological word constructed over these prefixes is removed (deleted) again under the appropriate morphological conditions. The other exception is the suffix *in-*, which assimilates to following consonants as in *illegal, irregulär, impotent*. Under identity of the prefix-final and the base-initial consonants, there is probably only one, ambisyllabic, consonant. Again, this prefix is not syllabified independently. (The fact that obligatory assimilation and degemination takes place between prefix and base is another strong indication of the special status of *in-* with respect to ω-hood; see § 7.3.6.)

Crucially, however, the derivational suffixes in (55*d*) are syllabified in a way that morphological boundaries are not co-terminous with syllable boundaries. This is a puzzle since there is no systematic morphological difference between these suffixes and those of (55*b*). The generalization is that derivational suffixes starting with a vowel are syllabified with one or more consonants from the preceding stem as the consonantal onset. If the phonotactics allow for more than one consonant to be syllabified with the vowel-initial suffix, this is certainly done, as in *Fil.tr+at, mö.bl+ier+en*, and optionally in *Han.dl+ung*.

The initial consonant in *+lich* and the lack of such a consonant in *+ig* is responsible for the different syllabification in *lieb.+lich* versus *ne.bl+ig*. Those derivational and inflectional suffixes that consist of a consonant only (or of schwa plus a consonant, see § 7.4.2) are also integrated with the preceding material; see (55*e*) for examples and (3) and (4) in § 5.2.1 for extensive lists of suffixes of both types. The conclusion from these observations is that for any configuration of morphemes and words it is possible to indicate where the syllable boundaries are placed.

Given that the domain of syllabification is predictable, but that there is no morphological unit which provides this domain for all cases, we may go on to find some other unit which delineates the domain of syllabification directly. I will follow the hypothesis that the *phonological word* is the unit in question. As suggested by its name, it bears a strong affinity to the word in the morphological sense (at least in German), but is itself a unit within the phonological structure.

There are two tasks in order to substantiate the hypothesis. First, it has to be shown how a string with the necessary morphological and phonological information can be subdivided into phonological words. In other words, an algorithm for the construction of phonological words has to be specified. Second, if possible, the hypothesized unit has to be defended by providing independent evidence for its existence. That is, the case for the phonological word will be much stronger if it can be shown that it functions as more than only a domain of syllabification.

Since phonological words are meant to provide the domains for syllabification, they must be constructed before syllables are assigned. The algorithm for the construction of a phonological word, under this assumption, should only depend on the morphological structure and on the underlying featural information.[33]

It seems that it is indeed possible to devise such an algorithm. The most direct approach seems to be the following: if a suffix either starts with a vowel (+*ung*, +*ität*, and others enumerated in § 5.2.1) or does not bear a syllable of its own (as with +*t*, +*st*, +*n*), it is integrated into the preceding phonological word. Members of all other morphological categories (stems, prefixes, suffixes) are dominated by their own phonological word. Suffixes beginning with a consonant followed by a vowel ([+ consonantal] [– consonantal]) are the only suffixes which license a phonological word.

Thus, we can assume that the status of a phonological word is automatically assigned to all morphemes except for those suffixes (not stems!) which are vowel-initial or vowelless.[34] In (56) and (57), this is illustrated for the two relevant cases—vowel-initial and consonant-initial suffixes. To avoid confusion with other bracketings, I use curly brackets to denote boundaries of phonological words.

(56) *a.* Ver+sicher+ung+en   morphemes
      b. {Ver}{sicher}ung+en   assignment of phonological words
      c. {Ver}{sicherungen}   integration of remaining material

(57) a. lieb+lich+er   morphemes
      b. {lieb}{lich}er   assignment of phonological words
      c. {lieb}{licher}   integration of remaining material

This discussion answers the question how phonological words are built on the basis of phonological and morphological information. The crucial condition for suffixes (namely that the suffix must start in the segmental sequence [+ consonantal] [– consonantal]) looks somewhat arbitrary, but it should be noted that suffixes with more initial consonants do not exist in German, and that it thus allows phonological words over only those suffixes which provide a segment for a syllabic onset. Furthermore, the resulting syllable has a CV . . . -shape, that is,

---

[33] If phonological words were to be constructed on the basis of prior syllabification and foot construction, then the ordering paradox pointed out by Inkelas (1989: § 3.3.1) would result, since phonological words also provide the domains for syllabification.

[34] Incidentally, this distinction cuts across the distinction between derivation and inflection. Inflectional suffixes happen to be of a shape which prevents them from forming a phonological word of their own, but derivational suffixes can be of both kinds. In § 7.4.2, I will argue that affixes starting (sometimes) in schwa are in fact vowelless underlyingly. For present purposes, it is not important whether the plural suffix in (56) is represented as /ən/ or /n/. The suffixes +*chen*, +*sel*, +*ler* contain schwa as a vowel and behave as those with a full vowel; see below for some details.

one which appears to be unmarked universally. It is worth noting that Southern variants seem not to include the consonant-initial suffixes as triggers of phonological words, given that respective words are syllabified across the boundary, as in *far.b+los*. It must also be stressed that syllabification across the phonological words as just defined is possible in German (that is, syllabifications such as [liː.blɪç] *lieb+lich* are in fact found), but it is definitely not as common as in other languages such as English.

As additional evidence supporting the claim that consonant-initial suffixes are phonological words, one can point out that all such suffixes are either homophonous to existing independent words (compare +*schaft* to *Schaft*, +*los* to *Los*, +*bar* to *Bar*) or are only minimally different from such words; cf. +*heit* to *Scheit*, +*sam* to *Scham*, +*lich* to *dich*). That is, there is no difference in the segmental make-up between these suffixes and either existing or potential words of German.[35] This generalizaton does not hold for the other class of suffixes.

The second question asked above was whether phonological words serve other functions besides specifying the domains of syllabification. The answer is affirmative, but the argument to this conclusion can only be sketched at this point, by drawing on the next identifiable function of the phonological word. I will briefly show here that a number of phonological rules, especially those of assimilation and degemination, take the phonological word as their domain of application. To start with assimilation, we note that this rule can only apply between segments if the two segments belong to the same phonological word. Taking the rule of Nasal Assimilation as an example (for details see § 7.3.4), this is unproblematic in clearly word-internal cases such as those in (58*a*). More interesting is the application of this assimilation across morpheme boundaries as in (58*b*), or even word boundaries as in (58*c*). In both of these cases, the assimilation is optional.

(58) *a.* Ta[ŋ]go, Ta[ŋ]k; Da[m]pf, Am[bloss
     b. U[ŋ]glück, A[ŋ]kunft
     c. i[m] Bonn, a[m] Peter; ei[ŋ] Glück,   vo[ŋ] Göttingen
         'in Bonn   'to Peter' 'a (piece of) luck' 'from Göttingen'

Here I propose to express the optionality not by applying the rule of Nasal Assimilation in an optional mode, but by making the construction of phonological words optional, in the sense that prefixes and function words such as prepositions and articles can either be dominated by their 'own' phonological words or be integrated into the phonological words constructed over their right word neighbours. The reason for doing it in this way is that the optional (and not obligatory) construction of phonological words is needed for other purposes independent of Nasal Assimilation, as for the optional cliticization of articles and pronouns (see § 7.4.3) and for the characterization of the domain of syllabification. All of these (and other) cases have in common that a property generally attributed to the phonological word may stretch over a larger domain.

---

[35] The one problematic suffix is diminutive +*chen*, which, I argue, constitutes a phonological word of its own in spite of its schwa vowel.

The simplest and most unified way of accounting for this observation seems to be to allow for the construction of 'larger' phonological words.

One of the present claims is that consonant-initial suffixes are dominated by a phonological word of their own. An argument for this claim derives from the fact that geminate (contrastively long) consonants are not found in Modern Standard German. If a geminate happens to be created within a phonological word through inflection as in *reit+et* or *rät* (see (17)–(19)) degemination of consonants or schwa epenthesis occurs. However, no such degemination is obligatory in words such as *Schrift+tum* and *Papst+tum*, *fehl+los*, and *glaub+bar*. This follows if their prosodic structure is $_\omega$[*schrift*] $_\omega$[*tum*], and so on, but not *$_\omega$[*schrift tum*]. (It must be said, though, that other consonant-initial suffixes do not seem to allow their base to end in the consonant with which the suffix begins. This is true for *+lich* and *+schaft*. There is thus more interaction between adjacent phonological words than assumed in the restricted theory here.)

The analysis of the phonological word as presented here also has obvious consequences for the treatment of the famous pair of *Kuchen* vs. *Kuh+chen* (Bloomfield 1930 and many others), in which the medial fricative in the former word assimilates to preceding /uː/, while it does not in the latter word. This non-application of the Dorsal Fricative Assimilation (see § 7.3.3) in *Kuh+chen* is explained by the fact that this word breaks down into two phonological words ({Kuh}{chen}); see below for an argument to this conclusion.

The phonological word also plays a role in the regularities of word stress (the topic of Ch. 8). Words in German show a pattern of prominence defined over the syllables of a word. One of the basic rules that holds for these patterns is that one of the three last stressable syllables in a phonological word receives the most prominent stress. Since this is true for the phonological word as just defined and no other unit, it provides further compelling evidence for this unit.

Next I turn to a particular class of 'gapping' phenomena which seems to provide more compelling evidence for the Phonological Word, and in fact for other prosodic categories too. Consider the phrases of conjoined expressions in (59), where one part of the word is missing in some sense.[36] The missing part is invariably interpreted as being identical to the corresponding part (in bold print) in the sister word in the coordinative phrase. From (59*b*) it appears that derivational suffixes can be left out under certain circumstances, while (59*d*) shows that another group of derivational suffixes does not allow for the deletion. The examples in (59*c*) show that prefixes can also be left over in this reduction.[37]

---

[36] This argument for the phonological word and for the existence of a phonological deletion rule is taken from Booij (1985), whose analysis differs in details. Höhle (1982: § 5) discusses this deletion to show that composition and derivation are not fundamentally different. He proposes strong and weak boundaries (#*lich* vs. +*ig*) to account for the differences between the suffixes; see page 74. Wiese (1992) contains a more complete discussion of the regularities around the deletion studied here.

[37] Some of the examples are taken from the large corpus of examples provided by Müller (1990), whose main concern is normative acceptability. The two suffixes noted above to be exceptional in their behaviour in syllabification (*her-*, *in*) behave as expected in deletability: **herein und -aus* 'in and out', **illegal und -regulär* 'illegal and irregular'.

(59) *a.* Tief- und Hoch**ebenen** ('low plains and high plains'), konsonant- oder
        schwa**final** ('consonantal-final or schwa-final'), Herbst- und Frühlings**blumen**
        ('autumn flowers and spring flowers'), termin- und qualitäts**gerecht**
        ('according to schedule and according to quality conditions')
   b. mütter- und väter**lich** ('motherly and fatherly'), Heiser- oder Übel**keit**
        ('hoarseness or sickness'), Ritter- und Bauern**schaft** ('knighthood and
        peasantry'), Piraten- und Banausen**tum** ('piracy and philistinism')
   c. Ur- oder Ururoma ('great-grandmother or great-great-grandmother'), Psycho-
        und Sozio**linguistik** ('psycholinguistics and sociolinguistics'), Über- oder
        Unter**bau** ('superstructure or substructure'), pro- und anti**amerikanisch** ('pro-
        American and anti-American')
   d. *winz- oder ries**ig** ('tiny or huge'), *Komponist- und Lehrer**in** ('composer (f.)
        and teacher (f.)'), *Versicher- und Verwalt**ungen** ('insurances and
        administrations'), *maler- und romant**isch** ('picturesque and romantic'),
        *Meine Dam- und Herr**en** ('my ladies and gentlemen')
   e. *male- oder wähler**+isch** ('picturesque or choosy'), *Verwal- und
        Bearbeit**+ung** ('administration and handling')
   f. Väter- und Mütter**chen** ('father (dim.) and mother (dim.)'), Brüder- oder
        Schwester**chen** ('brother (dim.) or sister (dim.)')

I hasten to add that not all words of the right kind of structure can be treated
in this way. The illformedness in other cases (?*Freund- oder Feindschaft*, ?*glaub-
oder ehrenhaft*) is apparently due either to a difficulty in parsing these sequences
because of local ambiguities or to another prosodic factor: many speakers only
find those reduced words acceptable where the remaining part is at least bisyllabic.
Also, the impossible reductions in (59*d, e*) are markedly worse than those of (59*b*)
even if these and similar expressions are not totally acceptable to some speakers.

The main point is that no single morphological factor seems to be responsible
for the pattern of deletability found in (59). Furthermore, comparing (59*b*) with
(59*d*), it is striking that the pattern found for syllabification is seen again. Exactly those strings which constitute domains for syllabification can be deleted.
The examples in (59*e*), again very bad, demonstrate that the deletion does not
operate on the syllables as such, but only if corresponding to the proper type of
morpheme. Notice finally that the deletability of +*chen* demonstrated in (59*f*)
argues for the claim made above that +*chen* constitutes a phonological word of
its own, a fact to which I return in § 7.3.3, since it is of crucial significance for
the treatment of the alternation of the dorsal fricative.

The most natural conclusion is that a deletion of a phonological word is possible
under certain specifiable circumstances. But the deleted item must indeed be a phonological word of the type described above. Under the assumption of such a category, the forms in (59*a–c*) can be derived by the following optional rule of deletion.

(60) Word Deletion
      Delete a phonological word,
      if it occurs adjacent to a phrase boundary, and
      if a phonologically identical phonological word exists in an adjacent sister
        phrase in the coordinative structure.

The first *if*-clause in this rule is necessary since it can be shown that the phonological word cannot be deleted if material intervenes between its position and the phrase boundary. I return to the issue of the rule's phrasal context in the next section. In (61*a*), deletion is possible, while it is not permitted in (61*b*), where the deleted element is not adjacent to the boundary (assuming that the conjunction is part of the second phrase).

(61) *a.*   Peters   Apfel- und Annas   Orangen**saft**
          (lit.) 'Peter's apple- and Anna's orange-juice'
    b.   *der Apfel- von Peter und der Orangen**saft** von Anna
          (lit.) 'the apple- of   Peter and the orange-juice of   Anna'

Finally, it should be mentioned that deletion of *right-hand* constituents is also made possible by rule (60). That this is in accordance to the facts is demonstrated in (62). If some right-hand neighbour of the conjunction has an identical counterpart in the first part of the coordination, it can be deleted as well, both in coordinated compounds (62*a*) and in prefixed words (62*b*).[38]

(62) *a.*   **Oster**sonntag oder -montag,   **Pfeifen**reiniger und -tabak
          (lit.) 'Easter Sunday or   Monday',   'pipecleaner   and tobacco'
    b.   **Ur**oma   und -opa,   **Pseudo**argumente und -lösungen
          (lit.) 'Great-grandma and -grandpa',   'pseudoarguments and -solutions'

These cases then also throw a different light on those phrases in which an independent syntactic word is deleted, as in *der Antrag des—oder der **Dozenten*** 'the petition of the teacher or of the teachers', in which the two occurrences of *Dozenten* are only phonologically identical, since they instantiate different sets of morphosyntactic features (singular and plural, respectively). In the present treatment, these cases are not handled by a syntactic rule at all, but by a word-deletion rule as part of the phonological component. As a proper phonological rule, it has no access to morphosyntactic features and is therefore capable of deleting one of two phonologically, but not morphologically, identical words. The example above and similar ones are used by Eisenberg (1973) and others to argue that phonological identity constitutes information to which syntactic transformations (here: deletion) must have access. Arguably, Deletion has no place in the syntactic component anyhow; especially not if the deletion rule in question refers to phonological information, namely phonological identity.

According to the original proposal by Booij, deletion is restricted to co-ordinative structures. This is most certainly too strong a condition, as Booij (1985: 159, fn. 11) points out himself. His example *Sie ersetzen Ofen- durch Zentral**heizung*** (lit.) 'They replaced stove- by central heating' strikes me indeed as grammatical. In (63), I offer more examples of this kind, taken partly from Müller (1990). Probably the phonological word to be deleted must simply be adjacent to a word which is not from one of the major lexical categories—noun, verb, or adjective. I return to a discussion of the conditions on the deletion rule

---

[38] Again, only complete phonological words may be deleted, cf. *Verehrte **Zuhörer** und -(r)innen* 'Dear listeners (male and female)'.

in § 3.5, in which I show that even this condition is probably of a derivative
nature and need not be mentioned in the rule.

(63) *a.* Sachsen entwickelte sich vom Herzog- zum Kurfürsten**tum**.
        'Saxony developed from a dukedom to an electorate.'
    b. Formen wir den Aktiv- in einen Passiv**satz** um.
        'We form the passive sentence from the active sentence.'
    c. . . . übernahm zum Fraktions- auch noch den Landes**vorsitz**
        '. . . taking over both the faction chair and the state chair'
    d. Weil Leitungs- von Mineral**wasser** unterschieden werden muß, . . .
        'Since tap water must be distinguished from mineral water, . . .'

    The notion of 'phrase' used in this discussion will be made clear in the
following section. Booij (1985) assumes that adjacency not to a phrase boundary
but to a conjunction is the crucial condition. There are reasons to doubt this: first
since the restriction to coordinative phrases is questionable, as we have just
seen; and, second, since phrases such as *Frühlings-, Sommer- und Herbstblumen*
'spring, summer and autumn flowers' are well-formed. Booij's formulation of
the rule must rely on the assumption that a deleted conjunction accounts for the
deletion in the first phrase.

    The preceding discussion presents evidence for the phonological word, in
that there is a recurrent unit for deletion which can hardly be defined in either
morphological or syntactic terms. For final consideration, I offer the claim that
the phonological word may also act as a domain for phonotactic constraints. In
the discussion of the syllable it was mentioned that certain segments, in particular final coronal obstruents, may be extrasyllabic, as in *Markt*. These additional
consonants cannot appear after every syllable but only in a position which can
be interpreted as final to the phonological word. Notice that vowel-initial suffixes will always turn a final consonant into an initial one, as in *Vermark.t+ung*.

    This section offers various pieces of evidence for the role of the phonological
word in German, while the preceding section attempts to establish the foot as an
equally necessary category. These two prosodic units are not always easy to
keep apart. This is witnessed by the fact that Booij (1985: 155), on whose
analysis the present discussion of the deletion of the phonological word is based,
also relates the occurrence of the glottal stop to the phonological word. But this
leads to the exclusion of glottal stops in positions that are clearly word-internal,
as in *The[ʔ]ater* or *Ru[ʔ]ine* (cf. (45)). The foot seems to be the more adequate
domain for the description of glottal stop insertion. The phonological word is a
different unit, demonstrated by the fact, for example, that word-final feet, as in
the two words just given, could never be deleted.

    A final problem for the analysis of phonological words lies in the treatment
of complex words, especially compounds. Given that Modern Standard German
allows virtually unlimited concatenation of words (to be more precise, largely,
but not exclusively, nouns, or noun stems) into compounds, what is the phonological structure related to such complex compound words? According to many

theories of word syntax, compounds should be characterized with recursive phrase structures as illustrated for a not very complex compound in (64).

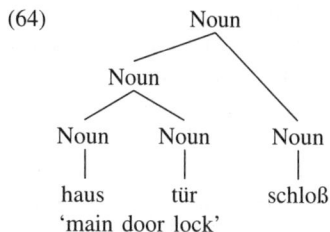

(64)

```
                        Noun
                     ╱        ╲
              Noun             ╲
            ╱      ╲            ╲
       Noun       Noun        Noun
        │           │           │
       haus        tür        schloß
            'main door lock'
```

It is true for the terminal words in structures such as (64) that they are domains for syllabification; follow certain stress regularities; and can be deleted. These properties follow, if the proposal made above is correct or almost correct, from the fact that these nouns correspond, in the prosodic structure, to phonological words. But what about the higher-level units? These do not show the properties characteristic of phonological words, and in fact follow stress regularities which are different from the ones found in phonological words (see § 8.4). They are also not phonological phrases or intonational phrases in the sense discussed in the following sections. Therefore, I simply assume that phonological words combine into higher-level units *of the same type*, as long as the word syntax specifies a branching structure. This would mean that for the compound in (64), each word node maps on to a prosodic node, which might be seen as a projection of the terminal phonological word (cf. (65)). The higher units are, in the language of phrase structure theory, categories which are one bar-level higher than the terminal ones but identical in other respects. The exact status of these nodes remains to be explored. Alternatively, phonological words within compounds may be analysed to combine into phonological phrases, the unit treated in the next section. This possibility is considered in § 8.4 in connection with certain stress patterns.

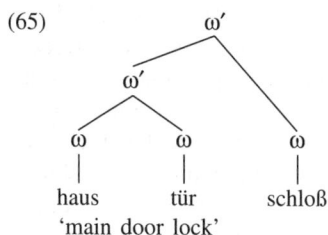

(65)

```
                        ω′
                     ╱      ╲
              ω′              ╲
            ╱    ╲             ╲
       ω         ω            ω
       │         │            │
      haus      tür         schloß
            'main door lock'
```

Words derived by those suffixes which correspond to their own phonological word provide a similar problem. If a suffix like +*lich* is dominated, as argued above, by its own phonological word, than a derived word such as *täg+lich* consists of two such ωs. Again, we must provide a prosodic category for the combination of these two items. An argument that this category is indeed the phonological word (which must therefore allow for a certain amount of recursiveness) derives from the fact that there is reason to assume that these derived words have a *foot* spanning both of the two elementary phonological words. It is a fact that *täg+lich* rhymes with *kläg+lich*, and if rhyming has anything to do with the foot, there must be a foot spanning the whole expression (as shown in (43b)). We are thus forced to the conclusion that higher-level ωs, such as those in (65), may directly dominate a foot. Otherwise, the lower-level ωs, as in a word such as ω[tägl]ω[lich], would be subordinated to the foot—contravening the prosodic hierarchy assumed here and in general.

The phonological word as understood in this section will play a role in later discussions of a number of phonological rules. It is also worth pointing out that the phonological word replaces some of the devices used in other theories of phonology. In various phonological theories, boundary symbols such as '+' and '#' are used to partition a phonological string into sub-strings. Roughly, a string demarcated by # on both sides in the *SPE* theory (Chomsky and Halle 1968: 367) corresponds to a phonological word. In prosodic phonology of the kind proposed here, the role of boundaries or junctures is taken over either by the morphological structure, as illustrated in (64) for a compound, or by the prosodic categories, in particular the phonological word.

3.5. THE PHONOLOGICAL PHRASE

Moving upwards from the phonological word, matters become even less well established.[39] Nevertheless, I will attempt to make a case for other prosodic categories. Phonological words can be supposed to combine into phonological phrases. Little, if anything, is known about this category in the phonology of German, but I will try to motivate this prosodic unit by taking up word deletion again and by studying phenomena of stress shift. Nothing will be said on the explicit derivation of phonological phrases. It may be sufficient for present purposes to assume that each syntactic phrase of the type noun phrase (NP), adjective phrase (AP), or verb phrase (VP) corresponds to a phonological phrase, if the phrase is expanded beyond the head word (noun, adjective, verb, respectively) by some complement or modifying expression. Prepositions, for example, do not normally lead to a separate phonological phrase, but are adjoined into the phrase they precede, that is, usually a noun phrase. It is problematic, however, to claim that prepositions in principle cannot head a phonological phrase. Intransitive prepositions, those without an object noun phrase, seem to form a phonological phrase of their own, as in *Das Wasser läuft über* 'The water is spilling'.

It seems also plausible to assume that there is a certain amount of variability in the construction of phonological phrases. A short, but complex, noun phrase such as *der Mann aus Bonn* 'the man from Bonn' is likely to form a single phonological phrase, while a long, but structurally equivalent, noun phrase such as

---

[39] For a general survey see in particular Nespor and Vogel (1986).

der Linguistikstudent aus Düsseldorf 'the linguistics student from Düsseldorf' is more likely to be broken up into two such phrases.[40]

Given these assumptions, a sentence such as that in (66) may be broken up into the phonological phrases as shown, without implying that the structuring shown is the only one possible. The phonological word is the lowest prosodic element given here; the phonological phrase will be denoted by Greek φ. Note that the first and the final adjectival phrase in this sentence are treated in different ways, as one and two phonological phrases respectively. The adjective phrase *besonders viele* heads its own φ, while the adjective phrase *alte* does not.

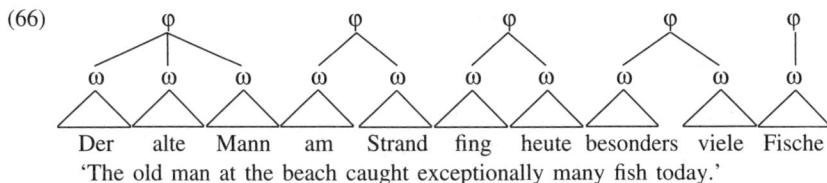

(66)

φ		φ	φ		φ		φ
ω	ω	ω	ω	ω	ω	ω	ω	ω	ω
Der	alte	Mann	am	Strand	fing	heute	besonders	viele	Fische

'The old man at the beach caught exceptionally many fish today.'

The variability of phonological phrasing can be treated in two principled ways. In one approach, the rules for the construction of φs are permitted to be sensitive to factors such as length of constituents. Short noun phrases or prepositional phrases, for example, are merged with neighbouring phrases to form a single phonological phrase. Note in this context that length (sometimes called *heaviness*) must be counted in terms of the number of subordinate prosodic units, such as syllables. This confirms the hypothesis that we have a genuinely phonological process here.

Alternatively, the phonological phrases are first constructed on the basis of purely syntactic information without any regard for other possible influencing forces such as heaviness. Subsequently, however, a *restructuring* of phonological phrases is permitted. All φs dominating little material are deleted optionally, and the subordinate material is adjoined to neighbouring phrases. While this second approach has the advantage of keeping the rules mapping the syntax into prosody free from referring to phonological factors,[41] this approach requires a restructuring of prosodic structure involving deletion of nodes.

One other question ignored here is how more than two phonological words are structured within the phonological phrase, and how several phonological phrases are connected. As for phonological words, phonological phrases probably require some amount of recursiveness. Leaving these questions open, I consider now the expressions in (67), partly taken from Giegerich (1985: ch. 4). They illustrate various types of *stress shift* in which a secondary stress is 'moved away' from an adjacent primary stress (denoted by "). In the left-hand column,

---

[40] As with the phonological word, we face the problem of saying what the unit is which groups together the phonological phrases. It seems inevitable to allow for some amount of recursiveness for phonological words and phrases.

[41] And also free from factors such as speech rate or formality of speech which may influence phonological phrasing.

stress is represented as it would appear for the word used in isolation or in other contexts.

(67) *a.* ˌPaderˈborn   ˈPaderˌborner "Uni
         'Paderborn'   'Paderborn university'
         ˌlineˈar   ˈlineˌare "Steigerung
         'linear'   'linear growth'
    b. ˈabˌnehmen   den "Hut ˌabˈnehmen
         'take off'   'take off the hat'
         ˈanˌziehen   den "Rock ˌanˈziehen
         'put on'   'put on the jacket'
    c. ˈNeuˌheit   "Buchˌneuˈheit
         'novelty'   (lit.) 'book novelty'
         ˈAufˌsicht   "Schulˌaufˈsicht
         'supervision'   'school supervision'
         ˈAufˌbau   Ver"suchsˌaufˈbau
         'layout'   'experimental layout'

At this point, discussion of the details of the analysis and the various factors that allow or prevent such a stress shift to take place in the different subcases will be postponed until § 8.5.2.[42] But it can be claimed that the elements (stresses) involved in this process have to be in the same phonological phrase. If the main stress causing the shift and the two reversed stresses are in different phonological phrases, stress shift does not take place. I illustrate this with some examples in (68), where the stress shift observed in (67) is not possible. These expressions are such that two phonological phrases, and not one, are constructed. Notice that quite different syntactic configurations either allow or disallow the stress shifts. In other words, a unified treatment of these phenomena in syntactic terms seems unlikely.

(68) *a.* ˌPaderˈborn und seine Uni
         'Paderborn and its university'
         ˌlineˈar war die Steigerung nicht.
         'The growth was not linear.'
    b. Den "Hut nicht ˈabˌnehmen!
         'Don't take off the hat!'
         Den "Rock kann er ˈanˌziehen.
         'The jacket, he can put on.'
    c. des "Buches ˈNeuˌheiten
         (lit.) 'the book's novelties'
         Er führt in der "Schule ˈAufˌsicht.
         'He is on supervision duty in the school.'

As in the case of other phenomena studied earlier, the phonological phrase is motivated by the fact that it provides the domain for the application of at least

---

[42] I left it open in the preceding section whether compounds such as *Buchneuheit* should be analysed as a single phonological word. Of course, members within a single phonological word also share a phonological phrase.

one phonological regularity, that of stress shift. To conclude this section, I offer another, perhaps more speculative, example of this kind.

In the preceding section, it was proposed that there is a special deletion rule operative in the phonology of Modern Standard German, which deletes a complete phonological word under conditions of identity. It was also mentioned there that the item to be deleted must be adjacent to a phrase boundary. I would now like to propose that the phrase referred to in rule (60) is the phonological phrase. In this analysis, the structures in which we find this deletion are such that two consecutive phonological phrases contain phonologically identical phonological words. The purely phonological categories used in this analysis provide the justification for classifying Word Deletion as a strictly phonological, as opposed to a syntactic, rule.[43] The two possible configurations for this rule to apply are given in (69). As demonstrated in (59) and (62), both left-hand and right-hand deletion is possible. Before a more principled solution becomes available, a deletion rule therefore needs two parts, here given in (69a, b).

(69) $a.$ . . . ω_i $]_\varphi$ $_\varphi[$ . . . ω_i . . .
$$\downarrow$$
$$\emptyset$$

$b.$ . . . ω_i . . . $]_\varphi$ $_\varphi[$ ω_i . . .
$$\downarrow$$
$$\emptyset$$

Analysed in this way, the rule fits quite naturally into the known types of phonological rules, since rules often refer to the *ends* of prosodic constituents. Rule (60), applying in the contexts stated in (69), is then one of the 'edge-related' rules so common in prosodic phonology. The observation that it often applies in coordinative structures is probably due to the coincidental fact that such structures, because of the necessary parallelism between the parts, are most likely to contain identical elements. I resume the discussion of ω-deletion once more in its relation to the intonational phrase.

3.6. THE INTONATIONAL PHRASE

Intonation is the phonological aspect of pitch movement (unless it is lexically distinctive, when it is called 'tone'). Intonation is clearly not to be captured as a local, segmental phenomenon. That is why it was hardly treated at all in those phonological theories which took the phoneme or the segmental feature as their

---

[43] I regard it as an open question whether this deletion must be distinguished from the, presumably syntactic, phenomenon called Verb Gapping as in *Hans liebt Maria und Peter____Inge* 'Hans loves Maria, and Peter Inge', regardless of whether Gapping is treated as an omission transformation or not. In other words, not all kinds of omitted constituents are necessarily subsumed under the rule of Word Deletion. But some confusion in the literature arises since *all* deletion is taken to be of a syntactic nature, either as deletion proper or as involving some other type of mechanism. Booij (1988), too, proposes to describe the context of Word Deletion by means of the phonological phrase, in modification of his earlier treatment in terms of syntactic boundaries.

primary (or only) categorial unit. On the other hand, approaches interested in global characteristics of speech and in the meaningful aspects of sound structures have usually turned to intonation as that aspect of the sound system which is relevant to their concerns. Studies under the name of 'discourse phonology', for example, predominantly turn to matters of intonation (see Selting 1995; Coulthard and Brazil 1982).

The need for a unit within which intonation is to be described is therefore not in doubt, and detailed studies involving this unit have been pursued for a while. The *intonational phrase* is the next unit of the prosodic hierarchy, and its existence is justified easily, if only because there must be some domain for intonational contours, distinct from syntactic units. This section reviews some arguments for this unit. As mentioned in Chapter 1, a thorough discussion of German intonation is not attempted in this book. The intonational phrase is also known as the *intonational group* (Fox 1984) or the *tone group* (Pheby 1981) in other treatments.

It is clear that one element of an intonational contour (i.e. the 'melody' of speech, the up- and downward changes of pitch over time) is the final part of this contour. At this point, pitch is either relatively high or relatively low. One part of the description of the closure of an intonational contour must be to determine where in a sentence this final tone of a contour can occur. It is easy to see that an intonational contour can stop before the end of a complete sentence; that is, a sentence may carry two or more intonational contours.

The question then arises whether the points for a potential intonational boundary can be characterized syntactically. If this is the case, then there is no room for a category of an intonational phrase as such. In the expression of the sentence given in (70), it will often be the case that there is a distinct intonational break before the relative clause modifying the noun phrase begins. In contrast, for the break to occur in front of the noun phrase is much less likely and requires special conditions. But, syntactically, the relative clause is just a part of the noun phrase. A structurally more important syntactic boundary occurs before the noun phrase.

(70)   intonational break
                            ↓

Ich vermisse [den Mann, der sonst die Zeitung gebracht hat]$_{NP}$
'I miss the man who used to bring the paper.'

This is a mismatch between intonationally relevant structure and syntactic structure, for which further examples can be given, even from simple sentences. In (71), the most natural point for an intonational boundary would be the transition between the verb and the object. But again, according to most syntactic theories, the structurally superordinate syntactic division is in a different place, namely after the subject noun phrase.

(71)   intonational break
                            ↓

Der Minister bestreitet seine Verantwortung für den Skandal.
'The minister denies his responsibility for the scandal.'

We may conclude from these examples that sentences are divided up into one or more intonational phrases. For an early approach to the formation of intonational phrases on the basis of syntactic structures see Bierwisch (1966). There is a considerable amount of freedom in this intonational division of sentences, in that the syntactic structure alone allows for many different intonational phrasings. This optionality in assigning prosodic structure is mentioned in this chapter at various points. Intonational phrases probably provide the clearest cases for this principle. On the other hand, parenthetical remarks, appositions, and extraposed phrases are always set apart as intonational phrases of their own. In (72), I give an example for each of these constructions and their divisions into intonational phrases.

(72) *a.* [Jakob hat], [wie du weißt], [schon lange aufs Rauchen verzichtet]
    (lit.) 'Jacob has, as you know, stopped smoking a long time ago.'
  b. [Mein Sohn], [dieser Schlauberger], [hat mich den ganzen Abend beschäftigt].
    'My son, the clever dick, has kept me busy the whole evening.'
  c. [Ich kenne ihn schon lange], [diesen Schuft].
    'I have known him for a long time, the bastard.'

In the theory of Nespor and Vogel (1986: § 7.2), there is a single rule for determining intonational phrases on the basis of syntactic structure, while subsequent restructuring may optionally break down an intonational phrase into a series of intonational phrases, according to factors of tempo, length of constituents, style, and perhaps others. Alternatively, one could construct the intonational phrases wanted directly on the basis of syntactic-semantic information such as the sense units proposed by Selkirk (1984*b*).

The transitions between phrases determined in this way can be characterized by particular suprasegmental phenomena, in particular a phrase-final intonational contour, a phrase-final lengthening, and, in some cases, a pause between two phrases. The following is an informal demonstration of these effects. The sentence *Er überredet sie zu kommen* 'He talks her into coming' was spoken in two different ways, so that one (73*a*) or two (73*b*) intonational phrases were realized for an otherwise identical sentence.

Intonational research relies either on auditive judgements of tonal contours or on acoustic measurement of intonation. Here I follow the second approach; see Pheby (1981) and Fox (1984) for exemplification of the first. The following diagram is a print-out of the fundamental frequency (F_0) contour as it is measured by a suitable instrument, in this case the DSP Sona-Graph and the Computerized Speech Lab (Kay Elemetrics Corp.). The printouts in (73) each show a tracing of the intensity (energy measured in decibels) in the upper part and an F_0 tracing in the lower part. The upper curve is shown only to facilitate the matching of the utterance to the time line. F_0 corresponds articulatorily to the rate of vibration of the vocal cords and is a relatively good measure of pitch as it is produced by the speaker and perceived by the hearer. The sentences produced and analysed here are written orthographically into the B part of the diagrams to show rough correspondences between the two tracings and the segmental aspects.

(73) *a.* [Er überredet sie zu kommen]

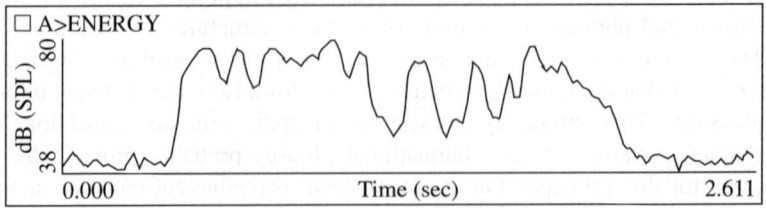

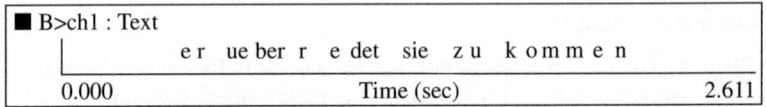

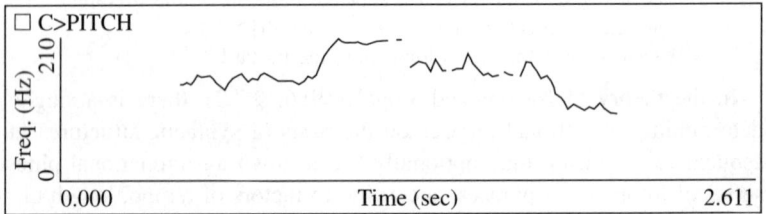

□ A>ENERGY

dB (SPL) 80 38

0.000 Time (sec) 2.611

■ B>ch1 : Text

er ue ber r e det sie zu k omm e n

0.000 Time (sec) 2.611

□ C>PITCH

Freq. (Hz) 210 0

0.000 Time (sec) 2.611

b. [Er überredet sie] [zu kommen]

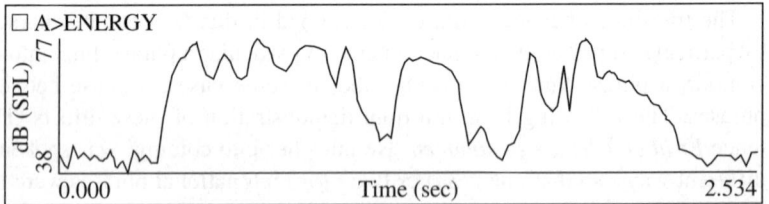

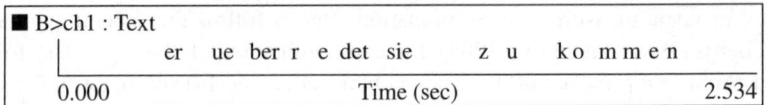

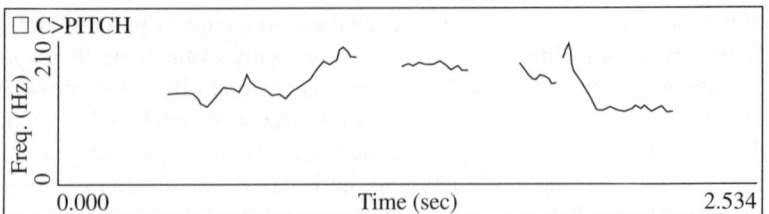

□ A>ENERGY

dB (SPL) 77 38

0.000 Time (sec) 2.534

■ B>ch1 : Text

er ue ber r e det sie z u ko mm e n

0.000 Time (sec) 2.534

□ C>PITCH

Freq. (Hz) 210 0

0.000 Time (sec) 2.534

Two points are visible in the pitch tracings in (73): the boundary between intonational phrases in (73*b*) is marked by a lengthening of the final syllable (*sie*), by keeping the tone on a constantly high level, and by a pause, a period of silence much longer than the corresponding section in (73*a*). Second, there is one syllable in each of the phrases which is salient in terms of pitch, length, and (perhaps) intensity pattern. In (73*a*), *re-* is uttered with the highest level of intensity and shows the peak in the F_0 contour. In (73*b*), the same observation can be made with respect to *re-* for the first intonational phrase. The accented syllable of the second intonational phrase is *kom-*, which is also prominent in its phrase. This is the so-called nuclear syllable, the syllable with the largest amount of stress, of which each intonational phrase has exactly one. In other words, (73*a*) displays one intonational peak, and (73*b*) two.

The F_0 contour of (73*a*) is also characterized by a gradual fall of the frequency from the accented high tone syllable (*re-*) to the end. This phenomenon is known as 'declination'. In (73*b*), the first intonational phrase ends, as noted above, on a high tone. In this example, the falling intonation can be observed in the second intonational phrase, as there is a steep fall within the final word *kommen*. Thus, the declination of intonation is clearly a property of intonational phrases.

To return to the description of the final part of the intonational contour, we can note disagreements on the number and nature of the distinctive pitch patterns necessary for the description of intonation in German. Pheby (1981: § 6.1.1.3) assumes (in line with traditional descriptions, for example by von Essen 1964) the following three patterns:

(74) *a.* pattern 1 (falling)
       b. pattern 2 (rising)
       c. pattern 3 (level)

In contrast, Fox (1984) identifies four intonational patterns, with two types of boundary tones grouped into two classes each:

(75) low-ending falling
                    rising-falling
       high-ending rising
                    level

The most important constraints for the formation of intonational phrases probably derive from the notion of focus (see Selkirk (1984*b*) in general and Uhmann (1991) and Féry (1993) for recent discussion with respect to German). Besides the characteristic pitch pattern and the existence of a nuclear syllable, the third main aspect of the intonational contour is its relation to the notion of *focus*. Focus may be thought of as an indicator of communicative salience. It is either a semantic-pragmatic feature or, according to other theories, a syntactic feature assigned to phrases, which has then both semantic and phonological consequences. For present purposes, it is only relevant since one hypothesis about the formation of intonational phrases is that each intonational phrase carries at least one feature of focus. In other words, the distribution of focus features over the constituents of a sentence (or over the semantic units) is largely responsible for the intonational phrasing.[44]

To summarize, intonational phrases are sense units not necessarily corresponding to syntactic structures which bear one or more pitch accents. One of these accents is called the nuclear accent; it is found on a focused element or on the final head. Intonational phrases are marked by final lengthening and boundary tones. Those pauses called *grammatical pauses* (since they are not interpreted as hesitations) also occur between intonational phrases.

After having reached a preliminary notion of intonational phrase, its function may be studied with respect to the phenomenon of a missing morpheme or word which I argued constitutes a case of Word Deletion. While the preceding section demonstrated that the two identical elements must be in adjacent phonological phrases, I would now like to claim that these two phrases must be contained in a single intonational phrase.

Consider the sentences in (76). Word deletion is impossible here, and this seems to be due to the fact that the two phonological phrases containing target and trigger of the deletion are not part of one single intonational phrase. This follows from the fact that subordinate clauses in general form intonational phrases of their own. Note that the two instances of *Blumen* in (76) are close enough to each other to be in adjacent phonological phrases.

(76) a. *[Er liebt alle Herbst-]$_{\text{IP}}$, [die sich von Frühlings**blumen** unterscheiden]$_{\text{IP}}$
          'He loves all autumn flowers which are different from spring flowers.'
      b. *[Er liebt alle Herbst-]$_{\text{IP}}$, [weil Frühlings**blumen** so schnell verblühen]$_{\text{IP}}$
          'He loves all autumn flowers, because spring flowers wither so quickly.'

The regularities involved in Word Deletion have proven to provide interesting evidence for a number of prosodic categories. In particular, the phonological word, the phonological phrase, and the intonational phrase seem all to be crucially involved in an adequate statement of the facts and regularities.

3.7. CONCLUDING REMARKS

This chapter's main aim is to introduce and motivate the prosodic categories of German, which serve a number of functions in the phonology of this language. These categories are the universally available building blocks of a prosodic structure which is hierarchical, but non-recursive. (A limited amount of recursion, however, is admitted by the stacking of identical categories proposed in (65) for the phonological word. In § 8.1, a similar way of extending the hierarchy will be allowed for the foot.) With the categories discussed here in some detail, the hierarchy takes the form given in (77) (disregarding branching at all levels and intrasyllabic structure).

---

[44] For more discussion on intonational phrases in German, see Wunderlich (1988); Uhmann (1991); and Féry (1993: ch. 2).

(77) intonational phrase
                |
      phonological phrase
                |
      phonological word
                |
             foot
                |
           syllable

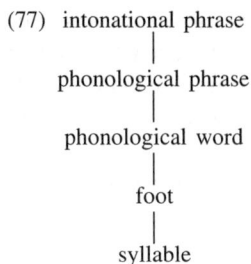

This proposal for prosodic structure must certainly be seen as minimal; there are other prosodic categories, which have been discussed in the relevant (general) literature. One such potential additional prosodic unit is the clitic group. Obviously, it could be relevant in the construction of reduced forms (Nespor and Vogel 1986: ch. 5). In § 7.4.3, I argue (following Prinz 1991) that the clitic group is not a relevant unit for German, not even in the description of cliticization. Strictly speaking, the subsyllabic categories of onset, nucleus, and coda have also been treated as parts of the prosodic hierarchy in § 3.2.

The main reason for not having included more categories in the preceding discussion is that no evidence has been found for these categories with respect to German.[45] But since it is quite probable that the only reason for this gap might be that no one has looked for the relevant type of facts, I conclude this chapter with an extended hierarchy of prosodic categories outlined in (78). Further research into German prosody is likely to unearth evidence for some of the additional categories in this tree, especially for the utterance as the highest unit in the prosodic constituent hierarchy.

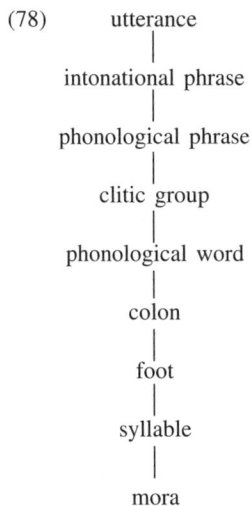

(78)   utterance
                |
      intonational phrase
                |
      phonological phrase
                |
         clitic group
                |
      phonological word
                |
             colon
                |
             foot
                |
           syllable
                |
             mora

---

[45] This is true also for the colon, a unit between the foot and the word argued to be necessary for the description of Hungarian stress by Hammond (1987).

A hierarchy of prosodic categories such as (78) is crucial for the study of phonological rules in the remainder of this book, since one of the tenets assumed here is the existence of a rather strict boundary between syntax (including word-internal syntax) and phonology. Following one line of research in phonology (see, e.g., Selkirk 1984*b*; Inkelas 1989; Hayes 1990; and the discussion in Zwicky and Kaisse 1987), I will maintain that phonological rules (perhaps with the exception of very specific lexical phonological rules, as will be introduced in Chapter 5) can refer only to the domains provided by prosodic structure, and not to those provided by syntactic structure (as assumed, e.g., by Kaisse 1985). Syntactic influence can only be indirect, through its relevance for the construction of prosodic structure.

It is also important to note that the prosodic units discussed in this chapter may derive in two different principled ways. One type, represented by the phonological word, the phonological phrase, and the intonational phrase, is derived by a syntax-phonology-mapping. That is, specific structural configurations for words or sentences allow for, or force, the construction of a particular prosodic unit. Feet and syllables, in contrast, represent the second type. They arise on the basis of purely phonological information, namely as the result of parsing a phonological domain such as the phonological word in particular ways as discussed for syllables in § 3.2.4 and for stress feet in § 8.1. This partitioning of prosodic units into two types also has the consequence that prosodic structure cannot be erected from the bottom up. Phonological words, for example, are defined (on the basis of morphology) before syllables and feet are constructed within a phonological word.

4

PROSODIC MORPHOLOGY

In this chapter, I attempt to demonstrate the presence and importance of prosodic structure for German morphology. In particular, I discuss a series of examples in which the wellformedness of complex words crucially depends on
prosodic conditions being fulfilled. Seen in this way, this chapter is a direct
continuation of the preceding one, because some of the prosodic categories
introduced there (namely the syllable, the foot, the phonological word) provide the elements on which some types of word formation can be shown to
depend.

The line of recent research exploring this relationship between phonology and
morphology is known as *Prosodic Morphology*.[1] It is largely associated with
phenomena such as reduplication, and the non-concatenative morphology in
languages like Arabic, where various morphemes (consonant patterns and vowel
patterns, for example) are interlocked with each other. The existence of a relevant group of prosodic regularities in the morphology of German is generally
neglected but, as I argue in the present chapter, very real. In the first section, it
is claimed that the constraints on some derivational affixations of German, in
particular noun derivation by the suffix *+ei*, prefixation with *ge+* and *be+*, and
the allomorphy between the suffix forms *+heit* and *+keit*, can only be described
in prosodic terms. I will then (§ 4.2) discuss a prosodic condition on compounding, and finally (§ 4.3), in some detail, the status and function of schwa in
various types of German inflectional morphology.

4.1. PHONOLOGY-DEPENDENT AFFIXATIONS

4.1.1. *+ei*

Consider the following series (1) of possible and impossible words all suffixed
by *+ei*.[2] The straightforward generalization to be drawn from (1) is that this suffix can only appear if two syllables precede the suffix of which the second is

---

[1] The ideas of Prosodic Morphology are put forward mainly in papers by McCarthy (1984), and
by McCarthy and Prince (1986; 1990). The more recent theory of *Optimality Theory* (McCarthy and
Prince 1993; Prince and Smolensky 1993) is not taken into account in the following discussion.

[2] Discussing *+ei*, Giegerich (1987) and Hall (1989*a*) argue for the need for a cycle in German
phonology. Their analysis differs from that given here, mainly because they consider *+ei* and *+erei*
to be allomorphs of the same morpheme. On this point see § 4.1.4. The cycle will be discussed in
§ 5.3.1.

a *schwa syllable* in the sense defined in § 3.2.4. (The reader should bear in mind that such a syllable may in fact contain a syllabic consonant instead of schwa.) The schwa may be stem-internal as in (1*a*), or it may be part of another suffix as in (1*b*). As the examples in (1*c*) reveal, the crucial condition seems to be that the base contains two final syllables with the stress pattern of 'strong–weak'. Note that none of the cases in (1*c*) is excluded on phonotactic grounds. Examples such as *Diskutier+er+ei* show that the total number of syllables in the base is also irrelevant.

(1) *a.* Segel+ei   *b.* Segl+er+ei   *c.* *Segl+ei
          Plauder+ei   Dieb+er+ei   *Dieb+ei
          Esel+ei   Schwein+er+ei   *Schwein+ei
         *Atem+ei   Atm+er+ei   *Atm+ei
         *Segen+ei   Segn+er+ei   *Segn+ei

Two presuppositions are being made in this presentation: first, there are two homophonous suffixes, one with a locative meaning (as in *Pfarr+ei, Detekt+ei, Bäcker+ei*) and the other of the same shape denoting an activity which is in some sense inferior or undesirable. Only the latter suffix, with the pejorative or diminutive meaning, is treated here; it happens, as the examples show, that the locative suffix is not subject to the phonological constraints. Words such as *Barbar+ei* or *Tyrann+ei* do not fall into this category of pejorative expressions either. The prosodic condition does not play a role, and the meaning is different.

Second, contrary to other treatments, no suffix variant or allomorph *+erei* is assumed. This raises no problems for words such as *Segl+er+ei*, where an existing word *Segl+er* can function as a base for the suffix. It is apparently more questionable for other formations, such as *Schwein+er+ei*, since *Schweiner* does not exist as an independent word. Nevertheless, in § 4.1.4, I argue that there are no reasons for the supposed morph of *+erei* nor for other strings of a similar kind. Instead, a sequence of two suffixes, *+er* and *+ei*, should be assumed in the analysis.

The ungrammatical words in (1*c*) and also *Atemei* and *Segenei* from (1*a*) cannot be excluded on phonotactic grounds alone, since in each case well-formed syllables would be built. Nevertheless, the generalization that a schwa syllable has to precede the suffix holds without exception. What kind of solution for this problem is available? For *+ei*, let us assume that it is not subcategorized (unlike most other suffixes) for a particular morphological category of the base, but for a prosodic one. This seems natural since the prosodic information constitutes the crucial constraint on this affix. In other words, the base for *+ei* is a foot of the type introduced in § 3.3—with the additional restriction that the final syllable must be a schwa syllable.

Suppose now that *+ei* is a suffix with the lexical entry as in (2). Like all suffixes, it has a specification as to its phonological shape (2*a*) and a subcategorization frame (2*b*), which states to what kind of bases it can be attached. The categorial features of the suffix (2*c*) are supposed to determine the result of the affixation, namely a feminine noun with [+ N, − V] as the standardly used features for the category of nouns.[3]

(2) Lexical entry for +*ei*

   a. phonology: F

                            /aɪ/

   b. subcategorization: [[F] ____]

                            σ σ

   c. categorial features: $\begin{bmatrix} + \text{N} \\ - \text{V} \\ + \text{fem} \end{bmatrix}$

Following Selkirk (1982) and other authors' work on word structure, I assume that the categorial features of a derivational affix, that is, those of (2*c*), percolate up to the root node of the tree of which it is the head. The foot node in (2*a*) ensures that +*ei* ends up with primary word stress (see § 8.1). Naturally, a lexical entry also has a component for semantic information, but since semantics is irrelevant for the problem under discussion, I will disregard all questions of meaning representation.

Affixes are lexical entries with subcategorization frames in the morphological model by Lieber (1981) and others. More unusual in (2*b*) is the claim that the complement to +*ei* is a particular *prosodic* constituent. In this the present proposal follows the proposals made by Booij and Lieber (1993) and Inkelas (1989) who define affixes as units subcategorized for prosodic and morphological information. The subcategorization frame here contains one crucial condition, namely that the base to which +*ei* can be attached has to end in a bisyllabic foot. This prosodic structure should be familiar from the discussion of the foot in § 3.3. Postulating it as a part of any base to which +*ei* can be suffixed provides exactly the information needed to explain all of the distinctions between the well-formed and ill-formed expressions found in (1), with the exception of the ungrammatical *Atemei* and *Segenei*, to which I return shortly. The stress pattern on the base for +*ei* is always of the 'strong-weak' type, but since the foot as defined in § 3.3 does not allow for any other stress pattern, this fact does not have to be stated explicitly in (2*b*). (What *is* missing in (2*b*) is the fact that the final syllable must be a schwa syllable and not just any weakly stressed syllable; I return to this recurring problem below.)

Consider now the way in which a word such as *Segel*+*ei* might be derived. The foot required in (2*b*) for the base is not part of the underlying base for the verbal root of *segel*. Furthermore, the final vowel in this root is schwa. As briefly mentioned in § 3.2.4 and more explicitly discussed in § 7.4.2, there are

---

[3] Later, [+ N, + V] will be used for categorizing adjectives, [+ V, − N] for verbs, and [− V, − N] for prepositions.

good reasons to assume that this vowel emerges via a rule of epenthesis, which goes hand in hand with syllabification.[4] The underlying entry for the root morpheme is given in (3a). Details of the segmental representation are irrelevant here.

In order for the affixation of +*ei* to take place, the entry will have to be assigned its prosodic structure. This step is sketched in (3b). The structure built up here matches the requirement specified in the entry for +*ei*, so that the affix can be added, see (3c). In a further step of the derivation, rules of prosody apply again, so that a structure such as (3d) is arrived at. Just as with other vowel-initial suffixes, a syllable built over +*ei* takes the preceding consonant(s) as its onset. This follows from the integration of this suffix into the phonological word constructed over its base (cf. (56) and (57) in § 3.4).

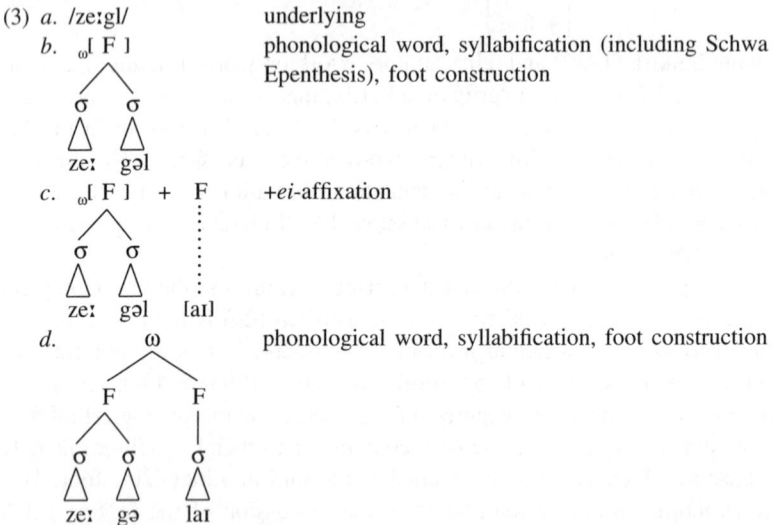

(3) *a.* /zeːgl/   underlying

   b. $_{\omega}$[F]   phonological word, syllabification (including Schwa
                          Epenthesis), foot construction

         σ   σ

       zeː gəl

   c. $_{\omega}$[F] + F   +*ei*-affixation

         σ   σ

       zeː gəl [aɪ]

   d.   ω   phonological word, syllabification, foot construction

        F   F

      σ   σ   σ

     zeː gə laɪ

For present purposes, the crucial point in this derivation is that the rules of phonology and morphology are not to be applied in two complete disjoint blocks of the grammar, as Giegerich (1987) and Hall (1989a) have already pointed out for the example under consideration. The affixation of +*ei* provides rather strong evidence that, first, the morphology needs access to categories such as the foot and the syllable, and, second, that certain phonological rules must apply prior to suffixation, that is, prior to the application of morphological rules. Construction of prosodic structure in (3b) must by necessity precede affixation in (3c). This is precisely the interaction between phonology and morphology which is postulated in the theory of Lexical Phonology, to be discussed in Chapter 5. The application of prosodic rules in (3b) and then again on a larger domain in (3d) is an instance of the use of a cycle in phonology.

---

[4] Some initial justification for the assumption that schwa is not part of the entry comes from the fact that in *Segl+er* and *segl+e* there is a no stem-internal schwa.

The ungrammatical *Atemei and *Segenei find a natural explanation in the framework proposed as well. As is proposed in § 7.4.2 on the distribution of schwa, the epenthesis of schwa in verb stems ending in a nasal consonant (here: /m/, /n/) follows a different pattern from that in stems ending in a liquid /l/ or /R/. To confirm this point, one may simply note the difference between the infinitival forms atm+en and segn+en on the one hand and ruder+n and segel+n on the other hand. In section 7.4.2 this is interpreted to mean that Schwa Epenthesis can take place before affixation of +ei with stems ending in a liquid, but it cannot take place before this affixation in the case of stems ending in a nasal (/m/ or /n/). Thus, the independently motivated distinction between two kinds of Schwa Epenthesis is sufficient to explain the ungrammaticality of those verbal bases ending in a nasal consonant.

To counter possible alternative proposals to that given here, one may add that this particular type of word formation with +ei is very productive. All roots with the right (semantic and prosodic) properties apparently can undergo this suffixation.[5] Lexically listing all words of this type thus does not appear to be a viable alternative. Moreover, it is also not plausible to assume that the prosodic structure required for the base is part of the lexical entries for stems (and not derived by rule), since, first, it is totally predictable, and second, some rule to change this structure would then be required for words such as Segl+er, where the root appears in a monosyllabic shape.

Given that the theory of prosodic morphology predicts the existence of the specific type of phonology–morphology interaction just studied and that alternative descriptions are not easily available, one may ask whether affixation of +ei is the only phenomenon of this kind. If this were the case, one would more willingly allow for an unorthodox mechanism for its description. It seems, however, that there are other word formations in German with a comparable phonological conditioning.

4.1.2. Unstressed prefixes be+ and ge+

Consider next a structurally similar example, the conditions for the unstressed prefixes be+ and ge+. I deal first with one subcase for the occurrence of one of these two prefixes, the past participle of verbs. Past participles of all verbs in German are formed from verb stems by suffixing either +(e)t or +en. The choice between these suffixes is not completely predictable. The major generalization is that members of the class of weak verbs never take the +en affix. Since strong and mixed verbs as irregular verbs are those which take either +(e)t or +en (cf. ge+rann+t vs. ge+fund+en), some lexical marking is necessary, probably in such a way that the strong verbs are marked for taking +en, with all other verbs

---

[5] It remains to be explained why adjectives apparently cannot occur as bases of ei-affixation. Possibly, the bases to ei-affixation must be verbal roots in the productive formations, contrary to the assumption made above.

(mixed or weak) taking +(*e*)*t* as the default marker for past participles.[6] The distribution of schwa in the suffixes +(*e*)*t* is governed by the nature of the stem-final segment: final /t, d/ cause schwa to be inserted between stem and suffix, as in *ge+arbeit+et, ge+red+et*.

In addition to the suffix, some of these participle forms are also marked by a prefix *ge+*. Closer study of the conditions on the appearance of this prefix reveals a very peculiar distribution. All verbs in (4), those obligatorily taking the prefix (see the ungrammaticality of the corresponding *ge*-less forms in (7)) are either monosyllabic or, if not monosyllabic, show a word-stress pattern such that the first syllable following *ge+* bears the primary stress.

In contrast, past participles with primary stress on some other syllable in the word cannot be prefixed by *ge+*, cf. (5) and (6). It seems therefore that word stress is the crucial factor determining the distribution of the prefix (cf. *schma'rotzen* vs. *'kiebitzen*). Here and in other cases, the foreign origin of some words cannot be responsible for the distinction, although it is true that more of the words in (5) are loan-words than in (4). Finally, at least *liebkosen* occurs with two different stress patterns (partly for different speakers). If it bears initial stress, the past participle must be *ge'liebkost*; with final stress, it must be *lieb'kost*.[7]

(4)	geredet	(5)	diskutiert
	gesucht		versucht
	gefallen		entfallen
	gepredigt		krakeelt
	gearbeitet		palavert
	gekiebitzt		schmarotzt
	geheiratet		applaudiert
	getriangelt		trompetet
	ge'liebkost		lieb'kost
(6)	*gediskutiert	(7)	*redet
	*geversucht		*sucht
	*geentfallen		*fallen
	*gekrakeelt		*predigt
	*gepalavert		*arbeitet
	*geschmarotzt		*kiebitzt
	*geapplaudiert		*heiratet
	*getrompetet		*triangelt
	*gelieb'kost		*'liebkost

It is instructive to see how these facts are treated in the existing literature. In one of the earliest studies of German within generative phonology, Kiparsky

---

[6] The question of rule-governedness in the participle system of German is discussed extensively by Marcus et al. (1995).

[7] The two possibilities for (*ge*)*liebkost* are already cited by Bloomfield (1933: 230), although in a context in which he intends to show that the past participle (of *liebkosen* in this case) is formed by a circumfix consisting of *ge+* and *+t*. I do not follow this common analysis of a discontinuous morpheme in participle formation, mostly because, as shown in (5), many past participles do not show the prefix in question. That is, the suffix *+t* or *+n* is quite sufficient as an affix to form the verbal past participle. This is also the view expressed by Giegerich (1985: 178).

(1966) not only drew attention to the facts outlined in (4) to (7), but also provided an analysis within the model available to phonologists at the time. The solution offered involves two steps: first, every past participle receives the prefix *ge+* within morphology. Second, a rule of truncation is proposed.[8] Informally, this rule should say that *ge+* is deleted if not followed by a syllable bearing primary stress. Within the assumptions of generative phonology of that period, such a rule could not be stated directly. Instead, a formulation such as that in (8) was necessary (Kiparsky 1966: 69). The rule deletes two segments (the second one being an unstressed vowel), if a complex set of morphological and phonological conditions holds. '§' and '#' refer to special morphological boundaries, 'A' to a stress feature [accent] (in addition to 'U' [unaccented]!), while 'X' is any phonological or morphological material before the end of the verb. 'K' refers to the feature [consonantal].

(8)
$$[+ K] \begin{bmatrix} - K \\ + U \end{bmatrix} \rightarrow \emptyset \; (\S \underline{\hspace{1cm}} \#) \; [+K]_0^n \begin{bmatrix} - K \\ + A \end{bmatrix} X)_v$$

This rule is not only complex (and inelegant, for some people), but also subject to other objections. First, it is transformational in the sense that it presupposes an unrestricted set of possible operations on the phonological representation. If a single rule is possible which deletes two segments, there seems to be hardly any limit on what a rule can do. Second, the intuition expressed in the informal formulation of the truncation appears in the formal rule only very indirectly, namely through a judicious use of boundaries in the context.

Finally, the whole idea of truncation may well be questioned. Should the grammar have the power of first introducing a morpheme and then deleting it without a trace? How could morphological regularities be learned if such operations were possible? Does deletion of morphemes not lead to a multiplication of possible analyses for any word, since a word may contain numerous morphemes which are first introduced and then deleted? In what follows, I will assume that truncation is indeed not a possible operation in grammar (following Kiparsky 1982*b*: 23–4).

If a truncation analysis is questionable, there seems to be only one alternative, namely prefixation of *ge+* according to the proper prosodic condition(s). One could assume that a *ge*-prefixation rule such as (9) applies. This rule is proposed by Giegerich (1985: 178) and states that a morpheme *ge+* is inserted if followed by a word stress S which is primary in its domain (= DTE, designated terminal element), some other material (X), and either the morpheme {t} or {n}, the latter two symbols being indications of the fact that the rule applies to past participles.

(9) *ge*-Attachment

$$\emptyset \rightarrow \{ge\text{-}\} / \underline{\hspace{1cm}} + S \; X \begin{Bmatrix} \{t\} \\ \{n\} \end{Bmatrix}$$

where S = DTE

---

[8] Truncation is defined as a special kind of deletion, namely as the deletion of all segments (or other phonological material) of a morpheme.

There are certainly technical problems with the rule as given, in that the stress feature /S/ should not be supposed to precede other material. In what sense does S (for strong) precede the segments as parts of the base, for example? But more importantly, in this formulation Giegerich assumes that monosyllabic participles such as *lernt* carry an internal stress pattern (strong-weak), of which the second, weak, element is realized on a non-realized syllable, the null syllable. As I argue in Chapter 8, stress should be seen as being strictly relational, that is, it is only defined if there are two non-empty units between which such a relation may exist. Accordingly, a monosyllabic formative such as *lernt* does not carry a stress pattern if looked at in isolation. Nevertheless, this form and all other monosyllabic participles receive the *ge*-prefix, as shown in (4). A modification of rule (9) is thus not available to describe the distribution of *ge*+.[9]

Closer inspection of the prosodic structure of the relevant cases reveals the crucial factor. In (10), a number of possible participles are displayed with the prosodic categories argued for in the preceding chapter. The stress relation (s-w) for 'strong-weak' is added to the prosodic structure, but it becomes apparent that there is another simple difference between the participles requiring *ge*+ (10*a*, *c*) and those which do not (10*b*, *d*): words containing only one foot receive the prefix, words with more than one foot do not. This analysis presupposes the particular (stress-initial) foot assumed in § 3.3, but this (and only this) type of foot has been assumed for independent reasons anyhow.

(10) *a.*   *b.*   *c.*   *d.*

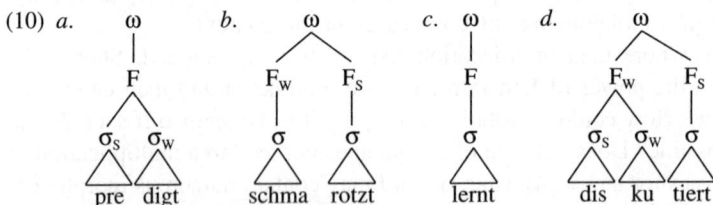

We may now take advantage of the asymmetry in prosodic structure between stress-final and stress-initial bisyllabic forms. Let us assume that the prefixation of *ge*+ is described by the 'rule' stated in (11), written again in the form of a subcategorization frame for *ge*+. It states that the prefix can be added (in the position indicated by the blank) if two conditions of subcategorization are fulfilled. First, a monopedal[10] phonological word is required as a base, and second, a past participle must be present. That is, (11*a*) and (11*b*) set requirements on two different, but parallel structures. The prefix is inserted if the requirements stated are met in both of these structures.

(11) *ge*-Prefixation

    a. $_\omega[$ _____ $_F[$]]

    b. [_____ [V]$_{[+ \text{part} \atop + \text{past}]}$]

---

[9] For a brief discussion of *ge*-Prefixation and the conclusion that '/ge/ only attaches to stems that bear initial stress', see also Anderson (1992: 282–3).

[10] The adjective *pedal* as referring to feet is a useful one, once the foot category becomes prominent in the phonological discussion.

No provision is made in (11) for the result of this concatenation to be different from the input. In other words, *ge*-prefixation is assumed to have no morphological or semantic consequences. This seems to be a plausible analysis. Compared to the rule for +*ei*, the rule is more complex, since there is morphological as well as phonological information in the subcategorization frame for *ge*+. This type of prefixation refers to two structures, the morphological and the prosodic, which can be assumed to coexist.

The derivation of a past participle such as *gepredigt* proceeds, then, as shown in (12). What is crucial here is the order between steps (12*b*, *c*) and (12*d*). Only after assignment of prosodic structure (application of a phonological rule) has provided the prosodic information, can *ge*+ be prefixed to the participle. Only then are the two conditions stated in (11) fulfilled.

(12) *a.* /pRE:dig/ lexical entry

   b. $_\omega[_F [pRE:dig]]$ prosodic structure assignment

   c. $[[pRE:dig]_V t]_{[+ part \atop + past]}$ formation of participle

   d. $_\omega[gX _F [pRE:dig] t]$ *ge*-Prefixation (11)

In (12*d*), only *ge*+ adjoins to the foot which has been formed in a previous step of the derivation. At this point it must also be mentioned that the underlying phonological representation of the prefix is assumed to be /gX/, that is, to have an empty skeletal position finally. This will be realized as [ə], as in other comparable cases treated in §§ 6.1 and 7.4.2. The step illustrated in (12*d*) must of course be followed by another cycle of phonological rule application (leading to the structure in (15*b*) below).

The preceding discussion leads to the conclusion that stress, in spite of being the apparent crucial condition, is neither necessary nor sufficient in the description of *ge*-prefixation. Rather, direct reference to prosodic structure is needed. As with the preceding example of +*ei*, a possible objection might be that the prosodic structure could be a part of the underlying entries and not be assigned by rule. In this case, morphology would be sensitive to the phonological information provided by the morphemes but not to the application of 'proper' phonological rules. But the prosodic structure is clearly a part of the predictable information. In general, the foot and the phonological word are not regarded as being phonemic or part of underlying structure (in German).[11]

Note also that verbs can be morphologically complex and derived by suffixation of +*ier*. In these cases, prosodic structure is derived as well. In particular, verbs derived by the suffixation of +*ier* must receive prosodic structure by rule, since it is always the suffix which carries primary stress. The resulting verbs follow the pattern of distribution for *ge*+ just like any other verb. Only if the general prosodic condition is provided as it is through the subcategorization for *ge*+, can *ge*-prefixation take place (or not take place).

It is also noteworthy that newly coined verbs follow the pattern without

[11] Underlying feet may be used to represent exceptional stress; see Hayes (1986) and my proposals for the treatment of word stress in § 8.2.

exception. The denominal verb *computer+n* (an *ad hoc* formation) would have the past participle *com'puter+t*, while *trigger+n* would (and does) have a past participle *ge+'trigger+t*. Only the difference in prosody can account for the different behaviour with respect to *ge*-prefixation.

An interesting additional set of cases are those with morphologically complex verbs as given in (13). The morphological structure of such verbs is actually a matter of some debate (see Stiebels and Wunderlich 1994), but fortunately this does not affect the argumentation here. While, on first sight, it might seem that examples such as *ge+ohrfeig+t* constitute counterexamples to the analysis proposed in (11), this turns out not to be the case. The relevant domain for the requirement in (11a) is the first phonological word only. It does not require the whole participle form to consist of only one phonological word. That is, the prefix is added to the whole participle as a morphological whole, but, if there are several phonological words as in {ohr} {feigt}, the prosodic condition as stated in (11a) applies only to the first phonological word.

(13) a. ge+wallfahrt+et   b. ent+fall+en   c. ein+ge+atm+et
    ge+ohrfeig+t   ver+such+t   durch+ge+fall+en
    ge+frühstück+t   zer+stäub+t   über+ge+stülp+t
    ge+kennzeichn+et   miss+glück+t   vor+ge+sung+en
                         er+leb+t

The forms in (13b) are participles of the so-called prefix verbs of German, with the prefixes belonging to a small class of morphemes which usually signal a change in the argument structure of the underlying verb; see Olsen (1986: § 3.2.4). Main stress is on the verb in these cases, but the vowel in the prefix, as argued below, is not reduced.

Prefixation of *ge+* is not possible here; in fact there is a complementary distribution between the prefixes in (13b) and *ge+*. I propose to account for these facts by assuming that these forms have a bipedal structure. The prefixes (*ver+* etc.) are headed by a foot, but not by their own phonological word. Since these prefixed participle forms do not meet the requirement in (11), *ge*-prefixation cannot occur. Stress in prefixed verbs is discussed again in § 8.3.2.

The so-called separable particle verbs, of which some examples are given in (13c), behave differently. Here, *ge+* appears between the separable particle and the verb, if the condition on the verb is met (i.e. *ge+* does not occur in *durch+diskutiert*.) Note also that the stress pattern is reversed in these cases: there is initial stress as in *'durchge,fallen*, and this is the general pattern of compounds. It therefore seems reasonable to assume that in these cases two free words, a preposition and a verb, are compounded. The rule of *ge*-prefixation applies before this composition, since *atm+et*, and so on, is a participle form subject to rule (11). On the other hand, *wallfahrten*, and so on, from (13a) as a whole is a verb. If turned into a participle, *ge*-prefixation can apply to the whole form only.

The particle verbs contrast with those prefix verbs in which a prefix segmentally identical to a particle cannot be separated: *,über'setzt* 'translated' vs. *'überge,setzt* 'carried over'; *₁durch'fahren* 'crossed' vs. *'durchge₁fahren* 'driven through'. That is, with respect to stress and occurrence of *ge+* the prefix verbs *₁über'setzen* and *₁durch'fahren* pattern with the forms of (13*b*), and their counterparts with those of (13*c*). These prefix verbs certainly require a foot on the prefix, since bisyllabic prefixes with an internal stress pattern (strong-weak, as in *'ü₁ber*) occur.

In § 3.4, word deletion was established as a test for phonological word-hood. The claims just made about the prefixes can actually be verified by the means of this test. As the examples in (14*a*, *b*) demonstrate, the prefixes claimed to be dominated by feet cannot be deleted, while the separable particles in (14*c*) can in principle be deleted, as they should (given that they are phonological words). See (15*c*) below for the structure of *vor+ge+spiel+t*.[12]

(14) *a.* **ge**liebt und -heiratet,   **be**suchen oder -sichtigen
       'loved   and married'   'visit   or   inspect'
    b. **ver**liebt und -heiratet,   **zer**stäuben oder -streuen
       'in love and married'   'spray   or   disperse'
    c. **vor**gesungen und -gespielt,   **ein**atmen oder -saugen
       'sung and played in front of somebody' 'breathe or   suck in'

The claim that *ge+* is prefixed to participles with monopedal phonological words can also be justified on the grounds that the rule is very natural and gives a certain unity to all participial forms. To see this, consider the result of *ge*-prefixation. I have not yet stated what the resulting prosodic structure is supposed to be. But rule (11) states that a past participle can be expanded by *ge+* if the base consists of one foot only. The simplest conclusion would then be that the expansion adds exactly one more foot; a monopedal phonological word is turned into a bipedal one.

This view of ge-Prefixation is eminently sensible in view of the observation that prosodic structures are generally binary in the unmarked case. We have already observed in this and the preceding chapter that the binary foot is the preferred form for feet and that a number of morphological and phonological rules conspire to create such feet, for example in the plural forms of nouns (§§ 3.3.2, 4.3.1). It is now possible to make an analogous statement about the shape of past participles: in Modern Standard German they must consist of two feet in the (first) phonological word.[13]

More formally, (15*a*) may be postulated as a template which past participles must satisfy. This is a special case of the 'minimal word requirement' often referred to in Prosodic Morphology. In Modern Standard German, however, only past participles minimally require a bipedal phonological word; all other words are sufficiently structured by the assignment of a single foot. In (15*b*), the

---

[12] The same test demonstrates that the verbal base to the prefixes is apparently not a phonological word either: **ver- oder geheiratet*. The pattern changes, however, if the prefixes are stressed: *be- und entladen* (see also fn. 14). Note that the rule proposed in § 3.4 for erecting phonological words will make every prefix correspond to a phonological word.

[13] Alternatively, the first phonological word for a participle is simply required to have *branching* structure. The prefixes would directly attach to the phonological word, without an intervening foot node.

result of ge-Prefixation is illustrated for gepredigt. Postulating a constraint such as (15a) is in fact crucial to make ge-Prefixation obligatory for the relevant cases. Rule (11) by itself would not prevent a past participle such as *predigt, since morphological rules are generally regarded to apply in an optional mode. Constraint (15a), in effect, makes (11) obligatory. The rule of ge-Prefixation (11), on the other hand, has to apply to make a participle conform to the requirement expressed in (15a), since, as mentioned above, application of the rule has no morphological or semantic consequences. The rule's function appears to be purely prosodic.

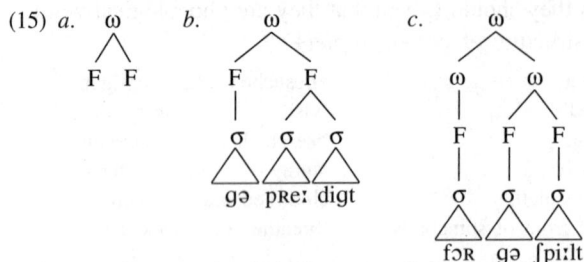

(15) *a.* ω   *b.*   ω   *c.*   ω

         F F   F   F   ω   ω

                    σ   σ σ   F   F   F

                    gə pʀeː digt   σ   σ   σ

                                          fɔʀ gə ʃpiːlt

If *ge+* (and, identically, *be+*) are usually headed by (stressless) feet, they contrast, in the way predicted by the analysis, with these same prefixes when under exceptional stress. It has been noted that even these prefixes containing schwa can be stressed, if the right communicative conditions are present (Wurzel 1970). Contrast or correction of misunderstandings provide such conditions, in which regular lexical stress is overridden, as shown in (16).[14]

(16) 'be- und 'ent,laden
    'load and unload'
    Ich sagte 'ge,fallen und nicht 'be,fallen.
    'I said "'ge,fallen" and not "'be,fallen".'

Based on the observation that the participial stress pattern is reversed in these cases, and that the resulting stress pattern is that of compounds, one may argue that here the prosodic structure is that of forms such as *'vorge,spielt* illustrated in (15c) and argued above to consist of two phonological words. This conclusion is almost inevitable on the basis of the fact that the deleted material in *'be- und 'ent,laden* must also be a phonological word. If the stressed *'be-* were not headed by its own phonological word, deletion of *laden* alone would not be possible.

How would a theory which treats morphology and phonology as components which do not interact in the way proposed here handle such cases? Classical generative grammar constitutes such a theory, since morphemes are assumed to

---

[14] These examples are usually quoted in connection with the phonological status of schwa. The claim is that *be+* and *ge+* under this sort of stress are not pronounced with a vowel [ə], but with a long [eː]. This is then used to argue that schwa derives from /eː/ (see Wurzel 1970: 182–3). But a pronunciation with [ə] is actually quite common under these circumstances; ['bə,falən] and ['beː,falən] both seem possible. On the proposed derivation of schwa from /eː/, see § 7.2.3.

be concatenated by morphological (or syntactic) rules. All phonological rules apply subsequently *en bloc* to the string of underlying phonemes as they are provided by the concatenation of morphemes. This approach was discussed above with reference to Kiparsky's deletion rule (8).

The particular conditions for the prefix *ge+* could alternatively be expressed with the help of filters: one such filter would only allow prefixed participles with primary stress on the following syllable or with a monosyllabic shape; another one would admit non-prefixed participles with primary stress in some other position. All other forms generated by the morphology would be marked as ill-formed. While such a filter approach seems to be possible in principle, it should be clear that it not only produces a massive overgeneration of ill-formed words, but also posits filters in the phonology which duplicate information that seems to belong somewhere else, namely to information about the distribution of *ge+*. Finally, these filters necessarily contain both phonological as well as morphological information. They are thus at least very marked parts of the phonological components. (Note, in contrast, that it is normal for lexical entries such as that for *ge+* to contain phonological as well as morphological information.)

It is also instructive to consider other instances of the prefixes *ge+* and *be+*. These two prefixes have a number of different (sometimes idiosyncratic and opaque) functions within the morphology of German. Looking at the verbs in (17) and the nouns in (18), which I will not analyse in detail, it becomes clear that the prosodic restriction analysed above for *ge+* in participles holds for all occurrences of the prefixes *ge+* and *be+*. In other words, the two schwa-final prefixes may only occur if the following phonological word is monopedal. The examples in (18*a*) alone would provide only weak evidence for the claim, since the group of *ge*-formations of this type is limited anyhow. But the general picture clearly is that the prosodic constraint holds not only for the 'empty' *ge+* in participles, but also for cases where the prefixes are markers with important morphological and semantic constraints and functions (see Wunderlich (1987) on *be*-verbs and Olsen (1991) on *ge*-nouns). The numerous discussions of these prefixes seem to have largely ignored this point.[15]

(17) beantworten, befragen, betriangeln ~ *bediskutieren, *bepalavern, *betrompeten

(18) *a.* Gebüsch, Geschrei, Geplapper ~ *Gepalaver, *Gespektakel
    b. Gerede, Gepredige, Gerenne ~ *Gediskutiere, *Getrompete, *Gespaziere

In the present account, there is no explanation for the fact that of all prefixes only *ge+* and *be+*, the prefixes with final schwa, are subject to such prosodic constraints. The other prefixes, whether carrying main stress or not, are not constrained in this way. Whether the prosodic constraint on *ge+* and *be+* can be

---

[15] Olsen (1991: 353, fn. 7) mentions the prosodic constraint on *ge+*, and that for some speakers, as for some of my informants, *Ge+diskutier+e* or *Ge+telefon+ier+e* are marginally acceptable. She also points out that the nominal *ge*-prefixation illustrated in (18*a*) must be distinguished from the (completely productive) type in (18*b*). For this latter formation, she proposes a complex affix (i.e. circumfix) *ge____e*. This analysis is perhaps unnecessary. The prefix *ge+* might be regarded as a predictable prefix analogous to the analysis provided above for the past participles.

tied to their segmental properties (i.e. the vowel schwa), remains to be explored. Claims to the contrary notwithstanding, it seems reasonable to assume that of all prefixes in Modern Standard German, only *ge+* and *be+* constitute reduced syllables. All other prefixes contain a full vowel, at least underlyingly. Especially in *er+*, *ver+*, *zer+*, the rhyme sequence [ɛʀ] may be reduced optionally to a vocalized [ɐ] in a fast or informal mode of speech. But this does not hide the fact that these suffixes would rhyme with *sehr* and *Meer*, but not with the final syllable of *Vater* or *Lehrer*.

4.1.3. Allomorphy of +*heit* and +*keit*

As a final example for phonology-dependent morphology within derivation, I shall consider yet another type of affixation in German. In (19), the distribution of the two suffix forms +*heit* and +*keit* is displayed. Both of these forms derive abstract nouns from adjectives; but they are in an (almost) strict complementary distribution: +*heit* can appear if and only if the preceding unit ends in a monosyllabic foot (19*a*). In contrast, (19*b*) demonstrates that +*keit* appears if the base ends in a branching (binary) foot. Again, for independent reasons, the base for +*heit* is such that its final syllable carries main stress if polysyllabic (see § 8.1). Contrary to the standard description (Fleischer 1982, for example) it is assumed here that there are two suffixes +*ig* and +*keit* in formations such as *Neuigkeit*. The common assumption that there is an allomorph of +*keit* in the shape of +*igkeit* will be argued against in § 4.1.4 below.

(19) *a.* Neu+heit   *b.* Neu+ig+keit
           Frei+heit   Frei+heit+lich+keit
           Schön+heit   Höf+lich+keit
           Privat+heit   Ewig+keit
           Ge+spann+t+heit   Ver+ständ+ig+keit
           Mark+ier+t+heit   Ge+lehr+sam+keit
           Interess+ant+heit   Ehr+bar+keit

We may diagnose the same familiar type of prosodic conditioning as in the preceding cases. It can therefore be expressed by the same means. The prosodic subcategorization frame for +*keit* as given in (20*b*) is the crucial part that expresses the regularity observed here. This suffix attaches to adjectives ending in a branching, polysyllabic foot. It is obvious that the conditions expressed in the subcategorization frame are very similar in type to the one for +*ei* presented in (2) and for *ge+* in (11). Affixation of +*heit* has no comparable phonological condition, but the same set of other morphological input and output conditions. It can therefore be assumed to act as the default case with respect to +*keit*.[16]

---

[16] It is not the case that +*keit* only attaches to morphologically complex bases: *fähig* and *ewig* in *Fähig+keit*, *Ewig+keit* are certainly simplex words; see also examples in (21*c*).

(20) +*keit*
    a. phonology: /kaɪt/
    b. subcategorization: *a.* [$_\omega$[... F] _____]

$$\overset{\displaystyle\bigwedge}{\text{s} \quad \text{w}}$$

                       b. [[ ]$_{\left[\substack{+ N \\ + V}\right]}$ _____]

    c. categorial features: $\begin{bmatrix} + \text{N} \\ - \text{V} \\ + \text{fem} \end{bmatrix}$

As shown in (21), there is only one class of words disturbing the clear picture. If the adjectival base ends in a syllable containing schwa (or, of course, a syllabic consonant), either of the suffixes can appear. In these cases, both suffixes are possible, and near-minimal pairs such as *Heiser+keit* vs. *Sicher+heit* can be found. It seems as if the affixation of +*keit* may be 'blind' to the presence or absence of the schwa syllable. Thus, it looks as if the rule attaching the suffix has a 'choice'. It can either 'see' the schwa as an unstressed vowel, an option which leads to +*keit*, or else ignore schwa, an option leading to +*heit* since then the preceding stem will be monosyllabic and thus be headed by a non-branching foot. The special status of schwa syllables has been mentioned a few times already. Arguably, the suffix may be added either before or after schwa syllables are built up. Even more in accordance with the distributional pattern for schwa is the fact that schwa is in general inserted 'earlier' if the roots end in /l/ or /ʀ/, and not in /n/ (see § 7.4.2).

(21) *a.* Selten+heit, Offen+heit, Albern+heit, Nüchtern+heit
    b. Sicher+heit, Dunkel+heit
    c. Heiser+keit, Sauber+keit, Übel+keit, Dunkel+keit

The distribution of +*heit*/+*keit* is apparently not completely random even here. Adjectives ending in /n/ always take +*heit* (i.e. **Offen+keit* could not occur), while those ending in /l/ or /r/ seem to take +*keit* as the unmarked option. This would mean that *Sicherheit* and *Dunkelheit* in (21*b*) are lexicalized exceptions to the general pattern illustrated in (21*c*).[17] It will be shown later that schwa often behaves differently with respect to stem-final nasals versus liquids, as we have already seen in the discussion of +*ei*-affixation.

Another question arising here is whether +*heit* and +*keit* are two separate morphemes or two allomorphs of one morpheme.[18] Given that no difference

---

[17] *Dunkel+heit* should block the regular *Dunkel+keit*, but does not, as various dictionaries contain both forms. This illustrates that blocking 'in derivational morphology [...] can hardly be considered more than a general tendency' (Kiparsky 1982*b*: 6–7). The reverse dictionaries of German by Mater (1983) and Muthmann (1988) give more entries for words with stem-final /ʀ/ followed by +*keit*. For stem-final /l/ the quantitative evidence is unclear; however, new formations such as *Simpel+keit* seem better than *Simpel+heit*.

[18] An *allomorph* is one of several variants of a morpheme, usually one where the shape is not predictable on the basis of general phonological rules. The relationship between +*heit* and +*keit* seems to be an exceptionally good example of allomorphy in German.

seems to be detectable in the behaviour of words suffixed by either of the two forms, an allomorph solution is quite plausible. Under such an analysis, the information stated in (20) would not be the subcategorization frame for the morpheme +*keit*, but for one of its two allomorphs, while the other allomorph would not be prosodically restricted. Under the allomorph analysis, the traditional three morphemes or allomorphs +*heit*, +*keit*, and +*igkeit* can be collapsed into one morpheme with two prosodically conditioned allomorphs.

All in all, the dependence of derivational affixation rules on the assignment of prosodic structure, and thereby perhaps on the prior application of phonological rules, seems well established in German. Of course, German is not unique in this respect. There are well-known examples from English: noun-forming suffixation of +*al*, as in *revers+al*, is only possible with stress-final bases. The German examples studied in this chapter have the advantage of being very productive and predominantly exceptionless cases of this sort from different parts of morphology. These facts may be used as arguments not only for the model of Prosodic Morphology, but also for the cycle as an important mechanism in the interaction of morphology and phonology. Only by applying morphological and phonological rules 'from the inside out' and feeding these types of rules into each other can a considerable number of the possible word forms in German be derived. The concept of the cycle is taken up again in Chapter 5.

4.1.4. **On some supposed allomorphies**

In the preceding analyses of the conditions for +*ei* and +*heit* two crucial assumptions were made. Contrary to standard descriptions (in particular Fleischer 1982: § 2.2), no allomorphs +*erei* and +*igkeit* are postulated here. Instead, these strings are broken down into two affixes, +*er+ei* and +*ig+keit*, respectively. Thus, while Fleischer (1982), Giegerich (1987), and Hall (1989*a*) would break down the word *Backerei* into two morphs, *back* and *erei*, here this word is treated as consisting of three morphs, in spite of the fact that the word *backer* (not to be confused with *Bäcker*) does not exist in the vocabulary of German. The issue comes down to a principled problem on the domain of morphology: should the object of morphology be the set of existing words in a language, or is morphology concerned with the set of *possible* words in a language?

Consider, first, the two sets of words given in (22). In some cases, (22*a*), the potential base for the affix +*keit* is not acceptable, or at least does not exist. These are the words for which the morphological handbooks and descriptions postulate a morpheme or an allomorph +*igkeit*, so that *Neu+igkeit* would be bimorphemic. The complex words in (22*b*) are structured as given here, that is, they involve a derivation with +*ig* and another with +*keit*.

(22) *a.* Neu+ig+keit ~ *neu+ig   *b.* Farb+ig+keit ~ farb+ig
      Geschwind+ig+keit ~ *geschwind+ig   Verständ+ig+keit ~ verständ+ig
      Schlaf+los+ig+keit ~ *schlaf+los+ig   Zufäll+ig+keit ~ zufäll+ig
      Müd+ig+keit ~ *müd+ig   Flüss+ig+keit ~ flüss+ig

This analysis has several disadvantages, however. First, it assumes an allomorph which is absolutely identical in shape to the sequence of two other affixes, namely *+ig+keit*. This is rather unexpected, given that the well-established kinds of allomorphy usually consist of an alternation between segments, where the change described in the alternation cannot be accounted for by a general phonological rule of the language in question.

Second, it is simply not the case that adjectives can never be affixed by *+ig* to coin another adjective. As shown in (23), some adjectives of this sort exist, where the base form and the adjective derived with *+ig* usually differ, at least slightly, in meaning.[19] Given these forms, the word *Lebendigkeit* actually is structurally ambiguous: [[[lebend]ig]keit] and [[lebend]igkeit] must both be possible structures for it under the analysis interpreting *+igkeit* as a single morph.

(23) *a.* wahrhaft ~ wahrhaft+ig   *b.* lebend ~ lebend+ig
    c. elend ~ elend+ig   *d.* stet ~ stet+ig

These facts again raise the question about what kinds of objects should be studied in morphology. Should morphological rules account for the fact that *wahrhaftig* is a word in Modern Standard German, while **schlaflosig* is not? Various authors have come to the conclusion that a sensible and well-defined object of morphology could only be the set of *possible words* of some language (cf. Halle (1973), Kiparsky (1982*b*: 25–8) as against Aronoff (1976) who argues that morphology describes relations between the existing words of a language). There are simply too many gaps which can only be regarded as accidental in a word-based approach.

Furthermore, the non-existence of some words can be explained by reference to *blocking*, to be discussed further in § 5.3.1. It seems to be a principle of morphology that completely synonymous words are avoided (and thus blocked from being generated). This would mean that **schlaflosig* is only possible if it differs in meaning from *schlaflos* in some minimal way, as in fact *wahrhaft* differs from *wahrhaftig*. But the principle of synonymy avoidance is a metaprinciple in morphology; it presupposes that the rules of morphology (whatever these are) are able to generate words which might be synonymous if the words do not acquire idiosyncratic properties. (I assume that the affixation of *+ig* by itself only specifies the category of the word as an adjective, but does not necessarily have any further semantic consequences.)

The claim is that the word grammar of German should in fact be allowed to generate the starred forms in (22*a*). These words are potential words, which however do not exist. Being synonyms of their bases, they are superfluous. In other words, the use of the asterisk in (22) is problematic, since it is too strong to claim that the words are ill-formed. They may well be potential words of Modern Standard German.[20]

---

[19] A *wahrhafter Freund* is a 'true, real friend'; a *wahrhaftiger Freund* is a 'truth-adhering or -loving friend'. Fleischer (1982: 239) presents some more examples. On the vowel alternation in *leblɔlnd* vs. *leblɛlndig* see § 7.2.4.

[20] For a slightly different view on *ig*-affixation see Olsen (1990: fn. 5).

The problem presented by the supposed allomorph +*igkeit* is not at all an isolated one in the morphology of German. The case of +*er*+*ei* vs. +*erei* (with the latter form as an allomorph of +*ei*) was mentioned above. Again, the allomorph analysis has to assume an allomorph suspiciously identical to a sequence of affixes occuring independently in other words. It is clearly preferable to assume that the suffix +*er* as in *Schwein*+*er*+*ei* is semantically empty and serves a purely prosodic function similar to *ge*+ in past participles. It is not restricted to the position before +*ei*, since it also occurs in *läch*+*er*+*lich*, *wein*+*er*+*lich*, *geist*+*er*+*n*, *wild*+*er*+*n*, and others. This recurrence strengthens the point that it is a morpheme in its own right. I will take no stance at this point on its morphological properties, such as word-class features. To weaken the observation made above that *schweiner* is not an existing word, one may also note that an adjective *schweinern* does exist, and that the logic of the present argumentation would lead to *schwein*+*er*+*n* as its structure.

In (24), some more structurally analogous cases are given, here involving +*at*, +*is*, and +*ik*. Once again, the common assumption is that +*ator*, +*iker*, +*ation* are single morphemes (Fleischer 1982: § 2.2). Giegerich (1985: 40) follows Fleischer in taking +*iker* as in *Akademiker* to constitute a single morpheme. Again, I dispute this analysis. While *Akademik* does indeed not exist as an actual word, it is easy to imagine a possible usage of such a word (e.g. as the study of academies or of academics).

(24) *a.* Ventil+at+or, Reform+at+or (*Ventil+at, *Reform+at)
      b. Akadem+ik+er, Theoret+ik+er (*Akadem+ik, *Theoret+ik)
      c. Rot+at+ion, Organis+at+ion (*Rot+at, *Organis+at)
      d. national+is+ier(en), elektr+is+ier(en) (*national+is, *elektr+is)

None of the starred examples in (24) exists in the German vocabulary without the final morpheme. But there are also other words which include the pre-final morphemes of (24) (which would not be a morpheme in the standard treatments) with or without a following morpheme. Examples are given in (25). Only +*is* is special in that it never ends a word, but this in itself is not reason enough to deny morpheme-hood.[21]

(25) *a.* Imit+at+or, Dikt+at+or (Imit+at, Dikt+at)
      b. Botan+ik+er, Krit+ik+er (Botan+ik, Krit+ik)
      c. Deriv+at+ion, Form+at+ion (Deriv+at, Form+at)

We may safely draw the conclusion that the starred words in (24) do not exist, but are *possible*. Word formation in general is about *possible* words in a language, and not actual words. Which of the possible words are in actual use depends on extralinguistic factors that cannot be dealt with successfully in theories of grammar. On this assumption, the inventory of derivational suffixes for

---

[21] Inkelas (1989: § 5.3.2) proposes to handle such affixes with a bidirectional subcategorization frame, i.e. one which requires a left- and a right-neighbouring morpheme. This would allow treating sequences such as +*ist*, +*ismus*, +*isieren* as involving a morpheme +*is*, which is followed by one or more other affixes. If followed by a tautosyllabic consonant, /i/ in this suffix is also shortened ([. . . ɪstl] vs. [. . . iː.ziː.ʀənl]) according to the rule discussed in § 7.1.2.

Modern Standard German can be simplified considerably. In particular, allomorphs with the shape of a sequence of two other suffixes are broken down into these two suffixes. At the same time, the morphological and/or phonological regularities governing the derivations become quite transparent.

4.2. A PROSODIC CONSTRAINT ON COMPOUNDS

The most generally accepted model for the analysis of compounds states that such expressions should be described by reference to a binary phrase structure tree with lexical category nodes governing free morphemes. More specifically, for German it is assumed that all major lexical categories can occur as left-hand elements in such a tree, while only nouns and adjectives can be placed in the right-hand or head position. Verbal compounds (*abfahren*, *sicherstellen*) occur, but because of their different properties cause a number of problems and may be assumed to arise from different sources.[22] In (26), I give illustrative examples for each case, including the controversial verbal compounds.

(26) *a.* N N: Haus+mann, Frauen+haus   *b.* N A: blut+rot, bild+schön
      A N: Rot+wild, Dunkel+kammer   A A: taub+stumm, wohl+geformt
      V N: Seh+hilfe, Hör+funk   V A: lauf+gerecht, trief+nass
      P N: Zwischen+fall, Über+sicht   P A: über+reif, über+groß

      c. N V: staub+saugen, rasen+mähen   *d.* N P: *
         A V: gut+tun, sicher+stellen   A P: *
         V V: mäh+dreschen, web+stricken   V P: *
         P V: auf+räumen, durch+laufen   P P: *

A corresponding phrase structure rule for compounding (excluding verbal compounds) might be that in (27), assuming that the category level of compounding is that of the stem. That stems and not words enter composition is a traditional assumption further discussed in §§ 5.2.2 and 5.2.3. Basically, it is motivated by the fact that irregular inflection can be found compound-internally, while regular inflection (word inflection) is impossible within compounds. The variable X can take N and A as values, while Y may take any of N, A, V, and P.

(27) $X^{stem} \rightarrow Y^{stem}\ X^{stem}$ (X = [+ N])

To my knowledge, prosodic constraints on compounding in Modern Standard German have not been discussed in the relevant literature. However, there is at least one relatively clear case of such a condition. The relevant examples are given in (28) to (31). The initial adjectives in (31) have a final stress pattern of strong-weak, and since this stress pattern seems to be the only property they have in common, we must look for a prosodic explanation of the constraint.

---

[22] The separability of the parts of a verbal compound constitutes one such problem (*er fährt ab* 'he drives off'); regular compounds cannot be taken apart within a sentence. (On complex verbs in German see Wunderlich 1987 and Stiebels and Wunderlich 1994.)

(28) Schwarz+brot
      Rot+wein
      Grau+schopf
      Groß+mut
      Weich+spüler

(29) Dunkel+ziffer
      Sauber+mann
      Sieben+gebirge
      Besser+wisser
      Trocken+dock

(30) To'tal+verdunkelung
      Ro'sé+wein
      Ak'tiv+posten
      Simul'tan+dolmetscher
      Bi'när+code
      Pri'vat+dozent

(31) *'Farbig+graphik
      *'Rosa+wein
      *'Rötlich+schopf
      *Ro'mantisch+kirche
      *'Gleichzeitig+dolmetscher
      *'Ewig+student

While (28) to (30) demonstrate that adjectives can in principle appear in the non-head position of compounds, a limitation exists according to which adjectives must conform to a specific prosodic pattern. It appears from (31) that adjectives as first element in noun compounds are not acceptable if they end in a bisyllabic foot,[23] that is, for compounding to take place, the final foot of the left-hand part must be monosyllabic. That the restriction is indeed confined to adjectives is shown by countless noun-initial examples such as 'Kaffee+bohne, 'Arbeits+kraft, in which no comparable constraint is found.

Once more, reference to the foot category is sufficient to account for all the data in a unified way. We may write this down as in (32); morphological structures of the type specified in (32), that is, adjective-noun compounds, must fulfil the implicational condition stated here. The constraint to the right of the double arrow is understood as stating that the final foot in the initial phonological word must be monosyllabic.[24] This condition is fulfilled in the examples of (28) and (30), but not in those in (31).

(32) [A N] $\leftrightarrow$ $_\omega$[... $_F$[σ]]

---

[23] I should mention that a number of such compounds exist in which the final syllable of the adjective contains the final sequence /ɪg/: *Niedrig+wasser*, *Billig+ware*, *Fertig+gericht* are clear counterexamples to the claim made here. Nevertheless, many speakers agree that other, similar words to those given in (31) are not felicitous. The precise formulation of the constraint and its strength need further inquiry.

[24] Adding a left bracket '$_\varphi$[' to the rule would be one way of clarifying that the initial phonological word is the relevant one.

A number of apparent counterexamples to the constraint seem to exist, as shown in (29) above and in (33). In (29), cases can be found where the initial adjective ends in a schwa syllable. This structure has already been shown to be exceptional with respect to other regularities (e.g. with respect to the allomorphy of +*heit/keit*, see (21)). Again, we may simply suppose that schwa syllables do not 'count' for this regularity. In § 7.4.2, this invisibility will be related to a rule of Schwa Epenthesis.

The compounds in (33) demonstrate that the prosodic constraint holds for nominal compounds alone. Adjectival compounds (33*a*) are not subject to it. Neither are the verbal compounds (33*b*), but this is not surprising, given that they may be of a different structure altogether. Finally, my analysis leads to the claim either that the apparent adjective-noun compounds in (33*c*) are in fact adjective-verb compounds which have been subjected to further nominalization by affixing +*ung* ([[richtig$_A$ stell]$_V$ ung]$_N$) or that deverbal nouns do not enter the constraint formulated in (32). In any case, the differences found for verbal compounds motivate the claim that they derive from different structural configurations.

(33) *a.* lila+farben
        zwanzig+teilig
     b. richtig+stellen
        rosa+färben
     c. Richtig+stell+ung
        Rosa+färb+ung

The prosodic constraint found here is a very specific and marked one; it applies to one class of compounds only; and furthermore, it requires a non-branching foot. Since prosodic structure may be regarded as branching in the unmarked case, condition (32) explicitly disallows the unmarked structure in favour of a marked one.

4.3. INFLECTION, SCHWA, AND PROSODIC STRUCTURE

Having explored prosodic dependencies in derivation and compounding, I will now discuss some aspects of inflectional morphology. Prosodic phonology enters this area mostly through alternations of inflectional suffixes with and without the vowel schwa. We have come across several examples of this sort already, and in § 3.3.2, I argue that an argument for the foot category in German is provided by the fact that plural nouns (of most kinds) must be such that they end in a bisyllabic foot of which the second syllable is a schwa syllable. As I show in the present section, the presence or absence of schwa (rather, a schwa syllable as defined above) in many cases is to be regarded as an indicator of prosodic constraints, and these constraints are treated differentially within different lexical categories. We will therefore have to study nouns, verbs, and adjectives separately.[25] In each case, however, the distribution of schwa can be described in very simple prosodic terms.

4.3.1. Schwa in nouns

In looking at schwa in noun inflection, the argument for the foot presented in § 3.3.2 is repeated and extended here. The analysis of plural inflection is also taken up again in § 5.3.2, where the relationship between the different rules of affixation and other plural formations is in the focus of the discussion.

Consider first the nouns in (34), which are given in their singular and plural forms. These words, all of masculine or neuter gender, do not receive one of the plural suffixes, and are therefore identical in their singular and plural forms, except for a possible umlauting of the vowel.

(34) *Singular*   *Plural*
     Filter   Filter
     Computer   Computer
     Vater   Väter
     Onkel   Onkel
     Segel   Segel
     Vogel   Vögel
     Segen   Segen
     Beben   Beben

This pattern is one reason for postulating that plural nouns in Modern Standard German must end in a bisyllabic foot, with the second syllable being a schwa syllable. The unique behaviour of these words is recognized in studies of German morphology by postulating 'pseudo-suffixes' +*el*, +*er*, +*en* (Augst 1979; Köpcke 1988). The present prosodic analysis avoids such pseudo-entities and relies on independently motivated categories.

Another observation strengthens the point: only nouns of the type given in (34) have plural forms without any explicit suffix, that is, a zero-marking of plurality. All other nouns, those not ending in a schwa syllable, must receive one of the plural suffixes. I am not aware of any exception here.[26]

Taking these cases together with the suffixed plural nouns, it is a noticeable fact about all noun plurals that the suffixes and schwa occur in such a way

---

[25] The distribution of schwa in German has been the subject of a vigorous recent discussion with a number of analyses differing in details. In this section, I rely on proposals by Giegerich (1985; 1987), Wiese (1986, 1988: ch. II, pt 2), Hall (1992*b*), Féry (1991), Noske (1993: ch. 5), and Kleinhenz (1991). Note that all of these proposals share the assumption that schwa is basically a phenomenon of epenthesis. I regard the present section plus § 7.4.2 as a contribution to the debate and as an answer to some of the criticisms raised to my earlier proposals. For a very brief discussion of alternative proposals see § 4.3.4.

[26] The regularity is not bidirectional. That is, words of the type given in (34) may receive the plural marker /n/: *Vetter* vs. *Vetter+n*, *Muskel* vs. *Muskel+n*. I argue that this is an exceptional plural pattern (for non-feminines) in § 5.3.2.

that the constraint ('a final sequence consisting of a stressed syllable plus a schwa syllable') is obeyed almost without exception. If the noun in the singular form ends in a stressed syllable, either schwa or schwa plus a consonant is suffixed. Only if the noun already contains a final schwa syllable (either in the stem or in a derivational suffix), can plural nouns without suffixes appear, see (34).

Note that I disregard nouns taking an *s*-plural. These will be argued to belong to a totally different class in § 5.3.2. Two words seem to be exceptional in that they do not take schwa in the plural formation although they should: *Nachbar+n*, *Ungar+n* (as 'Hungarians'). In these cases, we might want to say that the syllable *bar/gar* is unstressed. This could be interpreted in such a way that the foot-based constraint described above is in fact valid here. But other bisyllabic nouns with the same stress pattern behave differently: *Arbeit* vs. *Arbeit+en*, *Tugend* vs. *Tugend+en*. However, schwa must be inserted into these words for phonotactic reasons alone: /tn/ and /dn/ are totally impossible as word-final consonant clusters. This analysis is plausible, since, as we will see in § 7.4.2, schwa is often inserted to break up combinations which would be unsyllabifiable otherwise.

The presence or absence of a plural suffix is one element in this prosodic constraint; another aspect is provided by the alternation of the suffix forms. The plural suffix /n/, which will be shown to be the unmarked suffix for feminine nouns in § 5.3.2, addresses this point, since it appears as [ən] if the foot constraint is not met, and as [n] if there already is a schwa syllable (see (35)). All examples in (35) are feminine, while the nouns in (34) are of masculine or neuter gender. In (36), a number of feminine nouns which are either monosyllabic or end in a stressed syllable show that the suffix /n/ indeed surfaces as [ən]. Since the orthography of Modern Standard German quite consistently indicates the presence of schwa by the letter *e*, no other transcription is needed in this discussion.

(35) Steuer+n
     Mauer+n
     Nummer+n
     Kammer+n
     Tafel+n

(36) Uhr+en
     Jagd+en
     Fabrik+en
     Figur+en
     Idee+en

Within the present approach, one can state a prosodic condition which nouns marked for plural must fulfil. This condition can be formulated as in (37), in which the final foot of a phonological word corresponding to a plural noun is required not only to be bisyllabic, but also to end in a schwa syllable. This is another, morphologically conditioned, minimal word requirement. Tentatively, I assume that the schwa syllable referred to so often can be represented as a syllable with adjacent onset and coda, that is, without a nucleus.[27] Note that the syllabification rules of § 3.2.4 can indeed create a schwa syllable as a syllable without a nucleus, since syllabification rule (34b) is not applicable. This problem will be discussed further in connection with the question of schwa epenthesis in § 7.4.2.

(37) $\begin{bmatrix} + \text{N} \\ - \text{V} \\ + \text{plural} \end{bmatrix} \Rightarrow {}_\omega[\ldots {}_F[\sigma \quad \sigma]]$
$\qquad\qquad\qquad\qquad\qquad\quad \overset{\displaystyle\wedge}{\text{O} \quad \text{C}}$

Condition (37), to be discussed again in the context of the plural system of Modern Standard German in § 5.3.2, seems like an attractive alternative to past descriptions. In these descriptions, either a suffix /e/ was postulated which was then deleted (Wurzel 1970; Rettig 1972), or a zero-suffix was assumed (Augst 1979). No such questionable units are required in the present analysis. This may be seen as an indication of how non-linear phonology avoids pitfalls of earlier structuralist or generative approaches.

The discussion so far has been restricted to plural marking of nouns. Matters become more complex when case markings, especially the dative plural and the genitive singular, are considered. I will only sketch the facts and the treatment in the present framework.

In a number of words, schwa in case endings is optional, as the examples of (38), with genitive and dative forms for such words, demonstrate. Here, schwa may or may not appear. Generally, the forms containing schwa are regarded as more formal or even slightly archaic. There are also a number of other factors favouring one or the other variant (see Helbig and Buscha 1987: 237). In present-day Standard German, schwa is obligatory only if the word-final segment is /s/, as in *Haus+es*. With final /ʃ/ (as in *Busch* vs. *Busch+es*) the variant [əs] is strongly preferred. This finds a natural explanation in the feature model proposed in § 3.1, where /s/ and /ʃ/ are both [Coronal] but differ in the presence or absence of the feature [high].

(38) Mann(e)s, Mann(e)
      Hut(e)s, Hut(e)
      Buch(e)s, Buch(e)
      Baum(e)s, Baum(e)

On the other hand, schwa never appears if the genitive marker /s/ is added to one of the bisyllabic nouns in (34): *Filter+es*. Because of the absolute exclusion of such forms, I argue that the prosodic condition given in (37) is *optional*

---

[27] Other ways of marking the non-existence of the vowel or the vowel position (such as crossed association lines to indicate emptiness) are problematic, since they rely on a purely diacritic marking. The only potential problem of the present proposal is, as noted in § 3.2.4, that the generation of a syllable node without a nucleus must be ensured.

for the genitive and dative singular forms.[28] If the condition is satisfied, Schwa Insertion is impossible. Finally, note that not every noun inflection may lead to the creation of a schwa syllable. Suffixation of /n/ as the marker for dative attached to plural nouns never appears as [ənl], unless the plural form already ends in schwa: *Männ+er+n, Onkel+n, Hüt+e+n*. There simply exists no prosodic condition, analogous to (37), for the morphological features of dative case. Comparison of *Herrn* 'gentleman (dat. sg.)' to *Herren* 'gentlemen' (recall (32) in § 3.2.4) illustrates the same point.

4.3.2. Adjectives

The prosodic structure of adjectives follows a different rule from that for nouns. As with nouns, schwa occurs in interaction with inflection, but in a more general and simpler pattern. The pattern is that all inflectional endings to adjectives must form a schwa syllable. In (39) this fact is illustrated for *rot* and *roh* with respect to the endings for case, number, and gender in the so-called strong declension. The weak declension can be ignored because it is a much simpler system which illustrates the same point: all inflected adjectives display schwa. Orthographic *e* in bold print signifies schwa.

(39)

	Masc.	Neut.	Fem.	Pl.
Nom.	roter	rotes	rote	rote
	roher	rohes	rohe	rohe
Acc.	roten	rotes	rote	rote
	rohen	rohes	rohe	rohe
Dat.	rotem	rotem	roter	roten
	rohem	rohem	roher	rohen
Gen.	roten	roten	roter	roten
	rohen	rohen	roher	rohen

(39) shows that schwa is indeed omnipresent in adjectival inflection. The second of the two adjectives is vowel-final (/ʀoː/); it demonstrates that the presence of schwa in adjectives is independent of any phonotactic constraints. Forms such as **rohr, *rohn* are acceptable (see *Rohr*), but not as inflected forms of the adjective. Adjectives possessing stem-internal schwa again are no exception: see *trocken+es*, but not **trocken+s*. (The conditions for this stem-internal schwa are a different matter, see § 7.4.2.) Since the comparative suffix +er and the present participle ending +end are also realized as a schwa syllable, adjectives with stem-internal schwa or present participles may end in up to three schwa syllables, as shown in (40).

---

[28] Instead of the feature [+ plural] used in (37), it seems necessary to refer to the presence of *any* inflectional feature, the same constellation as found for adjectival inflection below.

(40) trocken+er+es
     entscheid+end+er+e

It is thus not the case that inflected adjectives must end in a bisyllabic foot, as (most) plural nouns must. The adjectival paradigm in (39) and the stacking of schwa syllables in (40) show that adding any morphological feature to an adjective leads to an additional schwa syllable. The generalization present in these cases can be captured by stating that for any adjectival ($[+ N, + V]$) inflectional suffix the presence of a final schwa syllable is required. This is the intended interpretation of (41), analogous to rule (37). The rule or condition reapplies for any additional suffix as examples in (40) demonstrate, which provides an argument for the cyclic nature of this rule.[29] It may eventually be possible to replace 'F' (a cover symbol for any inflectional feature) by more specific information, if the theory of inflectional features becomes more elaborate. The prosodic structure preceding this syllable is irrelevant, as we have seen above. In particular, there may already be a schwa syllable.

(41) $\begin{bmatrix} + \text{N} \\ + \text{V} \\ + \text{F} \end{bmatrix} \Rightarrow {}_\omega[\ldots \sigma]$

$\qquad\qquad\qquad\qquad\quad$ O C

4.3.3. Verbs

Inflectional schwa in verbs is morphologically similar to that in nouns. Again, we can diagnose the requirement of a final bisyllabic foot under specific morphological conditions. To see an example of this, consider first the verb forms from relevant classes as displayed in (42). Schwas are again emphasized.

(42)						
a.	Infinitive:	denken	leiten	segeln	segnen	diskutieren
b.	1 sg.:	denke	leite	{ segle	segne	diskutiere
				segele		
c.	3 sg.:	denkt	leitet	segelt	segnet	diskutiert

Infinitives always end in the bisyllabic foot known from the analysis of noun plurals. Schwa is distributed precisely in a way that such structures result, as is demonstrated by the alternation between stem-internal (*segel+n*) vs. inflectional schwa (*segn+en*) in (42*a*). This pattern holds for the infinitival forms of all verbs in Modern Standard German except for the infinitives of the two high frequency verbs *tun* and *sein* (which however are often bisyllabic in colloquial speech).

Looking at (42*c*), it appears that the bisyllabic foot requirement does not hold for all verb forms. Schwa can appear here, but only if it is required phonotactically. This point will be taken up in connection with phonotactic regularities in § 7.4.2. It has nothing to do with a prosodic requirement of the morphology itself. The first-person singular forms in (42*b*) are slightly more complex, especially since

---

[29] 'Cyclic' means an application of a rule to increasingly larger domains; see discussion in § 5.3.1.

the final +e, as a marker for first-person singular, may also be missing (*denk'*, *leit'*, *diskutier'* but not **segn'*, which would be ruled out phonotactically). The bisyllabic foot found in final position seems to be due to the fact that the suffix consists simply of [ə], which may also be missing, so that *segeln* actually has three forms for the first-person singular: *segele, segle, segel*.

It appears that the bisyllabic foot requirement holds without exception for exactly those forms with a suffix of the shape /n/, that is, the infinitive and the first- and third-person plural forms. Here, in fact, the forms are always identical to each other for any given verb except for the suppletive forms of *sein*: *sind* (1 or 3 pl.). Even the past participles end in a bisyllabic foot if the suffix is /n/: *gesehen* and examples in (4) to (13) of this chapter.[30] As with adjectival inflection, it is not sufficient to refer to phonotactic requirements: **brau+n* or **seh+n* would be acceptable phonological forms, but, as inflected verb forms, surface as *brau+en* and *seh+en*.

The prosodic requirement then is subject to a further—a segmental— condition. In (43) the condition is stated formally, using the same notation for schwa syllables as above. Note that a conjunction of two conditions must be satisfied for the implication to hold.

(43)
$$\begin{bmatrix} + V \\ - N \end{bmatrix}, {}_\omega[\ldots /n/] \Rightarrow {}_\omega[\ldots \sigma]$$

The condition as formulated holds for present-day Modern Standard German only; both older stages of German and present-day dialects follow other rules. In the history of German, there is a clear tendency to reduce the number of contexts for schwa. That is why the presence of optional schwa as in (38) makes the forms appear archaic to many speakers. Many, if not all, dialects of German are ahead of Modern Standard German in this respect. (On schwa in Viennese German, see Rennison 1980.)

I take the variable realization of first-person singular forms (*denke* vs. *denk'*) to be due to the optionality of the affixation of +e (or rather, its underlier). Alternatively, there might be a rule deleting final schwa, but at least for reasons of simplicity I propose the former analysis. It is not easy to choose between these two options given that final schwa is always a suffix. In connection with the present discussion of prosodic constraints in morphology, however, not much hinges on this choice.

Finally, it is instructive to study the distribution of schwa in subjunctive verb forms. The relevant forms of the verbs *geh+en, lieb+en, segel+n, ruder+n* are displayed in (44). The first verb belongs to the class of 'strong' verbs, the others to the 'weak' verbs.[31]

---

[30] And even for the other exceptional verb, *tu + n*, it is true that all of its forms suffixed by /n/ do not have to be bisyllabic. That is, the exceptional nature needs to be stated for the root *tun* only once, not for each of its inflected forms.

[31] The fact that some subjunctive forms are rare and that others are systematically identical to the indicative forms does not invalidate the analysis.

(44) Subjunctive verb forms

		Present	Past
1sg.	a.	gehe	ginge
2sg.		gehest	gingest
3sg.		gehe	ginge
1pl.		gehen	gingen
2pl.		gehet	ginget
3pl.		gehen	gingen
1sg.	b.	liebe	liebte
2sg.		liebest	liebtest
3sg.		liebe	liebte
1pl.		lieben	liebten
2pl.		liebet	liebtet
3pl.		lieben	liebten
1sg.	c.	segele	segelte
2sg.		segelst	segeltest
3sg.		segele	segelte
1pl.		segeln	segelten
2pl.		segelt	segeltet
3pl.		segeln	segelten
1sg.	d.	rudere	ruderte
2sg.		ruderst	rudertest
3sg.		rudere	ruderte
1pl.		rudern	ruderten
2pl.		rudert	rudertet
3pl.		rudern	rudertet

Looking at the first two verbs, a possible conclusion would be that the sub-junctive marker for German verbs is the vowel schwa between the stem and the (possible) personal ending. Because schwa is present throughout the subjunctive forms, it, or whatever its underlier is assumed to be, constitutes an affix in the inflectional paradigm. In other words, a typical verb form from the subjunctive subparadigm would consist of three morphs as in {lieb} {e} {st}. The relevance of the liquid-final verbs given in (44c, d) is that they require a different analysis. Since schwa here occurs stem-internally and not following the stem, it is hardly the affix just proposed. (The final schwa in the past-tense forms is required independently, to break up the sequence of two obstruents or to allow syllabi-fication in the case of /t + n/.)

What unifies the two types of subjunctive forms is the word-final prosodic pattern. Again, we find the foot of the strong-weak type as discussed above. The vowel schwa appears precisely if such a structure is not already present for other reasons. In the case of verbs such as *segeln* or *rudern*, these other reasons are the phonotactic restrictions which require a bisyllabic form to accommodate all of the segments from /zeːgl/ and /ʀuːdʀ/.

From these considerations, it follows that schwa in the subjunctive forms (44a, b) is not an affix, but simply the reflex of yet another prosodic requirement. This requirement, formulated in (45), is either met for independent reasons or not met in the input. Only then is a schwa inserted. (45) assumes, without implying the ultimate correctness of the claim, that a feature [subjunctive] characterizes subjunctive verb forms.

$$(45) \quad \begin{bmatrix} +\text{V} \\ -\text{N} \\ +\text{subj} \end{bmatrix} \Rightarrow [\ldots \underset{\text{O} \quad \text{C}}{\bigwedge}]_\omega$$

Assuming that this rule applies once in the morphology–phonology interaction as soon as its input condition is met, the formulation here does not exclude the possibility that further suffixation leads to more than final schwa syllable, a situation amply illustrated in (44). In the present context, the main point to be made is the following: given that the prosodic morphology approach to the subjunctive forms is able to describe all verb forms in a unified way, this approach is clearly preferable to those which postulate a subjunctive suffix.

4.3.4. **On various approaches to inflectional schwa in German**

In the preceding sections, I gave an account of so-called inflectional schwa. Giegerich (1987) contrasts this type of schwa with the stem-internal 'prosodically conditioned' schwa. In the present account, both types of schwa are prosodic in that they can be dependent on prosodic conditions and in that they create specific prosodic structures.

As the data above demonstrate, inflectional schwa is subject to different morphological and segmental conditions in nouns, verbs, and adjectives. From this fact it does not follow, however, that a general rule of Schwa Epenthesis in German is impossible, as some authors have concluded. The account above postulates a number of prosodic schemata, prosodic configurations which must be satisfied for a given morphological configuration. The insertion of the vowel schwa simply is a way (usually the only one) to satisfy these conditions.

According to the analyses presented here, Schwa Epenthesis itself is a completely general rule: the reference to morphology is provided neither by a whole series of such rules, each annotated with the necessary morphological information (Giegerich 1987; 1989; Hall 1992b: § 1.2.6; Kleinhenz 1991), nor by including schwa (or its underlier) into the representation of the inflectional morphemes, as Féry (1991) and Noske (1993: ch. 5), essentially following Issatschenko (1974), propose.

Both of these approaches suffer from a lack of generality: first, of the sixteen vowels of German, it is always the vowel schwa which is inserted; second, in the various schwa insertion rules, crucial information on the position of schwa is repeated again and again. The inclusion of schwa in the representation of suffixes suffers from the same problems. If, for example, all adjectival endings include schwa, then schwa is completely predictable from the context and should not be interpreted as part of the underlying representations of these suffixes.[32]

The proposal made here avoids this problem by claiming that inflection has to obey a number of prosodic conditions which are tied to (sometimes general, sometimes very specific) morphological specifications. All rules apply freely and optionally; but if the prosodic conditions are not met in the output of the phonological component, the word is simply not well formed. By separating the morphology-dependent prosodic conditions from the rule of Schwa Epenthesis itself, a single such rule (see § 7.4.2) is sufficient.

I would like to conclude this chapter with a very general remark which is perhaps superfluous for some readers: phonology is occasionally connected to properties of spoken language (speech), and, implicitly or explicitly, excluded from considerations of written language. Given the dependence of (productive) morphology on clearly phonological conditions, this association of phonology with spoken language alone is unwarranted. Obviously, the prosodic conditions analysed above are independent of the modality of linguistic expressions; they hold equally well for written and for spoken German. The same observation can also be made with respect to the prosodic nature of the word deletion studied in Chapter 3; the relevant phenomenon actually is more typical for written than for spoken German.

From this fact we must conclude that phonology is just one of the components involved in the structural description of a language, to a large extent without regard to the modality of its realization. Phonology is an integral part of the grammar of natural languages. The connection to spoken language derives mainly from the requirement that phonological categories (in particular the atomic features) are (and must be) phonetically interpretable.

---

[32] This criticism also applies to work on the syntax or morphology of the inflectional endings, in which the underlying forms are usually assumed to contain schwa; see Zwicky (1985).

5

ASPECTS OF LEXICAL PHONOLOGY AND MORPHOLOGY

The preceding chapter demonstrates the close relationship between phonological representations and the structure of words. In pursuing this topic further, the main aim of this chapter is to discuss the theory of Lexical Phonology as an interesting framework for major aspects of the phonology of German, aspects which are largely orthogonal to the issues of rules and representations which are the focus of most discussions. Lexical Phonology, as developed mainly by Kiparsky (1982a, b; 1983; 1985), is primarily a theory of the interaction of phonology with morphology. It also constitutes an attempt to rule out excessively abstract solutions to phonological problems, and it interacts closely with theories of non-redundant representations and non-linear phonology.[1]

The first part of this chapter will introduce some basic notions and proposals of Lexical Phonology, providing motivation for these ideas through a description of relevant phenomena of German. This introduction is followed by some more considerations on the morphology and the lexicon of German, couched in terms of Lexical Phonology (which can be named 'Lexical Morphology' with equal justification). In particular, derivational affixes and the classes they are associated with, lexical levels, and nominal and verbal inflection are discussed in some detail, mostly illustrating the application of principles formulated in Lexical Phonology.

Lexical Phonology is basically a theory of how the formal shape of words is incrementally built up in the component of grammar called the 'lexicon', following restricting principles on the application of rules. In the lexicon, the morphology supplies the principles and rules of combining the constituent morphemes of a language, and the phonology supplies both general as well as language-specific wellformedness conditions for phonological representations as far as they hold within the word domain. A large part of this build-up involves the accumulation of feature values that are not part of the underlying entries for morphemes. In this respect, Lexical Phonology adopts the theory of underspecification, as discussed in the chapter to follow.

---

[1] Kiparsky (1982a) is an abbreviated version of Kiparsky (1982b). Kaisse and Shaw (1985), Booij and Rubach (1992), Durand, Goldsmith, and Jensen all provide introductory texts to this theory, the last three, by some coincidence, each in ch. 5 of their 1990 textbooks; a list to which Kenstowicz (1994: ch. 5) is the most recent addition. Spencer (1991) is a good source for an introduction to all related problems within a wider frame of morphological theory and also introduces Lexical Phonology in § 4.3. Mohanan (1986) also compares Lexical Phonology to preceding theories. For earlier applications of Lexical Phonology to German see Giegerich (1985), Wiese (1988a), Hall (1989a, b).

5.1. LEXICAL PHONOLOGY AND MORPHOLOGY

On one popular view on the relationship between morphology and phonology, words are built up by the application of morphological rules. After these rules of morphology have applied, phonological rules generate the correct phonological shape of the words, by specifying the phonemes for each morpheme, and perhaps also by altering the phonological structure of morphemes according to the context the morpheme appears in. Under such a 'syntax first' approach, morphological rules can never be directly dependent on the prior application of a phonological rule.

Lexical Phonology offers a different view of the phonology–morphology interaction. As diagrammatically shown in (1), it is assumed that morphology interacts with phonology in such a way that after the application of each morphological rule a part of phonology (called *lexical phonology* as opposed to *postlexical phonology*) is checked for the possible application of a phonological rule. If there are such rules, they are indeed applied. The result of the application is handed back to the morphology for the possible application of another morphological operation. Of course, adding another layer of morphological structure would cause a further round of phonological rule application.

(1) A simple model of the lexicon

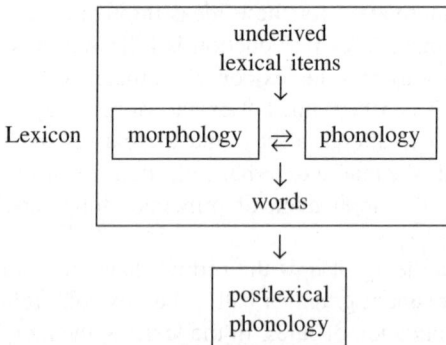

Models of the type (1) vary as to whether underived lexical items enter a first phonological cycle before entering the system of morphological rules. The evidence from German is rather against such a pre-morphological cycle; see discussions in §§ 7.3.5 and 7.4.2. Notice also that many underived roots are not syllabifiable until they have undergone suffixation. That is, the top-most vertical arrow in (1) should point to the morphology box, and not in between or to the phonology box. Phonological rules are applied only after some morphological rule has applied. In § 5.2.3 below, I discuss how this might be possible even for morphologically simple, apparently underived words.

The mode of applying a set of phonological rules to a string of increasing length (or to some other kind of representation, if the string character of representations is rejected) is known as *cyclic* rule application. In this way, complex words are derived in a specific component of the grammar, the *lexicon*. Postlexically, that is, in a postlexical component of grammar, these words may, following different principles, be affected by other (or the same) rules of the phonology.

A different interpretation of the same claim would be to say that the lexicon acts as an interface between phonology and morphology. The proposal that morphology and phonology interact in the lexicon to derive word forms is the first fundamental aspect of Lexical Phonology. According to this concept, the lexicon is much more than a list of words existing in a language or for a particular speaker. First, it must contain an inventory of all morphemes or at least their unpredictable, idiosyncratic properties. Second, the *possible* words of a language must be characterized, possibly by word-formation rules.[2] Finally, the phonological rules, as far as they state phonological generalizations holding for the shapes of simple or complex words, are also considered to be part of the lexicon.

As shown in (1), Lexical Phonology proposes that there are two 'places' for phonology in the organization of a grammar. Phonological rules may in principle apply in the lexicon and outside it. More specifically, it is possible for the same phonological rule to apply in the lexicon, determining the shape of morphemes or words, or outside the lexicon, in the *postlexical phonology* of (1), functioning at a phrasal level. The rule of Nasal Assimilation, which is explored in greater detail in § 7.3.4, may be used to illustrate the point. Basically, the rule states that the place features of a nasal are identical to those of the following consonant. On the one hand, the rule may account for the fact that a labial consonant can only be preceded by a nasal which is also labial. In other words, intramorphemically no sequences such as */nb/ or */ŋp/ can occur. In these cases, the rule of Nasal Assimilation clearly operates within the lexicon, since it specifies the types of phoneme sequences which can make up a morpheme in Modern Standard German. This kind of rule is known as a *morpheme structure condition*, but in Lexical Phonology it can be assumed to be a normal phonological rule.

On the other hand, this very rule accounts for the fact that words ending in a nasal can be observed to alternate in a way that /n/ may optionally surface as [m] if a labial consonant starts the following word: see i[n/m] *Bonn* 'in Bonn' or ei[n/m] Boot 'a boat' and a wider range of cases presented in § 7.3.4. This rule cannot be lexical since it operates not on a single word, but rather on adjacent words within a phrase whose nature must be explored. Given that the change and the structural conditions for Nasal Assimilation are identical in the lexical and the non-lexical rule, it seems adequate to assume that there is only

---

[2] The difference between actual and possible words has been touched upon in § 4.1.4, where I argued that morphological regularities refer to possible, and not actual, words. However, the existence of unproductive morphology and the fact that speakers have some intuition on whether they 'know' a particular word or not, forces us to acknowledge that the lexicon also lists some of the actual words for a speaker, or at least their unpredictable properties.

one single rule. To be sure, there are important differences between the lexical and the postlexical variant of Nasal Assimilation. One of these is the possibility of *free variation*, the optional application noted for the postlexical case. The same rule in the function of a morpheme structure condition applies obligatorily, though sometimes with lexically specified exceptions. But the theory of Lexical Phonology relates these differences to principles of the grammatical components in which the rules happen to operate, and not to information directly encoded with the rule itself. In Chapter 7 on the phonological rules of Modern Standard German, I note for each rule whether it is supposed to be a lexical rule, a postlexical rule, or, possibly, both.

The next major aspect of the theory is the close 'cooperation' of morphology and phonology mentioned above and also illustrated in (1). Why assume this kind of interaction? Apart from numerous other considerations, rather compelling evidence is provided by cases where a phonological rule feeds a morphological rule, that is, the output of a phonological rule provides a necessary ingredient of the input to a morphological rule. Any model which treats morphology independently of phonology, for example by applying all morphological rules before all phonological rules, will have difficulties with such phenomena. In the preceding chapter, it is claimed that the constraints on some affixations of German, in particular noun derivation by the suffix +*ei*, prefixation with *ge*+ and *be*+, and the allomorphy between the suffix forms +*heit* and +*keit*, provide exactly such cases. Phonological rules creating prosodic structure are necessarily applied prior to the application of morphological rules. This range of facts provides strong evidence for the particular use of the cycle made in Lexical Phonology, although I will discuss a slightly different interpretation in § 5.2.3 below.

It should be mentioned at this point that I am not committed to the claim, often made with respect to English, that only the so-called *major categories* of nouns, verbs, and adjectives are subject to affixation and to lexical rules in general. There is, in German, clearly affixation of and to other categories, such as adverb-forming +(*e*)*n* or +*s*; consider *inn+en*, *gester+n* and *recht+s*, *nacht+s*. In addition, articles and possessive pronouns are inflected just as adjectives are.[3] On the phonological side, it is hard to see why prepositions and conjunctions, in particular the bisyllabic ones, can be assumed to be exempt from the rules assigning word stress. The rules of word stress being a clear case of a lexical rule, we must conclude that all words, including the function words, are derived in the lexicon. Finally, prepositions also occur in compounds, as we saw in (26) of § 4.2. Since compounding takes place in the lexicon, the conclusion that the lexicon is a component for all classes of words in German becomes rather compelling.

As a final general remark, I should add that there is, on first sight, a contradiction between two claims made in the present work; above it is said that phonological rules in the lexicon apply to strings as they are defined by morphological

---

[3] Possessive pronouns (*mein, dein*) are inflected just like adjectives. In Wiese (1988*b*) I argue that the inflectional endings even for the definite articles (*der, die, das*) are virtually identical to those for strongly inflected adjectives. These observations argue against a non-lexical treatment of the respective word classes.

rule application. Earlier, in § 3.7, I claimed that phonological rules can only apply within phonological domains as provided by prosodic structure. How can this conflict be resolved? I will follow the proposal made by Inkelas (1989) that the first phonological rule triggered by the application of a morphological rule is the formation of a prosodic constituent.[4] This prosodic constituent containing the material of the morphological units (in my interpretation the phonological word ω as introduced in § 3.4) then provides the domain for the application of all other phonological rules, segmental alternations as well as rules of prosodic structure. The basic steps of this procedure are sketched in (2). This version of Lexical Phonology has been named *Prosodic Lexical Phonology* by Inkelas (1989).

(2) *a.* $[[\ ]_A]_B$ derivation of morphological constituent B
    b. $[X]_\omega$ derivation of phonological word
    c. $[Y]_\omega$ application of phonological rules to X

5.2. MORE ON MORPHOLOGY AND THE LEXICON OF GERMAN

5.2.1. Two classes of morphology

In the preceding chapter, it was shown how, in a number of different cases, phonological rules can and must feed morphological rules. Ultimately, this is due to the fact that morphological rules may be seen to operate partly on phonological representations. Lexical Phonology as sketched in (1) allows precisely such interactions. We now turn to a further aspect of Lexical Phonology, the partitioning of word-derivational processes into several distinct sets on both morphological and phonological grounds.

A first approximation to the issues related to this topic is the fact, well known from studies of English morphology (Siegel 1974; Kiparsky 1982*a*, *b*), that the derivational affixes of this language can be divided into two sets, on the basis of their relative position in a word and their behaviour with respect to phonological rules such as Stress Assignment. As pointed out by Giegerich (1985), the same division can be assumed for German. I will briefly consider the observations that lead to the postulation of class I and class II morphology. Some of the affixes of German will be assigned to different classes from those used in previous treatments. For example, Giegerich (1985: 28, 105) treats +*isch* and (nominal) +*er* as class II suffixes. I argue below that they should be classified as class I. On the basis of their behaviour in plural suffixation, +*ling*, +*nis* and +*tum* are also, in § 5.3.2, argued to belong to class I. The lists below are long, but not totally exhaustive.[5] The various ways of derivation without an explicit affix (zero-affixation or conversion) are not considered. I also ignore those root-adjacent suffixes which seem to behave like the so-called theme vowels in other languages, such as /u/ in *sex+u+ell*, *grad+u+ier+en* or /i/ in *offiz+i+ell*, *Mobil+i+ar*.

---

[4] Instead of the general rule of prosodic constituent formation, there may be a more specific rule leading, for example, to two phonological words.

[5] On +*is* as a suffix, see fn. 21 in Ch. 4. It seems reasonable to assume that +*iz* (/its/) is its shape variant before +*ität*, see *Elektr+iz+ität*. On nominal +*er*, which is listed twice, see also below.

The proposed assignment of derivational suffixes to the two classes is as shown in (3) and (4), with a classification according to the resulting word class and with examples of words derived with each suffix. Inflectional suffixation for nouns and verbs will be analysed in § 5.3 below.

(3) Suffixes of class I

    a. Noun-forming

+a	Dram+a, Skal+a
+age	Spion+age, Report+age
+and	Doktor+and, Konfirm+and
+ant	Demonstr+ant, Protest+ant
+anz	Akzept+anz, Konst+anz
+ar	Archiv+ar, Bibliothek+ar
+at	Kandid+at, Magistr+at
+at	Dekan+at, Filtr+at
+ei	Mogel+ei, Plauder+ei
+ent	Präsid+ent, Absolv+ent
+enz	Assist+enz, Frequ+enz
+er	Bäck+er, Mal+er
+eur	Fris+eur, Installat+eur
+ie	Phantas+ie, Biolog+ie
+ik	Linguist+ik, Mus+ik
+ion	Produkt+ion, Funkt+ion
+is	Sozial+is+t, real+is+ier+en
+ität	Neutral+ität, Total+ität
+ling	Schäd+ling, Sträf+ling
+nis	Verständ+nis, Vermächt+nis
+o	Tri+o, Kommand+o
+on	Elektr+on, Stadi+on
+or	Profess+or, Direkt+or
+tum	Eigen+tum, Piraten+tum
+um	Stadi+um, Sanatori+um
+ur	Korrekt+ur, Konjunkt+ur
+us	Radi+us, Typ+us

    b. Adjective-forming

+abel	vari+abel, diskut+abel
+al	diagon+al, radik+al
+är	reaktion+är, vision+är
+ant	interess+ant, mark+ant
+ell	kommerz+i+ell, manu+ell
+esk	kafka+esk, ballad+esk
+isch	fantast+isch, kind+isch
+iv	akt+iv, relat+iv
+os/ös	grandi+os, nebul+ös

    c. Verb-forming

+er	geist+er+n, löch+er+n
+ier	produz+ier+en, diskut+ier+en
+(e)l	tänz+el+n (from tanz+en), deut+el+n (from deut+en)

The suffixes +*a*, +*um*, +*us* are special in that they are replaced by +*en* in the plural form of the nouns: *Dram+a* vs. *Dram+en*, and so on. This might be handled by marking these suffixes explicitly with [− plural], while the other noun suffixes are literally unmarked in that they are unspecified with respect to the number feature. For these latter words, plural suffixes add [+ plural], and non-suffixed forms are [− plural] by default. Final +*i* as in *Vati*, *Bubi* (see (52) and (53) in § 3.3.3) is not regarded as a suffix here. Rather, it is a prespecified segment as part of the foot template which serves as the basis in the prosodic morphology of these words.

(4) Suffixes of class II

a. *noun-forming*		b. *Adjective-forming*		c. *Verb-forming*	
+er	Physik+er, Gewerkschaft+er	+bar	ess+bar, durchführ+bar	?+ig	rein+ig+en, pein+ig+en
+heit/keit	Ganz+heit, Höflich+keit	+haft	glaub+haft, formel+haft		
+sal	Müh+sal, Trüb+sal	+ig	farb+ig, niedr+ig		
+schaft	Wissen+schaft, Wirt+schaft	+lich	weiß+lich, verständ+lich		
+ung	Prüf+ung, Bezieh+ung	+los	farb+los, hoffnungs+los		
		+sam	kleid+sam, spar+sam		

There is a marked difference in the number of available affixes, especially between those for creating nouns and verbs. The single verb-deriving suffix +*ig* of class II is certainly somewhat dubious, since it may in fact be seen as the adjectival suffix +*ig*, with a zero derivation of the verb. This is not the standard analysis (presumably because adjectives *reinig* and *peinig* do not exist), but given that such a derivation is certainly the correct one for cases such as *kräft+ig*$_A$ > *kräft+ig+en*$_V$, and that in § 4.1.4 I argue for similar cases in which intermediate derivations are not actual words, there is nothing wrong in principle with assuming an adjective *rein+ig* (although it does not exist); see in particular the remarks on adjectives derived by affixation of +*ig* in § 4.1.4 above. The form simply is not a lexicalized word because of the availability of both *rein* and *rein+lich* with very similar meanings. *reinig+en* or *kräftig+en* are then equally a result of conversion. While on this topic, I note that the evidence for +*er* in (3c) as a verb-forming suffix is similarly doubtful. In this analysis, it remains unclear why this suffix is found only if the plural suffix of the embedded noun is also +*er*; compare *Geist+er*, *Löch+er*. Fleischer (1982: 322) treats this verbal derivation as zero derivation with plural nouns as its base.

I add a list of some affixes which are neither clearly derivational in nature, nor unambiguously assigned to single levels. In particular, they do not change the word category of the base. But because of their failure to form the paradigms so typical for inflection, and because they do not specify categories relevant in syntax, they are not clearly inflectional either. The distinction between derivation and inflection is of no fundamental importance in Lexical Phonology; I therefore tentatively include the suffixes below among the derivational ones.[6] For the noun suffixes this can be justified by referring to the observation that the suffixes determine the gender of the words just as other derivational affixes do. The suffixes in (5) might be argued to belong to class II, since they seem to follow all derivational suffixes of classes I and II.[7] However, +in will be argued to interact with word stress rules of German in § 8.3.1, and may therefore be a level 1 suffix in these cases. Similarly, Iverson and Salmons (1992) argue that +chen is a suffix of class I as well as II; see also § 7.3.3.

(5) Inflectional/derivational suffixes, class II

a. Noun-modifying	b. Adjective-modifying
+in Linguist+in, Lehr+er+in	+er schön+er, rund+er
+chen Wört+chen, Tisch+chen	+st schön+st, rund+est
+lein Tisch+lein, Büch+lein	

In the general case, it is true that the suffixes classified as belonging to class I are non-native morphemes, which have been borrowed from Latin, Greek, or the Romance languages. This correlation, however, is by no means perfect. Furthermore, most speakers of German will have no access to the information whether suffixes such as +ei, +isch, or +iv are native or not.[8] Note that it is not the case in Modern Standard German that (non-)native affixes attach to (non-)native stems only, see pedant+isch vs. kind+isch or (with +ei in the local meaning) Pfarr+ei vs. Kanzl+ei. A second criterion which is not behind the classification is that of productivity. Although it is true that class II suffixes tend to be more productive than those of class I, in both groups, both highly productive suffixes (+ei, +ung) and very unproductive ones (+o, +schaft) can be found.

The true reasons for the division into the two classes lie in a number of morphological and phonological regularities. For a first argument leading to the classification proposed above, the examples given in (6) are relevant, in which a series of affixes occur. There are some affixes which recurrently can be found immediately after the roots and before some other affixes.

(6) Protest+ant+in
    Mark+ier+ung
    kontinu+ier+lich
    phantas+ie+los
    Präsid+ent+schaft
    Relat+iv+heit

The suffixes directly following the respective roots are classified above as class I, those in the final position as class II. But for any pair of affixes (suffixes)

---

[6] Participle-forming suffixes +end (present participle) and +t/+en (past participle, see §§ 4.1.2 and 5.4) probably also belong to this group, although their status is different.

[7] Diminutive suffixes also exist within class I; see +ett(e) and +in(e) as in Statu+ett+e, Sonat+in+e.

[8] The suffix +ei derives from Medieval Latin and French īe and eia, while +isch is a dependent of Old High German +isc. +iv again derives from Latin and French +ivus and +if. Olsen (1986: 95) classifies +ei and +ier as native suffixes synchronically, presumably on the basis of their productivity. But on the basis of their stress behaviour, they would be classified with the non-native suffixes.

in (6), the reverse order never occurs. On the morphological side, there is thus a constraint to the effect that certain affixes always occur before certain other affixes, and the first affixes are those of class I, the second those of class II. The ordering is independent of the distinction between derivation and inflection, since all the affixes studied are probably derivational affixes. The generalization to make, then, is that affixes of class I are added before any affixes of class II are.

Another observation is that the 'root-close' affixes, those of class I, are also able to attach to *bound roots*, roots which never surface by themselves, without being suffixed. That is, a large number of roots such as *präsid*, *diskut*, and *demonstr* may occur in connection with a number of class I affixes, but neither unaffixed nor with class II affixes alone. Later, in § 5.2.3, I argue that this property follows from the fact that class I affixes attach to bases classified as roots, while class II affixes attach to stems.

At the same time, affixes from one of the classes may occur, in principle, in any order. In (7) this freedom is illustrated for class I, in (8) for class II. Because independent semantic, morphological, and stylistic restrictions exist for any morpheme combination, the number of actual cases is not very high. Nevertheless, examples of free morpheme order *within* a class exist, while no examples are known of such a free ordering relation *between* classes. In (7), I give examples of alternative orderings from class I suffixes, in (8), from class II.

(7) *a.* Dikt+at+or ~ Rekt+or+at
     Medit+at+ion ~ Pens+ion+at
   b. Prakt+ik+ant ~ Rom+ant+ik
     afr+ik+an+isch ~ Rom+an+ik

(8) *a.* Zier+lich+keit ~ obrig+keit+lich
   b. Gewerk+schaft+er ~ Handwerk+er+schaft

Next, it must be noted that the affixes behave very differently with respect to word stress. Class I affixes may either carry word stress and/or influence stress on their base. Class II affixes, in contrast, never attract word stress and never even influence the stress pattern on the preceding syllables. As (9a) demonstrates, each successive class I affix may cause word stress to move, while the series of class II affixes in (9b) has no comparable effect on word stress. (There exists some stress variation for class II words depending on pragmatic and/or semantic factors: in some adjectives derived through class II affixation, optional stress shift can be found; see 'un+möglich vs. un+'möglich. This shift is due to postlexical stress shift rules, see § 8.3.)

(9) *a.* Na't+ion ~ nat+io'n+al ~ Nat+ion+a'l+ist
   b. Frei ~ 'Frei+heit ~ 'frei+heit+lich ~ 'Frei+heit+lich+keit

If these stress regularities hold for the two sets of affixes, it also follows that +*isch* and +*er* belong to class I, as stated in (3). It should be noticed that adjective-forming +*isch* seems to require either that the preceding syllable is stressed or that it is a syllable containing schwa: *fan'tast+isch*, *itali'en+isch*, *'mal+er+isch*. This is the reason why it is classified here as belonging to class I.

In word pairs such as *'Alkohol* vs. *alko'hol+isch*, *'Japan* vs. *ja'pan+isch* it seems to induce a shift of word stress on its bases. Again, since word stress is, by hypothesis, exclusively affected by class I affixes, *+isch* must be diagnosed to belong to this class. (However, in § 7.3.5 on /g/-Deletion I note a problem with this hypothesis.)

Note that the agentive or instrumental suffix *+er* is listed twice, in (3*a*) and (4*a*). It appears that both verb roots (*back, mal*) and noun stems (*Physik, Gewerkschaft*) may act as bases for this suffix. Since in the latter case *+er* may also be outside of class II suffix *+schaft* (see (8*b*)), this variant must be diagnosed as part of class II as well. But *+er* as a suffix to a verb root may precede both *+isch* and *+ei*, and is consequently also assigned to class I. In (10), a number of examples are given. I propose an analysis of such dual attachments in § 5.2.3 below.

In *Ja'pan+er* from *'Japan* and *'Mus'ik+er* from *Mu's+ik*, there is also the shift of word stress which can, according to the theory, only be caused by class I suffixes. This seems to be in conflict with the fact that *+er* here is the noun-forming affix supposed to belong to class II. In § 8.3.1, I argue that the stress shift is a property of their respective bases, that is, of *Japan* and the suffix *+ik*, and only superficially caused by the suffix *+er*.

(10) *a.* mal+er+isch, verrät+er+isch
  b. Bäck+er+ei, Mal+er+ei

A brief look at the prefixes is also in order, since analogous relationships can be shown to hold. The prefixes listed (without any claim to exhaustiveness) in (11) may be regarded as class I prefixes, those in (12) as belonging to class II. (12*b*) lists those prepositions which can also occur as inseparable prefixes; see also § 4.1.2 for discussion.[9]

(11) Prefixes of class I
  in+   in+stabil, il+legal
  sub+   sub+versiv, sub+atom+ar
  re+   re+kultivieren, Re+form
  ex+   ex+poniert, ex+klus+iv
  dis+   Dis+harmonie, dis+kret
  ge+   ge+brauch+en, Ge+bäud+e
  be+   be+halt+en, be+haupt+en

(12) Prefixes of class II

a. un+	un+genau	*b.* durch+	durch+'laufen
ver+	ver+stärken	über+	über+'setzen
er+	er+fahren	unter+	unter+'suchen
ent+	ent+fernen	hinter+	hinter+'gehen
miss+	miss+trauen	um+	um+'fahren
zer+	zer+setzen		

---

[9] The classification of *ver+, er+, ent+, miss+, zer+* as class II prefixes is very preliminary. It is possible, for example, that *ver+* attaching to nouns is a class I prefix; see the morphological bracketing of [[Ver+ständ] nis].

The argument for the assignment to the two classes is quite parallel to the one above. First, class II prefixes can appear outside of class I prefixes, as in *un+sub+stantiell*, while the reverse order is not possible. This is analogous to the ordering constraints found above for suffixes. Secondly, there is an alternation for the nasal of the prefix *in+*, which assimilates the nasal to the following consonant, as in *il+legal, ir+regulär, im+potent*. The respective rule does not apply to the prefix *un+* (see *un+logisch, un+reif, un+parteiisch*), which can be interpreted to mean that the assimilation rule in question is a rule restricted to class I. Assigning *un+* to class II will then automatically prevent it from undergoing the assimilation rule.

Notice that unstressed *ge+* and *be+* are taken to be elements of class I.[10] Evidence for this move comes from the fact that roots can be subcategorized for these two prefixes: *Ge+fahr, be+haupt+en*. Also, class II prefixes may occur outside of *ge+* and *be+*, but not in reverse order: *un+ge+fähr+lich, un+be+ständ+ig*. This treatment of these two suffixes does not extend to *ge+* in past participles as discussed in § 4.1.2. In general, it may turn out to be neither necessary nor sufficient to assign each affix to exactly one of the classes. A complete lack of class assignment for this particular prefix is argued for in § 5.2.3 below.

As expected, several prefixes can be stacked on top of each other. The ordering constraint built into the class distinction above never seems to be violated; prefixes of class I are closer to the root than those of class II. There also exist some (limited) ways for permuting prefixes belonging to the same class, as shown in (13). This is again as predicted: disregarding the existence of other possible constraints, order of prefixes is constant between the two classes, but open within classes.

(13) *a.* un+ver+einbar ~ ver+un+reinigen
      un+ver+dient ~ ver+un+treuen
  b. Vor+über+legung ~ über+vor+teilen

We can summarize at this point some of the properties associated with the two classes in question: class I affixes are such that they may be accompanied by some non-automatic phonological rules, such as Assimilation. They also attract word stress and/or induce a stress shift, while on the morphological side they are always closer to the word's root than class II affixes. In the following section, these differences will be accounted for by reference to two different parts of the lexicon.

As mentioned already, all cases can be diagnosed unambiguously, and I will now refer to a few cases of uncertainty. One of the puzzling cases is noun-final schwa. Apart from its function as an inflectional marker for nouns, verbs, and adjectives in word-final position, schwa occurs in nouns such as those in (14). While this is often ignored, there are good arguments to assume that in

---

[10] If this is correct, as it seems to be on the basis of the ordering facts, it proves again the impossibility of reducing the class distinction to foreignness or a feature [± native].

noun-final position schwa is a derivational suffix, as proposed by Wurzel (1970: § 2.1). One such argument is that +*e*, just like any other derivational suffix, determines its plural marker: all nouns ending in +*e* have a corresponding plural suffix +*en*. The assignment of this suffix to a class I or II is difficult because it does not co-occur with any other derivational suffix. Therefore, no ordering relation can be established. As shown in (14*a, c*) vs. (14*b, d*), it also attaches equally well to native and foreign stems.[11]

(14) *a.* Wies+e   *b.* Statu+e
        Katz+e   Melon+e
        Freud+e   Raket+e
     c. Aug+e   *d.* Interess+e
        Ries+e   Phonolog+e
        Glaub+e   Kolleg+e

Note that I regard *all* noun-final schwas as instances of a noun-forming suffix. Another argument for the suffix status of word-final schwa would be that it does not occur if another derivational suffix occurs (see different types of examples with stems taken from (14) in (15)). While it is possible, of course, to assume that schwa is deleted under certain circumstances (see analyses by Kloeke 1982, Strauss 1982), it seems preferable to assume that schwa is simply not suffixed if another noun-forming suffix is chosen. Deleting +*e* as a morpheme would also be a case of truncation against which I argue on principled grounds in § 4.1.2.

(15) *a.* Ries+in   *b.* Äug+chen   *c.* interess+ant
        Phonolog+in   Kätz+chen   statu+ar+isch
        Kolleg+in   Melön+chen   ries+ig

With Harnisch (1994), I assume that the plural suffix +*en* is in paradigmatic contrast to +*e*. That is, +*e* marks the singular, and +*en* the plural for this class of nouns. However, this does not imply truncation of +*e* to describe the alternation: both +*e* and +*en* attach to stems unmarked for number and fix the values of this category. For the time being, +*e* will be taken as a class II suffix. A very similar suffix is +*en* in words such as *Gart+en, Brunn+en, Daum+ en*. These words are of masculine gender, and the suffix +*en* is not present in derivations such as *Gärt+chen, Brünn+lein, Däum+ling*.

Some, perhaps apparent, problems in the assignment of suffixes to classes are caused by the derivational suffixes +*or* and +*ik* because of their behaviour with respect to word stress. Words derived by +*or* bear stress on the syllable preceding the suffix, but only if no other suffix follows: *Pro'fess+or, Dik'tat+or*. If another suffix follows, stress is shifted so that the suffix itself may receive stress: *Profes's+or+en, dikta't+or+isch*. For closer inspection of the stress patterns involved in +*or*-suffixation see § 8.3.

---

[11] Words in (14*a, b*) (the large majority) have feminine gender, those in (14*c, d*) masculine or neuter gender. That is, this suffix does not completely determine the gender of the stem as most other suffixes do. The suffix +*tum* has the same property, though: a few cases are of masculine gender (*Irr+tum, Reich+tum*), the large majority are neuter.

Facts relating to +*ik* are slightly more complex. A closed set of words, those given in (16*a*), shows this suffix with final stress. All other words with final +*ik* display penultimate stress. That is, the words in (16*b*) illustrate the productive case. Also, when further suffixation occurs (16*c*), stress is on the syllable preceding +*ik* in all cases.[12]

(16) *a.* Mathema't+ik, Mu's+ik, Phy's+ik, Poli't+ik
     b. Lingu+'ist+ik, Gram'mat+ik, Sta'tist+ik
     c. Gram'mat+ik+er, 'Mus+ik+er, Mathe'mat+ik+er

It is not the aim of the present chapter to account for the stress regularities of derived words in German. Rather, I defer this discussion to § 8.3. For the present purposes, it is sufficient to note that the two suffixes interact with stress in complex ways. Since +*or* and +*ik* bear main word stress under certain conditions, we may conclude that they are both class I suffixes.

5.2.2. Level ordering in the German lexicon

The observations on class I and II morphology in the previous section have led to the proposal that the lexicon (of German) contains two ordered blocks, two sub-lexica so to speak, in which morphological and phonological rules are applied. In Lexical Phonology, this distinction has been generalized by postulating that a lexicon may in principle be divided into a number of lexical components called *levels* or *strata*. These may be seen as ordered sub-lexica with which morphological and phonological rules are associated. The properties associated above with class I morphology (closeness to roots, word-stress assignment) are taken to be properties of the first level in the lexicon, those of class II of a subsequent, second, level. Obviously, the ordering relation between the two classes follows immediately, if a word derivation requires the application of all level-1 rules before application of level-2 rules.

While the analysis of the derivational suffixes leads to the postulation of two lexical levels, this is not a statement on the complete range of relevant facts. Inflection and compounding must also be considered. Including both of these domains leads to a richer structure of the lexicon, as I will now try to demonstrate.

Compounding (for a survey on compound types in German see § 4.2) can be shown to interact with class II affixation. Words affixed by class II affixes may occur as left elements in compounds, as shown in (17*a*).[13] But compounds may also undergo class II derivation; see (17*b*). Examples are somewhat more difficult to find because of a potential structural ambiguity. With affixes on the right-hand heads of compounds, it is hard to decide whether the affix takes the whole compound or its right-most subpart. The structure of *Farbenblindheit* could be [[farben][blind+heit]] or [[farben blind]heit]. However, for the examples given in (17*b*), the first type of structure does not seem to be motivated. Note, though,

---

[12] Of course, stress-attracting suffixes such as +*al* cause the word stress to fall on a position further to the right: *phys+i'k+al+isch*, *mus+i'k+al+isch*.

[13] The *Fugenmorpheme* (*s*, *en*) appearing within compounds are discussed in § 5.3.3 below.

that +*tum* is classified in (3*a*) as a class I suffix and see the remarks on bracketing paradoxes in § 5.4.

(17) *a.* [Neu+ig+keits] [wert]
      [Verhandl+ungs] [basis]
      [Eigen+tums] [recht]
   b. [[gegen ständ] lich]
      [[Spieß bürger] tum]
      [[ober lehrer] haft]

In other words, class II affixation and compounding may feed each other; there is no fixed ordering between the two processes. In Lexical Phonology, this mutual feeding of class II affixation and compounding is accounted for by assigning both of these sets of rules to a common level in the lexicon. This level of compounding should be one level earlier than the final level because the larger part of inflection cannot be found inside compounds. In particular, verbs as left-hand non-heads in compounds occur only as pure stems; see [V X] compounds in (26) of § 4.2.

If it is true that a large portion of the inflectional markers, notably in verbal inflection, only occurs outside all other word formation, the general model of morphology must reflect this. Lexical Phonology accounts for this fact by postulating a level in the lexicon which is ordered after the levels on which derivation and compounding take place. These considerations lead to the postulation that the lexicon for Modern Standard German is composed of three lexical levels as diagrammed in (18), in accordance with a proposal by Kiparsky (1982*b*) for English.[14] For the sake of concreteness, some morphological and phonological rules mentioned so far are assigned to their respective levels. The status of the irregular inflection on level 1 will be clarified in the discussion of plural formation in § 5.3.2. Schwa Epenthesis is distributed in intricate ways over the grammar of German; one of its occurrences is with regular inflection of nouns and verbs; see § 7.4.2.

(18) Lexicon of German

	morphology	phonology
level 1	irregular inflection class I affixes	⇄ Word Stress
level 2	compounding class II affixes	⇄ Compound Stress
level 3	regular inflection	⇄ Schwa Epenthesis

Evidence for such a three-level lexicon for Modern Standard German comes from various sources. The ordering and feeding relationships between sets of morphological processes (derivation, compounding, inflection) have just been

---

[14] Researchers disagree widely on the number of lexical levels to be assumed for language-particular lexica. Proposals for English, for example, range from two to four lexical levels (cf. Kiparsky 1985; and Halle and Mohanan 1985). And, of course, the need for distinguishing lexical levels can be denied altogether; see Sproat (1985) or Fabb (1988).

discussed. Blocking effects within inflection, where application of a rule on an early level blocks the application of a similar rule on a later level, will be introduced in § 5.3. The feeding relationships between various phonological rules as discussed in Chapter 7 add more details to the proposal. Compound stress, for example, respects word stress. That is, the syllable which is strongest in the prominent element of a compound surfaces as the strongest syllable in the whole compound. The interaction of inflection and compounding as predicted by the model in (18) will be demonstrated in the discussion of the *Fugenmorpheme* in § 5.3.3.

5.2.3. **Lexical levels or lexical categories?**

Traditional models of morphology distinguish between the notions of *root, stem,* and *word* which are hierarchically related to each other. That is, a word will contain at the deepest level a (single) root, which is embedded in a stem and, finally, a word. This division is obviously reminiscent of the proposal of a three-level lexicon expressed in (18). That is, it might be possible to associate level-1 processes with root-related regularities, level 2 with the stem, and level 3 with the word.

To give a concrete example, it would be quite natural to suppose that *kontinu* is a root to which *+ier* is added as a suffix which is subcategorized for roots; see (19). (A possible morphological analysis of *kontin+u* is ignored here. Both *kontin+* and *kontinu+* are bound, i.e. non-free, roots.) The verbal root *kontinuier* also acts as a stem, to which a stem-related suffix *+lich* may be attached. On the word level, the adjective may be inflected, for example by *+es*. The resulting structure would be as in (19). This description presupposes a rule schema for the syntax of words which generally allows a root to be dominated by a stem, and a stem by a word.

(19) *kontinu+ier+lich+es*

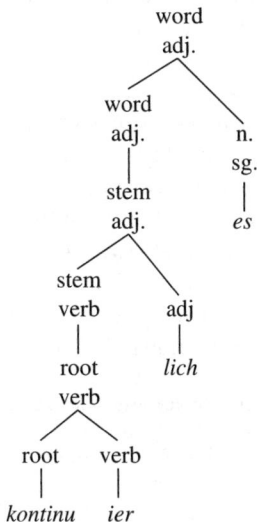

The first affixation illustrated in (19) thus leads to a *derived* root, which is perhaps a less common notion. It is, however, necessary in the present framework to assume that the affixes do not change the lexical category of their bases, since affixes such as +*ier* may be attached to roots directly or to roots bearing other affixes already, as in a verb root *nat+ion+al+is+ier*. There is no reason to assume that we are dealing here with two homophonous affixes with the shape of /iːʀ/ or with one affix with two subcategorization frames. In general, I will assume that roots, stems, and words are recursive categories, reflecting the fact that several word-building processes are possible on each of the lexical levels discussed above.[15] As illustrated in (19), roots may be (but need not be) unspecified for lexical categories.

Similar proposals, identifying levels with categories such as root, stem, and word, have been made by other authors, notably Selkirk (1982), Giegerich (1988), Inkelas (1989), and Goldsmith (1990); although, to my knowledge, in each of these analyses only two out of the three categories—root, stem, and word—have been made use of.[16] These proposals, including the present one, see lexical level ordering as being primarily or exclusively grounded in the morphology, while other approaches (in particular Mohanan 1986; Halle and Mohanan 1985) base level ordering on phonological regularities.

To illustrate the usefulness of a category approach, I consider the relationship between the noun-final schwa discussed above and its disjunctive relationship to other derivational suffixes in § 5.3.1 below. One of the problems for the level-ordering hypothesis noted several times before might be less severe under the category approach: certain affixes seem to belong not uniquely to one particular level, but attach at two different levels. Aronoff (1976) and Selkirk (1982) claim this to be true for +*ment* in English, which has different properties in *experi+ment* (level 1) and *employ+ment* (level 2). But if affixes are simply subcategorized for taking roots, stems, or words, then it would only be a marked case if an affix had to be subcategorized for two such categories. The mechanism of subcategorization allows for such multiple subcategorizations in any case. The nominalizing suffix +*er* was diagnosed above to be exactly of this kind: it accepts both verb roots and noun stems. (The prefix *ver+* may exemplify the exact reverse, taking noun roots and verb stems; as in *Ver+stand* vs. *ver+un+sicher+n*.) In the model proposed here, such affixes would have, as part of their lexical entry, two corresponding subcategorization frames. Given that the morphological and semantic properties of the two variants of each suffix seem identical, this solution is to be preferred over one which assigns two such suffixes to two different levels in the lexicon. The existence of such suffixes is expected in the present framework and may be used to counter some of the level-ordering paradoxes pointed out by authors such as Aronoff and Sridhar (1987).

---

[15] As Giegerich (1994) points out, such a model of level ordering in the lexicon can be seen as *base-driven*, in contrast to the usual description of level ordering as being *affix-driven*.

[16] Goldsmith (1990: § 5.1.4) recognizes root, stem, and word as necessary categories for the description of Bantu languages, but proceeds to propose two lexical strata.

A further possibility is instantiated by *ge+* in past participles. The treatment of this prefix in § 4.1.2 avoids mentioning any level assignment. Instead, other morphological and prosodic information was implemented in the subcategorization frame of the prefix. The result is that *ge+* will affix to any suitable participle, regardless of level. As argued by Marcus et al. (1995), it is indeed the case that participles are formed on verbal roots in the case of irregular verbs, and on stems in the case of regular verbs. If this is correct, the features for roots, stems, or words should not be mentioned in the rule for *ge*-Prefixation. The suffix is free to attach to any of these categories. Level-free suffixes are again not anomalous in the present proposal.

If the sketch given here is correct, another question arises: do lexical rules (morphological or phonological) refer to roots, stems, and words, because they are assigned to levels 1, 2, or 3, or is it the other way round? In other words, is it the lexical levels or the lexical categories which are primary? This is not a question devoid of empirical and theoretical content, although it might at first appear that the replacement of levels by the lexical categories is no more than a terminological change, bringing the terminology more in line with that of traditional morphology.

One reason for shifting the approach from a level-ordered to a category-based lexicon might be that it becomes easier under the second approach to formulate regularities in terms of *features*. Root, stem, and word as categories can more readily be decomposed into a non-arbitrary featural description than levels 1, 2, and 3. The lexical category system might, for example, be interpreted in a way similar to systems of X'-syntax. For X'-syntax, featural encodings are available, as by Muysken (1986).

These considerations might also lead to a new description of compounding in German. First, compounds of the type *Psycho+logie*, *Spektro+graph*, *Thermometer* can be interpreted as root compounds. Note, for example, that the parts in such compounds do not have to exist as free morphemes. Second, the typical (nominal and adjectival) compounds of German can be seen as compounded stems. For these, we find that regular inflection does not occur compound-internally, as is to be expected for a stem. For illustration and discussion, see the following section. Finally, the separable particle verbs of German such as *auf+hören* can be regarded as involving words, which would make the separability of its parts a natural consequence.

Stating all morphological and (lexical) phonological regularities in feature structures including features for the lexical categories leads to another central aspect. In Chapter 4 and in the present one I argue that phonology must be allowed to operate cyclically, given that phonological rules may depend on the prior application of morphological rules. Conceivably, however, the case for the cycle is much weaker under the assumption that the types of regularities covered here are definable as wellformedness conditions expressed in feature structures. It would then be possible to allow the application of a rule at any point where its featural conditions are met. A rule requiring a stem, for example, will only apply when the stem features have been introduced, while a root-related rule will cease to be applicable at this point. No other statement on rule ordering seems necessary.

Finally, note that the approach sketched here will treat a lexical entry surfacing as a seemingly underived word as much richer in morphological structure. A simple noun such as *Bett* will emerge from the lexicon as $_{word}[_{stem}[_{root}[Bett]]]$. Because of this fact, a derived environment (in the technical sense used in § 5.3.1) is created for all underlying entries. It is for this reason that the claim that some phonological rules must apply to underived forms is not necessary in the present framework.

I leave these speculations as an area for future research. The sections on nominal inflection below give some substance to what I mean by rules and well-formedness conditions which have to be fulfilled on various levels or, alternatively, for various lexical categories.

5.3. LEXICAL PRINCIPLES AND THE SYSTEM OF NOMINAL INFLECTION

Lexical Phonology postulates a number of principles or constraints, which ensure a restricted system of rules and representations. I will attempt to illustrate and discuss the major examples of such principles as they are formulated mostly in the work by Kiparsky (1982*a*, *b*; 1983, 1985) by presenting an analysis of some relevant cases from German. I then turn towards a consideration of nominal inflection in German. Since nouns in Modern Standard German display a relatively rich system of inflectional categories, endings, and allomorphic variants of these endings, there is a wide testing ground for the ideas developed within Lexical Phonology.

The concept of the lexicon developed here assumes that all word-structure formation including inflection takes place in the lexicon. This is a controversial claim, in that at least inflection is often assigned to the syntactic component (see, e.g., Anderson 1982; 1988; Chomsky 1991). I therefore present another line of evidence for the model of Lexical Phonology, this time involving patterns in inflectional suffixation, in particular the plural formation of German nouns.

5.3.1. **Principles in Lexical Phonology**

A basic motivation for the principles of Lexical Phonology derives from the concern to rule out excessively abstract solutions to problems of phonological analysis. To this purpose, a number of conditions constraining the application of phonological rules have been formulated. I will now briefly introduce these principles.

Consider the *Umlaut* rule fronting back vowels in Modern Standard German, the subject of § 7.2.1. If not constrained in some way, we might propose that any fronted vowel with a back counterpart is the output of this rule. Thus, in *f*[y]*r*, *sch*[ø]*n*, [ε]*cke*, the vowels would derive from /u/, /o/, /a/, respectively. Since the Umlaut rule exists independently, and since the latter vowels are unmarked compared to vowels from the first set (see (2) in § 6.1), this move might be argued to lead to a simpler grammar.

To be sure, either words surfacing with front vowels would have to be marked for undergoing the Umlaut rule, or words surfacing with back vowels would have to be marked for *not* undergoing this rule. Otherwise no back vowels would ever appear. But given that some amount of exception marking is necessary anyhow in the case of Umlaut, this does not drastically change the picture. Vennemann (1968) and Bach and King (1970), who actually proposed an analysis of this sort, made Umlaut dependent on a suffix and assigned such an umlaut-causing suffix to each root which they considered to undergo Umlaut. Thus, [fyːʀ] might be represented underlyingly as /fuːr+e/.

I have now demonstrated how, for the front vowels of German, an abstract solution of the kind proposed in *SPE* might be construed. As critics of such proposals have pointed out (e.g. Kiparsky 1973), it is counter-intuitive and problematic to assume this obligatory application of a rule to all instances of a morphological form. In addition to such analyses as the hypothetical one sketched here for umlauting vowels, it also allows for the postulation of underliers which never surface. This possibility leads to problems of learnability and an unwanted degree of arbitrariness.

What is needed, then, is a way of restricting certain phonological rules to cases of observable alternations. In a series of attempts to achieve this goal, Kiparsky proposed the *Strict Cycle Condition*, a principle requiring a derived environment for all structure-changing rules. It presupposes that a subset of phonological rules is cyclic. Cyclic rules, according to a theory first developed by Mascaró (1976), apply in a particular domain A, but not in a subdomain B, the material of which is already fully present in the previous cycle.

We may equate these cyclic rules with the lexical rules. The condition is then a constraint on the application of lexical phonological rules. The particular formulation of this condition in (20) from Kiparsky (1982*b*: 41) admits the application of both morphological and phonological rules as leading to a derived environment. Kiparsky offers another formulation of this condition, according to which the application of most phonological rules would not create a derived environment:

(20) Strict Cycle Condition (Kiparsky 1985: 89)
> *a.* Cyclic rules apply only to derived representations.
> *b.* Def.: A representation Φ is *derived* with respect to rule R in cycle j iff Φ meets the structural analysis of R by virtue of a combination of morphemes introduced in cycle j or the application of a phonological rule in cycle j.

We can see now how the Umlaut rule under the *Strict Cycle Condition* is excluded from an application to underlying /fuːʀ/ in order to derive [fyːʀ]. Thereby it enforces the non-abstract representation of these words, since there is no other way to derive the front vowels in underived words.[17] And indeed, application of Umlaut always requires 'a combination of morphemes'; see examples in § 7.2.1.

An even more important concept discussed in relation to Lexical Phonology (but not only there) is the *Elsewhere Condition*. Suppose there are two phonological or morphological rules with compatible input conditions, but different results (outputs). How do we know which rule to apply, and may both of them apply? The question is quite to the point, given the different rules for plural affixation in German already mentioned or the various rules discussed in Chapters 6 and 7 providing values for each phonological feature.

Kiparsky suggests that for some such rules their relationship is regulated by the Elsewhere Condition as stated in (21). The condition only refers to those rules whose environments stand in an subset relation to each other, and claims that, if two rules compete under such conditions, only one of the rules will apply, namely the more specific one.

(21) Elsewhere Condition (Kiparsky 1983: 138)
    Rules A, B in the same component apply disjunctively if, and only if,
    (i) the input of A is a proper subset of the input of B,
    (ii) the outputs of A and B are distinct.
    In that case A (the particular rule) is applied first, and if it takes effect, then B (the general rule) is not applied.

It has been pointed out that things could hardly be different from the way predicted by the condition stated in (21). If the more general rule had priority, the more specific rule would never have a chance to apply; it would simply not exist since no evidence for it could ever surface. Nevertheless, the Elsewhere Condition seems to work in stating the relationships between a number of rules, in particular in accounting for the phenomenon of blocking, already mentioned in § 4.1.4 above.

As a further example within morphology, consider the relationship between word-final schwa in nouns as illustrated in (14) and other suffixes. As shown in (15), this suffix does not appear if another noun-forming suffix is present. We may assume that schwa as a suffix represents the more general case if compared to the other suffixes. If this suffix +e is subcategorized for stems and adds no other features (except, perhaps, for gender), it is more general than other suffixes of this class, which are more specific, as they add other morphological features (noun, verb, diminutive, etc.).

The subcategorization schemata in (22) illustrate this point. As in Chapter 4, I assume that lexical entries for derivational suffixes state the conditions under which these suffixes may be inserted into abstract morphological structures, as

---

[17] Later in this section, I discuss the attempt to make the Strict Cycle Condition superfluous by letting it follow from the Elsewhere Condition and from a notion of the lexical entry according to which an underived lexical entry is a very special rule (Kiparsky 1982b: 46).

defined by very general word-formation rules. A specific 'rule' like the one in (22b) for the diminutive is given priority, by the Elsewhere Condition, over the rule introducing noun-final schwa as stated in (22a). Furthermore, once (22b) has applied, the rule introducing schwa may not be applied later.

(22) *a.* +*e*: $\begin{bmatrix} \begin{bmatrix} + \text{N} \\ - \text{V} \\ + \text{stem} \end{bmatrix} \underline{\hspace{1cm}} \end{bmatrix}$ *b.* +*chen* $\begin{bmatrix} \begin{bmatrix} + \text{N} \\ - \text{V} \\ + \text{stem} \end{bmatrix} \underline{\hspace{1cm}} \end{bmatrix}_{[+ \text{ diminutive}]}$

Within phonology, the Elsewhere Condition provides a way of capturing the mode of application between rules such as the different feature-filling rules discussed in the following chapter.

Lexical Phonology explicitly endorses a concept of rule in which both completely general regularities as well as phenomena with a very restricted range are covered as instances of a 'rule'. Consider how one might differentiate between rule-governed and non-rule-governed phenomena in a language. The more general a regularity is, the more willing we are to attribute the regularity to a rule. But there is no clear or well-defined cut-off point at which a rule stops and an exception begins. Does a rule have to apply to five or to fifty items before it is properly called a rule? Or, perhaps more to the point, how productive does a regularity have to be before it is properly described by means of a rule? Consequently, we might even think of a particular lexical entry as a rule, a rule on the phonological form of a single word. Thus, the statement expressing the fact that the German word for 'table' consists of the phoneme sequence /tɪʃ/ is simply a very specific rule in comparison to the very general rule stating that all vowels are voiced in German. In the words of Kiparsky (1982b: 55–6): 'Thus the lexical entries themselves are the end points of the above-mentioned hierarchies of successively more specific rules.'

At this point we can consider how this conception might make the stipulation of the Strict Cycle Condition superfluous. If a lexical entry of an underived lexical item such as *Turm* constitutes nothing but a specific rule (a lexical identity rule, see (23a)), then a phonological rule describing an alternation such as the Umlaut rule (informally stated in (23b); see § 7.2.1) stands in a disjunctive relationship to the former rule (see also Giegerich 1988). Thus, as required by the Elsewhere Condition, umlauting cannot apply to *Turm*. But the morphologically complex plural [[*turm*] *e*] as the output of (level 1) morphology is not a lexical entry, since derived lexical entries, by definition, arise through the completion of a morphological *and* phonological cycle. Thus, the form may undergo the Umlaut rule, and in undergoing this and possibly other phonological rules a derived lexical entry is created.

(23) *a.* /tʊʀm/ → /tʊʀm/
   b. Umlaut: front final vowel

Rules such as syllabification, which assign prosodic structure, on the other hand, should not be banned from applying to underived lexical items. Obviously both *Turm* and *Türme* undergo syllabification. But taking the Elsewhere Condition literally, it appears that a rule assigning syllable structure does not lead to an output which is distinct from the input. Therefore, a syllabification rule does not stand in a disjunctive relationship to the 'rule' specifying the phonological form of individual entries, and may apply freely. In other words, rules of prosodic structure are cyclic, but without being subject to the Strict Cycle Condition.

The Elsewhere Condition is thus a general organizing principle, in the lexicon but perhaps also in other domains, plus, possibly, a principle used to make the Strict Cycle Condition a derivative concept.

Another important constraining principle proposed by Kiparsky (1982; 1985) is that of *structure preservation*. It claims that during the whole course of the lexical derivation, only those phonological features which are distinctive may be introduced by or mentioned in a rule. That is, no lexical phonological rule may refer to a feature which is not a bearer of phonological contrast in that language. In German, for example, a lexical rule could not refer to the features of aspiration (i.e. [spread glottis]), assuming that aspiration (of stops) is not distinctive in German. On the other hand, the Umlaut rule may be a lexical rule, since it refers to the distinction of front vs. non-front vowels, and this is a contrastive distinction, see /u/ vs. /y/.

On the basis of the Dorsal Fricative Assimilation, Hall (1989*b*; 1992*b*) has argued against the principle of structure preservation. In § 7.3.3, I will give this rule a different analysis, with the consequence that Hall's argument against structure preservation does not appear to be valid any more.

Structure preservation as a principle may be thought to follow naturally from the fact that the lexicon is considered as the system responsible for the derivation of *words*. Given that the contrastive features are those which play a role in establishing the phonemic contrasts, things could hardly be otherwise. Note that the contrasts expressed by phonemes or contrastive features are usually defined as *lexical contrasts*.

5.3.2. Plural formation

It has already become apparent in Chapters 3 and 4 that plural formation in Modern Standard Grammar displays rather complex and seemingly untidy properties. I will now show that this impression is only partly true, and that the regularities which hold for plural formation can be stated in the optimal way if the lexical principles described above are considered. In (24), a number of simplex nouns are shown with their plural affixes, separately for the three genders. Whenever possible, I give an umlauted and a non-umlauted noun in its plural form.[18] However, in the following discussion all umlauting of vowels is disregarded, since Umlaut will be treated as a lexical phonological rule in § 7.2.1.

---

[18] Plural suffix +(*e*)*n* never co-occurs with umlaut. Instead, I give a row of nouns with schwa syllables, illustrating the allomorphy of /ən/ vs. /n/.

(24)

	Masculine	Neuter	Feminine
+e	Bäum+e	Flöß+e	Städt+e
	Tisch+e	Schiff+e	
+er	Männ+er	Häus+er	
	Geist+er	Brett+er	
+(e)n	Fürst+en	Bett+en	Frau+en
	Muskel+n		Schwester+n
Ø	Väter	Klöster	Mütter
	Computer	Segel	

Suffix-derived words have basically the same possibilities, as (25) shows. The derivational suffixes determine the shape of their plural suffixes just as nouns do, which provides one argument for treating them analogously in the lexicon. The nouns in (25a) taking +n as plural markers are all feminine. As noted, noun-forming suffix +e also leads to +n as the plural marker. The suffixes +tum, +ling, +nis, and +ar seem to be the only ones taking +er or +e as plural affixes. Suffixes creating a schwa syllable such as +chen or +en may lead to zero suffixation, as discussed in § 4.3.1.

(25) a. Beschreib+ung+en, Neu+heit+en, Wissen+schaft+en
      b. Reich+tüm+er
      c. Sträf+ling+e, Hinder+niss+e, Archiv+ar+e
      d. Blüm+chen, Gärt+en, Lehr+er

In addition to these types of plural nouns, there are words taking +s as a plural marker. Although this type of plural marking is traditionally regarded as non-native and peripheral to the inflectional system of German (see Rettig 1972), the number of nouns taking +s as plural markers is high altogether and several groups can be distinguished. Besides the few consonant-final common nouns illustrated in (26a), which represent various kinds of borrowings, there is a slightly larger group of nouns all ending in a vowel, of which examples are given in (26b)). Additionally, personal names (26c) and abbreviations (26d) take +s as the plural marker.[19] The suffix +o (26e) apparently is the only suffix taking an s-plural.

(26) a. Park+s, Bar+s, Tipp+s, Auto+s, Labor+s,
      b. Büro+s, Kanu+s, Kino+s, Oma+s, Cowboy+s, Eskimo+s
      c. Wiese+s, Dominik+s, Martina+s
      d. AKW+s, LP+s, LKW+s
      e. Tri+o+s, Kommand+o+s

It should be stressed at this point that plural marking by +s cannot be regarded a simple transfer (borrowing) of the English or French plural marker. This can

---

[19] Names and abbreviations ending in +s are special; since gemination of /s/ (as of any other consonant) is not allowed, they take /n/ as an intermediary (empty) suffix, to which the plural marker +s can be added: (die) Hans+en+s, Schmitz+en+s.

be seen from several facts: first, *s*-plurals are in fact older than English (or French) borrowings, see Öhmann (1961–2). Second, new word coinages generally receive this plural ending: take, as an example, the plural of the recent reduplicative formation of *Schickimicki*, which is *Schickimicki+s*; the foot-based clippings presented in § 3.3.3 also invariably show an *s*-plural. Furthermore, there is no reason why the large stock of Germanic personal names (26c) or a suffix such as *+o* should receive a plural ending borrowed from English or French. In this context it is important to stress that the status of *+s* as a borrowed entity is radically different from other borrowed plural markers briefly mentioned below.

Finally, *+s* is overgeneralized in the acquisition of German plurals by children (see Clahsen et al. (1992) for review and data). As Köpcke (1988) shows, this plural marker is also used by adults when they are asked to produce a plural form for a nonsense word (*(der) Treika* vs. *(die) Treika+s*).[20]

Drawing particularly on the fact that names invariably, borrowings and new coinages usually, take the *s*-plural marker, I propose that this suffix is a default plural marker, one that can be added on the final level of the lexicon, the word level. The special categorial status of names and abbreviations is consistent with this assumption: while regular nouns are entered in the lexicon as roots, stems, and words simultaneously (disregarding possible redundancy considerations), names and abbreviations behave as words, but not as roots or stems. To witness this, note that names and abbreviations cannot undergo category-changing derivational processes. From their word status, it follows that names and abbreviations can only take the word-level plural suffix. Note again how naturally these relationships are formulated in a morphological category approach.[21]

To return to the nouns in (24) to (25), there seems to be a strong tendency for feminines to take *+n* as a plural suffix. In (27), a number of word pairs is listed, each in its singular and plural form, where identical strings happen to exist as words with different genders.[22] Nouns in (27a) are masculine or neuter, those in (27b) are feminine. It is obvious that the feminine forms all receive *+n* as a plural marker, in one of its two shapes according to the foot constraint discussed in § 4.3.[23] The non-feminine forms either surface unchanged, if ending in a schwa syllable, or else receive schwa as a plural marker. All of this is as predicted. Additionally, one could propose that *+e* is a regular marker for non-feminine forms, especially masculines. I leave this possibility open, since relevant evidence is rather weak.

[20] For vowel final forms, *s*-plural was actually the dominant form in Köpcke's (1988) study, but it was found to occur under all other conditions.

[21] For normal common nouns of German, *+s* is a very infrequent plural marker. The importance of this suffix lies precisely in the fact that it acts as a default suffix in spite of its low frequency; see Marcus et al. (1995) and Clahsen et al. (1995) for more discussion and empirical evidence. Janda (1990) also concludes that *+s*, in spite of its low frequency with common nouns of German, is the default plural marker in this language.

[22] Some examples are taken from Helbig and Buscha (1987: 275). All of the thirteen suitable pairs listed by these authors follow the constraint.

[23] It is not the case, as proposed by Wurzel (1990: 206–8), that /n/ is the default plural for *monosyllabic* feminine nouns only.

(27) *a.* das Partikel ~ Partikel   *b.* die Partikel ~ Partikel+n

das Partikel ~ Partikel	die Partikel ~ Partikel+n
das Steuer ~ Steuer	die Steuer ~ Steuer+n
das Koppel ~ Koppel	die Koppel ~ Koppel+n
der Kiefer ~ Kiefer	die Kiefer ~ Kiefer+n
der Leiter ~ Leiter	die Leiter ~ Leiter+n
das Mark ~ Mark+e	die Mark ~ Mark+en
der Flur ~ Flur+e	die Flur ~ Flur+en
der Marsch ~ Märsch+e	die Marsch ~ Marsch+en

The pattern apparent from (27) I consider to be evidence for the claim that the regular plural for feminines is +*n*, regardless of the shape of the stem. It is also noteworthy that the observation made in (26*d*) on abbreviations unexceptionally only holds for non-feminine forms: feminine pluralized abbreviations such as *KPen*, *AGen*, or *NPen*, in which we find the suffix +*n* again, are possible (with some speaker variation or uncertainty).[24] In addition, the above examples provide further evidence for the shape constraint discussed several times before: all the plural forms end in a schwa syllable. Note that words with a final schwa syllable in their singular form do not take the *s*-plural, even if they are recent borrowings: (*die*) *Computer* is the only plural form of this word.

Summarizing these observations, I suggest that there are three rules involved in the formation of *regular* plurals in Modern Standard German, formulated in (28) to (30). (29) is repeated from § 4.3.1. I return to the question of level assignment of these rules in a moment. These plural formations may all be called regular in that no exception features or lexical listings are required. In this respect, the present analysis differs from that of Janda (1990) which makes the *s*-plural the only regular plural.

(28) Insert /n/ in $\left[\begin{bmatrix} + N \\ - V \\ + fem \end{bmatrix} \underline{\quad\quad} \right]_{[+plural]}$ (level 2)

(29) $\begin{bmatrix} + N \\ - V \\ + pl \end{bmatrix} \Rightarrow {}_\omega [\ldots {}_F[\sigma \quad \sigma]]$ (level 2)

                            O C

(30) Insert /s/ in $\left[\begin{bmatrix} + N \\ - V \end{bmatrix} \underline{\quad\quad} \right]_{[+plural]}$ (level 3)

I assume here that inflectional suffixes are represented in the lexicon differently from derivational suffixes. Somewhat speculatively, I propose that only the latter suffixes are encoded as lexical entries. That is, while the derivational suffixes are represented as lexical entries with all the necessary conditions for their use written into the entry (see (22*a*, *b*) as examples), inflectional suffixes arise through morphological rules such as (28) to (30), which state the

---

[24] Gender of abbreviations is determined by the gender of the head of the unabbreviated word. KP abbreviates *Kommunistische Partei*, NP *Nominalphrase*, and AG *Arbeitsgemeinschaft*, in which *Partei*, *Phrase* and *Gemeinschaft* are feminine.

morphological and phonological conditions of their insertion.[25] In this conception of morphology, abstract morphological structures are freely generated according to the principles of morphology, while the rules inserting the inflectional
suffixes (or stating other operations) apply obligatorily.

For confirmation that rules (28) to (30) are adequate for the facts of pluralization
of German nouns, see Mugdan (1977: ch. 10). The quantitative results given
there show that:

noun plurals must end in a schwa syllable, unless pluralized with +s,
feminines very predominantly take +(e)n,
+e and +en may occur with all genders occasionally, +er only with masculines
and neuters.

The rules suffixing n and s, respectively, stand to each other in the relationship expressed in the Elsewhere Condition: the input to (28) is a subset of the
input to (30), and the two outputs are distinct. Thus, the Elsewhere Condition
may be held responsible for the fact that the two general rules of plural affixation
(28) and (30) do not both apply to a form. At the same time, both of these rules
are more general than the lexical markings for the other, 'irregular' suffixes;
again, no word receives both an irregular and a regular suffix.[26] That is, nouns
for which a plural form has been derived in level 1 or 2, by whatever means,
are blocked for being pluralized again through rule (30), assigned to level 3. The
inability of plural nouns to undergo /s/-suffixation is a particularly clear case of
the blocking phenomenon in German.

On the other hand, rules (28) and (29) do not stand in the relationship required
by the condition, since the output of the two rules is not distinct in the technical
sense. Thus, the rules should both be applicable to forms with the right properties. And indeed, the large majority of feminine nouns undergo both rules, as
shown in (27). A final schwa syllable is either present for phonotactic reasons
or created by inserting schwa before /n/. Rules (29) and (30), finally, cannot
conjunctively apply to a form, because plurals from an earlier level are blocked
for reapplication of pluralization at level 3, as we have just seen.

In other words, the system of rules proposed here together with the constraints
provided by the Elsewhere Condition correctly predict that no two suffixes
combine in the same plural form. But it is in fact the case that plural nouns can
be marked in two different ways, by the suffix plus by the umlauting of a vowel
(for examples, see (24) and (25) above). The system allows for this double
marking of plurals under the assumption that umlaut is not a morphological, but
a phonological rule applying in contexts defined partly by the morphology.

By assuming three default rules for plural formation and not just one, I extend
an earlier analysis, in which only +s was regarded as a regular case (Wiese

---

[25] See Anderson (1982) and Kiparsky (1982b: 6–7) for inflectional rules in a similar format for
English.
[26] North German dialects have forms such as *Jung+en+s* which look like doubly marked plurals.
This needs further inquiry. In particular, it has to be established that +en is indeed a plural marker
here. See also the analysis of *Herz+ens+lust* in § 5.3.3 below.

1988*a*: pt II, § 2.3; Clahsen et al. 1992).[27] The present analysis seems to have a number of descriptive advantages besides the ones mentioned already: the fact that only nouns ending in a schwa syllable may have a suffix-less plural form is expressed as well as the fact that in language acquisition overgeneralization of suffixes is restricted to the *en-* and *s*-plurals.

For nouns receiving one of the unpredictable plural suffixes, the following rules may be assumed. Here, the nouns and noun-forming suffixes explicitly listed as members of the classes undergo one of the suffixations. In (31*b*), X, a skeletal position, is the underlier of schwa as the plural ending (cf. (9) in § 6.1). All rules in (31) provide information on 'irregular' plurals, since the relevant nouns must be explicitly listed. For the same reason, these rules are more specific than (28) and (30) and are therefore given priority via the Elsewhere Condition. All nouns or suffixes in N_c of (31*c*) are of course non-feminine, since for feminine nouns the *n*-plural is the default form.

(31) *a.* Insert /ʀ/ in [N_a ____]$_{[+ \text{plural}]}$ for N_a = {*Buch, Haus, Wurm, +tum*, ... }
       b. Insert /X/ in [N_b ____]$_{[+ \text{plural}]}$ for N_b = {*Tisch, Schiff, Turm, +nis*, ... }
       c. Insert /n/ in [N_c ____]$_{[+ \text{plural}]}$ for N_c = {*Bett, Fürst, Muskel, +or*, ... }

The rules in (31) are assumed to apply at level 1. One argument for this assignment is the fact that level-2 derived words (see (4*a*), (5*a*)) never undergo these pluralizations. As for +*e* as plural marker, there is a special prosodic condition on it as well as on other affixes with this shape: as Vennemann (1991*a*: 98) observes, final +*e* always seems to require an immediately preceding stressed syllable, not only within noun inflection. Only for some words with root-final vowels is this condition relaxed, see 'Studi+e, 'Statu+e, and so on, where stress is on the antepenultimate syllable. Arguably, the root-final vowels here are extrametrical, in the sense to be discussed in § 8.2.

As an alternative to the present analysis, it could be assumed that the lexical entries for the nouns taking 'irregular' plurals are enriched by information on the shape of the plural suffix. The rule approach is chosen here as there are even more irregular ways of plural formation. A number of nouns can be used in borrowed plural forms; see *Tempo* vs. *Tempi*, *Thema* vs. *Themata*, *Cherub* vs. *Cherubim* as examples. Apart from the fact that these forms are rare and not known to all speakers, the crucial difference to the plural formation analysed in (31) is that only the forms just illustrated are replaced by other plural forms, such as *Tempos, Themen, Cherubs*. Note also that *s*-plurals, although they may sometimes be borrowed from English, are not replaced by supposedly more native forms. Rather, +*s* may itself serve as a replacing plural marker. This observation again confirms the default status of +*s*. On the other hand, feminine plurals such as *Bar+s* appear to be exceptional (borrowed) forms in line with the learned borrowed plurals just mentioned.

---

[27] This analysis is criticized by Wurzel (1990: 214–15, fn. 6) for ignoring the regularity of *n*-plurals; he, in turn, acknowledges the regular status of the *s*-plural only for vowel-final words. Other large groups of words are ignored.

The preceding considerations and the proposals on morphological rules for plural nouns can be summarized as in (32). Modern Standard German makes use of three levels or strata in the lexicon. On level 1, all irregular inflectional suffixes, that is some of the plural markers for nouns and strong verbal inflections, are assigned, in conjunction with phonological rules such as word-stress assignment.

Level 2 provides the domain for n-plurals of feminine nouns, probably also for the rule stating the constraint (29) requiring an unmarked foot. Level 3 is the seat of regular (default) inflection (s-plural and dative plural $+n$ for nouns, weak verbal inflection). The phonological part is largely left empty in (32), assuming that in fact very few, if any, phonological rules must be explicitly assigned to one of the levels. Following the discussion on lexical categories in § 5.2.3, one could alternatively say that there are plural markers for roots, for stems, and for words. This is reminiscent of a proposal by Wurzel (1970: pt I, ch. 2), in which he argues that these suffixes are not plural markers, but stem-forming suffixes. The present proposal claims that they are both.

(32) Plural formation in the lexicon

	morphology		phonology
level 1	irregular inflection: $+er$, $+e$, $+(e)n$, $+s$	$\rightleftarrows$	Word Stress
level 2	$+(e)n_{[\text{fem.}]}$ foot construction	$\rightleftarrows$	Compound Stress
level 3	regular inflection: $+s$	$\rightleftarrows$	

All plural suffixes not assigned by one of the regular rules are defined as irregular. Consequently, $+(e)n$ is irregular for non-feminines, and $+s$, as in $Bar+s$, is a representative standing for the completely irregular plurals. If further analysis should come to the conclusion that $+e$ for masculines, or $+s$ for vowel-final stems is a regular case, as the quantitative results by Mugdan (1977: ch. 10) suggest, more defaults can be stated, and the number of irregular plurals would shrink correspondingly. Basically, the model would not change through such elaborations.[28] For two feminine nouns, *Mutter* and *Tochter*, it seems to be necessary to mark the lack of any plural suffix lexically.

Pluralization of German nouns is often regarded as a linguistic phenomenon which is not rule-governed and defies formal description. In the words of MacWhinney and Leinbach (1992: 137): 'none [of the plural suffixes] can be characterized as being "the regular ending". In a situation such as this, there is simply no regular pattern at all.' The present description leads to a different

---

[28] Bloomfield (1933: 211) takes it for granted that in German plural nouns /ə/ for masculines and neuters alternates with /ən/ for feminines. This is his example for a 'regular grammatical alternation'. Children, at least, do not recognize this putative default status of $+e$ for non-feminines. Their overgeneralizations are restricted to $+en$ and $+s$.

conclusion: there are several regular endings; and the existence of several regular patterns is simply an argument for an intricate hierarchy of regularity, and a corresponding system of formal rules.

The particular assignment of plural markers to levels as specified in (32) is also in agreement with the pattern of plural markers with derivational suffixes: all suffixes previously assigned to level 2 take *+en* as their plural suffix, and never a level 1 plural (cf. (25)). On the other hand, noun-forming suffixes assigned to level 1 can be found with plural markers from any of the levels. The model predicts that a noun-forming suffix from level 2 cannot take a level 1 plural marker. Such a case does indeed not exist.

One final argument for the distribution of pluralization over the lexical levels as stated in (32) comes from word-internal inflection. Note that the proposal made predicts that level 1 and level 2 inflection may occur within compounds, as inflection on the left element. The following discussion of the *Fugenmorpheme* will demonstrate that this prediction is actually borne out.

5.3.3. **On the status of the *Fugenmorpheme***

In connection with plural formation and the treatment of German inflection in Lexical Phonology, a number of elements should be discussed which have escaped adequate analysis in other frameworks. These are the so-called *Fugenmorpheme* or *linking morphemes*. A careful study of these units is important since it may shed light on the interspersing of inflection and compounding, and thereby on the range of facts to be treated as lexical. As illustrated in (33), there are a number of such units occurring compound-internally.

(33) *a.* Kind+er+wagen, Büch+er+wurm
   b. Gäns+e+stall, Schwein+e+braten
   c. Frau+en+haus, Schwester+n+liebe
   d. Tag+es+zeit, Mann+s+bild

I will continue to refer to the segments between compounded words as *linking morphemes*, but with no commitment as to their morphemic status. These linking morphemes are not generally predictable. That is, any given word can occur with or without a linking morpheme in a compound. For a number of words, it is even possible to find three different forms, or four, if one takes the two variants of *s* into account, see (34). For other compounds, speakers may vary in their use of linking morphemes. It is, however, true that certain regularities can be found. For a number of words derived by particular suffixes, for example, it is true that they always receive the linking morpheme *+s* or *+n*; see (35) for *+ung*, *+or*, and *+e*. Furthermore, all linking morphemes adding a schwa syllable may be thought of as having a prosodic motivation: they create preferred prosodic structures, namely branching feet.

(34) *a.* Kind+frau, Kind+s+kopf, Kind+es+alter, Kind+er+wagen
   b. Mann+loch, Männ+er+stimme, mann+s+dick, Mann+es+kraft

(35) *a*. Versicher+ung+s+vertreter, Öffn+ung+s+zeiten
     b. Blum+en+duft, Tasch+en+messer
     c. Profess+or+en+versammlung, Mot+or+en+geräusch

The large number of such words in German constitutes a problem for any theory which assumes that inflection must follow compounding—presupposing that the linking morphemes are indeed inflectional markers. But there is at least one argument that this is the case: the set of linking morphemes as illustrated in (33) to (35) is identical to the set of plural affixes. No linking morphemes occur which are formally distinct from plural markers. Furthermore, the linking morphemes illustrated in (33*a*–*c*), though not in those in (33*d*), are identical to the plural suffixes which the preceding noun would bear in isolation, that is, if not in a compound. If the linking morphemes, especially given the unpredictability of their occurrence, were not identical to the plural markers, this would be a highly unlikely coincidence.

On the other hand, there are two arguments against the interpretation of linking morphemes as plural markers. First, there is no sense in which the nouns modified by linking morphemes receive a plural interpretation. A *Kinderwagen* (usually) is a pram for one child, and a *Schweinebraten* is pork stemming from a single pig. Second, +*s* as a linking morpheme is much more problematic, in that its distribution is not identical to that of the normal plural marker. In fact, it often occurs compound-internally with feminine nouns, which can never receive an +*s* as an inflectional marker. This also argues against an interpretation of linking-*s* as a genitive marker.

I have now sketched the reasons leading to the widespread uncertainty which is found in the literature on the status of the *Fugenmorpheme*. The solution I propose here claims that these units are not forming a homogeneous class. Rather, there is one class of completely 'regular' plural suffixes, namely +*er*, +*e*, +*en*. On the other hand, +*s* as a linking morpheme is not a morpheme at all. It surfaces as an inserted consonant through a rule of *s*-Insertion.

Consider, first, the semantic argument against the morphemic status of linking morphemes. The indisputable fact that linking morphemes do not contribute to a plural interpretation does not necessarily lead to the conclusion that a plural morpheme cannot be present. In morphological theory, left and right parts of compounds are usually assigned a very different status, that of non-head and head position, respectively. The crucial property of heads is that their features must agree with that of the whole morphological unit. For example, if a construction has a nominal head, then the whole structure has the features of a noun.

The features of non-heads do not contribute in the same way to the featural composition of the resulting structure. While morphological theories differ in the exact formulation of feature percolation for heads vs. non-heads (see Williams 1981; Selkirk 1982; Lieber 1981), it is a natural consequence of such models that a non-head's morphological feature does not contribute to the features of the whole word. This seems to be precisely the situation we find for the linking morphemes. But if the lack of a plural interpretation for plural-marked nouns in compounds is accounted for by the principles of feature percolation for non-heads, the semantic counterargument to the plural-marker interpretation of the linking morphemes evaporates.[29] Analogously, the presence of a singular noun form does not imply the necessity of a singular interpretation: an *Auto+händler* is by no means a person who would sell only a single car.

Non-suffixed, but umlauted plural forms may also appear in initial position of compounds: *Mütter+beratung*. In general, highly exceptional plural forms such as *Mütter* (feminine, but no +n) or *Hund+e* (no umlaut) are found in compounds. Again, these cases would constitute a problem, unless we assume that plurals may freely occur in the compound-initial position. For compounds such as *Maus+e+fall+e*, in which no umlaut is observed in spite of umlaut in the plural form *Mäus+e*, the same lexical listing of exceptions as for the non-umlauting plural *Hund+e* may be assumed (see § 7.2).

The objections to the morphemic interpretation of compound-internal *s* are much more compelling. Consider how a word such as *Schwingung+s+zahl* would be derived. According to the general model assumed here, morphological structures are built up cyclically, roughly following the steps indicated in (36).

(36) *a.* schwing+ung   derivation
   b. schwingung+s   affixation
   c. schwingungs+zahl   compounding

The result of the hypothetical derivation in (36*b*) is an ill-formed morphological structure. Neither plurals of +*ung*-nouns nor genitives of any feminine noun can ever be suffixed by +*s*. Note that this is not the type of 'ungrammaticality' seen earlier on several occasions, where intermediate morphological structures were diagnosed as possible but not lexicalized or actual words. Only if we attribute to the grammar the power to look ahead and 'see' that a compound is to be formed on the next cycle, can words such as the one in (36*b*) not be ruled out as ungrammatical. Current morphological theory does not give this look-ahead power to grammatical rules. In addition, since there is no necessary plural or genitive interpretation for the nouns marked with +*s*, there is no basis for a decision whether the plural or the genitive affix should be chosen. Given this indeterminacy, avoiding a decision would seem to constitute the optimal strategy.

There is another, morphophonological, argument against identifying the *Fugen-s* with any inflectional morpheme. +*s* as an inflectional marker for genitives is subject to the alternation discussed in § 4.3.1, in which the morpheme may appear as [s] or [əs], depending in part on the ending of the preceding stem. As shown again in (37*a*), there is a certain degree of optionality involved in the genitive case, while the shape of the linking-*s* is lexically conditioned.[30]

---

[29] For parallel cases in Modern Hebrew, Borer (1988: § 4) invokes a notion of semantic and syntactic opacity to ensure that the plural marking on non-heads in compounds is not available for interpretation.

[30] In an informal register, the genitive marker +*s* may be absent for words ending in +*s*: (*des*) *Witz*, (*des*) *Bus*. Again, since this optional absence does not occur with the linking-*s*, the two units should not be collapsed.

(37) *a.* genitives   Mann+(e)s, Tag(e)s
     b. plurals   Männ+er, Tag+e
     c. linking morphemes   Mann+s+bild (*Mann+es+bild), Mann+es+alter
                                (*Mann+s+alter), Tag+es+zeitung, Tag+e+blatt

The important observation is that the distribution of schwa is quite different for genitives, plurals, and the linking morpheme. The optionality to be found for genitives is not possible in the case of linking-*s*, where, lexically conditioned, either [əs] or [s] is obligatory.

A final argument against the interpretation of *Fugen-s* as the plural marker is provided by the fact that nouns taking +*s* as plural suffixes never seem to display a *Fugen-s*, that is, a compound-internal /s/.[31] Compounds such as *Auto+s+ versicherung 'car insurance' or *LKW+s+gebühr 'truck fee' are non-existent, although we would perhaps expect that the number of such forms is actually large, given the high frequency of *Fugen-s* in general. I conclude from this survey that there is no basis for identifying linking-*s* with a plural marker or any other suffix such as the genitive marker. Instead, we may assume that this segment arises, synchronically, through a rule of Consonant Epenthesis, which will be discussed briefly in § 7.3.7.

To confirm the claim that such rules of consonant epenthesis exist in German, it may be pointed out that a similar rule must be postulated to account for the /t/ in the words given in (38). As in the case of linking-*s*, it does not seem possible to identify this segment with any independently motivated morpheme from the inventory of Modern Standard German. A phonological (or rather, morphophonological) solution therefore seems preferable.

(38) *a.* wesen+t+lich, orden+t+lich, eigen+t+lich, namen+t+lich
     b. allen+t+halben, mein+et+wegen

The conclusion above with respect to the linking morphemes +*er*, +*e*, +*en* is that they constitute the plural markers of the nouns to which they attach. This leads to a model of the lexicon as in (18) and (32), which allows some part of inflection to occur inside derived and compounded words. This conclusion is also of some relevance for those grammatical theories (Anderson 1988; Chomsky 1991) which propose to assign inflection (but not derivation and compounding) to the syntactic component. On the basis of the present result on the *Fugen-morpheme*, such models must be regarded as problematic.

There is further evidence that word-internal inflection is possible. We have not yet seen cases in which inflection for plural precedes derivation. The level-ordered lexicon as specified in this chapter allows for this constellation, which does indeed exist, although it is not very common. Two relevant cases are presented in (39). The plural suffix +*er* may precede the diminutive suffixes;[32]

---

[31] The (near-)impossibility of plural-*s* in compounds in English was used by Kiparsky (1982*a*, *b*) as an argument for level-ordering and for assigning plural-*s* to a level ordered after the level of compounding. However, counterexamples such as *buildings inspector* or *parks commission* are known to exist. The case for such a model seems to be much stronger from the German data.

[32] Interestingly, *Kind+er+chen* and *Kind+er+lein*, are always plural nouns, in contrast to *Kind+chen*, *Kind+lein*, which allow for a singular and plural interpretation. The formations in (39*a*) do not come from a very productive class, but see *Ei+er+chen*, *Ding+er+chen*.

and all plural suffixes assigned to levels 1 and 2 may precede noun-forming suffix +*schaft*. As expected, plural +*s* never precedes a derivational suffix. Again, if the material in front of the derivational suffixes were not the plural suffixes, but just epenthesized segments, we would find a highly unlikely formal identity of these segments to the plural suffixes as they are found elsewhere.

(39) *a.* Kind+er+chen, Kind+er+lein
     b. Student+en+schaft, Ärzt+e+schaft, Völk+er+schaft

There is even a class of compounds in which the two types of phenomena called *Fugenmorpheme* coexist. Consider the nouns in (40), where both +*en* and /s/ are added to the left-hand units. While *Herzens* is the (exceptional) genitive form of *Herz*, the genitive singular forms of *Schmerz* and *Mensch* are *Schmerz+es* and *Mensch+en*, respectively, and thus not identical to the form found in the compound.

(40) Herz+en+s+lust, Schmerz+en+s+geld, Mensch+en+s+kind+er

Under the present analysis, there is no reason why the two phenomena, plural affixation and /s/-epenthesis, should not co-occur within one and the same expression. Thus, I propose that the non-heads in the compounds of (40) have been subject both to the plural affixation as well as to the epenthesis of /s/.

The major empirical problem for the present proposal derives from those compounds in which [ən] occurs as a *Fugenmorphem*, but cannot be identified with the plural suffix. In (41), I give a number of examples. The proper plural marker of all left-hand nouns in these compounds is schwa, so that +*en* cannot be regarded as the plural suffix. The actual number of such cases is not high, and some are regarded as somewhat archaic.

(41) Stern+en+glanz, Instrument+en+bauer, Hahn+en+fuß

Several options are available for these cases, such as treating /(ə)n/ as a further example, alongside /s/, of an epenthesized consonant, or allowing plural nouns inflected for the dative case as non-heads in compounds. (The left-hand nouns in (41) are the actual dative plural forms of the respective nouns, modulo the lack of umlaut in the final example.) I will take no stance on this issue here. However, as +*n* is the regular dative plural suffix for nouns, and is used for all nouns except those with the plural suffix +*s*, it is plausible to assume that the rule affixing +*n* for dative plural forms is a level 2 rule. Its (occasional) appearance in compounds would then be accounted for, as well as its non-appearance with *s*-pluralized forms.

5.4. ON SOME OPEN PROBLEMS

The preceding discussion has concentrated on plural inflection for nouns including the status of the so-called linking morphemes. The wide range of other relevant morphological and phonological phenomena does not allow for an exhaustive treatment of all morphological problems of German, not even when phonological issues are at stake. Instead, I close this chapter by discussing a few areas in which problems of principle may possibly arise.

Leaving the subject of morphophonology and level orderings it must be acknowledged that not all problems for the description of morpheme order can be solved by reference to the lexical levels (or categories). Obviously, the splitting-up of the lexicon into a small number of levels is not sufficient to describe all the constraints on the ordering relations of affixes. In fact, the number of cases in which both orders can be found, for some pair of morphemes from the same level, is quite small. In (7) and (8) all relevant morpheme sequences are listed which I could find with the help of a reverse dictionary (Mater 1983).

Second, there is a number of cases in which a morphologically complex word seems to show evidence for two different structures simultaneously. These are the well-known bracketing paradoxes, often exemplified in the literature by the word *ungrammaticality*, in which the class I prefix *un+* should attach to the adjective *grammatical* before the class I suffix *+ity*, since *un+* is prefixed to adjectives and not nouns, at least in the general, productive case. But this means that the structure of this word should be seen as [[un [grammatical]] ity], with the class II prefix closer to the root/stem than the class I suffix. The theory of Lexical Phonology explicitly disallows such a configuration.

In (42), I simply illustrate potential cases from German of such bracketing paradoxes. In all of these examples, the semantic composition argues for the left-hand bracketing (*Maulheldentum* is the characteristic of being a *Maulheld*), while the fact that the unproductive suffix *+tum* combines independently with *Helden* (as it does with *König*) argues for the right-hand bracketing. Note also that *+isch* is classified in (3b) as a class I suffix, while compounding is argued to be part of level 2. This ordering makes the derivation of [[*mengen theoret*] *isch*], which seems like the structure required for semantic reasons, impossible.

(42) *a.* [[Un [grammatikal]] ität] ~ [Un [[grammatikal] ität]]
       [[mengen theoret] isch] ~ [mengen [theoret+isch]]
   b. [[Wahl könig] tum] ~ [Wahl [könig+tum]]
      [[Maul helden] tum] ~ [Maul [helden+tum]]

For such bracketing paradoxes, various solutions have been proposed (Kiparsky 1983; Pesetsky 1985; Spencer 1988), usually admitting two types of structures for a single word.[33] I will not discuss this issue here, but only mention that any morphological theory faces a challenge by the existence of these and other bracketing paradoxes. Some of the cases, in particular those illustrated in (42a), may receive a solution by formulating regularities which refer to either the morphological or the prosodic structure of the words in question. As repeatedly shown in Chapters 4 and 5 (see also § 8.4 for compounds), these two structures are not necessarily isomorphic. Also, affixes are allowed to subcategorize not for morphological, but for prosodic structures.

---

[33] Spencer (1991: ch. 10) provides a useful review on the problems of bracketing paradoxes and the various solutions proposed in the literature.

The preceding discussions are intended to show that there are many open questions within Lexical Phonology, in general and in its application to German. At the same time, I hope to have demonstrated that the attempt to propose a restricted model of the morphology–phonology interaction is a necessary and fruitful part of a theory of phonology. I also ask the reader to bear in mind that Lexical Phonology is a framework, a family of theories, and not a single, unified set of statements. If the specific proposals advanced here prove to be insufficient for some aspects, as they most certainly will, a different version of the description within the same overall framework may well provide a better solution.

UNDERSPECIFICATION: AN ANALYSIS OF MARKEDNESS AND DEFAULTS

The preceding two chapters were devoted to some aspects of the phonology–morphology interaction. The present chapter turns to an aspect more directly related to matters of phonological representation, namely the treatment of distinctive versus redundant phonological features. It is clear that any featural characterization of the segments in a language will contain redundant information. For example, saying which segments are voiced and which are voiceless in some language will usually—perhaps always—lead to redundant statements, since the feature [voice] will hardly ever be a distinctive feature for all segments of this language.

German is quite typical in that respect, in that [voice] is distinctive for the obstruents only, as inspection of (7) in § 2.3.2 reveals. Vowels and sonorant consonants are always voiced.[1] In other words, for these segments, voicing is predictable, and including [+ voice] in the specification for these sounds is redundant. From the phonemic perspective, [voice] gives only non-distinctive information. The idea that such redundant information does not belong to the phonemic representation had already put forward by Trubetzkoy through his concept of the phoneme, when he offered the theory that 'das Phonem die Gesamtheit der phonologisch relevanten Eigenschaften eines Lautgebildes ist' (Trubetzkoy 1939: 35). In such a conception, only the obstruent phonemes of German would contain a specification for voicing.

The conception of the lexicon as introduced in the preceding chapter is naturally connected to the idea that only distinctive or non-redundant information should be part of all underlying representations, following the principle that 'the lexicon is minimally redundant' (Kiparsky 1982b: 25). This means that all redundant feature specifications are to be introduced by rules which apply later in the derivation, partly in the lexicon, partly in the postlexical component, and perhaps even later, by means of phonetic rules. To give this move some plausibility, consider what a person knowing a language has to know about a word or lexical entry. Any distinctive feature or phoneme will certainly be part of such lexical information; that the word for the German language (*deutsch*) begins with /d/ is not predictable from any other information. Also one has to know about the application of morphophonological rules, namely those rules

---

[1] This statement is not true on the phonetic level, where partial devoicing often may occur.

whose applications are not completely predictable on the basis of phonological or other information. But to take up the example of voicing, for *deutsch* only the first consonant in this word is distinctively and non-redundantly voiced; the diphthongal vowels are predictably [+ voice], and the final cluster /tʃ/ is, at least on the surface, necessarily voiceless.

The insight that only a subset of all features actually carries a distinctive function in contrasting lexical entries is taken literally in Lexical Phonology. It is interpreted to mean that all non-distinctive feature values are absent. This is the concept of *underspecification* which is pursued in the following sections for vowels, consonants, and major class features, respectively. That phonological representations cannot be fully specified in the general case seems to be a notion about which most current phonology is in agreement. In a few studies of German, such as Hall (1989*b*) on Dorsal Fricative Assimilation, it has also been shown that underspecification is an important ingredient of an optimal analysis of phonological rules and alternations in this language.

Unfortunately, there is no agreement in the current literature on the principles that underspecification should adopt. I will propose a particular version of the model, relying to some extent, though not completely, on the model of *Radical Underspecification* as proposed by Archangeli (1988). I will also briefly consider an alternative theory called *Contrastive Underspecification* in § 6.1.2. Section 6.1 analyses the vowel system, and § 6.2 the place features of the consonant system. The so-called major class features and other features, particular those of /ʀ/ and the laryngeals, are analysed in § 6.3.

6.1. THE VOWEL SYSTEM UNDERSPECIFIED

In § 2.3.1, a specific featural analysis was proposed for all vowels which play a role in the phonology of Modern Standard German. Since this analysis (enriched by the considerations on feature geometry in § 3.1) is crucial for the following argumentation, it is repeated here in (1). It may be useful to recall that [high] and [low] are features dependent on the articulator node [Tongue Position], while [front] and [back] are dependent on [Dorsal], and [round] and [ATR] on [Labial] and on [Radical], respectively. All the features in (1) except for [long] are part of the feature hierarchy within and below the root node R (as illustrated in (2) and (4) of Ch. 3). Length, as may be recalled, is actually represented as an underlying association of one R to two prosodic positions, X X.

All features in (1) potentially may be distinctive, but it is clear that there is a high degree of redundancy in this matrix. For example, vowels with the specification [+ ATR] are always, phonologically, [+ long] (though not vice versa), and, of course, high vowels cannot be low and vice versa. In addition to these considerations of economy and parsimony, there are further rather compelling

arguments for assuming a level of description where many values of phonological features are simply not present, as I try to show in the discussion of some
of the rules treated in Chapter 7.

(1) Features of the vowel system

	iː	ɪ	eː	ɛː	ɛ	aː	a	oː	ɔ	uː	ʊ	yː	ʏ	øː	œ	ə
consonantal	−	−	−	−	−	−	−	−	−	−	−	−	−	−	−	−
high	+	+	−	−	−	−	−	−	−	+	+	+	+	−	−	−
low	−	−	−	−	−	+	+	−	−	−	−	−	−	−	−	−
front	+	+	+	+	+	−	−	−	−	−	−	+	+	+	+	−
back	−	−	−	−	−	−	−	+	+	+	+	−	−	−	−	−
round	−	−	−	−	−	−	−	+	+	+	+	+	+	+	+	−
ATR	+	−	+	−	−	−	−	+	−	+	−	+	−	+	−	−
long	+	−	+	+	−	+	−	+	−	+	−	+	−	+	−	−

There are several ways of approaching the goal of removing predictable feature
specifications from lexical entries using features as specified in (1). A first, difficult, step consists in deciding which features are distinctive at all, and which are
totally redundant. This problem is discussed in Chapter 2, where I indicate which
features I propose to select as providing the necessary distinctions.

A first argument for choosing 'gaps' in (1) comes from the values for the
vowel [ə] which behaves quite differently from all other vowels. It is a much
discussed fact in the vowel phonology of German that schwa must be set apart
from all other vowels, on the basis of its predictability in many instances, of its
role in alternations where it seems to appear and disappear again, and of the fact
that it occurs in non-stressed syllables only. All these properties, partly discussed
in preceding chapters, may be taken as indications that schwa is a default vowel
of German, a vowel filled in under special prosodic circumstances. But according to the reasoning of Underspecification Theory, it should then have no underlying feature specifications.

Notice now that in (1) [ə] has only negative values. It may be concluded from
this, together with the attempt to make schwa an 'empty' vowel, that negative
values are in principle excluded from underlying representations. Thus, it is
postulated here that only positive values can be distinctive. This is a very restrictive hypothesis on phonological structure: it directly ties together markedness,
distinctiveness, and the form of representations.

This move does not disturb the distinctions to be made, since all gaps can be
interpreted as negative values. But there are other dependencies between values,
even among the positive ones. These can be expressed in a large number of
alternative ways; I will therefore simply present the system I came to choose.
This is the analysis as displayed in (2).

(2) A radically underspecified vowel system

	iː	I	eː	ɛː	ɛ	aː	a	oː	ɔ	uː	ʊ	yː	Y	øː	œ	ə
high	+	+								+	+	+	+			
front	+	+	+	+	+							+	+	+	+	
round								+	+	+	+	+	+	+	+	
ATR				−												
long	+		+	+		+		+		+		+		+		

In (2), all features are eliminated which are not regarded as carrying underlying values. Compared to (1), these are [consonantal], [low], and [back]. Also, as proposed above, negative values do not occur (except for [ATR], to which I return shortly). The first of the redundant features, [consonantal], is of course negative for all vowels. The next two features, [high] and [low], involve more intricate considerations.

With regard to the elimination of the feature [low], it might appear that the move towards non-redundancy has gone too far in this analysis, since /a/ and /ə/ are not distinct, as far as the information in (2) goes. This is due to the fact that [low] is not regarded as a distinctive vowel feature. As (2) in § 1.4 and (1) above make clear, the value for [low] is taken to be the only featural difference between the two vowels [a] and [ə]. The reasoning for eliminating [low] will become clear in the discussion of Umlaut in § 7.2.1. For now it should suffice that a more systematic treatment of the umlauting vowels [a] and [ɛ] is possible if the former vowel is not specified as being [+ low]. Note that its counterpart in the umlaut alternation, [ɛ], is [− low].

Fortunately, in the present framework [a] and [ə] can be distinguished by other representational means. Recall that a feature structure was introduced in § 3.1 according to which a distinction was made between positions on the skeletal tier, the root node R, and the features dependent on this root node. The role of these elements is often neglected in studies of underspecification. But it is clear, for example, that associations between segments and skeletal positions are also a matter of relative markedness. In other words, while segments are usually short, they may be long (linked to two positions) in the marked case. The theory proposed here will express this judgement by representing underlying length, and by introducing the usual one-to-one relationship between segments and skeletal positions via a default rule which assigns a skeletal position to a root node.

Now, if skeletal positions may be present or absent underlyingly, the same may be said for the root nodes. The proposal here will be that the vowel /a/ is specified underlyingly by an *empty root node* R (see (6a)), while a schwa (if underlying at all) is represented as an *empty* X (see (9a)). That is, in both cases, a highly underspecified structural category exists, but different levels of structure are addressed. In the case of /a/, the proposal expresses the judgement that this vowel is the least marked segment of all distinctive segments. In the case of /ə/, the analysis treats this vowel as a pure prosodic position, X, as defined in 3.2.1.1, to which a complete default segment may be attached postlexically. It must be added that an 'empty' category is just that: a phonological category symbolized as R, X, σ, and so on (hopefully to be reanalysed by suitable features in later theories) with no other features attached to it either directly or indirectly.

Similar problems arise with the two features for the back–front distinction. In contrast to the path usually taken (not only) in Underspecification Theory (see Archangeli 1988), I remove [back] and choose [front] as the distinctive feature. The featural system proposed in (2) for the vowels of Modern Standard German thus follows the argumentation by Schane (1973: 174) that 'tongue position (*frontness*) is primary for vowels such as *i, e, æ*, whereas lip shape (*rounding*) is primary for vowels such as *u, o, ɔ*'.[2] While the claim made here is primarily one for the German vowel system, the case for /a/ as a back vowel seems not very convincing in general. Note that apparent cases of a [+ back] grouping of /a/ may well be reanalysed as a [− front] patterning.

The features [ATR] and [long], or similar features, are certainly necessary to bear out all contrasts in the system. At this point we may recall that a default rule for skeletal positions has already been introduced in § 3.2.4: in (33) I proposed that every segment (i.e. root node) receives a skeletal position, X. Short vowels are default cases in contrast to long vowels (X X underlyingly) and to the underlying X surfacing as schwa.[3]

We now come to that part of the model in which the missing values in (2) are derived. To achieve this, a distinction must be introduced which will be useful in several areas: some values, namely the positive, must be specified before others, the negative values. Furthermore, if the negative values are generally interpreted as the unmarked values, then they should be inserted whenever no value is given either by virtue of the lexical entry or by some other mechanism, normally some phonological rule. In other words, negative values are the last resort, the defaults on which the system may always fall back.

In contrast, the marked, positive, values, if redundant, may be introduced by more specific rules. I will call this latter type of rule *markedness rule*, simply because these rules insert marked values. In (3), a number of such rules are given. These rules are such that they introduce the missing positive values for the vowels in (2).

---

[2] The system proposed here has other similarities to Schane's ideas. First, Schane too gives a redundancy rule analogous to our [+ round] → [+ back] (3a), and not the more common implication from [back] to [round]. Second, Schane, in the final section, suggests that the feature [front] should be used to encode the primary frontness quoted above.

[3] Underlying X is necessary only for those schwas for which the distribution is unpredictable. Other skeletal positions arise through Schwa Epenthesis (§ 7.4.2).

(3) Markedness rules[4]

    a. [+ round] → [+ back]

    b. empty R → [+ low]

    c. [+ long, − low] → [+ ATR]

The first of these rules ensures that round segments are back vowels. Markedness rules as well as other rules cannot change existing values, neither can they override the fundamental constraint that an articulator cannot move in two opposite directions at the same time; this ensures that the segments marked [+ round, + front] cannot be subject to rule (3*a*). Rule (3*b*) ensures that the empty segment surfaces as [a]; another way of seeing this rule would be to say that the unspecified vowel is the maximally open vowel. This rule is not as arbitrary as it might appear; since only vowels can have a totally empty root node (see (25) below), the rule says that the unmarked vowel is maximally open, which seems to be the optimal state for a vowel.[5] Finally, (3*c*) makes all long, non-low vowels tense, that is, [+ ATR], except of course for /ɛː/, for which underlying [− ATR] cannot be overwritten. Recall that the *a*-sounds were judged to be lax in § 1.4. As far as possible, the present analysis takes [ATR] to be predictable from length; for an argument that this is the right direction of predictability, see the discussion of vowel shortening in § 7.2.2.

Rules in (3) provide positive values; they are complemented by a set of maximally simple default rules, stated in (4) for the features considered necessary for vowels. The rules presented here can of course be summarized by the rule schema in (5), which says that for any feature F not specified the negative value is to be chosen. Schema (5) is applicable to all features with the binary values '+' and '−'. Since the articulator features and organizing nodes are not assumed to have these values, the default rules cannot apply.

(4) Default rules

    a. [high] → [− high]

    b. [front] → [− front]

    c. [back] → [− back]

    d. [round] → [− round]

    e. [ATR] → [− ATR]

    f. [low] → [− low]

(5) Default schema

    [F] → [− F]

Example (2), the entries for underlying vowels, contains only positive values, with the exception of /ɛː/. Because of this property, an alternative interpretation

---

[4] The reader familiar with Generalized Phrase Structure Grammar-style grammars may note that the markedness rules are similar to *feature cooccurrence restrictions* in GPSG, while the default rules used here are the *feature specification defaults* of that theory. In phonology, Lodge (1992) uses a similar distinction under the labels of *predictive rules* and *default rules*.

[5] This is a notion already expressed by Jakobson (1941: 104), who calls /a/ the *optimal vowel*. Formally, (3*b*) is perhaps more problematic. It requires reference to the *absence* of phonological structure. The predicate 'empty' in (3*b*) is hard to formalize within the present theory. A notation such as '®', used by many authors, does not change this fact.

of the phonological features seems available on first sight: instead of seeing features as two-valued, with the values '+' and '–', features could be unary (or monovalent), where only the presence or the absence of a feature counts. This concept, first proposed for some features by Trubetzkoy (1939) and subsequently by other authors, such as Goldsmith (1985) and van der Hulst (1989), makes it impossible to use the negative value ([– F]) to mark a property—precisely what is implemented, with one exception, in (2).

On the other hand, phonological representations also have the task of characterizing vowels (as well as consonants) with respect to their phonetic properties by the use of features. Under a unary feature concept, a vowel such as schwa would never be related to any feature, rather it would remain empty throughout the derivation. There is no way of saying, for example, that schwa is non-high or that /iː/ is not labial, since the concept of a negative value is simply not available. Of course it would be possible to interpret empty cells in the feature matrix in this way, but this move would in fact reintroduce the concept of binarity. For this reason, I assume that features are binary, with the exception of articulator nodes (see § 2.3.2).

One important aspect of the theory proposed here is that feature values are linked to the concept of markedness in the following simple way: marked values are positive (+), unmarked values are negative (–). This simple and natural connection between feature representation and markedness is not widespread in phonology, but is taken for granted in theories of morphological features (see Jensen (1990: 48–9) for some discussion). In phonology, usually a more elaborate relationship between markedness and positive/negative values is assumed. I do not consider this question settled, however, since a change in the features chosen may often result in a different constellation. A simple replacement of [sonorant] by [obstruent] with a reversal of values, for example, leads to a difference exactly in this respect. Note that (2) embodies the claim that /yː/ is the most marked vowel in the vowel system of Modern Standard German.

The exceptional marking of /ɛː/ in (2) by a negative value could perhaps be taken care of by choosing a feature other than [ATR]. On the other hand, the exceptional representation neatly reflects the special status of this vowel phoneme. As noted in § 2.2.5, this vowel often merges with /eː/, to the extent that it has been considered not to be a sound of Modern Standard German any more. The marginal status of /ɛː/ is predicted in the present proposal from its highly marked featural representation.[6]

As a summary, I specify some different types of vowels (/aː/, /ʏ/, /ə/) in their underlying representations and their further specification by means of markedness and default rules. Note that these rules (like all other rules to be treated in the next chapter) do not change values (the reason why rule (3a) is not applicable in (7b)), and affect only one feature each. I further adopt the convention

---

[6] This view presupposes that markedness is computed on underlying representations.

that the introduction of a terminal feature automatically creates the structure above it. Features not mentioned in (1) (major class and manner features) are not considered here. I refer to § 6.3 for the treatment of these features; but we may note at this point already that vowels receive the default values for all of these features, except for [voice]. Of course, the segmental hierarchy introduced in § 3.1 is used as the representational format for the vocalic features.

(6) /aː/

   a.

$$\begin{array}{c} \text{X} \quad \text{X} \\ \diagdown\!\diagup \\ \text{R} \end{array}$$

underlying

   b.

$$\begin{array}{c} \text{X} \quad \text{X} \\ \diagdown\!\diagup \\ \text{R} \\ | \\ \text{Supralaryngeal} \\ | \\ \text{Tongue} \\ \text{Position} \\ | \\ \text{[+ low]} \end{array}$$

markedness rule (3*b*)

   c.

defaults (4)

$$\begin{array}{c} \text{X} \quad \text{X} \\ \diagdown\!\diagup \\ \text{R} \\ | \\ \text{Supralaryngeal} \end{array}$$

Place   Tongue Position

Labial   Dorsal   Radical   [− high]   [+ low]

[− round]   [+ ATR]

[− front]   [− back]

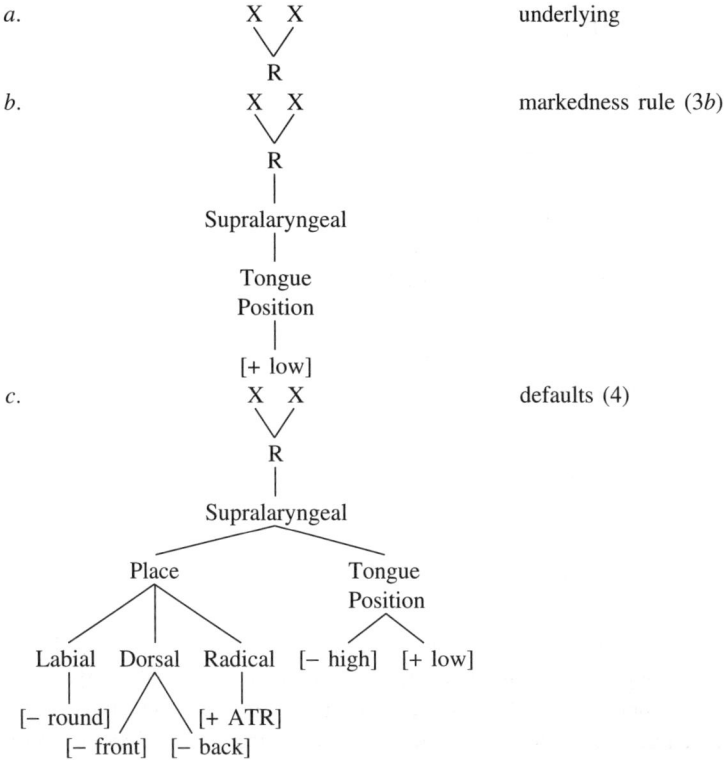

The derivation of schwa is particularly important, since schwa is here assumed to be, in most cases, a vowel of epenthesis. For schwa, an additional default rule is required, one which creates a root node for an empty skeletal position. (A separate rule is needed, since the convention that hierarchically higher structure is automatically created cannot apply here.) This default rule given in (8) for the creation of segments is a late rule, just like other default rules. For this reason it counterfeeds the markedness rule (3*b*), and no low vowel is derived.[7] Instead, only default values are specified eventually.

---

[7] Two rules A, B are said to be in a feeding relationship if rule A creates the environment necessary for B to apply, and if the rules actually apply in the order A, and then B. If rule A is in a feeding relationship to B, but A is actually applied *after* B, this is called a counterfeeding relationship.

(7) /ɤ/

a. 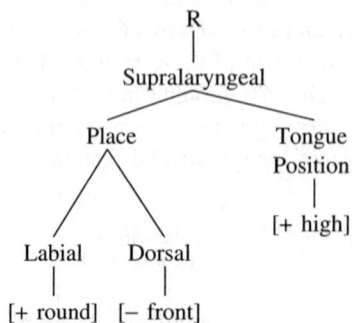   underlying

b.   ——   markedness rules (3)
c.   R   defaults

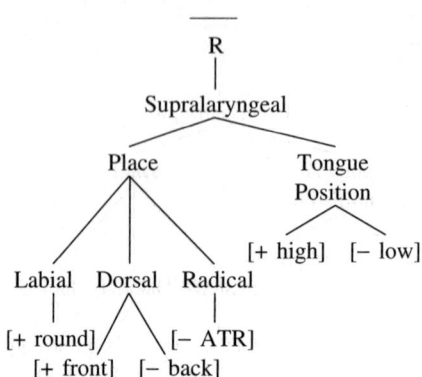

(8) Default segment
   X → X
       |
       R

As (9) shows, the derivation of the neutral vowel, schwa, is straightforward, once the root node is present. It is pertinent to note here that schwa may be called an epenthetic vowel for two reasons: first, the vowel receives all of its segmental features through default rules, as illustrated in (9). Second, the prosodic slot, X, may itself be inserted (epenthesized). This latter aspect is dealt with in § 7.4.2.

Adopting the concept of Radical Underspecification, it seems impossible to insert all default values only after all other values (i.e. those via either representation in entries, by markedness rules, or by 'regular' phonological rules) have been derived. Rather, a principle such as (10) is needed. It is proposed by Archangeli (1984; 1988) and makes it possible for an 'early' rule to refer to a value provided by one of the default rules which would normally apply much later in the derivation, presumably at the end of the phonological component. I return to this topic in § 6.3.2 and at various other points below, where it will turn out that it seems necessary to state regularities referring to default values and also to both values of a feature. Of the rules given so far, (3c) is such that it requires this or a similar principle, since it refers to the negative value of [low].

(9) /ə/

a.	X	underlying or by epenthesis
b.	——	markedness rules
c.	X	default segment (8)

```
          X
          |
          R
```

d. X   defaults (4)

```
          X
          |
          R
          |
     Supralaryngeal
       /        \
    Place      Tongue
    /|\\       Position
   / | \        /\
  /  |  \  [- high]  [- low]
 Labial Dorsal Radical
   |    /\      |
[- round] / \ [- ATR]
[- front] [- back]
```

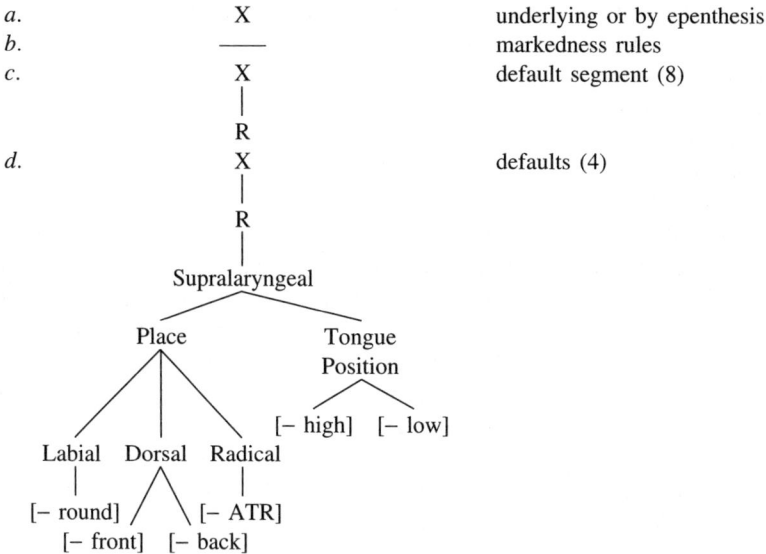

(10) Redundancy Rule Ordering Constraint
   Insert default values as late as possible (unless needed by another rule).

The Redundancy Rule Ordering Constraint may turn out to be objectionable for formal reasons. It is not clear that a formally constrained system should possess the power to look ahead and refer to values provided by later rules. It also seems necessary to check first on all other rules before it can be determined whether a default rule is actually applicable. In the general case as well as for German, it must be said that the evidence for the level of application for default rules is inconclusive.

6.1.1. The diphthongs

I will argue in this section that the diphthongal system of German is much more constrained than the superficial facts suggest, and that the version of Underspecification proposed above for the vowels seems to be confirmed by the diphthongs. On the surface, Modern Standard German has three falling diphthongs which can best be transcribed as [au̯], [ai̯], and [ɔy̯].[8] Some authors (e.g. Wurzel 1981: § 7.3.3) instead choose a transcription indicating non-high vowels for the non-syllabic glide segments: [ae̯], [ao̯], [ɔø̯]. Furthermore, [ɔi̯] is sometimes used instead of [ɔy̯]. The variant in transcriptions might reflect some phonetic variability in the realizations of three different off-glides, but it seems correct to assume, as most scholars of German phonology do, that the sounds indicated in the first series of transcriptions above are the articulatory targets intended by the speakers (see also Vennemann 1982: 275). In general, non-syllabic vowels are often articulated

---

[8] Rising diphthongs such as [jo] exist as well and will be treated in § 7.4.1.1.

such that the target values of the articulatory features are not as fully and clearly realized as they are in syllabic vowels. This is a point to be taken up below (§ 6.3.1) in the discussion of vocalized /ʀ/.

Given this, it may be asked why, of all possible combinations, only the three sequences enumerated above can occur. Even if a falling diphthong is defined as a sequence of a non-high vowel followed by a high vowel, many other combinations would become possible, and would be expected to occur.[9]

To answer this question, it can first be noted that for every short high vowel of German, there is exactly one diphthong ending in such a vowel. One diphthong ends in [ɪ], one in [ʏ], and one in [ʊ]. This part, at least, is remarkably regular. Turning to the first vocalic segment, the syllabic part, it seems as if [ɔʏ] is the odd member of the set, since the other two diphthongs start with low [a]. The set of diphthongs would be completely regular and homogeneous if it could be shown that [ɔʏ] is a surface form of the underlying diphthong /aʏ/. In such a case, every possible diphthong in German would consist of low /a/ followed by one of the short, high vowels /ɪ/, /ʏ/, and /ʊ/, as represented in (11), an analysis first suggested by Ramers and Vater (1991: § 4.3.4).

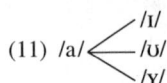

$$(11) \quad /a/ \overset{\displaystyle /ɪ/}{\underset{\displaystyle /ʏ/}{\longleftarrow /ʊ/}}$$

In fact, it can be shown quite clearly that the diphthong [ɔʏ] is indeed derived from /aʏ/, and that the desirable systematic description of Modern Standard German diphthongs is not only possible, but also unavoidable. Two groups of facts point in this direction.

For the first line of reasoning, we note, following Hall (1992b), that there are many intramorphemic vowel sequences in German other than diphthongs. Some examples illustrating the wide range of combinations are given in (12a). I ignore all distinctions of vowel length and/or tenseness; see Hall (1992b: § 3.1) for a more complete list and discussion. The noticeable fact is that, apart from other systematic gaps such as the exclusion of completely identical vowels (12b), no clear case of a sequence of two round vowels can be found, as indicated in (12c).

	Vowel sequences	Examples				
(12) a.	/i o/	Bio, Lioba	b.	*/i i/	c.	*/o u/
	/e o/	Theo, Deo		*/e e/		*/u o/
	/o a/	Boa, Kroate		*/ɛ ɛ/		*/y u/
	/o e/	Poet		*/u u/		*/u y/
	/i a/	Ria, Tiara				
	/u i/	Ruine				
	/i u/	Triumph				
	/y ɛ/	Hyäne				

---

[9] The existence of /ʊi/ in the two interjections *hui* and *pfui* was mentioned in § 3.2. It may be significant that many speakers also pronounce the adjective *ruh+ig* as [ʀʊiç]. Presumably, vowel shortening of the type studied in § 7.2.2 leads to diphthongization.

The few apparent counterexamples to (12c) can all be analysed as being derived in morphologically complex words, see (13):[10]

(13) a. /u o/ Du+o   (compare Du+ett, Tri+o)   b. /o u/: Droh+ung
       /y o/ My+om (compare my+o+gen, Karzin+om)   /u o/: virtu+os
                                                           /y u/: Bemüh+ung
                                                           ·
                                                           ·
                                                           ·

The examples in (13b), to which many others can be added, show furthermore that the constraint responsible for the exclusion of two adjacent round vowels must be a constraint on the underlying form of morphemes, not of words. We are dealing here with a *morpheme structure condition*. Its precise formulation is not the issue at this point (see Hall 1992b: § 3.1), so we assume it has the form given in (14). Two adjacent specifications of [+ round] are prohibited.

(14) Morpheme structure condition

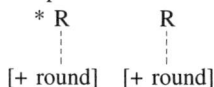

       * R   R
         ┊   ┊
         ┊   ┊
    [+ round]   [+ round]

The important point here is that morphemes with the diphthong [ɔʏ] would provide the only systematic (and highly frequent) exceptions to the regularity, since this diphthong consists of two round vowels. It seems, then, that there is good reason not to allow such a diphthong in the underlying representation of morphemes. What, if not /ɔʏ/, could be the representation of this diphthong?

Its behaviour in the functioning of the Umlaut rule, discussed in detail in § 7.2.1, can give a clue to its nature. For now, we note that one of the umlaut examples is the change from /aʊ/ to /ɔʏ/, as in *Baum* vs. *Bäume*. As proposed by Kloeke (1982: 17), a uniform treatment of umlaut in all its instances becomes possible, if it is assumed that in the umlauting of the diphthong, the change from /ʊ/ to /ʏ/ is the, totally regular, result of the Umlaut rule. The change in the first segment, from /a/ to /ɔ/, however, has nothing to do with Umlaut itself. It is, instead, the result of a special rounding rule which spreads the roundness feature from /ʏ/ to preceding /a/. These two rules, Umlaut and Rounding Assimilation, interact furthermore with the default rules. As will be demonstrated in (11) of § 7.2.1, the result is the derivation of [ɔʏ] from underlying /aʏ/.

I have now given two reasons for assuming underlying /aʏ/ for [ɔʏ]. First, /ɔʏ/ should not occur since it is ruled out by a well-motivated Morpheme Structure Constraint. Second, to derive [ɔʏ] from /aʏ/ in umlauting pairs of words, an account which includes a Rounding Assimilation seems optimal as it brings umlauting of the diphthong in line with all other umlauting vowels. The respective rule is stated in (10) of § 7.2.1. Finally, we also note again (although this would not be sufficient as an argument by itself) that under this approach the

---

[10] If these words are not analysed as being morphologically complex, the words in question are exceptions to the Morpheme structure condition (14). This type of exception is admitted in the theory; morpheme structure conditions may be violated in lexical exceptions. It is interesting, however, that a deeper morphological analysis of these words leads to the elimination of a phonological exceptionality.

system of diphthongs in Modern Standard German is as systematic and symmetric as it could possibly be: any sequence of low /a/ followed by one of the short high vowels (/ɪ/, /ʊ/, /ʏ/) is a well-formed (falling) diphthong.

These two (or three) arguments may be sufficient to justify the claim that Modern Standard German allows an underlying diphthong only if it consists of /a/ followed by a high vowel. No other statement is necessary which lists the three diphthongs to the exclusion of other combinations.

It may even be asked if it could follow from other principles that the three diphthongs discussed above (i.e. those beginning in /a/) exhaust the possibilities. It is here that the underspecification model proposed above comes into play. The description is confirmed by the underspecification analysis in (2) in so far as here the vowel /a/ is empty of all features. Recall that in § 3.2.4 a model for syllabification was proposed in which the nucleus dominates all and only the vowels of a syllable, that is, short vowels, long vowels, or a diphthong. With the model of underspecification as proposed here, the nucleus of a syllable would dominate maximally one value per feature, never more, since /a/ carries no specifications. There is evidence that syllable constituents such as onset, nucleus, coda can each contain (license) only one specification for place features (see Goldsmith 1990: § 3.4). For the nucleus in Modern Standard German, this theory can be upheld only if a model of Radical Underspecification is adopted in which /a/ is an empty vowel. Note that this reasoning presupposes that syllabification must operate on radically underspecified segmental structure.

6.1.2. On Contrastive Underspecification

The approach to underspecification developed above relies heavily on a notion of minimal specification. An alternative model, proposed in particular by Steriade (1987), stresses the notion of *contrastive* values of features. I will now examine this model of *Contrastive Underspecification* and the results it yields for Modern Standard German.

The values in (15) are derived by applying the algorithm for contrastive underspecification as proposed by Steriade (1987).[11] Starting from the fully specified matrix, one determines for any pair of segments whether the segments in this pair contrast in only one feature. For every such pair, feature values that are used contrastively in this sense are retained in the matrix, while all others are eliminated. Thus, as /iː/ and /eː/ contrast only in [high], [+ high] for /iː/ and [– high] for /eː/ are kept as contrastive features.

The decision about which features are the contrastive ones has of course to be taken prior to the application to the algorithm. In (15), the same features as in (2) are being used. Inspection of the result shows that Contrastive Underspecification leads not only to more features and feature values in the

---

[11] See also the discussion by Archangeli (1988: 192).

matrix (and thereby to redundancy), but also to a different picture as far as markedness is concerned. In particular, note that neither /ə/ nor /a/ emerges as an unspecified vowel, although /aː/ comes close to such an empty vowel. In general, there seems to be no good fit between the markedness of vowels as determined by other criteria and the degree of specification in (15). Short /ɛ/, for example, does not seem to be a very marked vowel in German, although (15) treats it as such a segment. A different choice of features before applying the algorithm does not fundamentally change this picture.

(15) Contrastive Underspecification

	iː	ɪ	eː	ɛː	ɛ	aː	a	oː	ɔ	uː	ʊ	yː	ʏ	øː	œ	ə
high	+	+	−		−			−	−	+	+	+	+	−	−	
low							+									−
front				+		−	−	−		−		+	+	+	+	−
round	−	−	−	−								+	+	+	+	
ATR			+	−												
long	+	−		+	−	+	−	+	−	+	−	+	−	+	−	

On the other hand, long /ɛː/ is clearly very marked within the vowel system of German, to the extent that it is neutralized with (and towards) /eː/ in many dialects. The analysis in (15) does not predict this outcome at all. The logic behind Contrastive Underspecification basically is that a segment bears as many feature values as it has minimal contrasts to other segments in a language.[12] The results yielded by the discussion in this section seem to indicate that it is not a hypothesis which works for German.

6.2. THE CONSONANT SYSTEM UNDERSPECIFIED

The preceding section on vowels has given a tentative answer to the question which features and feature values are distinctive, and which are redundant and predictable. Answering the same set of questions about underspecification for the consonants of German is somewhat more difficult, first, because the set of segments and features involved is larger. There are also more consonantal alternations, which often may give a clue as to the underspecification of the segments in question. Consequently, though I aim to motivate a complete underspecification analysis for consonants, the following discussion is less than complete.

Again, I will first repeat Table (7), § 2.3.2, for the consonants. This table does contain some gaps already, but these come about because some features are

---

[12] In this respect, Contrastive Underspecification implements a Trubetzkoyan concept of the phonemic contrast. Note also that degree of specification is completely dependent on the particular linguistic system.

defined only with respect to their dominating features.[13] Also, /h/ and /ʔ/ as the laryngeal segments lack a Supralaryngeal node, and hence all Place specifications. In addition, all features regarded as completely redundant, such as [lateral], have been removed from (16).

(16) Features of the consonant system

voice −	p	t	k	f	s	ʃ	ç	x	χ						h	?
voice +	b	d	g	v	z	ʒ	ʝ	ɣ	ʁ	m	n	ŋ	l	ʀ		
consonantal	+	+	+	+	+	+	+	+	+	+	+	+	+	+	+	+
obstruent	+	+	+	+	+	+	+	+	+	−	−	−	−	−	+	+
continuant	−	−	−	+	+	+	+	+	+	−	−	−	−	+	+	−
nasal	−	−	−	−	−	−	−	−	−	+	+	+	−	−	−	−
spread glottis	−	−	−	−	−	−	−	−	−	−	−	−	−	−	+	−
constricted glottis	−	−	−	−	−	−	−	−	−	−	−	−	−	−	−	+
Labial	+			+						+						
Dental		+														
Coronal		+			+	+					+		+			
Dorsal			+				+	+	+			+		+		
front			−				+	−	−			−		−		
Tongue Position	+	+	+	+	+	+	+	+	+	+	+	+	+	+		
high	−	−	+	−	−	+	+	+	−	−	−	+	−	−		
low	−	−	−	−	−	−	−	−	+	−	−	−	−	+		

Table (17) is identical to Table (16) as far as the segments and features are concerned. But in (17), all redundancies from that matrix are removed. In other words, it represents the underspecification analysis of the German consonant system. I put into parentheses those segments and features of (16) which are hypothesized not to be part of underlying representations. Capital X is a notation for the common underlier of the dorsal segments alternating in the Dorsal Fricative Assimilation, discussed in § 7.3.3. The other parenthesized segments do not need an underspecification analysis, since they are not underlying segments.[14]

Notice that the goal of using only positive values as underlying specifications has been achieved here. In what follows, the particular choices made leading to (17) are justified, sometimes simply by referring to rules and regularities formulated elsewhere in this book. This section concentrates on the Place features under the Supralaryngeal node which express the contrasts between elements of the same major class. Remaining features, the major class features understood in a broad sense, are analysed in the following section.

---

[13] This is the 'inherent underspecification' mentioned by Archangeli (1988: 190).

[14] This does not mean that they are fully specified once they emerge during the course of derivation. On [ʝ] see § 7.4.1.1, on [ʁ] see § 7.4.4.

(17) Consonant underspecification

X

	p	t	k	f	s	ʃ	(ç	x	χ)						h	(?)
	b	d	g	v	z	ʒ	(j	ɣ	ʁ)	m	n	(ŋ)	l	ʀ		
voice	+	+	+	+	+	+										
consonantal													+			
obstruent	+	+	+	+	+	+	+	+	+							
continuant				+	+	+	+	+	+				+			
nasal										+	+					
spread glottis															+	
(constricted glottis)																
Labial	+			+						+						
(Dental)																
(Coronal)																
Dorsal			+				+	+	+							
(front)																
Tongue Position						+							+			
high						+										
low													+			

Several strategies used in § 6.1 on vowels also apply in determining consonant underspecification. As one result, no negative values are included in (17). In addition, some necessary or factual implications from feature values to others are exploited. For example, since obstruents can be nothing but consonants, [+ consonantal] is only required for the non-obstruents. On a language-specific level, only obstruents can be either voiced or voiceless, while sonorants are voiced. Constraints on feature cooccurrences such as these justify markedness rules in the sense introduced above. Rules (26a) and (26b) apply to the facts just mentioned.

With regard to features for place of articulation, the first task is to determine whether there is an unmarked (and therefore unspecified) place of articulation and what it is. In the present framework, this makes necessary a study of the relationship between the three nodes under the Place node, that is, [Labial], [Coronal], and [Dorsal].

6.2.1. On coronals

One of the conclusions to be drawn from (17) is that the coronal consonants are not specified underlyingly for place of articulation. In other words, alveolar is taken to be the default place of articulation for consonants. This is formally expressed by the lack of a Place node and thereby specification for [Coronal] in (17), and is formally expressed by the default rule (18). The laryngeals [ʔ, h]

are characterized as segments without any Place features, that is, without a
Supralaryngeal node, while all other consonants except for the laryngeals have
a node [Supralaryngeal] in underlying representations. As with earlier rules, it
is assumed that the rule specifies a value if there is none so far.[15] Note that
palato-alveolar /ʃ, ʒ/ receive the feature [Coronal] through rule (18), although
they are already specified as [+ high] under [Tongue Position]. The separation
of [Tongue Position] from [Place] allows the differentiated treatment of the two
feature complexes.

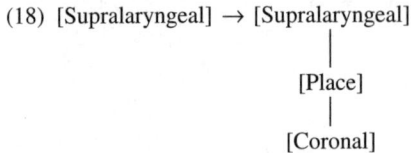

(18) [Supralaryngeal] → [Supralaryngeal]
                                    |
                                [Place]
                                    |
                               [Coronal]

There is good evidence that the hypothesis of the coronal articulator as a
default value is correct both in German and in other languages; see, for example,
Avery and Rice (1989) or contributions in Paradis and Prunet (1991). While the
default character of coronal consonants seems well established, authors disagree
on the range of what belongs to [Coronal]. Keating (1991) and others include
palatal consonants such as [ç] under the coronal articulator. The patterns found
in German (especially Dorsal Fricative Assimilation studied in § 7.3.3) seem to
speak against such a grouping in this language.

For the special status of alveolars in German, consider the following examples
of assimilations in place of articulation, taken from Kohler (1990c: 76). Given
that the examples in (19) are all the cases listed by Kohler, it is noticeable that
only alveolar consonants ([n, t, d]) are assimilated. Indeed, assimilation of labial
or dorsal consonants does not seem to be well formed.[16]

(19) *a.* Progressive assimilation of place
      [vaːgn] → [vaːgŋ]   *Wagen*
      [gəhɔlfn] → [gəhɔlfm̩]   *geholfen*
      [gəgeːbn] → [gəgeːbm]   *gegeben*
    b. Regressive assimilation of place
      [bɪn mɪt] → [bɪmmɪt]   *bin mit* 'am with'
      [mɪtm] → [mɪpm]   *mit'm* 'with a/the'
      [hat mɐ] → [hap mɐ]   *hat mir* 'has me'
      [jeːdm] → [jeːbm]   *jedem* 'every'
      [tseːn maɐk] → [tseːm maɐk]   *zehn Mark* 'ten marks'
      [hastn mɔmɛnt] → [haspm mɔmɛnt] *hast (du) 'n Moment* 'have you a
                                       moment'

---

[15] There is a gap in the present theory: 'no articulator' means 'none of [Labial], [Coronal], or
[Dorsal]'. The present model only partly accounts for their special status, as the articulator [Radical]
is also believed to be subsumed under [Place node].

[16] There is also the unexpected fact that /l/, /s/, and /z/, although coronal, are never subject to
assimilation, at least not beyond the coronal articulator as one would expect. See [haspm] in the final
example of (19*b*), which could not become *[hafpm].

Following Yu (1992*b*: § 4.1.1), I argue on the basis of this asymmetry between coronals and labials/dorsals that coronals lack a Place specification. Coronal consonants have other properties setting them apart from other consonants. In particular, they are the only consonants which can appear at the extreme right side of the syllable, in a position as in [*Mark*]$_\sigma t$ which is sometimes interpreted as being *extrasyllabic*; see § 3.2.3 and Wiese (1991) for discussion of extrasyllabicity in German. Suppose that no place of articulation can be specified for the extrasyllabic position. The defaults will then provide a consonant in this position with the values of the coronal place of articulation. Even if the concept of extrasyllabicity is not accepted, the fact remains that the consonants in this position can only be coronal.

The palato-alveolar consonants /ʃ, ʒ/ bear a feature ([+ high]) dependent on [Tongue Position]. They must therefore be specified underlyingly by this feature and by its superordinate articulator. Given the feature structure of § 3.1, they do not require an underlying Place node [Coronal]. In this respect, they are just like /s, z/.

6.2.2. Other place features

Articulators were not discussed in the preceding section on vowels, where it was not made explicit that the place features of the vowels are dependents of [Dorsal] and [Tongue Position]. The rules for vowels, especially the one introducing [+ low] for /a/, will automatically create the Tongue Position node (as part of higher structure), if it is not present already. But more generally, it seems that the coronal articulation provides the default articulation for consonants, while vowels always involve the Dorsal articulator. Furthermore, /ʀ/ is always dorsal in standard German. This regularity may be represented by stating rule (20). The feature combination [− obstruent, + continuant] applies precisely to the set comprising the vowels plus /ʀ/. For justification of the place features assumed here for /ʀ/, see § 6.3.1 below.

(20) $\begin{bmatrix} - \text{ obstruent} \\ + \text{ continuant} \end{bmatrix} \rightarrow$ [Dorsal]

Little must be said at this point on the articulator-dependent features. The negative values arise through the default schema given in (5). Of the positive values, some enter the representations through rules of assimilations, as for [χ] and (partly) [ʃ]. If it is correct to treat the dorsal segments /k, g, ç, x, ŋ/ as [+ high], the rule in (21) provides this value.

(21) $\begin{bmatrix} + \text{ consonantal} \\ \text{Dorsal} \end{bmatrix} \rightarrow$ [+ high]

Of the dorsal fricatives [ç, x, χ], palatal [ç] acts as the default consonant (for Modern Standard German, see § 6.4), as this consonant appears in all contexts where assimilatory properties are absent. This motivates the following rule (22*a*), which provides the value [+ front] for this consonant. Under the conditions of

assimilation discussed in § 7.3.3, the other variants appear. Rule (22*b*) is responsible for introducing the articulator [Dental] which is only needed for labiodental
/f, v/.

(22) *a.* $\begin{bmatrix} + \text{obstruent} \\ + \text{continuant} \\ \text{Dorsal} \end{bmatrix} \rightarrow [+ \text{front}]$

　　 b. $\begin{bmatrix} + \text{obstruent} \\ + \text{continuant} \\ \text{Labial} \end{bmatrix} \rightarrow [+ \text{Dental}]$

It is not clear whether the feature [lateral] plays any role in the phonological
system of Modern Standard German. In so far as the property of a lateral release
is also seen as a place feature required at least for the phonetic description of
/l/, the feature has to be included in the present discussion. I propose that [lat-
eral] should be inserted under the Coronal node. In some other proposals, this
feature is seen as belonging higher up in the segment tree; but since [lateral]
invariably denotes a coronal gesture (the sides of the tongue blade are lowered
to release the airstream), these alternative proposals are hard to defend. Given
the 'low' status of this feature, not much depends on this. Obviously, only
[l] is positive for this feature, which is actually one reason for not regarding
[lateral] as a distinctive feature. The markedness rule in (23) gives /l/ the positive value for this feature; all other sounds are [− lateral] by application of the
default schema.

(23) $\begin{bmatrix} - \text{continuant} \\ - \text{nasal} \\ - \text{obstruent} \end{bmatrix} \rightarrow [+ \text{lateral}]$

The lateral release for /l/ may be regarded as an inevitable consequence of the
fact that the sound is specified as a sonorant, and thereby as a voiced segment.
A lateral lowering of the tongue and the consequent release of the airstream is
perhaps the only way to ensure the voicing to continue in view of the blockage
of the mid-sagittal and the nasal airstream.

To demonstrate how the place features of fully specified consonants are created,
I illustrate the rules proposed here by the derivation of /t/ in (24), as this segment
is one of the alveolar consonants (of German) claimed to be void of all place
specifications.[17]

6.3. THE MAJOR CLASSES AND THEIR FEATURES

Phonological regularities are often stated in terms of subclasses of all segments
such as 'consonants' or 'vowels', 'fricatives' or 'liquids'. These are the *major
classes* of phonological theory. There are many open questions surrounding the
analysis of the major classes, also because the phonetic evidence for the features
assumed in this area is particularly weak or completely lacking.

---

[17] It is necessary here to pre-empt rules on major class features discussed in the following section.

(24) /t/

    a.

          R: [+ obstruent]   underlying
          |
   Supralaryngeal

    b.

$$R: \begin{bmatrix} + \text{obstruent} \\ + \text{consonantal} \end{bmatrix} \quad \text{markedness rule (26}a\text{)}$$

          |
   Supralaryngeal

    c.

$$R: \begin{bmatrix} + \text{obstruent} \\ + \text{consonantal} \end{bmatrix} \quad \text{markedness rule (18)}$$

          |
   Supralaryngeal
          |
      Place
        |
     Coronal

    d.

$$R: \begin{bmatrix} + \text{obstruent} \\ + \text{consonantal} \end{bmatrix} \quad \text{defaults}$$

          |
   Supralaryngeal

  Place   Tongue Position
    |
 Coronal   [− high]   [− low]

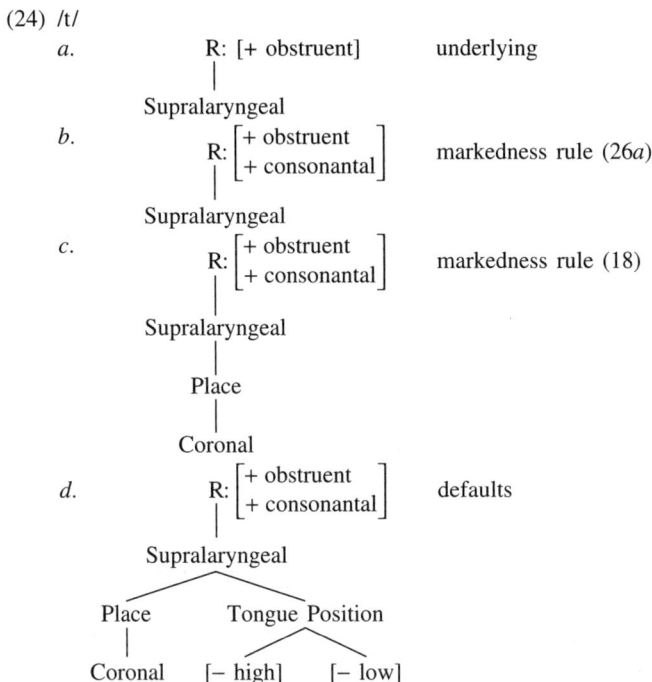

For a number of reasons involving mostly considerations of syllable structure and syllabification, the features listed in (25) will be assumed to hold in German. The feature [syllabic] may also be seen as a major class feature, but this was analysed as a feature belonging to the prosodic skeleton in (15) of § 3.2.1. For the place of the features treated here in the prosodic hierarchy, see (2) in § 3.1. Notice that major class features are generally those which are high in the segmental tree (i.e. close to the R node). This property may in fact be taken as the defining property of major class features.[18] That is, major class features are those which are not bound to a supralaryngeal articulator, and this may be a major reason why it is so difficult to establish phonetic correlates for these features.

In (25), the major classes playing a role in the phonology of Modern Standard German are listed and specified by the values which are needed in a highly underspecified analysis of the relevant major class features. The laryngeals are [h] and [ʔ], with [h] bearing [+ spread glottis] and [ʔ] bearing [+ constricted glottis]. /ʀ/ and /l/ are both members of singleton classes, each of which has its own phonotactic properties (see § 7.5.1). The voice feature is distinctive for fricatives and plosives, these segments are thus either unmarked or [+ voiced] in underlying representations, a principle already followed in (17). [Constricted glottis] cannot be part of the underlying structure, since it is only positive for [ʔ], which is an inserted segment (see below).

---

[18] The feature of voice, in accordance with this statement, does not really differentiate between the major classes of segments. It is included in the underspecification analysis below, since it interacts closely with the proper major class features.

(25) Underspecification of major classes

	Vowels	/ʀ/	/l/	Nasals	Fricatives	Plosives	Laryngeals
consonantal			+				
obstruent					+	+	
continuant		+			+		
voice					(+)	(+)	
nasal				+			
spread glottis							(+)
constricted glottis							

(25) includes only those values which are taken to be underlyingly present. Such an underspecification analysis of the major class features is often neglected in discussions of underspecification. One immediate conclusion from this may be that vowels are the least marked class of segments, while voiced fricatives are the most highly marked category. Notice further that [h] and [ʔ] have no special status according to this analysis with respect to the obstruents. [h] is included among the fricatives; [ʔ], among the plosives. The special properties of these two segments must derive from the fact that there is no Supralaryngeal node for these two segments, as explained in § 2.3.2. The laryngeal features of these segments are taken up again in § 6.3.2.

It is a somewhat surprising consequence of the analysis proposed here that /l/ emerges as being as underspecified as /t/, bearing only the specifications [+ consonantal, Supralaryngeal node]. While /l/ does not appear to be a very marked consonant, it is not usually seen as the least marked consonant either. I finish this section by simply pointing out this potential problem. It is interesting, however, that /l/ is universally a very common consonant, and that it is cross-linguistically clearly dominant among the liquids (see Maddieson, 1984: 73–8). Note also that the high degree of underspecification for [consonantal] contrasts with the use of this feature in the rules proposed for syllabification in § 3.2.4. If both of these proposals are (nearly) correct, then again a principle such as the Redundancy Rule Ordering Constraint (10) is needed. The rule constructing phonological words (sketched in § 3.4) even refers to both values of the feature [consonantal].

6.3.1. The feature phonology of /ʀ/

In (17) and (25), /ʀ/ is extremely underspecified in that [+ continuant] is its only feature specification except for a minimal place specification of [+ low]. I will now argue for this proposal by discussing the values given to, or left out for, /ʀ/. Some of the rules governing the appearance of different variants of this segment under specific conditions will be discussed in § 7.4.4.

There is probably no other segment with such a large set of realizations as /ʀ/. At least the following dimensions are included in the variability.

While the major place of articulation is uvular in Standard German, alveolar articulation can be found as well, especially in southern dialects such as Bavarian. But the place of articulation seems to be constant for any particular dialect and a given prosodic position. Variation between these places of articulation is interdialectal variation, but not allophonic or other variation within a given system. Presupposing that, in a universal perspective, the uvular articulation of the *r*-sounds is the marked one compared with the alveolar articulation, specifying the former place of articulation in underlying representations seems plausible.

The amount of constriction can vary (both within dialects and across) from fricative to vocalic. In the general case, /ʀ/ in Modern Standard German can best be described as an approximant in the sense used by the IPA classification or Ladefoged (1982). (See also ch. 1, fn. 4 on transcription.) Expressed in features, approximants are defined as [+ consonantal, − obstruent, + continuant]. Note that this definition sets /ʀ/ apart from /l/ and the nasal consonants.

In postvocalic position, /ʀ/ usually becomes vocalized to a considerable extent. In northern dialects and probably the standard language, /ʀ/ is totally vocalized. In these cases, it may sometimes completely merge with preceding /a/; consequently, a word-final sequence of /a/ plus /ʀ/ is difficult to distinguish from final /a/ alone: *Honorar* [hono'ʀaɐ̯] vs. *hurra* [hʊ'ʀaː]; near-neutralization may also occur between syllabic, vocalized /ʀ/ as in *Oper* [oːpɐ] and /a/ as in *Opa* [oːpa].[19]

The fricative version /ʁ/ can be found in initial position. As Hall (1993) observes, in certain dialects of German along the Lower Rhine, this fricative variant may extend to other positions.

Applying the logic of underspecification to these observations, it may be concluded that /ʀ/ has hardly any major class features; it is simply [+ continuant]. This is indeed the only property which remains constant across all *r*-realizations. In contrast, the features [consonantal] and [obstruent] receive varying values under specifiable circumstances. In its non-Southern versions, the place of articulation can be described as uvular and as very close to the vowel [a]. Taking this observation seriously means that /ʀ/ should bear place features similar to or identical with /a/. Thus, it is also [+ low]. This is the argument leading to the particular assignment of dependent place features given in (16) and (17). That /ʀ/, in the present analysis, is not completely underspecified like the vowel /a/ might be regarded as an indication that underspecification for /ʀ/ has not gone far enough.

On the other hand, it is, in German as in other languages, the alveolar place of articulation which can be claimed to constitute the unmarked place of

---

[19] The final vowel in *Opa* may be judged to be half-long, however. The pronouncing dictionary by Krech et al. (1982) avoids the problem by transcribing vocalized /ʀ/ as [r], unless it is the syllabic vowel. More on the transcription and classification problem in § 7.4.4.

articulation. Note, however, that rule (20) is assumed to apply to /ʀ/. This rule can be regarded to take precedence over (18). /ʀ/ is thus protected against the application of default rule (18) which would assign the articulator [Coronal] to it. Also, (21) cannot apply to /ʀ/ because of the incompatibility of [+ high] and [+ low]. The feature specification of vocalic /ʀ/, that is, [ɐ], will be taken up again in the discussion of r-Vocalization in § 7.4.4.

6.3.2. **Markedness rules and defaults**

As for other articulatory features, in addition to all negative values missing from the underspecified matrix, some positive values are also predictable.

A first set of redundancy rules refers to the feature [obstruent]. It seems natural to assume that obstruents must be consonants. In other words, we may predict [+ consonantal] on the basis of [+ obstruent]. This is done in (26a). Likewise, sonorants are, as mentioned, voiced, and accordingly, voicing is predicted through (26b) for all sonorants. Finally, all vowels are continuants, and rule (26c) expresses this relationship. These statements, given formally as markedness rules of the type familiar by now, are probably true for most languages, although, for example, voiceless vowels may be found occasionally.

(26) Markedness rules
    a. [+ obstruent] → [+ consonantal]
    b. [− obstruent] → [+ voice]
    c. [− consonantal] → [+ continuant]

In (26a) and (26b), two quite uncontroversial rules are stated which require the opposite values for the same feature [obstruent] as input. This is precisely the situation alluded to in § 6.1 on vowels, when some doubt was cast upon the assumption that default rules could always be made to apply at the last level of the phonology. The Redundancy Rule Ordering Constraint (10) or a similar mechanism is required for exactly such cases.

Assuming that [+ consonantal] is predictable for /ʀ/ and the nasals, two more markedness rules are necessary:[20]

(27) *a.* [+ continuant] → [+ consonantal]
    b. [+ nasal] → [+ consonantal]

The remaining gaps in (25) are easy to fill; the required values are all negative and can be provided by either the default rules in (28) which are instantiations of the simple schema [ØF] → [− F] proposed in (5) above.

(28) Default rules
    a. [consonantal] → [− consonantal]
    b. [obstruent] → [− obstruent]
    c. [voice] → [− voice]
    d. [continuant] → [− continuant]
    e. [nasal] → [− nasal]

---

[20] Some mechanism is needed to prevent (27a) from applying to vowels (which are [+ continuant] because of rule (26c)). If no satisfying mechanism (such as application of markedness rules to underlying entries only) can be found, it may be necessary to mark /ʀ/ as a consonant and drop (27a) In this case, the rule of r-Vocalization (§ 7.4.4) would require a different treatment.

6.3.3. **Laryngeals**

The two segments [h] and [ʔ] can be characterized as laryngeal sounds, since the articulatory gesture characteristic for them is performed by the glottal folds in the larynx. This specification of the respective laryngeal gesture seems to be sufficient for these sounds, since no other supraglottal property, no constriction in the oral or nasal tract, is characteristic for these segments.[21] Accordingly, [h] and [ʔ] are treated in featural terms as particular states of the laryngeal node, as first indicated in § 2.3.2. It was also stated there that [h] as well as aspiration requires a glottal state which can be described as 'spread glottis', while the glottal stop [ʔ], quite in accordance with its name, should be analysed with a feature of glottal constriction. The resulting typology of segments with reference to the laryngeal features is that in (29).

(29)

	/h/ aspirated consonant	ʔ	All others
spread glottis	+	−	−
constricted glottis	−	+	−

It may be unnecessary to state at this point that glottis features are also subject to underspecification. As a consequence, underlyingly, only [+ spread glottis] is present as a feature specifying /h/. This gives the minimal distinction needed between, say, *Haus* and *aus*. While the negative values for [spread glottis] and [constricted glottis] are accounted for by the normal default schema (5), [+ constricted glottis], as the crucial feature for [ʔ], requires a special rule. All that is required is to replace '[ʔ]' in the insertion rule (47) of § 3.3.1 by this feature. The result is given in (30).

(30) Glottal Stop Insertion
Insert [+ constricted glottis] / $_F$[_____ [− consonantal]

To ensure a complete underspecification for the laryngeals, their major class features must be introduced by means of markedness rules such as those in (31). Other rules formulated above will then apply.

(31) Markedness rules
  a. [+ constricted glottis] → [+ obstruent]
  b. [+ spread glottis] → [+ obstruent]
  c. [+ spread glottis] → [+ continuant]

In (32) the derivation of a completely specified [ʔ] from such an inserted glottis feature is illustrated. The segmental structure above it is automatically created by following the convention mentioned above. Notice that since there is no rule or principle to specify the Supralaryngeal node or its subordinate features, it never comes into being.

---

[21] Usually, the other articulators are in the position required for the following segment, which is, in German, always a vowel. Therefore, there is no oral-nasal constriction narrower than that for a high vowel.

(32) [ʔ]

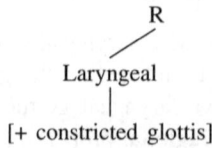

a.   R   Glottal Stop Insertion
                          ╱   (30), segmental
                  Laryngeal   structure
                      |
            [+ constricted glottis]

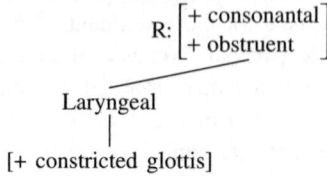

b.   R: $\begin{bmatrix} + \text{consonantal} \\ + \text{obstruent} \end{bmatrix}$ markedness rules (31),
                                                                                                            (26a)
                          ╱
                  Laryngeal
                      |
            [+ constricted glottis]

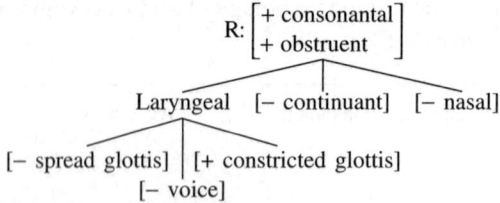

c.   R: $\begin{bmatrix} + \text{consonantal} \\ + \text{obstruent} \end{bmatrix}$ default rules
                              ╱ | ╲
                  Laryngeal   [− continuant]   [− nasal]
              ╱ |
    [− spread glottis] | [+ constricted glottis]
              [− voice]

To conclude this section, it may be worthwhile to compare those segments of
MSG which are, more than others, stripped of particular distinctive features,
either because they are default segments or because they display so much variation that reducing their phonological substance to a minimum is justified. (33)
represents the features for these sound segments either at the underlying levels
or at the first level where the segment is introduced.

(33) *Segment*   *Representation*
     ə   X (underlying or inserted)
     a   R
     t   R, [+ obstruent], Supralaryngeal
     h   [+ spread glottis]
     ʔ   [+ constricted glottis] (by foot-initial insertion)

Before moving on to the 'proper' phonological rules of German, that is, those
which account for systematic alternations, in Chapter 7, it may be worth considering the status of the rules proposed in the present and in earlier chapters. The
theory assumed here assigns a minimum set of non-predictable phonological
specifications to lexical entries. Phonological rules describing alternations will
usually specify additional values, according to their context descriptions. Only
when such rules are not available, are underspecified values provided by markedness and default rules as given in this chapter. There is thus the hierarchy of
rules as in (34), in which the bottom rules only apply if higher rules have not
already done so. Recall in this connection the remarks in § 5.3.1 on the treatment
of lexical entries as very specific rules. The relationship between rules as specified here will usually, if not always, fall out of the Elsewhere Condition.

     The discussion above has not been very explicit about the point at which all
values must be specified. Given that there do not seem to be clear cases showing

that all features must bear a specification at a specific point, I will assume that the default rules apply as late as possible. Some values may actually be part of the phonetic implementation, that is, never specified during the lexical or postlexical phonology. On this point, see also the remarks on phonetic forms of assimilation in § 7.3.4. On the other hand, it appears that default rules actually must apply before the application of phonological rules proper. For example, the *s*-Voicing rule to be discussed below requires the presence of [+ voice] for the vowel following /s/. As voicing of vowels is a clear case of a default assignment, we are forced to admit that here the default rule which assigns [+ voice] to a vowel applies before other rules do.

(34) Hierarchy of specifications
　　 a. Lexical entries
　　 b. 'Proper' phonological rules
　　 c. Markedness rules
　　 d. Default rules

6.4. SOME OPEN QUESTIONS

The above attempt to provide an underspecification analysis for the segments of Modern Standard German aims at removing all redundant features and values from lexical entries, and at formulating the system of rules and principles which derives the full specifications. It must be stressed that such an enterprise is not primarily a formal exercise: the approach is motivated by such empirical considerations as the need for a more adequate treatment of the dorsal fricatives (see § 7.3.3) and of the umlauting of vowels (§ 7.2.1). Furthermore, for theoretical reasons it seems to be desirable to express markedness formally by the degree of underspecification. Nevertheless, the specific proposals above are likely to be subject to alternative solutions. In view of this I now turn to some such problems and alternative directions which warrant discussion.

It should be noted that, in the analysis given, all the markedness and default rules given are context-free, in the sense that none of the feature-filling rules takes into account the context of the segment in question. It is not clear whether or not this is a desirable property of the analysis.

For an example of a plausible context-sensitive markedness rule, consider vowel length. In the system proposed here, vowels are unmarked if short, while long vowels, without exception, are marked underlyingly (by two skeletal positions). However, as noted earlier, German words cannot end in a short vowel. Thus, all word-final vowels will be long (except for schwa).[22] For this reason, it is possible to remove all length representations from word-final vowels. Instead, they can receive the proper value (two skeletal positions) from a rule such

---

[22] The actual vowel length varies and is dependent on stress. But given the correlation between vowel length and tenseness expressed in (3c), it can be concluded that vowels must be long in word-final position, since lax vowels do not occur here. Hall (1992b: § 1.2.5) proposes a vowel-length analysis of this kind.

as (35), assuming that the word to be considered here is actually the phonological word ω.

(35)   X   X
                              \   /
                               \ /
     R: [− consonantal] → R: [− consonantal] / _____]$_\omega$

In a similar vein, consider the restriction against voiceless /s/ in word-initial position. Words such as *Sonne* and *sehen* have no counterparts with voiceless /s/ in the word-initial position before a vowel. Loan words such as *Sex* or *Samowar* usually assimilate in the direction of initial /z/. In the approach to underspecification presented above, words would be represented simply with an initial /z/, and so the generalization that voicing is predictable here would go uncaptured.[23] We may therefore propose a (simplified) rule such as the following, in which word-initial /s/ receives voicing. There is in fact evidence that ω, the phonological word, is the correct context here. The two suffixes +*sam* and +*sal* (see (4) of § 5.2.1) begin in /z/, while no suffix beginning with /s/ and containing a full vowel exists. According to the model of the phonological word proposed in § 3.4, the suffixes in question, being consonant-initial, will form their own phonological word, but they are obviously not words in the morphological sense. On the other hand, a syllable may well start in /s/ if word-internal; for example, *reißen* [ʀaɪ̯.sən] or *dreißig* [dʀaɪ̯.sɪç]. (One of the few minimal pairs available is *reis+en* [ʀaɪ̯.zən] vs. *reißen* [ʀaɪ̯.sən].)

(36) /s/ → [z] / $_\omega$[_____

(36) is a context-sensitive underspecification rule. This rule is inadequate, however, since it disregards cases such as *Skelett* [skelɛt], *Slalom* [slaːlɔm] with initial /s/ plus consonant, and *Zahn* [tsaːn], *Psalm* [psalm], with initial affricates /ts/ or /ps/. Here, /s/ is voiceless in various word-initial contexts. These examples demonstrate that the exclusion of voiceless /s/ is restricted to a position which is adjacent to both a word boundary and a vowel. While it is possible to simply add [− consonantal] as a right-hand condition to the context of rule (36), another solution is also available: the specification [+ voice] for /z/ may derive from the following vowel, which is always (redundantly) voiced. Again abbreviating on the format of the rule, (37) is the alternative to a modification of (36). For the use of the broken line, see § 7.1 below. The lack of voicing assimilation found in further examples of /s/-initial loans such as *Smoking*, *Slalom*, or *Sri Lanka* with a following voiced consonant suggests that the triggering element must indeed be a vowel.

(37) *s*-Voicing
     $_\omega$[/ s/ [− consonantal]
           \ |
            \   ↓
            [+ voice]

---

[23] Voicing is unpredictable only in some morpheme-final positions as in *reis+en* vs. *reiß+en*, where the actual voicing depends of course on the applicability of Final Devoicing.

This rule assigns [+ voice] to an /s/ immediately preceding the vowel. Note that the adjacency required here of the word boundary, /s/, and the vowel prevents the application of the rule in *Skat* or *Psalm*. Rule (37) belongs to the type of spreading rules usually not classified as redundancy rules, although it does provide an otherwise unspecified value. If (37) is preferable over (modified) (36), then it should be an element of the list of proper phonological rules treated in the following chapter.

These examples show how context-sensitive underspecification can lead to further elimination of redundancies, and that it is not always clear whether a redundancy rule or a spreading rule of the type introduced in the following chapter provides the correct analysis. I leave such questions to further studies.

In pursuing such questions, one might reflect on the various strategies applied above to arrive at underspecified representations. Basically, two arguments were used to propose a particular gap in the feature matrix. First, values regarded as unmarked were ruled out from underlying representations and filled in by rule. This strategy leads to the desirable result that markedness of segmental information can be immediately read off from the number of feature markings. But a second strategy, applied in the case of /ʀ/ and the vowels, was to remove those values from the representations which vary, that is, which can be observed to alternate through the effect of a phonological rule such as Umlaut or *r*-Vocalization. It is this strategy which makes it possible to disallow all feature-changing rules, an equally desirable move on theoretical grounds. It is not clear whether the two approaches (relying on markedness and relying on alternation) always yield the same or congruent results.

Finally, I have largely left open the universal vs. language-particular aspects of the analysis. In general, it is clear that some of the rules are at least good candidates for universal statements, while other rules are clearly valid for German, but not for all languages. Rules (18) and (26) are examples of the former, rules (22), (36), and (37) of the latter sort. (22) makes the palatal place of articulation the default case for the dorsal fricatives. This seems to be a language-specific fact of Modern Standard German, given that a related language such as Dutch has velar articulation in analogous cases. Similarly, voiceless /s/ in word-initial position is a common property of other Germanic languages, while German /s/ is subject to the voicing rule, as we have just seen. Finally, the set of rules 'conspiring' to make schwa the default vowel of German cannot be regarded as universal, given that different languages have different default vowels. In the light of such facts, I see no way to formulate the markedness or default rules in such a way that all of them express universal regularities or even tendencies.[24]

---

[24] Mohanan (1991) requires all statements on markedness to be universal statements. It seems to me that there is a good case for markedness relative to an individual linguistic system. With respect to (36) and (37), the language-particular nature of the constraint may be used as an argument against its inclusion among the redundancy rules.

PHONOLOGICAL RULES AND ALTERNATIONS

> That's not a regular rule; you invented it just now.
> *(Lewis Carroll, Alice in Wonderland)*

In a way, all the preceding proposals for the categories and the structure of phonological representations and for the place of phonology in grammar have been preliminaries to the content of the present chapter. The adequate formulation of phonological rules and alternations in Modern Standard German is highly dependent on phonological representations (as developed in Chs. 3 and 6) and the organization of grammar (Chs. 4 and 5), and thus provides the litmus test for the hypotheses formulated there for these fundamental aspects of phonology.

This chapter attempts to cover what is known about the major (and some of the minor) phonological rules of Modern Standard German. The term *alternation* is often used for a (more or less) systematic variance of two sounds which are both phonemic in the specific language, while *rule* is used for allophonic variation. I use the concept of 'rule' in a relatively broad sense, encompassing all observable variants of well-formed expressions in German. Within this rather broad range, I have little to say on the two very extreme forms of such alternations: the irregular, lexicalized changes such as the root changes in verb forms (*bring+* vs. *brach+t*)[1] will not be treated as effects of phonological rules; and those rules which create a gradient output and are often applied optionally, never involve distinctive oppositions and will be assumed to belong to the domain of phonetics (see § 7.6 for discussion).

There still remains a large number of phenomena to be covered, some of which are well studied, while others are not. In this chapter, after a brief discussion of formalism and notation in § 7.1, I cover rules operating on vowels in § 7.2, and rules operating on consonants in § 7.3. Syllable-related rules in German which cross the consonant–vowel boundary are treated separately in § 7.4, while phonotactic constraints are the subject of § 7.5. The final section discusses the problems of separating phonology from phonetics in the formulation of rules, and of assigning rules to the lexical or postlexical component of grammar.

According to the model of grammar presented here, phonological rules can apply both within and outside of the lexicon, as discussed in Chapter 5. This is particularly true for rules of epenthesis, degemination, assimilation, and deletion

---

[1] Although there is at least one obvious regularity about the so-called ablaut: the onset consonants are, with very few exceptions, not affected. One particular case of ablaut (raising of /e/ to /i/) will be briefly treated in § 7.2.1. For a recent systematic treatment of ablaut patterns, see Wunderlich and Fabri (1993).

in the phonology of Modern Standard German. The important role of these rules and their different behaviour lexically and postlexically will be stressed. Starting from the notion of underspecification developed in the preceding chapter, it will also be shown that all the rules proposed here do not have the power (in contrast to previous descriptions) to change values of a feature. Instead, they usually insert values, that is, they are blank-filling. At most, rules can be destructive, that is, remove values for some feature.

7.1. RULE FORMALISM

In an explicit account of phonological phenomena, phonological rules have to be stated in a framework which is as precise and formal as possible. It is therefore advisable to state a format for phonological rules. In classical generative phonology, rules are written according to the format

A → B / C ____ D

('The (complex) symbol A is rewritten as the (complex) symbol B in the environment left context C and right context D'). This framework uses an explicit notation for phonological rules, but the transformational format in effect means that such rules have the power to change phonological representations in an arbitrary way, to add or delete material, or to reorder it.

In this respect, theories such as the one proposed by Chomsky and Halle in *SPE* were totally unconstrained. Rules could manipulate the featural matrices in any way possible. The overall concern to formulate restricted theories of grammar has led phonological theory to a more constrained concept of rules. The concept of rules used in this study relies on the idea that phonological representations may be affected in only two ways: information may be added or deleted. In other words, no rule may change feature values or reorder units. All apparent structure-changing rules must be reinterpreted as deletion plus (possibly) addition of relevant phonological material. As the rule responsible for the addition must be independently motivated, this decomposition is more than a purely formal exercise.[2]

It would be even more in the spirit of Underspecification theory as developed in the last chapter, if all phonological rules were to add information. However, as I argue in this chapter on the basis of several examples, such a conception does not seem to be viable. Note that one of the (few) rules stated so far, the rule of Word Deletion given in (60) of § 3.4, provides a clear example of a deletion rule. The rules of Vowel Shortening, Final Devoicing, and g-Deletion, to be discussed later in this chapter, provide further, well-motivated cases. I will,

---

[2] Computational phonologists such as Coleman (1995) or Walther (1993) insist that the power of a system containing feature-changing rules is not reduced by allowing only rules which either add or remove feature values. Therefore I emphasize that, on a non-formal level, such decomposed rules must be independently motivated by taking part in other regularities.

therefore, assume that phonological rules are free to either add or delete featural information, but that addition is the unmarked option.

Rules which seem to be changing the representation by changing feature values must be decomposed, following a proposal first made by Poser (1982), into one rule of removing a value and another rule of adding a value. Such processes are therefore necessarily more complex than structure-building operations. As Kiparsky (1993) points out, simplicity of grammar alone will ensure that adding information will be the standard case. Under the present concept of phonological rule, each single rule is also restricted to performing only *one* of the possible operations. It cannot do two things at once.

In a semi-formal way, the present proposal may be expressed by the convention that in phonological rules, lines of association in phonological representations are either inserted or removed. The first type of rule is illustrated in (1), in which (1*a*) is a common abbreviation of (1*b*). Broken lines are to be interpreted as representing association lines added as a result of the application of the rule.

(1) Association

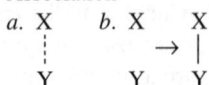

$$a.\ \text{X} \qquad b.\ \text{X} \qquad \text{X}$$
$$\vdots \qquad\qquad \rightarrow\ \vert$$
$$\text{Y} \qquad\quad \text{Y} \qquad \text{Y}$$

Compared to the addition of a line of association, removing an association line probably constitutes the marked case. This type of rule is notated as in (2), again given here in an abbreviated (2*a*) and a more explicit (2*b*) form. Given the existence of rules such as Word Deletion, delinking seems to be possible between phonological categories of any kind and position within the prosodic hierarchy.

(2) Deletion of association line (*delinking*)

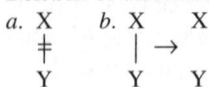

$$a.\ \text{X} \qquad b.\ \text{X} \qquad \text{X}$$
$$\neq \qquad\qquad \vert\ \rightarrow$$
$$\text{Y} \qquad\quad \text{Y} \qquad \text{Y}$$

The values '+' and '−' are the terminal nodes in the featural representation of segments as developed in § 3.1. Strictly speaking, they may also be conceived as being linked by association to the features of which they are values. But as a further shorthand notation, one may follow (as I have done so far) the common convention whereby these two elementary values are notated simply to the left of their features. (3*a*) notes this equivalence of notations; (3*b, c*) demonstrates its use in the two types of phonological rules assumed above. But in order to uphold the claim that all rules either add or remove a line of association it is important to acknowledge these equivalences.

In writing down rules, I use a different abbreviatory convention, simply to conserve space. If intermediate categories can be left out without ambiguity, I will sometimes connect relevant feature structures by dotted lines. That is, for example, (4*a*) will be represented by (4*b*). Note that the dotted line has a different meaning from the broken line.

(3) Shorthand notation

    a. F: [α F], with α = +, −
       |
       α

    b. F: [F] → [α F], with α = +, −
       ⋮
       α

    c. F: [α F] → [F], with α = +, −
       ‡
       α

(4) *a.*   R   *b.*   R
           | ⋮
    Supralaryngeal   Dorsal
           |
       Place
         |
      Dorsal

In the rest of this chapter, I treat rules pertaining to vowels and to consonants separately, although there are important phenomena of transitions between these two classes of sounds, as we will see in § 7.4.

7.2. RULES OF VOWEL ALTERNATION

Within the vowel system of Modern Standard German, the number of rules describing actual alternations between vowels is relatively small. I begin with the much discussed rule of Umlaut and then proceed to a discussion of a few lesser-known vowel rules.

7.2.1. **Umlaut**

The rule named *Umlaut* is the central rule in the Modern Standard German vowel system. Indeed, as Wurzel (1970: 105) remarked, an understanding of Umlaut involves practically all aspects of the phonology of Modern Standard German including its interaction with morphology. Its fame is also responsible for the retention of the German term *umlaut* in the international phonological terminology.[3] Some of the decisions made in the specification of vowel features in § 6.1 have been justified by reference to the Umlaut rule. In the following, the purely phonological aspects of the Umlaut rule will be treated before we deal with its interaction with morphology. As by-products, a rule of Rounding Assimilation within diphthongs and a rule of Vowel Raising will be developed as well. I also discuss alternative accounts of Umlaut to a greater extent than those of other rules to be discussed later.

---

[3] A non-German term for vowel alternations of all kinds is *apophony*.

(5) gives a number of typical examples of what is called *umlaut* in Modern Standard German. The list of vowel pairs given here is complete, and the vowel in the second word of each pair has undergone the rule of umlauting to be discussed. The examples also illustrate the large range of morphological contexts in derivation and inflection for this vowel alternation.[4] We also note that the umlauted vowel always appears in a morphologically derived form.

(5) *a.* /uː/ ~ /yː/   Huhn ~ Hühn+er, Gruß ~ grüß+en
     b. /ʊ/ ~ /ʏ/   dumm ~ dümm+lich, Hund ~ Hünd+in
     c. /oː/ ~ /øː/   hoch ~ höch+st, Vogel ~ Vögel
     d. /ɔ/ ~ /œ/   Glocke ~ Glöck+chen, Holz ~ hölz+ern
     e. /aː/ ~ /ɛː/   Europa ~ europä+isch, (ich) sah ~ säh+e
     f. /a/ ~ /ɛ/   Stand ~ ständ+ig, lach+en ~ läch+el+n
     g. /aʊ/ ~ /ɔʏ/   (ich) lauf+e ~ (er) läuf+t, sauf(en) ~ Säuf+er

Setting aside the last pair of vowels in which a diphthong is the subject of the rule, we note that the result of umlauting is invariably a front vowel. In fact, the umlauted vowel is usually identical to its non-umlauted counterpart—except for the feature [front]. The pairs of vowels in which /a/ alternates with /ɛ/ are apparent exceptions to the generalization: /a/ is [+ low], and /ɛ/ is [− low]. A solution for this problem is suggested in the discussion of underspecification of vowels in 6.1: if [low] is not an underlying distinctive feature, but introduced by the operation of markedness rules or some similar device, the irregularity may disappear.

As for the diphthongal pair (5*g*), the second segment is identical to that in (5*b*). Again, nothing but a fronting of the vowel, that is, umlaut, must be assumed. The change in the initial segment, however, cannot be covered under the umlaut alternation. But in § 6.1.1 it was argued that it is necessary for independent reasons to assume a rule of Rounding Assimilation within diphthongs. The diphthong /ɔʏ/, according to that reasoning, can never be underlying, and the underlying initial segment should be taken as /a/.

Note, finally, that long vowels umlaut in a uniform way, just as short vowels do. This fact provides an argument against the treatment of long vowels as sequences of short vowels, such as /aa/. Not only would Umlaut have to apply twice in the case of long vowels; more problematically, under such a representation, we might expect umlauting of only one of the vowels, as in the case of the diphthong /aʊ/. Since this never happens, the 'gemination' approach to vowel length mentioned in § 3.2.1 does not seem to make the right prediction. Umlaut provides an example of the fact that long segments behave uniformly in quality-sensitive rules, that is, they confirm the appropriateness of separating quality features from the features of length.

With these preliminary remarks, the path is cleared for a formulation of the Umlaut rule covering all cases traditionally subsumed under this name. Umlaut is always the fronting of a vowel. 'Fronting' is to be taken literally here; it is the feature value [+ front] which is assigned in this rule.

---

[4] For more discussion of the morphological contexts see Wurzel (1984).

(6) Umlaut

$\qquad$ R: [− consonantal]

$\qquad$ ⋮

$\qquad$ Dorsal

$\qquad\qquad$ [+ front] $\rfloor_\omega$

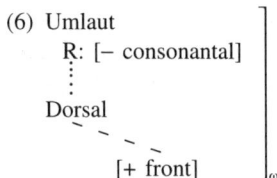

In rule (6), first proposed in a similar form by Wiese (1987), the feature of fronting is associated with the right-most vowel within a domain which is taken to be the phonological word (see p. 191 below). That the affected vowel is indeed always the right-most one is indicated by the fact that cases such as *Europa* vs. **euröpa+X* are unattested, but compare *europä+isch*.[5] Besides numerous roots, one nominal suffix also umlauts: *Reich+tum* vs. *Reich+tüm+er*, *Volks+tum* vs. *volks+tüm+lich*. Of course there is no reason why the lexical entry for an affix could not contain a floating [+ front].

The Umlaut rule proposed in (6) differs from the traditional rule-oriented approaches to German umlaut (e.g. King 1969; Wurzel 1970; Lieber 1981; Kloeke 1982) in that it postulates a *floating* feature [+ front] as part of underlying entries of roots. The Umlaut rule only associates such a feature with a suitable root node. In other words, only lexical entries containing such a feature may umlaut. Also, in the present formulation the rule is not dependent on particular phonological information in the following suffix. For discussion of some alternative conceptions, also involving a floating feature, see below. The use of [+ front] instead of [− back] in the more *SPE*-oriented proposals is justified by the fact that umlauted vowels are indeed front, and not just central, vowels. Notice in particular that umlauted /ɔ/ leads to (front) /œ/, and not to (central) /ǝ/, a round counterpart of schwa. Also, as the *a*-sounds are assumed to be [− back], only fronting can umlaut these segments (to /ɛ/ and /ɛː/ respectively).

This proposal is meant to account for one part of the well-known fact that umlauting has a number of morphologically conditioned irregularities. The extent of these irregularities is such that various authors have questioned or denied the possibility of a *phonological* rule of Umlaut for Modern Standard German, but the preceding remarks are also intended to demonstrate that in terms of the featural changes found in the process itself, Umlaut is in fact very regular and simple.

The ω-boundary in (6) replaces morpheme boundaries in earlier proposals. The reference to a prosodic constituent first follows from the hypothesis that all phonological rules can only apply within phonological domains, and nowhere else. Second, this conception will turn out to have a major advantage over those proposals referring to morphological structures; see discussion of examples in (14) below. Conceivably, the ω-boundary in (6) can be left out, if it can be

---

[5] This pair also illustrates a difficulty with the common claim that, in spite of *'Bischof* vs. *'Bischöf+e*, only stressed vowels may umlaut. In *Eu'ropa*, it is the penultimate vowel which carries stress, while in *euro'pä+isch* the same vowel, now umlauted, is stressed. The clause that only stressed vowels are subject to umlaut is usually meant to exclude umlaut on schwa. But to achieve this, it is sufficient to assume that schwa is not present when the Umlaut rule applies.

shown that association between features and segment nodes in all cases proceeds from right to left within the domain of the phonological word. More precisely, if the phonological word turns out to be the unmarked domain of rule application (as I claim in the discussion of some consonantal rules below), only domains other than ω will have to be mentioned.

At this point, we only note that it is always the right-most vowel which umlauts; if there is a vowel to the right of the umlauting vowel in the same phonological word, it is either schwa or a front vowel of the suffix. Of course, word-final schwa presents no problem if simply presumed absent. In fact, Lieber (1987: § 2.3) takes the irrelevance of schwa in umlauting as an argument for a description involving schwa epenthesis. It happens that vowels do not umlaut if there is a non-front vowel in the same phonological word. In particular, with affixes containing a non-front vowel (such as +*ung*) no umlauting is ever found. Possibly, this fact represents a remnant of older forms of German, in which umlauting was related to the presence of a high front vowel.

The factors complicating the picture and the reasons for treating umlaut as a stem alternation is illustrated by the word pairs in (7). The examples demonstrate that umlaut co-occurs with suffixation of +*lich*, +*chen*, +*t*, and (comparative) +*er*, but not without exception. The back (or non-front) vowels in *rund, Onkel, ruf*(*en*), or *dumpf* could umlaut for purely phonological reasons, but do not, either in the present examples or under any other conditions, that is, derivational or inflectional processes. That is, potential umlaut in *rund+er* (comparative), *rund+en* (de-adjectival verb), and so on, does not in fact occur.

(7) *a.* lang ~ läng+lich, rund ~ rund+lich
  b. Vater ~ Väter+chen, Onkel ~ Onkel+chen
  c. laufen ~ läuf+t, rufen ~ ruf+t
  d. dumm ~ dümm+er, dumpf ~ dumpf+er

Rule (6) is designed precisely to handle the distinction illustrated here. The fact that stems such as *rund, Onkel, ruf*(*en*), and *dumpf* and many recent borrowings never undergo umlauting under any morphological condition is accounted for by the lack of a floating [+ front] in their respective representations. Since neither the suffixes nor any other factor such as a rule are available to change these representations, no umlauting can ever take place.

Before we turn to more complications, the analysis may be summarized in the following way. There are three types of relevant vowels: in a first set of vowels, front vowels never alternate. These vowels in words such as *für* [fyːɐ̯], *schön* [ʃøːn], *Bär* [bɛːɐ̯], and *Heu* [hɔy] are not derived via the Umlaut rule; they invariably have the structure given to them according to the model of featural representation developed in Chapters 3 and 6.[6] The second set of vowels is that of the umlauting vowels; they surface as [− front] vowels if not being subjected

---

[6] Classical generative studies of Umlaut such as Vennemann (1968) or Bach and King (1970) would indeed derive /fyːʀ/, etc. from /fuːʀ/. In § 5.3.1, I stated how such 'free rides' of front round vowels by the Umlaut rule are blocked in Lexical Phonology.

to the Umlaut rule (6). The final set is identical to the second set with respect to the segmental structure; they never umlaut, only because the morphemes in which the vowels appear do not have the floating feature [+ front]. Their vowels are invariably [− front]. In (8), these types of phonological forms are illustrated, neglecting other details of segmental representations.

(8) *a. für* /fyʀ/   *b. lang* /lang/   *c. rund* /ʀʊnd/

[+ front]   [+ front]

After these clarifications, the application of rule (6) can be studied in its interactions with the markedness and default rules for vowels. In (9), the singular and plural forms of *Kamm* are derived step by step, again ignoring all details for other segments and most of the intrasegmental structure. Recall that the representation of /a/ is proposed in § 6.1.1 to consist of an empty root node, R, and observe how, by ordering the Umlaut rule before the markedness rule introducing the feature specification [+ low], the difference in vowel height between [a] and [ɛ] is taken care of. I also propose to assign the Umlaut and markedness rules to the lexical phonology as defined in Chapter 5, and the other rules to the postlexical domain of phonology. In (9*d*), the terminal features of the full representation are simply listed.

(9) *Kamm*   ~   *Kämm+e*
   lexically
   a. /k R m/   /k R m + ə/   underlying
      [+ front]   [+ front]
   b. ——   /k R m + ə/   Umlaut rule (6)

               [+ front]

   c. /k R m/   markedness rule (3*b*), § 6.1

      [+ low]
   postlexically
   d. /k R m/   /k R m + ə/   default rules

$$
\begin{bmatrix} + \text{low} \\ - \text{high} \\ - \text{front} \\ - \text{back} \\ - \text{round} \\ - \text{ATR} \end{bmatrix} \qquad \begin{bmatrix} - \text{low} \\ - \text{high} \\ + \text{front} \\ - \text{back} \\ - \text{round} \\ - \text{ATR} \end{bmatrix}
$$

     ([a])   ([ɛ])

The other umlauting vowels can be derived analogously. As mentioned, the complication in the case of the umlauting diphthong /aʊ/ will be accounted for by a rule of Rounding Assimilation. If the reasoning on the vowel features and their constraints in § 6.1.1 is correct, this rule is independently motivated.

We can now formulate the rule of Rounding Assimilation postulated for the derivation of [ɔʏ]. The rule must be restricted to this diphthong, since [aʊ] and not [ɔʊ] (or some other initial round vowel in this diphthong) is found in German (see also Kloeke 1982: 17, 221). The rule, as formulated in (10), spreads the articulator node [Labial] (and its dependent feature [+ round] which need not be represented) to an immediately preceding root node if both root nodes are adjacent vowels, and the second one a front vowel. Note that the absence of [Labial] for /ɪ/ prevents any spreading in the case of /aɪ/. Rule (10) is not only a language-specific rule of Modern Standard German; it also does not hold for many other German dialects which often have other diphthongal systems.[7]

(10) Rounding Assimilation

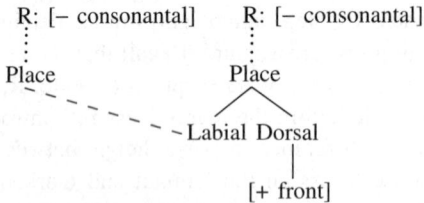

R: [− consonantal]   R: [− consonantal]

Place   Place

Labial Dorsal

[+ front]

Having added this rule to the available mechanisms, we can demonstrate the application of the rules and principles in the alternation of [aʊ] vs. [ɔY] as in *Baum* vs. *Bäum+e* or the examples of (5*g*). The diphthong /aʊ/ is represented at the underlying level as an empty root node for /a/ followed by the feature structure assumed for /ʊ/. Again, since Rounding Assimilation (10) applies before the markedness and default rules in (11*c*), the correct vowel sequences emerge. In not applying Umlaut to the left form in (11*b*), I assume that the floating [+ front] effectively disappears; it is not available any more.

The present analysis of umlaut claims that the possibility for Umlaut is encoded as the appropriate floating feature for individual lexemes on a one-by-one basis. Confirmation of this view comes from empirical studies by Augst (1971) and Köpcke (1988): when subjects are asked to form comparative forms of nonsense adjectives (Augst) or to form plural forms of nonsense nouns (Köpcke), the percentage of umlauted forms is generally quite small, although in the real lexicon the number of umlauting forms is very high for some of the subgroups. This can be interpreted to mean that speakers need positive evidence for the umlaut alternation in the existing vocabulary before they add the [+ front] to the representation of a lexical entry. The authors named take their results as evidence against a phonological (generative) treatment of umlaut. Their counterargument from nonsense formations does not apply to the present treatment which insists on Umlaut as a phonological rule but postulates a (non-arbitrary) trigger belonging to individual roots.

---

[7] Because of the existence of the sequence /i ø/ in words such as *seriös* it may be necessary to restrict the rule of Rounding Assimilation to either tautomorphemic or tautosyllabic (i.e. diphthongal) vowel sequences.

(11) *Baum*   *Bäume*

  lexically

  a. /b R   R m/   /b R   R m + ə/   underlying

$$\begin{bmatrix} + \text{high} \\ + \text{round} \end{bmatrix}$$
  [+ front]

$$\begin{bmatrix} + \text{high} \\ + \text{round} \end{bmatrix}$$
  [+ front]

  b. /b R   R m/   /b R   R m + ə/   Umlaut (6)

$$\begin{bmatrix} + \text{high} \\ + \text{round} \end{bmatrix}$$

$$\begin{bmatrix} + \text{high} \\ + \text{round} \\ + \text{front} \end{bmatrix}$$

  c. ——   /b R   R m + ə/   Rounding Assimilation (10)

$$\begin{bmatrix} + \text{high} \\ + \text{round} \\ + \text{front} \end{bmatrix}$$

  d. /b R   R m/   /b R   R m + ə/   markedness rule (3*a*), § 6.1

$$\begin{bmatrix} + \text{high} \\ + \text{round} \\ + \text{back} \end{bmatrix}$$

  [+ back]
$$\begin{bmatrix} + \text{high} \\ + \text{round} \\ + \text{front} \end{bmatrix}$$

  e. /b R   R m/   ——   ——   markedness rule (3*b*),
                                                          § 6.1

  [+ low]
$$\begin{bmatrix} + \text{high} \\ + \text{round} \\ + \text{back} \end{bmatrix}$$

  postlexically

  f. /b R   R m/   /b R   R m + ə/   default rules

$$\begin{bmatrix} + \text{low} \\ - \text{high} \\ - \text{front} \\ - \text{back} \\ - \text{round} \\ - \text{ATR} \end{bmatrix} \begin{bmatrix} - \text{low} \\ + \text{high} \\ - \text{front} \\ + \text{back} \\ + \text{round} \\ - \text{ATR} \end{bmatrix}$$
       ([a   ʊ])

$$\begin{bmatrix} - \text{low} \\ - \text{high} \\ - \text{front} \\ + \text{back} \\ + \text{round} \\ - \text{ATR} \end{bmatrix} \begin{bmatrix} - \text{low} \\ + \text{high} \\ + \text{front} \\ - \text{back} \\ + \text{round} \\ - \text{ATR} \end{bmatrix}$$
       ([ɔ   ʏ])

Historically, present-day Umlaut derives from a vowel harmony rule of Old High German, in which, disregarding well-known complications, a final high front vowel or glide caused the preceding stressed vowel to be a front vowel, as in the pair *gast* vs. *gest+i* ('guest' vs. 'guests'). The analysis proposed here assumes that concomitantly with the reduction and/or loss of the final vowels (roughly around the transition from the Old High German to the Middle High German period) the fronting alternation had to be reanalysed as a feature of the relevant stem (see Wiese (1987) and Lodge (1989) for more details, and Scheutz (1989) and Wiese (1989*b*) for discussion).

The following data illustrate complications in the application of the Umlaut rule beyond those given in (7). It appears from (12) that identical morphological contexts do not always have an identical, predictable outcome. These sets of words demonstrate that particular roots and/or affixations may lead to an umlauted vowel or not. That is, although +*er*-nominalization can induce umlaut, as shown by *Bäcker* in (12*a*), *Fahrer* does not umlaut, and this in spite of the fact that *fahr* belongs to those roots which may umlaut, as the final pair reveals. The examples in (12*b, c*) show basically the same point, but dependent on a particular root; particular morphological contexts may lead to umlaut in one case, but fail to induce umlaut in other cases of an umlauting stem.

(12) *a.* back ~ Bäck+er, fahr ~ Fahr+er, fahr+e ~ fähr+t
     b. Maus ~ Mäus+e, Maus ~ maus+en, Luft ~ lüft+en
     c. Hund ~ Hünd+in, Hund ~ Hund+e, Turm ~ Türm+e

While postulating a floating [+ front] is sufficient to explain the variation between umlauting and non-umlauting stems, the non-predictable variation shown in (12) seems non-amenable to a phonological solution. The question is how much should be made of the fact that some suffixations (such as diminutive +*chen*) almost always lead to umlaut, while in the context of other suffixations umlaut is not a regular process, as with +*in* or +*ig*. The first class was called *umlauterzwingend* ('umlaut conditioning') by Wurzel (1970: 118 ff.), the second, *umlautbewirkend* ('umlaut variable') (see also Lieber 1987: 100). There are practically no suffixes, however, which always cause umlaut on suitable bases: for diminutive +*chen*, for example, see *Onkel+chen*, *Hund+chen* or a potential new formation such as *Computer+chen*.[8] Conceivably, the difference in frequency noted by several authors could be relied upon in the expression of the umlaut regularities, but it remains a fact that some amount of lexical conditioning exists for practically all suffixes. Speakers have to learn exceptions, that is, mark them in their lexicon, while it is not clear at all whether speakers have access to the frequency patterns observed in the literature.

All exceptions to Umlaut will therefore, as I presumed, have to be marked lexically. This means that the lexical entry for a noun such as *Hund* will be marked for having *Hund+e*, and not the expected form **Hünd+e*, as the plural. The lexical entry for *Turm*, in contrast, needs no particular marking for the plural form, since the 'regular' *Türm+e* appears. The marking in the lexicon should be done, according to the principles of underspecification, in a minimal way, but at least partly on an entry-specific basis.

In this connection, we may also reconfirm that Umlaut must be a lexical rule

---

[8] The one suffix which really does not seem to occur with non-umlauted bases is +*lein* as in *Mütter+lein, Häus+lein, Knäb +lein*. It would be interesting to find a common explanation for this fact and for the several exceptions with this suffix noted elsewhere in this book: it does not attach to bases with final /l/ nor does it cause degemination (see *Vög+lein* or *Vöge+lein*, derived from *Vogel*), and it does not require a final schwa syllable in the plural form.

as according to Lexical Phonology for a number of reasons: it is a cyclic rule operating in a derived environment only; it has, as just noted, lexical exceptions; and it is structure-preserving in that it creates an output which is itself a distinctive segment in the sound system of Modern Standard German.

The cyclicity of the Umlaut rule can be confirmed by the following fact: as noted by Strauss (1982: 135) the second suffix in a series of suffixes is not capable of undoing the effects of a preceding suffix. That is, if umlaut occurs or does not occur with a first suffix (as in *mächt+ig* vs. *wolk+ig*), no further suffix can cause umlaut or lead to a non-umlauted form: *Mächt+ig+keit*, *Wolk+ig+keit*. For Strauss, this fact is expressed by stating that exception features for umlaut cannot extend further than the suffix immediately following the relevant root. But by using the concept of the cycle as introduced in § 5.3.1, no such stipulative statement is necessary. The Umlaut rule will apply (if possible) after the application of each morphological rule, and there is no mechanism to undo the effects of Umlaut.[9] Furthermore, adding the next suffix does not create a derived environment in the sense of (20*b*) of § 5.3.1, since the context needed is not crucially created by that suffixation (but by the previous suffixation).[10]

A further question is whether umlaut is restricted to a particular level in the lexicon. While it seems to be true that umlaut never occurs in connection with morphological operations assigned to level 3 (word level) in Chapter 5, it is not altogether clear whether umlaut can be restricted to level 1. Umlaut can be found with a number of suffixes from the lists in (4) and (5) of § 5.2.1. Counterexamples to the hypothesis restricting umlaut to level 1 formations are those in (13), where a level 2 suffix co-occurs with an umlauted vowel.

(13) *a.* röt+lich, läng+lich, brüder+lich
 b. gött+lich, ver+ständ+ig, Hüt+chen

The umlauting visible in connection with level 2 suffix +*lich* must be assigned to level 2. Conceivably, derivations of words in (13*a*) proceed from the de-adjectival verbs *röt(en)*, *läng(en)*, *(ver)brüder(n)*, but as the formation of such verbs (by conversion or zero-derivation) must be placed on level 2, as can be shown from the fact that zero-derivation of denominal verbs is possible with compounds such as *Schrift+steller* (> *schrift+steller(n)*), we are again left with a level 2 process.

Umlauting in the words in (13*b*) is even more straightforwardly related to level 2 morphology. Therefore, I can offer the confinement of umlaut to the first lexical level (the root level) as a speculation only. The issue is not closed, however; as noted before, it has been proposed by Iverson and Salmons (1992) that +*chen* is both a level 1 and level 2 suffix; in particular, it is level 1 if umlaut-inducing. Note in this context the difference in meaning between

---

[9] I ignore the small, but interesting, set of cases of the type *nerv+ös* vs. *Nerv+os+ität*, where something like anti-umlaut seems to take place.

[10] In contrast to Strauss (1982) and others, I do not assume that prefixation ever leads to umlauting. That is, umlaut in *ver+ächt+lich* (cf. *be+acht+lich*) is totally due to the suffixation triggering the umlaut. For more examples of such variation, see (14).

Hünd+chen 'dog (dim.)' and *Hund+chen* 'dog (endearment)', a difference recurrently found in such pairs.

One may note further that with all plural suffixes (+ *(e)n*, +*s*) assigned to
levels 2 and 3 in § 5.3.2, umlaut is not found, while it occurs commonly with
level 1 plurals (see (24) of § 5.3.2). If regular verbal inflection is to be located
at level 3, and irregular verbal inflection at level 1, it appears that umlaut in
connection with inflection is indeed restricted to level 1 of the lexicon.

I now turn to a set of cases which I regard as constituting an argument for the
claim made in (6) that the phonological word provides the relevant domain for
umlauting. Lieber (1981; 1987) discusses word pairs such as those given in (14)
in which particular root-affix combinations can be found with or without umlaut.
In Lieber's account, these alternations are evidence for a lexical representation
of the umlaut alternation: all affixes which cause umlaut in a variable manner
are represented twice, once with the non-front ([back] for Lieber) vowel *and*
once with the umlauted front vowel. All of the umlaut-variable suffixes, then,
have two allomorphic representations in the grammar.[11] How the affix (and not
the root) is the carrier of the umlaut feature in this model is explained below.
Second, the particular forms (with or without umlaut) are simply the result of
lexicalization. Both forms are possible, and in the course of language acquisition
a speaker may learn either of them or both.

(14) *a.* ver+trag+lich ~ ver+träg+lich   *b.* [blut+ig] ~ [[voll+blüt]+ig]
           gegen+stand+lich ~ gegen+ständ+lich   [mut+ig] ~ [[groß+müt]+ig]

The word pairs in (14*a*) are such that particular concatenations of morphemes
occur with and without umlauting. In (14*b*), it appears that particular affixations
do not cause umlaut if attached to simplex bases; but the same affixes cause
umlaut with complex (compounded) bases. Significantly, the reverse to the pattern
in (14*b*) is not found. This by itself is a hint that more than arbitrary choice of
allomorphs is involved.

Two aspects of the problem have to be distinguished: first, there is the lexical
conditioning of umlaut, which means that Umlaut may be blocked for individual
lexical items. This is the case only for the left-hand examples in (14). More
interesting is the observation indicated in (14*b*): the blocking of Umlaut for a
lexical item does not carry over to a more complex word of which the blocked
stem is a part.

In general, Umlaut follows a principle of morphological locality (alongside
the phonological locality) in that it is always the immediately following suffix
which causes the rule to apply. Compare, for example, *größ+er* to *blut+ig+er* or
Bäck+er to *Fahr+er+chen*. The final suffixes +*er* and +*chen* cannot 'undo' the
blocking of Umlaut in connection with the first suffixes. This condition is
apparently violated in the examples of (14*b*) since Umlaut applies to part of a
structure not immediately followed by the affix triggering the rule. Consider, for
example, the morphological structure of these words before Umlaut applies (or

---

[11] As I have stressed above, there are practically no umlaut-conditioning suffixes. Thus, all suffixes
ever co-occurring with umlaut would have to display this allomorphy.

does not). Taking the first word pair from (14*b*), these words will be represented morphologically as the bracketing there indicates. This gives an unexpected twist to the conditions of applications for the Umlaut rule: it seems as if Umlaut cannot apply across an intervening suffix, but that the presence of morphological structure itself (i.e. more than one morphological boundary) has no such blocking effect.

Intervening suffixes (as opposed to boundaries) also block umlaut if the suffix consists of schwa (plus consonant) only, as in *mal+er+isch*, where forms similar to **mäl+er+isch* are not attested. This means that the presence of schwa as a phonological entity alone cannot be the crucial factor, since we know from cases such as *Bauer* vs. *bäuer+lich*, *Vater* vs. *Väter* that schwa in final position may be 'skipped' in umlauting.

In the model presented here, the Umlaut rule (6) is triggered partly by morphological features, but nevertheless operates on phonological structures. This means that the examples in (14) are not problematic. There may be two morphological boundaries before the umlaut-triggering affixes in [[[ver] [trag]] lich], but what the Umlaut rule can see is the phonological structure of {ver} {trag} {lich}. In the same spirit, *vollblütig* is represented as {voll} {blutig}, with the suffix even part of that phonological word in which umlaut occurs.

The regularity appearing in (14*b*) may be accounted for in the following way: the umlaut-triggering suffixes in (14) attach to the complex word, and not to its final part, as perhaps suggested by the bracketing in (14). The interpretation of these words confirms this view. *Vollblütig* is the property of being a *Vollblut*, and not the property of being full of blood. The information blocking Umlaut is attached to *blut+ig* as a lexical entry. Thus, because this latter entry never plays a role in the derivation of *vollblütig*, the blocking cannot take effect.

I would finally like to discuss two alternative analyses to the one presented here. The first is the one current in older stages of generative phonology; the second is a possible non-linear alternative. Consider first the rule given in (15), taken from Kloeke (1982: 219).[12]

$$
(15) \quad
\begin{bmatrix} + \text{consonantal} \\ <+ \text{low}> \end{bmatrix}
\rightarrow
\begin{bmatrix} - \text{back} \\ - \text{low} \\ <- \text{tense}> \end{bmatrix}
\Bigg/
\left[\overline{} \atop + \text{U} \right]
C_0 \, (\text{eR}) \Bigg] \ldots
$$

In formulations such as these, umlaut is regarded as a feature-changing process which changes the value of [back] and, possibly, [low]. The statement in angled brackets (if the segment is [+ low], the output is [− tense]) is not necessary under the present account because of the interaction of umlauting with underspecified segments and the role of markedness and default rules (see examples (9) and (11)). In the context of (15), the vowel must bear the diacritic feature [+ U], simply as a mark indicating that the form belongs to those which may umlaut. The role of this feature is taken over here by the existence of the floating [+ front]. In other words, the present proposal has one (independently

---

[12] Kloeke draws on the series of proposals by Zwicky (1967), Wurzel (1970), King (1971), and Lieber (1981).

motivated and therefore non-diacritic) feature [+ front], where rule (15) has [+ U] plus the features [− back, − low, − tense]. The /eR/-part in brackets is needed since Kloeke represents words with a final schwa syllable as ending in /eR/. Umlaut is then required to 'skip over' this sequence. Of course, if there is no such final vowel as in the present account (and in that of Lieber 1987), Umlaut may always affect the final vowel. In fact, the rule could not very easily be formulated if the alternating vowel were not the final (or initial one) in the domain, and, as Lieber (1987) noted, this may be taken as an argument for the autosegmental formulation of the umlaut regularity.

The ellipsis in (15) indicates the omission of the long and complex list of morphological conditions for umlauting as they have been stated by Wurzel (1970: 163); see also Wurzel (1984) and others. I leave open the question of how the problem of tying the phonological rule to the rather idiosyncratic morphological conditions should be solved. Note that I propose to solve one part of this, namely how to encode the lexical exceptions to Umlaut, by marking these in the lexical entries themselves, a solution compatible with the mechanisms available in Lexical Phonology. A possible solution is proposed by Zwicky (1987), who distinguishes between morphological operations and morphological rules. Operations are processes such as umlaut (or affixation, or whatever). Rules of derivation or inflection may call upon any number of operations. In such an account, there would still be a place for a single formulation of the Umlaut rule, perhaps in the form of (6).

In older stages of German, umlauting of vowels was triggered, as mentioned above, by following high, front vowels, in particular by /i/. This is obviously a case of *vowel harmony* (that is, of the identity of vowels in a word with respect to one or more of their features), in that a feature of one segment (/i/) is adopted by another segment (the preceding umlauting vowel). While such a harmony analysis can no longer be motivated for Modern Standard German, one fact remains which might lead to the consideration of yet another analysis of Umlaut: suffixes including a non-front vowel never trigger the umlauting of the preceding vowels. Such suffixes include +*ung*, +*at*, +*o*, and +*schaft*. It is as if a suffix vowel containing [− front] is not compatible with the [+ front] required for umlaut. The account given above has no explanation for this fact, since the [+ front] as part of the stem in no way excludes a back vowel in the suffix.

But if the specification [+ front] were assumed to be a part of the suffix, things would be different. In such an analysis, a rule similar to (6) could be stated, but one in which the feature of fronting, although underlyingly part of the *suffix*, would be linked through association to the final *root* vowel. In pairs such as *Vater* vs. *Väter*, there would not be zero-affixation, but instead a suffix consisting solely of [+ front]. Precisely such analyses of Umlaut have been proposed by Lieber (1987: § 2.3) and Lodge (1989), whose analyses differ in many details from each other and from the present proposal.[13]

---

[13] For Lieber, though, the floating umlauting feature is either an element of a suffix (such as +*lich*) or of the stem, for other cases such as *Vater*. The various alternatives are discussed further in Wiese (1996).

While the advantage of such an approach might be in its ability to express directly which suffixes are umlaut-inducing and which are not, it loses the ability to account for the fact that umlaut is variation not in the suffixes, but in their bases, that is, in roots or stems, with a number of bases never undergoing the rule. The findings on newly coined words referred to above are also in better agreement with the base-variant approach: if the umlaut feature were to be part of the suffixes, why should new formations (with old suffixes, of course) not be umlauted? Note that such words cannot, by their very nature of not yet being listed in the lexicon, have exception features. In a theory beyond the scope of the present one, it might be possible to combine the two models discussed here. An umlaut would then appear if a suitable property of the stem *and* of the suffix were available. (Such a proposal was actually developed by Zwicky 1967.)

I conclude this discussion of umlaut by asking (as many authors have done before) whether umlaut belongs to the domain of phonology or of morphology. On the one hand, I have attempted to show that in terms of the featural contribution, umlaut is a completely regular and simple phonological process, namely the fronting of a vowel. On the other hand, the list of unrelated morphological conditions on umlaut and its function in signalling morphological markings (as for plural) seem to assign umlaut to the morphological domain of Modern Standard German. The claim that umlaut is morphologically conditioned is somewhat weakened, though, by the fact that no morphological features as such cause or prohibit umlaut. Rather, it is the presence or absence of particular suffixes which plays the crucial role. Compare umlauting in connection with plural suffixes +*er* and +*e* and non-umlauting with plural suffixes +*en* and +*s*. That is, a morphological rule of Umlaut would refer to rather shallow information. Taken together with the observation that the umlaut alternation appears exclusively in morphologically derived environments, it might be more appropriate to interpret Umlaut as a prototypical example of a lexical phonological rule.

It must be added that, in the light of the results of Chapter 4, the distinction becomes less important, if not irrelevant. If a part of morphology, the so-called *prosodic morphology*, is heavily dependent on phonology and operates on phonological categories, then we may very well argue that no principled distinction can be drawn between phonology and morphology. For such a view, the question of putting umlaut into one of the two components is of less importance than for theories which presume a strict boundary between the two components.

In going beyond the umlaut facts, consider the alternations exemplified in (16). The right-hand forms are those which appear in the second- and third-person singular forms in present tense: *ich esse* 'I eat', *du ißt* 'you (sg.) eat', *er ißt* 'he eats'. The vowels /e, ɛ/ in a moderately large number of irregular verbs (the strong verbs) alternate with /i, ɪ/. The conditioning factor is the presence of the morphological features [− past, − plural, − 1].[14]

---

[14] I assume that [−1] is the feature representation for second and third person.

(16) ess(en) ~ iss+t, stehl(en) ~ stiehl+t, geb(en) ~ gib+t, nehm(en) ~ nimm+t, vergess(en)
      ~ vergiss+t

This alternation is clearly one of vowel raising, traditionally called *breaking* (*Brechung*). I take these phenomena as evidence that umlaut is only the major type of alternation in Modern Standard German for which an analysis in terms of adding a feature may be the most adequate one. (17) may be regarded as a first attempt to treat this alternation systematically. On the basis of (5) in § 6.1, the reader may convince him- or herself that just as adding [+ front] to /u, o, a/ yields the umlauted vowels /y, ø, ɛ/, adding [+ high] to /e, ɛ/ yields /i, ɪ/. In both cases, tenseness or length distinctions are ignored. As with umlaut, it is always the last (full) vowel in a phonological word which is raised.

(17) Vowel Raising

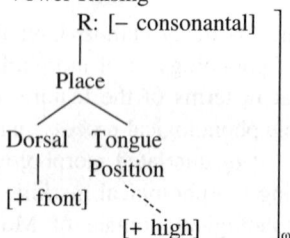

$$
\left.
\begin{array}{l}
\text{R: } [- \text{ consonantal}] \\
\quad\mid \\
\text{Place} \\
\quad\diagup\diagdown \\
\text{Dorsal} \quad \text{Tongue} \\
\quad\mid \qquad \text{Position} \\
[+ \text{ front}] \qquad \diagdown\diagdown \\
\qquad\qquad [+ \text{ high}]
\end{array}
\right]_\omega
$$

This rule of Vowel Raising provides an opportunity to discuss briefly the problem of rule-governed vs. phonologically arbitrary alternation. In the present model, a phonological rule is proposed if the alternation to be observed can be stated by means of an elementary operation on the feature structure. Both Umlaut and Vowel Raising fall under this category. Thus, a rule may be proposed even if there is morphological or lexical conditioning (as is the case for Umlaut and Vowel Raising). The facts of the quantitative distribution are comparatively irrelevant; there are, according to Wunderlich and Fabri (1993), about thirty-three verbs undergoing the alternation of Vowel Raising, while five other verbs do not (see *bewegen*). This distribution alone does not provide a strong argument for or against postulating a phonological rule.

On the other hand, alternations such as those of the strong and mixed verbs, cannot be subsumed under such elementary operations of adding or removing single units of phonological structure, and are treated consequently as listed lexical entries. Note that this position on what may count as a rule of phonology lies between the positions of, for example, Halle and Mohanan (1985), who write phonological rules for the alternations of English strong verb roots, and of those who deny Umlaut the status of a phonological rule (e.g. Anderson 1985; 1992; Wurzel 1984; Janda 1987; Lieber 1992; in contrast with Wiese 1994).

7.2.2. Vowel shortening

The set of regularities discussed in this section has received much less attention than Umlaut. Nevertheless, vowels of Modern Standard German show a set of alternations in length, sometimes with a concomitant variation in tenseness ([ATR] in the present feature system). We deal briefly with each of these shortening processes.

The first set of shortening alternations can be observed in words as given in (18). The vowel in the left word of each pair is long. Two observations must be added: first, the shortening is generally optional, that is, it may or may not occur.[15] Second, there is a large amount of lexical variation. Speakers of the North German vernacular, in which this shortening can be found, have various sets of words undergoing the rule.

(18) sieben ~ s[ɪ]bzig, Räder ~ R[a]d, Gräser ~ Gr[a]s, Gase ~ G[a]s,
     Flüge ~ Fl[ʊ]gzeug, Städte ~ St[a]dt, grobe ~ gr[ɔ]b

The long vowels in the lefthand-side forms must be assumed to be the underlying forms, first, because the vowel in the righthand-side forms is only optionally short, and second, for words with short vowels no lengthening can be observed. That is, in assuming an open-syllable lengthening for *sieben*, and so on, a large number of words would have to be exceptionally marked as not subject to this rule.[16] This observation, together with the fact that shortening appears to be optional, motivates the shortening analysis.

As demonstrated in (18), for shortening to take place, a long vowel must be followed by a consonant (more precisely an obstruent) in the same syllable. If these observations provide the relevant conditions, the rule in question is an instance of closed syllable shortening and can be formulated as in (19). This rule illustrates several of the representational means developed earlier: long vowels are associated with two positions. Thus, the distinction between the prosodic position and the segmental information makes it possible to describe shortening as a delinking in the sense of (2).

(19) Vowel Shortening

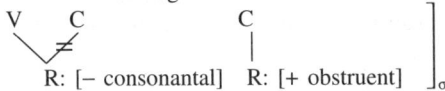

$$\left[\begin{array}{ccc} V & C & C \\ \diagdown\!\!\!\!\diagup\!\!\!\!\!{\neq} & & | \\ R: [- \text{consonantal}] & & R: [+ \text{obstruent}] \end{array} \right]_{\sigma}$$

The problem with this rule is mentioned above: it seems to be completely lexically conditioned. While there are straightforward phonological conditions— those included in (19)—the applicability of the rule is determined on a lexeme-by-lexeme basis, with quite a bit of speaker variability. Its precise status needs further inquiry with respect to its lexical or postlexical position. The lexical conditioning argues for a lexical rule, but it must be noted that it applies in non-derived forms only. That is, it is not a cyclic rule. Apparently, this rule provides straightforward evidence for the claim by Kiparsky (1993) that cyclicity of a rule and its application in non-derived environments are independent of each

---

[15] In *Stadt*, the vowel is always short. For some speakers, however, the vowel is also short in the plural form *Städt+e*.
[16] Historically, it is indeed open-syllable lengthening which leads to the present situation. Middle High German short, syllable-final vowels were reanalysed as long vowels (see Reis 1974).

other. Rather, Vowel Shortening may apply to non-derived forms such as those in (18) because it is a delinking, and thus structure-changing, rule.

It must be mentioned here that there are further sets of words in which vowel shortening of different kinds may be observed. In (20), I illustrate such formations; (42) of § 7.3.2, in connection with obstruent spirantization, gives more examples. Here, shortening depends on morphological information, in particular on the presence of a suffix with the shape of /t/. I leave open the nature of this suffix (perhaps several suffixes). A possible corresponding rule is given in (21). Note that the formulation given relies on morphemes and morpheme boundaries; therefore, the rule does not conform to the hypothesis that phonological rules must operate in an environment specified purely in phonological terms.

(20) Phant/aː/sie ~ Phantſaſ+t
     abstr/aː/hieren ~ abstrak+t
     drei ~ dri+tt (but: zweit)

(21) Vowel Shortening

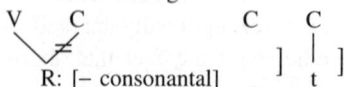

$$
\begin{array}{ccc}
V & C & C \quad C \\
\diagdown\!\!\!\!\diagup & & | \\
\text{R: } [-\text{ consonantal}] & &] \quad \underset{t}{|} \;]
\end{array}
$$

It might be thought that words in (20) are simply subject to a size constraint disallowing a sequence *VVC/t/. That this is not the case is shown by the examples in (22), all of which display a long vowel plus at least two following consonants, but no tendency to shorten.

(22) Arzt, Dienst, Obst; Mond, Freund, Feind

For another case of shortening, we can look at one of the subclasses of ablauting (strong) verbs. In this (moderately large) class of verbs the vowel /iː/ in the present-tense form of the root alternates with /o/ in the past-tense and participle forms of the root. But there is an exceptionless alternation of vowel length: /o/ is short if a voiceless obstruent follows as in (23b), and long else-where, as in (23a).

(23) a. /iː/ ~ /oː/ ~ /oː/
          bieg+en ~ bog ~ ge+bog+en, schieb+en ~ schob ~ ge+schob+en
      b. /iː/ ~ /ɔ/ ~ /ɔ/
          schließ+en ~ schloß ~ ge+schloss+en, riech+en ~ roch ~ ge+roch+en

If we wanted to treat the shortenings illustrated in (18) and (23) with the same rule, it would actually be possible to claim that it is not the syllable boundary, as assumed in rule (19), but the voicelessness of the obstruent which is respons-ible for the shortening alternation. All that would be required for such an approach to work would be to claim that for the ablauting verbs the shortening rule operates *before* the rule of Final Devoicing, while for the underived nouns of (18), shortening applies *after* Final Devoicing. At least the former clause is required anyhow, given that in *bog*, and so on, of (23a), the final obstruent is voiceless on the surface due to Final Devoicing. That is, any description of this alternation must refer to a level at which Final Devoicing has not yet applied.

This is also the place to introduce yet another vowel-shortening rule often discussed in the literature, one that ties vowel length to degrees of stress. Consider a word with a series of open syllables as in (24). The numbers above the vowels refer to degrees of stress (with a decreasing order from 1 to 4) in the numerical representation explained in § 8.1. Thus, in a word such as the one given, there are syllable-final vowels under four different degrees of stress. Expressions with more stress levels can be easily found, but the degree of specification needed then is one of the problems encountered by such models of stress.

(24) Philosophiestudium: [fi lo so fiː ʃtuː di ʊm]

It is true that the length of the vowels under such conditions depends on the degree of stress. But given the large number of stress degrees, it is obvious that there are more than two degrees of length involved here. Furthermore, there is no way even of determining an upper bound to the number of stresses, and consequently, length distinctions.

This would then mean that we are dealing with a fine-tuning of vowel length which goes beyond the representational means of phonology (and those of phonetic transcription, even if the convention of notating half-length as '·' is adopted). In other words, the shortening found in open syllables is a phonetic phenomenon, one which phonology cannot and should not deal with. This issue is taken up again in §§ 7.6 and 8.2.1.

In addition, it must be asked how short the so-called short, tense vowels in unstressed syllables really are. Ramers (1988) and others find that they are still longer than the short, lax vowels; furthermore, Ramers found practically no tendency to shorten the vowels if they follow stressed vowels, as in *Demut* (['deːmuːt]).

Vowels which have been shortened in the categorial way described at the beginning of this section (see (18)), are invariably lax ([− ATR]), although their long underlier surfaces as a tense vowel (except for /aː/ and /ɛː/, of course). This observation is important in that it gives further justification for the claim that [ATR] is a largely redundant feature, the values of which depend on vowel length. In addition, the shortening of lax /aː/ and /ɛː/ confirms the independent existence of vowel shortening. That is, formulating a laxing rule instead of a shortening rule would seem to be inadequate in that an additional shortening rule for these two vowels is still needed. Furthermore, in an underspecification framework like the one proposed in Chapter 6, no change of values for [ATR] is required to accommodate the apparent shift from tense to lax.

The difference between short, tense vowels and short, lax vowels also helps to distinguish the phonological type of vowel shortening from the phonetic one. Phonological vowel shortening is followed by specification of [ATR] values. We thus have derivations such as /eː/ → /e/ → [ɛ], as in [mɛtal]. On the other hand, phonetic vowel shortening has no such consequences for vowel tenseness.

Finally, we observe that the length contrast for vowels is not very stable in the position before /ʀ/. Meinhold and Stock (1980: 180 f.), following the pronouncing dictionaries (Duden 1990, Krech et al. 1982) judge the vowel in *Art, Schwert, Fahrt* to be long, while the vowel in *Ort, Furcht, hart* is supposed to be short. The factual basis of this presumed distinction seems very questionable. In my own dialect, there is no length difference in the examples quoted. Judgements on vowel length in front of /ʀ/ which is itself vocalized are problematic, in particular if low /a/ precedes. Note that laxing of the vowel is predicted to take place in shortened vowels; it does indeed seem to go hand in hand with the vowel shortening in many cases.

7.2.3. Alternations with schwa

While the large topic of the regularities around the vowel schwa will mostly be dealt with in other sections, one issue should be taken up at this point. Schwa can be observed to alternate with other vowels in a few cases. While I regard this as a minor regularity, it still belongs among the vowel-related rules. Apart from the schwa/zero alternation, schwa alternates with two other vowels, as shown in (25) and (26).[17]

(25) leb+[ə]nd ~ leb+[ɛ]nd+ig, Itali[ə]n ~ itali[eː]nisch

(26) b[ə]+laden ~ b[eː]- und entladen

The first alternation is used as a standard argument in order to derive schwa from the underlier /ɛ/ (see Wurzel 1970: pt III, ch. 3; Kloeke 1982: §1.2.4) or to treat schwa as an allophone of /ɛ/ (Moulton 1947). It must be emphasized, however, that the pair *leb+end* vs. *leb+end+ig* in (25) is totally unique. No other participle allows an affixation of *+ig*, so that *lebendig* is highly exceptional on morphological grounds. Basing any argument for the status of schwa on this alternation is therefore, to say the least, very weak.

The word *itali[eː]nisch* may be formed in analogy with all other geographical adjectives on *+isch*: *brasili'an+isch, chil'en+isch*. The generalization is that in geographical terms derived by *+isch* the syllable preceding this suffix always carries primary stress.[18] Again, *itali[eː]nisch* is unique in that it is the only word in which [eː] alternates with schwa in this particular environment.

Nevertheless, in spite of the extreme rarity of the cases quoted in (25), the phenomenon is more general. This is shown by the alternations in (26), in which the schwa syllable receives exceptional stress for reasons of contrast or clarification. If a schwa syllable, which is lexically always stressless, is subject to such an exceptional stressing for reasons of emphasis or contrast, the vowel is usually, though not always, /eː/ in open syllables, and /ɛ/ in closed syllables.

---

[17] Alternations of schwa with /i/ (*Jubel* vs. *Jubil+ar*) or with /u/ (*Muskel* vs. *Muskul+atur*) are found in addition in a closed set of words; see Kloeke (1982: 21).

[18] As noted in § 5.2.1 and to be taken up again in § 8.3, *+isch* requires either a preceding schwa syllable or a main stressed syllable. Apparently, for some adjectives in the geographical domain, the choice between the two options is lexically restricted to the latter one.

This is the same distribution of vowels as found in cases of (25), which confirms the unity of the alternation. Consequently, the task remains to account for the relationship between [ə] on the one hand and [eː, ɛ] as its counterparts under stress on the other hand. In this connection it is also noteworthy that [e] in unstressed syllables tends to be reduced to schwa in words such as *e'gal*, *e'norm*, or articles *den*, *dem*; see Ramers (1988: ch. 3). That is, a special relationship between the *e*-sounds and schwa undoubtedly exists; but this is not necessarily a reason to derive the latter from the former segment.

That one of the vowels ([eː]) is long immediately follows from the constraint that open syllables in Modern Standard German must end in a long vowel, especially (but, as I claim here, not only) if the syllable is stressed. Nothing more needs to be said here. The underspecified features of the vowels in question are given in (2) of § 6.1. It appears that the difference between schwa and the two other vowels is only that the latter two are specified by [+ front], and by this feature alone. That is to say that the change from schwa to [eː] or [ɛ] is as minimal as possible. It consists in adding exactly one of the distinctive features for vowels. There is also, given the German vowel system, only one other way of achieving such a minimal change, namely the addition of [+ round] which would lead to the vowel /o/. (Note that [low] was argued not to be among the distinctive vowel features in § 6.1. This might explain why schwa does not change into low [a], which would otherwise also constitute a plausible, and minimal, change.)

These considerations have reduced the problem considerably. It only remains to account for the fact that [+ front], and not [+ round], is chosen as the feature added to the vowel. Conceivably, schwa is perceptually closer to the front vowels [eː, ɛ] than to back and round [oː, ɔ]; [front] might be chosen for this reason. Alternatively, an explanation may be found in the lower functional role of [round] in general. That this is the case has been established empirically by Berg (1990), who finds that of all (1,074) impure rhymes in the works of nineteenth-century poet Wilhelm Busch, 90 per cent concern the feature [round] alone. Berg concludes that vowel pairs in rhymes differing in rounding are not categorized as impure by the author.[19]

On the basis of these considerations, schwa must surface under stress as [ɛ, eː] because of simplicity ('add the minimal number of specified features') and because of prominence of features ('choose a salient feature'). The choice between [ɛ] and [eː] is completely determined by syllable structure: the former variant appears in closed and the latter variant in open syllables.

7.3. RULES IN THE CONSONANT SYSTEM

The phonological alternations to be observed within the consonant system of German are more numerous than those found for vowels. This fact also opens

---

[19] The excerpt from a poem by Schiller ((25), § 3.2.2) shows the same phenomenon. But in contrast to Schiller, Busch came from a dialect area where rounding in front vowels is (and was) distinctive.

the possibility to observe more intricate interactions of rules, where several rules operate on the same underlying segment. More phonological rules affecting (or, in fact, creating) consonants are covered in § 7.4.

7.3.1. Final Devoicing

The rule of Final Devoicing is, next to Umlaut, the other classical phonological rule of Modern Standard German.[20] The name refers to a particular neutralization of the voicing distinction for obstruents in final position. That it is indeed the feature [voice] which is affected here is not altogether clear. Kloeke (1982) and other authors propose that not voice but tenseness of obstruents is affected in 'Final Devoicing'. There is also a tradition in German studies to use a fortis/ lenis opposition here. As I will show below, the fricatives demonstrate more clearly than the stops that Final Devoicing is indeed a voice-related alternation. Often, the 'voiced' stops are transcribed as lax but voiceless ([b̥, d̥, g̥]), while the fricatives are interpreted phonetically as properly voiced [z, v, ʒ]. Because of the lack of a better featural analysis, I will continue using the feature [voice] in formulating the rule for the alternation.

Final Devoicing describes alternations as exemplified in (27), with the voiceless member of the pair in final position. The list of segment pairs given here is complete.

(27) Lo[p] ~ Lo[b]es
  Ra[t] ~ Ra[d]es
  Sar[k] ~ Sär[g]e
  akti[f] ~ akti[v]e
  Gra[s] ~ Grä[z]er
  oran[ʃ]e ~ Oran[ʒ]e

 Occasional statements to the effect that /v/ vs. /f/ is not involved in Final Devoicing (e.g. Philipp 1974: 60) are in error. The group of words ending in /v/ includes common items such as *brav*, *Archiv*, *naiv*. Even within native words, pairs such as *Lö[v]e* vs. *Lö[f]+chen* can be found. The large group of words built on the suffix *-iv* is also subject to Final Devoicing very regularly (see *akt+iv* in (27)). Notice also that the adjective *ewige* has a bisyllabic alternant (for metrical reasons) in poetic language: *e[f]'ge*. Again, Final Devoicing applies automatically, and at the syllable edge.

 Applications of Final Devoicing to /ʒ/ are very rare because of a lack in relevant morphemes. The recent formation of the colour adjective *orange* ([oːˈʀaŋʃ]) formed from the fruit name *Orang+e* ([oːˈʀaŋʒə]) and the fact that Final Devoicing applies to /ʒ/ in the former word is important, since it demonstrates the role of a featural description. By simply listing the segments to which Final Devoicing applies there would be no way of predicting that /ʒ/

---

[20] An extensive review of the various analyses of Final Devoicing in German and its relevance for phonological theory is now available by Brockhaus (1995), who also discusses the choice of an adequate feature.

also undergoes the rule. Before this segment entered the relevant context through morphological backformation, we would have had no reason to include /ʒ/ in the list of segments.[21]

(28) is a first attempt to formulate the rule, one to be revised in (34) below. The restriction of Final Devoicing to obstruents is obvious from (27), while the claim that it is found exactly in syllable-final position needs justification. From the much-mentioned pair of pairs *bunt* vs. *bunte* vs. *Bund* vs. *Bunde* we can also conclude that the voiced segment should be assumed as the underlier, since otherwise we would have no way of predicting under what circumstances the alternation occurs.

(28) Final Devoicing (first version)
      [+ obstruent] → [– voice] / ——]$_\sigma$

The application of this rule is illustrated in the following example. In (29) *Lo*[p] (nom. sg.) is derived, while in (30) the suffixation of /s/ (for gen sg.) with its subsequent assignment of /b/ to the onset of the second syllable prevents Final Devoicing from applying.

(29) *Lob*   (30) *Lob+es*
  a. /loːb/   a. /loːb/   underlying
  b. —   b. /loːb + əs/   suffixation
  c.   c.   Syllabification

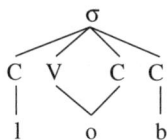

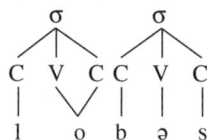

  d.   d.   Final Devoicing (28)

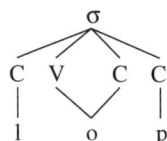

                                            ——

Final Devoicing, as formulated in (28), is restricted to apply to a segment in the syllable-final position. In the literature a number of other proposals has been made. While some agreement has been reached that the syllable is the crucial domain (Vennemann (1968) and Kloeke (1982) make use of morphological boundaries), it is often (Vennemann 1978; 1982; Hall 1989*b*; Rubach 1990) proposed that Final Devoicing must be assumed to apply in the syllable coda, the category discussed in § 3.2.2. The cases on which this claim is based involve a series of obstruents in the coda. Since voiced obstruents do not occur in the coda, this formulation expresses a valid generalization. Given this situation, it is hard to see how (28) can be defended. I will first confirm the basic claim that

---

[21] Since all obstruents seem to undergo Final Devoicing, we may conclude that /ʀ/ is not a fricative. If it were, it should undergo Final Devoicing, given that fricatives are obstruents. But in Modern Standard German, it never does. This is an example of how behaviour in rules justifies featural specifications. The apparent circularity is circumvented by the recurrence of such patterns. /ʀ/, for example, behaves as a non-obstruent in other ways, as in the phonotactics.

Final Devoicing must be related to the syllable in general, and then proceed to justify the more specific idea that only the syllable edge might be needed as an environment for this rule.

For evidence of the syllable (either its right edge or the coda) as the relevant domain, see the alternations in (31). In each of these morphologically diverse cases, the voicing alternation occurs, but not in a morpheme- or word-final position. Rather, the obstruents may optionally occur in a position which can be characterized as syllable-final. In this environment, they are invariably voiceless. That is, I assume, following Vennemann (1968), a syllabification of, for example, either [eː.dlə] or [eːt.lə]. Final Devoicing, if confined to the syllable-final position, then gives a correct account of the distributions.[22]

(31) e[d]el ~ e[d/t]l+es
      han[d]eln ~ Han[d/t]lung
      schmu[g]el+n ~ Schmu[g/k]l+er
      nör[g]el+n ~ Nör[g/k]l+er
      Ei[g]en+tum ~ Ei[k/g/ç]n+er
      Re[g]en ~ re[k/g/ç]n+en

The last two examples in (31) provide the most convincing evidence for this claim. Here, the rule of g-Spirantization (to be discussed in § 7.3.2) can apply optionally in the colloquial speech of Northern speakers. If it does apply, the fricative [ç] appears which is clearly voiceless. Also, because of the restriction of g-Spirantization to the syllable-final position, the co-variation of the outputs of the two rules (voiced but spirantized /g/, i.e. [ɣ], does not occur) is accounted for. Furthermore, determining whether the obstruent is voiced or voiceless is perceptually easier for the fricatives than for the stops.

Eisenberg (1992), who basically agrees with the syllabification patterns given in (31), claims that the same possibilities for syllabifications exist for *Nör[.g]l+er/ Nör[k.]l+er* as for *Gebir[.g]+ler/Gebir[k.]+ler*. Note that morpheme boundaries vary in the two cases. It seems to me that only the latter syllabification is acceptable for the latter word (along with colloquial *Gebir[ç.]+ler* in which g-Spirantization has applied), which would confirm the point made in § 3.4 that the suffixes *+chen* and *+ler* behave as corresponding to a phonological word of their own. One must, however, agree with Eisenberg that judgements on placement of syllable boundaries become problematic and perhaps overly subtle in this area.

In one set of cases, syllable-final obstruents are not devoiced: *Bagger, Kladde, Robbe*, and others are pronounced with *voiced* intervocalic stops. We may relate this fact to the idea that these consonants are ambisyllabic (§ 3.2). Ambisyllabic consonants in these words close the initial syllable, a fact which should force the segments to undergo Final Devoicing. To prevent ambisyllabic consonants from

---

[22] I depart from Rubach's (1990: 83) view that the syllabification in which the obstruents are syllable-final and voiceless may be neglected as 'performance problems'. Rather, we have two alternative modes of word-internal syllabification, one leading to a maximized though sometimes marginal onset such as /dl/, and one in which no such cluster appears, but in which the onset is not maximized.

undergoing the rule, it is necessary to involve the principle of 'exhaustiveness' alluded to in connection with Syllabification, which requires that categories must fulfil structural constraints, as stated in a rule, exhaustively (see the *Linking Constraint* formulated by Hayes 1986: 472). As ambisyllabic obstruents are both syllable-initial and syllable-final, the condition is not met.

On the question of syllable-final position vs. syllable coda as the relevant context for Final Devoicing we may recall that certain consonants were argued in § 3.2.3 to be extrasyllabic. I will now demonstrate that under such an assumption the rule formulation in (28) may be upheld.

Consider *Jagd* as in (32). From the alternations of its verbal root *jag* we know that the root ends in /g/ and from the plural form *Jag+d+en* we conclude that the underlier of the final segment must be /d/. This latter segment represents an unproductive noun-forming suffix.

(32) Jag+d: [jaːkt] ~ jag+en: [jaːgən] ~ Jag+d+en [jaːkdən]

How can both final obstruents become voiceless? Considering the syllabification mechanisms proposed in § 3.2.4, we find that a first attempt at syllabifying the string will result in something like (33*b*). The /d/ remains extrasyllabic, but /g/ is final and must be devoiced, as in (33*c*). But the extrasyllabic segment will eventually be integrated into the syllable, perhaps through an adjunction like the one specified in (41) of § 3.2.4. At this point, Final Devoicing must reapply, if we assume that this rule is free to apply whenever syllabification rules have operated. The final result is that both segments have been devoiced by one rule applying at the syllable edge.

(33) Derivation of [jaːkt]

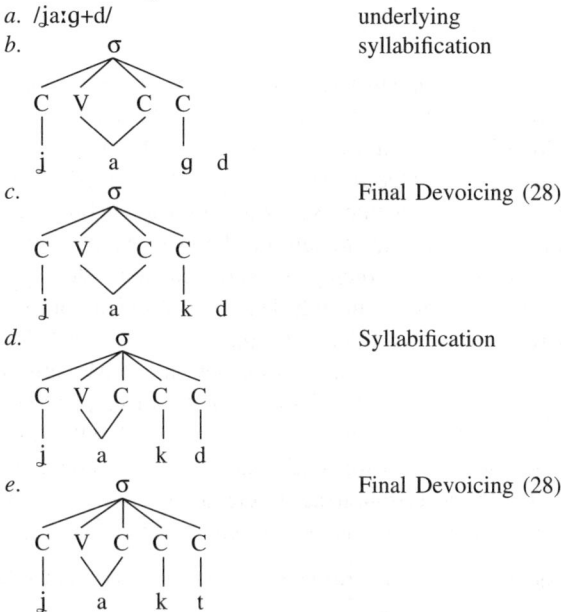

   a. /jaːg+d/   underlying

   b.   σ   syllabification

```
              σ
          ___/|\___
         /  / |   \
        C  V  C    C
        |  \ /     |
        j   a   g  d
```

   c.   σ   Final Devoicing (28)

```
              σ
          ___/|\___
         /  / |   \
        C  V  C    C
        |  \ /     |
        j   a   k  d
```

   d.   σ   Syllabification

```
               σ
          ___/|\\___
         /  / |  \ \
        C  V  C  C  C
        |  \ /  |  |
        j   a   k  d
```

   e.   σ   Final Devoicing (28)

```
               σ
          ___/|\\___
         /  / |  \ \
        C  V  C  C  C
        |  \ /  |  |
        j   a   k  t
```

This discussion is meant to demonstrate that it is sufficient in the formulation of Final Devoicing to apply the rule only to the syllable-final segment. Hall (1992*b*: § 2.13) argues that Final Devoicing must indeed be restricted in such a way, but that any preceding obstruents are devoiced through a rule of Voicing Assimilation.

Rule (28) is insufficient in two ways: first, given the apparatus for writing rules proposed in § 7.1, it is simply not a rule admitted in this framework, since it is a rewriting rule which turns [+ voice] into [− voice]. Second, on a more factual level, it can be asked why this rule (in German as in a number of other languages) leads to the *voiceless* obstruent, the unmarked member of the pair. Linguists have often pointed out that this does not seem to be an accidental part of this alternation. Yet the rule as stated in (28) in no way expresses this asymmetry. The rule would be equally simple if it required syllable-final obstruents to be [+ voice], thus changing segments bearing [− voice] into their [+ voice] counterparts.

The alternative analysis, which is in accordance with the formal theory of phonological rules sketched in § 7.1, regards Final Devoicing as *delinking* of the disallowed feature value for voice. This analysis can exclusively rely upon a mechanism proposed there, and avoids the feature change of (28). The revised rule will then be as in (34).

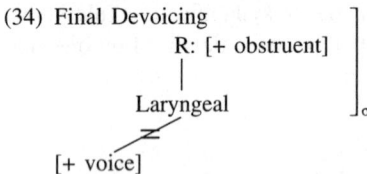

(34) Final Devoicing

$$
\left.
\begin{array}{c}
\text{R: } [+ \text{ obstruent}] \\
| \\
\text{Laryngeal} \\
\diagup\!\!\!\diagup \\
[+ \text{ voice}]
\end{array}
\right]_\sigma
$$

Of course, delinking by itself is not sufficient to derive the voiceless obstruent. But, perhaps not quite by chance, there exists a default mechanism available to supply [− voice]. In (28) of § 6.3.2, it was proposed that the general default schema, which gives the negative value for any feature not specified otherwise, also applies to [voice]. The delinking rule (34) is a complete account of Final Devoicing if it works in tandem with this default mechanism. At the same time, the neutralizing character of Final Devoicing is expressed more clearly, since removing a lexically distinctive value can only lead to neutralization. Starting from a syllabified structure, these two rules will apply to *Lob* as in (35).

Final Devoicing is the prime example of a phonological rule of Modern Standard German, given its purely phonological character and its exceptionless and automatic applicability.[23] From these criteria and from the fact that the rule may never apply before the addition of a vowel-initial suffix we may conclude that it is a postlexical rule. Its characterization as a rule of neutralization has recently been questioned by a number of studies trying to demonstrate that the

---

[23] This is why Final Devoicing is part of the stereotype for Germans pronouncing a foreign language such as English.

neutralization is not absolute. These results are rather tentative, however, given that the recognition of non-neutralized *Devoicing* was found in a minority of cases only. For references and critical discussion, see also Fourakis and Iverson (1984), who conclude that the apparent incomplete neutralization is probably a phenomenon of a hypercorrect spelling pronunciation used in reading word lists.

(35) *a.*   σ   Syllabification

```
              σ
          ╱ ╱ ╲
     C   V   C   C
     │   ╲╱      │
     l   o       R: [+ obstruent]
                 │
              Laryngeal
             ╱
     [+ voice]
```

b.   σ   Final Devoicing (34)

```
              σ
          ╱ ╱ ╲
     C   V   C   C
     │   ╲╱      │
     l   o       R: [+ obstruent]
                 │
              Laryngeal

     [+ voice]
```

c.   σ   default

```
              σ
          ╱ ╱ ╲
     C   V   C   C
     │   ╲╱      │
     l   o       R: [+ obstruent]
                 │
              Laryngeal
             ╱
     [− voice]
```

There is more evidence for the postlexical status of Final Devoicing from the interaction of this rule with cliticization of personal pronouns. These pronouns may, under specific conditions discussed in § 7.4.3, be syllabified with the preceding word, often the finite verb. Observe now that there is an optional application of Final Devoicing to the verb form *hab* if a cliticized vowel-initial personal pronoun is to follow: [habɪçl/[hapɪçl or [habəsl/[hapəsl for *hab ich* 'have I', *hab es* 'have it', respectively. This variation requires Final Devoicing to apply either before or after attachment of the clitic. However, since clitic attachment is postlexical, especially for fast-speech clitics like the ones given here, Final Devoicing must be postlexical as well.[24]

---

[24] Cliticization must be postlexical since the clitic pronouns are in the positions assigned to them by the syntactic rules. There is no special clitic position in German. For more discussion of clitics see § 7.4.3.

7.3.2. g-Spirantization

Another consonantal rule, interacting with Final Devoicing, is that of g-Spirantization. This section will first present an analysis of g-Spirantization, and then briefly treat other spirantizations operating in Modern Standard German. As the data in (36*a*) demonstrate, /g/ appears as a palatal fricative if preceded by /i/ and in final position. That the underlying segment must be /g/, may be inferred from the contrast between (36*b*) and (36*c*): medial /ç/ is possible as well as medial /g/. Only from underlying /g/ is it possible to predict the occurrence of spirantization. It is not the case that final [ç] changes to [g] if in medial position.

(36) *a*. König[ç] ~ Köni[g]e, weni[ç] ~ weni[g]e, belieb+i[ç] ~ belieb+i[g]e
      b. Tei[ç] ~ Tei[g]e, Zwei[ç] ~ Zwei[g]e
      c. Tei[ç] ~ Tei[ç]e, Lei[ç]nam ~ Lei[ç]e

In Modern Standard German, this spirantization of /g/ is restricted to a context in which /i/ immediately precedes /g/, though it is not restricted to the suffix +*ig*, as *Köni*[ç] or *Honi*[ç] demonstrate. Spirantization after non-syllabic [i̯], as in (36*b*), is already excluded in the formal register of Modern Standard German. In Northern colloquial speech, however, the narrow context for g-Spirantization is extended to include, with an increasing distance from the standard language, non-syllabic [i̯], other vowels than [i] (see (37*a*, *b*)), and even consonantal contexts (37*c*).[25]

(37) *a*. We[ç] ~ We[g]e, lü[ç] ~ lü[g]en, Zu[x] ~ Zü[g]e
      b. zo[x] ~ zo[g]en, Ta[x] ~ Ta[g]e
      c. Tal[ç] ~ Tal[g]e, Sar[ç] ~ Sär[g]e

Note that in (37*b*) and in the final example of (37*a*) the fricative is [x], and not [ç], a fact that will be of importance in the discussion below. The second context condition for g-Spirantization to apply is that /g/ must be in syllable-final position. Examples demonstrating the correctness of this claim have been given in (31) above, where *re*[ç].*nen* and *re*.[g]*nen* were supposed to differ precisely in the syllabification of the medial obstruent. Notice that, as with Final Devoicing, 'end of syllable' cannot be understood in an absolute sense. The genitive form of *König*, for example, is *Köni*[ç]+*s*, where g-Spirantization is just as obligatory as in the simple form. This does not provide a problem if either g-Spirantization applies before affixation of +*s* or /s/ is taken as extrasyllabic.

In the present framework, the rule describing the regularity may be expressed abbreviating on the segmental feature structure, as in (38). As can be seen from (17) in § 6.2, /g/ has the features given in the context part of (38) and is not specified for [continuant]. It will receive [– continuant] via the default schema —unless rule (38) applies. I leave out the vowel restriction valid for the standard

---

[25] For phonotactic reasons, only [l] and [ʀ] may appear in this position before [g]. Other dialects of German display g-Spirantization even in initial position.

language, since, as will be seen, more interesting interactions with other rules can be observed if the generalized version is studied.

(38) g-Spirantization

$$[\text{continuant}] \rightarrow [+ \text{continuant}] \;/\; \left[\begin{array}{c} \overline{} \\ \left[\begin{array}{l} + \text{voice} \\ + \text{obstruent} \\ \text{Dorsal} \end{array} \right] \end{array} \right]_\sigma$$

The formulation proposed here relies on an analysis using underspecified segments and is in this respect an alternative to the more common formulation (see Meinhold and Stock 1980; Wurzel 1981) in which fully specified /g/ is directly changed into fully specified [ç]. But in such a rule certain information is redundantly specified. In particular, the change from [+ voice] to [– voice] can be taken care of by the independently well-motivated rule of Final Devoicing, and the change in place of articulation may also be described by independent rules of place-feature assignment discussed in the next section. Furthermore, the latter change is not found in all cases, as the examples from colloquial speech in (37b) demonstrate. The rule account using full specification will therefore need a second spirantization rule in order to describe these (colloquial) forms.

Consider now how g-Spirantization, in conjunction with Final Devoicing, will operate on the final segment of *König*. As (39c) demonstrates, the segment derived is actually velar [x], and not palatal [ç], as required.

(39) *a.* /k øː n i g/   underlying
     b.   Syllabification

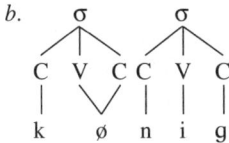

     c.   Final Devoicing (34), g-Spirantization (38)

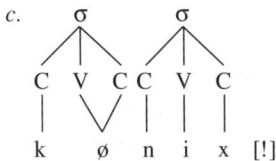

This apparent problem for the account of g-Spirantization offered here will be taken care of in the next section, where the rule of Dorsal Fricative Assimilation is discussed. Note that the two rules (g-Spirantization, Final Devoicing) will correctly derive the velar fricative present in the examples of (37b).

Hall (1992b: § 5.3) considers to treat g-Spirantization as a *spreading* process, in which [+ continuant] spreads from the vowel to following /g/. Such an analysis would provide some phonetic motivation to the process by treating it as an assimilation of a manner feature, but it fails in cases of (colloquial) [talç] *Talg*, in which the preceding consonant /l/ is [– continuant]. Nevertheless, g-Spirantization is found here.

The rules of g-Spirantization and Final Devoicing must apply in the order just mentioned. Consider the result of applying them in a different order, as demonstrated in (40). Since devoiced /k/ is not an input to g-Spirantization, the surface form would be *[veːnik].[26]

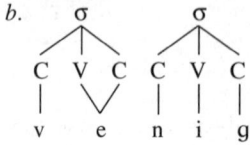

(40) a. /veːnig/   underlying
      b.   σ   σ   Syllabification

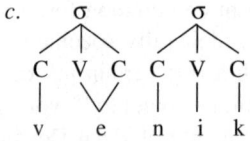

            C V C   C V C
            | \ / | | |
            v   e   n i g

      c.   σ   σ   Final Devoicing (34)

            C V C   C V C
            | \ / | | |
            v   e   n i k

      d.   ——————   g-Spirantization (38)

   How can we ensure that the two rules apply only in the order g-Spirantization
—Final Devoicing? Three solutions for this problem seem possible. The first
simply states that the two rules are ordered in the required way. This is the
concept of explicit rule ordering, used for the problem at hand by Wurzel
(1970) and Hall (1989b; 1992b). While explicit rule ordering cannot be excluded as a possibility, it seems somewhat undesirable on a priori grounds. It
certainly puts a considerable burden on the learners of a language if they have
to figure out the correct ordering of rules from all the theoretically possible
sequences.

   Another line of reasoning might claim that it is generally the case that feature-
filling rules apply before feature-removing rules. Since g-Spirantization adds a
value, while Final Devoicing removes one, their respective order would be fixed
through such a general principle. As principles of this kind have, to my knowledge, not been proposed in the literature, I leave this version in its speculative
status.

   Finally, it is not implausible to argue that g-Spirantization is a lexical rule,
while Final Devoicing is postlexical. Again, the ordering of the two rules would
follow automatically from the assignment of the rules to different components
of this grammar. The basis of this claim is the observation that Final Devoicing
is an exceptionless rule, while g-Spirantization has a set of exceptions exemplified in (41).

(41) köni[kl]lich, ledi[kl]lich

   Forms in (41) would have two successive rhymes ending in [iç] if g-
Spirantization applied. At least the pronouncing dictionaries require g-
Spirantization not to apply in such a case. While speakers even of the standard
pronunciation certainly do not follow this normative rule in all cases, it may be

---

[26] This is the correct form for non-Northern dialects, which do not have the rule of g-
Spirantization.

sufficient to demonstrate that g-Spirantization can in principle be subject to marking of exceptions, and therefore has a status in the grammar of Modern Standard German different from that of Final Devoicing.

While spirantization is the topic of discussion, it should be mentioned that there are more phenomena to be covered under the term 'spirantization'. Here, not only /g/ spirantizes, but also other obstruents. On the other hand, this rule applies in a heavily restricted set of contexts, namely before the suffixes /t/ (apparently with various functions) and noun-forming /ɪoːn/. In (42a, b), the rather restricted set of examples in relation to noun-forming /t/ is given. This suffix is unproductive and the morphological relation in some of these word pairs is rather opaque, as with geb(en) vs. Gift.[27] (42c) lists verb-related cases of spirantization.

(42) a. heben ~ Hef+t; schreiben, schrieben ~ Schrif+t; halb ~ Hälf+t+e; Grube ~ Gruf+t; geben, gib ~ Gif+t

b. tragen ~ Trach+t; pflegen ~ Pflich+t; schlagen ~ Schlach+t; biegen ~ Buch+t

c. mögen ~ möchte; denken ~ dachte; bringen ~ brachte; taugen ~ tüchtig; schweigen ~ beschwichtigen

(43) heben ~ hebt; schreiben ~ schreibt; laden ~ lädt; mögen ~ mögt

As the contrast between verbs in (42c) and (43) shows, this type of spirantization is not a general phenomenon. Furthermore, it is part of the verbal alternation called *ablaut*, which should be treated as a matter not of phonological rules, but of entry-specific representation, as argued by Wunderlich and Fabri (1993) and Wiese (1996). It is significant, however, that in the verbal paradigm it is restricted to /g/, and thus is not incompletely independent of the g-Spirantization studied above.

The spirantization depending on suffixation of +*ion* is more general than the one just discussed in that it always applies to root-final /t/. Without going into details of possible analyses, I give a few examples illustrating the alternation in (44).

(44) diskut+ier+en   Diskut+ant ~ Diskuss+ion
     Produkt   produkt+iv ~ Produk[ts]ion
     Fabrik+at   Fabrik+at+or ~ Fabrik+a[ts]ion

One possible treatment of this spirantization would assign the spirantizing property ([+ continuant]) to the suffix +*ion*, and then allow this feature to spread to the root-final (or suffix-final, in the case of +*at*) consonant.

7.3.3. Dorsal Fricative Assimilation

As noted in the sections on the segments of Modern Standard German, [ç], [x], and [χ] can be found as a set of voiceless fricatives which have in common the articulator [Dorsal]. It is well known, however, that these sounds should not be

---

[27] In (42), the shortening of vowels before +*t* discussed in § 7.2.2 can also be observed. The set of cases illustrated in (42) is also discussed by Kloeke (1982: 210).

taken as phonemes of German. Rather they constitute the best (though disputed) example for complementary distribution of two or three allophones.[28] The discussion of this allophony has been somewhat simplified, as Kohler (1977; 1990a) has pointed out. It is not, as commonly assumed, just an alternation between palatal [ç] and velar [x], but between the three fricatives listed above. While palatal [ç] occurs after front vowels, velar [x] is found after non-low back tense vowels (i.e. [oː] and [uː]), and uvular [χ] after low vowels. After [ʊ] and [ɔ], there is, according to Kohler's findings, variation between [x] and [χ], but [χ] predominates. Words in (45) exemplify the basic pattern of the alternating dorsal fricative for the postvocalic position, (45a) for short, lax vowels including glides, (45b) for long vowels, and (45c) for front vowels with no back counterpart. I will assume that this pattern is indeed the correct one. It is a rule-governed pattern of allophony, with a small amount of free variation between [x] and [χ] due to optional application of the respective rule ((54) below).

(45) a. Da[χ] ~ Dä[ç]er   b. n[aːχ] ~ n[ɛːç]ste   c. rie[ç]len
     Lo[χ/x] ~ Lö[ç]er   h[oːx] ~ h[øːç]stens   Tri[ç]ter
     Flu[χ/x]t ~ flü[ç]tig   B[uːx] ~ B[yːç]er   rei[ç]
     Bau[χ/x] ~ Bäu[ç]e   Tü[ç]ler

Palatal [ç] appears, without the alternations visible in the postvocalic position, in a number of additional contexts, as illustrated in (46). If preceded by consonants (46a) or if morpheme-initial (46b, c), the velar or dorsal alternants do not occur. Note that [ç] is syllable-final in *durch, manch, solch*, but syllable-initial in *Kirche, München, Kolchose*. Syllable boundaries seem to play no role in Dorsal Fricative Assimilation.

(46) a. dur[ç], Kir[ç]e; man[ç]; Mün[ç]en; sol[ç]; Kol[ç]ose
    b. Chirurg, Chemie, China, +chen: [ç]
    c. Charisma, Cholesterin: [ç]

As shown in (46c), I assume, contrary to some of the literature and the pronouncing dictionaries, that a back (non-front) vowel *following* the dorsal fricative does not lead to a velar articulation of the fricative. Pronunciations for foreign names such as [x]*abarowsk*, [x]*uan*, [x]*losé* are required by the pronouncing dictionaries, but strike me (and others) as unassimilated forms.[29] Some of the words spelt with initial *ch* such as *Charisma* are pronounced with initial /k/ by many speakers; Southern speakers avoid the initial dorsal fricative altogether and replace it generally by /k/, see [kiːna] *China* or [kemiː] *Chemie*. Other speakers tend to replace standard [ç] by [ʃ].

The outline of the facts given here implies, contrary to other accounts, that velar [x] is a very rare form. There is indeed additional evidence that the velar fricative is highly exceptional. First, we may note with Hall (1992b: 234, fn. 1) that only two underived roots with /oː/ followed by the dorsal fricative exist,

---

[28] Hall (1992b: ch. 5) provides the latest survey of the bulky discussion of this topic.
[29] Krech et al. (1982: 353) propose *Kol[ç]ose*, but *Kol[x]os* besides *Kol[ç]os*. The latter word *Kolchos* is clearly the one which is integrated into Modern Standard German to a lesser extent.

namely *hoch* and *Bochum* (a town name). Second, *hoch* displays an irregular alternation in that in the inflected forms of this adjective the dorsal fricative simply disappears: *hohe*, *höher*, and likewise for all other members of this paradigm. Thus there is a strong tendency to avoid velar [x] before the non-high long back vowel.

While the data above speak for a straightforward treatment of complementary distribution, the examples in (47) are well known as crucial for a proper theory of the phenomenon. We will return to them below on page 217.

(47) brau[x]en ~ Frau[ç]en, tau[x]en ~ Tau[ç]en, Ku[x]en ~ Kuh[ç]en

To introduce the rules discussed in the literature, let us temporarily assume that the alternation is only one between palatal [ç] and velar [x]. One possible rule to describe the alternation is then given in (48). In similar format, it can be found in Wurzel (1970: pt III, § 3.2) and Kloeke (1982: 208). Words in parentheses on the right illustrate its application in the three contexts.

(48)

$$/x/ \rightarrow [ç] / \left\{ \begin{array}{ll} \begin{bmatrix} - \text{consonantal} \\ + \text{front} \end{bmatrix} \underline{\hspace{1cm}} & (\textit{ich, euch}) \\ [+ \text{front}] \underline{\hspace{1cm}} & (\textit{durch, manch, solch}) \\ \# \underline{\hspace{1cm}} & (\textit{Chemie, +chen}) \end{array} \right.$$

The arguments against this rule are fairly straightforward. On the formal level, there is a three-part disjunction of the type that usually raises the suspicion that some generalization has not been captured. Why should the rule be applicable in exactly the three contexts given in (48)? The rule might be acceptable as a statement expressing regularities in the morphophonemic domain, with exceptions, sub-regularities, and so on. But the rule of Dorsal Fricative Assimilation is not of this type. It is an exceptionless, natural rule of German. Furthermore, the assumed underlying form /x/ occurs only in one context (namely after back vowels) which has all the appearances of a context of assimilation. The rule does not express this assimilatory behaviour of [x].

Such considerations have led authors such as Wurzel (1981) and Dressler (1985) to a different proposal, summarized in the rule given in (49). Here, the velar fricative is derived from the palatal in a context of assimilation. The implication of the rule is, correctly, that [ç] occurs under all other circumstances.

(49) $/ç/ \rightarrow [x] / \begin{bmatrix} - \text{consonantal} \\ - \text{front} \end{bmatrix} \underline{\hspace{1cm}}$ (*acht*)

However, this rule fails in cases of interaction with the rule of g-Spirantization as discussed in § 7.3.2. In the standard language /g/ is spirantized only after /i/, with [ç] as the result. If g-Spirantization only changes the value of [continuant] and Final Devoicing applies subsequently (as I argue in the preceding section), then the change effected is not one leading from /g/ to [ç], but from /g/ to /x/; see the steps in the derivation of (39) and repeated in (50a). This reveals an apparent advantage of the first rule, the one introduced in (48), since, making use of this rule, /x/ can be changed to the final form

[ç], while the rule (49), which seems to have better motivation in other respects, fails here. (50b) shows that in (colloquial speech) *Zug* no change in
the place features is found (except for the fact that the fricative is actually
uvular).

(50) *a.* Köni[ç] ~ Köni[g]e   /g/ → /ɣ/ → /x/ → [ç]
     b. Zu[x] ~ Zü[g]e   /g/ → /ɣ/ → [x]

In the recent discussion of this alternation, agreement has been reached that
the alternation provides excellent evidence for underspecification of the relevant
feature. Jessen (1988), Hall (1989b; 1992b: ch. 5), and Yu (1992b: § 4.5.4) all
propose *not* to specify the alternating feature, thereby avoiding the pitfall of
earlier analyses, which had to choose between /x/ or /ç/ as the underlying segment. I will take up this argumentation and present a similar analysis, which
differs from those by the aforementioned authors empirically in its consideration
of the threefold allophony and theoretically in the features chosen.

As (16) of § 6.2 shows, the difference between [x] and [ç] is to be expressed
in the value of [front] (as a dependent feature of [Dorsal]), while most earlier
authors follow the *SPE* tradition in expressing the difference by values of the
feature [back]. In addition, [low] (dependent on [Tongue Position]) functions to
distinguish uvular from velar articulation. The three sounds thus need the underlying features given in (51a), with the minimal amount of specification, while
the fully specified surface segments have the features given in (51b). I use 'X'
as an abbreviatory symbol for the underlier of the dorsal fricatives. The feature
[high] need not be considered here, as it is taken care of independently of Dorsal
Fricative Assimilation by rule (21) given in § 6.2.

(51) *a.* X: $\begin{bmatrix} + \text{obstruent} \\ + \text{continuant} \\ \text{Dorsal} \end{bmatrix}$ *b.*

voice	−	ç	x	χ
	+	j	ɣ	ʁ

consonantal	+	+	+
obstruent	+	+	+
continuant	+	+	+
nasal	−	−	−
Coronal	−	−	−
Labial	−	−	−
Dorsal	+	+	+
front	+	−	−
Tongue Position	+	+	+
high	+	+	−
low	−	−	+

On the basis of this featural analysis, the following treatment is derived. There
is, first, a rule of assimilation, the one given in (52). It spreads [− front] from
a vowel to a following dorsal fricative. The result is the class of segments
/x, χ/.

(52) Dorsal Fricative Assimilation

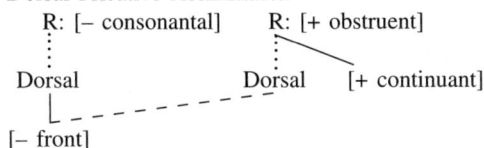

R: [– consonantal]　　R: [+ obstruent]

Dorsal　　　　　　Dorsal　　[+ continuant]

[– front]

This rule provides the first example of a spreading rule.[30] The operation called *spreading* is a crucial element of non-linear phonology. It transmits featural information from one site to another, adjacent node. Note that it is a special case of the mechanism called association in § 7.1.

Rule (52) must be complemented by the rule already stated in (22*a*) of § 6.2.2. It is repeated here in (53) and states that the dorsal fricative is articulated with a fronting movement of the tongue body. Because of the Elsewhere Condition, this rule applies only if (52) does not, so that it applies in all contexts of non-assimilation, namely those illustrated in (46) and in the right-hand examples of (45*a*).

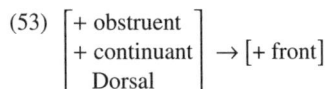

(53) $\begin{bmatrix} + \text{ obstruent} \\ + \text{ continuant} \\ \text{Dorsal} \end{bmatrix} \rightarrow [+ \text{ front}]$

Finally, the alternation between [x] and [χ] must be taken care of by a rule introducing [+ low] if the preceding vowel is [– ATR]. This rule, dubbed *Dorsal Fricative Lowering*, is formulated in (54). Given that [o] and [u] are the only back vowels which are [+ ATR], this is the simplest statement on the distribution.

(54) Dorsal Fricative Lowering

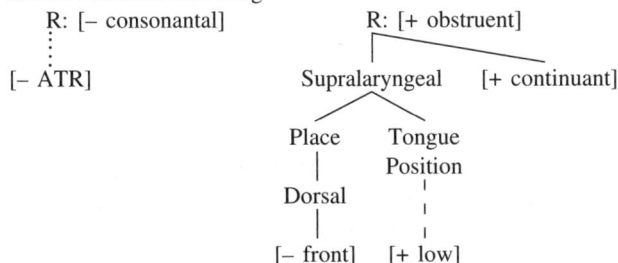

R: [– consonantal]　　　　　R: [+ obstruent]

[– ATR]　　　　　Supralaryngeal　　[+ continuant]

Place　　Tongue
　　　　　Position
Dorsal

[– front]　[+ low]

The tie between the features [low] and [ATR] is somewhat unexpected in the present featural geometry and may eventually provide grounds for a different treatment of this regularity.[31] The rule does however describe the generalization that [χ] only occurs if [ʊ, ɔ, a, aː] precede. It is also not implausible to assume a lowering effect of [– ATR] vowels.

However, as shown in (45*b*), the lowering rule (54) can also apply if the preceding vowels are [oː] or [uː]. To account for this, we must regard the condition on the Radical node of the vowel ([– ATR]) as optional. That is, the rule

---

[30] Actually, the *s*-Voicing rule (37) of Ch. 6 was also formulated as a spreading rule.

[31] To my knowledge, the distribution of uvular [χ] in Modern Standard German has never been discussed in a feature-based model before.

applies optionally if the vowel is [+ ATR]. If in rule (54) the condition that the preceding vowel must be [– ATR] has not been removed the feature [– low] for [x] results from the default schema.

We are now ready to illustrate a fairly complex interaction of relevant rules in the derivation of the dorsal fricatives. The derivation of palatal [ç] in *dich* (55) is not regarded as an example of assimilation between vowel and fricative; therefore this derivation is identical to that of all other occurrences of [ç]. In (56) and (57), respectively, the two pronunciations possible for *hoch* are exemplified.

(55) *dich* [dɪç]

    a. / d ɪ $\begin{bmatrix} + \text{obstruent} \\ + \text{continuant} \\ \text{Dorsal} \end{bmatrix}$ /   underlying

    b. / d ɪ $\begin{bmatrix} + \text{obstruent} \\ + \text{continuant} \\ \text{Dorsal} \\ + \text{front} \end{bmatrix}$ /   rule (53)

    c. / d ɪ $\begin{bmatrix} + \text{obstruent} \\ + \text{continuant} \\ \text{Dorsal} \\ + \text{front} \\ + \text{high} \end{bmatrix}$ /   rule (22*a*), § 6.2.2

    d. / d ɪ $\begin{bmatrix} + \text{obstruent} \\ + \text{continuant} \\ \text{Dorsal} \\ + \text{front} \\ + \text{high} \\ - \text{low} \end{bmatrix}$ /   default

The most complex interaction between a fairly large number of rules, most of them treated in this chapter, can be demonstrated in the derivation of the phonetic form [tsʊχ] for *Zug* in (58). This pronunciation is found not in the standard language (where it would be [tsuːk]), but, as mentioned above, in the closely related Northern colloquial form, in which g-Spirantization is not restricted to preceding /i/. In the same dialect, the word is also one of those to which Vowel Shortening (19) applies. In the derivations here, I abbreviate for reasons of space on the subsegmental feature structure. Syllable structure, once it is assigned in (58*b*), is also not indicated in the subsequent derivation.

The large number of rules participating here allows the study of rule interactions and rule orderings. Note that g-Spirantization, which itself is by necessity preceded by syllabification, must precede all rules applying to the dorsal fricative. On the other hand, the ordering of Final Devoicing is not particularly relevant, except that it should bleed g-Spirantization. If Vowel Shortening feeds lowering rule (54), the obligatory application of this latter rule is ensured. The hypothesis considered in § 7.3.2, that g-Spirantization is a lexical rule, is not invalidated by the present derivation. All other rules are perhaps postlexical, with syllabification applying ubiquitously.

(56) *hoch* [hoːχ]

a. / h oː $\begin{bmatrix} + \text{obstruent} \\ + \text{continuant} \\ \text{Dorsal} \end{bmatrix}$ /   underlying

b. / h oː $\begin{bmatrix} + \text{obstruent} \\ + \text{continuant} \\ \text{Dorsal} \\ - \text{front} \end{bmatrix}$ /   rule (52)

c. / h oː $\begin{bmatrix} + \text{obstruent} \\ + \text{continuant} \\ \text{Dorsal} \\ - \text{front} \\ + \text{low} \end{bmatrix}$ /   Dorsal Fricative Lowering (54), ignoring [– ATR] condition

d. / h oː $\begin{bmatrix} + \text{obstruent} \\ + \text{continuant} \\ \text{Dorsal} \\ - \text{front} \\ + \text{low} \\ - \text{high} \end{bmatrix}$ /   default

(57) *hoch* [hoːx]

a. / h oː $\begin{bmatrix} + \text{obstruent} \\ + \text{continuant} \\ \text{Dorsal} \end{bmatrix}$ /   underlying

b. / h oː $\begin{bmatrix} + \text{obstruent} \\ + \text{continuant} \\ \text{Dorsal} \\ - \text{front} \end{bmatrix}$ /   rule (52)

c. / h oː $\begin{bmatrix} + \text{obstruent} \\ + \text{continuant} \\ \text{Dorsal} \\ - \text{front} \\ - \text{low} \end{bmatrix}$ /   default

d. / h oː $\begin{bmatrix} + \text{obstruent} \\ + \text{continuant} \\ \text{Dorsal} \\ - \text{front} \\ - \text{low} \\ - \text{high} \end{bmatrix}$ /   default

(58) *Zug* [tsʊχ]

a. /t s uː $\begin{bmatrix} + \text{voice} \\ + \text{obstruent} \\ \text{Dorsal} \end{bmatrix}$ /   underlying

b.   σ   Syllabification

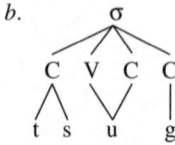

c. /t s uː $\begin{bmatrix} + \text{voice} \\ + \text{obstruent} \\ \text{Dorsal} \\ + \text{continuant} \end{bmatrix}$ /   g-Spirantization (38)

d. /t s uː $\begin{bmatrix} - \text{voice} \\ + \text{obstruent} \\ \text{Dorsal} \\ + \text{continuant} \end{bmatrix}$ /   Final Devoicing (34), default

e. /t s uː $\begin{bmatrix} - \text{voice} \\ + \text{obstruent} \\ \text{Dorsal} \\ + \text{continuant} \\ - \text{front} \end{bmatrix}$ /   Dorsal Fricative Assimilation (52)

f. /t s ʊ $\begin{bmatrix} - \text{voice} \\ + \text{obstruent} \\ \text{Dorsal} \\ + \text{continuant} \\ - \text{front} \end{bmatrix}$ /   Vowel Shortening (19)

g. /t s ʊ $\begin{bmatrix} - \text{voice} \\ + \text{obstruent} \\ \text{Dorsal} \\ + \text{continuant} \\ - \text{front} \\ + \text{low} \end{bmatrix}$ /   Dorsal Fricative Lowering (54)

h. /t s ʊ $\begin{bmatrix} - \text{voice} \\ + \text{obstruent} \\ \text{Dorsal} \\ + \text{continuant} \\ - \text{front} \\ + \text{low} \\ - \text{high} \end{bmatrix}$ /   default

We also find that the problem noted in connection with (39) has now been solved: spirantized /g/ is input to the rules deriving palatal [ç] for *König*. This presupposes, however, that /g/ is specified for [Dorsal] only, with no other place features. That is, the underspecification approach in its present form ensures the identity of underlying /g/ and /X/ with respect to their place features.

Bloomfield (1930) was among the first to propose that the difference between the simplex word *Ku*[x]*en* and the complex word *Kuh*+[ç]*en* should be accounted for by analysing the latter as a compound. The solution proposed here is in the spirit, though not the letter, of that proposal: phonologically, *Kuh*+*chen* and in fact all words involving the diminutive suffix +*chen* are complex words.[32] An argument for this claim is developed in § 3.4 where I demonstrate that +*chen* is deletable just like other words and suffixes claimed to have the status of phonological words. But since in a morphological perspective the diminutive words are single words with affixes, the difference between their morphological vs. phonological compound nature should be preserved.

In the present analysis, +*chen* is a phonological word; and the non-application of Dorsal Fricative Alternation to +*chen* follows directly from the assumption that this rule like (perhaps all) other rules of assimilation operates within the phonological word but not across its boundaries. No special treatment, for example, is necessary to explain the stability of [ç] in connection with the umlauting, that is, fronting, of the preceding vowel; compare *Kuh*+[ç]*en* to *Küh*+[ç]*en*, which are both possible diminutive forms of *Kuh*.

In contrast, under Lieber's account (1987: 107–8), it is the floating feature [– back] postulated as part of the suffix +*chen* which accounts for the umlauting of the preceding vowel, and which also changes /x/ to [ç] in the suffix. No such mechanism is required here. An account such as Lieber's would have to provide underlying /ç/ in *China, Kolchose*, and other words containing a non-assimilating dorsal fricative. That is, the dorsal fricatives would not be derived from a single underlier, but from two, in violation of the predictable nature of *all* instances of this set of sound segments.

Hall (1989*b*; 1992*b*: ch. 5) argues that Dorsal Fricative Assimilation must be a lexical rule since it operates intra-morphemically. It cannot be postlexical because information on morpheme boundaries is not available outside of the lexicon. *Kuchen* as a single morpheme is thus subject to the rule, while the morpheme boundary in *Kuh*+*chen* prevents the application of the rule. In the present account, Dorsal Fricative Assimilation may safely be claimed to belong to postlexical phonology, in accordance with the fact that it introduces non-phonemic distinctions between segments. The principle of structure preservation (see § 5.3.1), claimed to be valid for the lexical part of phonology, therefore forces the alternation to be postlexical. The classification of Dorsal Fricative Assimilation as a lexical rule is also doubtful because it has no lexical exceptions. Under the appropriate circumstances, the rule is applied automatically and exceptionlessly. In the present analysis, we simply assume that the rule of Dorsal Fricative Assimilation operates postlexically, before the default rule creating [ç],

---

[32] If Iverson and Salmons (1992) are correct, this is true only for one class of words affixed with +*chen*, those (the minority) in which no umlaut appears.

within the domain of ω (i.e. the phonological word). In this connection, it is perhaps worth noting that the prosodic categories are assumed to be available lexically as well as postlexically.

7.3.4. Nasal Assimilation

Nasal consonants in German, as in many other languages, have a remarkable tendency to adjust to neighbouring sounds with respect to their features of place of articulation.[33] Furthermore, the asymmetries to be observed there point to particular configurations in their featural representation. This section is about two rules of Nasal Assimilation, one of which will be demonstrated to interact closely with the rule of g-Deletion to be discussed in the following section.

Two types of assimilation have to be distinguished: nasals assimilating to a following consonant (regressive assimilation) and nasals assimilating to a preceding consonant (progressive assimilation). The status of nasal assimilation is somewhat unclear with respect to the classes of consonants triggering the two types of assimilation. I will start with a particularly clear subgroup, namely regressive nasal assimilation to stops, and then discuss other cases.

As the nasal consonants in (59) demonstrate, alveolar [n], velar [ŋ], and labial [m] are found before stops which are themselves alveolar, velar, or labial, respectively. The phonetic forms given in (59a) for *Ding* and *lang* are impossible in Standard German, but possible in colloquial Northern pronunciation. In Modern Standard German, the assimilatory behaviour of [ŋ] is partly obscured by the rule of g-Deletion to be discussed in the following section. Nasals and the following stops in (59) are all tautomorphemic.

(59) *a.* Ba[ŋ]k, Fi[ŋ]k, de[ŋ]ken; Di[ŋk], la[ŋk]; Ta[ŋ]go, fi[ŋ]gieren
     b. Hand, Stunde, Kind, Kante, ganz
     c. impfen, Rumpf, Amboss, Tempo
     d. Amt, Hemd, Wams, Samstag; Lemgo, Imker
     e. */n [Labial]/, */n [Dorsal]/
     f. */ŋ [Labial]/, */ŋ [Coronal]/

It is not the case that all nasals are homorganic with the stop following them. As (59d) shows, labial nasals are found before alveolar and velar stops. (Though the latter configuration is rare, there is no tendency to avoid a sequence of labial-dorsal or to assimilate it.) The other two nasal consonants, however, are only found before a homorganic stop, a fact indicated in (59e, f). This means that there is not only nasal assimilation to be taken care of. The asymmetry in the assimilatory behaviour of different nasal consonants must also be considered. Note also that /ŋ/ cannot occur before coronal stops and fricatives, while /m/ can, as (59d) demonstrates. However, the sequences /mk/ and /mg/ are decidedly rare; the two examples in (59d) are the only cases known.

---

[33] In (19b) of § 6.2.1, I gave examples of non-nasal, coronal consonants assimilating in place of articulation. Such assimilation certainly exists, but it is not as clear-cut and obligatory as nasal assimilation. I therefore ignore it in this chapter.

Briefly, the following analysis will claim that there is a rule of Nasal Assimilation on the basis of which the place features of a stop spread to the preceding nasal if the nasal is unspecified for these place features. I will also argue that the two relevant segments must be in the same phonological word, and that the particular underspecification proposed earlier explains the asymmetries in assimilatory behaviour.

We may begin by looking at the features of the nasal consonants. As stated in (17) of § 6.2, alveolar /n/ has no place features underlyingly, while /m/ is characterized by [Labial] and /ŋ/ by [Dorsal]. In addition, they share the specification [+ nasal], which sets these segments apart as a natural class. We also note that the stops triggering the assimilation have completely analogous place features.

Therefore, the assimilation is most naturally seen as the spreading of the place features of the stop to the preceding nasal—provided that the nasal does not itself bear a Place node. The respective rule, called Regressive Nasal Assimilation, is given in (60).[34] The need for the use of the label 'regressive' will become apparent below.

(60) Regressive Nasal Assimilation

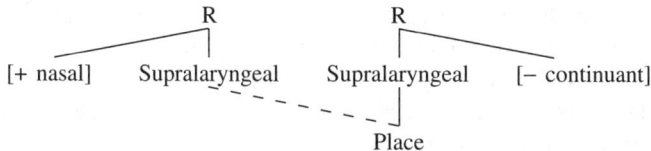

Of course, this rule of Nasal Assimilation is complemented by the default rule for place features. That is, a nasal not subject to (60) will surface as the alveolar nasal [n], as discussed in § 6.2.1. The respective default rule is repeated here in (61).

(61) Default rule

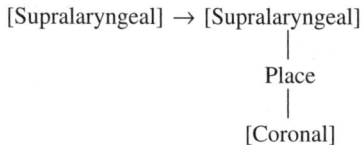

[Supralaryngeal] → [Supralaryngeal]
|
Place
|
[Coronal]

A further crucial assumption of the present analysis is that no velar /ŋ/ exists underlyingly, but that it is in all instances generated through assimilation. The velar nasal will be discussed further in the following section; here we just note that the non-existence of velar /ŋ/ in underlying forms immediately explains that it is never found before labial or coronal stops; see (59f). On the other hand, labial /m/ will surface unchanged, while underspecified /n/ will inherit the place features of the right-hand neighbour.

Strictly speaking, the features in (60) on the context segment include the nasal

---

[34] The present proposal is not fundamentally different from those by Hall (1992*b*: § 4.2) and Yu (1992*b*: § 4.5.2).

consonants since nasals are also [– continuant]. This seems to be correct, given the data in (62). If in these words schwa is not pronounced, the assimilation of the first nasal to the second seems obligatory, while a sequence of /nm/ is not possible. Given the limited distribution of [ŋ], the only other non-homorganic nasal sequence which could be found is /mn/ (as in *Omnibus* or *Anamnese*), in which, parallel to examples in (59*d*), no assimilation occurs.

(62) ein+em   [aɪnəm]/[aɪmm̩]/*[aɪnm̩]
     dünn+em   [dʏnəm]/[dʏmm̩]/*[dʏnm̩]

By studying the (abbreviated) derivations of [ŋ], [m], and [n] in (63), it is possible to see how the differential behaviour of the nasal consonants is explained: it is the asymmetry in the segmental specification together with the strictly structure-building character of the assimilation rule which yields the results required by the facts. Capital 'N' here and in the following stands for a nasal unspecified for place features.

(63) *a*. /b a N k/   /t ɛ N p o/   /b a N d/   underlying
     b. /b a ŋ k/   /t ɛ m p o/   ——   Nasal Assimilation (60)
     c. ——   ——   /b a n d/   Default (61)

Turning from the structural part of Regressive Nasal Assimilation to its contextual condition, I take up the claim made earlier that the domain of Nasal Assimilation as of other rules is the phonological word ω. This position, also held by Hall (1992*b*) and Yu (1992*b*), contrasts with those which assume morpheme-internal application of the rule.

A further set of assimilatory phenomena which address the choice between these two domains is illustrated in (64). In the expressions given here, nasal and stop consonants are separated by boundaries of various types, morpheme and word boundaries. Nevertheless, assimilation is found across the boundaries. It must be added, though, that the assimilation in (64) is generally *optional*, that is, pronunciations displaying the non-assimilated nasals are also possible.[35]

(64) *a*. U[ŋ/n]glück, Ei[ŋ/n]gabe; A[ŋ/n]kunft, u[ŋ/n]kundig
     b. Un+tat, in Sachen, in Tübingen
     c. A[n/m]pfiff, u[n/m]billig; i[n/m] Berlin, ei[n/m] Pass
     d. um+tun, Um+sicht
     e. i[ŋ/n] Göttingen/Kassel, ei[ŋ/n] Gruß/Kuss
     f. Um+gebung, um+kleiden, um+tun

The pattern of assimilation, apart from the optionality, is exactly identical to that in (59). In particular, the velar nasal is only found before velar stops, and the coronal nasal before coronals, while labial [m] may be found in an assimilatory context and elsewhere. Given the identity of the assimilation process, the same rule should be made responsible for the alternation. Otherwise,

---

[35] An unexpected fact remains: assimilation of coronals to velars seems to take place more readily than does the same assimilation to labials. I have ordered transcription symbols in (64) correspondingly.

a generalization would go uncaptured. But under this requirement, the domain of Nasal Assimilation (60) cannot be the morpheme.

The usual approach to the assimilation across boundaries is to allow the respective rule to operate within the domain delimited by boundaries and also optionally across these. I will pursue a different approach here. Recall that rules such as Nasal Assimilation are claimed to apply within phonological words. For the intra-word assimilations in (59), no problem arises since trigger and affected nasal are clearly situated within one phonological word. In (64), however, nasals and following stops are, in each single case, in different phonological words, because all morphemes here qualify as being assigned a separate phonological word according to the rule set up in § 3.4.

But it seems plausible to suppose that under specific conditions certain phonological words are reanalysed to form a phonological word with the following unit. This is illustrated in (65).[36] Words and 'small phrases' such as *ungenau* or *in Berlin* may optionally form a single phonological word.

(65) *a.* [in+kompetent] ~ [in] [kompetent]
     b. [un+genau] ~ [un] [genau]
     c. [in] [Berlin] ~ [in Berlin]

Apparently, only 'small' words such as prepositions, pronouns, and prefixes can be reanalysed as losing their status as phonological words; see more illustrative examples in (64) and the discussion of clitics in § 7.4.3 below. There is a contrast in the readiness to undergo Nasal Assimilation between *man kommt* (optionally realized as [maŋ kɔmt]) 'one comes' and *Der Mann kommt* 'The man comes'. The coronal nasal in *Mann* will tend to resist assimilation, thus leading to a rendering as [dɛɐ man kɔmt]. The cautious wording in these remarks is due to the fact that, first, there is little systematic study of such differences, and, second, at the tempo of fast speech, assimilation is certainly possible in the latter example. The reanalysis of phonological words proposed here is parallel to that of phonological phrases discussed in § 3.5.

One relevant observation is that even the non-native prefix *syn+* must not necessarily undergo Nasal Assimilation. That is, for *syn+chron* two possible pronunciations exist: [zʏn.kʁoːn] and [zʏŋ.kʁoːn].[37] Such a non-assimilation of /n/ before /k/ is impossible morpheme-internally. As for the assimilated form, we may assume that the optional restructuring of two phonological words into one has taken place.

Given that the expanded phonological words in (65c) can be formed only postlexically, Nasal Assimilation also cannot be exclusively lexical. I will assume that this rule is not restricted to the lexical or postlexical domain. Rather, it applies whenever a relevant context is created within a single phonological word.

---

[36] Note that it is in principle possible to delete *un+*: *ungenau und -exact* 'vague and inexact', which proves the phonological-word status of this prefix. I assume that the reanalysis is the preferred option for prefixes, but not for prepositions. The examples in (65) are ordered correspondingly.

[37] The pronouncing dictionaries actually require the non-assimilated version.

Assimilation triggers in the preceding discussion were limited to non-continuants. There is, however, a not quite clear-cut assimilation of nasals to fricatives in Modern Standard German. Some examples with labiodental [f] are illustrated in (66). Generally, the assimilated versions seem to occur at a faster tempo of speech, but even then are not obligatory. Also, assimilation may (but need not) be complete. That is, a labiodental fricative causes the nasal to be labiodental, as shown in (66a). Such assimilation seems not possible across word boundaries, see (66c).

(66) *a.* Se[n/ɱ]lf, Ha[n/ɱ]lf, fü[n/ɱ]f
   b. U[n/ɱ]+fall, Ko[n/ɱ]+flikt
   c. *i[ɱ] Frankfurt 'in Frankfurt', *ei[ɱ] Fall 'a case'

Particular attention must be paid to the fact that no assimilation occurs, not even optionally, before palatal fricative [ç] and palatoalveolar [ʃ], as exemplified in (67).[38]

(67) *a.* Mensch, Flansch, Wunsch
   b. manch, Mönch (*ma[ɲ]ch, *Mö[ɲ]ch)

The first of these types of non-assimilation is immediately accounted for by rule (60): as alveolar and palatoalveolar segments bear an identical Place node, and differ only in the separate node [Tongue Position], assimilation to [ʃ] is not possible. The non-assimilation to palatal [ç] remains a problem. A possible solution would be to subsume palatals under the Coronal node, an option found in the literature (e.g. Keating 1991) but not taken here; see § 3.1. Alternatively, we may assume a phonetic kind of assimilation, as with the labiodental [ɱ].

The mirror-image type of Nasal Assimilation, Progressive Nasal Assimilation, is illustrated by the examples in (68). Basically the pattern is that there is a clear and obligatory assimilation to stops and nasals (i.e. to segments specified as [− continuant]), while the assimilation to fricatives is again dubious or variable. The right-hand alternative pronunciations in (68c) strike me as optional fast-speech forms. There is no assimilation to liquids, in particular not to uvular /ʀ/. (Because /l/ is alveolar, we cannot test whether it triggers assimilation. In the sequence /lm/ as in *Halm*, assimilation is expected not to occur because assimilation is generally restricted to segments which are not specified for place features.)

(68) Progressive Nasal Assimilation
   a. Stops   *geben* [geːbml̩], *tragen* [tʀaːgn̩], *leiten* [laɪtn̩]
   b. Nasals   *kämmen* [kɛmml̩], *ringen* [ʀɪŋn̩], *kennen* [kɛnn̩]
   c. Fricatives   *raufen* [ʀaʊfn̩]/[ʀaʊfm̩], *braven* [bʀaːvn̩]/[bʀaːvm̩], *rasen* [ʀaːzn̩],
                     rauschen [ʀaʊʃn̩]/—, *reichen* [ʀaɪçn̩]/[ʀaɪçɲ̩], *rauchen* [ʀaʊχn̩]/
                     [ʀaʊχŋ̩]
   d. Liquids   *wollen* [vɔln̩], *kehren* [keːʀn̩]

Wurzel (1970: 219) assumes that the nasal assimilates to a preceding velar/uvular fricative, but not to a palatal: [ʀaʊχŋ̩], but not *[ʀaɪçɲ̩]. The facts are not so clear, however. It seems to be true that the nasal does not easily assimilate

---

[38] IPA conventions do not even provide a symbol for a palatoalveolar nasal.

to either of these fricatives. Also, while assimilation to the stop in [geːbm̩] appears to be almost obligatory, the labial fricative in *laufen* does not cause the assimilation of the nasal with an identical force. Hall (1992*b*: ch. 4) therefore restricts this assimilation to stops as triggers. I will simply assume here that the assimilation is a phonetic phenomenon of (optional) co-articulation with all fricatives as triggers, but a true regularity in the phonological domain with preceding non-continuants. The rule required will then be that in (69): a nasal unspecified for place features receives these from a preceding non-continuant. See below in regard to the presence of the nucleus node.

(69) Progressive Nasal Assimilation

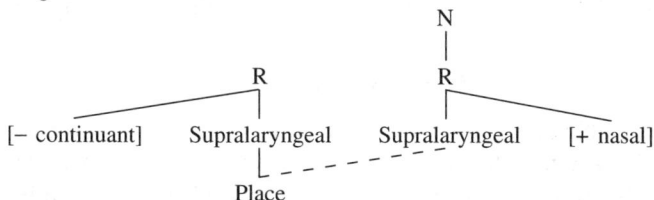

The claim that Progressive Nasal Assimilation (just like Regressive Nasal Assimilation (60)) is triggered by all non-continuants (and not just oral stops, as in descriptions by Hooper 1976 and Yu 1992*b*: § 4.5.2) is based on examples such as those in (68*b*). Here, the infinitival suffix /n/ surfaces as an assimilated [m] or [ŋ] in the appropriate contexts. Most importantly, the two nasals may only interact if there is no intervening schwa vowel. Further data from adjectival inflection with the two suffix forms /n/ and /m/ are given in (70). As the form [dʏmm̩] demonstrates, the inflectional suffixes may be the trigger as well as the object of Nasal Assimilation. Progressive Nasal Assimilation applies in the left-hand forms, while Regressive Nasal Assimilation applies to derive [dʏmm̩] *dünn+em* or [aɪmm̩] *ein+em*.

(70)

| | Suffix | |
	/n/	/m/
dünn	[dʏnn̩]	[dʏmm̩/ʔdʏnm̩]
lang	[laŋŋ̩]	[laŋm̩]
dumm	[dʊmm̩]	[dʊmm̩]

While Regressive Nasal Assimilation (60) is the exact mirror image of Progressive Nasal Assimilation (69) in terms of the feature structure of affected segment and the trigger, the context condition is different. As shown in (71), not all nasals immediately following a potential trigger assimilate. Here, orthographic *n* represents a phonetic [n].

(71) *a*. Hypnose, Akne, Signal
    b. Amnestie, Hymne

In these examples, the syllable boundary lies immediately before the second nasal. Compare also the assimilated nasal in [tʀɔkŋ̩] *trocken* to the non-assimilated one in [tʀɔk.nɐ] *Trockn+er*. But even within syllables, nasals in a syllable onset are not subject to Progressive Nasal Assimilation, as the illustration of the range of phonotactic combinatorial possibilities in (121) below shows.

The crucial condition seems to be that the affected nasal must be in a nucleus position, see also Hall (1992*b*: § 4.2.1). As the assimilated nasals are always syllabic nasals, and the trigger segments can then only be in the preceding onset, it is difficult to tease apart the necessary conditions from the accidental circumstances. This problem actually emerges for Regressive Nasal Assimilation as well. Notice that all nasals assimilating to their right-hand neighbours in (59) and (64) are placed in the coda. It is unclear whether this should be seen as a necessary condition. There is at least one form among the examples considered here, [aɪmm̩] in (62), where the assimilated nasal is in the onset of its syllable.

7.3.5. g-Deletion

The segment /g/, which may spirantize under conditions discussed in § 7.3.3, is the subject of yet another alternation. In the preceding section it was claimed that the velar nasal [ŋ] is always the result of nasal assimilation from a following dorsal non-continuant. I will now try to substantiate this claim, which is by no means new but remains controversial. By looking at the words given in (72), we find that the *g*s written (in orthographic form!) in words of (72*a*, *b*) are actually pronounced, while the highlighted *g*s of (72*c–g*) are not part of the pronunciation of their respective words. However, the nasal preceding this orthographic *g* is always the velar nasal [ŋ].

(72) *a.* fing+ier+en, Tang+ent+e, restring+ier+en, Ing+o, Ing+a
     b. Tango, Ungarn, Hangar, Singular
     c. Finger, Hunger, Bengel
     d. läng+lich, Lang+finger
     e. Ding(+e), Säng+er, lang(+er), Ing+e,
     f. Be+ding+ung+en, Ver+läng+er+ung+en
     g. Angelsachsen ~ angloamerikanisch, Diphthong ~ diphthongieren

Note that the presence or absence of a following morpheme boundary cannot be held responsible for the difference, as /g/ may (72*a*) or may not (72*d*) appear before a morpheme boundary. The pairs of words in (72*g*) are of particular relevance as they refute the claim that the 'unrealized' /g/ never alternates with actual [g]. In the few pairs as in (72*g*), such an alternation can be demonstrated. For other reasons to be discussed shortly, the set of facts given here has motivated a number of authors from Issatschenko (1963) to Hall (1992*b*) to propose a rule of g-Deletion. This rule may be formulated as in (73): a segment /g/ is delinked from its skeletal position if a nasal precedes and a syllable boundary follows immediately. This particular proposal will be defended below.

(73) g-Deletion

    C   /   [+ nasal] ____]$_\sigma$
    ⧺
    /g/

This rule, yet another rule sensitive to syllable boundaries, will operate as exemplified in (74), assuming that it may always apply, but that syllabification, just like all other phonological rules, will not apply to roots which have not undergone any derivation. The latter condition is needed to prevent g-Deletion from applying to the root-final /g/ in the roots in (72a); for discussion, see p. 228 below. That is, some morphological process is always needed to trigger the first round of phonological rule application. It is not necessary to stipulate the 'morphology-first' principle for g-Deletion; there are good arguments that it is a general feature of the morphology–phonology interaction as discussed in § 5.1. The derivations in (74) of *Dinge* and *Tango* also exemplify the interaction of g-Deletion and Nasal Assimilation. Recall also that X, an empty prosodic position, is the proposed underlier of schwa.

(74) *a.* /dɪNg/ /taNgoː/ underlying

b. /dɪng + X/ —— suffixation

c.
```
      σ                σ          σ
   ⟋⟋⟍⟍           ⟋⟋⟍         ⟋⟋⟍
  C V C C  X      C V C  C V C
  | | | |         | | |  | \ /
  d ɪ N g         t a N  g  o
```
Syllabification

d.
```
      σ
   ⟋⟋⟍⟍
  C V C C  X
  | | | ‡
  d ɪ N g
```
—— g-Deletion (73)

e.
```
      σ                σ          σ
   ⟋⟋⟍            ⟋⟋⟍         ⟋⟋⟍
  C V C  X        C V C  C V C
  | | |           | | |  | \ /
  d ɪ ŋ           t a ŋ  g  o
```
Nasal Assimilation (60)

f.
```
      σ       σ
   ⟋⟋⟍      ⟋⟍
  C V C C  V
  | | \ /  |
  d ɪ  ŋ   ə
```
—— Syllabification

In the derivation of [dɪŋə], it is tacitly assumed that the final suffix (X) remains unsyllabified in the first pass of syllabification;[39] this situation makes /g/ syllable-final and thereby subject to g-Deletion. Analogously, any final consonant in monomorphemic words such as *Engel* [ɛŋəl] or *Anger* [aŋɐ] would be extrasyllabic at this point, thus causing the preceding /g/ to delete syllable-finally. In contrast, the right-hand derivation of [taŋ.goː] illustrates the non-applicability of g-Deletion to syllable-initial /g/. The non-syllabification of consonants which eventually surface in schwa syllables is crucial within the

---

[39] Syllabifications of *Ding+e* and *Tango* in (74c) are nevertheless both triggered by a first round of morphology. This is obvious for the former word, while for *Tango* we may assume that the root-to-stem conversion discussed in § 5.2.3 provides the morphological input to the first phonological cycle.

present description; it also enables the deletion of /g/ in monomorphemic words like those given in (72c).

The non-syllabification of X in (74c) (or of other extrasyllabic consonants), causing the deletion of preceding, syllable-final /g/, contradicts the view used in Chapter 4 that schwa syllables are present in the lexicon as reduced syllables. In the discussion there, a number of prosodic constraints in various parts of morphology were expressed by making use of a representation of schwa syllables as weak elements in a foot. There is thus a contradiction between an optimal description of the patterns found in the area of prosodic morphology and the optimal formulation of the rule of g-Deletion: one set of facts seems to require syllabification of final material, while another set of facts seems to argue, with equal force, for its extrasyllabic, or at least invisible, status.

I leave this conflict unresolved. It would however be possible to change the description of the prosodic requirements in the following way: certain morphological configurations require extrasyllabic material word-finally. Thus, a plural noun would have to have a structure of the form [. . . σ] X, with X being an unsyllabified skeletal position. Note that *Dinge* in (74c) is of precisely this form.[40] Words of the type given in (72c) can be treated the same: initial syllabification leads to [. . . ŋ g]$_\sigma$ X, and subsequent rules applying to this form involve g-Deletion, Nasal Assimilation, Schwa Epenthesis and rules of syllabification.

It is easy to see now how the claim that [ŋ] is always a product of Nasal Assimilation can be upheld against surface falsification: postulating a /g/, but one which may be deleted, provides the necessary trigger for place assimilation of the nasal.

One crucial aspect of the particular formulation of g-Deletion here is that it does not require the rule to be ordered with respect to Nasal Assimilation. In (74), Nasal Assimilation was ordered arbitrarily after g-Deletion. Such a rule-ordering is required in other approaches, because a deleted /g/ is obviously unable to provide the place features for the preceding nasal.

Consider the deletion rule in (75), taken from Hall (1989a). (The simpler rule given by Wurzel (1970: 210) deleting any voiced consonant following a nasal can only work since Wurzel explicitly disregards words containing a sequence [ŋg] as in *Tango*.) This rule literally removes /g/. Thus, it cannot be available for Nasal Assimilation, as it can in the non-linear framework assumed here.

(75) Linear formulation of g-Deletion

   $g \rightarrow \emptyset$ / [+ nasal]____]$_\sigma$

What has been achieved here is the elimination not of rule-ordering in general, but of a particular instance of it. While the theory assumed here allows for the sequential application of rules (see the interaction of Dorsal Fricative Assimilation, g-Spirantization and Final Devoicing as displayed in (58)), no stipulated rule-ordering is needed with respect to Nasal Assimilation and

---

[40] For arguments against the alternative move, in which g-Deletion would take place in a number of different contexts (syllable-final or before schwa), see Hall (1992b: § 4.4).

g-Deletion. The description developed here thus contributes to the reduction of 'the unfortunate degree of language-specific rule ordering' (Goldsmith 1990: 2) characteristic for classical generative phonology.

The linear formulation of g-Deletion as in (75) also runs into a paradox if it is assumed to be a lexical rule. As Kaisse and Shaw (1985) point out with respect to the analogous rule of English phonology, g-Deletion exhibits a certain ambiguity in its assignment to lexical vs. postlexical phonology. On the one hand, phonological analysis of the type just given argues that it must be a lexical rule, on the other hand, some properties of the /g/ in question cast a doubt on this analysis. In particular, deleted /g/ is always present in the orthographic forms (of English and German), although lexical phonological changes are generally reflected in writing.[41] Second, there is evidence that /g/ may participate in speech errors. As there are arguments (particularly from Mohanan 1986) that speech errors require sounds to be available at the level of output from the lexicon, it follows apparently that /g/ should not be deleted within the lexicon. Finally, speakers are unaware of g-Deletion. In this respect, g-Deletion is not unlike Final Devoicing, but very much unlike typical lexical rules such as Umlaut.

These paradoxes with respect to the placement of g-Deletion may be resolved if, first, the rule is supposed to be a lexical rule with the formulation given in (73), and if, second, the deassociation in this formulation is taken literally. This means that the features of /g/ are not actually deleted but only delinked from its skeletal position. They are thus available throughout the lexicon as triggers of assimilation, as segments corresponding to graphemes, and as possible participants in speech errors. A general principle of *stray erasure* (as suggested e.g. by McCarthy 1979 and Steriade 1982) forbids the phonetic realization of any material that is not linked, in the appropriate way, to the phonological representation. This principle will then be responsible for the non-realization of the deassociated segment.

Consider next the earliest possible application of g-Deletion in the lexicon. Hall (1989*a*) proposes to apply this rule 'early at level 2 before the suffixes of this level are added'. The motivation for this restriction is the need to prevent the deletion of /g/ in root-final position. As seen in (72*a*), such a /g/ is kept. On the other hand, g-Deletion must take place before suffixation of +*ung*, as shown by [lɛŋʊŋ] (*Läng+ung*) and all similar words.[42]

However, Hall's proposal requires an otherwise unmotivated pre-cyclic application of a phonological rule. It is thus desirable to find an alternative.[43] Such an

---

[41] In Wiese (1989*a*), I argue that sound–letter correspondences in German are best described on the output level of lexical phonology. That is, while lexical rules are (or may be) reflected in writing, postlexical rules are not. Compare the rules of Umlaut and Final Devoicing in that respect: while umlaut is faithfully represented in the spelling, Final Devoicing leaves no trace.

[42] Note that the suffixes +*ung and* +*ling* themselves undergo Nasal Assimilation and g-Deletion.

[43] Allomorphy rules are often seen as phonological or morphological rules applying *before* the morphology (see e.g. Spencer 1988). But the criteria for rules of allomorphy (lexical or morphological conditioning of the alternation) are not fulfilled by g-Deletion. Hall (1992*b*: § 4.3.2) comes to a conclusion identical to the one proposed here.

alternative is in fact available if we follow the hypothesis made earlier that underived roots do not form an input to phonological rules. This restriction fulfils the same function of preventing g-Deletion from applying to the final segment in *restring+*, and similar bound roots. At the same time, /g/ will be deleted before +*ung*, given that this suffix is a level-2 suffix, and that going from level 1 to level 2 is to be interpreted as creating a derived environment (see § 5.2.3). In short, it seems most adequate to allow the application of g-Deletion on all lexical levels without any restriction, except for the application to underived roots. We again call upon the 'morphology first' principle here.

Finally, observe how g-Deletion may work in the context of an extended final consonant cluster. As shown in (76*a*), word-final coronals as in the words given here are not a problem if the extrasyllabicity hypothesis is assumed to make /g/ syllable-final. In other cases, following consonants are extrasyllabic in the sense of not syllabifiable, again leaving /g/ at the syllable edge. Note that here g-Deletion must again be assumed to operate before further suffixation. If, in the derivation of [huŋʀɪç] in (76*b*), g-Deletion were suspended until after affixation of +*ig*, syllabification would form a syllable-initial cluster /gʀ/, leading to the wrong form of *[huŋ.gʀɪç].

(76) *a.* Hengst, Angst: [hɛng]$_\sigma$st, [ang]$_\sigma$st
    b. hungr+ig: /hungʀ/ → [hung]$_\sigma$ʀ → [huŋ]$_\sigma$ʀ → [huŋ]$_\sigma$ʀ + /ig/ → [huŋ]$_\sigma$[ʀɪç]$_\sigma$

A further well-known argument for the rule of g-Deletion is provided by those colloquial northern forms of German in which words such as *lang* or *Ding* may be pronounced as [laŋk] and [dɪŋk] instead of the standard forms [laŋ] and [dɪŋ]. Note that the speakers of this dialect will still say [lɛŋɐ] (*länger*) and [dɪŋə] (*Dinge*). It would thus be wrong to conclude that speakers of such dialects have no rule of g-Deletion. Instead, it is much more plausible to claim (as Wurzel (1970) was the first to argue) that in this group of dialects Final Devoicing and g-Deletion may optionally have an order of application as illustrated in (77), which is the reverse of that assumed in (74). The point at which to apply Regressive Nasal Assimilation is arbitrary again.

(77) *a.* /laNg/   underlying
    b.   σ   Syllabification
           ⟋⟋⎺⟍
          l a N g
    c.   σ   Final Devoicing (34), Nasal Assimilation (60)
           ⟋⟋⎺⟍
          l a ŋ k
    d. ——   g-Deletion (73)

The ordering of g-Deletion after Final Devoicing in this derivation forces g-Deletion into the postlexical part of phonology, as there is no evidence that Final Devoicing is a lexical rule in this variety of German. Note that g-Deletion was taken to be a lexical rule in the standard language.

A further set of facts motivating the analysis of [ŋ] as including a rule of g-Deletion stems from the phonotactic behaviour of this nasal. There are well-known exceptionless phonotactic constraints pertaining to the occurrence of [ŋ]. First, in Modern Standard German [ŋ] never occurs word-initially. Second, [ŋ] does not occur after long vowels or diphthongs. (If it occurs here, it is only as the result of an /n/ assimilated to become [ŋ], as in [aɪŋkaʊfən] *ein+kaufen*.) A grammar not recognizing the derived status of [ŋ] would have to include the statements in (78), which indicate how the velar nasal under the two conditions mentioned might be disallowed. Furthermore, these statements are rather arbitrary, since they simply claim that the velar nasal behaves differently from the other two nasals. But this difference is precisely what is in need of explanation.

(78) *a.* * [ŋ . . .
  b. * vv ŋ]$_\sigma$

Assuming that the sequence /ng/ underlies [ŋ], these two filters are superfluous, and no arbitrariness is found. The first filter follows from independently motivated claims that /ng/ is exluded as an initial cluster just like any parallel cluster consisting of a nasal plus a stop such as /nd/. Secondly, the phonotactics of the syllable also disallow two vocalic positions, that is, a long vowel or a diphthong, followed by two consonants (except for extrasyllabic coronals; see § 3.2). Thus, a structure such as /. . . aːng/ is ruled out independently of any statement such as (78*b*).

In summary, [ŋ] behaves 'as if' it were the sequence /ng/, and a phonological description involving rules of Nasal Assimilation and g-Deletion acknowledges this fact.[44] This is not to say that the alternative treatment of treating [ŋ] as an underlying segment could not work; rather, the advantage of the present approach seems to be that it allows for a unified analysis of a body of observations which would otherwise require a set of seemingly unrelated regularities. Furthermore, a non-linear treatment of g-Deletion makes ordering between these two rules unnecessary.

7.3.6. Degemination

Degemination was mentioned in § 3.2.1.2 in connection with the treatment of affricates. It has, however, a wider range of occurrence in the phonology of Modern Standard German. First, it is found as a consequence of verbal inflection. As shown in (79), for a number of verbs, the suffixes /t/ and /st/ may 'fuse' with preceding root-final consonants. As the verbal base and the suffix each contribute a consonant from their underlying forms, and as there is clearly only

---

[44] The argument for an *abstract* solution to the description [ŋ] has long been recognized; for statements to this effect from authors not usually favouring abstract solutions to phonological problems see Dressler (1981) and Lass (1984: § 9.2).

one consonant in the surface form, we may assume some kind of degemination of the consonants.[45]

(79) *a.* (er) rät: [Rɛːt], tritt: [tRɪt], hält: [hɛlt]
    b. (er) lädt: [leːt],
    c. (du) reißt: [raɪst], lässt: [lɛst], sitzt: [zɪtst]
    d. (du) liest: [liːst], (du) reist: [raɪst]

The conditions for degemination clearly involve identity of the two adjacent consonants. It is never found, for example, with root-final /k/, /f/, or /p/. It must be noted, however, that strict identity of segments is not required, as /d/ and /t/ as well as /z/ and /s/ also degeminate to a single /t/ or /s/. One question arising here is how to determine which verbs display degemination, and which display schwa epenthesis instead of degemination. There is the fact that degemination always correlates with umlaut or ablaut in the verbal root. For this reason I will assume without further discussion that degemination takes place at level 1, the lexical level at which umlaut and ablaut are also possible. As argued in § 5.4, verb inflection of regularly inflected forms may be placed on level 3. Assuming further that schwa epenthesis is possible at this lexical level, the particular disjunction between degemination and schwa epenthesis is then accounted for.

For a similar case of degemination, consider inflection of nouns for dative plural. It is plausible to assume that *all* nouns in their plural form (except for those plural-marked by /s/) receive a suffix /n/ as a marker for the dative case.[46] As (80) shows, with the dative plural forms given on the right of each pair, this suffix does not surface with all nouns ending in /n/, regardless of whether the /n/ is a (plural or other) suffix itself (80*a*) or a root consonant (80*b*).

(80) *a.* Nam+en+n > Nam+en   *b.* Zeichen+n > Zeichen
      Gärt+en+n   > Gärt+en   Wappen+n > Wappen
      Muskel+n+n > Muskel+n   Orden+n > Orden

It would be possible to claim that the dative plural marker /n/ is not suffixed to bases ending in /n/, but a more plausible alternative, if just for reasons of simplicity, seems to be to allow the degemination rule to apply here, as this is a rule needed on independent grounds.

Another rather narrowly circumscribed case of degemination is found with the diminutive suffix +*lein*. If the preceding base for this suffix ends in a schwa syllable ending in /l/, this base-final consonant is fused with the suffix-initial consonant; see (81) for examples. This degemination is obligatory, but restricted to this particular configuration: degemination is not obligatory for the suffixes +*los*, +*bar*, whereas the diminutive suffix +*lein* is prohibited for other stems

---

[45] One unique case of degemination of /st/ is provided by (*du*) *birst+st* > *birst*.

[46] This proposal has been made by Wurzel (1970) and Lieber (1987). To take up the discussion of level ordering again, it would be possible to assign dative-plural suffixation to level 2. As speculated in the discussion of linking morphemes in § 5.3.3, rare forms such as *Stern+en+schein* suggest such a treatment anyhow.

ending in /l/, that is, those which do not end in a schwa syllable. *Bäll+lein*, *Krokodil+lein*, and so on, are not acceptable. Instead, +*chen* is chosen as the diminutive suffix under such circumstances.[47] The precise extent of this phenomenon needs further study, as there are also apparently no words formed with the suffixes +*lich* and +*sam*, in which the base ends in a consonant identical to the prefix-initial consonant.

(81) Diminutive +*lein*
    Engelein, Vögelein, Eselein, Schlüsselein
    (Engel+lein, Vogel+lein, Esel+lein, Schlüssel+lein)

A different type of degemination is found at the compound-internal boundary. Again, adjacent identical consonants may be degeminated, but it is generally assumed that this is not obligatory as for the cases introduced above, but an optional process which is more likely to apply at faster speech rate. (82*a*) gives examples of words in which this type of degemination is possible but not mandatory. Prefixed words in (82*b*) seem to behave like compounds, except that here the degemination is perhaps the preferred option. This is particularly clear for words with the prefix *in*+, where both degemination and assimilation are mandatory.[48]

(82) *a.* Schiff+fahrt, wahl+los,
    b. un+nahbar, il+legal, an+nehmen, Ver+rat

The preferred application of degemination across the prefix–stem boundary is reminiscent of the treatment of prefixes with respect to Nasal Assimilation. As in the case of that rule, we may propose that prefixes (and also shorter compound-internal words) are optionally reanalysed as not being dominated by a phonological word of their own. Given that the inflectional suffixes are, as established for quite independent reasons, also integrated with the preceding phonological word, and that the diminutive suffix +*lein* also does not behave in all respects as a phonological word in its own right, the most straightforward account of the domain of application for degemination would require that this rule is restricted to the domain of phonological words. If two stems or other morphemes are dominated by a single phonological word, degemination of consonants applies automatically. If the two (nearly) identical segments belong to different phonological words, no degemination takes place. The degemination process itself is then relatively straightforward and can be expressed as the

---

[47] The suffix +*lein* has one other exceptional property: as argued in § 5.3.2, plural nouns in general must end in a schwa syllable. But nouns ending in +*lein* do not require a suffix if the noun is realized as a plural form, in spite of the fact that /laɪn/ is a non-reduced syllable. That is, *Tisch+lein*, *Vöge+lein* are ambiguous with respect to their number. In general, the two diminutive suffixes behave differently from the way expected from their segmental make-up.

[48] The orthographic system of Modern Standard German reflects the difference between optional and obligatory degemination very precisely: while optional degemination is not reflected in the spelling of words, only one consonant grapheme is found in cases of obligatory degemination. This is why orthographic forms are sufficient in transcribing the degeminated forms in (79) to (81). (However, if the two consonant graphemes are themselves distinct (as in *läd+t*), both letters are retained.)

delinking rule given in (83). As in other cases of delinking, the empty C-slot cannot be realized. Note in this connection that no default rule is available to provide a consonant out of nothing.

(83) Degemination:

$$\begin{array}{cc} C & C \\ | & \# \\ R_i & R_i \end{array}$$

Regularities of this type are sometimes characterized as the *fusion* of identical, adjacent nodes (see Avery and Rice 1989). The present account prefers a description in terms of delinking. Admittedly, the choice of the segment to be deleted is arbitrary at present. Restricting this rule to consonants or C-slots is necessary as two identical vowels may occur next to each other. At least in complex words, sequences of such vowels are occasionally found; see *Kana.an*, *Zo.o+log+e* with identical vowels across a syllable break.

The application of the Degemination rule to relevant cases is illustrated in (84), where use is made of the assumptions about the deletion of ω-nodes motivated above. That is, ω-deletion is obligatory for +*lein*, and optional for +*los*. The rules of Umlaut and Schwa Epenthesis are also assumed to have applied in (84*b*).

(84) *a.* /laːd/ + /t/   /eːzl/ + /laɪn/   /vaːl/ +/loːs/   underlying
     b. [/leːdt/]   [/eːzəl/] [/laɪn/]   [/vaːl/][/loːs/]   ω-Formation
     c. ——   [/eːzəl laɪn/]   [/vaːl loːs/]   ω-Deletion
     d. [/leːt/]   [/eːzəlaɪn/]   [/vaːloːs/]   Degemination

7.3.7. Consonant epenthesis

In § 5.3.3, it was proposed that the so-called *Fugen-s* is not a morpheme, but an inserted consonant, similar to the /t/ inserted under other conditions; see (33) to (38) in that section. To substantiate the claim, I will state the two necessary rules at this point. (85*a*, *b*) are both rules inserting the segmental content of /s/ and /t/, respectively, into the required context. s-Insertion seems to apply in the case of certain nouns in the non-head position of compounds only, while t-Insertion is restricted to morphological formations in which the left-hand side ends in /n/.

(85) *a.* Ø → /s/ / X]_N ___[for X a member of {+*ling*, +*ung*, ...}
     b. Ø → /t/ /...../n/] ____ [X   for X a member of {+*lich*, *wegen*, *halben*}

The mixture of phonological, morphological, and lexical conditions in these two rules reveals their marked status. X is a variable for those morphemes for which insertion is obligatory. Other compounds have to be listed for undergoing this rule; see the examples in § 5.3.3. To uphold the claim that all phonological rules apply in phonological contexts, the morphological brackets in (85) should be replaced by phonological-word brackets. While this is possible, the reference to morphological information cannot be avoided in the statement of these rules.

Note that the two inserted consonants are alveolar obstruents. That is, as extrasyllabic consonants they can be attached within a wider range of phonotactic contexts than any other consonant could be.

A very different kind of epenthesis is found inside some particular consonant clusters. In realizing words as in (86), speakers are found optionally to produce an epenthetic consonant, the so-called *intrusive stop* or *Sproßkonsonant*. That this consonant is not present in the underlying forms is revealed in the plural forms given in (86c), in which the clusters are broken up through syllabification. No intrusive stop is possible here.

(86)	a.	b.	c.	
Gans	[gans]	[gants]	[gɛn.zə]	Gänse
Wams	[vams]	[vamps]	[vɛm.ɐ]	Wämser
Hals	[hals]	[halts]	[hɛl.zə]	Hälse
Vers	[fɛʀs]	——	[fɛʀ.zə]	Verse
Balkons	[bal.kɔŋs]	[bal.kɔŋks]	[bal.kɔŋə]	Balkone
Mensch	[mɛnʃ]	[mɛntʃ]	[mɛn.ʃən]	Menschen
Ramsch	[ʀamʃ]	[ʀampʃ]	[ʀam.ʃən]	ramschen
falsch	[falʃ]	[faltʃ]	[fɛl.ʃən]	fälschen
Marsch	[maʀʃ]	——	[mɛʀ.ʃə]	Märsche

Crucially, as noted by Clements (1987) for English and Hall (1992b) for German, no intrusive consonant is possible after /ʀ/. In other words, a *Sproßkonsonant* is inserted between tautosyllabic clusters of a sonorant consonant (except for /ʀ/) and a fricative. The account of this distribution is maximally simple if we rely on the feature analysis proposed in § 2.2, especially for /l/. Note that /l/ is treated as a non-continuant there. Consequently, we can argue that the intrusive stop is found after segments specified as [– continuant]. The difference in place of articulation between /l/ (alveolar) and /ʀ/ (uvular) cannot be made responsible for the possibility of having an intrusive consonant; such a consonant can also be found in *Balkons* (see (86)) involving a velar nasal.

Under such an analysis, the phenomenon can be treated completely as an imprecise timing of relevant articulatory features: the stop articulation (i.e. [– continuant]) is prolonged into the part in which the following fricative is articulated. In other words, the epenthetic segment is a stop since the *preceding* segment always is non-continuant. It is an obstruent with particular place features because the *following* segment invariably carries this information. The optionality of the phenomenon also derives from the contingency of the timing facts. Such an analysis seems to be the optimal one, but it presupposes the non-continuancy of /l/.

Concluding these sections on the consonantal alternations found in Modern Standard German, I should point out that all rules have indeed been treated as association or delinking rules as introduced in § 7.1. The insertion rules just formulated are no exceptions; they can be stated as rules associating a segment with the syllable. Furthermore, all rules are constrained in performing only one operation; that is, they affect a single feature or featural node. On a more substantial level, it must be noted that the segment /g/ is remarkably prone to be subject to alternations. There are two major rules treated above, namely g-Spirantization (38) and g-Deletion (73), which are uniquely defined for this segment. Hall (1992b: § 4.1.2) also points out that /g/ (and again only /g/) can undergo an optional nasalization rule in informal registers. *Signal* may be realized as [ziɡnaːl] or [ziŋnaːl]. Naturally, this state of affairs leads to the question of a possible explanation. What makes /g/ particularly apt for undergoing alternations? To confirm the relevance of the question, note that many dialects of German display g-Spirantization not only syllable-finally, but also in any onset position: [juːt] *gut*, [jənaʊ] *genau*, [liːjən] *liegen*.[49] Also, /g/ seems highly susceptible to phonological processes, in particular spirantization, not just in German, but also in many other languages (see e.g. Foley 1977). There are thus many observations confirming the special status of /g/ with respect to its readiness to undergo alternations.

One possible explanation I can offer is that /g/, as a segment bearing the features [+ voice] and [Dorsal], is in these respects quite close to the features of vowels. Phonetic theory, now, claims that within syllables the articulation of consonants and vowels should be maximally distinct, since this allows for an independent movement of their respective articulators (see Lindblom 1983).[50] In syllables of the shape ₒ[g V . . .] or ₒ[. . . V g] this requirement is not met, since the tongue-body (dorsum) first has to reach the target position for /g/ (or the vowel). Only afterwards can the tongue-body as the major articulator move towards the target for the next segment, that is, the vowel or /g/. In addition, the articulation of [g] requires complete closure, while vowel articulation requires no obstruction in the articulatory tract. For these reasons, sequences of /g/ and vowels are avoided. If this account is correct, we may conclude that the rules related to /g/ arise from grammaticalizations of phonetic preferences.

7.4. SYLLABLES AND RELATED MATTERS

There is an idea going back to at least Saussure's *Cours* (1916) that the phonetic shape of a segment is a function of both its inherent properties and its place in a syllable. I will pursue this idea here by discussing some processes by which segments are considerably shaped and modified through syllabic conditions. Segments may change their status from vowels to consonants and vice versa, or they may be inserted or deleted under specific prosodic conditions as in the case of clitics. As pointed out in § 3.2, the existence of these facts also provides compelling evidence for the systematic place of the syllable in the phonology of German. With respect to the phonology of /ʀ/, I also argue that the phonetic shape of this sound is only very incompletely determined by its segmental featural make up.

---

[49] The resulting voiced fricative is palatal, and not velar, again confirming an analysis which makes palatal articulation the default one for dorsal fricatives (in Modern Standard German).

[50] And, of course, segments in a syllable are not articulated one after the other like beads on a string. Independent articulatory gestures for consonants and vowels therefore lead to an economy of articulation.

7.4.1. Consonant–vowel transitions

At the beginning of § 3.2, a particular complementary distribution was introduced briefly: non-syllabic [ɪ] and [j̯] are found in complementary contexts. It is argued there that the relevant context is the syllable edge. The voiced fricative [j] is found syllable-initially, while [ɪ] cannot appear in this position. This description seems to be correct, since [j] is indeed found only syllable-initially. Furthermore, it cannot be found in any consonant clusters, neither pre- nor postvocally (see (122) and (128)). This particular distribution indicates that, contrary to assumptions in the majority of the literature, /j/ is not a distinctive segment of Modern Standard German. Rather, it is, as authors from Trubetzkoy (1939) to Hall (1992b) have argued, a positional variant of /ɪ/. (Diphthongal [i̯] is, of course, also a positional variant of /ɪ/.) Treating [j] as an allophone of /ɪ/ is not generally accepted in the pertinent literature, although Trubetzkoy (1939: 64) is already quite explicit in claiming that the fricative is a 'kombinatorische Variante des Vokals *i*'.

In the following discussion, I shall make some particular assumptions on the phonetic characteristics of the relevant sound segments. Articulatorily, the transition from vowels to consonants consists in a greater constriction of the vocal tract. But this narrowing (traditionally: hardening) proceeds not in one, but in several steps. In general, only three such constriction degrees are presupposed in work on the phonetics/phonology of German in the relevant domain. This view distinguishes maximally open vowels such as [ɪ] from non-syllabic vowel [ɪ̯] from fricative [j].[51]

But as inspection of (1) in § 1.4 will tell, phonetic description as codified in the IPA conventions allows for a slight extension of this scheme. Palatal and labial (-velar) approximants [j, ʋ] are also part of the two series. We can, for a given place of articulation, distinguish at least four degrees of opening, where each degree of opening (or constriction) corresponds to a major class as provided by feature theory. In (87), I illustrate this situation with examples from the palatal and the velar (labial) point of articulation. Note that transcription conventions often collapse some of these distinctions, and how the featural description groups the sounds into several intersecting natural classes.[52]

(87)

Palatal series	Labiovelar series	Featural description
ɪ	ʊ	[− consonantal, − obstruent, + syllabic]
ɪ̯	ʊ̯	[− consonantal, − obstruent, − syllabic]
j	ʋ	[+ consonantal, − obstruent, − syllabic]
j̯	v	[+ consonantal, + obstruent, − syllabic]

[51] Of course, among the vowels [ɪ] is not maximally open. Also remember that [j] is the new IPA symbol for the voiced palatal fricative where earlier versions had [j], which is now the symbol for the corresponding approximant.

[52] The segments in the labiovelar series are partly labial, in so far as rounding is present for the vocalic members of the set, and as the obstruent [v] is labiodental. The vowels are velar in the sense of being back vowels. The reasons for the changes in place features and a possible treatment of them are discussed below.

I make the further factual assumption that the initial sounds in *jung, Wand,* and in similar words, are the fricatives of the two series, to be transcribed as [ʝ] and [v], respectively. Here, I follow the pronouncing dictionaries and Hall (1992*b*), while Kohler (1990*a, b*) takes the palatal segment in question to be an approximant [j].[53] On the other hand, prevocalic, but not syllable-initial, glides as in *Nation* [naː.tsjoːn] will be taken as being represented by the approximant. In other words, all on-glides are consonants, some obstruents and some sonorants, while all off-glides are vowels. Thus, the whole range of palatal segments given in (87) above are claimed to exist in Modern Standard German. I will return to the labiovelar series below.

7.4.1.1. *Palatal vowels and consonants*

Concentrating on the palatal series first, the important point for the analysis is that the four sound segments have a number of place features in common, but occur in mutually exclusive contexts. The complementary relationship of the four segments to each other suggests that the sounds should be related by rule. According to the analysis of underspecification in § 6.1, /ɪ/ is assigned the specification [+ high, + front]. These features are indeed shared by all the segments studied here. The question now arises of what the structural conditions are which restrict [j] and all other segments in its occurrence. In order to state the necessary rules, it is crucial to define the structural configurations under which the variants appear. As already suggested in (87) through the use of [syllabic], factors of syllable structure play an important role. More precisely, I claim that the palatal segments under discussion appear in the contexts given in (88). The syllable-structure context for approximants and fricatives is identical in (88*c, d*). However, the approximant is always preceded by another consonant in the same onset.

(88) *a.* Full vowel [ɪ]   *b.* Glide [ɪ̯]

         V   N

         | |

  [− consonantal]   C

                          |

                  [− consonantal]

   c. Approximant [j]   *d.* Fricative [ʝ]

         O   O

         | |

         C   C

         | |

  [+ consonantal]   [+ obstruent]

The difference between [ɪ] and [ɪ̯], represented in (88*a*) vs. (88*b*), can be seen to be a direct consequence of syllabification, as taken care of by rule (34) in § 3.2.4. Recall that the V-position is defined as containing the feature [+ syllabic]. This part requires no further discussion.

---

[53] Duden (1990) first notes the distinction between [j] and [ʝ] and then, somewhat confusingly, uses 'j' as the symbol for the fricative segment; cf. Duden (1990: 13–44).

The other two palatals, represented in (88c, d), are consonants claimed to occur in syllable onsets only. One important observation is that both [j] and [ʝ] are restricted to prevocalic positions. That is, they are not found morpheme-finally (where the obstruent would be devoiced to [ç] under the appropriate circumstances). Furthermore, [j]/[ʝ] are generally excluded in front of the vowels [iː, ɪ].[54] The list of words in (89) illustrates the distribution of [ʝ] word-initially (89a) and in intervocalic position (89b). The words in (89c) are (perhaps the only) exceptions to the restriction against the sequence of [ʝi].

(89) *a.* Jugend, Josef, jeder, jagen, jäh
    b. Boje, Kajüte, Kajak
    c. jiddisch, Yin, in+jizieren

The exclusion of final [j] and [ʝ] follows immediately from the assumption that they are both reflexes of an underlying /ɪ/. As the consonantization postulated here occurs only in onsets, [ʝ] and [j] have no chance to be found anywhere else. For examples illustrating the approximant and its context, see (5) in § 3.2 and (92) below.

The question to be answered now is what types of rules are necessary to provide the features required here, that is, [+ consonantal] and [+ obstruent]. I will propose two rules, High Vowel Consonantization and Desonorization, respectively, which derive [j] and [ʝ] from /ɪ/. As vowels are not specified for the values of [consonantal] and [obstruent] according to the model of underspecification proposed in § 6.3, the rules simply add specifications in the proper contexts. These rules turn a non-syllabic, prevocalic glide (note the presence of a C) first into an approximant and then, if the context of the segment matches that specified in rule (91), into a fricative. Note that (90) applies to any segment specified as [+ high] in an onset, while (91) requires syllable-initial position.

(90) High Vowel Consonantization
    [consonantal] → [+ consonantal] /O
                          |
                          C
                          |
                        R: ___
                        [+ high]

(91) i-Desonorization
    [obstruent] → [+ obstruent] /σ[C
                              |
                         R: ___
                       [+ high]
                       [+ front]

---

[54] As Hall (1992*b*: § 3.3.1) notes, [ʝ] is also rare before [yː, ʏ, øː, œ]. Furthermore, some of the exceptions have vowels derived from /uː, ʊ/, see *jung→ jüng+er, Jud+e→ jüd+isch*. I leave open the status of non-high front vowels. Actually /eː/ is also not very common after [ʝ].

High Vowel Consonantization initially looks too general in that it also applies to /ç/, /ʃ/ and also to the high vowels /ʊ, ʏ/. As this does no harm, I leave the rule as general as possible. The round high front vowel /ʏ/ never occurs as a prevocalic glide, while the rule will be shown to be valid for /ʊ/ in onsets in the following section.

To a form such as /ɪʊŋ/, both rules will apply, deriving the desired surface form [jʊŋ], while in the examples in (92) only High Vowel Consonantization (but not i-Desonorization) has a chance to apply. There are some cases in which, depending on the syllabification of the preceding consonant, both variants are possible, see (92*b*). In any case, approximant [j] only appears in non-initial position.

(92) *a.* [ʀeː.gjoːn] Region, [ak.tsjə] Aktie
    b. [bɪl.joːn]/[bɪljoːn] Billion, [mɪl̯jaɐ̯.də]/[mɪl̯jaɐ̯.də] Milliarde
    c. [i.di.oːt]/[i.djoːt] Idiot, [ʀe.li.gi.oːn]/[ʀe.li.gjoːn] Religion
       [ʃpaː.ni.ən]/[ʃpaː.njən] Spanien

A third kind of alternation is illustrated in (92*c*), that between a full vowel and a prevocalic glide. Words of this kind are treated quite inconsistently by the pronouncing dictionaries,[55] a fact probably reflecting the optional application of the rule of Vowel Shortening discussed in § 7.2.2. Only after shortening can /iː/ become part of an onset and so can undergo consonantization. Incidentally, this implies that the vowel shortening here results from the phonological (as opposed to the phonetic) rule of shortening.

The overall result is that neither /j/ nor /j̊/ are elements of the set of underlying segments of German. The restricted distribution of the palatals allows (or forces) the conclusion that all their occurrences are derived from [ɪ], which, in turn, is simply a particular version of /ɪ/. In fact, this special relationship between [ɪ], [ɪ̯], [j], and [j̊] is one of Saussure's examples for syllable-based modification of speech sounds. The segments' surface features are determined only partly (in these cases, minimally) by their own underlying representation.

7.4.1.2. *Back vowel desonorization*

The labiovelar series postulated in (87) above behaves similarly, but not totally identically. There exists a general assumption, both in the pronouncing dictionaries and the phonological literature, that the clusters represented orthographically as *schw*, *zw*, or *qu* as in *schwarz, zwei, Quatsch* are pronounced with [v], the labiodental voiced fricative, as the second element. The facts are more complex, as is pointed out by Kurka (1965), and provide justification for the claim to be made here that the sound in question is underlyingly not to be identified with /v/, which undoubtedly is a distinctive segment in the German phonology in other contexts, as we will see shortly.

Kurka's phonetic study first shows that a large number of postconsonantal labiodental fricatives are not voiced, but voiceless, even when speakers made an

---

[55] See also the discussion by Vater (1992: § 2.2.1).

attempt to meet the norms of the *Hochsprache*. On the other hand, Kurka (1965: 56–7) presents oscillograms of *w*-realizations which are voiced, but show no fricative (noisy) components (his figs. (4) and (5)). These sounds can be interpreted as representing voiced approximants, [ʋ], in analogy to [j], the voiced palatal approximant from the discussion above.

The labiovelar series of sounds displayed in (87) is then found in Modern Standard German. Besides short syllabic [ʊ] there is the non-syllabic [ʊ̯] in the diphthong [aʊ̯]; and the two consonants [v] and [ʋ] exist as well. The claim to be defended here is that the latter segment is always, and the former segment is sometimes, derived from underlying /ʊ/. But the status of a distinctive /v/ in general is not in question. In that respect, as well as in the precise formulation of the rule of u-Consonantization, the facts for the back vowel are not identical to those found above for /i/.

To motivate the phonemic status of /v/, it must be pointed out that the limited distribution found above for /j̯/ does not hold for /v/. In particular, it may be followed by /uː/ or /ʊ/ in a large number of words, such as *Wunder*, *Wunsch*, *Wut*, *Wurm*. Furthermore, /v/ occurs morpheme-finally in *brav*, *aktiv*, and others, where it is subject to Final Devoicing (see § 7.3.1). Palatal /j̯/, as we saw above, does not occur morpheme-finally.

As indicated above, however, it is most likely wrong to identify the labio-velar segment following /k/ with the fricative labiodental /v/. The reasons are twofold. First, the range of phonetic segments found here consists of [v], [f], [ʋ], and [ʊ̯]. That is, a word such as *Quatsch* may be pronounced in the four different ways transcribed in (93).

(93) Realizations of *Quatsch*
    [kvatʃ], [kfatʃ], [kʋatʃ], [kʊ̯atʃ]

Of these pronunciations, the first is the one given by the pronouncing dictionaries. There is however little doubt that this is not the only version to be found, as Kurka's study demonstrated. All words in which /v/ (or some of the other segments given in (93)) is preceded by /k/ behave in the way just illustrated; words supposedly beginning in /ʃv/ (*Schwatz*, *schwer*) and, more rarely, /tv/ and /tsv/ seem to display the same alternation. The question is, then, how to account for such a variety of possible forms, especially given that such a variation does not occur with words beginning in /v/ or with intervocalic /v/ (*Löwe*, *Lava*).

Let us assume that the sound in question is not /v/, but some unknown distinctive segment /*v/, whose nature needs clarification. A second relevant observation in this connection is that words with initial /k*v/ or /ʃ*v/ do not generally allow the vowels /uː, ʊ/ to follow the clusters in question. More precisely, while a wide range of vowels can follow both /k*v/ and /ʃ*v/, as (94a) shows, no example is found of the type */kvu . . . /, */kvy . . . /, */kvø . . . /, with either a long or a short round vowel. However, a few cases, all unassimilated Latin words, with /kvo . . . / exist, as (94b) demonstrates. Apart from these, there is a fair generalization that round vowels are excluded here; see Hall (1992*b*: § 3.3.2) for additional discussion.

(94) *a*. Quirl, quieken, quer, quäken, Quatsch, quaken
     b. Quorum, Quodlibet, Quote
     c. Schwur, Schwung, Schwund, schwul

The restriction against /ʃ*vu/ is less severe, as shown by the words in (94*c*). However, only the last of these words is clearly underived, while the others are words derived by the ablauting of vowels (i.e. from *schwören, schwingen, schwinden*). An immediate answer to the question why /*v/ should be restricted in the way illustrated here is to claim that it is in fact the underlying vowel /ʊ/. As established earlier (see § 6.1.1), sequences of two round vowels are generally not well formed. Assuming that the segment underlying [v], [f], [ʋ], and [ʊ] is in fact the vowel /ʊ/ thus leads to an immediate explanation for the phonotactic restriction just noted. Furthermore, the observations on the different variants of /*v/ can be accommodated as well and are accessible to a principled description on the model of analysis for the palatal series above.

On the basis of these arguments, the derivation of the variants from underlying /ʊ/ requires the following steps. Recall that the surface segments in question are [ʊ̯, ʋ, v, f], with their phonological representation given in (87) with an additional devoicing for [f]. The first of these variants, [ʊ̯], needs no further discussion as a member of the diphthong [aʊ̯]. It will derive through regular syllabification, as rule (34) in § 3.2.4 is designed especially for diphthongs.

The other three segments are consonants, or even obstruents. As with the palatal segments, we observe that they occur in syllable onsets. For the mechanism needed to assign the features [+ consonantal] or [+ obstruent] instead of the defaults [− consonantal, − obstruent] we can thus rely on the rules proposed in the preceding section. The difference from the palatal series is that all four labiovelar segments occur in the same environment, that is, after the consonants /k, ʃ/, to take only the more frequent cases. In other words, we are dealing with free variation here.

But apart from its optional application in the case of the labiovelar series, High Vowel Consonantization (90) is completely sufficient to derive [ʋ] from an /ʊ/ in onset position.[56] For the desonorization of [ʋ] to [v], a rule of u-Desonorization is needed, as formulated in (95). As it applies not only syllable-initially like i-Desonorization, it is apparently not the same rule. Again, it is an optional rule, to account for the variation found here and illustrated in (93).

The vowel having undergone these changes may finally be rendered voiceless, as in [ʃfɪmən] *schwimmen*. This alternation probably results from a voicing assimilation within the onset. As the devoicing here may well be partial and

---

[56] As far as underlying /v/ is concerned, it will be [+ consonantal] anyway, because of markedness rule (26*a*) of § 6.3.2.

gradient, the respective rule might be part of the phonetic implementation. I therefore refrain from stating a phonological rule here.

(95) u-Desonorization

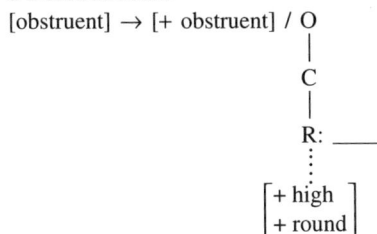

$$[\text{obstruent}] \rightarrow [+\ \text{obstruent}] \ / \begin{array}{c} \text{O} \\ | \\ \text{C} \\ | \\ \text{R:} \ \underline{\quad} \\ \vdots \\ \left[\begin{array}{c} +\ \text{high} \\ +\ \text{round} \end{array} \right] \end{array}$$

We must now discuss the fact that in the series of labiovelar segments, the place features are not identical. Underlying /ʊ/ bears the features [+ high, + round] and thereby the higher nodes of Tongue Position, Labial, Place. Note however that /ʊ/ is not specified as Dorsal.[57] Going from /ʊ/ to /ʋ, v/, we observe that these consonants are not [+ high, + round] any more. On the other hand, the configuration of the major articulators is exactly the same as that of the underlying vowel. Observe further that consonants which are Labial *and* [+ high, + round] simply do not exist in the German consonant system. The change in place features is thus not totally random or unnatural: the features which do not fit into the consonants derived through application of the two rules are eliminated, but only terminal features need to be removed. I leave the question open whether a rule is needed to achieve this result. The only other changes are independently motivated, in particular the addition of [Dental] to make [ʋ, v, f] labiodental, see (22*b*) of § 6.2.2.

We are now ready for an illustrative application of the rules discussed here. In (96), the phonetic form [kfatʃ] *Quatsch* is derived by going through all the major steps proposed above. I have abbreviated completely the subsegmental feature structure. Note that the onset rule in § 3.2.4 is not restricted to consonants as members of an onset. (96*b*) is thus a well-formed structure, and stopping at any point in the derivation here will produce one of the outputs claimed to exist in (93).

As a final argument for the analysis of /*v/ as /ʊ/ proposed here, note that hypothetical /*v/ is in fact the only obstruent which can appear in the position after another initial obstruent—not counting affricates such as /ts/, /pf/. As other sequences of the type ₛ[[+ obstruent] [+ obstruent] . . .] do not occur (and should not, given standard assumptions on the sonority sequencing; see § 7.5.1), it would be a welcome move to be able to exclude the clusters /kv/ and /ʃv/ from the structures which must be considered in phonotactic descriptions of German. The present proposal in fact constitutes such a move: as there is no prohibition against sequences of the type /k ʊ V . . . / or /ʃ ʊ V . . . /, a seeming irregularity has been accounted for.

---

[57] Rule (20) of § 6.2.2 gives [Dorsal] for those vowels which do not yet bear it.

(96) *a.* / k ʊ a t ʃ/   underlying

   b.   σ   Syllabification

```
              O    N    Cd
             / \   |    |
            C   C  V    C
            |   |  |    /\
          / k   ʊ  a    t  ʃ /
```

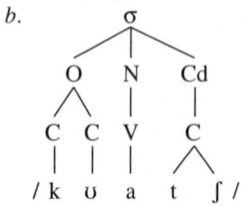

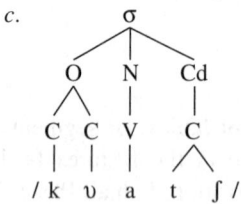

   c.   σ   High Vowel Consonantization (90)

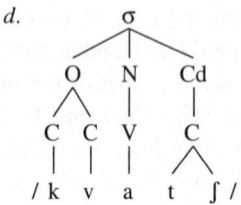

```
              O    N    Cd
             / \   |    |
            C   C  V    C
            |   |  |    /\
          / k   ʋ  a    t  ʃ /
```

   d.   σ   u-Desonorization (95)

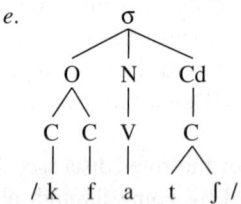

```
              O    N    Cd
             / \   |    |
            C   C  V    C
            |   |  |    /\
          / k   v  a    t  ʃ /
```

   e.   σ   Voicing Assimilation

```
              O    N    Cd
             / \   |    |
            C   C  V    C
            |   |  |    /\
          / k   f  a    t  ʃ /
```

   The two cases of desonorization and consonantization discussed above fit in
well with the *preference law* stated by Vennemann (1988: 13–21) on the strength-
ening of consonantal onsets. The main difference between Vennemann's syllable theory and the present treatment is that the latter argues for a synchronic
rule-based alternation between underlying vowels and surface consonants.

   Having found two rather clear cases of consonant–vowel transitions in German, we may conclude that the principle used during the course of the present
book of having one set of features for describing consonants *and* vowels is
sound. Not following this principle would require an arbitrary number of featural
changes in going from vowels to consonants (or vice versa, as in the case of r-
Vocalization discussed below).

7.4.2. The distribution of schwa

Different treatments of schwa in German within *SPE*-type analyses have been
presented by Bach and King (1970), Wurzel (1970), Kloeke (1982), and Strauss
(1982). For critical discussion of those approaches see Wiese (1986, 1988*a*: pt

II, ch. 2), Kleinhenz (1991: § 3.4), and Hall (1992a). As proposed throughout this book, schwa in Modern Standard German should generally be treated as a vowel of epenthesis and not as an underlying vowel (of whatever kind). The one general exception is word-final schwa as in *schön+e, Ros+e, glaub+e*, which represents, as argued in § 5.2, invariably a grammatical morpheme with a number of functions. As this morpheme must contain some underlying phonological material (surfacing as schwa), this type of schwa cannot be solely due to epenthesis.

The discussion at this point concentrates on the phonotactic distribution of schwa in monomorphemic words. In this connection, we will nevertheless have to consider morphology–phonology interactions once again. The special nature of the schwa vowel lies partly in its limited contexts of occurrence, as we had opportunity to observe in Chapters 4 and 5.

Consider now the well-known alternations between schwa (italicized *e*) and 'zero' in (97).[58] As exemplified here, schwa (represented once again by ortho-graphic *e*) appears within a number of word-final consonant clusters, but does not appear in a number of specific derivations of the same roots or stems. These alternations motivate a rule of Schwa Epenthesis, as schwa generally appears in the monomorphemic nouns or adjectives where it is required phonotactically, for the reason that the consonants surrounding schwa (/gl, tʀ, gn, tm/ in (97a)) cannot be final in their syllable. The alternative treatment of deleting schwa from underlying forms containing either schwa or some other vowel misses this generalization.

(97) *a.* Segel ~ Segl+er   *b.* dunkel ~ dunkl+es
     Filter ~ Filtr+at   sauber ~ saub(e)r+es
     Segen ~ segn+en   trocken ~ trock(e)n+es
     Atem ~ Atm+ung

A rule of Schwa Epenthesis may have, somewhat simplified, the shape pro-posed in (98). The rule comes in two parts; the first inserts a position before an unsyllabified position X, while the second turns this new position into a syllabic position and fills it with the features of the vowel schwa. It seems that ω, the phonological word, provides the bounding domain for the rule.

(98) Schwa Epenthesis
     a. 0 → X / ___ X]$_\omega$
     b. X → V
          |
          [ə]

Part (*b*) of the rule (98) is given for illustrative purposes only; strictly speak-ing, it is superfluous given the apparatus for syllabification in § 3.2 and for default vowels in § 6.1. These rules are such that an empty position will be

---

[58] As earlier, I here disregard the fact that the presence of the vowel schwa is often equivalent to a syllabic sonorant. The alternation between the actual vowel [ə] and sonorant syllabicity as in [zeːgəl] vs. [zeːgl̩] is a different phenomenon, to be discussed below.

automatically filled with schwa. Also, there is the alternative to (98*b*) presented below in (103). There are thus good reasons to separate the two aspects of schwa epenthesis. The rules operate as in (99). Note that its application is sandwiched in between two rounds of syllabification. I leave the question open whether the second round of syllabification must actually be regarded as a resyllabification (of /g/).

(99) *a.* /z eː g l/   underlying
      b.   σ   Syllabification

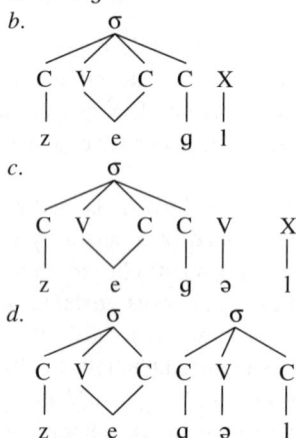

      c.   σ   Schwa Epenthesis (98)

      d.   σ   σ   resyllabification

While schwa in monomorphemic words is largely confined to the position specified in the epenthesis rule (i.e. the pre-final segmental position in the word), not all schwas are predictable in the way sketched here. In some cases, there must be an underlying schwa, or rather, the phonological structure supposed to surface as schwa. As argued before, this underlier is taken to be the unspecified prosodic position X. As the words in (100*a*) show, schwa sometimes appears in a position in which it is not phonotactically predictable, and where rule (98) would not insert schwa. In other words, *Dromdar* is a possible (though non-existent) word in German, and instead of *hundert*, we could just as well have *hundret* (cf. English *hundred*!). Note that these unpredictable schwas occur in positions other than the pre-final one in which the phonotactically motivated schwa is found usually.

(100) *a.* Drom[ə]dar, hund[ə]rt
       b. sag+e, Ros+e, groß+e

The second type of unpredictable schwa is exemplified in (100*b*). Here, schwa itself represents a morph occurring with a large number of diverse functions. Clearly, schwa as a morphological marker is unpredictable from the phonology alone (which does not exclude the possibility that such markers sometimes occur to fulfil prosodic requirements; see Chapter 4).

The obvious solution in the present framework is to allow empty skeletal nodes X to occur in underlying forms. As Xs also occur to represent distinctive vowel length, the formal inventory is not even enlarged through this move.

Again, such an X will be turned into V through syllabification and then be filled through the default rules; the resulting vowel is again [ə].

Following recent theories developed in phonology (Itô 1989; Noske 1993), one attractive alternative to the description just sketched would be to claim that there is no schwa epenthesis at all; instead, the insertion of the schwa vowel would be a direct consequence of syllabification. That is, rule (98a) would follow from independent principles of syllabification (or rather, be replaced by these), while (98b) is simply the application of the default rules needed on independent grounds.

There is at least one argument that Schwa Epenthesis in the sense of rule (98a) must be regarded as a proper rule in the phonology of Modern Standard German and not simply as a concomitant phenomenon of syllabification: it occurs only morpheme-finally (more precisely, before the morpheme-final consonant) and not, in connection with syllabification, at any arbitrary point within the word. In other words, roots such as /aːtm/ exist, but roots such as /ktb/, as found in the Semitic languages, do not. An across-the-board application of epenthesis-by-syllabification would predict the existence of such forms, because they could then surface as [kətəb]. Secondly, the syllabification approach to schwa would require syllabification to be sensitive to rather subtle morphological differences. While this is not a straightforward argument against this theory, it nevertheless changes the general concept of syllabification considerably.[59]

Schwa Epenthesis, finally, is sensitive to the morphological categories of word formation in Modern Standard German. As seen earlier in this work with other cases of morphology–phonology interactions, there are regularities which do not hold across the whole lexicon of German, but rather for small, though well-defined, subgroups. On the other hand, in all of these subgroups, in which there is an alternation of a vowel with 'zero' (i.e. no vowel), it is the vowel schwa which appears.[60] Also, the alternation between schwa and its absence always occurs one consonantal position away from the right-hand word boundary. It is the existence of these two facts which argues strongly for the unity of schwa epenthesis in German.

One of the contrasts between simplex (nouns, adjectives) and derived (verbs) words is given in (101). In order to characterize the distribution of schwa properly, we need to distinguish between the word classes of verb, noun, and adjective on the one hand, and between final sonorant consonants from various classes on the other.[61]

---

[59] It is largely for this reason that Noske (1993) postulates underlying schwa in these cases, as for the schwa co-occurring with adjectival inflections.

[60] There is a very limited group of words in which other vowels (/i/ and /u/) alternate with the absence of a specified vowel, see *Omen* vs. *omin+ös*, and the list of cases by Kloeke (1982: 21). This alternation may be regarded as a morphologized version of vowel epenthesis, in which more than just the default vowel is inserted.

[61] Verbs do not really exist uninflectedly; the infinitive forms in the right-most column of (101) show the differences between liquid-final and nasal-final verbs.

(101)

	Noun	Adjective	Verb
[+ nasal]	Segen Atem	trocken	trockn+en atm+en
[− obstruent, − nasal]	Segel Ruder	dunkel sicher	segel+n sicher+n

In derived words, schwa distribution becomes more complex. Some, but not all, of the relevant cases have been treated in Chapters 3 to 5; see also the literature referred to at the beginning of this section. The general picture, again illustrated in (102), is always the same: particular affix-root combinations may require schwa (as part of the root or of the suffix) even where the general phonotactic regularities do not require its presence, or where, as in the case of *arbeit+et* and similar verb forms ending in a coronal stop, degemination would be an alternative. In these cases, combinations of morphological and phonological factors require Schwa Epenthesis, which is, in other cases, an independently motivated general rule.[62]

(102) Derived words

a. Atm+er	*b.* trocken+e	*c.* Trockn+ung	*d.* arbeit+et
Eign+er	eigen+e	Eign+ung	leid+et
Segl+er	dunkl+e	Umsegel+ung	leg+t
Ruder+er	sicher+e	Sicher+ung	läuf+t

The distributional pattern for schwa is different in each column of (102). For the degree of specificity needed here, compare *Segl+er* to *Ruder+er*. There are two verbal bases with the same suffix. The difference between final /l/ and /ʀ/ is sufficient to require Schwa Epenthesis in the latter case, but not in the former. These applications of Schwa Epenthesis under specific, partly morphological, conditions are certainly part of the lexical phonology, while the application of Schwa Epenthesis under the general conditions stated in (98) is perhaps a postlexical rule application.

In discussing schwa distribution, one further topic to be dealt with is the alternation of schwa with syllabic consonants. As pointed out first in (5) of § 2.2.5, schwa plus a sonorant alternates with the same sonorant as a syllabic consonant; see (62), (68), and (70) for examples. In the present framework, this means that we must provide two ways of deriving a phonetic form from an empty skeletal position X.

Suppose that the syllable nucleus can be filled with segments specified as [− consonantal] in lexical syllabification. But postlexically, this condition (followed in the syllabification algorithm of § 3.2.4) is relaxed somewhat so that a nucleus can now hold all segments which are [− obstruent]. Such a weakening

---

[62] In Wiese (1986; 1988*a*: pt, II, ch. 2), I attempted to distribute the various contexts for Schwa Epenthesis over the lexical levels postulated for German. This approach may be able to explain part of the patterns.

of structural constraints in the postlexical domain is quite common. It allows us to formulate a spreading rule (103) which lets the features of the coda sonorant be shared with the nucleus.

(103) Sonorant Syllabicity

$$\begin{array}{cc} V & C \\ \diagdown \ \diagdown \ | \\ \end{array}$$
R: [− obstruent]

This rule will apply optionally if a sonorant follows an empty V, and obligatorily if the sonorant happens to be /ʀ/. This obligatory application follows because /ʀ/ can surface as a vocalized [ɐ]; see § 7.4.4. This segment will automatically become the syllabic vowel, if there is no other such vowel already. The two ways of deriving schwa syllables are illustrated in (104) and (105).

(104) *a.* ... V ...   underlying or by Schwa Epenthesis (98*a*), Syllabification

    b. ... V ...   rule (8), § 6.1
          |
          R

    c. ... V ...   default rules
          |
          R
          △
          ə

(105) a. ... V   C   underlying or by Schwa Epenthesis (98*a*),
          | Syllabification
        R: [− obstruent]

    b. ... V   C   Sonorant Syllabicity (103)
          &diagdown; &diagdown;|
        R: [− obstruent]

The pattern of schwa distribution also provides evidence for the claim indicated in the introductory discussion to Lexical Phonology in Chapter 5, namely that phonological rules including Syllabification and Schwa Epenthesis operate strictly cyclically, that is, only after the application of some morphological rule. For evidence for this 'morphology first' principle, consider the alternation between schwa and zero in the following structures. To the form (106*a*), Syllabification and concomitant Schwa Epenthesis must not take place before suffixation of *+isch*. Otherwise, **bäuerisch* instead of *bäurisch* would be derived. On the other hand, suffixation of *+er* in (107) must trigger Schwa Epenthesis to prevent the derivation of **mal+r+isch*.[63] Finally, it must be ensured that schwa can be inserted into the non-suffixed form *Bauer*. This is achieved by the system of morphological rules proposed in § 5.2.3, according to which each independent root entry will be dominated, through rules of word formation, by a stem. As

---

[63] Note that both of the starred forms are phonotactically possible. The analysis assumes that *Bauer* is not morphologically complex (**Bau+er*). This is justified precisely because of the form *bäurisch*. The suffix *+er* always surfaces as a schwa syllable.

soon as the stem category is added, as in (108*b*), the form is not underived any more.

(106) *a.* /baʊʀ/   root
      b. /baʊʀ/ + /ɪʃ/   suffix
      c. [bɔʏ]$_\sigma$ [ʀɪʃ]$_\sigma$ Syllabification, (Umlaut)

(107) *a.* /maːl/   root
      b. /maːl/ + /ʀ/   suffix
      c. [maː]$_\sigma$ [lɐ]$_\sigma$ Syllabification, schwa
      d. [maː]$_\sigma$ [lɐ]$_\sigma$ + /ɪʃ/   suffix
      e. [maː]$_\sigma$ [lɐ]$_\sigma$ [ʀɪʃ]   Syllabification

(108) *a.* /baʊʀ/   root
      b. /baʊʀ/   stem
      c. [baʊ]$_\sigma$ [ɐ]$_\sigma$ Syllabification, schwa

In other words, the contrast of *bäurisch* to *malerisch* as well as to *Bauer* is taken care of—provided that underived roots are not input to phonological rules. The non-application of Schwa Epenthesis in *bäurisch* does not require a diacritic marking of being an exception or some similar mechanism.

7.4.3. Some clitic forms

Particular classes of words in Modern Standard German can be found both in a full and a reduced form. Such reduced forms are generally called *clitics* (although they may be of a diverse nature); and I will deal briefly with some clitic phenomena here. Clitics are tough problems in many languages (for a survey of data and problems see Spencer 1991: ch. 9), since there seem to be syntactic and morphological, as well as phonological, aspects to their description.

The most obvious clitics in German are the reduced forms of personal pronouns and articles, and I will deal with each of these in turn. In (109), the paradigm of personal pronouns is displayed, distinguishing number, person, and case as relevant dimensions. The full forms of personal pronouns are then contrasted with their respective reduced forms.[64]

(109) gives only those reduced forms which are acceptable in non-rapid informal speech. (Formal speech has no clitics here.) That is, more clitics may be found in faster speech. Restricting ourselves to those clitics given in (109), and assuming that these are a complete and homogeneous set of cases in the colloquial register of (Northern) Standard German, leads to the generalization that personal pronouns in the nominative and accusative case and ending in a segment specified as [− obstruent] have a clitic alternant. In addition, *es* can be cliticized; but here we note that [s] is one of those consonants which can be added to almost any syllable (see § 3.2.3 on extrasyllabic consonants), and is thereby distinct from [ç] and [ns]. Consequently, *dich* has no clitic form as it ends in an obstruent, while *dir* instantiates the dative case. As nominative/accusative

---

[64] Personal pronouns in the genitive case are identical to possessive pronouns; gender distinctions only exist for third-person pronouns.

case contrasts with dative/genitive case by means of the feature [± oblique], the clitics can be claimed to be restricted to the pronoun forms bearing [– oblique] case.

(109)

		Singular		Plural	
		Full	Reduced	Full	Reduced
First person					
Nom.		ich		wir	[vɐ]
Acc.		mich		uns	
Dat.		mir		uns	
Second person					
Nom.		du	[də]	ihr	[ɐ]
Acc.		dich		euch	
Dat.		dir		euch	
Third person					
Nom.	m.	er	[ɐ]	sie	[zə]
	f.	sie	[zə]		
	n.	es	[(ə)s]		
Acc.	m.	ihn	[n̩]	sie	[zə]
	f.	sie	[zə]		
	n.	es	[(ə)s]		
Dat.	m./n.	ihm		ihnen	
	f.	ihr			

It is often hypothesized that clitic forms cannot (or should not) be derived from the full forms by rule, as the clitic is not predictable on the basis of the full form, and as the range of words in which the putative rule applies is either too small or again unpredictable (see Kaisse 1985; Klavans 1985; Berendsen 1986). But the personal-pronoun clitics given here are systematically related to the full form. On the basis of the observation that neither initial consonants (if any) nor final consonants (if any) are missing in the clitic form, but that vowels are invariably reduced to schwa or to the vocalic /ʀ/, it is sufficient to propose the rule of Vowel Deletion (110). All the clitic forms in (109) can be derived from rule (110), together with the independently stated rule of Schwa Epenthesis, and the default rules. Note that Vowel Reduction is another rule removing information. As the full vowel varies from pronoun to pronoun, we cannot predict the shape of the full vowel from any other information. But schwa (or vocalized /ʀ/) is indeed predictable.

(110) Vowel Reduction

X
⧺
R: [– consonantal]

It is true that this rule applies in non-fast speech only to non-oblique personal pronouns with final sonorants under specific contextual conditions, but, nevertheless, it still applies uniformly in a set of cases which can be characterized in a straightforward fashion. The rule also plays a role in the derivation of a second type of clitic in Modern Standard German to which I now turn.

The patterns of reduction found for the definite and indefinite articles are slightly more complex. In (111), reduced forms of definite and indefinite articles are exemplified together with the corresponding full forms, assuming that the reduced forms given in (111a, b) are the only ones which are acceptable (and even obligatory in some contexts) in the standard language. The only reduced forms of the definite articles are those in which prepositions merge with following definite articles.[65] A large additional group of clitics is found in informal registers, such as *in'e* [ɪnə] instead of *in die*.

(111) *a.* an dem   am   'at the'   *b.* an das   ans   'at the'
        bei dem   beim   'near the'   auf das   aufs   'onto the'
        in dem   im   'in the'   hinter das   hinters   'behind the'
        von dem   vom   'from the'   in das   ins   'into the'
        zu der   zur   'to the'   ⋮
        zu dem   zum   'to the'   ⋮
     c. ein   [n̩]
        eine   [nə]
        einen   [nən]/[n̩]
        einem   [nəm]/[m̩]
        ⋮

The pattern according to which definite articles reduce is very simple: only final consonants are kept, and are syllabified together with the preceding preposition. Furthermore, if unacceptable final clusters (/nm/) result from the reduction, final consonants of the preposition are deleted. We can thus assume that rule (110) is complemented here by a rule deleting initial (but not final) consonants of the articles. The indefinite article *ein* displays two patterns of reduction, as illustrated in (111c): either only the vowel is deleted, or the stem-final consonant in *ein* also disappears.

A second aspect of clitics which needs mention is their distribution. As with most other types of clitics known, the clitics introduced here are not free to appear in every context. That is, not every full form can be replaced by (or changed to) a reduced form. The most obvious contextual constraint is that a clitic always needs some item to which it attaches. This item is called the *host* of the clitic. The obligatoriness of such a host immediately explains why clitics cannot be alone in an utterance.

---

[65] They are often called *Verschmelzungsformen* in German grammars. Note that there are standard orthographic forms for these, but not for other clitics. The list in (111a) contains dative forms of articles and is complete, while the forms in (111b) display accusative cases and only exemplify the pattern. More discussion of these and other clitics can be found in Wiese (1988a: § 3.2.2) and Prinz (1991: ch. 3). More syntactically oriented approaches are formulated by Hinrichs (1986) and Raffelsiefen (1987).

Generally, the contextual conditions for the two principal types of clitics in German introduced above can be described either in syntactic or in phonological terms. Not surprisingly, I will argue that it is the phonological representation which provides the background for the characterization of clitic contexts.[66] Briefly, the argumentation is as follows. First, there is no uniquely definable syntactic context for the clitic personal pronouns; they can occur with finite verbs, conjunctions, other nouns, and pronouns as hosts on their left-hand side. (112) gives an example for each of these cases. It is hard to see how a unified syntactic description of the clitic contexts can be construed.

(112) *a.* Hat [ɐ] (er) das Buch gelesen?
      'Did he read the book?'
    b. Wenn [də] (du) damit fertig bist, . . .
      'If you are finished with it, . . .'
    c. Wenn Peter [s] (es) geschafft hat, . . .
      'If Peter has made it, . . .'
    d. Hat [ɐs] (er es) gefunden?
      'Did he find it?'

Second, clitics are never initial in what can be characterized as a phonological phrase in the sense of § 3.5.[67] The phonological unity thus consists in the fact that clitics are always preceded by at least one phonological word in some phonological phrase, and that the clitics themselves are not dominated by their own phonological word. The clear evidence for this latter claim lies in the stresslessness of the clitics and in the fact that they are syllabified with their host. They must therefore be subsumed under the phonological word of the host. The situation with the definite articles is slightly more complex; however, it might be sufficient to claim that articles lose their status as phonological words only after suitable prepositions (in the standard language). Again, they are then syllabified with the prepositional hosts.

Nespor and Vogel (1986: ch. 5) suggest that the host-clitic combination forms a special prosodic category: the *clitic group*. However, there seems to be no evidence for such a category in Modern Standard German. Rather, host-clitic combinations never have properties different from those of the phonological word. Thus, they are phonological words constructed in the postlexical phonology (as opposed to base-affix combinations).[68] Clitics are integrated into their preceding phonological words, just as those affixes which do not form their own phonological word are (see (56), (57) of § 3.4). Host-clitic differ from the phonological words considered so far in that the latter are generally part of the lexical derivation.

---

[66] This is a claim made for German, not for clitics in other languages such as the Romance languages.

[67] This statement requires qualification, as the indefinite article *ein* can occur proclitically, i.e. with the host to the right, as in *'n Haus* 'a house'. Southern dialects of German generally allow proclitic forms of pronouns and articles.

[68] Booij (1995: ch. 8) makes the same point with respect to Dutch clitics.

If a clitic were attached to its host within the clitic group, we would expect the clitic group to consist of two phonological words (as prosodic units are assumed to dominate exclusively units of the rank one step lower). However, as just noted, clitics do not carry the properties of distinct phonological words. Above all, clitics in German are syllabified with their host. Furthermore, they are unstressed. This justifies the conclusion that host and clitic share a common phonological word, since the phonological word was argued in § 3.4 to be the domain for syllabification, and also is a stress-bearing unit. If the putative clitic group acts as a domain for syllabification and has no other differentiating properties, so should be considered indistinguishable from the phonological word, that is, is identical to it.

7.4.4. r-Vocalization

The extensive allophony of /ʀ/ has been mentioned in § 2.2 and is used there to argue for a specific feature structure in § 6.3.1. We are now ready to describe more precisely the distribution of some of the various sounds systematically related to /ʀ/.

The precise description of the occurring /ʀ/-sounds in segmental terms provides quite a puzzle. Let us first assume (following Meinhold and Stock 1980: 131–3) that there are two main variants of /ʀ/, besides alveolar /r/, which occurs in Southern dialects and is generally regarded as being on the decline diachronically. One of the uvular variants can be transcribed as [ʀ], denoting an approximant, uvular sound. It is not usually trilled or vibrant in the standard language, although here again dialectal variation may be found. The other variant is transcribed either as [ʌ] (Moulton 1962: 35–40; Hall 1992b; 1993), as [A] (Meinhold and Stock 1980; Fox 1990; Basbøll and Wagner 1985: 56–7), as [əʳ] (Wurzel 1981: 926), or as [ɐ] (Ulbrich 1972; Kohler 1977; Krech et al. 1982). It is characterized as 'vocalized r' (Meinhold and Stock 1980: 131), or as 'a more open variety of the /ə/' (Fox 1990: 38), or as 'lower mid unrounded vowel between central and back' (Moulton 1962). I will follow IPA convention by making use of 'ɐ' as the transcription symbol for this segment and discuss its featural analysis below. It is important to note that this vowel sound is monosegmental and stands in phonemic contrast to schwa, as demonstrated by pairs such as Lehr[ə] vs. Lehr[ɐ], Kutt[ə] vs. Kutt[ɐ].

The fricative variant of the uvular r-sound ([ʁ]) can be found as well, although not regularly in the standard language. Although Ulbrich (1972) claims to have found a majority of fricative realizations for /ʀ/ in onset positions (see Hall (1993) for recent summary), I regard his description as problematic. His classification of non-vocalic /ʀ/-realizations only distinguishes vibrants (rolled r) from fricatives. That is, an approximant non-vibrant realization is simply not regarded as a possibility and therefore not recorded. As a consequence, the number of fricative tokens is probably largely overestimated, as vibrant realizations are indeed rare for many speakers of German. In contrast to Ulbrich and others, I will assume that fricative realization of /ʀ/ is rare in Modern Standard German and too gradual to be admitted into the domain of phonology.

The claim that there is a systematic correspondence between the vowel transcribed [ɐ] and the consonant [ʀ] is supported by numerous alternations in which, depending on context, one or the other variant appears. (113) gives examples of both syllabic and non-syllabic [ɐ] compared to [ʀ] in other derivations of the same words.[69]

(113) *a.* [ɐ]   ~   [ʀ]   *b.* [ɐ̯]   ~   [ʀ]

    [gʀøː.sɐ]   ~   [gʀøː.sə.ʀə]   [tyːɐ̯]   ~   [tyː.ʀən]
    größ+er   größ+er+e   Tür   Tür+en

    [laɪ.tɐ]   ~   [laɪ.tə.ʀɪn]   [ʃveːɐ̯]   ~   [ʃveːʀɐ]
    Leit+er   Leit+er+in   schwer   schwer+er

    [ʀuː.dɐ]   ~   [ʀuː.də.ʀɐ]   [fɛːɐ̯t]   ~   [faː.ʀən]
    Ruder   Ruder+er   fähr+t   fahr+en

The distribution of the variants of /ʀ/ can be described as follows: vocalic [ɐ] predominates after long vowels (as in *Heer* [heːɐ̯]) and in the prefixes *er-*, *her-*, *ver-*, and *zer-* (where it is less clear whether the vowel is long). [ʀ] predominates initially, that is, in onsets, and (sometimes, see below) after short vowels as in *Herr* [hɛʀ]. It is, as mentioned above, a uvular approximant which may be trilled occasionally. Alveolar [r] occurs in Southern German dialects. In some of these, alveolar [r] does not seem to be vocalized. This is exactly as it should be, given that vowels (like uvular consonants, but unlike alveolars) are assumed to be dorsal. However, other southern dialects do vocalize alveolar /r/, against the prediction made.

The four relevant classes that must be distinguished for uvular /r/-realizations in Modern Standard German are illustrated in (114). The most straightforward generalization seems to be that /ʀ/ is consonantal in onsets, and vocalic elsewhere (or in rhymes). This clear picture is however disturbed by the consonantal realization of /ʀ/ after short vowels (114*d*).

(114) *a.* syllable-onset   [ʀaːt] Rat, [ʃtʀaɪt] Streit, [aː.ʀi.ə] Arie
    b. syllabic vowel   [laɪtɐ] Leiter, [zɪçɐ] sicher
    c. non-syllabic vowel   [viːɐ̯] wir, [veːɐ̯t] Wert, [vaːɐ̯] war
    d. after short vowels   [naʀ] Narr, [ɪʀt] irrt

The realization of /ʀ/ after short vowels (114*d*) is subject to more variation than is found in the other environments. The claim that /ʀ/ is not vocalized after short vowels is based on the pronouncing dictionaries, while, contrary to this claim, in actual use vocalization will often occur (see Ulbrich 1972; Kohler 1977: 170). As pointed out by Hall (1993), there are also dialects in which /ʀ/ will be a fricative (and be devoiced) in precisely this context.

---

[69] In some colloquial dialects there is a 'double' realization of /ʀ/ in words such as *größere* or *Leiterin*: [gʀø.sɐ.ʀə]. A single underlying /ʀ/ is realized here as the heterosyllabic sequence [ɐ.ʀ]. These cases remain problematic for the present account (as probably for others), which has no means of providing one segment with more than one, and therefore contradictory, value (here, [− consonantal] [+ consonantal]). I leave the question open whether it is necessary under these circumstances to 'split' one /ʀ/ into two segments, or whether there are other means of analysis.

The non-vocalization of /ʀ/ after a short vowel (as opposed to a long vowel) must be regarded as surprising, given that /ʀ/ after a long vowel (and even in a vowel-less context as in (114*b*)) is usually vocalized. We are clearly dealing here with a marked state of affairs. On grounds of naturalness, just the opposite might be expected: a short vowel is more likely to be continued in a vocalic glide than a long vowel. For confirmation, note that the regular diphthongs of German always begin in a short vowel. On the other hand, we note that an /ʀ/ after a short vowel is precisely the one which will be ambisyllabic if /ʀ/ is followed by another vowel: [naʀən]. Ambisyllabic [ʀ] is not vocalized, not even optionally.

This observation actually provides an argument for assuming r-vocalization in rhymes rather than r-consonantization in onsets. As just noted, the presence of /ʀ/ in an onset has priority over its presence in a rhyme. That is, the r-Vocalization rule introduced shortly is blocked by the double linking of /ʀ/, as it should be blocked according to the principle of *Linking Constraint* proposed by Hayes (1986) and introduced in § 3.2 (fn. 20). However, the putative rule of r-Consonantization would have to apply to ambisyllabic /ʀ/, in order to make it consonantal, and this would be in violation of this constraint.

In order to give a precise description of the variants and their distribution, we must provide feature specifications for all members in the set, including the vocalized /ʀ/. Embarrassingly on first sight, there is no room for a segment characterized in the way assumed here in the feature system proposed in Chapters 2, 3, and 6 (nor in any other system I am aware of). If [ɐ] is a central vowel occupying the space between [a] and [ə] in terms of vowel height, then the three possible vowel-height distinctions provided by the features [high] and [low] leave no room for such a vowel. However, I will argue now that [ɐ] should be identified in its phonological features with the vowel [a].

Consider first the facts presented in (115). As first discussed in § 6.3.1, there is a tendency to neutralize the distinction between [a(ː)], [aɐ̯], and [ɐ]. That is, *Oda*, *Radar*, and *Oder* have final syllables which are perceptually very similar, and are nearly or completely identical in some dialects. Recall that the actual vowel length of unstressed open syllables is an open issue, leading some authors to assume 'half-length' here. However, final schwa and vocalized [ɐ] are the only vowels which are unambiguously short in open syllables.

(115) Ode [oːdə], Oder [oːdɐ], Oda [oːdaˑ], Radar [ʀaːdaɐ̯]

The other reduced vowel, [ə] as in *Ode*, is quite distinct from the other variants under consideration here. This observation argues against the treatment of vocalized /ʀ/ as an r-coloured schwa (see [əʳ], p. 252), and for a strong overlap in feature structure between /a/-sounds and the vocalized variant of /ʀ/. Suppose we even proceed to claim that there is *no* difference between /a/ and vocalized /ʀ/, and that all differences arise from factors external to the segmental composition of these two sounds. This position seems untenable at first sight: the basic function of feature representations is to classify objects; entities judged to be distinct must receive different featural representations. Given that [a] and [ɐ] are

very similar, but at least *can* be differentiated, there must be different representation for them in terms of features.

However, segment-internal features are not the only means available to us
for the purpose of differentiation here. By analogy with the treatment of palatal
and labiovelar vowels, glides, and consonants in § 7.4.1 above, we can make
use of higher levels of structure. Similarly, it is possible to distinguish vocalized
variants of /ʀ/ from /a/ by structural, syllabic representations. Ignoring long /
aː/ which is different simply because of its association with two skeletal positions, (116) gives the structural environments for the three sound types under
discussion.

(116) *a.* [a]:   V   C   *b.* [ɐ]:   V   *c.* [ɐ̯]:   C

           | | |

          /a/   /a/   /a/

As the vowel classification in (2) of § 1.4 shows, the vowel [ɐ] is placed between [a] and [ə]. That is, it is assumed to be somewhat higher in terms of tongue
position than the low vowel; but arguably, this is just a reflex of its glide status
in the case of [ɐ̯]. Non-syllabic vowels in general display their articulatory
features in a less salient and steady manner; typically such vowels are, with
respect to the articulatory space, centralized. It is for this reason that the categorization (and subsequent transcription) of glides in diphthongs is a matter of
debate, as we noted in § 6.1.1. However, I submit that this observation should
not subtract from the phonological categorization of these items. That is, we
may classify the second segment in the diphthong [aɪ] as /ɪ/, although its realization may in fact be close to [e̞]. Analogously, I propose to assign identical
segmental feature specifications to [a] and [ɐ̯], namely those of /a/.

The difference between the two syllabic vowels [a] and [ɐ] is more subtle. In
(116*a*) a skeletal C is given to hint at the fact that short [a] never appears syllable-
finally, while [ɐ] often does appear in this context. In fact, if there are following
consonants as in *scheiter+t*, *sicher+n*, these are usually exponents of inflectional
morphemes. In other words, syllable-final [a] is different from [ɐ] because it is
long, or at least longer than a short vowel. The remaining case is that exemplified
by *Bad* ([bat], if the vowel is shortened) vs. *Ebert* ([eː.bɐt]). I regard it as an open
question whether there actually is any segmental distinction between the two *a*-
like vowels beyond that of the difference in amount of stress.

An additional argument for the identity of the sounds discussed stems from
a remark by Ulbrich (1972: 55), who notes that it is practically impossible for
German speakers to utter [ɐ] in isolation.[70] But why should this be the case for
a very frequent vowel of German? I suggest that its featural identity to [a] provides the answer: outside of a word context, [ɐ] cannot be distinguished from [a].
(Note that it is comparatively easy for German speakers to utter [ə] in isolation.
That is, the stresslessness of syllables containing schwa or [ɐ] is not responsible
for the observation.)

---

[70] Ulbrich (1972) also describes vocalized /ʀ/ as a sound articulatorily intermediate between [ʀ]
and [a].

For the sake of concreteness, I illustrate the featural content of the /a/- and /R/-sounds at this point in the complete featural tree given in (117). As the place features are assumed to be identical for the consonants and vowels involved, only [consonantal] is a feature with variation in its value.[71] Recall also that underlyingly, of these features, only [+ low] and [+ continuant] are present (and ensure that /R/ is different from /a/ at this level).

(117) Featural content of /R/ and /a/

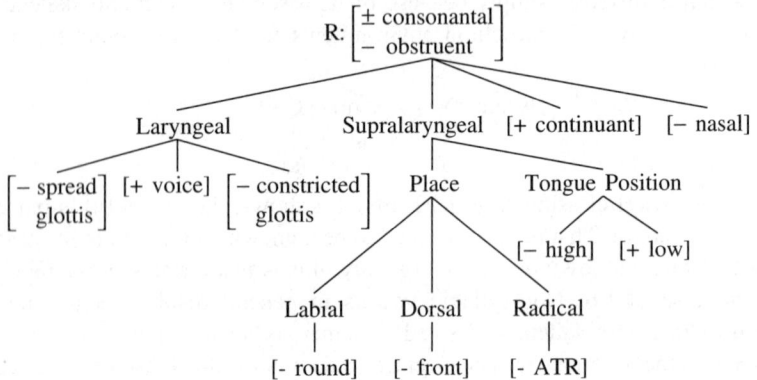

$$
\text{R:} \begin{bmatrix} \pm \text{ consonantal} \\ - \text{ obstruent} \end{bmatrix}
$$

Laryngeal   Supralaryngeal   [+ continuant]   [– nasal]

$$\begin{bmatrix} - \text{ spread} \\ \text{glottis} \end{bmatrix}$$ [+ voice] $\begin{bmatrix} - \text{ constricted} \\ \text{glottis} \end{bmatrix}$ Place   Tongue Position

[– high]   [+ low]

Labial   Dorsal   Radical

[- round]   [- front]   [- ATR]

On the basis of the preceding discussion, we are ready to state a rule of r-Vocalization. As /R/ is not assumed to be specified underlyingly for the feature [consonantal], the rule (118) only needs to provide the negative value for this feature in the right context. This context is the rhyme of a syllable; if, and only if, /R/ is placed in the rhyme, it is (usually) vocalized. The fact that vowels also fall under the input condition of (118) does no harm, as vowels are of course non-consonantal under all conditions. Vocalization rule (118) applies to any /R/ in a rhyme, independent of its position in the nucleus or in the coda.

(118) r-Vocalization

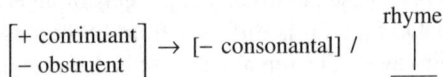

$$
\begin{bmatrix} + \text{ continuant} \\ - \text{ obstruent} \end{bmatrix} \rightarrow [- \text{ consonantal}] \ / \ \overset{\text{rhyme}}{\mid}
$$

The non-vocalization of /R/ after short vowels (see (114d)) might perhaps be taken care of by a *dissimilation* rule, operative only within nuclei. This rule would make /R/ consonantal within a nucleus, precisely because there already is a non-consonantal segment in that constituent. An argument for this proposal is provided by the fact that /R/ in a schwa syllable (i.e. in the absence of a vowel) is always vocalized. That is, it is the presence of and the close contact with a vowel which causes the non-vocalization, and not its position in the nucleus alone.

As dissimilation is generally regarded as a marked rule (compared with assimilation) we would also have accounted for the marked and unstable status

---

[71] One unexplored consequence of the present view is that the feature [ATR] (or [tense]) might be a feature relevant for consonants as well.

expressed by this rule. The alternative treatment proposed by Hall (1993) and Giegerich (1992*b*) makes r-Vocalization optional after short vowels, but obligatory in other contexts. This type of account appears to be less adequate in expressing the marked status of the result of the application of the rule.

Finally, we are also ready to look at the interaction of r-Vocalization (118) with other rules. Of particular interest here is the relationship of this rule to the rule of Dorsal Fricative Assimilation (52). Recalling that this rule assimilates the dorsal fricative to a back (rather, non-front) vowel, we find that there is no assimilation of the fricative to a vocalized /ʀ/, see [dʊ̯ɐç] *durch* or [zaɐç] *Sarg*. (There are dialects in which the facts are different. Certain dialects of the Ruhr area have [dʊ̯ɐχ], [zaɐχ] here, *pace* Ronneberger-Sibold 1988.) As shown in (119) for *durch*, this requires a particular ordering between r-Vocalization and Dorsal Fricative Assimilation: applying the two rules in this order (a feeding relationship) leads to the dialectal forms just mentioned, but not to the correct forms of Modern Standard German. What is required instead is a counterfeeding relationship (see Kenstowicz and Kisseberth 1979: 315), in which the application of r-Vocalization *after* Dorsal Fricative Assimilation prevents the dorsal fricative from becoming uvular.

(119) *a.* / d ʊ R X /   underlying

                /‾‾‾‾‾‾‾‾‾‾‾

      Supralaryngeal   [+ continuant]

       |

      Tongue
      Position

       |

      [+ low]

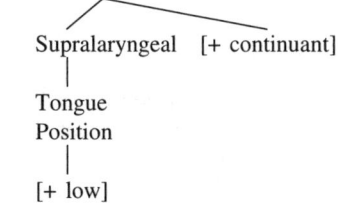

   b. not applicable   Dorsal Fricative Assimilation (52)

   c. / d ʊ R: [– consonantal] X /   r-Vocalization (118), after Syllabification

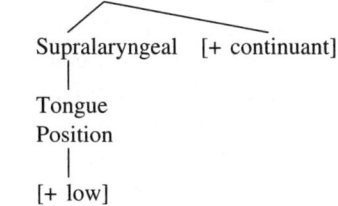

                /‾‾‾‾‾‾‾‾‾‾‾

      Supralaryngeal   [+ continuant]

       |

      Tongue
      Position

       |

      [+ low]

   d. / d ʊ R: [– consonantal] ç /   rule (22*a*), § 6.2.2

                /‾‾‾‾‾‾‾‾‾‾‾

      Supralaryngeal   [+ continuant]

       |

      Tongue
      Position

       |

      [+ low]

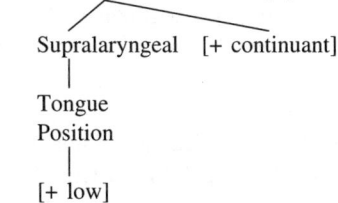

The ordering relationship illustrated here seems to constitute one of the clearest cases for a stipulated ordering of rules. The two rules in question are very much of the same type, as they are both automatic, allophonic rules, both dis-allowing exceptions. Avoiding rule ordering for this case seems hard to achieve; one possible way might be to exploit the fact that Dorsal Fricative Assimilation does not depend on prior syllabification, while r-Vocalization clearly does.

7.5. PHONOTACTIC CONSTRAINTS AND PRINCIPLES

In § 3.2, a basic model of the syllable is presented which may serve as a frame-work in which the question of phonotactic possibilities and constraints can be discussed. In this section, I take up the description of the syllable-internal sequencing of sounds and give a more detailed picture. In general, I follow the strategy of breaking up the large number of cases to be considered here into what appear to me to be the natural classes. That is, instead of providing one large unified account of phonotactics, I give detailed solutions to specific sub-problems. First, the presumed overall conditions on segmental sequencing within the syllable are discussed. In the following section, I present an analysis of syllable-initial and syllable-final consonantal clusters, and also take up again the question of the complex segments.

7.5.1. **The sonority hierarchy**

Most attempts to characterize the structure of syllables, especially for languages like German which allow relatively elaborate clustering of consonants, have incorporated some notion of *sonority* and of a *sonority hierarchy*. This concept, dating back to the phonetics of Sievers (1901) and Jespersen (1904), depends on the observation that syllables are built up in such a way that segments at the edges of syllables are of relatively little inherent loudness or perceptibility, while segments in the centre of a syllable will be of much higher inherent loudness. Obviously, a stop such as [p] is of low sonority in that practically no noise is audible, at least during the closure period, while a vowel [a] is of high sonority in that no obstruction is blocking the airstream. It is no accident, ac-cording to this reasoning, that [a] will always be found in the centre of a syllable, whereas [p] will (almost) never be found in this position, but (almost) exclu-sively at the left or right margin of a syllable. Segments occurring between the central (core) segment of a syllable and the peripheral segment will be inter-mediate in inherent loudness, according to this model. The consonant [l] would be an example of an intermediate segment; and indeed, both [pla] and [alp] are possible syllables in German, while *[lpa] and *[apl] are not. Note that in the former two syllables the assumed inherent loudness decreases monotonically from the vowel to the consonant [p]. This is not the case in the structures marked as ill formed, which thus cannot be monosyllabic. The property of 'loudness' used here is generally referred to as *sonority*.

The next step in this reasoning involves setting up a complete and exhaustive hierarchy, which specifies the sonority value for each segment or segment class. A syllable may then be seen as a pattern of *crescendo* (increasing sonority) from the beginning towards the peak or nucleus, followed by a *decrescendo* (decreasing sonority) from the peak to the end of this syllable. The combinatorial possibilities of segments within a syllable are then considerably, though not totally, explained by reference to the sonority hierarchy.[72]

Plausible though this argument may appear, the details are far from settled. While various proposals for a sonority hierarchy (or, equivalently, consonantal strength) have been discussed (see, with reference to German, Vennemann 1982; 1988; Wiese 1988*a*: 91; Butt 1992; Hall 1992*b*: § 2.6), a number of problems remain open. First, the phonetic basis of the alleged sonority difference between segments is questionable. While Ladefoged (1982: 222) presents a diagram representing sonority values for a number of sounds, it has been stated repeatedly that no coherent phonetic evidence for sonority differences exists. But if the sonority hierarchy is based on observations of possible or preferred phonotactic patterns alone, then the explanation of the phonotactic patterns by reference to the sonority hierarchy obviously proceeds in a vicious circle.

Secondly, even if this problem can be solved, it is not obvious whether there is a single sonority hierarchy which holds without exception. It is in fact easy to show that both 'sonority reversals' and 'sonority plateaus' (in the terminology of Clements 1990) exist. For example, most specific proposals claim fricatives to be more sonorous than plosives. This would seem to make sense phonetically, and is consistent with the fact that many combinations of a fricative and a plosive appear syllable-finally, as in *Luft*, *Kiosk*, *Herbst*. But plosive-fricative sequences would be predicted to occur in syllable-initial position. The affricates /ts/ and /pf/ partially bear out this prediction, but the reverse combinations, for example /sk, ʃt/, are more frequent, as is in fact demonstrated in (132) below.

Also, plosive-fricative sequences are common syllable-finally both in monomorphemic and in complex words. Such words containing these sequences would constitute either direct counterexamples to this variant of the sonority hierarchy or lead to the conclusion that the initial fricatives are extrasyllabic. Extrasyllabic segments should not 'count' for the sonority hierarchy as well as for all other syllable-internal constraints.

Here I will pursue yet another analysis. In §§ 3.2.1.2 and 7.5.2, it is proposed that a plosive and a fricative can be joined under a single skeletal position. Given that such combinations appear in either order both initially and finally in the syllables of German, a safe conclusion is that sonority is not calculated on the segment level, but on the skeletal level. On this level, complex segments count as one single unit, and it is this unit which is relevant for the combinatorial potential, at least in German.

On this view (proposed by Hall 1992*a*, *b*) obstruents form one single class in

---

[72] Clements (1990) gives a valuable discussion of all relevant concepts and proposals on sonority and the sonority hierarchy. I also follow the theory developed by Clements in breaking down the uniform sonority hierarchy into a number of featural constraints, although the details differ.

the sonority hierarchy. A sonority hierarchy for German can then be represented as in (120), where the direction of the arrow indicates decreasing sonority. High vowels are lower in sonority than other vowels, since in diphthongs it is always the non-high vowel which appears in the nucleus. /ʀ/ is more sonorous than /l/ since *Kerl* is a possible monosyllabic word, while *Keller* is not, but becomes disyllabic by the means of schwa epenthesis. More generally speaking, while /ʀl/ constitutes a possible syllable-final sequence, /lʀ/ never does.

(120) Sonority hierarchy for German

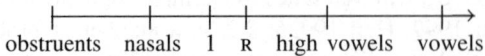

```
├──────────┼───┼─┼───────┼──────────┼──→
obstruents  nasals  l  ʀ  high vowels  vowels
```

A very similar hierarchy is proposed by Clements (1990). It ranks obstruents, nasals, liquids, glides, and vowels as being increasingly sonorous. Note, however, that the liquids /ʀ/ and /l/ seem to be different in sonority (as demonstrated *by Kerl* vs. *Keller*), and that glides are usually not in the V-position of the syllable because of their lesser sonority rank than a neighbouring vowel. That is, we may want to predict the glide status of a vowel from its sonority value.

Applying the sonority hierarchy in (120) to German words and syllables reveals no really glaring violations (see (122) and (128) below), given that affricates and the structures called suffricates (i.e. items such as /pf/ and /sk/) are assumed to be single units, and that final extrasyllabicity of a coronal obstruent is assumed for *Markt*, and many similar items. One additional problematic case would be provided by the initial clusters of [kv] and [ʃv], as these clusters involve two obstruents, in the latter case even two fricatives. But, fortunately, these sequences have been argued to be realizational variants of underlying /kʊ/ and /ʃʊ/ in § 7.4.1.2. Being analysed in this way, they do not constitute evidence against the sonority hierarchy. This also makes reference to voiceless vs. voiced obstruents (cf. Vennemann 1988; Eisenberg 1989) in stating the sonority hierarchy superfluous. As the voicing opposition does not generally lead to a difference in clustering potential, this is a welcome result. In fact, [kv] and [ʃv] are the only syllable-internal obstruent clusters in which a voicing difference (nonvoiced consonants outside voiced ones) is possible.

Note, finally, that this reasoning implies, unexpectedly, that the sonority constraint does not apply to the surface of syllables, but to more abstract structures. The sonority-based description is thus not part of the phonetic description of syllables, but part of the characterization of phonological patterning.

The overall conclusion from these considerations is that a sonority hierarchy provides at best a necessary, but certainly not a sufficient, condition on the shape of syllables. Further constraints must be formulated. Assuming that the sonority hierarchy given in (120) is the correct one, we can also proceed to break it up into featural constraints on syllable-internal phonotactics. Adapting a proposal made by Giegerich (1992a: 152) for English to the present featural system, I suggest the hierarchical feature structure in (121), in which, at each level, one value is subdivided further by another feature. The resulting classes are those specified in the original sonority hierarchy (120) and are exemplified in the bottom line of the tree.

(121)

This approach contrasts with those which postulate an autonomous multivalued feature of sonority (Selkirk 1984a) and relies on independently needed features instead. As we would expect from an adequate feature system, the classes required for the sonority ranking can be expressed as natural classes (conjunctions of feature specifications). Note finally that [obstruent], and not [consonantal], is the feature providing the most basic distinction for German phonotactics: a non-obstruent is always placed inside an obstruent in a syllable, and while all non-obstruents can form a syllabic nucleus, an obstruent cannot.

7.5.2. Consonant clusters and complex segments

This section covers some problems of detail in the description of German phonotactics. In doing this, I presuppose, first, that the general patterning of segments within syllables is covered by a sonority-related description as presented in the preceding section, and, secondly, that there are extrasyllabic consonants, namely /t/, /s/, /st/, or /d/ in word-final position. It is important to bear in mind that I explicitly deal with the phonotactics of the syllable only, and not of the morpheme. Morpheme structure conditions exist (see Wurzel 1981: § 7.5; Kloeke 1982; or Hall 1992b for a treatment of some of them), but are set aside here.

The discussion of German syllable structure in § 3.2 has revealed as a minimum assumption that the language allows maximally two consonants each in the onset and in the nucleus or coda position. We now turn to a more detailed study of the combinatorial possibilities within syllable onsets and codas.

In (122), only those consonants are mentioned which occur in at least one consonantal cluster in an onset. Most obstruent-obstruent clusters are disregarded here because they are either, like /pf/ and /ts/, seen as affricates,[73] that

---

[73] There are more phonetic affricates (such as [dʒ, ks, ps]), but these never form clusters with other consonants. Other obstruents not found in initial clusters are /z, X, h, ʔ/. On /h, ʔ/, the laryngeals, see the discussion on page 268.

is, as one complex segment as introduced in § 3.2.1.2, or are, more controversially, interpreted as suffricates with a mirror-image shape (/ʃp, ʃt, sk/). Initial voiceless /s/, as in *Slalom* or *Smoking*, is also ignored at this point, but will be discussed below. Bracketed pluses are those which are decidedly rare in Modern Standard German. Nevertheless, if they occur, they do not seem to be changed in the direction of some other cluster or broken up or simplified in some way. Examples for these rare but real clusters are *Pneu, Twist, Khmer, Xaver, Gmünd, Wladimir.*

(122) Onset clusters

	Sonorants				Obstruents	
	l	R	n	m	s	v
Obstruents						
p	+	+	(+)	−	+	−
t	−	+	−	−	−	(+)
k	+	+	+	(+)	(+)	+
b	+	+	−	−	−	−
d	−	+	−	−	−	−
g	+	+	+	(+)	−	−
f	+	+	−	−	−	−
v	(+)	+	−	−	−	
ts	−	−	−	−	−	+
pf	+	+	−	−	−	−
ʃ	+	+	+	+	−	+

Of the (few) obstruent-obstruent clusters, the two cases /ps/ and /ks/ may be subsumed under the category of affricates, that is, as complex segments. The remaining cases, /tv, kv, tsv, ʃv/, are familiar from the discussion of back vowel desonorization in § 7.4.1.2 above. The analysis established there for /kv, ʃv/ may be extended to the rarer forms /tv/ and /tsv/. The two arguments for an underlying /ʊ/, namely the lack of a following /ʊ/ and the variability in the realization, apply to the two new clusters as well. This argumentation, then, has taken care of all obstruent-obstruent clusters in (122). Remaining clusters are all sequences of obstruents plus sonorants, which are predicted as well formed by the sonority hierarchy in (120).

However, this sonority hierarchy also admits sonorant-sonorant clusters with increasing sonority (such as /n l/, /m R/, /l R/) as well formed. As these never occur (in onsets!), we must find some means of excluding them. It appears to be sufficient to state that the first position in an onset must be filled by an obstruent. The template in (123) states this restriction. The sonority restriction as formulated in (120), (121) will then correctly determine that the second onset position can only be filled by a sonorant (if filled at all).

(123)   O

         C   C
         |
         R: [+ obstruent]

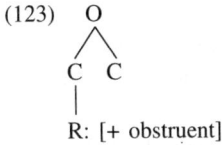

It remains to account for the unacceptable cases, the minuses in (122), within the obstruent-sonorant clusters. Inspection of the table reveals that many such gaps may arise from a principle ruling out identical place specifications for the two consonants. This is formulated as a filter in (124). Note that, first, the crucial condition here is identical specification of the Place node only, and that, second, the presence of two C-positions ensures the non-applicability of the rule to affricates (which are, as we have seen, homorganic in the unmarked case).

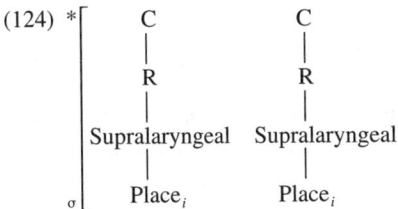

(124) *⎡   C   C
       ⎢ | |
       ⎢   R   R
       ⎢ | |
       ⎢ Supralaryngeal   Supralaryngeal
       ⎢ | |
      σ⎣   Place$_i$ Place$_j$

Template (124) correctly rules out many of the non-occurring clusters in (121), namely those repeated in (125a–c). Note that for most of these homorganic clusters at each of the major places of articulation there exist similar clusters, which are non-homorganic and at least marginally acceptable, see (125 d, e).[74] However, the clusters repeated in (126) and (127) are homorganic, but nevertheless well formed (although marked in the case of (126a)) and therefore provide apparent counterexamples to the claim made in (124).

(125) a. *[pm, bm, fm, vm]
      b. *[tl, dl, zl, tn, dn, zn]
      c. *[kŋ, gŋ]
      d. Khmer, Tmesis
      e. [klug, blau]

(126) a. [sl, sn]
      b. [ʃl, ʃn]

(127) [kʀ, gʀ]

One possible solution might be to note that the alveolar consonants /l/ and /n/ are treated in Chapter 6 as being unspecified for features under the Place node. Furthermore, /ʀ/ is also not specified, according to the model of underspecification developed in § 6.3.1, for any of the articulators [Labial], [Coronal], [Dorsal]. Recalling that the distinctive features of /ʃ/ and /ʀ/ are, respectively, [high] and [low], which are dependent on [Tongue Position], we can simply conclude that features under the node of Tongue Position do not count in determining homorganicity. The clusters in (126) and (127) are therefore not real

---

[74] Initial clusters involving [ŋ] are impossible in principle, a fact providing one of the arguments for the non-phonemic status of this segment, see § 7.3.5.

counterexamples to (124) (which requires identity of the Place node!) or the observation behind it. Again, this argumentation on the regularities involved in onset clusters relies on the assumption that the regularities are computed on underspecified representations.

The problem with the account just outlined is that it is unable to explain the fact that (125*b*) lists a number of alveolar onset clusters which are ill formed. The underspecification approach implies the absence of the Place node in these cases as well. The different behaviour of /s/ and /ʃ/ with respect to allowing homorganic clusters may actually be taken as an argument for interpreting these segments as being extrasyllabic. I argued against initial extrasyllabicity in § 3.2.3, but the argumentation is actually one against extrasyllabicity with respect to the fricative-stop clusters discussed below in this section.

We now turn to coda clusters, which are presented in (128). In general, they are more systematic than onset clusters, as analysis of the table reveals. The hypothesis expressed through the sonority hierarchy proposed is more directly verified by the coda clusters than it is by the onset clusters. Note that the segments in the first row and the left-most column are ordered according to their ranking on the sonority hierarchy. It appears from (128) that, generally speaking, elements with higher sonority values may cluster with elements lower on this hierarchy, in this order. Question marks in cells in (128*a*) are those combinations which would be expected to exist were it not for the Nasal Assimilation rule (60). Rare clusters such as those in *Ramsch* (ImʃI), *hübsch* (IpʃI), *orange* (IŋʃI), or *Lisp* (IspI) are simply included in either of the two tables.[75]

(128) Coda clusters

a. sonorant-obstruent clusters

	R	l	m	n	f	s	ʃ	ç	p	t	k
R	−	+	+	+	+	+	+	+	+	+	+
l	−	−	+	+	+	+	+	+	+	+	+
m	−	−	−	−	+	+	+	−	+	+	−
n	−	−	−	−	+	+	+	+	?	+	?
ŋ	−	−	−	−	−	+	+	−	−	+	+

b. obstruent-initial clusters

	R	l	m	n	f	s	ʃ	ç	p	t	k
s	−	−	−	−	−	−	−	−	(+)	+	+
f	−	−	−	−	−	+	−	−	−	+	−
X	−	−	−	−	−	+	−	−	−	+	−
ʃ	−	−	−	−	−	+	−	−	−	+	−
t	−	−	−	−	−	+	+	−	−	−	−
k	−	−	−	−	−	+	−	−	−	+	−
p	−	−	−	−	+	+	+	−	−	+	−

---

[75] A truly marginal cluster is IʃkI, occuring in the surname *Waschk*. The dorsal fricative is transcribed as Içl in the first row, as it always surfaces in this way after consonants (see § 7.3.3), but as IXI in the first column, as it may occur in various allophones. In general, note again that (128) covers syllable-final clusters, but not morpheme-final clusters.

As for the sonorant-obstruent clusters, we note that [ŋ] may occur with extrasyllabic alveolar consonants, if the nasal is derived from underlying /ng/, or with [k], if the underlying nasal is /n/ (cf. [dɪŋs] *Ding+s*, [oʀaŋʃ] *orange*, [lɛŋt] *läng+t*, [baŋk] *Bank*). Other sequences are predicted not to be possible. The gaps found for the sequences */mç/ and */mk/ point to an interesting restriction confirmed by the obstruent clusters: of the three articulators [Labial], [Coronal], [Dorsal], only [Labial] or [Dorsal] can be found within a coda, while [Coronal] can be combined with one of the others. Assuming that [Coronal] is absent by virtue of underspecification, we can formulate this restriction by simply saying that a coda allows only one of these articulators. Again, this claim presupposes that /ʀ/ is not specified for such an articulator.

The obstruent-obstruent clusters of (128*b*) demonstrate, first, the correctness of the prediction made by the sonority hierarchy that sonorants cannot follow obstruents syllable-finally. Second, the unlimited possibility of adding /s/ and /t/ to another obstruent is obvious.[76] This observation provides the argument for the extrasyllabic status of these coronals in word-final position. As extrasyllabic elements, these segments simply do not count in phonotactic matters such as those described by the sonority generalization. The small number of other possible clusters falls largely under the category of affricates and suffricates, as first discussed in § 3.2.1.2, and to be taken up again here.

As these two types of complex segments have opposing sequential values for the feature [continuant], sequences of two stops (/tp/ etc.) or two fricatives (/sç/ etc.) are generally excluded, unless the final segment is extrasyllabic. The remaining gaps found are of two basic types. One set, that of /fk, Xp, kf, pç/, can conveniently be related to the coda principle suggested, namely the exclusion of two specifications of [Labial] and [Dorsal] in a single coda. What remains to be done is to find some way of excluding the sequences /fp, Xk, kʃ, kç, ʃp/, which are mostly homorganic. There is no principled explanation available at present, so I will leave this matter here. In general, finding interesting constraints which contribute to a principled description of the data is perhaps more important than formulating a number of rules which, in arbitrary ways, aspire to cover the whole ground of the phonotactic patterns, an area which has, as we have seen, fuzzy boundaries in any case.

The account presented here for both onset and coda clusters crucially depends on the correctness of the claim that fricative-stop clusters are suffricates which take up only a single skeletal position and consequently count as a single unit for the purposes of determining sonority values. Here is another argument demonstrating the special nature of these obstruent-obstruent clusters. As (129) shows, such segment clusters can, in principle, occur both in syllable-initial and in syllable-final position. This observation with respect to the affricates (129*a*) is one of the classical arguments for their special (i.e. monophonemic) status; but the fact that it equally holds for the mirror-image sequences in (129*b*) provides a strong case for the equivalence of these two types of sequences. Furthermore,

---

[76] The one general restriction is that gemination, i.e. doubling a consonant, is not possible.

no obstruent-sonorant clusters have the property of occurring in both orders syllable-initially and syllable-finally. For these, we almost invariably find the mirror-image sequences of the initial clusters in final position (a fact complicated by the differences found with respect to homorganicity; see discussion above).[77]

(129) *a.* /ts/: Zahn ~ Latz
       /pf/: Pfad ~ Kopf
       /tʃ/: Cembalo ~ Rutsch
       /ks/: Xaver ~ Lachs
       /ps/: Psychologie ~ Schnaps
   b. /ʃp/: Sport ~ _____
       /sp/: Spezies ~ Lisp
       /ʃt/: Stein ~ Gischt
       /st/: Stil ~ List
       /sk/: Skat ~ Kiosk
       /ʃk/: (Schkeuditz ~ Waschk)

The symmetrical behaviour of both kinds of obstruent-obstruent clusters receives a straightforward account on the basis of two assumptions: first, they are associated with a single C-position; and secondly, syllable constraints are computed over such skeletal positions, and not over segments. In summary, we have arrived at a description of three-consonantal clusters in German in which a template such as that given in (130), admitting three syllable-initial consonants, is not necessary. Rather, a number of independent principles of phonotactics, such as the sonority hierarchy, the admittance of complex onsets, and the branching segment structure allowed for obstruents interact to yield this type of onset.

(130) C C C V
         |
       [ʃ]

Finally, another aspect of detail for the descriptions of fricative-stop clusters, to which I now turn, is the distribution of initial /s/ vs. /ʃ/. (131*a*) lists all possible combinations of word-initial /s/ and /ʃ/ with following consonants, with (131*b*) providing an example for each combination. Given that initial /s/ and /ʃ/ have very similar distributions, but that there are combinations which are marked compared to other similar combinations, I highlight the combinations judged to be marked cases by the use of bold face.

(131) *a.*

	p	b	f	v	m	t	d	s	z	n	l	ʃ	ʒ	j	ç	k	g	x	ɣ	ŋ	ʁ	h
s	+		+		+	+				+	+					+					+	
ʃ	+			+	+	+				+	+					+					+	
ts				+																		

   b. Spezies, Sphäre, Smoking, Stil, Snob, Slogan, Skat, Sri Lanka
      Spiel, schwer, Schmuck, Stadt, Schnee, schlecht, Schkopau, Schrank
      zwei

---

[77] The last example in (128*b*) is bracketed because of its extreme rarity. Note, however, that even here there is again no distinction between initial and final /ʃk/.

In (131), four groups of combinations with /s/ and /ʃ/ can be distinguished. (We will ignore initial /ts/ here because of its limited occurrence.) There are combinations of /s, ʃ/ with sonorants, combinations of /s, ʃ/ with voiceless plosives, and combinations of /s, ʃ/ with /f, v/. All other combinations are ill formed.

The following generalizations seem to hold for the sequences marked as possible in (131a), with some noticeable exceptions:

If the cluster consists of two obstruents, both members are voiceless, /ʃv/ and /tsv/ being the only exceptions. From the analysis of back vowel desonorization developed in § 7.4, it follows that [v] is underlyingly not an obstruent.

The initial fricatives studied here cannot be combined with any other fricatives, except for combinations with /f/ and /v/. The model allowing for suffricates admits the combination with non-fricatives. However, the cluster /sf/ as in *Sphäre* remains as an example of a cluster defying any description so far. Fortunately, it is decidedly rare and can be set aside as an exception.

In relation to the lexical inventory of German, combinations starting with /ʃ/ are unmarked, except for /sk/, where /ʃk/ is clearly the marked variant. The latter is attested for two town names only, *Schkeuditz* and *Schkopau*. Nevertheless, as there is no tendency to change this cluster into a different one, I regard it as a marked, but real element of German phonotactics. Words with initial /s C . . . / are largely loan-words, and are probably felt to be somewhat foreign by native speakers. Nevertheless, the clusters /sl, sr, sn, sm/ are not normally assimilated towards /ʃl, ʃr, ʃn, ʃm/.

In (132a), the overall pattern for the remaining fricative-stop clusters is exemplified again. Different from what was just noted on /s, ʃ/ combinations with sonorants, there is a strong tendency to replace marked clusters by their unmarked counterpart.

(132) a. Unmarked	Marked	b.		ʃ p	s p
Spiel	**Sp**ezies	high		+ −	− −
Stein	**St**il			ʃ t	s t
Skat	**Schk**euditz	high		+ −	− −
				s k	ʃ k
		high		− +	+ +

In (132b), the values for the feature [high] are given for the segments in question. On the basis of these featural descriptions proposed earlier, it turns out that the patterns represented in (132a) are far from arbitrary. If /p/ and /t/ are distinguished from /k/ as being [− high], this featural analysis offers the possibility to formulate a straightforward rule of *Dissimilation* for the syllable-initial fricative-stop clusters. /ʃ/ appears before a following stop precisely if this leads to a difference in the value for [high]. Otherwise, nothing happens; see /sk/. The rule needed, formulated in (133), adds [+ high] to the featural structure of /s/ if the following stop is [− high].

(133) Obstruent Dissimilation

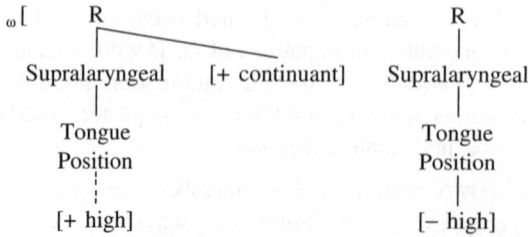

As far as is known at present, the context for this rule is provided, once again, by the phonological word. This ensures its application in the words noted above; on the other hand, the rule will not apply word-internally as in *fest, feist, Fenster,* and *Raspel,* regardless of the precise placing of the syllable boundary in the last two examples.[78] Again, if (133) cannot apply, the initial fricative will surface, unchanged, as [s]. This is also the case for non-assimilated loans as in (131*b*). Their marked nature consists precisely in the non-application of rule (133); underlyingly, they contain a fully specified /s/ or /ʃ/. A matter of formal interest is that we have here an example of a dissimilation rule which must still be formulated as a rule *adding* information. Generally, dissimilation rules are supposed to be rules *removing* pieces of phonological representation; see (2) in § 7.1.

One final case of a very restricted phonotactic environment to be discussed here is provided by /h/: in § 3.3, I claimed that /h/ can occur only foot-initially. But there is a further, very strong, constraint on the distribution of this sound which has been noted (Seiler 1962) but has not received systematic treatment: this segment never clusters with any other consonant. This fact is unexpected, given that all other fricatives have a wide range of possibilities for building clusters, as we have just seen.

The problem is not solved by assigning /h/ to a major class different from the one chosen here. Wurzel (1970; 1981) and Kloeke (1982: 53) follow *SPE* in classifying /h/ as [– consonantal, – sonorant], that is, as a glide. But glides, in contrast to /h/, may be followed or preceded by other consonants, so this classification does not provide the grounds for a principled solution. It is, however, important to realize that [ʔ] follows the same constraint: it occurs only foot-initially (§ 3.3.1) and allows no other consonant to precede or follow it within the same syllable. That means that we are obviously dealing with a constraint on the segments classified as laryngeals in § 6.3.3.

The feature structure assumed here, in particular the subsegmental hierarchy introduced in § 3.1, provides at least a partial explanation of this phonotactic gap. The most significant property of the class called laryngeals in terms of featural representation is the *absence* of any information on their place features. In the present framework, we may take advantage of this property and conclude

---

[78] A number of dialects such as Hessian or Swabian have a wider context of application for this rule, and may in fact dissimilate /s/ before /t, p/ in any context.

that the phonotactic potential of segments is calculated on the basis of features not present in the case of [h, ʔ].

As [h, ʔ] are assumed to be devoid of all supralaryngeal features, that is, without a Supralaryngeal node, there is no way to calculate their place features. But as we have seen in the discussion of coda clusters, whatever the correct account of the combinatorial possibilities of consonants in a German syllable is, it will have to check on features appearing as structure below the Supralaryngeal node. In the absence of such information, the laryngeal sounds must remain isolated in the onset of the syllables in which they may appear.

Alternatively, and perhaps more interestingly, we may even speculate that laryngeals do not appear within onsets, and thereby syllables, at all. They lack the featural information required for syllabification. Rather, they are only admitted within the higher category of the foot. I shall leave this line of reasoning open for the time being.

7.6. PHONOLOGY OR PHONETICS?

The preceding discussion has implicitly assumed that the rules treated are indeed phonological rules, while other rules may belong to a different domain, that of phonetics. I now discuss some ways of treating the phonology–phonetics distinction and some phenomena which are not easily classified as being phonological or phonetic in nature. The difficult question of the relation between phonetics and phonology as two related but separate aspects of human speech and language will not be treated here as a general topic; see, for example, Pierrehumbert (1990), Browman and Goldstein (1990), and Keating (1990) for discussion.

One plausible criterion might be to see that the phonological system involves discrete (usually binary) categories, and the phonetic system non-discrete ones. In the discussion of vowel length in § 7.2.2, this criterion was in fact used to argue against a phonological rule of vowel shortening which would assign an arbitrarily large number of length values to some vowel of German.

Continuing this discussion, consider, first, how length is treated in the pronouncing dictionaries. These works necessarily face the problem of deciding on a proper transcription of length, since they do not intend to transcribe strictly predictable aspects of phonetic form. While Duden (1990) transcribes only two degrees of length, Krech et al. (1982) have a convention of notating *half-length* by means of a single raised dot (ˈ). Thus, compare the following transcriptions, taken from this latter work.

(134) *a.* [maˈlaːriaˈ], [ˈmaltaˈ]
　　　　 b. [naturaˈlɪsmʊs], [naˈturalizaˈtsioːn]
　　　　 c. ˈHannɪoˈ], Hanˈnɪoːlver, Hannɪolveˈraner

Krech et al. (1982: 27) declare the vowels to be half-long in the following two contexts: first, word-final vowels are half-long, as shown in (134a) and with the

exception of final schwa; secondly, a vowel occurring at least four syllables before the accented syllable, as in *Meteorologie* [ˌmeˈteoʀoloˈgiː] or *Bibliothekar*
[ˌbiˈblioteˈkaːɐ] or the example in (134*b*). But in fact there is neither phonetic
nor phonological evidence for half-long vowels. Phonetically, there are more
than three degrees of length, and phonologically, half-long vowels seem to have
no special status whatsoever. What is right about the proposal is that the length
of vowels in open syllables depends on stress, and that vowels in phrase-final
position may be lengthened somewhat. (Of course, final vowels of isolated words
are actually phrase-final.)

Assuming half-length as part of the phonological distinctions would furthermore imply a rather roundabout derivation of vowel length in a number of
complex words. Thus, in *Pol*, the vowel would be long, and in *pol+ar* it would
be shortened, while in *Polarisation* the corresponding vowel would be half-
lengthened again. For all of these reasons, I conclude that the actual length of
vowels must be a matter of phonetic specification. To introduce a notion of half-
length is to do nothing more than recognize the situation.

A potential phonological rule of Modern Standard German which is not
covered in this chapter is that of *aspiration*. It is well known that voiceless
plosives are either aspirated ([pʰ, tʰ, kʰ]) or not. Since this difference never
contributes to a distinction of morphemes, it is regarded as an allophonic difference or a result of a feature assignment by rule, whatever the perspective of the
theory happens to be. More problematic, however, is the decision about which
segments are aspirated and which are not. Generally, the voiceless stops /p, t, k/
are said to be aspirated if standing alone in the onset of a syllable. That is,
neither in [ʃtaːp] *Stab* nor in [tʀaʊm] *Traum* does [t] acquire aspiration. But
furthermore, aspiration is not categorial; as Kohler (1990*b*: 49) remarks, 'the
aspiration is strongest before a stressed vowel, weakest in unstressed function
words'. Current feature theory has no means of expressing such a scale of
aspiration, and it is questionable whether it should have those means. Consequently, I have refrained from formulating a rule of aspiration. For a recent
phonological treatment of aspiration, see Hall (1992*b*: § 2.4.2). Hall argues that
stops are categorially aspirated foot-initially and before a pause, that is, in the
final position of an intonational phrase. In positions which are syllable-initial but
not foot-initial, Hall allows for a phonetic assignment of aspiration.

Another area of competition between phonetics and phonology is that of
deletion. While there are deletion phenomena which seem to fall under the
rubric of phonological rules by all sensible criteria, other cases may call for a
different treatment. In particular, there may be partial deletions not easily captured in phonology. Examples are provided by the gradual reduction of schwa
syllables with a syllabic sonorant. A schwa syllable can be reduced to such an
extent that it is not always clear whether the syllable still exists; see *rennen* or
legen which may be rendered mono- or bisyllabically. [ʀɛnn̩] or [ʀɛn], [leːgn̩]
or [leːŋ] are the usual transcriptions of such words, but in actual fact matters

may well be more gradual. Phonology might be well advised to stay clear of an area displaying gradience in the presence or absence of a category.

Consider, next, the place assimilation which can be observed for dorsal consonants. Dorsal Fricative Assimilation (§ 7.3.3) finds a parallel in the articulatory position for the realization of /k/ in various contexts. It is well known that [k] is articulated in the palatovelar region if preceded or followed by a front vowel, as in *Kind*, *dick*, *Kegel*, and *Ecke*. If followed or preceded by a back vowel, the place of articulation is considerably further towards the back, even in the uvular region. Interestingly, this variation is often acknowledged, but it is not treated in the same way as Dorsal Fricative Assimilation. This stems, perhaps, from an implicit judgement or an intuition that the two variations are not of the same kind or nature. It may be the case that the assimilation of the dorsal fricative is categorial, while the dorsal stops (i.e. /g/ and /k/) assimilate in a more gradual and variable manner.[79] If this difference could be verified phonetically, it would provide good evidence for treating Dorsal Fricative Assimilation as a phonological, and the assimilation (rather, coarticulation) of [k] as a phonetic process.

This conclusion might receive confirmation from another criterion, that of the language-dependent nature of a process: the fronting of [k] is a result of a process which is not under the control of either the speaker or the sound system of German. Rather, it derives from universal phonetic tendencies of coarticulation. The assimilation of the dorsal fricative, on the other hand, is a language-specific regularity of Modern Standard German. Even a language closely related to German like Dutch behaves differently (the dorsal fricative is always uvular, see Booij 1995: ch. 2). This would mean that Dorsal Fricative Assimilation as found in Modern Standard German cannot be derived directly from phonetic laws (although it may be grounded in these), and that it can and must be learned or suppressed by speakers of a particular language.

[79] This also offers the possibility that it is *perception* which is categorial for Dorsal Fricative Assimilation, while *production* is similar or equal for stops and fricatives.

WORD STRESS, COMPOUND STRESS, PHRASE STRESS

This chapter discusses some properties and regularities of stress in German, both for simple words and for more complex expressions. It is obvious that speakers of German perceive *patterns of prominence* in their speech, such that some parts of a linguistic unit are judged to be more prominent than other parts within the same unit. It also turns out, as we found in Chapter 4, that such patterns play a role in the grammar of German. A number of word-formation rules can be shown to depend on stress in various ways, as witnessed by the possible bases of the two allomorphs *+heit* and *+keit*. The following discussion will be largely concerned with the nature of this prominence relation and the rules according to which the prominence values are assigned. It will also be necessary to ask what the units are between which the stress relation exists. The discussion in the main part of this chapter starts from monomorphemic words (§ 8.2), proceeding to derived words and compounds in § 8.3, and then turning to phrasal stress in § 8.4.

8.1. REPRESENTATIONS FOR STRESS

A first and crucial presupposition for the treatment of stress concerns the nature of stress itself. It will be assumed that the perception of patterns of prominence referred to above rests on a system of *prominence relations* between various phonological units perceived by speakers of a language. This remark seems necessary since the phonetically elusive status of stress has led some authors to question the very existence of stress, especially of word stress. Phonetically, stress is realized in varying combinations of pitch, duration, intensity, and quality, sometimes only to a miniscule extent. But judgements of stress patterns are nevertheless possible and quite reliable for speakers of German, and are at least as valid as judgements on segmental matters.

A second presupposition concerns the representation and notation to be used. For stress, this is an unsettled question, and some phonological models of the past have treated stress in a less than convincing way. *SPE* phonology formalized the structuralist notion of stress levels as a segmental feature [n stress]. Each vowel is assigned a value for this feature, where the values contrast with all other (binary) features in being taken from the set of natural numbers.

To illustrate, in discussing German compound stress Wurzel (1970) assigns to each vowel a value for the feature [stress]. Following the proposal of *SPE*, this (and only this) feature has the natural numbers as the range of values, that is, a value may be 0, 1, 2, ... '0' is the value of completely unstressed vowels, and stress decreases as the numbers increase from '1'. (1) illustrates the resultant stress representations. The example also illustrates the cyclic nature of stress assignment assumed for complex words. With the addition of each additional part of a compound, a new stress value (always 1) is assigned. There is a convention that under such conditions the stress value of all non-primary stresses is reduced by one.

(1) *a.* $\overset{1}{\text{rot}}$ $\overset{1}{\text{wein}}$ $\overset{1}{\text{punsch}}$ $\overset{1}{\text{trinker}}$ $\overset{0}{}$ isolated lexical items

    b. [$\overset{1}{\text{rot}}$ $\overset{2}{\text{wein}}$]   compounding

    c. [[$\overset{1}{\text{rot}}$ $\overset{3}{\text{wein}}$] $\overset{2}{\text{punsch}}$]   compounding

    d. [[[$\overset{1}{\text{rot}}$ $\overset{4}{\text{wein}}$] $\overset{3}{\text{punsch}}$] $\overset{2}{\text{trinker}}$] $\overset{0}{}$ compounding

The problems inherent in such an approach were pointed out early, for example by Bierwisch (1968) and Liberman and Prince (1977). Not only is [stress] the only multivalued feature within such a theory; its use also leads quickly to a large succession of increasingly higher (or lower) stress levels, such that nobody is able to discern the differences expressed by the notation. Finally, the stress rules responsible for the assignment of the correct stress values are inexplicably different from other phonological rules. While the latter rules were regarded as statements manipulating the binary values of features, stress rules enumerate increasingly higher values of n.

Numerical notations—of which the IPA notation, introduced in § 1.4, is a variant, in that it recognizes three or four degrees of stress—has been displaced in phonological theory by a relational treatment of stress. Liberman and Prince's seminal paper (1977) is the first of a number of proposals according to which stress is assigned, first, to units larger than single vowels, and in which, secondly, the stress feature itself is of a different nature.[1] Unfortunately, several versions of this approach exist, but there is no decisive argumentation for one proposal rather than the other.

The stress representation I use here rests on two fundamental assumptions. First, stress is a particular relation between the independently motivated units of prosodic structure. Thus, the stress relation can be found between syllables, feet, phonological words, or phrases. These are exactly the units of the prosodic hierarchy as introduced in Chapter 3. Secondly, and perhaps more controversially, stress is defined exclusively as a relational notion. Whenever we judge one unit to be *stronger* than its *weak* counterpart, we may say that the stress

---

[1] Hogg and McCully (1987) and Goldsmith (1990) provide introductory texts to these various theories. A thorough overview of descriptions of German word stress and the problems involved is given by Jessen (1994).

relation exists between these two units. Otherwise, stress must remain unde-fined. This model of stress representation is similar to that of Nespor and Vogel (1986), who also define prominence relations between prosodic categories. It is more distantly related to theories of the so-called grids or constituents-plus-grids, as used by Halle and Vergnaud (1987) or Hayes (1990). However, as a strictly relational notion, the present concept of stress is not compatible with an arbitrary number of grid marks on a single stress unit.

In (2), I illustrate this notion of stress with a representative set of examples from the word domain. The binary stress relation is notated by using the labels *s(trong)* and *w(eak)*. First, in (2a) the stress relation is undefined, since none of the units has a counterpart with which it can be compared.[2] Compare this to (1a), in which every item receives a stress value, even if monosyllabic.

(2) Prominence relations and prosodic categories

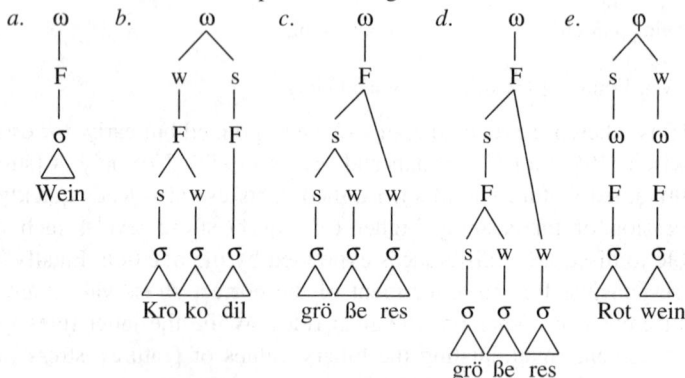

Words such as *Kroko'dil* in (2b) must display two feet, because the foot was defined in § 3.3 as either consisting of a single syllable or a sequence of a strong syllable followed by syllables with weaker stress. The hypothesis that phono-logical feet in German cannot be iambic (i.e. weak-strong) will be crucial in the discussion below. Notice that in (2b) the stress relation is expressed twice: once as the left-strong relation between the foot-internal syllables, and once as the right-strong relation between the two feet. I also remind the reader that bisyllabic words with final stress (as in *I'dee*, *Pa'last*) were argued in § 3.3.1, on the basis of the glottal-stop distribution, to contain two feet.

It is often claimed that there are two types of words with a bisyllabic strong-weak pattern: one in which the second (weaker) syllable is completely unstressed, and one in which this syllable carries some amount of secondary stress. Thus, words such as *Arbeit* and *Demut* supposedly contrast with *Hering* or *König*, which have unstressed final syllables (see e.g. Giegerich 1985). Analogously, suffixes such as *+bar*, *+haft*, *+heit* are claimed to carry stress, which shows up

---

[2] Of course, *Wein* as a phonological word may receive stress if it embedded in a larger unit such as a compound or a phrase. But the point remains that a monosyllabic unit cannot receive stress if stress is interpreted as strictly relational.

as secondary stress in *sicht+bar*, *glaub+haft*, *Neu+heit*, while *+lich* or *+isch* are unstressed. Accordingly, the two diminutive forms possible for *Kind* are notated as *'Kindchen* and *'Kind‚lein*, with an unstressed and a stressed suffix, respectively (Giegerich 1985: 107).

Speakers of German, however, have no clear intuitions that the stress pattern of *sicht+bar* is different from that of *sicht+lich*. Similarly, it is unclear whether there is a factual basis for a distinction in terms of secondary stress between *'säuber+lich* (strong-weak-weak) and *'säuber+‚lich+es* (strong-weak-strong-weak), as Eisenberg (1991: 56) claims. I will therefore dispute the reported distinctions and withdraw to the more cautious position that no such distinctions exist. The question will be relevant in the treatment of stress shifts in § 8.5.2.

The uncertainty with respect to the foot structure in sequences of syllables *after* the syllable bearing word stress has already been discussed in § 3.3: is there a secondary stress in, say, *'eigent+(‚)liche* or *'Lehre(‚)rinnen*? Similarly, is the stress pattern of *'unstatt‚haft* really different from that of *'unüblich*? I have adopted the position that secondary stresses do not exist in post-tonic positions within words. There is a long tradition confusing matters of stress with those of vowel status.

The present proposal then also entails that weak syllables in a foot are equally unstressed regardless of vowel quality. That is, *Inge* vs. *Inga* or *Bilder* vs. *Bildung* have equal stress patterns, the difference in the pairs being one of vowel quality alone. Usually, syllables containing full vowels are regarded as carrying some amount of secondary or tertiary stress. In the present model there is no place for this supposed stress distinction, which does not appear to fulfil any function for other regularities anyway.[3]

Assuming that the branching in prosodic structure is maximally binary, the two proposals given in (2c) and (2d) are reasonable attempts to represent stress within longer feet. A suspicious feature of (2c) is the unlabelled unit 's' dominating the first two syllables. Adhering to a strictly relational and binary model of stress necessitates such a grouping of two (or more) weak syllables. An alternative sometimes proposed in stress theory is the one in (2d). Here, an intermediate additional foot is introduced. This prosodic structure will not be used in what follows, since it assumes that a prosodic category such as the foot can contain a unit of the same category. Since in general this type of recursive structure is not found in prosody (syllables certainly do not contain syllables, etc.), descriptions such as (2d) will be rejected here. Additional solutions are available in principle, but will not be pursued for the moment, since nothing crucial in the treatment of German stress hinges on the precise internal form of polysyllabic feet. An obvious alternative would be to relax the binarity requirement of the stress relation and allow more than one weak sister to a strong node; see (42) in § 3.3.

---

[3] Note that schwa syllables are representationally different from full syllables in lacking a nucleus.

Two or more weak syllables following a strong one, as in (2c, d), cause another problem with respect to which metrical structure should be assumed. Such cases certainly exist in the stress system of Modern Standard German, since up to three schwa syllables may occur word-finally; see (3a). For full vowel syllables, the number of consecutive weak syllables seems to be restricted to a maximum of two, as in the examples of (3b) with initial stress. In longer words, there is also a tendency to have intermediate stresses which structure an otherwise unstructured series of syllables before the main stress by grouping them into feet containing two (or three) syllables; see examples in (3c) and the discussion later in § 8.3.1.

(3) a. ent'scheid+end+er+e, 'trocken+er+es
     b. 'Marzipan, 'Kimono, 'Talisman
     c. ˌBibliˌothe'kar, ˌMeteoˌrolo'gie

Finally, in (2e) the stress relation is illustrated with respect to the phonological words ω within a compound such as *Rotwein*. Here, the two phonological words (perhaps within the phonological phrase) are *strong* and *weak*, respectively.

Another formal ingredient of the stress model used below is *extrametricality*. Following Hayes (1982) and others, I will argue that certain prosodic units may be 'invisible' to stress rules. By analogy with extrasyllabicity, in which segments are outside syllables, syllables may stand outside the domain of stress. For a definition of extrametricality see (4a); in (4b) the notation for extrametricality, bracketing of the extrametrical unit, is indicated. Since extrametricality is used here to mark underlying entries, and since syllables are not part of underlying forms, root nodes of segments interpreted as extrasyllabic are marked in this way. This property will then be inherited by the respective syllable.

(4) Extrametricality
     a. 'A syllable is called *extrametrical* if it is ignored by the stress rules; that is, treated
         as if it were not there' (Hayes 1982: 227).
     b. Notation: (R)

It should be added that I follow the common assumption that extrametricality is restricted to a *single peripheral* unit of a domain.

8.2. SIMPLEX WORDS

Morphological structure and the influence of various affixes is one of the confusing issues in the German stress system. Therefore, the task of this section is to develop an account of stress for monomorphemic words. These words may be up to four syllables long in German and display a number of different stress patterns. This observation alone shows that word stress in Modern Standard German is not a simple matter. The regularities, which nevertheless exist, as we will see in a moment, are disrupted by the potential influence of syllabic complexity and/or vowel length. It is therefore necessary to discuss the influence of segmental and syllabic factors on stress assignment.

8.2.1. Vowel length and stress

The basic correlation between vowel length and tenseness was first discussed in § 2.3.1: long vowels are tense ([+ ATR]), and vice versa, with the exceptions of long /aː/ and /ɛː/, which are lax [[– ATR]]. Besides the two classes of vowels (long vs. short/lax), it is customary in Modern Standard German phonology to postulate a third class of vowels, those which are both short and tense. The three classes of contrastive vowels are illustrated in (5), following Wurzel (1981); see also Wurzel (1980), Kloeke (1982: § 1.2), Giegerich (1985: § 2.2.2), and Yu (1992b). The short vowels of class II presumably only occur in open syllables.[4]

(5) | *Short vowels I* | *Short vowels II* | *Long vowels* |
[– ATR]	[+ ATR]	[+ ATR]
Tenne	Te'nor	'Tenor
Mette	Metall	Metrik
locker	Biologie	Biologe
Kultus	kulinarisch	Kuli
Banken	Banause	Bake
Muster	Museum	Musen
dich	direkt	Diener
Syntax	Synagoge	Syrien

There can be no doubt that vowels in open syllables are longer if occurring in stressed syllables. But in the following, I will first argue that reference to vowel length is clearly insufficient to account for the stress variation found in German monomorphemic words. Vowel length is, at best, one of the factors involved. I will then continue the argument begun in § 7.6, that it is furthermore problematic to assume a binary length contrast within the group of tense vowels.

The class of 'short vowels II' is used, by the above-mentioned authors, to account for some of the stress differences found between words in German. The basic argument is that syllables ending in a short vowel are skipped by a stress rule such as that in (6).[5] Such syllables may be called light syllables. Rule (6) will stress the right-most non-light syllable in a word, but will not go beyond the third syllable from the right edge of the word, the so-called antepenultimate.

(6)   s
                     |
syllable → syllable /____((light syllable) light syllable)]_Word

---

[4] If it is correct that there is no tenseness distinction for the *a*-sounds, as I have argued in this study, the proposed distinction between the two classes of short vowels exemplified in (5) is even more problematic.

[5] The rule is taken from Giegerich (1985: 31). 's' means strong, as in the present notation.

Rule (6) will correctly single out the stressed syllable in the following examples—assuming that the vowels following the stressed syllable are all short. In (7), such short (tense) vowels, that is, the short vowels ɪɪ in (5), are illustrated with respect to their putative role in stress assignment. While the final vowels in (7a) are assumed to be short, the final vowels of (7b) are long and therefore attract stress. Words in (7c) have short vowels in the two final syllables. Stress must therefore fall onto the antepenultimate syllable.

(7) a. *Penultimate stress*   b. *Final stress*   c. *Antepenultimate stress*
     'Gummi   Etu'i   'Mimikry
     'Konto   Bü'ro   'Risiko
     'Akku   Ta'bu   'Kakadu
     'Kaffee   Ca'fé   'Kanapee
     'Sofa   Tra'ra   'Mafia

However, reference to vowel length is not sufficient to account for the stress differences in the word pairs given in (8) and (9). Word pairs in (8) have identical final rhymes, but initial stress in (8a) and final stress in (8b). (9) gives examples of those words which can be found with either initial or final stress ('*Dromedar* or *Drome'dar* etc.), though sometimes individual speakers have a preference for one of the alternatives. In both types of stress difference, reference to vowel length is clearly not sufficient to account for the placement of stress.

(8) a. 'Fazit   b. Gra'phit
     'Konsul   Mo'dul
     'Amok   Ba'rock
     'Ballast   Da'mast
     'Fakir   Pa'pier
     'Turban   ur'ban
     'Pinguin   Herme'lin
     'Tenor   Te'nor
     'Konsum   Kon'sum

(9) Dromedar
    Ballast
    Leopard
    Marzipan
    Motor

Stressed vowels in the left-hand column of (10) must be underlyingly long, since otherwise they would not receive stress according to the theories discussed here. In the right-hand column, their shortened counterparts appear, see [i] in [mu.zi.ka:lɪʃl.[6] There is, thus, good evidence for a process of vowel shortening. If the theory relying on underlying short and tense vowels were correct, not only

---

[6] I label these vowels as 'shortened' and not as 'short' here, since it is not clear in general that these vowels are as short as the short lax vowels. Ramers (1988) finds that tense vowels in pre-stress position tend to be as short as lax vowels in this position (cf. *Li'belle* to '*Lippen*); but in post-stress position tense vowels ('*Heimat*, '*Almosen*) are shortened only minimally. I discuss vowel shortening in § 7.2.2.

shortening, but also the converse, namely lengthening of short tense vowels under stress is required (see the rule stated in Wurzel (1981: 931), which relates length to stress by requiring a vowel with the feature [α stress] to have a length value [α long]).

(10) Har'pune   harpu'nieren
     Mu'sik   musi'kalisch
     Pa'rade   para'dieren
     Bio'loge   Biolo'gie

In other words, a complex net of relations between long and short vowels appears, where successive lengthening, shortening and lengthening of vowels is not impossible. In addition, the underlying value for the length of a vowel is hard to determine. What remains constant on the surface, however, is the relationship between length and stress for tense vowels.

A final argument for the basically quantity-insensitive nature of stress in German may be derived from words containing /aː/ as the final vowel. Suppose that it is indeed the case, as claimed in § 2.3.1 and by many authors before, that long and short /a/ are identical in their quality, that is, can only be distinguished by length (or some similar prosodic feature). There is a rather large set of words illustrated in (11), in which the final syllable contains the vowel /a/, with stress either falling on this syllable or not. The fact that a consonant follows the final /a/ makes it even more difficult to use extrametricality of final segments or lightness of syllables as the factor responsible for the stress differences.

(11) *a. (Initial stress)*   *b. (Final stress)*
        Turban   urban
        Balkan   Organ
        Japan   Kumpan
        Teheran   Koran
        Safran   Sopran
        Jordan   Sudan
        Pelikan   Vulkan
        Scharlatan   Titan

A quantity-sensitive rule will wrongly assign stress to the final syllable in all cases. Note also that the final syllables in (11*a*) are clearly distinct from those with really short vowels, as [ban] or [kan] in *Bann* and *Kanne*, or in *Ban'kett*, *Kan'tate*. To transcribe *Balkan* as [bal.kan] would hide this fact. If vowel quality for *a*-sounds is identical, only length (or some other prosodic property such as syllable-cut) can be made responsible for the distinction between the final vowels in (11*a*) and the vowels in *Bann, Kanne*. And furthermore, there is no way to treat the *a*-sounds in (11*a*) vs. (11*b*) as being different phonologically.

To demonstrate the frequency of such pairs, I have restricted the examples in (11) to those with final /aːn/. Other final consonants exist, however, as in *'Monat* vs. *Spi'nat*. In fact, as the vowel shortening rule (19) of § 7.2.2 may apply to *'Monat*, there are the two phonetic forms ['moː.naːt] and ['moː.nat], again demonstrating that unstressed vowels are not uniformly short.

The conclusion to be drawn and to be confirmed by the observations on loan-words below is that surface vowel length in German does depend on stress, but that stress does not depend on length. In other words, contrary to what most authors have proposed so far, a description of German word stress should work, on the assumption that stress in MSG is quantity-insensitive.[7] As far as the Vowel Shortening rule is concerned, I have argued in §§ 7.2.2 and 7.6 that we are dealing with a phonetic rule which is able to specify various (and certainly more than two) degrees of length.

Another correlation exists between schwa syllables and stress: schwa syllables are always unstressed. This correlation between syllabic status and stress is estab-lished by postulating here that only syllables containing a nucleus can bear stress. Since schwa syllables, in the present model, do not have a nucleus and are defec-tive in this sense, they are skipped in stress rules. Furthermore, if stress is forced to appear on a schwa syllable, there must be a nucleus corresponding to a full vowel (see the discussion on alternations between schwa and full vowels in § 7.2.3).

8.2.2. Marked and unmarked stress patterns

Under the closely related working assumptions that open syllables have long vowels and that tense vowels are uniformly long phonologically, a rather straight-forward account of the stress system of Modern Standard German can still be developed.

The outcome of an experiment concerning stress placement is pertinent here. In the pilot experiment, German speakers with no knowledge of Japanese read Japanese words and their stress placement was recorded.[8] Seven words each from the classes of bisyllabic, trisyllabic, and quadrisyllabic words were used. The num-bers in (12) refer to the number of speakers (a total of 10) using the respective stress pattern. The results clearly corroborate the evidence from data in (7) and (8), that stress on the penultimate syllable is the dominant pattern. More marked patterns occur, but there is regularity even in the exceptions: only the last and the antepenultimate syllable may receive main stress in this way.

(12)

Bisyllabic		Trisyllabic		Quadrisyllabic	
'Nippon	10	To'yota	10	Mitsu'bishi	10
'Honda	10	Su'baru	10	Kawa'saki	10
'Nissan	10	Sap'poro	10	Yoko'hama	10
'Tenno	10	Ya'maha	10	Naka'sone	10
'Nikko	10	Mi'shima	10	Take'shita	10
'Geisha	10	Wa'seda	10	Naga'saki	10
'Shogun	4	O'saka	9	Hiro'shima	5
Sho'gun	6	'Osaka	1	Hi'roshima	5

[7] Eisenberg (1991) and Kaltenbacher (1994) also argue for the basically quantity-insensitive nature of German word stress.

[8] This experiment was conducted by Katharina Micha. The subjects had no knowledge of Japanese and were familiar with various subsets of the words used. They were also not aware that stress was in the focus of the experiment.

Other Japanese loan-words in German follow the same pattern; see *Kami'kaze, Hara'kiri, Ka'buko, 'Sushi,* and *'Sake,* with which *Samu'rai* and *Kara'te* are in potential contrast as these latter words can bear final stress.

While most of the words are (or were at the time) reasonably well known, others, such as the word *Waseda,* were not known to any speaker. In Japanese, it receives pitch accent on the final syllable. Similarly, *Hi'roshima* with antepenultimate stress is not influenced by the Japanese stress pattern, since it happens that in Japanese this word has no tonal accent on any syllable. The point is that the stress patterns found above are practically independent of the Japanese patterns.[9] And, as for other languages, the treatment of loan-words in German is an area yielding rich insights into the phonological system.

It is therefore reasonable to assume that, in the absence of other sources of information on the stress patterns, speakers of German apply the stress rules for German to these words. We will now turn to these rules, which must express the unmarked nature of penultimate stress, with ultimate stress and antepenultimate stress as marked but possible deviations from the basic pattern. Note also that for the words with other than penultimate stress, there are always speakers using penultimate stress. This observation provides further confirmation that penultimate stress is indeed the unmarked case.

If it is correct that stress in these Japanese loan-words reveals properties of the German stress patterns, then it is also noteworthy that penultimate syllables receive word stress even if ending in a vowel. This contradicts claims by Vennemann (1991*a, b*; 1992) and Hall (1992*b*: § 1.2.4) to the effect that penultimate syllables (in the unmarked case) only receive main stress if not ending in a single vowel. The stress patterns emerging from (12) make such claims problematic. Note also the large number of words such as *La'metta* which have closed syllables only because of ambisyllabicity of /t/. If ambisyllabicity is not much more than a phonetic effect, then it could hardly interact with the stress patterns. Even if ambisyllabic consonants are a result of 'deeper' phonological rules, as Ramers (1992) argues, they are always the result of predictable rules, and therefore cannot regulate the appearance of exceptional stresses. The previous analyses which claim that closed syllables attract stress, while open syllables do not, are also unexpected on universal grounds, as stress systems are normally assumed to operate in just the reverse way (see Hyman 1985).

A statistical preference for penultimate stress in case of closed penultimate syllables certainly exists, as well as a preference for antepenultimate stress in the case of an open penultimate syllable; but it seems likely that the reason for this tendency may lie in the languages from which the respective words are borrowed. For Latin and Italian, for example, it is true that closed penults attract stress on a regular basis, while open penults do not (cf. *Ve'randa* to

---

[9] Japanese has a system of pitch (tone) accents which is phonologically and phonetically quite different from the stress accents found in Germanic languages. For example, words may be without any such pitch accent. For discussion see, e.g., Pierrehumbert and Beckman (1988).

'Kamera). Consequently, many words borrowed from these languages show this pattern.[10]

Undoubtedly, there are, besides the stress rules, other more or less well-pronounced tendencies at work, assigning words to stress patterns. This means that, by analogy with other, similar, words, a word may be likely to bear a specific stress pattern, marked or unmarked. For example, words ending in the vowel /a/ do not receive final stress, except in the case of exclamation words such as *Hur'ra, Tra'ra*. However, I would argue that all relevant observations express tendencies which may be violated to a greater or lesser extent. Furthermore, all such patterns are within the scope of stress rules, to which we now turn.

8.2.3. **Stress rules**

The two major descriptive observations made so far are that one of the last three syllables in a word receives main stress; and that, of the three potential locations of stress, penultimate stress is regular. Traditionally, word stress in German was considered word-initial—a view which gradually changed beginning with Kiparsky (1966). Kohler (1977: 191) notes the default status of penultimate stress. An additional generalization, as discussed in many previous sections, is that schwa syllables are never stressed.

The following system of stress rules for Modern Standard German can be proposed on the basis of these observations. The rules as formulated in (13) rely on the presuppositions that phonological words derive by a morphology–phonology mapping as discussed in § 3.4; that syllables and feet are built up on the basis of segmental information within a phonological word; and that stress rules (just like other rules) cannot perform structural changes. Furthermore, (13a) ensures that bisyllabic feet are constructed whenever possible. Otherwise, a monosyllabic foot is created. That is, the formulation of the foot rule (13a) expresses the claim that bisyllabic feet are preferred against monosyllabic ones. The right-to-left directionality of the Foot rule is motivated by the fact that the preferred binary foot is found at the right, and not the left, edge of words; see the trisyllabic words in (12). The Word rule (13b) simply makes the right-most foot stronger than preceding ones. Finally, the Adjunction rule (13c) allows for feet longer than two syllables. Again, the question how to characterize the internal structure of such feet is left open.

(13) Stress rules

    a. Foot rule Going from right to left, construct feet of the type F, or, if not possible,

       F.

                                             s   w

    b. Word rule In a phonological word, the right-most foot is strong.

    c. Adjunction rule Adjoin remaining syllables in a minimal way as weak members of a foot.

---

[10] Given the cultural background of Germany, knowledge of Latin and Romance languages is much more widespread than knowledge of Japanese. It is therefore not surprising that only words from the former languages are often (though by no means always) borrowed along *with* their stress patterns.

The rules in (13) are similar to those proposed by Liberman and Prince (1977: 266), Hayes (1981), Kiparsky (1982*a*, *b*), and Giegerich (1985: § 2.1.3) but are not identical to any of these precursors. Let us first see how these rules derive the stress pattern given for the Japanese loan words (12). In (14), *Fujiyama* represents a word displaying the unmarked stress patterns, while *Kimono* represents the type of word showing antepenultimate stress. Note that each of these words consists of a single phonological word. (The vowels in the underlying forms are probably all long, as argued in § 8.2.1, but this point is irrelevant and therefore ignored here.)

(14) Derivations of stress patterns

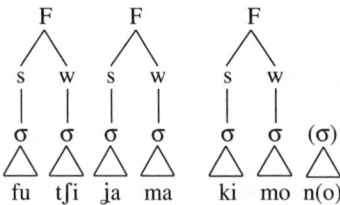

a. /futʃijama/   /kimon(o)/   underlying

b. F   F   F   Syllabification, rule (13*a*)

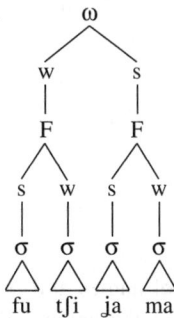

c.   ω   rule (13*b*)

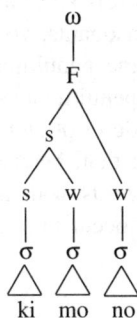

d.   ω   rule (13*c*)

The other type of marked stress diagnosed above is final stress. I propose to accommodate this pattern by associating the final vowel, underlyingly, with a foot.[11] Recall that, in the general case, prosodic units are assigned by rule. But

---

[11] See Kiparsky (1982*b*: 50) for the suggestion that exceptional stress may be represented by specifying the foot in the lexical entry.

it is not surprising that the foot may be more than a redundant prosodic unit. In the discussion of prosodic morphology in Chapter 4, several regularities demonstrated how foot structure may be called upon as a condition for morphological rules. In doing so, the present proposal does not expand the machinery available in the lexical morphology. (15) gives a relevant example, again from Japanese loan-words. The leading assumption here is that a foot cannot be altered once it is present via the underlying form or through the application of rule (13b). It is for this reason that the final, pre-specified foot remains monosyllabic. The Word rule (13b) ensures that this foot receives word stress. However, another foot must be built upon the first two syllables.

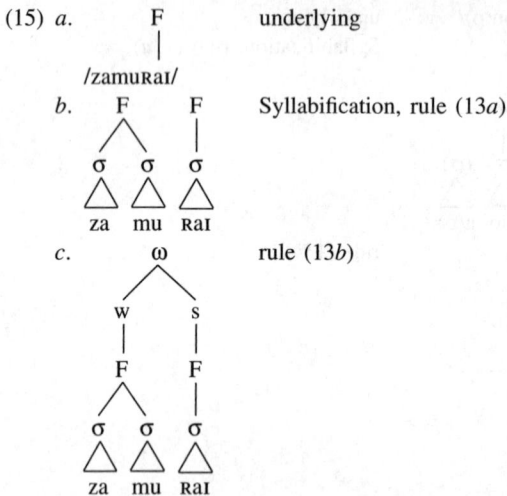

(15) a.   F   underlying
                   |
        /zamuRaɪ/

     b.   F   F   Syllabification, rule (13a)
            /\ |
           σ   σ   σ
           △   △   △
          za mu   RaɪI

     c.   ω   rule (13b)
                    /\
                  w   s
                  | |
                  F   F
                 /\ |
                σ σ   σ
                △ △   △
               za mu RaɪI

In (16), I present a few more words, from the domain of names and common nouns, where extrametricality of final vowels accounts for the antepenultimate stress pattern. Again, because of final consonants, vowel length cannot be held responsible for the pattern. Also, while the penultimate syllables in (16a) are open, the words in (16b) contain a closed penultimate syllable, one which should attract word stress according to the stress description by most authors (Giegerich 1985; Vennemann 1991a, b; 1992). Note that, here, we concentrate on monomorphemic words. Within this group, words with antepenultimate stress are not very common. Nevertheless, they can occur in principle with both open and closed penultimate syllables.

(16) a. E'lisab(e)th, 'Barbar(a), 'Theod(o)r
     b. 'Talism(a)n, 'Turand(o)t, 'Sigism(u)nd

In the system proposed here, exceptional stress on the final syllable is represented by the *existence* of a stress marker (the foot) for this syllable, exceptional stress on the antepenultimate syllable is represented by the *absence* of the final syllable for the calculation of stress through the means of extrametricality. In each case, only the final syllable is subject to such a lexical treatment. This can be related to a *peripherality condition* (Harris 1983) which disallows any markings of extrametricality or prosodic structure except on domain-final units.

The use of extrametricality here is different from that in the stress theories of Hayes (1981; 1982) and of others. In these theories, final segments or syllables are often made extrametrical by a rule. Such an approach seems unwarranted for German, given that there is no identifiable phonological or other factor which would make antepenultimate stress a predictable matter. Note, for example, that we cannot make extrametricality dependent on the number of word-final consonants. Words without (*'Risiko*), with one (*'Marzipan*), or with two (*'Leopard*) such consonants can all display antepenultimate stress.

The stress rules (13*a, b*) together with the two mechanisms of marking exceptional stresses ensure that the *Three-syllable rule* (Kiparsky 1966: 69; Vennemann 1992: 406: 'Only the last three full syllables can be accented') is obeyed. Note that bisyllabic words, such as those in (17), are examples from a not very large group of native words, but to which many names (*'Mozart, 'Richard*) could be added. In earlier accounts, these were generally regarded as problematic, since stress was predicted to fall on the final syllable, either because of its heaviness or because of the fact that a stressable syllable would remain even if the final consonant were assumed to be extrasyllabic: see *Arbei(t)* with a final diphthong.[12] In the present account, penultimate stress for these words simply follows from the stress rules. As noted at the beginning of this chapter, a stress distinction for the final syllables in these words is questionable.

(17) 'Arbeit, 'Heirat, 'Demut, 'Predigt, 'Kiosk

Counter-examples to the regularity of the Three-syllable rule can be provided from the set of words comprising grammatical terms.[13] Words such as *'Maskulinum, 'Femininum, 'Nominativ, 'Akkusativ* have three final syllables following the main stressed syllable. Note that the terms in question are always in contrast to some other term of the same grammatical dimension (gender, case, etc.). This means that an implicit notion of contrast is responsible for this deviation from the regular stress pattern. Vennemann (1992: 407) refers to this deviant pattern as 'paradigm accent'. The change of stress is not confined to quadri-syllabic words alone; note the stress difference between the grammatical term *'Aktiv* and the adjective *ak'tiv*. Not all grammatical expressions follow the pattern; see *Ge'rundium, Gerun'divum*.

Another set of deviant expressions are words prefixed by the non-native negative prefix *in*+: *'il+legitim, 'ir+regulär, 'in+kompetent*. Main stress falls on the prefix, which happens to be the fourth syllable from the right in the examples given. Again, this can be explained by reference to an implicit contrast between the negative form and its positive counterpart responsible. We note, without

---

[12] We have been using two separate notions, one of *extrasyllabicity* and one of *extrametricality*. While they refer to different domains, there may be a connection between these two types of externality.

[13] These words are all morphologically complex, but as I show in the following section, such derived words follow the restrictions of the stress rules.

exploring possible consequences, that the native negative prefix *un+* also attracts main stress precisely when the meaning of the prefixed word is the negation of the base (see § 8.3.2). Stress on the ante-antepenultimate syllable can result: *'unergiebig, 'unregelmäßig*.

Finally, it is instructive to observe the derivation of stress patterns for words containing schwa syllables. The word *Abenteuer* (with initial stress) has been mentioned as the only monomorphemic word violating the *Dreisilbengesetz*, the constraint that stress must fall on one of the three final syllables in a word (see p. 285). However, in this word, two syllables are schwa syllables in the sense used throughout this book: ['aː.bən.ˌtɔʏ.ɐl]. The first of these schwas cannot be derived by Schwa Epenthesis (§ 7.4.2 (98)), and therefore will be an underlying X. The second schwa need not have an underlier, and indeed should not, as it alternates with zero, see *Abenteur+er*. These considerations motivate the underlying form in (18a).[14] Assuming further that an empty X will not be syllabified in the lexical phonology (or lead to reduced, unstressable, syllables) the stress pattern is completely regular and proceeds according to (18b, c). Crucially, stress feet are not assigned to those parts of the string which later surface as schwa syllables. On the two full syllables of the word, a completely regular stress pattern can be constructed.

(18) '*Aben,teuer*
      a. /aːbXntaʏʀ/   underlying
      b.   F   Syllabification, rule (13a)

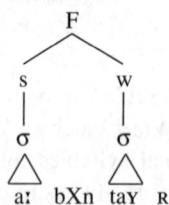

      c.   F   Schwa Epenthesis, rule (13c)

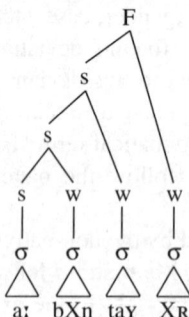

As shown in (18c), the description implies that there is only one stress foot in this word, contrary to what is implied by the stress marks in the transcription given above. The correctness of this claim is unclear. It is completely legitimate, however, to separate the effects of full vs. reduced vowels in the syllables from

---

[14] As argued in § 6.1.1, /aʏ/ must be the underlier of the diphthong [ɔʏ].

those of stress. The presumed secondary stress—that is, the claim that [tɔY] in ['aː.bən.ˌtɔY.ɐ] bears stronger stress than the neighbouring schwa syllables—may well be an artifact, a confusion resulting from mixing up stress and vowel quality.

8.3. COMPLEX WORDS

8.3.1. **Stress in suffixed words**

In accounting for stress in words derived by suffixation, two basic phenomena have to be dealt with: first, while some suffixes carry word stress, others never do, and a third class alternates with respect to stress.[15] Secondly, the stress patterns on an affix base can change or remain unchanged, depending on the particular affixation.

To illustrate briefly these two points, we consider first the alternations in (19). Similar examples are given in § 5.2.1. If a suffix is attached to one of the left-hand form, it takes word stress, while the stress pattern on the preceding base can change drastically. Under further suffixations, stress patterns are altered repeatedly. Often, suffixes which carry word stress when word-final lose this property under further suffixation. (Below, I discuss the suffix +*or*, which behaves in exactly the opposite way.)

(19) ˌDe'kan ~ ˌDeka'n+at
　　　ˌNa'tion ~ ˌnatio'n+al ~ ˌNation+a'l+ism+us
　　　ˌPro'dukt ~ ˌproduk't+iv ~ ˌProdukˌt+iv+i'tät
　　　ˌso'zial ~ ˌSozia'l+ist

Of course, not all suffixes behave in the way illustrated here. A list of relevant suffixes is given in (21*a*). All of the suffixes given there bear word stress if in word-final position, but not necessarily in non-final position. For the derivation of a form, that of ˌProdukˌt+iv+i'tät, see (26) below.

The properties of derivational suffixes with respect to stress can be summarized as in (20). Needless to say, a stressed syllable influences stress. Therefore, only three different types are instantiated. Stress neutral suffixes are all class II suffixes as listed in (4) of § 5.2.1.

(20)　　　　　　　　　　Stressed
　　　　　　　　　　　　+　　　−

		Stressed +	Stressed −
Stress-affecting	+	-ier	-er
	−	———	-lich

The large class of stress-affecting suffixes is equated in Chapter 5 with the class of class I (or root) affixes. It has different subsets which influence stress

---

[15] As the suffixes always carrying word stress are those which are not followed by any other suffixes of this type, we have no way of knowing whether they behave identically to the suffixes of the third type, those which alternate, usually under the influence of another stressed suffix.

in various and sometimes complicated ways. Suffixes in (21*a*) all bear word stress if in final position. Various stress-affecting suffixes, which are sometimes or always unstressed, are given in (21*b*). These are discussed to some extent below.

(21) Stress-affecting suffixes
    a. +ant, +at, +ie, +ist, +ur; +al, +är, +iv; +ier
    b. +er, +or, +ik; +isch

An additional class of relevant suffixes is provided by +*um*, +*us*, +*a* (and possibly others). These may co-occur with penultimate or antepenultimate stress as shown in (22). Of course, the existence of roots with the antepenultimate stress pattern (see examples of the *Kimono* type in (16)) almost leads to the prediction that suffixes of this type might exist as well, as roots and suffixes are treated in basically identical ways with respect to their status as lexical entries.[16]

(22) *a.* +um   'Stadi+um, 'Opi+um ~ Refe'rend+um, Al'pin+um
    b. +us   'Radi+us, 'Stimul+us ~ Pazi'fism+us, Euka'lypt+us
    c. +a   'Afrik+a, 'Pergol+a ~ Mar'tin+a, Vi'ol+a

Without going into details, I want to propose that *extrametricality* is operating in the case of those suffixes displaying antepenultimate stress. But what is extrametrical (i.e. invisible to stress rules) is not the suffixal vowel, but the vowel in front of it. That is, the vowel /i/ in the many words which pattern like those on the left in (22) and a number of other vowels is extrametrical, leading to antepenultimate stress under suffixation of suffixes which are themselves not marked for carrying stress. The extrametricality of this vowel seems to be independent of whether it is part of a suffix, as perhaps in *Stud+i+um* or in *Amer+ik+a*. No such suffixal vowel is present in words such as *Stimul+us*.

In (23), the effect derived from some of the stress-affecting (but unstressed) suffixes is illustrated. Note that stress in the right-hand examples invariably falls on the last syllable before the final suffix +*er* or +*isch*, regardless of the position of stress in the base. Schwa syllables are again exceptional; see '*Zauber+er* or '*maler+isch*.[17]

(23) *a.* 'Japan ~ Ja'pan+er, A'merik+a ~ Ameri'k+an+er
    b. 'Kanon ~ ka'non+isch, 'Arab+er ~ a'rab+isch

This pattern suggests that stress can be assigned to words in total disregard of the stress pattern of the base. For confirmation of this view, note the stress patterns on the words given in (19) with stress-attracting suffixes. Here, the stress patterns on the respective bases are completely reorganized after suffixation. There does not seem to be evidence that stress assigned in earlier cycles leaves behind any traces.

We must now account for two seemingly contradictory facts: on the one

---

[16] As suggested in § 4.1.1, these two categories are different in that suffixes carry a subcategorization frame ensuring that they do not occur on their own (as 'free morphemes' do).

[17] A counter-example to this observation is represented by '*norweg+isch*. But see *ka'nad+isch*, *brasil'ian+isch*.

hand, there is good evidence that attachment of stress-attracting suffixes requires the prior application of stress rules. Note, for example, that some of these
suffixes require a particular stress pattern on their base; see in particular the
discussion on stressed +*ei* in § 4.1.1.[18] This fact then provides one of the main
arguments for a cyclic application of the stress rules. On the other hand, the
same suffixations may lead to stress patterns radically different from those
given for the bases.

In § 5.1, the notion of the cycle in phonology was introduced. Cyclic phonology assumes that phonological rules apply to a representation with a hierarchical
structure from 'the inside out'. This means that a larger constituent becomes
available to phonological rules only when all of its subconstituents have been
subjected to the relevant rules. In consequence, information provided by rules on
an early cycle can be input to rules operating on a later cycle. This model, then,
can account for the stress sensitivity of some affixations.

On the other hand, some method of ignoring stress derived on previous cycles
is needed. Halle and Vergnaud (1987) and Halle and Kenstowicz (1991), following Liberman and Prince's (1977: 300) rule of 'deforestation', make the basic
assumption that *stress erasure* takes place in the cyclic domain of phonology,
while stress preservation is found in the non-cyclic domain. Adapting this proposal slightly to the present model of the lexicon, let us assume that each
reapplication of stress rules in the *root* (level 1) domain is preceded by the complete erasure of metrical structure assigned previously, while in other domains
all stress representations already present may not be altered. In consequence,
there are either no stress rules in these other lexical domains (as is the case for
word stress), or the rules (such as the Compound Stress rules discussed in § 8.4)
can only *add* to the representations already present.

Stress erasure in level 1 also provides an explanation of the following contrast
between stress-neutral and stress-affecting suffixes. In derived words containing
the latter class of suffixes only, the *Dreisilbengesetz* established in § 8.2 holds
as well as it does for simplex words: word stress is never found further to the
left than on the antepenultimate syllable. Thus, the pattern exemplified by
Journa'l+ist, *Pro'fess+or*, *'Stadi+um* exhausts the possibilities. No main word
stress anterior to the antepenultimate position ever occurs in these words. In this
respect, this class of derived words is exactly parallel to underived words. Stress
erasure prior to a re-application of stress rules can explain this fact, as the
application of the stress rules stated in (13) can only lead to final, penultimate,
or antepenultimate stress—given the existence of exceptional markings for final
and antepenultimate stress by a foot or by extrametricality. (The need for stress
erasure on the respective bases arises because of the distribution of secondary
stresses; see discussion of examples in (27).)

---

[18] If +*ei* is treated as a level 2 suffix, one could argue that all prosodic dependencies are such that
they require an assignment of word stress at level 1, available as input for level 2 morphology.
However, as +*ei* carries word stress itself, I assign it to level 1. Under this view, stress assignment
at level 1 must be cyclic.

Stress-neutral suffixes, on the other hand, can often lead to a stress pattern in which main word stress is not on one of the final three syllables. The examples in (24) can be further expanded by the affixation of a plural suffix /n/, to be realized as a schwa syllable. This pattern strongly suggests that level 1 morphology interacts with word stress, while level 2 morphology does not. Since level 2 morphology is independent of word stress, then, in the current derivational framework, word stress is derived prior to the operation of this part of morphonology.

(24) 'Frei+heit+lich+keit, 'Arbeits+los+ig+keit, 'Wissen+schaft+ler+in

The stress model is applied to each of the two types of suffixes: compare the derivation of *'Arbeits+los+ig+keit* in (25) to that of *Produkt+iv+i'tät* in (26). In the derivation of *'Arbeits+los+ig+keit*, we note that two of the suffixes lead to the creation of their own phonological words, due to their CV-shape (25*b*, *f*), while the remaining suffix, +*ig*, does not satisfy this condition. However, since no difference in stress is detectable between these two types of suffix, I assume that each is subject to the Adjunction rule (13*c*).

(25) *'Arbeits+los+ig+keit*[19]

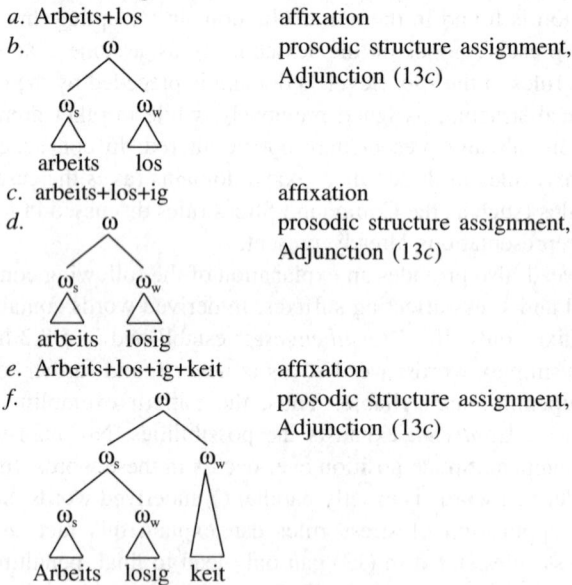

    a. Arbeits+los   affixation

    b. ω prosodic structure assignment,
                                    Adjunction (13*c*)

        ω_s ω_w

       arbeits los

    c. arbeits+los+ig   affixation

    d. ω prosodic structure assignment,
                                    Adjunction (13*c*)

        ω_s ω_w

       arbeits losig

    e. Arbeits+los+ig+keit   affixation

    f. ω prosodic structure assignment,
                                    Adjunction (13*c*)

       ω_s ω_w

    ω_s ω_w

   Arbeits losig keit

The prosodic structure assigned in (25) is also a good illustration of the recursiveness needed for phonological words. But the important point in the present discussion is that, by contrast with the derivation of *Arbeitslosigkeit*, the stress in *Produkt+iv+ität* changes from one affixation to the next. Note that

---

[19] As +*los* and +*ig* are both level 2 (stem) suffixes, their respective bases are assumed to receive prosodic structure before the affixation. However, this is not important for current purposes. The origin of the *Fugen-s* in *Arbeits* is also irrelevant here (but see § 5.3.3).

all lexical entries involved here bear a final foot as a marker for the exceptional final stress.

(26) *Produkt+iv+ität* [ˌpʀodʊkˌtivi ˈtɛːt]

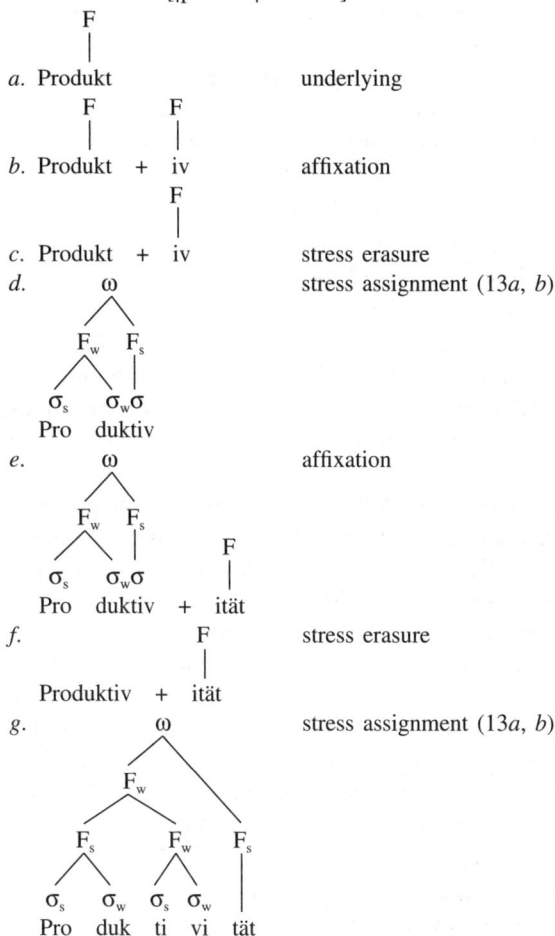

$$
\begin{array}{l}
\qquad\quad \text{F} \\
\qquad\quad | \\
a.\ \text{Produkt} \qquad\qquad\qquad \text{underlying}
\end{array}
$$

$$
\begin{array}{l}
\qquad\ \text{F} \qquad\ \text{F} \\
\qquad\ | \qquad\ | \\
b.\ \text{Produkt}\ +\ \text{iv} \qquad\qquad \text{affixation}
\end{array}
$$

$$
\begin{array}{l}
\qquad\qquad\quad \text{F} \\
\qquad\qquad\quad | \\
c.\ \text{Produkt}\ +\ \text{iv} \qquad\qquad \text{stress erasure}
\end{array}
$$

d.   ω   stress assignment (13a, b)

     F_w F_s

  σ_s   σ_wσ

  Pro duktiv

e.   ω   affixation

     F_w F_s   F

  σ_s   σ_wσ |

  Pro duktiv + ität

f.   F   stress erasure

               |

    Produktiv + ität

g.   ω   stress assignment (13a, b)

      F_w

   F_s   F_w   F_s

  σ_s σ_w σ_s σ_w

  Pro duk ti vi tät

The important difference is that word-stress rule (13*b*) may not be used in combination with the affixation of +*ig* and +*keit* in (25). Thus, word stress is not shifted, and is not located among the final three syllables. In contrast, the derivation in (26) requires the twofold application of this rule.[20] But it is only the rule assigning word stress which is thus restricted; all other rules assigning prosodic structures and the prominence (strong–weak) relations are free to apply whenever necessary. Otherwise, affixes of levels 2 (and 3) would in fact not be integrated at all into the prosodic structure of the respective word.

---

[20] Again, it is irrelevant for present purposes if stress is assigned prior to affixation of +*iv*. I have argued that such a pre-morphological cycle does not exist in Ch. 7 with respect to the rules of g-Deletion and Schwa Epenthesis.

A brief look at the secondary (i.e. non-primary) stresses in German words is also in order at this point. Secondary stresses within words are found to the left of primary stresses, which are, as we have seen, determined from the right edge of the word. Secondary stress then optimally occurs on each alternating syllable, counted from the location of main stress. In the distribution of secondary stress, there is thus further evidence that the bisyllabic foot is the preferred type of foot structure in German. Words with four or more syllables to the left of the main-stressed syllable optimally have bisyllabic feet in this string of syllables; see (27a) for further examples with four such syllables. (Numbers in (27) specify the number of syllables in each of the pre-tonic feet.)[21]

(27) *a.* ˌBibliˌotheˈkar, ˌZiviˌlisaˈtion, ˌafriˌkaniˈsieren, ˌEnzyˌklopäˈdie (2–2)
    b. ˌNatuˌralisaˈtion, ˌExisˌtenziaˈlismus (2–3)
    c. ˌMeteoˌroloˈgie, Akzeptaˌbiliˈtät, ˌOriginˌaliˈtät, ˌameriˌkaniˈsieren (3–2)

(27*b, c*) and (3*c*) above give examples with five syllables preceding the main-stressed one. In such a case, either a trisyllabic foot precedes the foot bearing word stress, and a bisyllabic one is formed word-initially, or the number of syllables in the feet preceding the main stress is reversed. Together, these patterns demonstrate that bisyllabic feet are preferred overall, while trisyllabic feet are preferred over monosyllabic ones. Additional evidence for the preference of trisyllabic over monosyllabic feet comes from the observation that three syllables occurring before the syllable bearing word stress are invariably grouped into a single pre-tonic foot; see examples in (28).

Furthermore, there is no evidence that the distribution of secondary stress is dependent on the segmental make-up of the respective syllables: the number of syllable-final consonants (0, 1, 2), or the presence of long vowels or diphthongs makes no difference, as (28) demonstrates. Secondary stress invariably falls on to the word-initial syllable, regardless of the syllable make-up. In (28*a*), all syllables are open, while in (28*b*) the second syllable is closed. In (28*c*), it is the first syllable which ends in a consonant, and in (28*d*), the third.

(28) *a.* ˌPhi.lo.so.ˈphie   ˌPho.no.lo.ˈgie
    b. ˌMe.lan.cho.ˈlie   ˌme.phis.to.ˈphe.lisch
    c. ˌFor.ma.li.ˈtät   ˌKan.di.da.ˈtur
    d. ˌEu.cha.ris.ˈtie   ˌma.ni.fes.ˈtie.ren

In summary, matters of foot structure (binarity) are clearly dominant in the patterning of secondary stress, while syllable structure does not seem to play any role. This, incidentally, may be taken as another argument for the quantity-insensitive nature of German word stress. Jessen (1994) reports phonetic evidence that secondary stress actually exists in German, refuting claims by Moulton (1962) that one of the differences between English and German is the non-existence of secondary stress in the latter language.

---

[21] For some words, an alternative distribution of secondary stresses to that given in (27) is possible; see *Enˌzyklopäˈdie*. In other cases, this seems impossible, as in **Masˌkuliniˈtät*. The details are not clear.

A further example of the intricacies of German word stress in derived words and of the way it yields to the kind of analysis proposed here, is given by the stress regularities of the noun-deriving suffix +*or*. This suffix belongs to the group of suffixes (21*b*) which affect stress, without carrying stress themselves. This is not the whole story, however, as (29) shows. Stress falls on the syllable preceding +*or* if there is no following suffix, or if the suffixes +*s*, +*chen*, or +*haft* follow. When other suffixes follow in the word, the +*or* receives stress unless the following suffix is stress-attracting, in which case, stress on +*or* is overridden; see (29*c*).[22]

(29) *a.* Pro'fess+or, Pro'fess+or+s, Pro'fess+or+chen, pro'fess+or+haft

　　　 b. Profes's+or+en, Profes's+or+in, profes's+or+en+haft

　　　 c. profess+o'r+al, Profess+o'r+at

The apparent paradox is that the suffix under consideration sometimes attracts word stress (29*b*), but causes word stress to fall on the *preceding* syllable under other conditions (29*a*). The question is whether there is a principled way of accounting for the difference found here.

We cannot simply make use of extrametricality for +*or*, and then claim that this extrametricality marking only holds word-finally. In this case, the ante-penultimate syllable should bear stress: *'*Profess+or* as in some of the words given in (22) above. Suppose then that +*or* is unusual among the class I suffixes in not being marked (by the presence of a foot) for word stress. Without any further stipulation, the stress patterns in (29*a*) are derived: stress is penultimate in the phonological word. (Recall that +*chen* and +*haft* are phonological words in their own right.)

Stress on +*or* as in (29*b*) is found only under further suffixation, in particular of plural +*en* and feminine +*in*. In other words, these two suffixes do not behave stress-neutrally here; they interact with the rules of word stress. For this reason, they must be grouped among the class I suffixes, a move which is independently motivated for +*en*, which was classified as an irregular plural suffix for non-feminines in the analysis of § 5.3.2. The stress assignment for *Profess+or+en* and *Profess+or+in* will then proceed as for all stress-affecting suffixes: upon suffixation of +*en* or +*in*, stress erasure on the base and subsequent reassignment of stress leads to main stress on the penultimate syllable, which happens to be +*or*. Assigning +*in* to level 1 is perhaps more dubious; however, there is some limited independent evidence that this suffix is not completely independent of stress: for a number of animal names with non-final stress, the female form derived by means of +*in* will have stress on the final syllable of the base, as in '*Pinguin* vs. *Pingu'in+in*.

8.3.2. Stress in prefixed words

The preceding discussion is limited to the stress patterns found for *suffixed* words. Prefixation can also have varying effects on stress, which I will describe

---

[22] The pattern is illustrated here for the root *profess* alone, but it must be stressed that it is completely general and applies to the complete range of words formed with the suffix +*or*.

briefly here. A fully worked-out theory of prefix stress would required a precise model of how the prosodic structure depends on the morphological (or partly syntactic) structure of such formations. While this is not possible at present, I will try to give at least a theoretically oriented survey of the phenomena and patterns. In dealing with prefixation, it is useful to distinguish prefixes for verbs and prefixes for non-verbs, that is, nouns and adjectives. In the non-verbal domain, one group of prefixes displays initial stress (30).[23]

	Nouns		Adjectives
(30) a.	'Un+glück	b.	'un+bekannt
	'Miss+gunst		'miss+gelaunt
	'Erz+feind		'erz+konservativ
	'Ur+zustand		'ur+wüchsig

The stress pattern found here is identical to that of compounds, to be discussed in the next section. There is no difference between a prefixed form such as *'Erz+feind* and a compound such as *'Erz+schicht*, where the prefix *erz-* and the noun *Erz* happen to be homophonous. We can therefore assume that the rule responsible for the stress pattern is the compound stress rule, and indeed, as far as the prosodic structure is concerned, there does not seem to be any difference between prefixed words such as those in (30) and compounds. To quote another example, the prefixed word *'Miss+gunst* and the compound *'Miss+wahl* are alike in prosodic structure. Whatever the difference may be between the two groups, it lies exclusively in the morphology, not in the phonology. We must note, however, that the adjectival forms often have alternative stress patterns, some of which are given in (31).

(31) un+'glaublich, un+'säglich, un+'menschlich

It has been noted that there is a particular emphatic meaning connected with this alternative stress pattern. In these words, the prefix *un+* does not simply mean negation of some sort, but, rather, expresses the fact that some event is contrary to prior expectations. In other words, *'un+menschlich* 'non-human' contrasts with *un+'menschlich* 'beyond reasonable human effort'.

For prefixed nouns, we note the following possibilities. In one class of nouns the 'prefixes' are actually free morphemes, usually prepositions. As in (30), stress is initial and, not surprisingly, identical with compound stress. These words partly relate to prefix or particle verbs (e.g. *über+'fallen* or *'vor+stehen*), but this does not seem to influence the stress pattern.

(32)	'Vor+stand	'Zwischen+fall
	'Über+fall	'Aus+sicht
	'Durch+gang	'An+fang

A second class of nominal words bears main stress not on the prefix, but on the base. In general, the prefixes are distinct from those in (32). The generalization

---

[23] The pattern for adjectives prefixed with *erz+* is in fact more complicated: if used predicatively, the adjective has stress on the base (*erz +'konservativ*); initial stress appears in attributive (prenominal) use. This is the pattern discussed for compound adjectives in § 8.5.2.

is that the prefixes *ver+*, *er+*, and so on (see (33)), are always unstressed. To this list *be+* and *ge+*, the two prefixes containing schwa as discussed in § 4.1.2, can be added. The prefix *miß+* constitutes a more complex case, analysed later.

(33) *a.* Ver+'sicher+ung *b.* Ver+'fall
      Er+'zähl+ung   Er+'laub+nis
      Ent+'gegn+ung   Ent+'leih+er
      Zer+'legung   Zer+'fall

However, all the nouns of the class illustrated in (33) are derived from verbs, or at least have a base which is verbal. In (33*a*), formations with *+ung* are clearly de-verbal, but there is no reason not to assume the same derivation for the variety of formations in (33*b*). The stress pattern is also transferred from the respective verbal base, that is, from *ver+sicher*, *er+leb*, *ent+gegn*, and so on. We might, therefore, consider basing the description of complex nouns as in (33) on a stress account of prefixed verbs. Note that nominalizations with *+ung* do not change the stress pattern in cases of complex verbs with final stress (like those in (34)) either; cf. *'Um+leit+ung*, from *'um+leit$_V$*, to *Über+'setz+ung*, from *über+'setz$_V$*.

To confirm this argumentation, there is, in addition, one class of 'prefixed' verbs without the bound prefixes given in (33), but with an identical stress pattern. These are the verbs listed in (34). Consequently, we now turn to pre-fixation in the verbal domain. Again, stress may fall either on the prefix or on the base. As first pointed out in § 4.1.2, there is a class of separable prefix (or particle) verbs with initial (i.e. prefixal) stress, and a class of inseparable prefix verbs with stress on the base to the prefix.

(34) unter+'schätzen
     über+'fahren
     durch+'laufen
     um+'manteln
     hinter+'treiben
     wider+'stehen

The prefixes in (34) are the inseparable ones; the set of such prefixes is restricted to the six given here. (35) gives a few examples of particle verbs, in addition to those presented earlier, in (13*c*) of § 4.1.2.

(35) 'auf+passen
     'durch+führen
     'ein+sehen
     'über+setzen

The basic problem here is whether to equate this stress pattern with that of compounds (see § 8.4) or with phrasal structures (as described later in § 8.5). The analogy with verbal phrases becomes obvious once it is realized that com-plex verbs such as *Klavier spielen* and *Rad fahren* bear initial stress as well. Given that the separability of the initial part is similar in these latter examples to that of particle verbs, the same structure and the same stress rule should be pertinent. The relevant rule is a rule to be discussed in § 8.5.1 which stresses the complement to a phrasal head.

Modifying proposals by Stiebels and Wunderlich (1994), we may assume that the structure of particle verbs is as in (36a). Particle verbs are minimal phrases of some sort, and the rules of phrasal stress are to be applied accordingly. The structure of prefix verbs and the relation of these verbs to stress rules are more difficult to identify. If their structure is as in (36b), there will be no reason for the compound rule not to apply. It would certainly be easy to write a separate stress rule for such complex verbs, but such a solution would not be very illuminating.[24]

(36) *a.* $_{V'}$[$_{PP}$[über] $_{V^0}$[setzen]]   ('übersetzen)
      b. $_{V^0}$[$_{P^0}$[über] $_{V^0}$[setzen]]   (über'setzen)

An alternative solution might be to make prefixes of this sort (the six identified in (34)) unstressable in some way, in analogy to the unstressed verbal prefixes given in (33). However, such an approach misses the point that only the true prefixes are always unstressed. As Stiebels and Wunderlich (1994) point out, nominalizations of the two kinds of structures behave differently: the stress pattern of *über+'nehmen* changes to *'Über+nahme*, while there is no such change when *ent+'nehmen* is nominalized to *Ent+'nahme*. As stated earlier, I leave the problem at this point.

Above it was noted that stress can vary for at least the prefix +*un*. Here is another case of stress variation, but this time dependent on the prosodic structure of the base.[25] As (37) shows, words prefixed with *miss*+ can have either initial stress (37a) or main stress on the base (37b).

(37) *a.* 'miss+ver,stehen   *b.* miss+'fallen
          'miss+be,hagen   miss+'brauchen
          'miss+interpre,tieren   miss+'trauen

The difference between the two patterns is obvious: forms in (37a) have at least one unstressed syllable in the initial position of the base of the prefixation, while bases in (37b) have initial stress. (Main stress in the bases of (37a) is indicated by the mark for secondary stress.) Thus, we have another case of an affix-related regularity which is conditioned by the prosodic pattern of the affix base.

8.4. COMPOUNDS

Compounds are concatenated stems morphologically (see § 5.2.3), and concatenated phonological words phonologically.[26] Compounding is both common

---

[24] The point to be made here is that the two types of complex verbs have different structures, and these structures may, *inter alia*, be responsible for the stress differences.

[25] Here, as in other cases, the discussion relies heavily on the insights provided by Kiparsky (1966).

[26] There are compounds of the type illustrated by *Psycho+logie* or *Thermo+meter*, which may be analysed as compounded roots (roots in the sense introduced in § 5.2.3). They are distinct from stem compounds in carrying stress on the final element of the construction (i.e. regular word stress!) and are treated only briefly below.

and productive in German. It is generally assumed that the unmarked stress pattern for simple binary compounds is strong–weak, see *Spiel+uhr* (38) as a representative example to which we could add other examples *ad libitum*. The range of compound structures found in German is illustrated in § 4.2. There, all the examples have initial stress with the exception of the [N A] cases in (26*b*), which are discussed later, in § 8.5.2. Complications arise first through the behaviour of more complex compounds and second through the counter-examples to the basic pattern illustrated here. Note that the root category of the structure in (38) has not been identified.

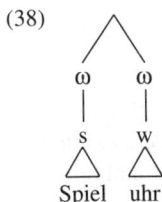

(38)

```
          /\
         /  \
        ω    ω
        |    |
        s    w
       /\    /\
      Spiel  uhr
```

Given the discussion of verbal prefixation in the preceding section, it is worth noting that complex compound verbs behave just as other compounds do; see (39). It is not possible to assign phrasal structures to these verbs, as in (36*a*), since many of the compound verbs cannot be separated and are highly lexicalized. Complex verbs thus display the full range of prosodic behaviour from reduced prefixes *be+* and *ge+*, to non-reduced but unstressed prefixes as in (33), to compound-like structures as in (39), to phrasal structures as in *Staub saugen* and *Auto fahren*.

(39) arg+wöhnen
      brand+marken
      not+landen
      mäh+dreschen

For compounds with more than two items, two stress patterns can be found, as illustrated in (40). Note that *Rot+wein+punsch* ('red-wine punch') is a drink made out of *Rot+wein* ('red wine'), while the *Stadt+bau+amt* ('city building office') is a *Bau+amt* ('building office') for, or of, the *Stadt* ('city'). Thus, the generalization is that compounds of the structure [A [B C]] (i.e. (40*b*)) have primary stress on B, and those with the structure [[A B] C] (like (40*a*)) have primary stress on A. There are exceptions to this pattern, which is generally regarded as the regular one, and these will be discussed briefly below.

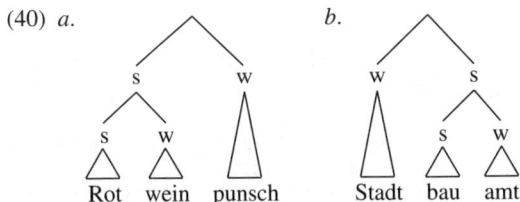

(40) *a.*

```
            /\
           /  \
          s    w
         /\    |
        s  w   |
       /\  /\  /\
      Rot wein punsch
```

b.

```
            /\
           /  \
          w    s
          |   /\
          |  s  w
         /\ /\  /\
       Stadt bau amt
```

The rule generally assumed in Metrical Phonology for stress in compounds is therefore that in (41).[27] It will correctly assign primary stress to an initial part A in a simple binary compound, as B does not branch. The large number of compounds with a left-branching structure [[A B] C] receive initial stress, the ones with a right-branching structure [A [B C]] receive final stress through this rule. (42) gives a list of additional examples of both left- and right-branching compounds.

(41) Compound rule

In a compound C, B is strong in [A B]$_C$, if, and only if, B branches.

(42) *a.* [[Fuß ball] feld]   *b.* [Regierungs [ober rat]]
     [[Welt bank] konferenz]   [Landes [zentral bank]]
     [[Rechen zentrums] leiter]   [Universitäts [rechen zentrum]]

In consequence of rule (41), identical strings of words may display different stress patterns depending on their structure. In a compound such as *Stadtplanungsbüro*, the main stress on *Stadt* or *Planung* dissolves the structural ambiguity of these words, as shown in (43). Words with a complex head bear main stress on the first part of that head (43*a*). Otherwise, main stress falls on the first word of the compound.

(43) *a.* [Stadt['planungs büro]] 'planning office of the city'
    b. [['Stadt planungs] büro] 'office for city planning'

So far, the discussion has treated compounds as objects with a particular morphosyntactic structure. But one of the general hypotheses of this study is that phonological rules (such as stress assignment) apply in phonological domains only. We are, therefore, forced to consider the nature of the phonological constituents involved. While the terminal unit involved in compounding is most certainly the phonological word ω, matters are less clear for higher nodes. Within the prosodic hierarchy first introduced in Chapter 3, the two available categories are the phonological word—used as a recursive category; and the phonological phrase—which would again be a recursive category, as there is always the possibility of another layer of compounding and, of course, the embedding of the compound in a phrase.

Starting from these prosodic categories and the word-syntactic compounding patterns introduced above, the following possibilities arise. Compounding can be regarded on the prosodic level as the conjunction of phonological words into either words (44*a*) or phrases (44*b*):

(44) *a.* [A B]$_\omega$ *b.* [A B]$_\varphi$
    | | | |
    ω ω   ω ω

Suppose that option (44*b*) is the unmarked case, usually chosen for compounds. Only root compounds such as *Psycho+logie* or *Thermo+meter*, briefly

---

[27] Such a rule was first formulated for English by Liberman and Prince (1977), taking up the basic insight from *SPE* and other work. For German compounds, see, in particular, Giegerich (1985: ch. 3), who offers a thorough discussion of compound stress within metrical phonology; and Benware (1987) for an alternative view.

mentioned in § 5.2.3, are of type (44a). These are indeed right-strong, as opposed to prototypical compounds of the type 'Spiel+uhr. We can then state that it is the left-hand phonological word in a phonological phrase which is strong.

Now consider more complex compounds. The possible alternatives are given in (45). Prosodically, a phonological word is adjoined either to a phrase on the left (45a) or to one on the right (45b). Finally, two phrases can be conjoined as in (45c).

(45) a. A [B   C]   b. [A   B] C   c. [A   B] [C   D]
        ω ω   ω   ω   ω ω   ω   ω   ω   ω
        [ω   ω]$_\varphi$ [ω   ω]$_\varphi$ C   [ω   ω]$_\varphi$[ω   ω]$_\varphi$
        [ω   φ]$_\varphi$ [φ   ω]$_\varphi$ [φ   φ]$_\varphi$

The resulting pattern is surprisingly regular and natural: the higher-level category φ will always be strong under adjunction of a phonological word, as in the final lines of (45a, b). If two such φs are combined as in (45c), the right-hand φ is strong. This will turn out to reflect the rule of phrasal stress which is discussed in the next section. But four-part compounds such as [[Kranken kosten] ['dämpfungs gesetz]] display the same pattern.

The three patterns found in compound stress can thus be summarized as in (46), with an illustrating example for each 'rule'. The statement on adjunction in (46d) is probably an instance of a general principle of adjunction: adjoining a category to a higher node means adjoining it as a weak node (see the application of (13c) in (14), (18), and (25)).

(46) a.   ω   (Psycho+lo'gie)
             /   \
           w   s
           | |
           ω   ω

     b.   φ   ('Spiel+uhr)
             /   \
           s   w
           | |
           ω   ω

     c.   φ   (Jahr+'hundert)
             /   \
           w   s
           | |
           φ   φ

     d. Adjoin ω as a weak member to a phrase φ.   ([' Rot wein] punsch)

With these new mechanisms for the description of compound stress available, let us look at some of the marked patterns mentioned above.

One group of exceptions to the general compound rules introduced here consists of simple binary compounds with final stress. This group contains several subgroups, some of which are illustrated in (47).

(47) *a.* Baden-'Württemberg, Sachsen-'Anhalt, Marxismus-'Leninismus
    b. Oster'montag, Jahr'hundert
    c. rot'grün, dunkel'rot
    d. Süd'afrika, Westber'lin, Ost'asien

Words in (47*a*) are usually coordinative compounds, which are regularly right-strong. For words in (47*b*), some kind of implicit or explicit contrast (as between *Ostermontag* and *Ostersonntag*) is usually held responsible for the deviating stress pattern. (This view is much less plausible for the other example in (47*b*), *Jahr'hundert*.) The compound adjectives in (47*c*) are partly of the coordinative type (e.g. *rot'grün*), but not generally (e.g. *dunkel'rot*). In fact, stress for these adjectives alternates, and is therefore compared to other, rhythmically conditioned, stress alternations in § 8.5.2. Words in (47*d*) represent a class of compounds which simply deviate from the general pattern, and which perhaps form a semantically coherent class, that of geographical terms modified by major points of the compass.

Words in (47) deviate from the general pattern in one direction, but another possible direction is also found. While words with the morphological structure of [A [B C]] are generally stressed on the B part, words in (48) show that this is not always the case.

(48) 'Hauptbahnhof, 'Sportflugzeug, 'Kinderfahrrad

Adapting a proposal by Giegerich (1985: § 3.4.2) we may argue that initial stress here is due to the fact that, for the cases under (48), the righthand-side word (*Bahnhof, Flugzeug, Fahrrad*) is analysed as consisting not of two phonological words but of only one. This reanalysis of a compound is obviously triggered by the non-transparency and the high degree of lexicalization of these complex words—very little of the meaning of *Hof* 'yard' or *Zeug* 'material' is retained in *Bahnhof* 'railway station' or *Flugzeug* 'aeroplane'; also, a *Fahr+rad* 'bike' is not a kind of *Rad* 'wheel'. Thus, as items consisting of only two phonological words, the words in (48) receive regular (left-strong) compound accent. However, it is difficult to distinguish stress effects due to inherent contrast from those of amalgamation of phonological words, as there seems to be a correlation between the bleaching of meaning (as for *Hof*) and the disappearance of the word status.

However, for other cases such a solution does not seem plausible. There is no evidence to indicate that *Teekanne* and so on in (49) are such that two phonological words are 'fused' into one. Nevertheless, main stress is clearly and reliably on the first part. In addition, contrast or particular emphasis does not seem responsible for the deviation from the general pattern.

(49) [Porzel'lan [tee kanne]]
    [['Straßen bahn] [fahr karte]]

And finally, the deviation cannot be due to the fact that *Porzellan* bears final stress; compare *Alu'minium+teekanne* with an identical stress pattern. For *Fahrkarte*, however, it has been suggested that lexicalization as in the case of

Hauptbahnhof might be responsible. The fairly large number of such compounds ([A [B C]] type with initial stress) has led Benware (1987) and Stötzer (1989) to propose that initial stress is regular for *all* compounds.

A further stress difference within the class of tripartite compounds is exemplified in (50). Here, it is presumably not the difference in morphological structure which can be held responsible for the stress difference. In all of these examples, the structure [[A B] C] is the most plausible. Nevertheless, examples in (50*b*) have main stress on part B.[28]

(50) *a.* 'Dreifarbstift   *b.* Drei'felderwirtschaft
     'Einmannboot   Drei'mädelhaus
     'Fünfuhrtee   Fünf'meilenzone
     'Zehnraumwohnung   Zehn'zimmerwohnung

One notable general property of compounds of the form [A B C] is that neither of the possible subconstituents [A B] or [B C] exists as an independent word with the exception of *Farbstift*. In consequence, one possible analysis of these compounds is to consider subconstituents of the form [A B] to be not words, but phrases. As phrases, they would receive final stress, that is, stress on B. However, this explanation fails to explain the stress pattern in (50*a*). It does not seem adequate to claim that *Dreizimmer* and so on in (50*b*) are phrases, while *Dreifarb* and so on in (50*a*) are not. In both groups (and not just in (50*a*)), we can find expressions which fail to constitute proper phrases in terms of agreement; see *Zwei'kammersystem*, in which the proper (plural) noun phrase would be *Zwei Kammern* 'two chambers'.

A second, more pertinent difference between compounds in (50*a*) and those in (50*b*) concerns the number of syllables of part B. B in (50*a*) is monosyllabic. Although there are exceptions, there is clearly a tendency for initial stress (i.e. on A) if B is monosyllabic. A possible solution might then be to claim that a binary phrasal[29] compound [A B] which consists of two monosyllabic parts, and which is embedded in another compound, undergoes some kind of a *de-accenting rule* for B. Stress is accordingly realized on A. That is, rule (46*c*) would treat [*Dreizimmer*] as a conjunction of phrases, while [*Dreifarb*] would be subject to de-accenting.

However, there are a few well-known exceptions to this pattern, given in (51).[30] Despite the fact that the most plausible (though not indisputable) structure of these words is [[A B] C] and that B is monosyllabic, main stress is still placed on B. We may suppose that de-accenting does not apply for these words. This process is also optional in the case of those words which were mentioned to allow for both stress patterns, that of *Fünf'uhrtee* and that of *'Fünfuhrtee*.

---

[28] For some words in (50*a*), main stress can alternatively be put on part B, as in *Ein'mannboot* or *Fünf'uhrtee*. This variation seems to be restricted to compounds of the type given in (50*a*), which might provide a reason to derive initial stress for these compounds by a more or less optional rule of stress shift.   [29] 'Phrasal' in the phonological sense; as specified in (46*b*).
[30] Recent discussions of such words can be found in Giegerich (1985) and Benware (1987).

(51) Rot'kreuzschwester
All'heilmittel
Groß'grundbesitzer

Rather disappointingly, this discussion of compound stress ends on an in-determinate mood. While clear-cut rules can be formulated (see (41), (46)), too many exceptions of an unclear nature must be acknowledged. Furthermore, the status of syntactic and/or semantic determinants of compound stress is also debatable. Reference to semantic properties is much less promising as a solution to the problems pointed out above than one might think. In English, some of the apparent vagaries of stress for compounds can be reduced by noting that, for compounds of the form [A B] in which A denotes the *material* of B, the stress is on B; for example, *steel pen, linen shirt* (see Liberman and Sproat 1992). However, there seem to be no such across-the-board generalizations of a semantic nature for German. In (47d), we noted that the geographic terms involving one of the cardinal points (*Nord* etc.) bear final stress. But even within such a small class as that, there are exceptions, for example, *'Nord+pol, 'Süd+pol*. (But as with words of the type (50a), the monosyllabicity of part B could be a relevant factor.)

8.5. PHRASAL STRESS AND STRESS SHIFTS

8.5.1. **Rules of phrasal stress**

We will now consider stress regularities outside the domain of the lexicon. Con-sidering stress in units larger than the lexical ones involves looking at stress phe-nomena which are not determined by lexical properties such as word structure or the properties of affixes. The question then is that of what properties deter-mine the stresses at this level, usually called the phrasal level. (However, com-pound stress and phrasal stress are probably not totally distinct, as we have seen above.) The representation I use here is again the metrical (strong-weak) model, following earlier discussions of phrasal stress in German by Jacobs (1982) and Giegerich (1985).

There seem to be three basic approaches to the derivation of phrasal stress: in the first approach, exemplified with respect to German by Kiparsky (1966), Jakobs (1982), and Cinque (1993), direct reference is made to the (surface) syntactic structure. Stress rules are formulated which assign stress values to particular syntactic constituents. In contrast, the second approach denies the relevance of syntactic structure. Rather, phrasal stresses are interpreted as mark-ers of focused vs. non-focused items, the items not necessarily being syntactic constituents, and the status of notions such as focus and background being determined in discourse (see Uhmann 1991). Finally, phrasal stress can be argued to occur in the units identified as phonological phrases in § 3.5. In this approach, syntactic structure is *indirectly* relevant to phrasal stress, as it constrains (but does not completely determine) the phonological phrasing. In view of the foregoing discussion, it is not surprising that I will follow the last approach. The alternative approaches will be addressed only briefly.

Phrasal stress is clearly distinct from compound stress, as shown in (52), where examples in (52*a*) are compounds and those in (52*b*) are phrases of various sorts.

(52) *a.* die 'Kranken+schwestern   *b.* die kranken 'Schwestern
      'the nurses'   'the sick sisters'
      die 'Armen+häuser   die armen 'Häuser
      'the poorhouses'   'the poor houses'
      'über+große   über 'große
      'over-sized'   'over big'
      'drei+farbig   drei 'Farben
      'three-coloured'   'three colours'

Such observations on stress in phrases have, directly or indirectly, motivated a syntactic approach to an analysis of phrasal stress, and led to the rule of phrasal stress such as that in (53). It is often called the *Nuclear Stress rule* (see *SPE*: 89 ff.) and it is meant to describe stress within phrases in the *unmarked* case. In phrases, it is more obvious than elsewhere that special conditions of focus, contrast, and so on, can lead to other patterns of stress. Generally, in these cases constituents in focus or under (implicit or explicit) contrast take stress. I disregard these cases, and assume that there is indeed room for a default stress. A relational version of the Nuclear Stress rule might be as in (53).

(53) Phrasal default stress (Nuclear Stress rule)
     In an expression $_c$[A B]$_c$, for C a phrase, B is strong.

More types of phrases with right-most stress are given in (54). All of these stress patterns are as predicted by (53). The correctness of the (admittedly superficial) phrase-structure labelling is not at issue here.

(54) N-NP   das Haus der 'Eltern 'the house of the parents'
     NP-N   Goethes 'Werke 'Goethe's works'
     N-PP   der Mann auf dem 'Dach 'the man on the roof'
     P-NP   über die 'Brücke 'over the bridge'
     V-NP   liest das 'Buch 'reads the book'
     V-PP   schaut über die 'Stadt 'looks over the city'
     Adv-Adj   sehr 'schön 'very nice'
     NP-VP   Friedrich 'singt 'Friedrich sings.'

That phrasal stress does not straightforwardly depend on the semantic relation between linguistic units can be demonstrated through such cases as those in (55), where there is invariably final stress, although the relationship between the two relevant units is identical, or at least very similar.[31]

---

[31] The final examples in (54) and (55) are simple but complete sentences. For these, a realization is also possible in *out-of-the-blue* contexts in which both subject and verb are stressed, and each constitute an intonational phrase. This version exemplifies the so-called hat or bridge pattern of intonational phrasing (see Wunderlich 1991 or Féry 1993).

(55) die stählerne 'Hand   die Hand aus 'Stahl
     'the steel hand'   'the hand made of steel'
     die blaue 'Forelle   die Forelle 'blau
     'the blue trout'   'the truite bleu'
     Peter 'kommt.   Kommt 'Peter?
     'Peter is coming.'   'Is Peter coming?'

However, not all types of phrases have right-most stress, as shown by the examples of phrases with left-most stress in (56).

(56) *a.* NP-P   die 'Straße entlang   des schlechten 'Wetters wegen
                    'down the road'   'due to the bad weather'
     b. V-Aux   'geben wollen   'lieben können
                    'want to give'   'can love'

The phrases in (57) illustrate, however, that phrasal stress is not exclusively dependent on linear (right–left) information. As the phrases here demonstrate, phrasal stress can be independent of its relative position.

(57) *a.* Erna will 'Klavier spielen.   Erna spielt 'Klavier.
         'Erna wants to play the piano.'   'Erna plays the piano.'
         Otto will aus dem 'Fenster schauen.   Otto schaut aus dem 'Fenster.
         'Otto wants to look out of the window.'   'Otto looks out of the window.'
     b. weil die Lehrer 'schimpfen wollen   Die Lehrer wollen 'schimpfen.
         'because the teachers want to scold'   'The teachers want to scold.'
         als die Kinder 'spielen durften   Die Kinder durften 'spielen.
         'when the children were allowed to play'   'The children were allowed
                                                     to play.'
     c. Erna will heute 'spielen.   Erna 'spielt heute.
         'Erna wants to play today.'   'Erna plays today.'
         Erna will fleißig 'üben.   Erna 'übt fleißig.
         'Erna wants to practise diligently.'   'Erna practises diligently.'

One possible approach to such stress regularities relies on the fact that the syntactic relation between the stressed constituent—object to verb in (57*a*), modal to main verb in (57*b*), and adverbial to verb in (57*c*)—is constant, while only the linear (right-to-left) relationship is changed. Such an approach is advocated by Cinque (1993: 271) who proposes that 'a phrase's main stress is located on its most deeply embedded constituent. This is ordinarily the innermost complement of the phrase head.' In the absence of a complement, the head of a phrase is most deeply embedded, and thus receives stress. The difference between the head-complement structure in (56*a*) and the head-modifier structure in (57*b*) is thus taken care of, as well as the irrelevance of the relative position of the two constituents.

While this simple rule ('stress the innermost constituent') works straightforwardly for a number of cases such as objects, it is less obvious that it is adequate for other cases such as compounds, which are also included in Cinque's model. Cinque argues that the syntactic surface structure of both phrases and compounds is indeed such that the rule proposed is obeyed. Pushing this argumentation to its limits, *Drei'zimmerwohnung* would be given a different syntactic analysis from *'Dreiraumwohnung*.

A further aspect of phrasal stress is the importance of the focus–presupposition dichotomy of sentences, a property which is relevant in the relation to the context of the sentence. As is well known, the focus–presupposition dichotomy influences the stress pattern of a sentence, usually in the way that the focused part of a sentence receives main stress. This is illustrated by pairs of sentences in (58), in which main stress is on the focused (as opposed to presupposed or given) part of the sentence.

(58) *a.* Ist jemand angekommen?
    'Has anybody arrived?'

    $\overset{1}{\text{O}}$tto ist $\overset{2}{\text{a}}$ngekommen.
    'Otto has arrived.'
  b. Was ist mit Otto?
    'What about Otto?'

    $\overset{2}{\text{O}}$tto ist $\overset{1}{\text{a}}$ngekommen.
    'Otto has arrived.'

One proposal has been to assign a focus feature, F, to syntactic constituents. It is then possible to postulate both the semantic and the phonological consequences of this assignment. One of the phonological consequences is that focused constituents with the focus feature (F) are strong. Rule (59) is a simple rule making any constituent (XP) which is marked F, strong. Of course, stress *within* such a focused, and thereby strong, constituent follows from other, independent, stress rules.

(59) Focus Stress Assignment
    $[\text{XP}]_F \rightarrow s$
          $|$
    $[\text{XP}]_F$

When discussing phrasal stress it is important to take into account the possibility of a clear but limited degree of free variation. In § 3.5, it was pointed out that the assignment of phonological phrases is not totally determined by the syntactic phrase structure. Rather, a certain amount of freedom exists. Assuming that a phonological phrase bears phrasal stress, it follows immediately that phrasal stress is not a deterministic event either. Consider the following example from Jacobs (1982: 157), where the focused constituent (as in answer to the question of what Peter gave to Gerda as a present) is identical in (60*a*) and (60*b*). For this reason, it becomes difficult to argue that a semantic difference is responsible for the two realizations.

(60) *a.* Peter hat ihr [eine 'Karte für die 'Oper geschenkt]$_F$
   b. Peter hat ihr [eine Karte für die 'Oper geschenkt]$_F$
     'Peter has given her a ticket to the opera.'

We are thus forced to conclude that for reasons which are unknown and probably extragrammatical, it is possible to realize a focused constituent as a single phonological phrase, as in (60b), or as a sequence of such phrases, as in (60a).

8.5.2. **Stress shifts**

Words and phrases do not always surface with the stress patterns assigned to them by the rules discussed so far. Stress shifts are discussed in § 3.5, where they are used in an argument for the phonological phrase, a category within which such changes seem to take place. In the present context, a rule describing these stress shifts is developed, and I explore the range of constructions in which stress shifts are possible.[32] A number of stress shifts are given as illustrations in (61). We may indeed assume that rhythm motivates these shifts, as all of these shifts create an alternating stress pattern (strong-weak-strong-weak). Such an alternation is the essence of rhythm as it occurs in non-linguistic human activities such as music or dance.

(61) Rhythmical stress shifts

    1   2   1 3   2
a. sichtbar ~ unsichtbar

    1   2   1 3 2
    Arbeiter ~ Gastarbeiter

    1   2   1 3   2
    Ausfall ~ Stromausfall

    1   2   1 3 2
b. abnehmen ~ den Hut abnehmen
    'take off' ~ 'take the hat off'

    1 2   1   3   2
    anziehen ~ den Rock anziehen
    'put on' ~ 'put the skirt on'

    2   1   2   3   1
c. Paderborn ~ Paderborner Uni
    'Paderborn (city)' ~ 'Paderborn University'

    2   1   2   3   1
    linear ~ lineare Steigerung
    'linear' ~ 'linear growth'

    2   1   2   3   1
    rationell ~ rationelle Tests
    'effective' ~ 'effective tests'

In each of these cases, a prosodic structure is created which is alternating to a larger degree than the original structure. The stress shift appears to be optional within syntactic phrases (see (61b, c)), but seems to operate obligatorily within compounds such as those in (61a). This stress shift changes a strong-weak pattern

---

[32] Of course, I am using the number notation for stress levels purely for reasons of space, without committing myself to the theory underlying it.

into one of weak-strong in (61a, b), while the mirror-image pattern is illustrated in (61c).

Translating the preliminary notation used in (61) into prosodic structures and the strong-weak (s-w) notation, we find the following pairs of prosodic patterns in these examples.

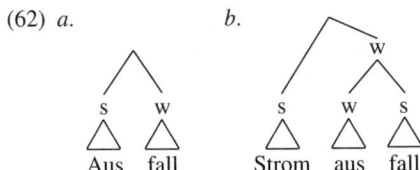

(62) a.   b.

```
        /\                      /        \
       /  \                    /          w
      s    w                  /          /\
     /\    /\                s          w   s
    Aus  fall              /\          /\   /\
                         Strom        aus  fall
```

This notation helps to clarify the pattern: the reversal consists in the avoidance of a 'clash' between two adjacent strong units, by reversing the strong-weak relation in the weaker element of the phrase. Thus, the following rule can be formulated (Liberman and Prince 1977: 319).[33] The rule comes in two parts (63a, b) which are mirror images of each other.

(63) Rhythmic Reversal

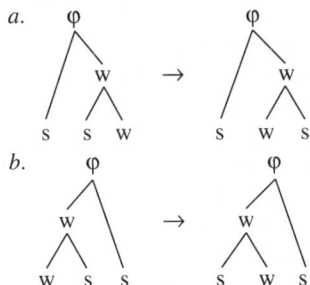

```
a.      φ                      φ
       /\                     /\
      /  w           →       /  w
     /  /\                  /  /\
    s  s  w                s  w  s

b.      φ                      φ
       /\                     /\
      w  \           →       w  \
     /\   \                 /\   \
    w  s   s               s  w   s
```

The two different cases (stress shift to the left, stress shift to the right) are then, with some simplification, represented as in (64). The stresses relevant for the stress shift are highlighted. Note that the relevant structure occurs at different levels of the tree. It is precisely one of the advantages of a non-linear stress notation that regularities can be represented in a local manner, disregarding the rest of the structure. (In (64b), I ignore the complication arising from the fact that the final schwa in linear+e, due to inflection, adds another layer of strong-weak relations.)

Finally, I turn to a particular domain of stress alternations which superficially also fall under the rubric of rhythmic reversals. There is a long-standing tradition in the phonological literature to treat the stress alternation of the examples in (65) as a rhythmic phenomenon. Kiparsky (1966: 94–5) was the first to formulate a stress-shift rule for compound adjectives, a rule changing main stress into secondary stress if the main stress comes into adjacency with another, stronger, main stress. In this tradition, compound adjectives are subject to

---

[33] Note that the decision in the preceding section to treat compounds prosodically as phonological phrases φ helps to unify the domain of stress shift. It is always a phonological phrase.

rhythmical stress shift just like the phrases discussed in (61) above and in (71) below.

(64) *a.*

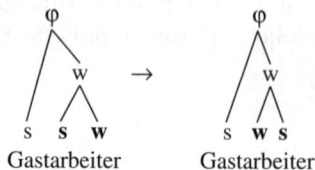

b.

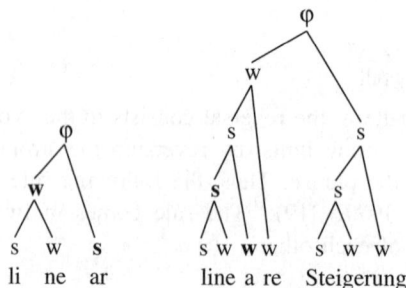

(65) *a.* Der Mann ist steinreich
'The man is immensely rich'

Der steinreiche Mann
'The immensely rich man'

b. Das Auto ist nagelneu
'The car is brand new'

Das nagelneue Auto
'The brand new car'

c. Das Kleid ist grasgrün
'The dress is grass-green'

Das grasgrüne Kleid
'The grass-green dress'

The stress-shift approach to these structures contrasts with those for prefixed adjectives. For adjectives, Kiparsky notes that adjectives with a prefix such as *un+* can have different syntactic structures, and that the stress patterns are partly determined by these syntactic structures. Thus, the two cases receive a different interpretation. Wurzel (1980: 311) treats all stress alternations as stress shifts, with a rule saying that a pattern '1 2' is replaced by '2 1', if the meaning of the compound is non-compositional. As the data in (64) and others below show, this regularity is true only for adjectives in predicative position. In a more recent account, Hayes (1984: 68) also equates adjectives as in (65) with such well-known English examples as *thir'teen* vs. *'thirteen "men.*

I now argue that the true stress shifts for rhythmical reasons have to be kept apart from the apparent stress shifts manifest in complex adjectives exemplified in (65). The latter are to be explained on the basis of the head-argument struc-ture of these compounds and the general stress rules for words and phrases.

The fact to be dealt with is the existence of a large class of compound adjec-tives with initial stress in attributive (prenominal) position and with final stress in predicative position. The difference between this class and the apparently similar English cases is that in this class the 'stress shift' is not dependent on the position of the main stress in the following word. As Prince (1983) and Hayes (1984) note, in English the stress shift does indeed depend on the closeness of the main stress in the phrase: compare '*thir,teen* "*men* to ,*thir'teen mathema"ticians*. But stress patterns in nouns following the adjectives in question have no influence on the stress in these adjectives, as (66) shows.

(66) der steinreiche Millionär   'the immensely rich millionaire'

   das nagelneue Automobil   'the brand new car'

   die grasgrüne Kombination   'the grass-green suit'

If the stress patterns of the prenominal adjectives were to be derived from the stress-final form by a clash-sensitive rule such as (63*b*), the stress movement should occur in (65), but not in (66). But no difference between these two groups can be observed. In fact, in both cases it seems possible to have final adjectival stress, for example, *der steinreiche Millionär* or *der steinreiche Mann*, although these are probably marked with respect to the patterns illustrated above.

It is important to note that there are two readings for some of the complex adjectives. The two readings correlate with a stress difference, but only in predicative position. As (67) and (68) show, the literal interpretation is available with initial stress, the metaphorically extended interpretation with final stress. Note that these readings cannot be disambiguated by stress alone in the case of the attributive adjectives. Here, primary stress is always initial, regardless of a literal or metaphorical reading.

(68) *a.* Das Kind ist blutarm.   'The child is very poor.'

   b. Das Kind ist blutarm.   'The child is anaemic.'

(69) *a.* Saudi-Arabien ist steinreich.   'Saudi Arabia is immensely rich.'

   b. Saudi-Arabien ist steinreich.   'Saudi Arabia is rich in stones.'

I will now argue that both the stress and the meaning difference between the (*a*) and (*b*) cases above can be accounted for on the basis of the word syntax: more precisely, the argument structure of the adjectives involved.[34] In examples (68*b*) and (69*b*) (with the literal interpretation and initial stress) argument structure is of relevance for the interpretation, with the head found on the right as usual. Both *reich* and *arm* are relational adjectives, that is, they have a possible argument, in contrast to other adjectives, such as *schön* or *grün*, which lack such an (internal) argument. If these latter adjectives form a compound, the first part can only be interpreted as an adjunct (modifier) to the head. See

---

[34] Wurzel (1980: 310) considers the semantics to be directly responsible for the stress alternation. In the present account, it is the semantic part of word syntax which is relevant.

bildschön, *grasgrün*, or *nagelneu* as examples. Of course, relational adjectives can have adjuncts as well, as *steinreich* and *blutarm* illustrate in their non-literal interpretation.

Let us suppose that 'being an argument' can be formally represented, for example as being a sister to an X^0 node.[35] An adjunct, in contrast, is a sister node to a higher-level node, say to an X^1 node. The two possible structures of *steinreich* can then be given as in (70), together with their corresponding prosodic structures. The structure in (70a) expresses the argument status of *stein* with respect to *reich*, while in (70b) *stein* is a modifier to the head of the compound.

(70) *a.* $_{X0}[$[stein] $_{X0}$[reich]] $\rightarrow$ $_{\varphi}[$ $_{\omega}[$] $_{\omega}[$]]

    b. $_{X1}[$[stein] $_{X1}$[reich]] $\rightarrow$ $_{\omega}[$ $_{\omega}[$] $_{\varphi}[$]]

It remains to be demonstrated that stress rules are (indirectly) sensitive to the head-argument structure of the complex words. In (57) above, we have already seen that a complement to a head is usually stressed, while adjuncts within a phrase are usually not. The same distinction is now found for compound adjectives, and the two cases should receive a similar analysis. Note that there are still two possible treatments: either the stress patterns are assigned in direct correspondence to the (word-)syntactic structure, or the syntax determines how prosodic structures are constructed, and the latter are then input to the stress rules.

In arguing that the two kinds of stress in adjectival compounds are not rhythm-based, I do not want to imply that there is no rhythm-related stress shift in German. In (71), further examples are given for rightward movement of stress in the context of a compound.

                1 2   1   3 2
(71) Mittag ~ Nachmittag

            1   2   1   3   2
        Marschall ~ Feldmarschall

            1   2   1   3   2
        Sparkasse ~ Stadtsparkasse

Finally, the compounds ending in *Arbeiter* in (72) provide a further argument for the rhythm-based nature of this alternation: the distance of the clash-producing main stress from the secondary stress is crucial; the further away (counted in the number of syllables) the main stress from the secondary stress, the less likely the stress shift is. That is, in *Gastarbeiter* (72b) the stress shift on *arbeiter* is (almost) obligatory, while it is optional in *Hafenarbeiter* (72c), which has one weak syllable between the clashing syllables. In *Flughafenarbeiter* (72d), stress shift clearly is the disfavoured option.

                1 2   1 3 2
(72) *a.* Arbeiter   *b.* Gastarbeiter

                    ⎧ 3   2 ⎫
                1 ⎨ 2   3 ⎬   1   2   3
                    ⎩   ⎭
        c. Hafenarbeiter   *d.* Flughafenarbeiter

---

[35] This is the word category of § 5.2.3.

If this description is nearly right, then we are clearly dealing here with truly rhythmic preferences, which are independent of the syntax-based phrasal stress alternations discussed above.

8.6. CONCLUDING REMARKS

Stress with its complexities in Modern Standard German is derived here from an interaction of (simple) rules and underspecified representations. Furthermore, only words displaying stress behaviour that has been diagnosed as being exceptional or non-regular have 'richer' underlying representations. This conception is certainly desirable on the theoretical grounds of parsimony, although the complexity of stress in Modern Standard German does not allow yet for a final evaluation.

To end this chapter on a speculative note, one may want to ask why there is such an apparently confusing array of stress patterns. The answer might be that there is actually a very good functional motivation behind most parts of it. Consider again the basic pattern found above for feet, words, compounds, and phrases. Feet are left-strong, that is, have stress on the *left*. As observed in this chapter, in words it is one of the three *final* syllables which is stressed. In compounds, in turn, it is usually the *first* part which receives stress (leaving out the complications). Finally, in phrases, it is again the *final* part which receives an additional layer of stress in the default case.

What we can thus observe is a very regular pattern: the location of main stress is reversed for each major level of structure. Seen in this way, stress can have an important function in indicating the level of the constituent expressed at a given point. In particular, the presence of a compound is signalled as against the presence of a word or phrase. In this way, discovering the stress relations can be of considerable help to the hearer in parsing an utterance.

It is of course quite natural to assume that stress functions as a device for emphasizing the beginning or ending of a particular type of linguistic entity, and it would add to the functionality of this device if it were to highlight the boundaries of constituents in an alternating fashion. Looked at in this way, stress in German is actually much less of a puzzle and much less exotic than it first appears to be. It provides another example of the *demarcative* function of stress, just as in other languages. (See Jakobson 1931 and Trubetzkoy 1939 for early discussions of this and other functions of stress.)

9

CONCLUDING REMARKS

> HIGGINS. *Tired of listening to sounds?*
> PICKERING. *Yes. It's a fearful strain.*
> (G. B. Shaw, *Pygmalion*)

The reader who has followed my *tour d'horizon* through the mazes of the phonology of German will undoubtedly have more questions to ask than I have answered in the present book. Furthermore, he or she will also not always accept the answers that I have ventured to propose.

Some of the open problems, I believe, are of a technical nature, that is, are problems of execution. Sharpening or slightly modifying the representational proposals, the model of phonology–morphology interaction, and the theory of phonological rules will often lead to solutions sufficiently different so that seemingly large difficulties are suddenly overcome with relative ease. Other problems are not so easily solved and may eventually require drastic changes in phonological theory. But I hope to have provided enough data and descriptions to have provided a starting point for work on other, more adequate analyses.

This book has served a useful purpose if it has demonstrated that the sound pattern of German (as of any other language) is part of the intricate structure underlying language, and must be part of the knowledge with which learners and users of this language are equipped. Seen in this way, the study of a phonological system becomes part of the scientific study of the human mind, a field of inquiry sometimes referred to as cognitive science. (From this characterization alone it is obvious that doing phonology does not consist of *listening to sounds* alone.) It is probably fair to say that phonology has as much to offer to the programme of cognitive science as any other domain of inquiry, because the systematic study of phonological patterns is a relatively well-established discipline. Much is known about possible phonological systems, their possible changes in history, and their relationship to other parts of grammar. As far as the phonology of the German language is concerned, the present book attempts to systematize this knowledge.

There are many, too many, ways of achieving this systematization, as I have become sometimes painfully aware during the course of writing the present book. Phonology is not so much in need of further tools of description, it has too rich an inventory of such tools. Finding more adequate ways of using only the right tools is the more pressing task for phonologists at present.

There are two general questions which are, to my mind, particularly outstanding in any further studies of this kind. The first question has been repeatedly addressed in the present book: the relationship between the *structure* of sound and the *matter* of sound, or, in terms of discipline, between phonetics and phonology. While a totally abstract conception of phonology, one which explicitly denies the grounding of phonology in phonetics, is hardly being pursued in current thinking, there are still many possible cut-off points between what is legitimately regarded as belonging to the domain of phonology, and what is phonetic. And there are consequences to particular answers: note that I have repeatedly 'solved' a phonological problem by postulating that it is really part of phonetics, and therefore not relevant for the rule at hand. Perhaps even more important is the question of whether a principled difference exists between the domains of phonetics and phonology. That is, are phonological rules and representations to be placed in a continuum ranging from the acoustic, articulatory, and auditory 'stuff' up to the highly abstract categories? Or is the abstract, cognitive domain of phonology shaply separated from the phonetic domain, with some kind of translation mediating between the two worlds?

The second question is the relation between the universal and the language-specific in phonology. This question, which arguably dominates modern theory-oriented linguistics more than any other, has to be faced at almost every point in the discussions of data in this book. For any feature, category, rule, or generalization, the following picture can be found: a cluster of properties that can be claimed to be universal is enriched, modified, or overlaid by additional language-specific properties. It is perhaps doubtful whether the study of the phonology of German in this book has paid proper justice to this state of affairs. After all, the rules and representations do not normally indicate what is universal and what is language-specific. (Recall from the discussion in § 1.1 that it is a basic assumption of generative phonology that representations 'matter'.) On the other hand, there is good reason to believe that in-depth studies of single languages, such as the present one, are among the few paths to find eventually an answer to this question.

POSTSCRIPT 2000

The present book attempts to formulate the generalizations found in the phonology of German within a rule-based and derivational framework. While some effort has been spent in order to both constrain the power of rules as well as to set limits on possible derivations, there is still reason to believe that such an approach has its own particular problems. These problems are twofold: on the one hand, feature-changing rules, working within serially-ordered derivations, allow for highly abstract and perhaps implausible derivations of surface forms from underlying entries. On the other hand, there has been increasing awareness among phonologists that many of the more interesting generalizations are to be found in the surface patterns of words and other phonological forms, and not within the rules. This book has in fact pointed to several such generalizations on the basis of the German language: the distribution of the vowel schwa, the prosodic patterns found for inflected and derived words, and the preferred patterns of word accent are all generalizations on output forms. In a rule-based framework, such surface-based generalizations appear as accidental by-products of a cleverly designed rule machinery.

For these and several other reasons, phonologists have turned to alternative ways of analysing the phonological systems of languages. One major attempt is clustered around a theory called *Optimality Theory* by its originators (see McCarthy and Prince 1993; Prince and Smolensky 1993). Optimality Theory offers a new perspective on the description of phonological systems, namely to treat the phonology of a language as a particular result of so-called *constraints* and their interaction. Constraints are universal well-formedness conditions, which are ranked (prioritized) according to a language-particular hierarchy. For example, while there is a general constraint saying that open (vowel-final) syllables are better than closed (consonant-final) syllables, and while German syllabification behaves according to this preference (onset clusters, and not coda clusters, are maximized in syllabification, see § 3.2.4), this constraint may have a rather low place in the rank order of constraints (witness the large number of closed syllables in the language, and the possibility of having remarkably complex codas).

Rules have no place in this theory. The two views are thus basically incompatible with each other, so I have refrained from integrating analyses done within Optimality Theory into the body of the book.

While an introduction to Optimality Theory (OT) is impossible here (and is available now from Archangeli and Langendoen (1997) and from Kager (1999)), I will discuss in this postscript how some of the facts and problems found in the phonology of German and presented in the preceding chapters of this book can be treated in OT, and what the current proposals are. (Because of the rapid development of the theory, these proposals and solutions are bound to be replaced by alternatives, but the general points should still hold.) I will structure these brief remarks in analogy to the progression of the book. That is, OT accounts of prosodic structure will be discussed first, then I will discuss some reinterpretations of phonological rules of German, before finally sketching some accounts of stress in German.

1. PROSODIC STRUCTURE

The interaction of prosodic structure, schwa deletion/epenthesis and morphological categories is the subject of Löhken's diachronic study (Löhken 1997). As we have seen in §§ 4.3 and 7.4.2, schwa epenthesis in Modern German seems to serve the purpose of making segments syllabifiable which would not otherwise be integrated into well-formed syllables. Furthermore, the position of schwa is category-specific, cf. nouns to verbs to adjectives. Such a scenario strongly suggests a constraint-based treatment, as the 'teleology' of schwa epenthesis is not really captured in a rule-based treatment. Löhken basically uses four types of constraints (each of which comes in a number of variants): one of *Morpheme Homogeneity*, to express the tendency of word forms within a paradigm to look alike; one of *Alignment*, to make the left and right boundaries of phonological and morphological fall together; one of *Prosodic Well-formedness*, to state preferred prosodic structures; and one of *Identity of Input and Output*, to prevent the deletion or epenthesis of segments. The various stages of the German language from Old High German to Modern Standard German undergo re-rankings of these constraints, so that vowel deletion, vowel (schwa) epenthesis, and morphological levelling within a paradigm play different roles in different historical stages.

The question of foot structure has been left somewhat undetermined in the present book, especially in §§ 3.3 and 8.2. Optimality Theory, in expressing preferred structures by means of constraints, and in relativizing these structures with respect to a particular ranking of the constraints, has the means of allowing a more flexible approach. It could well be that different situations prefer different types of feet, for example branching or non-branching feet, or feet allowing a heavy syllable in the weak element of the foot, or not allowing this configuration (see Alber 1997, 1998; Féry 1998a for discussion).

2. MORPHOLOGY AND MORPHOPHONOLOGY

The role of various types of morphemes and morphological categories was mentioned in Chapters 4 and 5 of this book. In OT, a particular version of constraints allows for a treatment of these categories by referring to their left and right boundaries: their edges. Golston and Wiese (1998) argue that the roots of German are quite pervasively marked at their edges by various features. For example, the feature [consonantal] is found at most roots' left and right edges. Therefore, Golston and Wiese propose that constraints of aligning left and right boundaries of roots by [consonantal] are operative here. Furthermore, other alignment constraints for roots combine to give German roots quite a uniform shape across a large database. To take up one other outstanding example: schwas are found in many German roots, but occur exclusively at the right edge, not at the left edge. This is explained by a constraint saying that the features of full vowels should be realized as much to the left as possible, that is, in the first syllable.

Golston and Wiese (1996) discuss a particular way of forming a noun plural in German dialects as found in parts of Hessia, namely by subtraction as in *Hond* (dog, sg.) vs. *Hon* (dog, pl.). They argue that this 'subtractive plural' stands in a complementary distribution to zero plural, and is predictable, assuming constraints of 'plurals end in a sonorant', and 'underlying features are realized on the surface' (the PARSE constraint). As the example shows, the place feature [coronal] is not deleted in the subtractive plural form, because it is still part of the final nasal /n/. And indeed, nouns without such identity of place between final consonants or vowel plus consonant have no subtractive plural forms (compare [hand̩] – [hɛn] 'hand, sg.' – 'hand, pl.', containing two final alveolar segments, with [ʃɪrm] – [ʃɪrm] 'umbrella, sg.' – 'umbrella, pl.'). The difference between this seemingly peculiar dialect and other variants of German is one of constraint ranking alone. (Holsinger and Houseman (1999) propose a re-analysis of these data which relies on lenition (cluster reduction) instead of the plural-specific constraint mentioned above.)

3. PROSODIC WORD FORMATION

Another area of rather extensive study within OT is that of Prosodic Morphology in German. In particular, hypocoristic truncations of the type mentioned in § 3.3.3, as with *Studi* from *Student* 'student', have been the subject of several analyses, by Féry (1997), Itô & Mester (1997), Wiese (2000). These analyses share the concern of predicting the specific form of these truncations from the interplay of three types of general constraints: those of prosodic well-formedness, of relationships between words (matching the properties of the base with those of the reduced form), and of a minimal amount of deletion. They differ in making use of different constraints within this set. (Neef (1997: 278–84) and Walther (1999) propose alternative constraint-based analyses, which do not involve the OT-particular domination, and therefore violability, of constraints.)

4. RULES VS. CONSTRAINTS

The celebrated rule of Final Devoicing in German (§ 7.3.1 in this book) has been the subject of some re-analyses, summarized by Féry (1998*b*). Two principled solutions seem available: either the requirement that the faithfulness to [+ voice] (or some other feature specification in the input) is more highly ranked in the onset of the syllable than elsewhere, or a use of constraint conjunction by which a combination of NoCoda with a ban on voiced obstruents is ranked higher than the faithfulness to the input feature. (Hahn (1998) presents a non-serious alternative to these explorations.)

As noticed in § 7.3, there is a remarkable cluster of 'rules' focussing more or less on the syllable-final consonants. These rules include Final Devoicing, ich/ach-alternation, g-spirantization, R-vocalization, and g-Deletion. Precisely because these rules have a focus in common, they can interact in interesting ways and exemplify the relationships between rules traditionally called 'feeding' and 'bleeding'. Allowing such rule-interactions leads to the phenomenon called 'opacity' of rules, because the effect of one rule can be made invisible by a later rule. Optimality-theoretic re-analyses must not only find analogues to the feature-changing rules operating in a serial order, but also come to terms with the fact that rule-orderings can produce the desired results. A re-analysis of the ich/ach-alternation is proposed by Merchant (1996) in terms of several constraints, among them a constraint disallowing a back vowel followed by a palatal fricative *in the same syllable*. In *Frau-chen* [fʀaʊ̯çən] 'woman, dimin.', the back vowel is not in the same syllable as the dorsal fricative. However, in order to prevent *rauchen* [{aʊ̯xən] 'smoke, v.' to surface with a palatal fricative, Merchant assumes that the fricative is ambisyllabic in the latter word; an assumption which may be problematic, and is not generally shared.

The interaction of Final Devoicing, g-spirantization, and g-Deletion is the topic of Itô and Mester (1999). Their solution depends on the 'local conjunction' of constraints, a mechanism of constraint combination proposed by Smolensky (1995). Thus, for example, the effects of g-spirantization are derived by combining one elementary constraint against voiced obstruents with one against segments in a coda with one against dorsal plosives. Only /g/ in a coda violates this conjoined constraint. By arranging such conjoined constraints on top of markedness constraints militating against deletion or feature change, the desired results emerge. However, the proper separation of the North German vernacular (the dialect allowing g-spirantization in all codas) from Standard German, and the deletion of /g/ in words such as *Ding-e* [dɪŋə] 'things', *Finger* [fɪŋɐ] 'finger', seems to remain a problem.

Other phonological 'rules' discussed in terms of OT include Umlaut (Féry 1994), and schwa-zero alternations (Löhken 1997; Raffelsiefen 1995).

5. STRESS PATTERNS

Stress, in particular word stress, is yet another domain of study in Optimality Theory. Relevant constraints are those requiring syllables of particular types to be stressed (heavy syllables) or unstressed (light syllables), and those which require a marking by stress of particular positions, either at the edge of larger constituents, or at the heads of such constituents. For German, Féry (1998a) has proposed an analysis of word stress which is based on a corpus of several thousand words in the CELEX database. Her proposal includes the following basic points: German word stress is quantity-sensitive, in that heavy syllables (those, in her interpretation, with either a long vowel plus a consonant or those with a short vowel plus two consonants) attract stress more easily than light (but non-schwa) syllables. Feet can consist of one heavy syllable or of two (left-strong) syllables. Within a word, the right-most foot is strong.

The issue of quantity-sensitivity appears to be crucial for a treatment of German stress in any type of framework. Note that I argue in § 8.2 of this book that stress in German cannot be quantity-sensitive, as syllables of all types are stressable as long as they contain a full vowel. But OT may allow for a more sophisticated decision in this case. Alber (1997, 1998) treats stress, in particular secondary stress, by constraints which include Weight-to-Stress, that is, a constraint requiring heavy syllables to be stressed. But by ranking this constraint somewhat low in the relevant hierarchy, the observation that German word stress often disobeys quantity-sensitivity is now taken care of: only under specific circumstances can quantity-sensitivity play a role. German turns out to be quantity-sensitive in this restricted way. The other issue of Alber's paper is stress preservation, whether word stress of complex (suffixed) words completely eradicates stress assigned in earlier cycles, or whether the stress-pattern of a stem is preserved after suffixation. Again, stress preservation can be found, but only at the cost of violating lower ranked constraints, and not at the cost of higher ranked constraints.

The acquisition of phonological patterns is the subject of Grijzenhout and Joppen's study (1999), in which they argue that the earliest utterances of a child learning German can be described by means of constraints favouring the maximal differentiation between consonants and vowels, and the realization of the place features for these consonants and vowels.

APPENDIX: WORD INDEX

Abenteuer adventure 286
Abenteurer adventurer 286
abfahren to drive off 103
Absolvent graduate 120
abstrahieren to abstract 196
abstrakt abstract 196
acht eight 211
Achtung attention 57, 65
Affe ape or monkey 10
Afrika Africa 46, 288
afrikanisch African 123
afrikanisieren to africanize 292
AG (abb.) > *Arbeitsgemeinschaft* 139
AGen (abb., pl.) > *Arbeitsgemeinschaft* 139
Ahorn maple 60
Akademiker academic 102
Akku (abb.) > *Akkumulator* 278
Akkumulator accumulator
Akkusativ accusative (case) 285
Akne acne 223
Aktie share 238
aktiv active 120, 200, 239, 285
Aktiv active voice (linguistics) 285
aktive (infl.) > *aktiv* 200
Aktivposten credit item or asset 104
AKWs (abb., pl.) > *Atomkraftwerke* 137
Akzeptabilität acceptability 292
Akzeptanz acceptance 120
Albernheit silliness 99
Alkohol alcohol 60, 124
alkoholisch alcoholic 124
allenthalben everywhere 146
Allheilmittel universal remedy 302
Alm Alpine pasture 10
Almosen charity 278
Alp Alpine pasture, nightmare 10
Alpinum alpine section in a botanical garden 288
Aluminiumteekanne aluminium teapot 300
Amboss anvil 68, 218
Amerika place name 288

Amerikaner an American 288
amerikanisieren to americanize 292
Amnestie amnesty 223
Amok amok 278
Amt office 218
Anamnese anamnesis 220
Anfang start, beginning 294
Angelsachsen (pl.) Anglo-Saxons 224
Anger meadow 225
angloamerikanisch Anglo-American 224
Angst fear 228
Ängste (pl.) fears 35
Ankunft arrival 68, 220
annehmen to suppose 231
Anpfiff kick-off 220
Antenne antenna 59, 60
Anton proper noun 59
applaudiert (part.) applauded 90
Araber Arab 288
arabisch Arabic 288
Arbeit work 107, 274, 285
Arbeiten (pl.) works 107
Arbeiter worker 306, 310
arbeitet he works 246
Arbeitsgemeinschaft working group 139
Arbeitskraft capacity for work 104
arbeitslos unemployed 290
Arbeitslosigkeit unemployment 290
Archiv archive 200
Archivar archivist 120
Archivare (pl.) archivists 137
argwöhnen to suspect 297
Arie aria 253
arm poor 309
Art type or kind 198
Arzt (medical) doctor 48, 196
Ärzteschaft medical profession 147
Asche ash 10
Assistenz assistance 120
äße he ate (cond.) 11
Atem breath 58, 59, 243, 246
atmen to breathe 34, 89, 246
Atmer (lit.) breather 246

Atmerei breathing 86
Atmung breathing 243
Atom atom 59
Atomkraftwerke (pl.) atomic power
    stations
aufhören to stop (doing something) 131
aufpassen to be alert (to) 295
aufräumen to clear 103
Äugchen (dim.) > *Auge* 126
Auge eye 126
aus out 10, 39, 173
Ausfall loss, cancellation 306, 307
Aussicht view 294
Auto fahren to drive a car 297
Autohändler car dealer 145
Automobil car 63
Autos (pl.) cars 137
Autoversicherung car insurance 146
Bach brook 10
Bäche (pl.) brooks 10
backen to bake 188
Bäcker baker 100, 120, 188, 190
Bäckerei bakery 86, 124
Bad bath 255
Baden-Württemberg place name 300
Bagger excavator 202
Bahn road, way, line 37
Bahnhof railway station 60, 300
Bake beacon, pole 277
Balkan the Balkans 279
Balken beam 50
Bälkchen (dim.) > *Balken* 50
Balkon balcony 12, 32
Balkone (pl.) balconies 233
Balkons (pl.) balconies 233
Ball ball 10
balladesk ballad-like 120
Ballast ballast 278
Banause Philistine or lowbrow 277
Band ribbon 220
Bank bank 37, 218, 220, 265
Banken (pl.) banks 277
Bankett banquet 279
Bann ban, spell 279
Bar bar 68
Bär a bear 184
Barbara proper noun 284
Barbarei barbarism 86

Bären (pl.) bears 17
Barock baroque 278
Barrel barrel 50
barren to hit horses in training 50
Barren ingot, parallel bars (sport) 50
Bars (pl.) bars 137, 141, 142
Bass bass 11
Bauch abdomen 210
Bäuche (pl.) abdomens 210
Bauer farmer 191, 247, 248
bäuerlich rural 191
Baum tree 61, 108, 161, 186, 187
Baume (dat.) > *Baum* 108
Bäume (pl.) trees 61, 137, 161, 186, 187
Baum(e)s (gen.) > *Baum* 108
bäurisch rural, rustic 247, 248
beachtlich considerable 189
beantworten to answer 97
Beben earth tremor 106
Bedingungen (pl.) conditions 224
Beeren (pl.) berries 17
Beet (flower) bed 11
befehlen to command 61
befragen to question 97
behalten to hold, keep 124
behaupten to claim 124
Bein leg 10, 37
beladen to load 95, 96, 198
beliebig any 206
beliebige (infl.) > *beliebig* 206
Bemühung effort 161
Bengel rascal, rogue 224
Berlin place name 220, 221
Bernhard proper noun 10, 15, 60
Bernward proper noun 10
Beschreibungen (pl.) descriptions 137
beschwichtigen to soothe 209
Besserwisser wiseacre, know-all 104
betriangeln to play the triangle (music)
    97
Bett bed 11, 132, 141
Betten (pl.) beds 35, 137
bewegen to move, stir 194
Beziehung relationship 121
Bibliothekar librarian 61, 120, 270, 276,
    292
biegen to bend 196, 206
Bienen (pl.) bees 11

Bier beer 17
bieten to offer 11
Bilder (pl.) pictures 275
bildschön pretty as a picture 103, 310
Bildung education 275
Billet billet, entrance ticket 34
Billigware low-priced goods 104
Billion billion (UK) or trillion (USA) 34, 238
Binärcode binary code 104
binnen within (a period of time) 11
Bio (abb.) > *Biologie* 160
Biologe biologist 277, 279
Biologie biology 120, 277, 279
Birne pear 17
birst you burst 230
Bischof bishop 183
Bischöfe (pl.) bishops 183
Biss bite 10, 11
bitten to ask for 11
blau blue 40, 263
Blümchen (dim.) flower(s) 137
Blumenduft floral fragrance 144
blutarm anaemic 310
blutig bloody 190, 191
blutiger bloodier 190
blutrot blood-red 103
Boa boa 160
Boden ground 10
bog he bent 196
Bogen bow 10
Boje buoy 237
Bojen (pl.) buoys 10
Bonn place name 68
Botanik botany 102
Botaniker botanist 102
brachte he brought 178, 209
brandmarken to brand, stigmatize 297
brasilianisch Brazilian 198, 288
brauchen to need 211
brauen to brew 111
brav honest, good 200, 239
braven (pl.) > *brav* 222
Bretter (pl.) boards 137
Brilliant cut-diamond, brilliant 34
bringen to fetch, bring 178, 209
brüderlich brotherly 189
Brunnen spring(s), well(s) 126

Brünnlein (dim.) > *Brunnen* 126
Bube lad 63
Bubi sonny 63, 121
Buch book 108, 141, 210
Buche (dat.) > *Buch* 108
Bücher (pl.) books 210
Bücherwurm bookworm 143
Buch(e)s (gen.) > *Buch* 108
Büchlein (dim.) > *Buch* 122
Buchneuheit (lit.) book novelty 76
Bucht bay 209
Bund association 201
Bunde (dat.) > *Bund* 201
Bundesdeutscher citizen of FRG 63
Bundi (abb.) > *Bundesdeutscher* 63
bunt colourful 201
bunte (infl.) > *bunt* 201
Büro office 278
Büros (pl.) offices 137
Bus bus 10, 145
Busch bush 108
Busches (gen.) > *Busch* 108
Café café 278
Cembalo harpsichord 266
Champagner champagne 34
Chaos chaos 59
chaotisch chaotic 59
Charisma charisma 210
Chemie chemistry 210, 211
Cherub cherub 141
Cherubim (pl.) cherubim 141
Cherubs (gen.) > *Cherub* 141
chilenisch Chilean 198
China China 10, 210, 217
Chirurg surgeon 210
Cholesterin cholesterol 210
Computer computer(s) 106, 137, 139
Computerchen (dim.) > *Computer* 188
computern to use a computer 94
computert (part.) used a computer 94
Cowboys (pl.) cowboys 137
Dach roof 210
Dächer (pl.) roofs 210
dachte I, he thought 209
Dahlie dahlia 34
Damast damask 278
Dampf steam 68
dann then 10

das (n.) the 10, 118
Daumen thumb(s) 126
Däumling thumb-stall, Tom Thumb 126
dein (sg.) your 118
Dekan dean 61, 287
Dekanat dean's office 120, 287
Demonstrant demonstrator 120
Demut humility 197, 274, 285
denke I think 110, 111
denken to think 110, 209, 218
denkst you (sg.) think 37
Deo (abb.) > Deodorant 160
Deodorant deodorant
der (m.) the 118
Derivat derivative 102
Derivation derivation 102
Detektei detective agency 86
deuteln (iter.) > deuten 120
deuten to indicate 120
deutsch German 34, 40
diagonal diagonal 120
dich (acc.) you 68, 214, 248, 249, 277
dick thick, fat 271
die (f. or pl.) the 118
Dieberei stealing 86
Diener servant(s) 277
Dienst service 37, 196
Diktat dictation 102
Diktator dictator 102, 123, 126
diktatorisch dictatorial 126
Dill dill 10
Ding thing 10, 218, 224, 225, 228
Dinge (pl.) things 224, 225, 226, 228
Dingerchen (dim.) > Dinge 146
Dings (gen.) > Ding 265
Diode diode 58, 59
Diphthong diphthong 224
diphthongieren to diphthongize 224
dir (dat. sg.) you 248, 249
direkt (adj.) direct 277
Direktor director 120
Disharmonie disharmony 124
diskret discreet 124
Diskussion discussion 209
diskutabel worth discussing 120
Diskutant discussant 209
diskutieren to discuss 110, 120, 209
Diskutiererei discussing 86

diskutiert (part.) discussed 90, 92
Doktorand doctoral student 120
Dominik proper noun 137
doof stupid 37
Dorf village 37
Drama drama 120, 121
Dramen (pl.) dramas 121
drauf upon 37
drei three 10, 196
Dreifarbstift three-colour pen 301
Dreifelderwirtschaft three-field system
    301
Dreimädelhaus (lit.) three-girl house
    301
Dreiraumwohnung three-room
    apartment 305
dreißig thirty 176
Dreizimmerwohnung three-room
    apartment 305
dritt third 196
Drohung threat 161
Dromedar dromedary 244, 278
Dschungel jungle(s) 40
du (nom.) you 249
Duett duet 161
dumm stupid 182, 184, 223
dümmer more stupid 184
dümmlich in a silly manner 182
dumpf dull, hollow 184
dumpfer duller, more hollow 184
dunkel dark 243, 246
Dunkelheit darkness 99
Dunkelkammer dark-room 103
Dunkelkeit > Dunkelheit 99
dunkelrot dark red 300
Dunkelziffer number of unreported cases
    104
dunkle (infl.) > dunkel 246
dunkles (n.) > dunkel 243
dünn thin 10, 223
dünnem (dat.) > dünn 220, 223
Duo duo 60, 161
durch through 39, 210, 211, 257
durchdiskutiert (part.) discussed
    thoroughly 94
durchführbar executable 121
durchführen to execute (a plan etc.)
    295

Durchgang passage 294
durchgefallen fallen through 94
durchlaufen to run through 103, 124, 295
dürr thin, skinny, arid 10
Ebert proper noun 255
Ecke corner 10, 133, 271
edel noble 58, 202
edles (n.) > *edel* 58, 202
egal alike, equal 59, 199
Ehrbarkeit respectability 98
ehrenhaft honourable 70
Eierchen (dim.) egg 146
eigene (infl.) own 246
eigentlich really 147
eigentliche (infl.) > *eigentlich* 275
Eigentum property 120, 202
Eigentumsrecht property law 128
Eigner owner(s) 202, 246
Eignung qualification 246
ein (n.) a, one 250
einatmen to inhale 59
eine (f.) a, one 58, 250
einem (dat.) a, one 220, 223, 250
einen (acc.) a, one 250
Eingabe input 220
eingeatmet (part.) breathed in 94
einkaufen to shop 229
Einmannboot (lit.) one-man boat 301
einsehen to have a look at 295
Ekel disgust 59
ekeln to be disgusted 50
eklen (infl.) disgusting 50
eklig disgusting 50
Elch moose 10
elektrisieren to electrify 102
Elektrizität electricity 119
Elektron electron 120
elend miserable 11, 101
elendig miserable 101
Elf a team of eleven 10
Elisabeth proper noun 64, 284
Elster magpie 35
Engel angel(s) 225
Engelein (dim.) > *angel* 231
enorm enormous 199
entfallen slipped 90, 94
entfernen to distance (oneself) 124

Entgegnung reply, retort 295
entladen to discharge 95, 96, 198
Entleiher borrower(s) 295
Entnahme withdrawal 296
entnehmen to withdraw 296
entscheidendere more decisive 110, 276
Enzyklopädie encyclopaedia 292
er he 249
erfahren to get to know 124
Erlaubnis permission 295
erlebt (part.) experienced 94
erstens firstly 35
Erz ore 45
Erzählung story, narration 295
Erzfeind arch-enemy 294
erzkonservativ arch-conservative 294
Erzschicht ore layer 294
es it 248, 249
Esche ash tree 10
Eselei tomfoolery 86
Eselein (dim.) donkey 231, 232
Eskimos (pl.) Eskimos 137
esse I eat 11
essen to eat 194
essbar edible 121
Etui case (for pencils, glasses, etc.) 278
euch (dat., acc., pl.) you 211, 249
Eucharistie Eucharist 292
Eukalyptus eucalyptus 288
Europa Europe 182, 183
europäisch European 182, 183
ewig eternal 98
ewige (infl.) > *ewig* 200
Ewigkeit eternity 98
Existenzialismus existentialism 292
exklusiv exclusive 124
exponiert (part.) exposed 124
extra extra 35
Fabrikat product 209
Fabrikation fabrication 209
Fabrikator manufacturer, producer 209
Fabriken (pl.) factories 107
fähig able 98
Fähigkeit ability 98
fahre I go, drive 188
fahren to go, drive 188, 253
Fahrer driver(s) 188
Fahrerchen (dim.) > *Fahrer* 190

Fahrkarte ticket 300
Fahrrad bicycle 300
Fahrt a drive 198
fährt he goes 188, 253
Fakir fakir 278
fallen to fall 10, 35, 36
falsch wrong 233
fälschen to falsify, counterfeit 233
fangen to catch 10
fantastisch fantastic 120, 123
Farbenblindheit colour blindness 127
farbig coloured 65, 100, 121
Farbigkeit colourfulness 100
farblos colourless 65, 66, 68, 121
Farbstift coloured pencil 301
Farn fern 50
Fazit result, upshot 278
fehlend missing 11
fehllos faultless 69
feil mercenary, venal 37
feilschst you (sg.) bargain 48
Feind enemy 48, 196
Feindschaft enmity 70
feist fat, chubby 268
Feldmarschall Field Marshal 310
Femininum feminine (gender) 285
Fenster window(s) 35, 268
Fertiggericht ready-to-serve meal 104
fest solid 268
Figuren (pl.) figures 107
Film film 37
Filter filter(s) 106, 243
Filtrat filtrate 52, 53, 54, 66, 120, 243
Finger finger(s) 224
fingieren to fake, simulate 218, 224
Fink finch 218
Fisch fish 10
Flanke flank 40
Flansch flange 222
Flöße (pl.) rafts 137
Flucht escape 210
flüchtig escaping 210
Flüge (pl.) flights 195
Flughafenarbeiter airport worker(s) 310
Flugzeug aeroplane 195, 300
Flur (m.) corridor, (f.) pasture 139
Flure (pl.) corridors 139
Fluren (pl.) pastures 139

flüssig liquid 100
Flüssigkeit a liquid 100
Formalität formality 292
Format format 102
Formation formation 102
formelhaft stereotyped 121
Frau woman 61
Frauchen (dim.) > *Frau* 211
Frauen (pl.) women 61, 137
Frauenhaus women's centre 103, 143
frei free 10, 123
Freiheit freedom 98, 123
freiheitlich liberal 123
Freiheitlichkeit liberality 98, 123, 290
Frequenz frequency 120
Freude joy 126
Freund friend 48, 196
Freundschaft friendship 70
Frikassee fricassee 36
Friseur barber 120
fühlen to feel 11
füllen to fill 11
Fundamentaler supporter(s) of
    fundamentalist ideas 63
Fundi (abb.) > *Fundamentaler* 63
fünf five 222
Fünfmeilenzone five-mile zone 301
Fünfuhrtee (lit.) five o'clock tea 301
Funktion function 120
für for 133, 184, 185
Furcht fear 198
Fürst prince 141
Fürsten (pl.) princes 137
Fußballfeld football pitch 298
Gans goose 233
Gänse (pl.) geese 233
Gänsestall (lit.) goose stall 143
ganz complete 218
Ganzheit completeness 121
Garage garage 12
Gärtchen (dim.) > *Garten* 50, 126
Garten garden 50, 126
Gärten (pl.) gardens 137, 230
Gas gas 195
Gase (pl.) gases 195
Gastarbeiter immigrant worker 306,
    308, 310
gearbeitet (part.) worked 90

Gebäude building 124
Gebein bones 11
geben to give 10, 11, 194, 209, 222
Gebirgler highlander 202
gebogen (part.) bent 196
gebrauchen to use 124
Gebüsch shrubbery 97
Gediskutiere discussing 97
gefallen to please, (part.) fallen 61, 190
gefrühstückt (part.) breakfasted 94
gefunden (part.) found 89
gegeben (part.) given 166
gegenstandlich with respect to an object 190
gegenständlich concrete 128, 190
Geheime Staatspolizei (lit.) secret state police 63
geheiratet (part.) married 90, 95
gehen to go 60, 111, 112
Geheul howling 50
geholfen (part.) helped 166
Geister (pl.) ghosts 121, 137
geistern to spook 102, 120
gekennzeichnet (part.) indicated 94
gekiebitzt (part.) spied 90
Geld money 11
Gelehrsamkeit learnedness 98
gelernt (part.) learnt 92
geliebkost (part.) caressed 90
Gemeinschaft community 139
genau exactly 61, 234
Genie genius 10, 12
Genius genius 10
geohrfeigt (part.) slapped 94
Georg proper noun 59
Georgien Georgia (in Caucasia) 59
Geplapper prattle 97
Gepredige preachings 97
gepredigt (part.) preached 90, 92, 93, 96
gerannt (part.) run 89
Gerede talk 97
geredet (part.) talked 90
Gerenne running 97
gern with pleasure 37
gerochen (part.) smelled 196
Gerundium gerund 285
Gerundivum gerundive 285
geschlossen (part.) closed 196

geschoben (part.) pushed 196
Geschrei shouting 97
Geschwindigkeit speed 100
gesehen (part.) seen 111
Gespanntheit tenseness 98
Gestapo (abb.) > *Geheime Staatspolizei* 63, 64
gestern yesterday 118
gesucht (part.) looked for 90
Getelefoniere telephoning 97
getriangelt (part.) triangled 90
getriggert (part.) triggered 94
gewallfahrtet (lit.) been on a pilgrimage 94
Gewerkschaft trade union 124
Gewerkschafter trade unionist(s) 121, 123
gib (imp.) give 209
gibt he gives 194
Gift poison 209
Gischt spray 266
glaubbar believable 69
glaube I believe 243
Glaube belief 126
glaubhaft credible 70, 121, 275
glaubst you (sg.) believe 48
glaubt he believes 48
Glöckchen (dim.) > *Glocke* 182
Glocke bell 182
Glück luck 40, 68
Gmünd place name 262
Gold gold 11
Göttingen place name 68, 220
Göttlich godly, divine 189
graduieren to graduate 119
Graf earl, count 10, 39
Grammatik grammar 127
Grammatiker grammarian 127
grandios grand 120
Graphit graphite 278
Gras grass 10, 195, 200
Gräser (pl.) grasses 195, 200
grasgrün grass-green 310
Grauschopf (lit.) grey-head 104
grob rough, coarse 195
grobe (infl.) > *grob* 195
große (infl.) big, large 244
größer bigger, greater 190, 253

größere (infi.) > *größer* 253
größeres (n., infl.) > *größer* 274
Großgrundbesitzer big landowner(s) 302
Großmut magnanimity 104
Grube pit, hollow 209
Gruft tomb, vault 209
grün green 309
Gruß greetings 182, 220
grüßen to greet 182
Gummi rubber 278
gut good 234
gutartig harmless 65
guttun to do good 103
Hafenarbeiter docker(s) 310
Hahn cockerel, rooster 11
Hahnenfuß crowfoot (plant name) 147
halb half 37, 209
halben half of something 232
Hälfte half 209
Halle hall 11
Halm stalk 222
Hals neck 233
Hälse (pl.) necks 233
hält he holds, stops 230
Hand hand 218
handeln to trade, act 202
handlich handy 57
Handlung act 66, 202
Handwerkerschaft (lit.) craftwork profession 123
Hanf hemp 222
Hangar hangar 224
Hanno proper noun 269
Hannover place name 269
Hannoveraner person from Hanover 269
Harmonika harmonica 61
Harpune harpoon 279
harpunieren to harpoon 279
harsch harsh 10
hart hard 10, 198
Haupt head, chief 48
Hauptbahnhof main railway station 300, 301
Haus house 10, 141, 173
Hauses (gen.) > *Haus* 108
Häuser (pl.) > *Haus* 137

Häuslein (dim.) > *Haus* 188
Hausmann houseman 103
heben to lift 209
hebt he lifts 209
Heer army 253
Heft copy-book 209
hehren (pl.) sublime, noble 17
Heimat home 278
Heirat marriage 285
Heiserkeit coarseness 99
heißen to be called, named 41
heißt you (sg.) are called 41
heitere (infl.) bright, fair 45
Helden (pl.) heroes 148
Hemd shirt 218
Hengst stallion 228
heran near to 66
Herbst autumn 37, 48, 259
Hering herring 274
Hermelin ermine, stoat 278
Herr mister, gentleman 50, 253
Herren (pl.) sirs, gentlemen 17, 50, 109
Herrn (dat. sg.) mister, gentleman 50, 109
Herz heart 45, 147
Herzens (gen.) > *Herz* 147
Herzenslust heart's desire 140, 147
Heu hay 184
hinaus out of, out from 66
Hindernisse (pl.) obstacles 137
hintergehen to betray 124
hintertreiben to prevent, thwart 295
hoch high 182, 210, 211, 214, 215
höchst highly, in a high degree 182
höchstens at the most 210
Hof yard 300
hoffnungslos hopeless 121
Höflichkeit courtesy 98, 121
hohe (infl.) high 211
höher higher 211
Höhle cave 11
Hokuspokus hocus-pocus 64
Hölle hell 11
Holz wood, timber 182
hölzern wooden 182
Honig honey 206
Honorar fee 171
Hörfunk radio 103

hübsch pretty 264
Huhn chicken 11, 182
Hühner (pl.) chickens 182
hui woosh! 52, 160
Hund dog 182, 188
Hundchen (dim.) > *Hund* 188, 190
Hündchen (dim.) > *Hund* 190
Hunde (pl.) dogs 145, 188
hundert hundred 244
Hündin bitch 182, 188
Hunger hunger 224, 228
hungrig hungry 228
hurra hurrah 171, 282
Hut hat 108
Hütchen (dim.) > *Hut* 189
Hute (dat.) > *Hut* 108
Hüte (pl.) hats 11
Hüten (dat. pl.) > *Hüte* 109
Hutes (gen.) > *Hut* 108
Huts (gen.) > *Hut* 108
Hütte hut 11
Hyäne hyena 160
Hymne hymn 223
Hypnose hypnosis 223
ich (nom.) I 211, 249
Ideal ideal 59
Idee idea 59, 60, 61, 274
Ideen (pl.) ideas 107
Iden ides 59
Idiot idiot 238
Igel hedgehog 58
ihm (dat. sg.) him 249
ihn (acc. sg.) him 249
ihnen (dat. pl.) them 249
ihr (infl.) her, you 249
ihren her, your 17
illegal illegal 66, 124, 125, 231
illegitim illegitimate 285
Imitat imitation 102
Imitator imitator 102
Imker bee keeper(s) 218
impfen to vaccinate 218
impotent impotent 66, 125
in in 39
Inga proper noun 224, 275
Inge proper noun 224, 275
Ingo proper noun 224
injizieren to inject 237

inkompetent incompetent 221, 285
innen inside 118
instabil unstable 124
Installateur plumber 120
Instrumentenbauer instrument maker(s) 147
interessant interesting 120, 126
Interessantheit interestingness 98
Interesse interest 126
irregulär irregular 66, 125, 285
irren to be mistaken 17
irrt he is mistaken 253
Irrtum mistake 126
isst he eats 194
Italien Italy 198
italienisch Italian 123, 198
Jagd hunt 203
Jagden (pl.) hunts 107, 203
jagen to hunt 203, 237
jäh suddenly 273
Jahrhundert century 299, 300
Japan Japan 124, 279, 288
Japaner a Japanese 124, 288
japanisch Japanese 124
jeder everybody, each 237
jiddisch Yiddish 237
Job job 10
Jordan Jordan 279
Josef proper noun 237
Journalist journalist 289
Jubel jubilation 198
Jubilar person celebrating his jubilee 198
Jude Jew 237
jüdisch Jewish 237
Jugend youth 10, 237
jung young 236, 237, 238
Jungens (pl.) boys 140
jünger younger 237
Jungsozialist Young Socialist 63
Juso (abb.) > *Jungsozialist* 63
Kaffee coffee 278
Kaffeebohne coffee bean 104
kafkaesk Kafkaesque 120
Kajak kayak 237
Kajüte cabin (on a ship) 237
Kakadu cockatoo 278
Kalb calf 10

Kalender calendar(s) 46
Kalk chalk 10
kalt cold 33
Kamera camera 282
Kamm comb 185
Kämme (pl.) combs 185
kämmen to comb 10, 222
Kammern (pl.) chambers 107
Kanaan Canaan 232
kanadisch Canadian 288
Kanapee sofa 278
Kandidat candidate 120
Kandidatur candidature 292
Kanne pitcher, pot 279
Kanon canon 288
kanonisch canonical 288
Kantate cantata 279
Kante edge 218
Kanus (pl.) canoes 137
Kanzlei office 122
Karzinom carcinoma 161
Kasse cash register 36
Kassel place name 220
Kätzchen (dim.) > *Katze* 126
Katze cat 126
Kegel cone, bowling pin 271
kehren to sweep 222
Keller cellar 10, 260
kennen to know 10, 222
Kenner expert(s) 10
Kerl lad 50, 260
Khmer proper noun 262, 263
kiebitzen to spy 90
Kiefer (m.) jaw, (f.) pine tree 139
Kiefer (pl.) jaws 139
Kiefern (pl.) pine trees 139
Kimono kimono 276, 283, 288
Kind child 10, 61, 218, 271, 275
Kindchen (dim.) > *Kind, Kinder* 146, 275
Kinder (pl.) children 61
Kinderchen (dim.) > *Kinder* 146, 147
Kinderfahrrad child's bike 300
Kinderlein (dim.) > *Kinder* 146, 147
Kinderwagen pram 143, 144
Kindesalter infancy, childhood 143
Kindfrau child-woman 143
kindisch childish 65, 120, 122

Kindlein (dim.) > *Kind* 146, 275
Kindskopf silly person 143
Kinos (pl.) cinemas 137
Kiosk kiosk 259, 266, 285
Kirche church 210
Kladde notebook, pad 202
kläglich wretched 74
Klavier spielen to play the piano 295
kleidsam flattering, becoming 121
klein small 39
klirren to clatter 40
Klöster (pl.) monasteries 137
klug clever 263
Knabe boy
Knäblein (dim.) > *Knabe* 188
Knäuel snarl, throng 50
Knie knee 39
Koch cook 10
Kolchose collective farm 210, 217
Kollege colleague 126
Kollegin (f.) colleague 126
Köln Cologne 50
Kommando command 120
Kommandos (pl.) commands 137
kommerziell commercial 120
Kommunistische Partei Communist Party 139
Konfirmand confirmand 120
Konflikt conflict 222
König king 148, 206, 207, 212, 216, 274
Könige (pl.) kings 206, 212
königlich royal 208
Königs (gen.) > *König* 206
Konjunktur economic situation 120
Konstanz constancy 120
Konsul consul 278
Konsum consumption, supermarket 278
kontinuierlich continual 122
kontinuierliches (n., infl.) > *kontinuierlich* 129
Konto bank account 278
Kopf head 10, 266
Koppel (n.) belt-buckle, (f.) meadow 139
Koppeln meadows 139
Koran Koran 279
Korrektur correction 120

KP (abb.) > *Kommunistische Partei* 139
kräftig powerful, strong 121
kräftigen to strengthen 121
Kräftigungen (pl.) strengthenings 55
krakeelt (part.) kicked up a row 90
Krankenkostendämpfungsgesetz law to reduce health-care costs 299
Krebs cancer, crab 48
Krimi (abb.) > *Kriminalroman* 63
Kriminalpolizei criminal police 63
Kriminalroman detective story 63
Kripo (abb.) > *Kriminalpolizei* 63
Kritik criticism 102
Kritiker critic(s) 102
Kroate Croat 160
Krokodil crocodile 274
Kuchen cake 69, 211, 217
Kuh cow 217
Kuhchen (dim.) > *Kuh* 69, 211, 217
Kühchen (dim.) > *Kuh* 217
Kuli a coolie 46, 277
kulinarisch culinary 277
Kultus cult 277
Kumpan companion 279
Kurzwort clipping 63
Kuss a kiss 10, 220
Kutte cowl, smock 252
Kutter trawler(s) 252
Labors (pl.) laboratories 137
lächeln to smile 182
lächelnd smiling 48
lachen to laugh 182
lächerlich ridiculous 102
Lachs salmon 266
laden to load 96, 209
lädt he loads 209, 230, 231, 232
lahm lame 10
lahmen to lame 10
Lametta tinsel 281
Landeszentralbank state central bank 298
lang long 184, 185, 218, 223, 224, 228
längen to elongate 189
langer (m., infl.) > *lang* 224
länger longer 228
Langfinger thief 224
länglich elongated, oblong 184, 189, 224
Längung elongation 227

längt he lengthens 265
Larifari nonsense 64
Last burden, load 14
lässt (sg.) you let, he lets 230
latschen to slouch along 10
Latz napkin 14, 266
Laub foliage 10, 11
Laubs (gen.) > *Laub* 48
laufe I run 182
laufen to run 184, 223
laufgerecht suited to running 103
läufst you (sg.) run 37
läuft he runs 182, 184, 246
Laute (pl.) sounds 11
läuten to ring 11
Lava lava 239
leben to live 10, 11, 65
lebend living, alive 101, 198
lebendig lively, alive 101, 198
Lebendigkeit liveliness 101
Leber liver(s) 10
lechzt you yearn for 48
lecken to lick 11
Leder leather(s) 10
lediglich merely 208
legen to lay 11, 270
legt he lays 246
lehnst you (sg.) lean 48
lehnt he leans 48
Lehre teachings, apprenticeship 11, 252
Lehrer teacher, teachers 11, 62, 65, 98, 137, 252
Lehrerin (f.) teacher 122
Lehrerinnen (pl.) > *Lehrerin* 275
Leib body 11
Leiche corpse 206
Leichnam corpse 206
leiden to suffer 10
leidet (infl.) he suffers 246
leiten to lead, to conduct 10, 110, 222
Leiter (m.) leader, conductor (f.) ladder 139
Leiter (pl.) leaders, conductors 139, 253
Leiterin (f.) leader, conductress 253
Leitern (pl.) ladders 139
Lemgo place name 218
Leonhard proper noun 60
Leopard leopard 278, 285

lernt he learns 92
lesen to read 41
Leute people 11
Libelle dragon-fly 278
Liebe love 7
lieben to love 10, 11, 111, 112
liebkosen to caress 90
liebkost (part.) caressed 90
lieblich sweet 7, 66, 68
lieblicher sweeter 67
liederliche (adj., infl.) negligent 57
liefen we, they ran 10
liegen to lie 234
liest you (sg.) read 41, 230
lilafarben violet 105
Lilie lily 34
linear linear 308
lineare (infl.) > *linear* 307, 308
Linguistik linguistics 120, 127
Linguistin (f.) linguist 122
Lioba proper noun 160
Lippen (pl.) lips 278
Lisp Lisp (computer language) 264, 266
List trick 11, 266
LKW-Gebühr toll for trucks 146
LKWs (pl.) trucks 137
Lob praise 10, 200, 201, 204
loben to praise 11
Lobes (gen.) > *Lob* 200, 201
lobst you (sg.) praise 37
Loch hole 210
Löcher (pl.) holes 121, 210
löchern to perforate 120
locken to lure 11
locker loose 277
lockern to loosen 50
lockren (infl.) > *locker* 50
Loggia loggia 10
Lohn reward, wage 10
Lok (abb.) > *Lokomotive* 63
Lokomotive locomotive 63
Los fate 10, 68
Lot plumb-bob 10
löten to solder 11
Lotta proper noun 10
Löwchen (dim.) > *Löwe* 200
Löwe lion 200, 239
LPs (pl.) long-playing records 137

Luft air 188, 259
lüften to air 188
lüg (imp.) tell a lie 206
lügen to lie 11, 206
Luise proper noun 58
Lust desire 11
mächtig powerful 189
Mächtigkeit power 189
Mafia mafia 278
Magistrat magistrate 120
Mahagoni mahogany 60
mähdreschen to combine-harvest 103, 297
Malaria malaria 269
Maler painter(s) 120
Malerei painting 124
malerisch picturesque 123, 124, 191, 248, 288
malerische (infl.) > *malerisch* 57, 58
Malta place name 269
manch some 210, 211, 222
manisfestieren to manifest 292
Mann man 108, 221
Manne (dat.) > *Mann* 108
Männer (pl.) men 137, 146
Männern (dat. pl.) > *Männer* 65, 109
Männerstimme male voice 143
Mann(e)s (gen.) > *Mann* 108, 146
Mannesalter manhood, virile age 146
Manneskraft manly vigour 143
Mannloch manhole 143
Mannsbild fellow 143, 146
mannsdick as wide as a man 143
manuell manual 120
Mappe portfolio 10
Mark (n.) marrow; (f.) march, mark 139
markant marked 120
Marke (pl.) marrows 139
Marken (pl.) marches, marks 139
Markiertheit markedness 98
Markierung marking 122
Markt market 48, 72, 167, 260
Markt(e)s (gen.) > *Markt* 48
Marsch (m.) march, (f.) marsh 139, 233
Marschall marshal 310
Märsche (pl.) marches 139, 233
Marschen (pl.) marshes 139
Martina proper noun 137, 288

Marxismus-Leninismus
MarxismLeninism 300
März March 45
Marzipan marzipan 276, 278, 285
Masche mesh 10
Maskulinum masculine (gender) 285
Masse mass 10
Mathematik mathematics 127
Mathematiker mathematician 127
Matte mat 10, 36
Matthias proper noun 36
Mauern (pl.) walls 62, 107
Maulheld braggart 148
Maulheldentum braggartry 148
Maus mouse 10, 188
Mäuse (pl.) mice 145, 188
Mausefalle mouse trap 145
mausen to catch mice 188
Meditation meditation 123
Meer sea 98
mein (sg.) my 118
meinetwegen on my behalf 146
Melancholie melancholy 292
Melönchen (dim.) > *Melone* 126
Melone melon 126
mengentheoretisch set-theoretical 148
Mensch human 147, 222, 233
Menschen (pl.) humans 147, 233
Menschenskinder man alive! 147
mephistophelisch Mephistophelean 292
Metall metal 46, 277
Meteorologie meteorology 270, 276, 292
Metrik metrics 277
Mette church mass 277
mich (acc. sg.) me 249
Michael proper noun 59
Michaela proper noun 59
Milliarde billion 34, 238
Mimikry mimicry 278
mir (dat. sg.) me 249
missbehagen to feel uneasy 296
missbrauchen to misuse 296
missfallen to displease 296
missgelaunt (part.) ill humoured 294
missglückt (part.) failed 94
Missgunst ill will 294
missinterpretieren to misinterpret 296
misstrauen to mistrust 124, 296

missverstehen to misunderstand 296
Misswahl beauty contest 294
mit with 39
Mittag midday 310
Mob mob 10
Mobiliar furniture 119
möblieren to furnish 66
möchte I, he would like 209
Modul module 278
Mogelei cheating 120
mögen to like 209
mögt you (pl.) like 209
Monat month 279
Mönch monk 222
Mond moon 48, 196
Mond(e)s (gen.) > *Mond* 48
Motor motor 278
Motorengeräusch engine noise 144
Müdigkeit tiredness 100
Mühsal toil 121
Mull gauze 11
Müll garbage 11
Mumps mumps 48
Mund mouth 10
München Munich 210
Murks something botched 48
Mus pap, mash 11
Musen (pl.) Muses 277
Museum museum 277
Musik music 120, 124, 127, 279
musikalisch musical 127, 278, 279
Musiker musician(s) 124, 127
Muskel muscle 106, 141, 198
Muskeln (pl.) muscles 106, 137, 230
Muskulatur muscular system 198
muss I have to, he has to 11
Muster pattern(s) 277
mutig courageous 190
Mutter mother 63, 142
Mütter (pl.) mothers 137, 145
Mütterberatung counselling for mothers 145
Mütterlein (dim.) > *Mutter* 188
Mutti mummy 63
myogen myogenic (medical term) 161
Myom myoma 161
nach after, to 210
Nachbarn (pl.) neighbours 107

Nachmittag afternoon 310
nächste (infl.) next, following 210
nachts at night 118
nagelneu brand new 310
nähren to nourish 17
naiv naïve 200
Namen (pl.) names 230
namentlich by name 146
Narr fool 253
Närrin (f.) fool 17
närrisch foolish 57
Nation nation 123, 236, 287
national national 123, 287
nationalisieren to nationalize 102, 130
Nationalismus nationalism 287
Nationalist nationalist 123
Nationalität nationality 7
Nationalsozialist national socialist 63
Naturalisation naturalization 269, 292
Naturalismus naturalism 269
Nazi (abb.) > Nationalsozialist 63
neblig foggy 66
nebulös nebulous 120
nehmen to take 194
nein no 11
nervös nervous 189
Nervosität nervousness 189
Neuheit novelty 98, 275
Neuheiten (pl.) novelties 137
Neuigkeit news 98, 100
Neuigkeitswert news value 128
neun nine 11, 37
Neutralität neutrality 120
niedrig low 121
Niedrigwasser low tide 104
nimmt he takes 194
Nominalphrase nominal phrase 139
Nominativ nominative (case) 285
Nord north 302
Nordpol north pole 302
nörgeln to nag 202
Nörgler nagger(s) 202
norwegisch Norwegian 288
Note note 10
notlanden to make a forced landing 297
NP (abb.) > Nominalphrase 139
Nüchternheit sobriety 99
Nummern (pl.) numbers 62, 107

oberlehrerhaft pedantic 128
obrigkeitlich authoritarian 123
Obst fruit 37, 48, 196
Oda proper noun 254
Ode ode 254
Oder river name 254
Ofen oven, stove 11
offen open 11, 58
Offenheit openness 99
offiziell official 119
Öffnungszeiten opening times 144
Omas (pl.) grandmas 137
Omen omen 245
ominös ominous 245
Omnibus omnibus 220
Onkel uncle 106, 184
Onkelchen (dim.) > Onkel 184, 188
Onkeln (dat. pl.) > Onkel 109
Opa grandpa 58, 171
Opal opal 10
Oper opera 171
Opium Opium 288
orange orange colour 200, 264, 265
Orange an orange 120, 200
Orden decoration, medal 230
ordentlich orderly, accurately 146
Organ organ 279
Organisation organization 102
Originalität originality 292
Ort place 198
Ostasien East Asia 300
Ostermontag Easter Monday 300
Ostersonntag Easter Sunday 300
Oval oval 10
Palast palace 274
palavert (part.) palavered, gabbled 90
Papier paper 278
Papsttum pontificate 69
Parade parade 279
paradieren to parade 279
Parfum perfume 12
Parks (pl.) parks 137
Partei (political) party 139
Partikel (n.) (grammatical) particle, (f.)
    particle 139
Partikel (pl.) (grammatical) particles 139
Partikeln (pl.) particles 139
Pass pass, passport 220

Pazifismus pacifism 288
pedantisch pedantic 122
Pein torment 10
peinigen to torture 121
Pelikan pelican 279
Pensionat boarding school 123
Pergola pergola 288
Pfad path 266
Pfalz Palatinate 42
Pfarrei parish 86, 122
Pfau peacock 10
Pfeil arrow 42
Pflanze plant 40
Pflaume plum 40
pflegen to care 209
Pflicht duty 40, 209
pflücken to pick 40
pfui phew! 52, 160
Phantasie fantasy, imagination 120, 196
phantasielos unimaginative 122
Phantast visionary 196
Philosophie philosophy 46, 292
Philosophiestudium studies of
    philosophy 197
Phonis (abb., pl.) > *Phonologe* 62
Phonologe phonologist 126
Phonologie phonology 34, 35, 292
Phonologin (f.) phonologist 126
Phrase phrase 139
Physik physics 124, 127
physikalisch physical 127
Physiker physicist 121
Pinguin penguin 278, 293
Pinguinin (f.) penguin 293
Piratentum piracy 120
Planung planning 298
Plauderei chatting 86, 120
Pneu pneumatic tyre 262
Poesie poesy 59
Poet poet 10, 59, 160
Pol pole 270
polar polar 270
Polarisation polarization 270
Politik politics 127
Pollen pollen 50
Porzellan porcelain 300
Porzellanteekanne porcelain teapot 300
Praktikant trainee 123

Präsident president 120
Präsidentschaft presidency 122
Predigt sermon 285
pricklig prickly 50
Privatdozent untenured university
    lecturer 104
Privatheit privacy 98
Produkt product 209, 287, 291
Produktion production 120, 209
produktiv productive 209, 287, 291
Produktivität productivity 287, 290, 291
produzieren to produce 120
Professioneller a professional 63
Professor professor 120, 126, 289, 293
professoral professorial 293
Professorat professorship 293
Professorchen (dim.) > *Professor* 293
Professoren (pl.) professors 126, 293
professorenhaft professor-like 293
Professorenversammlung professors'
    meeting 144
professorhaft professor-like 293
Professorin (f.) professor 293
Professors (gen.) > *Professor* 293
Profi (abb.) > *Professioneller* 63
Prolet (abb.) > *Proletarier* 10
Proletarier proletarian 63
Prolo (abb.) > *Proletarier* 63
Protestant Protestant 120
Protestantin (f.) Protestant 122
Prüfung examination 121
Psalm psalm 176, 177
Pschorr proper noun 40
Psychologie psychology 40, 131, 266,
    296, 298, 299
quaken to croak like a frog, to quack
    240
quäken to squeak, whine 240
Quatsch nonsense 238, 239, 240, 241,
    242
quer across 240
quieken to squeak 240
Quirl twirling-stick 240
Quodlibet quodlibet 240
Quorum quorum 240
Quote quota 240
Rabe raven 10
Rad wheel 195, 200

Radar radar 254
Räder (pl.) wheels 195
Rades (gen.) > *Rad* 200
Rad fahren to ride a bicycle 295
radikal radical 120
Radius radius 120, 288
Rage rage 10
Rahm cream 11
Rakete rocket 126
Ramsch trash 233, 264
ramschen to sell or buy junk 233
rasen to rage, race 222
Rasen mähen to mow the lawn 103
Raspel a rasp 268
Rat advice 253
rät he guesses, advises 41, 69, 230
raten to advise, guess 41
Rats (gen.) > *Rat* 14
Raub robbery 10, 37
raubst you (sg.) rob 37
rauchen to smoke 10, 222
raufen to tussle, wrangle 222
Raum room 11
rauschen to rustle, roar 10, 222
reaktionär reactionary 120
realisieren to realize 120
Realo (abb.) > *Realpolitiker* 63, 64
Realpolitiker supporter(s) of *Realpolitik* 63
Rechenzentrumsleiter computer-centre director 298
rechts right 118
recken to stretch 10
Referendum referendum 288
Reform reform 124
Reformator reformer 102
Regen rain 202
Regierungsoberrat title of government official 298
Region region 238
regnen to rain 35, 202, 206
reich rich 210, 309, 310
reichen to reach, suffice 10, 222
Reichtum wealth 126, 183
Reichtümer (pl.) riches 137, 183
rein clean, pure 121
reinigen to clean 121
reinlich clean, tidy 121

reisen to travel 10, 176
reißen to tear 10, 41, 176
reißt you (sg.) tear, he tears 41, 230
reist you travel 230
reitet he rides 69
reizen to provoke 10
Rektorat rector's office 123
rekultivieren to recultivate 124
relativ relative 120
Relativheit relativity 122
Religion religion 238
rennen to run 270
Reportage reporting 120
Restaurant restaurant 12, 32
restringieren to restrict 224
retten to rescue 10
Ria proper noun 160
Richard proper noun 285
richtigstellen to correct 105
Richtigstellung correction 105
riechen to smell 196, 210
Riese giant 126
riesig giant, gigantic 126
Riesin (f.) giant 126
Rind ox, bullock, or cow 10
ringen to wrestle 10, 222
rinnen to flow 10
Risiko risk 278, 285
Riss a tear, rip 10
Robbe seal 202
roch he smelled 196
roh raw 109
Rohr pipe 109
Romanik Romanesque period 123
Romantik romanticism 123
rosafärben to colour pink 105
Rosafärbung rose colouring 105
Rose rose 243, 244
Roséwein rosé wine 104
Röslein (dim.) > *Rose* 11
Ross horse
Rösslein (dim.) > *Ross* 11
rot red 10, 109, 273
Rotation rotation 102
rotem (dat.) > *rot* 35
röten to redden 189
rotgrün red-green 300
Rotkreuzschwester Red Cross nurse 302

rötlich ruddy 189
Rotwein red wine 104, 273, 274, 276, 297
Rotweinpunsch red-wine punch 273, 297, 299
Rotweinpunschtrinker red-wine punch drinker 273
Rotwild red deer 103
Ruck a jerk, shock 10
Ruder rudder(s), oar(s) 246, 253
Ruderer oarsman 246, 253
rudern to row 89, 110, 111
rudernd rowing 48
rufen to call 184
ruft he calls 184
ruhig calm 160
Ruine ruin 52, 59, 72, 160
ruinös ruinous 59
Rumpf (human or animal) trunk 218
rund round 184, 185
runden to round 184
runder rounder 122, 184
rundest roundest 122
rundlich round(ly) 184
Rutsch glide 10, 266
Saal hall 10
Sachen (pl.) things, matters 220
Sachsen-Anhalt place name 300
säen to sow 11, 17
Safran saffron 279
sage I say 244
sah I, he saw 182
sähe (cond.) I, he would see 182
Salat salad 61
Samowar samovar 176
Samstag Saturday 218
Sanatorium sanatorium 120
Sänger singer 224
Sarg coffin 200, 206, 257
Särge (pl.) coffins 200, 206
sauber clean 243
sauberes (infl.) > *sauber* 243
Sauberkeit cleanliness 99
säuberlich clean 275
säuberliches (infl.) > *säuberlich* 275
Saubermann 'Mr Clean' 104
saufen to drink hard, to guzzle 182
Säufer drunkard(s) 182

schadhaft defective 65
Schädling pest 120
Schaft shaft 68
Schal scarf 10, 11
schälen to peel 11
Schall sound 11
Schals (pl.) scarfs 48
Scham shame 68
Scharlatan charlatan 279
Scheit piece of wood 68
scheitert he fails 255
schellen to ring 11
Scherz joke 45
Schickimicki yuppie 64, 138
Schickimickis (pl.) yuppies 138
schicklich decent, proper 50
schieben to push 196
Schiff ship 141
Schifffahrt shipping 231
Schiffe (pl.) ships 137
Schkeuditz place-name 42, 266, 267
Schkopau place-name 42, 266, 267
Schlacht battle 209
schlaflos sleepless 101
Schlaflosigkeit sleeplessness 100
schlagen to strike, to beat 209
schlecht bad 266
schließen to close 196
schloss he closed 196
schluchzt you sob 48
schlucken to swallow 10
schlupfen to slip 10
Schlüssel key
Schlüsselein (dim.) > *Schlüssel* 231
schmarotzen to sponge 90
schmarotzt (part.) sponged 90, 92
Schmerz pain 45, 147
Schmerzes (gen.) > *Schmerz* 147
Schmerzensgeld compensation for pain, recompense 147
Schmuck jewellery 266
schmuggeln to smuggle 202
Schmuggler smuggler(s) 202
Schnaps strong liquor 266
Schnee snow 266
schob he pushed 196
schon already 11
schön beautiful 11, 37, 133, 184, 309

schöne (infl.) > *schön* 243
schöner more beautiful 122
Schönheit beauty 98
schönst most beautiful 122
schoss he shot 11
Schoß lap 11
Schote pod, husk 10
Schrank wardrobe, cupboard 266
schreiben to write 209
schreibt he writes 209
schrieben we, they wrote 209
Schrift writing 209
Schriftsteller author(s) 189
schriftstellern to be an author 189
Schrifttum literature 69
Schund trash 10
schwarz black 238
Schwarzbrot black bread 104
Schwatz chat 239
schweigen to be silent 209
Schweinebraten roast pork 143, 144
Schweinerei mess 86, 102
schweinern to mess up 102
schwer heavy, difficult 239, 253, 266
schwerer heavier, more difficult 253
Schwert sword 198
Schwester sister 62
Schwestern (pl.) sisters 62, 137
Schwesternliebe sisterly love 143
schwimmen to swim 240
schwinden to dwindle 240
schwingen to swing, oscillate 240
Schwingungszahl oscillation frequency 145
schwören to swear on oath 240
schwul gay, homosexual 240
Schwund decline 240
Schwung swing 240
Schwur oath 240
Segel sail(s) 35, 106, 137, 243, 244, 246
Segelei sailing 86, 87
segeln to sail 89, 110, 111, 112, 246
Segen blessing(s) 106, 243, 246
segle I sail 88
Segler sailor(s) 86, 88, 89, 243, 246
Seglerei sailing 86
segnen to bless 89, 110, 243

Segnerei blessing 86
sehen to see 11, 17, 111, 176
Sehhilfe visual aid 103
sehr very 98
sein to be 110
Seltenheit rareness 99
Senf mustard 222
seriös respectable 186
Sex sex 12, 176
sexuell sexual 119
sicher sure, safe 246, 253
sichere (infl.) > *sicher* 246
Sicherheit security 99
sichern to make safe 246, 255
sicherstellen to ensure 103
Sicherung protection 246
sichtbar visible 275, 306
sichtlich obvious 275
sie she, her, they, them 81, 249
sieben seven 195
Siebengebirge proper noun 104
siebzig seventy 195
Sigismund proper noun 284
Signal signal 223, 234
silbisch syllabic 7
Simpelheit simplicity 99
Simpelkeit simplicity 99
Simultandolmetscher simultaneous translator 104
sind we, you are 111
Singular singular 224
Sinn sense, meaning 10
Sitz seat 10
sitzen to sit 41
sitzt you (sg.) sit, he sits 41, 230
Skala scale 120
Skat name of card-game 42, 177, 266, 267
Skelett skeleton 42, 176
Sklave slave 42, 43
Sklerose sclerosis 43
Skrupel scruple 42
Slalom slalom 176, 262
Slogan slogan 266
Smaragd emerald 12
Smoking dinner jacket 176, 262, 266
Snob snob 266
Sofa sofa 278

solch such 210, 211
Sonatine sonatina 122
Sonne sun 176
Sopran soprano 279
sozial social 287
Sozialist socialist 120, 287
Spanien Spain 238
Spanier Spaniard(s) 34
Sparkasse savings bank 310
sparsam thrifty 121
Spaß fun 42
Speeren (dat., pl.) spears 17
Spektrograph spectrograph 131
sperren to close off 17
Spezies species 42, 266, 267
Sphäre sphere 12, 266, 267
Spiel game 42, 266, 267
Spieluhr musical clock 297, 299
Spießbürgertum bourgeois conformism 128
Spinat spinach 279
Spionage espionage 120
Spirans spirant 42
Splitter splinter(s) 42
Sport sports 266
Sportflugzeug sports aeroplane 300
Sprache language 42
Sprachwissenschaft linguistics 62
Sprachwissenschaftler linguist 62
Sprawis (abb.) > *Sprachwissenschaftler* 62
Spruch saying 43
spucken to spit 11
spuken to spook, haunt 11
Sri Lanka place name 176, 266
Stab stick 37, 270
Stadion stadium 120
Stadium stage 120, 288, 289
Stadt town, city 195, 266, 297, 298
Stadtbauamt (lit.) city building office 297
Städte (pl.) cities 137, 195
Stadtplanungsbüro city building office 295
Stadtsparkasse city savings bank 310
Stahl steel 11
Stall stable 11
Stand stand 182

ständig always 182
Standuhr grandfather clock 65
Statistik statistics 127
statuarisch according to statute 126
Statue statue 126, 141
Statuette statuette 122
Staub saugen to vacuum clean 103, 297
stehlen to steal 194
Steigerung increase 308
Steigerungen (pl.) increases 57
Stein stone 42, 266, 267, 310
steinreich extremely rich 310
Sternenglanz twinkling of the stars 147
Sternenschein starshine 230
stet continual 101
stetig continual, steady 101
Steuer (n.) helm, rudder, steering wheel, (f.) tax, (pl.) helms, etc. 139
Steuern (pl.) taxes 62, 107, 139
stiehlt he steals 194
Stiel handle, shaft 10
Stil style 10, 42, 266, 267
Stimulus stimulus 288
Stoiker Stoic 42
Sträfling prisoner 120
Sträflinge (pl.) prisoners 137
Straßenbahnfahrkarte tram ticket 300
streichst you (sg.) paint, strike 37
Streit quarrel 42, 253
Stromausfall power failure 306, 307
Struwwelpeter proper noun 36
Student student 63
Studentenschaft student community 147
Studi (abb.) > *Student* 63
Studie study 141
Studium studies 288
Stuhl chair 42
Stunde hour 218
subatomar subatomic 124
subversiv subversive 124
Südafrika South Africa 300
Südpol south pole 302
Sudan Sudan 279
Synagoge synagogue 277
synchron synchronous 221
Syntax syntax 277
Syrien Syria 277
Tabu taboo 278

Tafeln (pl.) tables 107
Tag day 206
Tage (pl.) days 146, 206
Tageblatt daily newspaper 146
Tag(e)s (gen.) > *Tag* 146
Tageszeit time of day 143
Tageszeitung daily newspaper 146
täglich daily 50, 65, 73, 74
Taifun typhoon 54
Taille waist 34
Tal valley 10, 11
Talg tallow 206, 207
Talge (dat.) > *Talg* 206
Talisman talisman 276, 284
Tangente tangent 224
Tango tango 68, 218, 224, 225, 226
Tank tank, container 68
tänzeln (dim., iter.) to dance, frisk 120
tanzen to dance 41, 120
tanzt you dance 41
Taschenmesser pocket knife 144
Tat deed, act, action 10, 11
Tau rope 10
taubstumm deaf and dumb 103
Tauchen (dim.) > *Tau* 211
tauchen to dive 211
taugen to be suitable for 209
Teekanne teapot 300
Teheran Tehran 279
Teich pond 206
Teiche (pl.) ponds 206
Teig dough 206
Teige (pl.) doughs 206
Teil part 11
Teint complexion 12
Tempi (pl.) tempos 141
Tempo speed 141, 218, 220
Tempos (pl.) speeds 141
Tenne threshing floor 277
Tenor tenor singer 9, 277, 278
Tenor tenor, substance 9, 277, 278
Thea proper noun 59
Theater theatre(s) 16, 59, 72
Thema subject, theme 141
Themata (pl.) themes 141
Themen (pl.) subjects 141
Theo proper noun 52, 54, 55, 160
Theoderich proper noun 59

Theodor proper noun 59, 284
Theoretiker theorist 102
Thermometer thermometer 131, 296, 298
Tiara tiara 160
Tiefebene lowland 65
Tier animal 11
Tierart species of animal 65
Tina proper noun 10
Tingeltangel music-hall, honky-tonk 64
Tipps (pl.) hints 137
Tisch table 10, 141
Tischchen (dim.) > *Tisch* 122
Tische (pl.) tables 137
Tischlein (dim.) > *Tisch* 122, 231
Titan titanium 279
Tochter daughter 142
Tod death 11
tot dead 10
Totalität totality 120
Totalverdunkelung total blackout 104
Tracht attire, costume 209
tragen to carry, wear 209, 222
Trara fuss, hullabaloo 278, 282
Traum dream 270
treten to kick 41
Trichter funnel(s) 210
triefnass soaking wet 103
triggern to trigger 94
Trio trio 54, 59, 120, 161
Trios (pl.) trios 137
tritt he steps 41, 230
Triumph triumph 160
trocken dry 223, 243, 246
Trockendock dry dock 104
trockene (infl.) > *trocken* 246
trockeneres (infl.) drier 110, 276
trockenes (n., infl.) > *trocken* 109, 243
trocknen to dry 246
Trockner dryer 223
Trocknung drying 246
trompetet (part.) trumpeted 90
Trübsal affliction, misery 121
Tscheche a Czech 10
Tübingen place name 220
Tücher (pl.) cloths 210
tüchtig capable, efficient 209
Tugend virtue 10, 107

Tugenden (pl.) virtues 107
tun to do 110, 111
Tür door 11, 253
Turandot proper noun 284
Turban turban 278, 279
Türen (pl.) doors 253
Turm tower 135, 136, 141, 188
Türme (pl.) towers 136, 188
Twist twist 262
Typus type 120
Tyrannei tyranny 86
Übelkeit sickness 99
überfahren to drive over 295
Überfall sudden attack 294
überfallen to attack suddenly 294
übergestülpt (part.) put on something, slipped over something 94
übergroß oversized 103
Übernahme take-over 293
übernehmen to take over 296
überreif overripe 95, 103
übersetzen to translate 124, 295, 296
übersetzen to carry across 295, 296
Übersetzung translation 295
Übersicht survey 103
übervorteilen to cheat on sb. 125
Übung exercise 58
Uhren (pl.) watches 107
Uhu long-eared owl 60
umfahren to drive around something 124
Umgebung surroundings 220
umkleiden to change (clothing) 220
umleiten to detour, divert 295
Umleitung diversion, detour 295
ummanteln to cloak, envelop 295
Umsegelung the sailing around something 246
Umsicht circumspection 220
umtun to put on 220
Unart bad habit 65
unbekannt unknown 294
unbeständig unsteady 125
unbillig unfair 220
unergiebig unproductive, unprofitable 286
Unfall accident 222
Ungarn (pl.) Hungarians 107, 224

ungefährlich dangerless 125
ungenau imprecise 124, 221
unglaublich unbelievable 294
Unglück misfortune 68, 220, 294
Ungrammatikalität ungrammaticality 148
Universitätsrechenzentrum university computing centre 298
unkundig uninformed 220
unlogisch illogical 125
unmenschlich inhuman 294
unmöglich impossible 123
unnahbar unapproachable 231
unparteiisch impartial 125
unregelmäßig irregular, uneven 286
unreif unripe, immature 125
uns (dat./acc. pl.) us 249
unsäglich unspeakable 294
unsichtbar invisible 306
unstatthaft forbidden 275
unsubstantiell insubstantial 125
Untat crime, outrage 220
unterschätzen to underestimate 296
untersuchen to enquire, to examine 124
unüblich uncommon 275
unverdient undeserved 125
unvereinbar incompatible 125
urban urban 278, 279
Uroma great-grandmother 65
urwüchsig original, native 294
Urzustand primal state 294
Vanille vanilla 34
variabel variable 120
Vater father 11, 62, 63, 98, 184, 191, 192
Väter (pl.) fathers 62, 106, 137, 191
Väterchen (dim.) > *Vater* 184
väterlich fatherly 191
Vati daddy 11, 63, 121
Ventilator ventilator, fan 102
verächtlich despisingly 189
Veranda verandah 281
Verantwortung responsibility 65
verbrüdern to fraternize 189
vereisen to freeze 59
Verfall decay 295
vergessen to forget 194
vergisst he forgets 194

Verhandlungsbasis base for negotiations 128

Verlängerungen (pl.) elongations, extensions 224

Vermächtnis bequest 120

Vermarktung marketing 72

Verrat betrayal, treason 231

verräterisch treacherous 124

Vers verse, stanza 233

Verse (pl.) verses, stanzas 233

Versicherung insurance 295

Versicherungen (pl.) insurances 67

Versicherungsvertreter insurance agent 144

Verstand reason 130

verständig reasonable 89, 100

Verständigkeit reason 98, 100

verständlich understandable 121

Verständnis understanding 120

verstärken to reinforce 124

versucht (part.) tried 90, 94

vertraglich by contract 190, 191

verträglich conciliatory, compatible 190

verunreinigen to pollute 125

verunsichern to make s.o. unsure of himself/herself 130

veruntreuen to embezzle 125

Vetter cousin 106

Vettern (pl.) cousins 106

viel much 10, 37

vier four 10

Viola viola 288

virtuos masterly 161

visionär visionary 120

Vogel bird 106, 182, 188

Vögel (pl.) birds 106, 182

Vögelein (dim.) > *Vogel* 188, 231

Völkerschaft (a) people 147

Volkstum national characteristics 183

volkstümlich popular, folkloric 183

Vollblut full-blooded, thoroughbred 191

vollblütig thoroughbred, full-blooded 190, 191

voran ahead 66

vorgespielt (part.) played s.th. to s.o. 95, 96

vorgesungen (part.) sung in front of somebody 94

Vorstand managing committee 294

vorstehen to project, precede 294

Vorüberlegung pre-consideration 125

Vulkan volcano 279

Wagen coach(es), car(s) 166

Wahl choice, election 166

Wahlkönigtum (lit.) electoral kingdom 148

wahllos indiscriminately 231, 232

wahrhaft true 101

wahrhaftig truthful 101

wallfahrten to go on a pilgrimage 94

Wams jacket 218, 233

Wämser (pl.) jackets 233

Wand wall 236

Wappen coat of arms 230

war was 253

waren were 10

Waschk proper noun 264, 266

waten to wade 10

webstricken to weave-knit 103

Weg way 206

Wege (pl.) ways 206

wegen because of 232

Weichspüler soft detergent 104

Wein wine 273, 274

weinerlich tearful 102

weißlich whitish 121

weitere (infl.) further, more 45

Welle wave 11

Weltbankkonferenz world bank conference 298

wenig few 206, 208

wenige (infl.) > *wenig* 206

Werft shipyard 48

Wert value 253

wesentlich essential 146

Wessi (abb.) > *Westdeutscher* 63

Westberlin West Berlin 300

Westdeutscher citizen of West Germany 63

widerliche (infl.) repugnant 57, 58

widerstehen to resist 295

widmen to dedicate 34

wiehern to neigh 50, 51

Wiese meadow 126

Wiese proper noun 137

wildern to poach 102

Wilhelm proper noun 60
Wille intention, determination 11
Willem proper noun 60
wir we 17, 50, 249, 253
wirfst you (sg.) throw 37
wirr confused 17
Wirtschaft economy 121
Wissenschaft science 121
Wissenschaften (pl.) sciences 137
Wissenschaftlerin (f.) scientist 290
Witz joke 145
Wladimir proper noun 262
wohlgeformt well formed 103
wolkig cloudy 189
Wolkigkeit cloudiness 189
wollen to want, intend 222
Wörtchen (dim.) word 122
Wunder miracle(s) 239
Wunsch desire 222, 239
Wurm worm 141, 239
Wut anger, rage 239
Xaver proper noun 40, 262, 266
Yin yin 237
zahm tame 10
Zahn tooth 42, 176, 266
Zauberer magician(s) 288
Zehnraumwohnung ten-room apartment 301
Zehnzimmerwohnung ten-room apartment 301
zehren to live on, live off 17

Zeichen sign(s) 230
Zerfall decay 295
Zerlegung dissection, disassembly 295
zerren to tug, strain 17
zersetzen to decompose 124
zerstäubt (part.) sprayed 94
Zierlichkeit daintiness 123
Zivi (abb.) > *Zivildienstleistender* 63
Zivildienstleistender (lit.) person who must complete his civil service 63
Zivilisation civilization 292
zog I, he pulled 206
zogen we, they pulled 206
Zonenbewohner citizen of East German zone 63
Zoni (abb.) > *Zonenbewohner* 63
Zoologe zoologist 232
zufällig accidental 100
Zufälligkeit coincidence 100
Zug train 206, 212, 214, 216
Züge (pl.) trains 206, 212
zumal especially since 46
zwanzigteilig consisting of twenty parts 105
zwei two 238, 266
Zweig branch 206
Zweige (pl.) branches 206
Zweikammersystem two-chamber system 301
zweit second 196
Zwischenfall incident 103, 294

REFERENCES

ALBER, BIRGIT (1997), 'Quantity Sensitivity as the Result of Constraint Interaction', in Geert Booij and Jeroen van de Weijer (eds.), *Phonology in Progress–Progress in Phonology. HIL Phonology Papers III* (The Hague: Holland Academic Graphics), 1–45.

—— (1998), 'Stress Preservation in German Loan Words', in Wolfgang Kehrein and Richard Wiese (eds.), *Phonology and Morphology of the Germanic Languages* (Tübingen: Niemeyer), 113–41.

ANDERSON, STEPHEN R. (1982), 'Where's Morphology?', *Linguistic Inquiry*, 13: 571–612.

—— (1985), *Phonology in the Twentieth Century: Theories of Rules and Theories of Representation* (Chicago: University of Chicago Press).

—— (1988), 'Inflection', in Michael Hammond and Michael Noonan (eds.), *Theoretical Morphology: Approaches in Modern Linguistics* (San Diego: Academic Press), 23–43.

—— (1992), *A-Morphous Morphology* (Cambridge: Cambridge University Press).

ARCHANGELI, DIANA (1984), 'Underspecification in Yawelmani Phonology and Morphology', Ph.D. dissertation, MIT.

—— (1988), 'Aspects of Underspecification Theory', *Phonology*, 5: 183–207.

—— and TERENCE LANGENDOEN (eds.) (1997), *Optimality Theory: An Overview* (Oxford: Blackwell).

ARONOFF, MARK (1976), *Word Formation in Generative Grammar* (Cambridge, Mass.: MIT Press).

—— and S. N. SRIDHAR (1987), 'Morphological Levels in English and Kannada', in Edmund Gussmann (ed.), *Rules and the Lexicon* (Lublin: Redakcja Wydawnictw Katolickiego Uniwersytetu Lubelskiego).

AUER, PETER and SUSANNE UHMANN (1988), 'Silben- und akzentzählende Sprachen. Literaturüberblick und Diskussion', *Zeitschrift für Sprachwissenschaft*, 7: 214–59.

AUGST, GERHARD (1971), 'Über den Umlaut bei der Steigerung', *Wirkendes Wort*, 21: 424–31.

—— (1979), 'Neuere Forschungen zur Substantivflexion', *Zeitschrift für germanistische Linguistik*, 7: 220–32.

AVERY, PETER and KEREN RICE (1989), 'Segmental Structure and Coronal Underspecification', *Phonology*, 6: 179–200.

BACH, EMMON and ROBERT D. KING (1970), 'Umlaut in Modern German', *Glossa*, 4: 3–21.

BASBØLL, HANS and JOHANNES WAGNER (1985), *Kontrastive Phonologie des Deutschen und Dänischen: Segmentale Wortphonologie und -phonetik* (Tübingen: Niemeyer).

BENWARE, WILBUR A. (1986), *Phonetics and Phonology of Modern German: An Introduction* (Washington, DC: Georgetown University Press).

—— (1987), 'Accent Variation in German Nominal Compounds of the Type (A(BC))', *Linguistische Berichte*, 108: 102–27.

BERENDSEN, EGON (1986), *The Phonology of Cliticization* (Dordrecht: Foris).

BERG, THOMAS (1990), 'Unreine Reime als Evidenz für die Organisation phonologischer Merkmale', *Zeitschrift für Sprachwissenschaft*, 9: 3–27.

BIERWISCH, MANFRED (1966), 'Regeln für die Intonation deutscher Sätze', in *Studia Grammatica VII* (Berlin: Akademie-Verlag), 99–201.

—— (1968), 'Two Critical Problems in Accent Rules', *Journal of Linguistics*, 4: 173–8.

BLOOMFIELD, LEONARD (1930), 'German ç and x', *Le Maître phonétique*, 20: 27–8.

—— (1933), *Language* (New York: Holt).

BOOIJ, GEERT E. (1985), 'Coordination Reduction in Complex Words: A Case for Prosodic Phonology', in Harry van der Hulst and Norval Smith (eds.), *Advances in Nonlinear Phonology* (Dordrecht: Foris), 143–60.

—— (1988), 'On the Relation between Lexical Phonology and Prosodic Phonology', in Pier Marco Bertinetto and Michele Loporcaro (eds.), *Certamen Phonologicum* (Torino: Sellier), 63–76.

—— (1995), *The Phonology of Dutch* (Oxford: Oxford University Press).

—— and ROCHELLE LIEBER (1993), 'On the Simultaneity of Morphological and Prosodic Structure', in Sharon Hargus and Ellen Kaisse (eds.), *Studies in Lexical Phonology* (San Diego: Academic Press), 23–44.

—— and JERZY RUBACH (1992), 'Lexical Phonology', in William Bright (ed.), *International Encyclopedia of Linguistics* (Oxford: Oxford University Press), 293–6.

BORER, HAGIT (1988), 'On the Morphological Parallelism between Compounds and Constructs', *Yearbook of Morphology*, 1: 45–66.

—— (1995) *Final Devoicing in the Phonology of German* (Tübingen: Niemeyer).

BROWMAN, CATHERINE P. and LOUIS GOLDSTEIN (1990), 'Representation and Reality: Physical Systems and Phonological Structure', *Journal of Phonetics*, 18: 411–24.

BUTT, MATTHIAS (1992), 'Sonority and the Explanation of Syllable Structure', *Linguistische Berichte*, 137: 45–67.

CHOMSKY, NOAM A. (1991), 'Some Notes on Economy of Derivation and Representation', in Robert Freidin (ed.), *Principles and Parameters in Comparative Grammar* (Cambridge, Mass.: MIT Press), 417–54.

—— and MORRIS HALLE (1968), *The Sound Pattern of English* (New York: Harper & Row).

CINQUE, GUGLIELMO (1993), 'A Null Theory of Phrase and Compound Stress', *Linguistic Inquiry*, 24: 239–97.

CLAHSEN, HARALD, GARY MARCUS, SUSANNE BARTKE, and RICHARD WIESE (1996), 'Compounding and Inflection in German child language', *Yearbook of Morphology 1995*: 115–42.

—— MONIKA ROTHWEILER, ANDREAS WOEST, and GARY MARCUS (1992), 'Regular and Irregular Inflection in the Acquisition of German Noun Plurals', *Cognition*, 45: 225–55.

CLEMENTS, GEORGE N. (1987), 'Phonological Feature Representation and the Description of Intrusive Stops', in Anna Bosch, Barbara Need, and Eric Schiller (eds.), *Papers of the Twenty-third Regional Meeting of the Chicago Linguistic Society: The Parasession on Autosegmental and Metrical Phonology* (Chicago: Chicago Linguistic Society), 29–50.

—— (1989), 'A Unified Set of Features for Consonants and Vowels', unpublished MS, Cornell University.

—— (1990), 'The Role of the Sonority Cycle in Core Syllabification', in John Kingston and Mary E. Beckman (eds.), *Papers in Laboratory Phonology I: Between the Grammar and Physics of Speech* (Cambridge: Cambridge University Press), 283–333.

—— and SAMUEL J. KEYSER (1983), *CV-Phonology: A Generative Theory of the Syllable* (Cambridge, Mass.: MIT Press).

COLEMAN, JOHN (1995), 'Declarative Lexical Phonology', in Francis Katamba and Jacques Durand (eds.), *Frontiers of Phonology: Atoms, Structures and Derivations* (London: Longman), 333–82.

COULTHARD, MALCOLM, and DAVID BRAZIL (1982), 'The Place of Intonation in the Description of Interaction', in Deborah Tannen (ed.), *Analyzing Discourse: Text and Talk* (Washington DC: Georgetown University Press), 94–112.

DI SCIULLO, ANNA MARIA and EDWIN WILLIAMS (1987), *On the Definition of Word* (Cambridge, Mass.: MIT Press).

DRESSLER, WOLFGANG U. (1981), 'External Evidence for an Abstract Analysis of the German Velar Nasal', in Didier L. Goyvaerts (ed.), *Phonology in the 1980s* (Ghent: E. Story-Scientia), 445–67.

—— (1985) *Morphonology: The Dynamics of Derivation* (Ann Arbor: Karoma).

DUDEN (1990), *Duden Aussprachewörterbuch: Wörterbuch der deutschen Standardaussprache*, 3rd edn (Mannheim: Dudenverlag).

DURAND, JACQUES (1990), *Generative and Non-Linear Phonology* (London: Longman).

EISENBERG, PETER (1973), 'A note on "identity of constituents"', *Linguistic Inquiry*, 4: 417–20.

—— (1989), 'Die Schreibsilbe im Deutschen', in Peter Eisenberg and Hartmut Günther (eds.), *Schriftsystem und Orthographie* (Tübingen: Niemeyer), 57–84.

—— (1991), 'Syllabische Struktur und Wortakzent: Prinzipien der Prosodik deutscher Wörter', *Zeitschrift für Sprachwissenschaft*, 10: 37–64.

—— (1992), 'Suffixreanalyse und Syllabierung. Zum Verhältnis von phonologischer und morphologischer Segmentierung', *Folia Linguistica Historica*, 13: 93–113.

ESSEN, OTTO VON (1951), 'Die Silbe—ein phonologischer Begriff', *Zeitschrift für Phonetik und Allgemeine Sprachwissenschaft*, 5: 199–203.

—— (1964), *Grundzüge der hochdeutschen Satzintonation* (Ratingen: Henn).

FABB, NIGEL (1988), 'English Suffixation is Constrained only by Selectional Restrictions', *Natural Language and Linguistic Theory*, 6: 527–39.

FÉRY, CAROLINE (1991), 'German Schwa in Prosodic Morphology', *Zeitschrift für Sprachwissenschaft*, 10: 65–85.

—— (1993), *German Intonational Patterns* (Tübingen: Niemeyer).

—— (1994), *Umlaut and Inflection in German*. Rutgers Optimality Archive: 34-1094.

—— (1997), 'Uni und Studis: die besten Wörter des Deutschen', *Linguistische Berichte*, 172: 461–89.

—— (1998a), 'German Word Stress in Optimality Theory', *Journal of Comparative Germanic Linguistics*, 2: 101–42.

—— (1998b), 'Final Devoicing and the Stratification of the Lexicon in German', Unpublished ms., Tübingen University. Rutgers Optimality Archive: 274.

FISCHER-JØRGENSEN, ELI (1975), *Trends in Phonological Theory* (Copenhagen: Akademisk Forlag).

FLEISCHER, WOLFGANG (1982), *Wortbildung der deutschen Gegenwartssprache*, 5th edn (Tübingen: Niemeyer).

FOLEY, JAMES (1977), *Foundations of Theoretical Phonology* (Cambridge: Cambridge University Press).

FOURAKIS, MARIOS and GREGORY K. IVERSON (1984), 'On the "Incomplete Neutralization" of German Final Obstruents', *Phonetica*, 41: 140–9.

FOX, ANTHONY (1984), *German Intonation: An Outline* (Oxford: Clarendon Press).

—— (1990), *The Structure of German* (Oxford: Oxford University Press).

GIEGERICH, HEINZ J. (1985), *Metrical Phonology and Phonological Structure: German and English* (Cambridge: Cambridge University Press).

—— (1987), 'Zur Schwa-Epenthese im Standarddeutschen', *Linguistische Berichte*, 112: 449–69.

—— (1988), 'Strict Cyclicity and Elsewhere', *Lingua*, 75: 125–34.

—— (1989), *Syllable Structure and Lexical Derivation in German* (Bloomington, Ind.: Indiana University Linguistics Club).

—— (1992a), *English Phonology: An Introduction* (Cambridge: Cambridge University Press).

—— (1992b), 'Onset Maximisation in German: The Case Against Resyllabification Rules', in Peter Eisenberg, Karl Heinz Ramers, and Heinz Vater (eds.), *Silbenphonologie des Deutschen* (Tübingen: Niemeyer), 134–171.

—— (1994), 'Base-driven Stratification: Morphological Causes and Phonological Effects of "Strict Cyclicity" ', in Richard Wiese (ed.), *Recent Developments in Lexical Phonology* (Düsseldorf: Heinrich-Heine-Universität), 31–61.

GOLDSMITH, JOHN (1976), *Autosegmental Phonology*, Ph.D. dissertation, MIT (Bloomington, Ind.: Indiana University Linguistics Club).

—— (1985), 'Vowel Harmony in Khalkha Mongolian, Yaka, Finnish and Hungarian', *Phonology Yearbook*, 2: 253–75.

—— (1990), *Autosegmental and Metrical Phonology* (Oxford: Basil Blackwell).

GOLSTON CHRIS and RICHARD WIESE (1996), 'Zero Morphology and Constraint Interaction: Subtraction and Epenthesis in German Dialects', in Geert Booij and Jaap van Marle (Hrsg.), *Yearbook of Morphology 1995*, 143–59.

—— —— (1998), 'The Structure of the German Root', in Wolfgang Kehrein and Richard Wiese (eds.), *Phonology and Morphology of the Germanic Languages* (Tübingen: Niemeyer), 165–85.

GRIJZENHOUT, JANET and SANDRA JOPPEN (1999), *First Steps in the Acquisition of German Phonology: A Case Study*. Rutgers Optimality Archive: 304-0399.

HAHN, AXEL (1998), *German Final Devoicing in Optimality Theory*. Rutgers Optimality Archive: 241-0198.

HALL, TRACY A. (1989a), 'German Syllabification, The Velar Nasal, and the Representation of Schwa', *Linguistics*, 27: 807–42.

—— (1989b), 'Lexical Phonology and the Distribution of German [ç] and [x]', *Phonology*, 6: 1–17.

—— (1992a), 'Syllable Final Clusters and Schwa Epenthesis in German', in P. Eisenberg, Karl Heinz Ramers, and Heinz Vater (eds.), *Silbenphonologie des Deutschen* (Tübingen: Narr), 208–45.

—— (1992b), *Syllable Structure and Syllable-related Processes in German* (Tübingen: Niemeyer).

—— (1993), 'The Phonology of German /R/', *Phonology*, 10: 83–105.

HALLE, MORRIS (1973), 'Prolegomena to a Theory of Word Formation,' *Linguistic Inquiry*, 4: 3–16.

—— (1977), 'Tenseness, Vowel Shift and the Phonology of Back Vowels in Modern English', *Linguistic Inquiry*, 8: 611–25.

—— (1983), 'On Distinctive Features and their Articulatory Implementation', *Natural Language and Linguistic Theory*, 1: 91–105.

—— (1992), 'Phonological Features', in William Bright (ed.), *International Encyclopedia of Linguistics* (Oxford: Oxford University Press), 207–12.

HALLE, MORRIS and G. N. CLEMENTS (1983), *Problem Book in Phonology* (Cambridge, Mass.: MIT Press).

—— and MICHAEL KENSTOWICZ (1991), 'The Free Element Condition and Cyclic Versus Noncyclic Stress', *Linguistic Inquiry*, 22: 457–501.

—— and K. P. MOHANAN (1985), 'Segmental Phonology of Modern English', *Linguistic Inquiry*, 16: 57–116.

—— and KEN STEVENS (1969), 'On the Feature "Advanced Tongue Root"', *MIT Quarterly Progress Report*, 94: 209–15.

—— and JEAN-ROGER VERGNAUD (1980), 'Three-dimensional Phonology', *Journal of Linguistic Research*, 1: 83–105.

—— (1987), *An Essay on Stress* (Cambridge, Mass.: MIT Press).

HAMMOND, MICHAEL (1987), 'Hungarian Cola', *Phonology Yearbook*, 4: 267–9.

HARNISCH, RÜDIGER (1994), 'Stammbildung im Singular—Stammflexion im Plural. Zum Bautyp der deutschen Substantivdeklination', in Klaus-Michael Köpcke (ed.), *Funktionale Untersuchungen zur deutschen Nominal- und Verbalmorphologie* (Tübingen: Niemeyer), 97–114.

HAYES, BRUCE (1981), *A Metrical Theory of Stress Rules* (Bloomington, Ind.: Indiana University Linguistics Club).

—— (1982), 'Extrametricality and English Stress', *Linguistic Inquiry*, 13: 227–76.

—— (1984), 'The Phonology of Rhythm in English', *Linguistic Inquiry*, 15: 33–74.

—— (1986), 'Inalterability in CV Phonology', *Language*, 62: 321–50.

—— (1989), 'Compensatory Lengthening in Moraic Phonology', *Linguistic Inquiry*, 20: 253–306.

HAYES, BRUCE (1990), 'Precompiled Phrasal Phonology', in Sharon Inkelas and Draga Zec (eds.), *The Phonology–Syntax Connection* (Chicago: University of Chicago Press), 85–108.

HEIKE, GEORG (1972), *Phonologie* (Stuttgart: Metzler).

HELBIG, GERHARD and JOACHIM BUSCHA (1987), *Deutsche Grammatik: Ein Handbuch für den Ausländerunterricht* (Leipzig: VEB Verlag Enzyklopädie).

HINRICHS, ERHARD (1986), 'Verschmelzungsformen in German: A GPSG Analysis', *Linguistics*, 24: 939–55.

HOGG, RICHARD and C. B. MCCULLY (1987), *Metrical Phonology: A Coursebook* (Cambridge: Cambridge University Press).

HÖHLE, TILMAN (1982), 'Über Komposition und Derivation: zur Konstituentenstruktur von Wortbildungsprodukten im Deutschen', *Zeitschrift für Sprachwissenschaft*, 1: 76–112.

HOLSINGER, DAVID J. and PAUL D. HOUSEMAN (1999), 'Lenition in Hessian: Cluster Reduction and "subtractive plurals"', in Geert Booij and Jaap van Marle (Hrsg.), *Yearbook of Morphology 1998*, 159–74.

HOOPER, JOAN B. (1976), *An Introduction to Natural Generative Phonology* (New York: Academic Press).

HULST, HARRY VAN DER (1989), 'Atoms of Segmental Structure: Components, Gestures and Dependency', *Phonology*, 6: 253–84.

HYMAN, LARRY (1985), *A Theory of Phonological Weight* (Dordrecht: Foris).

IIVONEN, AANTI K. (1987), 'Monophthonge des gehobenen Wienerdeutsch', *Folia Linguistica*, 21: 293–336.

INKELAS, SHARON (1989), 'Prosodic Constituency in the Lexicon', Ph.D. dissertation, Stanford University.

INTERNATIONAL PHONETIC ASSOCIATION (1949), *The Principles of the International Phonetic Association* (London: Department of Phonetics, University College).

—— (1989), 'Report on the 1989 Kiel Convention', *Journal of the International Phonetics Association*, 19: 67–80.

ISSATSCHENKO, ALEXANDER (1974), 'Das "schwa mobile" und "schwa constans" im Deutschen', in Ulrich Engel and Paul Grebe (eds.), *Sprachsystem und Sprachgebrauch: Festschrift für Hugo Moser zum 65. Geburtstag* (Düsseldorf: Schwann), 142–71.

ITÔ, JUNKO (1989), 'A Prosodic Theory of Epenthesis', *Natural Language and Linguistic Theory*, 7: 217–60.

—— and ARMIN MESTER (1997), 'Sympathy Theory and German Truncations', in Viola Miglio and Bruce Moréen (eds.), *University of Maryland Working Papers in Linguistics*, 5. Selected phonology papers from Hopkins Optimality Theory Workshop 1997/ University of Maryland Mayfest 1997: 117–39.

—— —— (1999), 'On the Sources of Opacity in OT: Coda Processes in German', in Caroline Féry and Ruben van de Vijver (eds.) (forthcoming), *The Syllable in OT* (Cambridge: Cambridge University Press).

IVERSON, GREGORY K. and JOE SALMONS (1992), 'The Place of Structure Preservation in German Diminutive Formation', *Phonology*, 9: 137–43.

JACOBS, JOACHIM (1982), 'Neutraler und nicht-neutraler Satzakzent im Deutschen', in Theo Vennemann (ed.), *Silben, Segmente, Akzente* (Tübingen: Niemeyer), 141–69.

JAKOBSON, ROMAN (1931), 'Die Betonung und ihre Rolle in der Wort- und Syntagma-phonologie', *Travaux du Cercle Linguistique de Prague IV*; reprinted in Roman Jakobson, *Selected Writings*, i, *Phonological Studies* ('s-Gravenhage: Mouton, 1962), 117–36.

—— (1939), 'Observations sur le classement phonologique des consonnes', *Proceedings of the 3rd International Congress of Phonetic Sciences*, 34–41.

—— (1941), *Kindersprache, Aphasie und allgemeine Lautgesetze* (Frankfurt: Suhrkamp, 1969).

JANDA, RICHARD D. (1987), 'On the Motivation for an Evolutionary Typology of Sound-structural Rules', Ph.D. dissertation, University of California, Los Angeles.

—— (1990), 'Frequency, Markedness, & Morphological Change: On Predicting the Spread of Noun-plural -s in Modern High German—and West Germanic', in *Proceedings of the Seventh Eastern States Conference on Linguistics* (1990): 136–53.

JENSEN, JOHN (1990), *Morphology* (Amsterdam: Benjamins).

JESPERSEN, OTTO (1904), *Lehrbuch der Phonetik* (Leipzig: Teubner).

JESSEN, MICHAEL (1988), 'Die dorsalen Reibelaute [C] and [X] im Deutschen', *Linguistische Berichte*, 117: 371–96.

—— (1994), 'A Survey of German Word Stress', unpublished MS, University of Stuttgart.

KAGER, RENÉ (1999), *Optimality Theory* (Cambridge: Cambridge University Press).

KAISSE, ELLEN M. (1985), *Connected Speech. The Interaction of Syntax and Phonology* (Orlando, Fla.: Academic Press).

—— and PATRICIA A. SHAW (1985), 'On the Theory of Lexical Phonology', *Phono-logy Yearbook*, 2: 1–30.

KALTENBACHER, ERIKA (1994), 'Typologische Aspekte des Wortakzents: zum Zusammen-hang von Akzentposition und Silbengewicht im Arabischen und im Deutschen', *Zeitschrift für Sprachwissenschaft*, 13: 20–55.

KAYE, JONATHAN (1989), *Phonology: A Cognitive View* (Hillsdale, NJ: Lawrence Erlbaum).

KEATING, PATRICIA (1988), *A Survey of Phonological Features* (Bloomington, Ind.: Indiana University Linguistics Club).

—— (1990), 'Phonetic Representations in Generative Grammar', *Journal of Phonetics*, 18: 321–34.

—— (1991), 'Coronal Places of Articulation', in Carole Paradis and Jean-François Prunet (eds.), *The Special Status of Coronals: Internal and External Evidence* (San Diego: Academic Press), 29–48.

KENSTOWICZ, MICHAEL (1994), *Phonology in Generative Grammar* (Cambridge, Mass.: Blackwell).

—— and CHARLES KISSEBERTH (1979), *Generative Phonology: Description and Theory* (New York: Academic Press).

KIENLE, RICHARD VON (1969), *Historische Laut- und Formenlehre des Deutschen* (Tübingen: Niemeyer).

KING, ROBERT D. (1969), *Historical Linguistics and Generative Grammar* (Englewood Cliffs, NJ: Prentice-Hall).

—— (1971), *Historische Linguistik und generative Grammatik* (Frankfurt: Athenäum).

KIPARSKY, PAUL (1966), 'Über den deutschen Akzent', in *Untersuchungen über Akzent und Intonation im Deutschen (Studia Grammatica VII)* (Berlin: Akademie-Verlag), 69–88.

—— (1973), 'Elsewhere in Phonology', in Stephen R. Anderson and Paul Kiparsky (eds.), *A Festschrift for Morris Halle* (New York: Holt, Rinehart, Winston), 93–106.

—— (1982a), 'From Cyclic Phonology to Lexical Phonology', in Harry van der Hulst and Norval Smith (eds.), *The Structure of Phonological Representations (Part I)* (Dordrecht: Foris), 131–75.

—— (1982b), 'Lexical Morphology and Phonology', in The Linguistic Society of Korea (ed.), *Linguistics in the Morning Calm: Selected Papers from SICOL-1981* (Seoul: Hanshin), 3–91.

—— (1983), 'Word Formation and the Lexicon', in Frances Ingemann (ed.), *Proceedings of the 1982 Mid-America Linguistics Conference* (Lawrence, Kan.: University of Kansas), 3–29.

—— (1985), 'Some Consequences of Lexical Phonology', *Phonology Yearbook*, 2: 83–138.

—— (1993), 'Blocking in Nonderived Environments', in Sharon Hargus and Ellen Kaisse (eds.), *Studies in Lexical Phonology* (New York: Academic Press), 277–313.

KLAVANS, JUDITH (1985), 'The Independence of Syntax and Phonology in Cliticization', *Language*, 61: 95–121.

KLEINHENZ, URSULA (1991), 'Die Alternation von Schwa mit silbischen Sonoranten im Deutschen', unpublished MA thesis, Cologne University.

KLOEKE, W. U. S. VAN LESSEN (1982), *Deutsche Phonologie und Morphologie: Merkmale und Markiertheit* (Tübingen: Niemeyer).

KOHLER, KLAUS J. (1977), *Einführung in die Phonetik des Deutschen* (Berlin: E. Schmidt).

—— (1990a), 'German', *Journal of the International Phonetic Association*, 20/1: 48–50.

—— (1990b), 'Comment on German', *Journal of the International Phonetic Association*, 20, no. 2: 44–46.

—— (1990c), 'Segmental Reduction in Connected Speech in German: Phonological Facts and Phonetic Explanations', in W. J. Hardcastle and A. Marchal (eds.), *Speech Production and Speech Modelling* (Dordrecht: Kluwer), 69–92.

KÖPCKE, KLAUS-MICHAEL (1988), 'Schemas in German Plural Formation', *Lingua*, 74: 303–35.

KRECH, EVA-MARIA (1968), *Sprechwissenschaftlich-phonetische Untersuchungen zum Gebrauch des Glottisschlages in der allgemeinen deutschen Hochlautung* (Basel: Karger).

—— et al. (1982), *Großes Wörterbuch der deutschen Aussprache* (Leipzig: VEB Bibliographisches Institut).

KUFNER, HERBERT L. (1971), *Kontrastive Phonologie Deutsch–Englisch* (Stuttgart: Klett).

KURKA, EDUARD (1965), 'Zur Aussprache der Lautkombination [kv]=qu im Hochdeutschen', *Phonetica*, 13: 53–8.

LADEFOGED, PETER (1971), *Preliminaries to Linguistic Phonetics* (Chicago: University of Chicago Press).

—— (1982), *A Course in Phonetics* (New York: Harcourt Brace Jovanovich).

—— and MORRIS HALLE (1988), 'Some Major Features of the International Phonetic Alphabet', *Language*, 64: 57–582.

—— and IAN MADDIESON (1990), 'Vowels of the World's Languages', *Journal of Phonetics*, 18: 93–122.

LAHIRI, ADITI and VINCENT EVERS (1991), 'Palatalization and Coronality', in Carole Paradis and Jean-François Prunet (eds.), T*he Special Status of Coronals: Internal and External Evidence* (San Diego: Academic Press), 79–100.

LASS, ROGER (1976), *English Phonology and Phonological Theory: Synchronic and Diachronic Evidence* (Cambridge: Cambridge University Press).

—— (1984), *Phonology: An Introduction to Basic Concepts* (Cambridge: Cambridge University Press).

LEVELT, WILLEM J. M. (1989), *Speaking: From Intention to Articulation* (Cambridge, Mass. and London: MIT Press).

LIBERMAN, MARK and ALAN PRINCE (1977), 'On Stress and Linguistic Rhythm', *Linguistic Inquiry*, 8: 249–336.

—— and RICHARD SPROAT (1992) 'The Stress and Structure of Modified Noun Phrases in English', in Ivan Sag and Anna Szabolcsi (eds.), *Lexical Matters* (Stanford: Stanford University), 131–81.

LIEBER, ROCHELLE (1981), *On the Organization of the Lexicon*, Ph.D. dissertation, MIT. [Published: Indiana University Linguistics Club.]

—— (1987), *An Integrated Theory of Autosegmental Processes* (Albany, NY: State University of New York Press).

—— (1992), *Deconstructing Morphology: Word Formation in Syntactic Theory* (Chicago: University of Chicago Press).

LINDBLOM, BJÖRN (1983), 'Economy of Speech Gestures', in Peter F. MacNeilage (ed.), *The Production of Speech* (New York: Springer-Verlag), 217–45.

LODGE, KEN (1989), 'A Non-segmental Account of German Umlaut: Diachronic and Synchronic Perspectives', *Linguistische Berichte*, 124: 470–91.

—— (1992), 'Assimilation, Deletion Paths and Underspecification', *Journal of Linguistics*, 28: 13–52.

LÖHKEN, SYLVIA C. (1997), *Deutsche Wortprosodie. Abschwächungs- und Tilgungsvorgänge* (Tübingen: Stauffenburg Verlag).

McCARTHY, JOHN (1979), 'Formal Problems in Semitic Phonology and Morphology', Ph.D. dissertation, MIT.

—— (1981), 'A Prosodic Theory of Nonconcatenative Morphology', *Linguistic Inquiry*, 12: 373–418.

McCarthy, John (1984), 'Prosodic Organization in Morphology', in Mark Aronoff and Richard T. Oehrle (eds.), *Language Sound Structure* (Cambridge, Mass.: MIT Press), 299–317.

—— (1988), 'Feature Geometry and Dependency: A Review', *Phonetica*, 43: 84–108.

—— and Alan Prince (1986), 'Prosodic Morphology', unpublished MS, University of Massachusetts/Brandeis University.

—— —— (1990), 'Foot and Word in Prosodic Morphology: The Arabic Broken Plural', *Natural Language and Linguistic Theory*, 8: 209–83.

—— —— (1993), 'Prosodic Morphology I: Constraint Interaction and Satisfaction', MS, University of Massachusetts, Amherst and Rutgers University.

MacWhinney, Brian and J. Leinbach (1992), 'Implementations are not Conceptualizations: Revising the Verb Learning Model', *Cognition*, 40: 121–57.

Maddieson, Ian (1984), *Patterns of Sounds* (Cambridge: Cambridge University Press).

Marcus, Gary, Ursula Brinkmann, Harald Clahsen, Steven Pinker, and Richard Wiese (1995), 'German Inflection: The Exception that Proves the Rule', *Cognitive Psychology*, 29: 189–256.

Martens, C. and P. Martens (1961), *Phonetik der deutschen Sprache* (Munich: Hueber).

Mascaró, Joan (1976), *Catalan Phonology and the Phonological Cycle*, Ph.D. dissertation, MIT (Bloomington, Ind.: Indiana University Linguistics Club).

Mater, Erich (1983), *Rückläufiges Wörterbuch der deutschen Gegenwartssprache* (Leipzig: VEB Bibliographisches Institut).

Meinhold, Gottfried and Eberhard Stock (1980), *Phonologie der deutschen Gegenwartssprache* (Leipzig: VEB Bibliographisches Institut).

Merchant, Jason (1996), 'Alignment and Fricative Assimilation in German', *Linguistic Inquiry*, 27: 709–19.

Mohanan, Karavannur P. (1986), *The Theory of Lexical Phonology* (Dordrecht, Reidel).

—— (1991), 'On the Bases of Radical Underspecification', *Natural Language and Linguistic Theory*, 9: 285–325.

Moulton, William G. (1947), 'Juncture in Modern Standard German', *Language*, 23: 212–26.

—— (1956), 'Syllabic Nuclei and Final Consonant Clusters in German', in Morris Halle, Horace G. Lunt, and Hugh McLean (eds.), *For Roman Jakobson* (The Hague: Mouton), 372–81.

—— (1962), *The Sounds of English and German* (Chicago: University of Chicago Press).

Mugdan, Joachim (1977), *Flexionsmorphologie und Psycholinguistik* (Tübingen: Narr).

Müller, Wolfgang (1990), 'Die real existierenden grammatischen Ellipsen und die Norm. Eine Bestandsaufnahme', *Sprachwissenschaft*, 15: 214–366.

Muthmann, Gustav (1988), *Rückläufiges deutsches Wörterbuch: Handbuch der Wortausgänge im Deutschen mit Beachtung der Wort- und Lautstruktur* (Tübingen: Niemeyer).

Muysken, Pieter (1983), 'Parametrizing the Notion Head', *Journal of Linguistic Research*, 2: 57–76.

Neef, Martin (1997), *Wortdesign. Eine deklarative Analyse der deutschen Verbflexion* (Tübingen: Stauffenburg Verlag).

Nespor, Marina and Irene Vogel (1986), *Prosodic Phonology* (Dordrecht: Foris).

Noske, Roland (1992), 'Moraic Versus Constituent Syllables', in Peter Eisenberg, Karl Heinz Ramers, and Heinz Vater (eds.), *Silbenphonologie des Deutschen* (Tübingen: Narr), 284–328.

—— (1993), *A Theory of Syllabification and Segmental Alternation: With Studies on the Phonology of French, German, Tonkawa and Yawelmani* (Tübingen: Niemeyer).

ÖHMANN, EMIL (1961–2), 'Die Pluralformen auf -*s* in der deutschen Substantivflexion', *Zeitschrift für deutsches Altertum und deutsche Literatur*, 91: 228–36.

OLSEN, SUSAN (1986), *Wortbildung im Deutschen: Eine Einführung in die Theorie der Wortstruktur* (Stuttgart: Kröner).

—— (1988), '*Flickzeug* vs. *abgasarm*: Eine Studie zur Analogie in der Wortbildung', in Francis G. Gentry (ed.), *Semper idem et novus: Festschrift for Frank Banta* (Göppingen: Kümmerle), 75–97.

—— (1990), 'Konversion als ein kombinatorischer Wortbildungsprozeß', *Linguistische Berichte*, 127: 185–216.

—— (1991), '*Ge*-Präfigierungen im heutigen Deutsch', *Beiträge zur Geschichte der deutschen Sprache*, 113: 333–66.

ORTMANN, WOLF DIETER (1983), *Materialien zur Didaktisierung der Phonemik des Deutschen. Teil 2: Minimalpaare* (Munich: Max Hueber Verlag).

PARADIS, CAROLE and JEAN-FRANÇOIS PRUNET (1991) (eds.), *The Special Status of Coronals: Internal and External Evidence* (San Diego: Academic Press).

PESETSKY, DAVID (1985), 'Morphology and Logical Form', *Linguistic Inquiry*, 16: 193–246.

PHEBY, JOHN (1981), 'Phonologie: Intonation', in Karl Erich Heidolph, Walter Flämig, and Wolfgang Motsch (eds.), *Grundzüge einer deutschen Grammatik* (Berlin: Akademie-Verlag), 838–97.

PHILIPP, MARTHE (1974), *Phonologie des Deutschen* (Stuttgart: Kohlhammer).

PIERREHUMBERT, JANET (1990), 'Phonological and Phonetic Representations', *Journal of Phonetics*, 18: 375–94.

—— and MARY E. BECKMAN (1988), *Japanese Tone Structure* (Cambridge, Mass.: MIT Press).

POSER, WILLIAM (1982), 'Phonological Representations and Action-at-a-Distance', in Harry van der Hulst and Norval Smith (eds.), *The Structure of Phonological Representations* (Dordrecht: Foris), 121–58.

PRINCE, ALAN (1983), 'Relating to the Grid', *Linguistic Inquiry*, 14: 19–100.

—— and PAUL SMOLENSKY (1993), *Optimality Theory: Constraint Interaction in Generative Grammar* (Rutgers University Center for Cognitive Science, Technical Report No. 2).

PRINZ, MICHAEL (1991), *Klitisierung im Deutschen und Neugriechischen: Eine lexikalisch-phonologische Studie* (Tübingen: Niemeyer).

—— and RICHARD WIESE (1991), 'Die Affrikaten des Deutschen und ihre Verschriftung', *Linguistische Berichte*, 133: 165–89.

RAFFELSIEFEN, RENATE (1987), 'Verschmelzungsformen in German: A Lexical Analysis', *Linguistic Analysis*, 17: 123–46.

—— (1995), 'Conditions for Stability: The Case of Schwa in German', in *Theorie des Lexikons: Arbeiten des SFB 282* (Düsseldorf: Heinrich-Heine-Universität), 69.

RAMERS, KARL HEINZ (1988), *Vokalquantität und -qualität im Deutschen* (Tübingen: Niemeyer).

—— (1992), 'Ambisilbische Konsonanten im Deutschen', in Peter Eisenberg, Karl Heinz Ramers, and Heinz Vater (eds.), *Silbenphonologie des Deutschen* (Tübingen: Narr), 246–83.

—— and HEINZ VATER (1991), *Einführung in die Phonologie* (Cologne: Gabel Verlag).

REIS, MARGA (1974), *Lauttheorie und Lautgeschichte: Untersuchungen am Beispiel der Dehnungs- und Kürzungsvorgänge im Deutschen* (Munich: Fink).

RENNISON, JOHN (1980), 'What is Shwa in Austrian German? The Case for Epenthesis, and its Consequences', *Wiener Linguistische Gazette*, 24: 33–42.

RETTIG, WOLFGANG (1972), *Sprachsystem und Sprachnorm in der deutschen Substantivflexion* (Tübingen: Narr).

ROCA, IGGY (1994), *Generative Phonology* (London: Routledge).

RONNEBERGER-SIBOLD, ELKE (1988), 'Verschiedene Wege der Phonemisierung bei Deutsch (regionalsprachlich) ç, x', *Folia Linguistica*, 22: 301–13.

RUBACH, JERZY (1984), 'Segmental Rules of English and Cyclic Phonology', *Language*, 60: 21–54.

—— (1990), 'Final Devoicing and Cyclic Syllabification in German', *Linguistic Inquiry*, 21: 79–94.

—— and GEERT BOOIJ (1990), 'Syllable Structure Assignment in Polish', *Phonology*, 7: 121–58.

RUSS, CHARLES (1990) (ed.), *The Dialects of Modern German: A Linguistic Survey* (London: Routledge).

SAGEY, ELIZABETH (1986), 'On the Representation of Complex Segments', in Engin Sezer and Leo Wetzels (eds.), *Compensatory Lengthening* (Dordrecht: Foris), 251–95.

SANDERS, WILLY (1972), 'Hochdeutsch /ä/—"Ghostphonem" oder Sprachphänomen', *Zeitschrift für Dialektologie und Linguistik*, 93: 37–58.

SAUSSURE, FERDINAND DE (1916), *Grundfragen der Allgemeinen Sprachwissenschaft* (Berlin: de Gruyter, 1967).

SCHANE, SANFORD A. (1973), '[back] and [round]', in Stephen A. Anderson and Paul Kiparsky (eds.), *A Festschrift for Morris Halle* (New York: Holt, Rinehart & Winston), 174–84.

SCHEUTZ, HANNES (1989), 'Umlaut im Deutschen als autosuggestive Beschreibungsharmonie: Anmerkungen zu einem Beitrag von Richard Wiese', *Zeitschrift für Sprachwissenschaft*, 8: 133–43.

SEILER, HANSJAKOB (1962), 'Laut und Sinn: Zur Struktur der deutschen Einsilbler', *Lingua*, 11: 375–87.

SELKIRK, ELISABETH O. (1982), *The Syntax of Words* (Cambridge, Mass.: MIT Press).

—— (1984a), 'On the Major Class Features and Syllable Theory', in Mark Aronoff and Richard T. Oehrle (eds.), *Language Sound Structure* (Cambridge, Mass.: MIT Press), 107–36.

—— (1984b), *Phonology and Syntax: The Relation between Sound and Structure* (Cambridge. Mass.: MIT Press).

SELTING, MARGRET (1995), *Prosodie im Gespräch: Aspekte einer interaktionalen Phonologie der Konversation* (Tübingen: Niemeyer).

SIEBS (1969), *Siebs. Deutsche Aussprache: Reine und gemäßigte Hochlautung mit Aussprachewörterbuch*, ed. Helmut de Boor, Hugo Moser, and Christian Winkler, 19th edn (Berlin: de Gruyter).

SIEBS, THEODOR (1898), *Deutsche Bühnenaussprache* (Ph.D. Thesis, Berlin: Ahn).

SIEGEL, DOROTHY (1974), 'Topics in English Morphology', dissertation, MIT.

SIEVERS, EDUARD (1901), *Grundzüge der Phonetik zur Einführung in das Studium der Lautlehre der indogermanischen Sprachen* (Leipzig: Breitkopf & Härtel).

SMOLENSKY, PAUL (1995), *On the Structure of the Constraint Component Con of UG*. Handout of talk at UCLA. Rutgers Optimality Archive: 86.

SPENCER, ANDREW (1988), 'Arguments for Morpholexical Rules', *Journal of Linguistics*, 24: 1–30.

—— (1991), *Morphological Theory: An Introduction to Word Structure in Generative Grammar* (Oxford: Basil Blackwell).

SPROAT, RICHARD (1985), 'On Deriving the Lexicon', Ph.D. dissertation, MIT.

STEMBERGER, JOSEPH P. (1983), 'The Nature of /r/ and /l/ in English: Evidence from Speech Errors', *Journal of Phonetics*, 11: 139–47.

STERIADE, DONCA (1982), 'Greek Prosodies and the Nature of Syllabification', Ph.D. dissertation, MIT.

—— (1987), 'Redundant Values', in Anna Bosch, Barbara Need, and Eric Schiller (eds.), *Papers of the Twenty-third Regional Meeting of the Chicago Linguistic Society: The Parasession of Autosegmental and Metrical Phonology* (Chicago: Chicago Linguistic Society), 339–62.

STIEBELS, BARBARA and DIETER WUNDERLICH (1994), 'Morphology Feeds Syntax: The Case of Particle Verbs', *Linguistics*, 32: 913–68.

STOCK, DIETER (1971), *Untersuchungen zur Stimmhaftigkeit hochdeutscher Phonemrealisationen* (Hamburg: Buske).

STÖTZER, URSULA (1989), 'Zur Betonung dreiteiliger Substantivkomposita', *Deutsch als Fremdsprache*, 26: 263–5.

STRAUSS, STEVEN L. (1982), *Lexicalist Phonology of English and German* (Dordrecht: Foris).

TOMAN, JINDRICH (1983), *Wortsyntax: Eine Diskussion ausgewählter Probleme deutscher Wortbildung* (Tübingen: Niemeyer).

TREIMAN, REBECCA (1983), 'The Structure of Spoken Syllables: Evidence from Novel Word Games', *Cognition*, 15: 49–74.

TRUBETZKOY, NIKOLAJ S. (1939), *Grundzüge der Phonologie* (Prague: TCLP 7), 6th edn (Göttingen: Vandenhoeck & Ruprecht, 1977).

UHMANN, SUSANNE (1991), *Fokusphonologie: Eine Analyse deutscher Intonationskonturen im Rahmen der nicht-linearen Phonologie* (Tübingen: Niemeyer).

ULBRICH, HORST (1972), *Instrumentalphonetisch-auditive R-Untersuchungen im Deutschen* (Berlin: Akademie-Verlag).

UNGEHEUER, GÜNTHER (1969), 'Das Phonemsystem der deutschen Hochlautung', in Siebs (1969), 27–42.

VATER, HEINZ (1992), 'Zum Silben-Nukleus im Deutschen', in Peter Eisenberg, Karl Heinz Ramers, and Heinz Vater (eds.), *Silbenphonologie des Deutschen* (Tübingen: Narr), 100–33.

VENNEMANN, THEO (1968), 'German Phonology', Ph.D. dissertation, University of California at Los Angeles.

—— (1972), 'On the Theory of Syllabic Phonology', *Linguistische Berichte*, 18: 1–18.

—— (1978), 'Universal Syllabic Phonology', *Theoretical Linguistics*, 5: 175–215.

—— (1982), 'Zur Silbenstruktur der deutschen Standardsprache', in Theo Vennemann (ed.), *Silben, Segmente, Akzente* (Tübingen: Niemeyer), 261–305.

—— (1988), *Preference Laws for Syllable Structure and the Explanation of Sound Change: With Special Reference to German, Germanic, Italian, and Latin* (Berlin: Mouton de Gruyter).

—— (1991a), 'Skizze der deutschen Wortprosodie', *Zeitschrift für Sprachwissenschaft*, 10: 86–111.

—— (1991b), 'Syllable Structure and Syllable Cut Prosodies in Modern Standard German', in Piermarco Bertinetto, Michael Kenstowicz, and Michele Loporcaro (eds.), *Certamen Phonologicum II: Papers from the Cortona Phonology Meeting 1990* (Turin: Rosenberg & Sellier), 211–45.

VENNEMANN, THEO (1992), 'Syllable Structure and Simplex Accent in Modern Standard German', in Michael Ziolkowski, Manuela Noske, and Daren Deaton (eds.), *Papers of the Twenty-sixth Regional Meeting of the Chicago Linguistic Society*, ii, *The Parasession on the Syllable in Phonetics and Phonology* (Chicago: Chicago Linguistic Society), 399–412.

WALTHER, MARKUS (1993), 'Declarative Syllabification with Applications to German', in T. Mark Ellison and James M. Scobbie (eds.), *Computational Phonology* (University of Edinburgh: Edinburgh Working Papers in Cognitive Science 8), 55–79.

—— (1999), 'German i-truncations'. Available online: http://pc0864.Germanistik-Kunst.uni-marburg.de/~walther/i-truncations.html

WÄNGLER, HANS-HEINRICH (1974), *Grundriß einer Phonetik des Deutschen: Mit einer allgemeinen Einführung in die Phonetik* (Marburg: Elwert).

WERNER, OTMAR (1972), *Phonemik des Deutschen* (Stuttgart: Metzler).

WIESE, RICHARD (1986), 'Schwa and the Structure of Words in German', *Linguistics*, 24: 695–724.

—— (1987), 'Phonologie und Morphologie des Umlauts im Deutschen', *Zeitschrift für Sprachwissenschaft*, 6: 227–48.

—— (1988a), *Silbische und Lexikalische Phonologie: Studien zum Chinesischen und Deutschen* (Tübingen: Niemeyer).

—— (1988b), 'The Proper Treatment of Inflection in the German Article System', *Wiener Linguistische Gazette*, Supplement 7: 32–4.

—— (1989a), 'Schrift und die Modularität der Grammatik', in P. Eisenberg and H. Günther (eds.), *Schriftsystem und Orthographie* (Niemeyer: Tübingen), 321–39.

—— (1989b), 'Umlaut im Deutschen: Richtigstellungen zu den Anmerkungen von Hannes Scheutz', *Zeitschrift für Sprachwissenschaft*, 8: 144–52.

—— (1990a), 'Towards a Unification-based Phonology', in Hans Karlgren (ed.), *Coling-90. Papers presented to the 13th International Conference on Computational Linguistics*, iii (Helsinki: Universität Helsinki), 283–6.

—— (1990b), 'Über die Interaktion von Morphologie und Phonologie: Reduplikation im Deutschen', *Zeitschrift für Phonetik, Sprachwissenschaft und Kommunikationsforschung*, 43: 603–24.

—— (1991), 'Was ist extrasilbisch im Deutschen und warum?', *Zeitschrift für Sprachwissenschaft*, 10: 112–33.

—— (1992), 'Prosodic Phonology and its Role in the Processing of Written Language', in G. Görz (ed.), *Konvens 92* (Heidelberg: Springer), 139–48.

—— (1996), 'Phonological vs. Morphological Rules: On German Umlaut and Ablaut', *Journal of Linguistics*, 32: 113–35.

—— (2000), 'Regular Morphology vs. Prosodic Morphology? – The Case of Truncations in German'. Unpublished ms., University of Marburg.

WILLIAMS, EDWIN (1981), 'On the notions "lexically related" and "head of a word"', *Linguistic Inquiry*, 12: 245–74.

WUNDERLICH, DIETER (1987), 'An Investigation of Lexical Composition: The Case of German be-verbs', *Linguistics*, 25: 283–331.

—— (1988), 'Der Ton macht die Melodie—Zur Phonologie der Intonation des Deutschen', in H. Altmann (ed.), *Intonationsforschungen* (Tübingen: Niemeyer), 1–40.

—— (1991), 'Intonation and Contrast', *Journal of Semantics*, 8: 239–51.

—— and RAY FABRI (1995), 'Minimalist Morphology: An Approach to Inflection', *Zeitschrift für Sprachwissenschaft*, 14: 236–94.

WURZEL, WOLFGANG U. (1970), *Studien zur Deutschen Lautstruktur* (*Studia Grammatica* VIII) (Berlin: Akademie-Verlag).

—— (1980), 'Der deutsche Wortakzent: Fakten—Regeln—Prinzipien. Ein Beitrag zu einer natürlichen Akzenttheorie', *Zeitschrift für Germanistik*, 3: 299–318.

—— (1981), 'Phonologie: Segmentale Struktur', in Karl Erich Heidolph, Walter Flämig, and Wolfgang Motsch (eds.), *Grundzüge einer deutschen Grammatik* (Berlin: Akademie-Verlag), 898–990.

—— (1984), 'Was bezeichnet der Umlaut im Deutschen?', *Zeitschrift für Phonetik, Sprachwissenschaft und Kommunikationsforschung*, 37: 647–63.

—— (1990), 'The Mechanism of Inflection: Lexicon Representations, Rules, and Irregularities', in Wolfgang U. Dressler, Hans C. Luschützky, Oskar E. Pfeiffer, and John Rennison (eds.), *Contemporary Morphology* (Berlin: de Gruyter), 203–16.

YU, SI-TAEK (1992*a*), 'Silbeninitiale Cluster und Silbifizierung im Deutschen', in Peter Eisenberg, Karl Heinz Ramers, and Heinz Vater (eds.), *Silbenphonologie des Deutschen* (Tübingen: Narr), 172–207.

—— (1992*b*), *Unterspezifikation in der Phonologie des Deutschen* (Tübingen: Niemeyer).

ZWICKY, ARNOLD M. (1967), 'Umlaut and Noun Plurals in German', in *Studia Grammatica* VI (Berlin: Akademie-Verlag), 35–45.

—— (1985), 'How to Describe Inflection', in *Proceedings of the Berkeley Linguistics Society* (Berkeley: Berkeley Linguistics Society), 372–86.

—— (1987), 'Morphological Rules, Operations, and Operation Types', in *Proceedings of the Fourth Eastern States Conference on Linguistics* (1987), 318–34.

—— and ELLEN KAISSE (1987) (eds.), *Syntactic Conditions on Phonological Rules. Phonology Yearbook*, 4: 3–263.

SUBJECT INDEX

ablaut 41, 178, 209
Advanced Tongue Root 20–1, 153–6, 197, 277
affix order 122–3, 125
affixes, *see* prefixes; suffixes
affricates 13–14, 40–3, 48, 259, 261, 265–6
allomorph 86, 99, 100–3, 227
allophones 16, 18, 210–11
ambisyllabic consonant 35–8, 46, 202, 254, 281
appendix, *see* extrasyllabicity
approximant 8 n., 246
Arabic 28 n., 85
aspiration 270
association line 28–9, 179–80
ATR, *see* Advanced Tongue Root

back 20–2, 31, 154–5
Bavarian 171
bleeding relationship 214
bracketing paradoxes 148

C-positions, *see* CV-phonology
clippings, *see* hypocoristics
clitic group 83, 251–2
clitics 205, 248–52
coda 44, 46, 53, 55–6, 201–2, 264–5
colon 83
colloquial pronunciation 2, 206, 248, 253 n.
complementary distribution 15, 211, 235–6
compound stress 128, 294, 297–302, 303
compounds 65, 72–3, 76, 103–5, 127–8, 131, 143, 147, 231, 232, 294, 296–302, 306
    verbal 103, 105, 295, 297
consonant clusters 262–7
Consonant Epenthesis 146, 232
consonantal 20, 23, 67, 165, 170, 235
consonants 22–6, 164–8, 242
continuant 23–4, 40–1, 170, 207, 233
coronal 23–4, 29–30, 108, 165–7
counterfeeding relationship 157 n., 257
CV-phonology 38–43, 51–5, 154, 255, 259
cycle 55, 85, 88, 93, 110, 115, 118, 145, 195, 289

default segment 158–9
    feature value 155–7, 215–16
    rule 140, 155, 166, 172, 175, 219
degemination 41, 229–32, 246
deletion rules 180
    see also Final Devoicing; g-Deletion;
    Vowel Shortening; Word deletion

dental 23–4, 29–30, 168
diminutive formation 68 n., 70, 122 n., 135, 146, 188, 217, 230–1
diphthong 14–15, 37–9, 159–62, 182
dissimilation 256, 267–8
dorsal 23–4, 29–30, 166–7, 212–13, 234
Dorsal Fricative Assimilation 69, 136, 209–17, 257, 271
Dorsal Fricative Lowering 213, 215–16
Dutch 177, 251 n., 271

Elsewhere Condition 134–6, 140, 174, 213
English 22, 65, 68, 100, 118, 137–8, 146, 204 n., 298 n., 302
extrametricality 276, 284–5, 288
extrasyllabicity 47–9, 55–6, 167, 226, 233, 285 n.

feature inventory 19–26, 29–33
feature structure 27–9, 33, 151, 157
feature theory 27, 151, 156, 200, 254, 270
feeding relationship 129, 157 n., 214
Final Devoicing 196, 200–5, 206–8, 228
focus 81, 302, 305
Focus Stress Assignment 305
foot 45, 56–65, 72, 74, 87, 92–4, 104, 108, 274–5, 282–4, 292
French 12, 32, 122 n., 137–8
front 20–2, 23–4, 29–31, 153–5, 168, 183, 185, 199, 213
fundamental frequency 79–81

g-Deletion 124, 218, 224–9, 234
g-Spirantization 206–9, 214–16, 234
ge-Prefixation 92–3, 96
Generalized Phrase Structure Grammar 155 n.
generative phonology 3–4, 27–8, 312–13
glides 39–40, 159–60, 236
glottal stop 58–60, 173–4
Glottal Stop Insertion 59, 173–4
glottis:
    constricted 23–5, 169–70, 173
    spread 23–5, 169–70, 173
Gothic 43

Hebrew 145
Hessian 268
high 20, 23–5, 153–4, 167, 194
High Vowel Consonantization 237–8, 240–2
Hungarian 83 n.
hypocoristics 62–4

i-Desonorization 237–8
inflection, *see* morphology, inflectional
intonation 3, 77–82
intonational phrase 78–82, 303 n.
  intonational phrase boundary 78, 81
intrusive stop, *see* Consonant Epenthesis
IPA conventions 7–8, 22, 35 n., 222 n., 235,
  252, 273
isochrony 65

Japanese 280–1

labial 23–4, 29–31, 166, 186
language acquisition 33, 64, 138, 208
laryngeals 23–5, 29, 164, 169–70, 173–4,
  268–9
lateral 24, 168
Latin 122 n., 281–2
level ordering 123, 125, 127–8, 130, 142–3,
  147–8, 189–90, 230 n., 246 n., 289,
  293
lexical levels, *see* level ordering
Lexical Phonology 115–17, 127–8, 132,
  148–9, 150–1
lexicon, *see* Lexical Phonology
Linking Constraint 52 n., 254
loanwords 12–13, 210, 280–2
long, *see* vowel length
low 20, 22, 23–4, 171, 213

major class features 168–71, 235
markedness 13, 152, 154–6, 163, 168, 172–3,
  177
Middle High German 50 n., 186, 195
minimal pairs 9–11, 176 n.
mora 47 n., 83
morpheme structure condition 117, 161
morphology, general 50, 88–9, 96–7, 100–1,
  115–17, 119, 144–5, 148, 188–93,
  245–6, 294
  derivational 98–9, 119–24, 188–90,
  287–91
  inflectional 61–2, 106–10, 113–14,
  136–43, 230

nasal 23, 170, 220, 224
Nasal Assimilation 68, 117–18, 166–7,
  218–24, 226, 229
non-linear phonology 28, 44, 108, 213, 226
Northern German vernacular 42 n., 195, 206,
  214, 218, 228, 248
notation 7, 28, 180–1
Nuclear Stress rule 303
nucleus 44–6, 52, 224

obstruent 23, 150, 170, 173, 235, 262–8
Obstruent Dissimilation 268
Old High German 122, 187

onset 44–5, 53, 253, 262
onset maximization 52–3
orthography, *see* writing system

phonemes 9–11, 16–18
phonetics 8, 178, 197, 223, 234, 241, 259,
  269–71, 292, 312–13
phonological phrase 74–7, 82, 251, 298–9,
  302–6, 307 n.
phonological word 51, 65–74, 92–5, 104,
  108, 110–11, 176, 217, 219–21, 251–2,
  274, 290, 298–300
phonotactics 34, 48, 229, 240, 258–61
phrasal stress 302–5
pitch, *see* intonation
plural formation, nouns 61–2, 106–9, 121,
  136–43, 144, 147, 190
postlexical phonology 116, 204, 215, 217–18,
  227
prefixes 66–7, 89–92, 94, 97, 124–5, 221,
  285–6, 293–6, 308
Progressive Nasal Assimilation 222–3
pronouncing dictionaries 1–2, 12 n., 34 n., 60,
  171 n., 198, 208, 210, 221 n., 236, 239,
  253, 269
prosodic hierarchy 56, 74, 83–4, 298–9
Prosodic Morphology 85, 100, 193

r-sounds 8 n., 18, 25, 170–2, 201 n., 252–7
r-Vocalization 171–2, 177, 254–7
radical node 32, 166 n.
Redundancy Rule Ordering Constraint 158–9,
  170, 172
reduplication 43, 64
Regressive Nasal Assimilation 219, 223–4
resyllabification 244
rhyme:
  poetic 44–5, 57–8
  syllabic 44–6, 47, 253, 256
rhythm 306–8, 310
Rhythmic Reversal 307
root 129–32, 193, 225, 228, 248, 289,
  296
  bound root 123, 129
root node 29, 51, 153, 155, 174
round 20, 153, 155, 199
  see also labial
Rounding Assimilation 161, 182, 185–7
Ruhr area dialect 257
rule:
  cyclic, *see* cycle
  formalism 179–81, 213, 226
  inflectional 139–41
  lexical vs. postlexical 188–9, 227; *see also*
    postlexical phonology

s-Insertion 144, 232
s-Voicing 175–7

schwa 16–17, 96 n., 99, 105–7, 109–12, 125–6, 152–3, 158–9, 184, 198–9, 242–4
Schwa Epenthesis 89, 113, 128, 226, 230, 243–7, 286
schwa syllables 50, 61–2, 86, 99, 106–10, 139, 143, 226, 247, 270, 275–6, 280, 286
secondary stress 275, 292, 307
segment structure, see feature structure
skeleton, see CV-phonology
sonorant, see obstruent
Sonorant Syllabicity 243 n., 247
sonority hierarchy 258–61, 262
SPE 19, 23, 27–8, 31, 33, 74, 133, 179, 183, 242, 268, 272–3, 303
standardization 1–2
stem 67, 103, 129–32, 193
stray erasure 227
stress, see word stress; compound stress; phrasal stress; secondary stress; stress representation; stress shift
stress representation 272–6, 311
stress shift 75–6, 306–10
Strict Cycle Condition 133–6
structure preservation 136
subcategorization frame 86–7, 92–3, 98–100, 102 n., 288 n.
suffixes 50, 57, 66–9, 85–7, 98, 102, 120–3, 126, 137–43, 190–3, 287–91, 293
Swabian 45, 268
syllabic 39, 52, 235
syllabic consonants 243, 246–7
syllabification 49, 51–6, 65–8, 201, 203, 225, 244–5, 247
syllable boundaries 35–7, 195, 201, 204, 224

syllables 33–49, 201–2, 234, 258–60, 261, 277, 292
syntax 71, 77–9, 84, 250–1, 296, 301, 302–5, 306, 309–10

tense 20–2
    see also Advanced Tongue Root
tongue position 23, 29, 33, 167, 263
truncation 91, 126

u-Desonorization 240–2
umlaut 41, 132–3, 135, 153, 181–94
underspecification 115, 152–76, 179, 212, 264
    Contrastive 162–3
    Radical 158, 162
utterance 83

V-positions, see CV-phonology
Viennese German 111
voice 23–5, 150–1, 169–70, 176, 200
vowel classification, see vowels
vowel length 20–2, 37–9, 153–5, 175 n., 195, 269–70, 277–8
Vowel Raising 193–4
Vowel Reduction 249
Vowel Shortening 194–8, 209 n., 269–70, 277–80
vowels 19–22, 152–3, 255

word boundary 65, 74, 91, 177
word deletion 69–72, 77, 82, 94, 180, 183, 232
word formation, see morphology
word stress 58, 69, 123–4, 126, 197, 276–86, 287–93
writing system 36 n., 227, 231